SOCIAL HISTORY OF THE DECCAN

SOCIAL HISTORY OF THE DECCAN

by

TEJASWINI YARLAGADDA

BHARATIYA KALA PRAKASHAN

DELHI (INDIA)

FIRST EDITION : 2004

ISBN : 81-8690-025-8

Published by : **C.P. Gautam**
for BHARATIYA KALA PRAKASHAN
3421-A, IInd Floor, Narang Colony,
Tri Nagar, Delhi-110035.
Phone : 27153083 (O), 27522129 (R)

Laser Typesetting by : Twinkle Graphics, Delhi-110094.

Printed at : Santosh Offset Press, Delhi.

CONTENTS

Acknowledgements .... (vii)

Transliteration Chart .... (ix)

Abbreviations .... (x)

List of Maps .... (xi)

List of Charts .... (xii)

Introduction and Sources **1-19**

Chapter I

Historiographical Context **20-51**

Chapter II

Geo-Political Context **52-89**

Chapter III

Social Context **90-185**

Chapter IV

Economic Context **186-255**

Chapter V

Spatial Context **256-326**

Chapter VI

Ideological Context **327-402**

Recapitulation and Conclusions **403-424**

Bibliography **425-449**

ACKNOWLEDGEMENTS

I wish to express my deep sense of gratitude to Dr. Aloka Parasher Sen, Professor, Department of History, University of Hyderabad, but for whose constant encouragement and inspiration, this work would not have been possible. The invaluable discussions which we have had, during the course of the work, have gone a long way in giving the ultimate shape to this book. Her scholarly erudition and the depth of her academic skills enthused in me a spirit of confidence at every stage of my work. I will look back on my association with Dr. Aloka Parasher Sen with a sense of pride and privilege.

I would also like to thank all the faculty of the Department of History, University of Hyderabad for the encouragement accorded to me throughout my academic career in the University of Hyderabad. In particulars, I wish to sincerely thank Prof. T.R. Sharma, Prof. S. Nagaraju, Prof. V. Ramakrishna and Prof. I.P. Gupta for their constant support. I am also grateful to Dr. P.V.P. Sastry, Deputy Director (Retd.) Dept. of Archaeology and Museums, Govt. of Andhra Pradesh, who patiently helped me with interpreting difficult epigraphic sources. In this regard I would also like to thank Dr. Subrahmanyam known popularly as Mysore Pandit, for the timely help extended to me during my field trip to Mysore. I would also like to acknowledge with thanks the help extended by Dr. Madhav N. Katti then Director, Epigraphy, ASI, Mysore, for permitting me to access the unpublished inscriptional data stored in the form of transcripts. Thanks are also due to Dr. N.S. Ramchandra Murthy and Dr. N. Mukunda Rao, Archaeology and Museums Department, Hyderabad, for allowing me to go through the transcripts available in their office.

I would also like to thank the staff of the libraries of University of Hyderabad, Osmania University, Directorate of Archaeology and Museums, Andhra Pradesh State Archives, Hyderabad, Adayar Research Institute, Madras, Office of the Government Epigraphist, ASI, Madras and the Office of the Department of Epigraphy, ASI, Mysore, for readily supplying all the required reading material. I wish to specially thank Mrs. M. Varalakshmi, Gazetted Librarian, for her prompt help in processing rare material in the Library of the Department of Archaeology and Museums, Hyderabad.

I would like to take this opportunity to express my gratitude to Dr. E. Siva Nagi Reddy, Sthapati, Dept. of Archaeology and Museums, Hyderabad, who has gone out of the way in extending his co-operation in bringout this work. I wish to also thank Ms. Sumabala and Dr. C.S. Vasudevan, for extending all the help during my stay at Madras and Mysore. My special thanks are also due to my friend Keiko Yamada who helped me in proof reading the final drafts of the book. I would like to extend my sincere thanks to Mr. Sudhakar and Mr. Siva Sankar Reddy for their patient co-operation in typing out the thesis in decent manner.

I am indebted to my entire family, whose spirited enthusiasm and constant inspiration formed the backbone of my research activity. In particular I wish to thank Mrs. Sashsi for her ever willing support. Harish, Sriram and my father-in-law Sri. Y. Sreeramulu need special mention for the amount of adjustments and accommodation they have made to enable me to complete this work as comfortably as possible. I wish to take this opportunity to thank my parents for laying the foundation to my academic career. Finally, I thank all the people who are directly or indirectly involved in bringing out this piece of work.

I thank to my publisher Shri C.P. Gautam, for Bharatiya Kala Prakashan, Delhi, for the good printing and excellent get up of the work and also his keen interest in my work.

Hyderabad **Tajaswini Yarlagadda**
Date : 1.4.2003

TRANSLITERATION TABLE

English	Devanagari	Telegu	English	Devanagari	Telegu
a	अ	అ	ṭh	ठ	ఠ
ā	आ	ఆ	ḍ	ड्	డ
i	इ	ఇ	ḍh	ढ्	ఢ
ī	ई	ఈ	ṇ	ण्	ణ
u	उ	ఉ	t	त्	త
ū	ऊ	ఊ	th	थ्	థ
e	ए	ఎ	d	द्	ద
ai	ऐ	ఐ	dh	ध्	ధ
o	ओ	ఓ	n	न्	న
ou	औ	ఔ	p	प्	ప
ṛ	ऋ	ఋ	ph	फ्	ఫ
k	क्	క	b	ब्	బ
kh	ख	ఖ	bh	भ्	భ
g	ग्	గ	m	म्	మ
gh	घ्	ఘ	y	य्	య
ṅ	ङ्	ఙ	r	र्	ర
c	च्	చ	l	ल्	ల
ch	छ्	ఛ	v	व्	వ
j	ज्	జ	h	ह्	హ
jh	झ्	ఝ	ś	श	శ
ñ	ञ्	ఞ	s	स्	స
ṭ	ट्	ట	ksh	क्ष्	క్ష

Anusvara: ṁ Visarga: ḥ

No diacritical marks have been used while describing the names of districts, towns and villages which have already become acceptable in modern English. However, these have been used to indicate ancient names of places, persons and in case of technical words in Sanskrit and other Indian languages.

ABBREVIATIONS

ABORI	Annals of the Bhandarkar Oriental Research Institute
APGAS	Andhra Pradesh Government Archaeological Series
ARE	Annual Report on Epigraphy
BDCRI	Bulletin of the Deccan College Research Institute
CSSH	Comparative Studies in Society and History
EA	Epigraphia Andhrica
EI	Epigraphia Indica
HAS	Hyderabad Archaeological Series
IA	Indian Antiquary
IESHR	Indian Economic and Social History Review
IHQ	Indian Historical Quarterly
IHR	Indian Historical Review
JAS	Journal of Asian Studies
JAHRA	Journal of the Andhra Historical Research Society
JBBRAS	Journal of Bombay Branch of Royal Asiatic Society
JESHO	Journal of Economic and Social History of the Orient
JIH	Journal of Indian History
JKU	Journal of Karnataka University
JOR	Journal of Oriental Research
JPS	Journal of Peasant Studies
JRAS	Journal of Royal Asiatic Society
MAS	Modern Asian Studies
PAPHC	Proceedings of Andhra Pradesh History Congress
PIHC	Proceedings of Indian History Congress
PKRBP	Progress of Kanada Research in Bombay Province
PSIHC	Proceedings of South Indian History Congress
QJMS	Quarterly Journal of Mythic Society
SIH	Studies in History
SII	South Indian Inscriptions

LIST OF MAPS

Map I : Area of Study 6

Map II : Delineation of Sub-Regions and Physiography 58

Map III : Areas of Political Control in the pre-10th century A.D. Period 63

Map IV : Areas of Political Control by Main Families 66
(1000 A.D–1200 A.D.)

Map V : Areas of Rule by Minor Dynasties
(1000 A.D.–1200 A.D.) 71

Map VI : Major Settlements (1000 A.D.–1200 A.D.) 279

(Acknowledgements : All the maps accompanying this work have been made by Dr. E. Siva Nagi Reddy, Department of Archaeology and Museums, Hyderabad based on Joseph E. Schwartzberg (ed.). A Historical Atlas of South Asia. The University of Chicago Press, Chicago and London, 1978 and C. Collin Davics, An Historical Atlas of the Indian Peninsula, OUP, Delhi, 1949.)

LIST OF CHARTS

Chart I : Sub-Regions A, B, C : Social Context 151

Chart II : Sub-Regions A, B, C : Economic Context 232

Chart III : Sub-Regions A, B, C : Spatial Context 306

Chart IV : Sub-Regions A, B, C : Ideological Context 384

INTRODUCTION AND SOURCES

While quoting one of the school boy rhymes 'Geography is about maps, History is about chaps'. Sabyasachi Bhattacharya[1] was underlining a very important point that no longer can history and geography be understood as two separate disciplines and entities. Historians have today come to willingly accept the inter-disciplinary approach for achieving a broader and total view of historical reality though some would argue, that this need not necessarily be the most objective. Hitherto, in these exercises into inter-disciplinarity, the relationship of history and geography has, at best, been one of a ritual introductory necessity rather than of being central to the historical analysis. A major departure in this regard has been the valuable contribution of scholars like Lucien Febvre and Marc Bloch who, as a major initiators of this trend in the historiography of the 'Annales' school, laboured consciously to make historical geography as central to their analysis of bringing about total history in the context of rural France.[2] However, as rightly pointed out by Baker, history is still given to play a superior role in this interpretation because it is endowed with the ability to synthesize[3] and explain historical patterns, processes and structures of the human interactions with physical space.

From our point of view the interpretative direction given by the 'Annales' school has become the motive for us to take up a regional study for historical analysis because it is in this arena alone that the right balance between the role played by physical space and human time in understanding the past can best be highlighted. This has necessarily entailed a moving away from the stage of a study of the rise and fall of historical empires in broad scales of time to the smaller localities of village settlements which, over lesser time spans, saw the rise and fall of rural elites in terms of their relationships to each other as also with their subordinate co-habitants. It would have been simple enough for us to narrate the local events in a linear fashion and end up with multiple strands of political histories each relevant in its own right. However, instead, we found it challenging to take up the historical aspect of highlighting social change in a spatial context which was rural but always in interaction with the larger geopolitical dimensions of its existence. Therefore, in the following pages of this book we endeavour to place the complex texture of social stratification as continually changing in time against the backdrop of a physical space that was also dynamic and changing because of its interaction with the former. It is the inseparability of these two variables–time and space–of historical analysis that hinges on all our discussions in the following chapters of this book.

Historical research undertaken by us in the present study essentially aims at an analysis of stratified social relationships as arising out of the interaction between the material and the cultural variables located within specific parameters of time (1000 A.D.–1200 A.D.) and space (South Western Deccan). Our choice of the study of society has been prompted by the fact that social groups and their relationships are the ultimate expression of an interplay of the structural phenomena (social, economic, political and ideological) of any given culture and these afford us with an effective perspective to analyze several issues crucial to our comprehension of historical reality. We have found in this context that the early medieval period (of which our period of study forms a crucial part) affords us a potential ground to realize our aim since it has been identified in Indian history as an important phase of transition from the ancient to the medieval, with fundamental changes having occurred in the social, economic, political and ideological arenas during this period.[4]

In such a study an analysis of the relationship of the changing social structure to its physiographic setting is fundamental to our comprehension of the larger issues at stake, namely, the historical processes of State formation. Such a realization is an out come of our understanding that it is basically the interaction of society with its natural surroundings that chiefly motivates the development of the economy in the first place, resulting in the specific formation of the socio-economic and cultural set up in a particular way for any given human settlement. Importantly, we have attempted to show that while changes in social structure are fundamentally related to the changes in land relations at the economic base we cannot, at the same time, establish that the social and economic change was totally independent of the dominant ideology and the nature of polity of the time. We argue in this context that the economic base itself was relational to change due to the social and political forces under operation which were expressed through the formation of kin groups, marital relationships established within them, wars fought by them, forms of legitimation adopted by them and so on. All these helped in unleashing forces of a religious and political dimension which, in turn, had a very significant impact of defining the nature of socio-economic change.

We have further observed in this regard that the above phenomena have to be posited against the backdrop of a rural spatial setting. The primary and crucial stages in the growth and spread of settlements, both horizontally and vertically, at times led to either, the formation of an important node in the cluster of settlements surrounding it or, more often, signified a specific stage in the growth of rural settlement hierarchy. This has significant implications for our comprehension of historical change during the period of transition which is under scrutiny. Such a study would entail an analysis of not just the nature of social relationships. established at the level of intra and inter settlement patterns, but more importantly, the variability of the concomitant social formations at every stage of the growth in settlement structures sub-regionwise. Thus, an examination of rural social relationships would enable us to strike at the very roots of historical change, and enable a comprehensive understanding of historical reality at the micro level. This has encouraged us to demarcate new regional and social boundaries of research particularly in relation to the study of state and society which defy any universalization of specific structural formations.

Hitherto, the major focus of historical analysis has been either, the northern part of India constituting the Gangetic basin as the core or, the extreme South constituting the Kaveri basin as the core.[5] This approach largely keeps in tune with the general trend of a greater emphasis invariably being laid on writing the history of "nuclear" areas.[6] Historiographical attention on the Deccan in a similar way has been dependent largely upon the degree of eminence that each of the physiographical entities that were part of it have achieved, corresponding to specific periods of historical time. Thus, north western Deccan and eastern Deccan, during the early historical period, have attracted the attention of scholars owing to the large scale socio-economic development under the rule of the Śātavāhanas and the Ikshvākus. Similarly, the Vengi region, with its core in the deltaic zone of Coastal Andhra had been a considerable area of attraction due to its fertility and thus, during the early medieval period it had emerged as a region of strategic and economic importance to become a widely contested area in history. Therefore, this part of the eastern Deccan came into historiographical prominence for the early medieval period too.

The south western region of the Deccan, which does not fall under the category of a 'nuclear' area has not attracted much historical scholarship in terms of the identification of its elements and nature of change for the early medieval period. This part of the Deccan which is substantially covered by the Raichur Doab, was an actively contested area under the Vijayanagara rulers but even this extremely fertile and strategic zone has, in a large measure, stood neglected in the historical scholarship of the early medieval period. When it did figure in the conventional historical literature as part of the Karnataka State or, at times on history of the state of Andhra Pradesh, it was largely projected either, as a warring zone or, was subsumed under the general descriptions of issues focussed elsewhere. Thus, the writing of chronologies, genealogies, political history and also, the social and economic aspects of it, have been worked upon from the inscriptional sources of this region from a descriptive point of view. However, information on how different social groups were integrated into the administration and the complex fabric of the socio-economic life has been left out or have been treated only marginally. For instance, when G.R. Kuppuswamy, while writing the economic history of the entire state of present day Karnataka for the early medieval period, opines that "some of the geographically unprotected but fertile regions such as Raichur district were more vulnerable to attacks and were often drenched in blood as a result of the violent rivalry between the empires",[7] he is focussing primarily on the how this economically viable zone was mainly the focus of military activity. On the other hand, cognizance has been taken of by various scholars on describing, to a certain extent, the temples located here.

This neglect has prompted us to take up the south western Deccan as our specific area of study as much remains to be done on identifying crucial elements of historical change in this region. Also, as mentioned above, if importance has to be given to historical geography in our analysis the choice of the south western Deccan as the specific area of historical analysis during the early medieval period stands justified because of its unique geographical situation and ecological features. This poses a requisite challenge for historians who wish to highlight geographical specificity in time. By taking up this study of an area, at a period of time when it had not emerged into prominence in terms of either, the rise of a large empire or, in terms of the attainment of a high degree of socio-economic development and advancement, we are doing away with the general trend of writing history which normally tends to focus upon 'nuclear' and by extension much researched areas of historical study during periods which usually coincide with the rule of great empires. In particular, the rise in importance of the Raichur Doab during the Vijayanagara period adds particular relevance to the present study. This is so because, since our focus is on the early medieval period prior to Vijajanagar rule, we can examine various ingredients of the historical processes that provided the crucial background for the rise and development of this area to become a viable zone of contestation and political focus during later medieval times. Further, this was not unrelated to the economic changes in the Raichur Doab during the early medieval period which was closely dependant on the spread of rural settlements located here prior to the period of Vijayanagara rule. Its location strategically between two major rivers, namely the Krishna and the Tungabhadra, has been studied by us in relation to its contiguous areas as part of the region defined by us as south western Deccan in order to compare and highlight the economic potential of this particular sub-region *vis-a-vis* the other two.

In doing so we wish to emphasize a significant historiographical departure. Surely, the present micro level study is a regional history and if we must accept the well formulated consensus amongst scholars that "regions are.... Products of history",[8] it is best that we identify and recognize the most meaningful territorial entities for historical analysis. The way we have proposed to do this in the following pages of this book is to identify regions as closely as possible to their technical geographical character, not simply in terms of their homogeneity but, also in terms of their heterogendity since the former is never absolute. Secondly, we have made a conscious attempt at underlining the features of historical continuity from one phase of the region's development to another so that here again, there is no erroneous impression left that regions are static in time. The boundaries of a region, are thus not rigid and may shift from time to time. However, if we are able to grapple with its historical specificity in terms of an appropriate level of spatial and political, economic and cultural homogeneity, this would enable us to move away from a parochialization and regionalization of history, and then the historian's construction of 'regions' is a positive endeavour. It allows a healthy possibility of exploring the historical interplay between economic, social, political and cultural factors at the micro level. By not adhering to a single administrative boundary giving preference to one region over the other, by not accepting a given ethnic criteria for defining our region of study and by not highlighting the political boundaries of one particular political dynasty of the past as the boundaries of our research subject, we hope to have been able to give direction and move away from such negative phenomena as 'regionalism' and 'communalism' that are used to define regions.

Our area of study **(Map I)** in terms of its present day administrative boundaries of modern India's linguistic states constitutes the eastern part of the Dharwar district, the southern parts of Bijapur and Gulbarga districts and the entire Raichur district located in the Karnataka State and the western part of the Mahaboobnagar and Kurnool districts of Andhra Pradesh. To overcome the rigid linguistic boundaries of consideration we have further attempted to classify our area of study into three sub-regions **(Map II)** which correspond largely to the local topographical variations. On this basis we have been able to identify potential zones of fertile tracts of early settlements at the micro level of space. In this context we have observed that settlement sites such as Badami, Pattadakal and Aihole of sub-region A and Alampur of sub-region C had emerged into historical prominence as temple sites much earlier to our period of study, *i.e.,* during the sixth century itself. This stands in contrast to the settlements of sub-region B which constitutes largely the Raichur Doab, including the eastern part of Dharwar district, most of which have their origins during our period of study. With a large number of inscriptions and temple sites concentrated here, we have taken up this area for special focus and discussion in our analysis as it affords as with an immense potential to comprehend various dimentions of rural social formations located within specific parameters of time (1000 A.D.-1200 A.D.). Further, recent spurt of micro level studies conducted with a non-Marxist approach for various regions of India have shown how positive processes of state formation took place

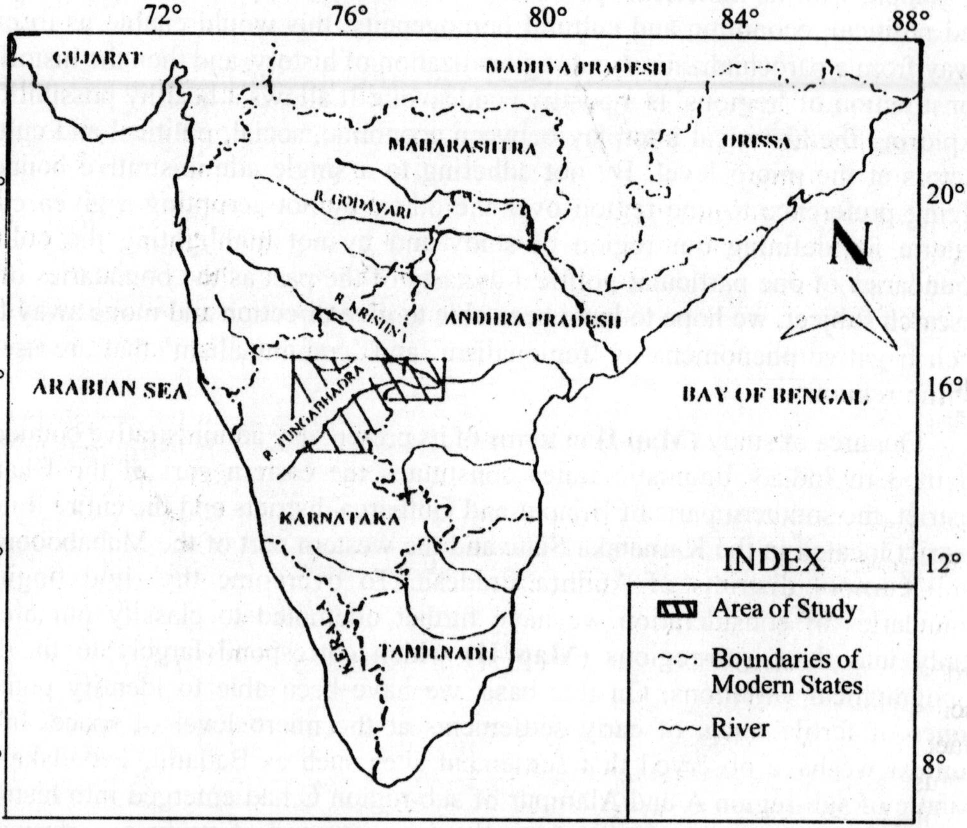

Map I : AREA OF STUDY

during the early medieval period to give rise to the multiple regional identities that India is composed of today. Importantly, these writings have put forth the paradigm of looking at the nature of state formation in the regions in terms of an integration of local bases of power which led to the emergence of overarching state systems.[9] This moves away from the view that the rise of regional kingdoms in the early medieval period should only be understood in terms of decentralization of a pan–Indian polity and therefore, state apparatus being imposed from above. It is in the light of the former view that we wish to align ourselves in conducting this regional study of state formation as representing a stratified social set up which was very much dependant on the spread of rural settlements. The ultimate aim in this book is to analyze the extent to which one can identify the factors that gave birth to a certain kind of social stratification and the reasons for the spread and development of rural settlements. The answer to both these agendas would enable us to define the particular nature of the growth of a regional identity in all its implications.

In order to tackle the complexities of social stratification and rural settlements in the context of our study, we have mainly relied upon the inscriptional sources of the period belonging to and issued by such dynasties as the Chālukyas of Kalyāṇi, the Kalāchuris of Kalyāṇi, the Yādavas of Devagiri and the Hoysalas of Dwarasamudra and innummerable local ruling families who ruled different parts of the south-western Deccan between the period 1000 A.D.-1200 A.D. A majority of the inscriptional data available to us for our area of study is in the Kannada language and characters which have been edited and some of them have translated. Apart from the Kannada inscriptions we have also used inscriptions in this book belonging to the Telugu and Sanskrit languages. We wish to underline in this regard that we have had to go beyond the published material and access the transcripts of inscriptional sources available at the Department of Epigraphy, Archaeological Survey India, Mysore and the State Department of Archaeology and Museums, Hyderabad.[10] Particularly those belonging to the Raichur district have not been published in the same organised manner as those belonging to the Dharwar and Bijapur districts of Karnataka. Similarly, the materials for the early medieval period in the western part of the Kurnool district and Gadwal taluq in the Mahaboobnagar district of Andhra Pradesh were found to be extremely scanty. It was difficult to locate any inscriptions in the Raichur taluq.[11] A majority of the inscriptions examined by us have, however, been collected from the major epigraphic journals/annual reports : (i) *Annual Reports on South Indian Epigraphy,* (ii) *Epigraphia Indica,* (iii) *Epigraphia Andhrica,* (iv) *South Indian Inscriptions* (Bombay-Karnataka Series), (v) *Indian Antiquary,* (vi) *Hyderabad Archaeological Series*, (vii) *A.P. Government Archaeological Series,* (viii) *Karnataka Inscriptions,* (ix) *Journal of Karnataka Historical Research Society*, (x) *Journal of the Bombay*

Branch of Royal Asiatic Society, (xi) *Journal of the Royal Asiatic Society of Great Britain,* (xii) *Journal of the Andhra Historical Research Society,* (xiii) *A Corpus of Inscriptions in the Kannada Districts of Hyderabad State,* (xiv) *Copper Plate Inscriptions of A.P. State Museum.* These inscriptions have been collected and edited since the year 1894 by eminent epigraphists like J.F. Fleet, Lionel D. Barnett, R.G. Bhandarkar, S.K. Dikshit, G.S. Gai, P.B. Desai, R.S. Panchamukhi, N. Lakshminarayana Rao and Krishna Sastri. As aids to further understanding the particular meaning of terms, D.C. Sircar's monumental work, *Epigraphical Glossary* (Delhi, 1966) and K. Ishwara Dutt's *Inscriptional Glossary of Andhra Pradesh* (Hyderabad, 1967) have been drawn upon. In particular, to aid our translations of the Kannada terms in the inscriptional sources of our study, we have made use of Kittel's *Kannada-English Dictionary* (London, 1894).[12] We have made use of these sources in particular to understand the literal meanings of various terms mentioned in the above inscriptions. Literary sources have only been marginally used mainly to draw upon the legal rules pertaining to property relations.[13]

The inscriptional sources of the early medieval period are nothing but legal documents recording the dominant economic activity of the period, namely, the land transactions. In the process we get to know about various social groups through the functions they performed and the rural settlements in the context of how and where these grants were made. We are well aware that the inscriptional sources available to us do not give any direct information regarding such issues as the nature of subjection of certain social groups we wish to enquire into. Further, not all aspects of social stratification of rural settlements are available in these sources in an explicit manner. This warrants, on our part, a critical and through analysis of the data available so as to delve into the implicit context of the source as a whole. We have further been cautioned in this regard that "inscriptions by their very nature tend to cause the historian to lay disproportionate stress on the institutions which house them namely the temples".[14] In fact, it would be a truism to stake that any historical fact whether literary or, epigraphic including archaeological,[15] cannot totally escape from some element of subjectivity. In our opinion, it is the approach or, the methodology adopted by the researcher that conditions the interpretation of the source and not vice-versa. We have found in the process of our study that the availability of a large majority of the data in the temple institutions itself is a significant pointer to the importance attached to the temple at a time when the temple building activity and the temple as an ideological institution was just gaining a concrete shape. It's popularity, at least among the dominant strata of the social groups, for various reasons described in the text cannot be sidelined as of no consequence to the larger issues at stake. But, this does not in any way mean that the entire economic and social activity during this period was temple-centric. That there did exist a productive social base outside the temple institution which can be culled out through the projection of the dominant economic activity itself in the context of various grants made to the temple. For example, in the case of a majority of commodities granted one can clearly gauge the crucial involvement of social groups who have not been mentioned in the inscription but who were clearly involved in the actual production of the commodities thus mentioned. Further, occasional mention of certain names of subject peasantry, or, the pastoral and hunting groups provide significant clues to comprehend several issues not directly related to the temple institutions from the inscriptional sources located in temples. It has been aptly and pertinently stated with regard to the nature of source material available for the early medieval period in India that a "document of the kind of the Fournier Register, on the basis of which Emmanuel le Roy Ladurie reconstructed the fascinating profile of peripheral village society in medieval France, is simply unavailable for a researcher on early medieval India".[16] In the face of these serious limitations, one is left with no choice but to make use of the inscriptional data in the best possible way to get across the historical reality during the early medieval period. It may also be stated at this juncture that these inscriptional sources are far more pervasive than individual historical chronicles and biographics. This is so mainly because of their distribution at various places. Often, their location in very small temples located in hitherto unknown village settlements sheds considerable light on the history of these small localities. Also, given the lack of historical literature of India as a whole, the inscriptions provide some of the rare data on linear historical events which would otherwise not be available for historical enquiry at all.

We have proposed to carry out our analysis of the inscriptional data at three levels. As a part of the first level of the data analysis we have taken up the following tasks.

Ia : First of all, in order to cull out the requisite information from the inscriptions, we have charted out what the inscriptions directly tell us on the basis of the main themes of analysis relating to the social, the economic, the spatial and the ideological. This information has been plotted out in charts accompanying the four chapters on these themes. The charts on social groups (I A B C) entitled 'Social Context' mainly depict various terms used in the inscriptional sources to describe them in the context of their political, economic and religious functioning. As such we have divided them on the basis of their roles as the main ruler, local potentate, state functionary, *brāhmaṇa, mahāhjana,* cultural groups in the temple and peasants. These are the coloumn headings given for this particular chart. Further, their mention in the capacity of donors and donees which forms a crucial clue to comprehend the economic, political and ideological power of these social groups has also been taken into account and marked out in the chart. To comprehend the economic aspect (II A B C) entitled Economic Context' of our study we made charts on the basis of the context in which the grants were made which includes the information in the various columns in this chart on the nature of grants made and various immunities attached to the grants. Coupled with this basic information, reference to revenue terms and taxes and the irrigation works have been taken note of. We have depicted all these against the columns on donor and donee so as to comprehend the status and the nature of the social groups in the larger economic setting.

Thirdly, to comprehend the physical space (III A B C) entitled 'Spatial Context' we have charted out the names of places and the categories which these belong to, indicated through the suffixes attached to them, such as *palli, vāḍa, ūr, grāma* and so on. Along with this information delineated in the columns of this chart through appropriate symbols, the contextual references of the space, whether rural or, urban, and the special status some of these were accorded, such as *agrahāra,* marked by the existence of temples in them, have been marked out in the chart so as to get a comprehensive understanding of the nature of space. Finally, the charts on ideology (IV A B C) entitled 'Ideological Context' have taken into account various aspects of the role of the temple and religious activity during this period. Importantly, we have attempted in these charts to list the patrons corresponding to the objects of their patronage such as the temples/deities, Vedic learning, priests and sects. Coupled with this information the specific purposes of the patronage extended to such aspects as the repairs and the construction of temple institutions, rituals and festivals performed in the temples and the names of various cultural groups involved in the services of the temple have been mentioned. Further, we have made use of common symbols (given at the end of each chart in the form of a *Key*) of various types to represent the data on hand so that the dominant trends of our analysis are indicted through a perusal of information across the different charts. We wish to underscore in this regard that having divided our study into various themes and categories, we do not however, propose to study these issues in compartments, independent of each other. All the above aspects have been integrated and correlated with each other in other to get a comprehensive picture of various dimensions in the textual analysis.

Ib : For the management of the inscriptional data thus chartered out we have made use of the computer. We have chalked a programme to enter all the above-mentioned direct data available from inscriptions into the computer. This has been then sorted out on the date and sub-regional basis to get a pattern of sequential analysis of the issues, both in terms of chronology and regional specificity.

II : At the second level our endeavours in depicting the inscriptional data in the form of various charts has been a natural corollary to our wider intention of comprehending the heterogeneity embedded in the inscriptional source as a whole. Thus we have basically attempted here to break the totality of the epigraphic source into various fragments of information with the hope that it would enable us to look even at the minutest details available in the sources. This is against the background of the first level of analysis which was divided into four categories of information such as the social, the economic, the spatial and the ideological. To further comprehend variations within each of the columns in these categories, we have divided it into several more pieces of information. This has been done because inscriptions do not give a uniform pattern of supplying information. Thus for example, to understand various aspects of social stratification among dominant groups, the different designations and the names of the individual persons/groups of persons that denote either their political, economic or social status have been used for classification. On this basis we have been able to classify the data on social groups into those belonging to the apex of the political structure such as the main ruling family chiefs designated mostly through such terms as *mahārājādhirāja*, who are then followed by the local potentates or, the supra local ruling groups designated through such as the *mahāmaṇḍaleśvaras* who are then followed by a variety of local level functionaries known through such terms as *gāvuṇḍas, heggaḍe, pergaḍe* and so on. Similarly, social groups mentioned in the context of their religious dominance have been comprehended separately under the category of the *mahājana,* various non-*Brahmanical* religious heads and so on. On similar lines, the direct information available for the individual/groups of artisans and the merchant groups who represent a socio-economic category, has been taken into account separately. Peasant groups represented through their corporated organizations have again been separated from other social groups. Finally the socio-cultural groups operating in the service of the temples have also been taken into account separately.

The data available for the economic structure of the period under study has been broken up into various pieces of information available for the nature of the grants made such as those of the land, villages, commodities, cash, gold, revenue and so on. Information available on the nature of soils, irrigation system and the immunities attached to the grants have been picked up simultaneously as depicting different strands of the nature of economy during the period of study. Next, we have comprehended the nature of space/settlement unit in as small a unit as possible. We have thus divided the nomenclature available for settlements into various categories of suffixes such as the *palli, vāḍa, ūr, grāma, pura, paṭṭana* and so on which has enabled us to graphically present the variety of ways through which physical space was conceived of during the period under study. Similarly, information available on the ideological dimension of the period has been classified into headings largely depending on the context in which it was mentioned. To list the various parts of the information available on ideology the names of various deities housed in the temple, local sects and priests, vedic learning and rituals performed in the temples, social groups involved in temple functions have all been minutely charted out. Through such a categorization we have attempted to comprehend the specific nature of information available to us which is strongly suggestive of the complex nature of the data on hand. Thus with the help of various designations and titles mentioned in the context of the social groups, we have been able to comprehend the basic levels of hierarchy present in them. Similarly, the specific nature of the grants made, depict the nature of the economic structure. On the other hand, various names of the places attached with a variety of suffixes highlight the multiple nature of settlement structures present in the area of our study. Similarly, one has been able to gauge in clear contours the heterogeneous belief systems present at this time with the help of the specific names of Gods, sects and priests that emerge at this level of data analysis. In particular the changing nature of all these aspects has been observed by us by positing them in chronological parameters. We wish to clarify at this juncture that we do not however, intend to take up the study of above elements as rigid entities totally divorced from each other. Importantly, we propose to comprehend these in close relation to each piece of information located within each broad category, which is then crucially linked up to the context in which all the above data find mentioned. Thus, the fragments of inscriptional data when tied up to each other and viewed in relation to their contextual mention, form the totality of the source and thus becomes crucial in reconstructing the specificities in historical formation.

III : As a part of the third level of data analysis we have therefore attempted an analysis of various terms culled out from the inscriptions under study and charted out as mentioned above at the first and second level of analysis. This has been done by correlating the direct information given to us through the inscriptions and understanding the contextual meaning of the various social groups and settlements. This had necessarily to be done in the light of what other scholars have written on the meaning of various terms as often, there are no single and absolute clearly acceptable meanings agreeable to everybody. This has further led on to arriving at certain conclusions over various issues of our study which differ in many ways from what earlier historians have written about the aspects taken up for study in this book. These conclusions have been elaborately presented at the end—**Recaptulation and Conclusions** so as to make a significant contribution to the existing state of knowledge on the subject.

First and foremost, to embark on this task we have, in **Chapter 1 : Historiographical Context,** ventured to point out the existing lacunae and question some of the existing methodological biases. A large part of this chapter deals with outlining the historiographical positions taken by earlier scholars. We have chosen to discuss these under four themes : society, economy, rural space or village communities and ideology. While attempting to test the specific data of the region under study with generalizations made by R.S. Sharma on the nature of the land grant economy, we propose to emphasize upon the study of the stratified society of the early medieval period, not merely in terms of descriptions of various social groups as determined by their economic status in the rural milieu of the period. But more importantly, we wish to align ourselves with the micro level studies conducted within a non-Marxist approach for various regions of India which have emphasized upon positive process of state formation during the early medieval period. It is pertinent to underscore at this juncture that this view describes society in terms of an integration of local bases of power into overarching state systems. It is against the background of these views delineated in this chapter that we wish to conduct this study as representing a stratified social set up of the rural settlements located at the level of a specific micro region within a small chronological parameter of 1000 A.D. to 1200 A.D. We have accepted in this regard to term this period as being part of what today scholars have defined as the early medieval period.

In **Chapter II : Geo-Political Context** we intend to elaborate upon the impact of the geographical configuration of our area of study which can be seen most conspicuously in the nature of the political power structure that evolved at this time. The rulers of the main ruling dynasties while basing themselves outside the area delineated for study, tried to control the fertile tracts between the rivers Krishna and Tungabhadra. It is chiefly in these processes of political control which the chiefs of the main ruling family tried to establish over their area of conquest, that one can see the south-western Deccan emerge as a zone for the legitimation of political power. It is in relation to these processes of state control exercised over the local bases of power that we shall try to correlate and integrate our analysis which primarily hinges on the theoretical stand taken by us that the social groups and their relationship to rural space was defined, to a large extent, by the existing geographical configurations. This chapter thus highlights the political levels of power structure which we intend to show was a necessary background for a study of several crucial issues regarding the social relations in the rural space. We highlight this against the background of recent writing on state-formation for the early medieval period.

Having outlined the regional dimension of local state formation in relation to our specific micro level space located within specific parameters of time (1000 A.D.-1200 A.D.) we next proceed to discuss the main body of the book in terms of how, given the intersection of time and space outlined in **Chapter II,** the specific forms of socio-economic and cultural formations emerge. All these aspects have been linked up by us to the pan-Indian cultural matrix as the formation of the region was not taking place in total isolation to the general trends in the socio-economic and cultural changes of the early medieval period on the Indian sub-continent as a whole.

We have, in **Chapter III : Social Context,** proceeded to comprehend the nature of social stratification as constituting relations of dominance and subordination which, we argue, are expressed in different forms and at various levels of social change. Thus, it is our intention to show how at the politico-economic level we have the emergence of several dominant social groups at the local and supra local level of state power expressed through various designations and titles conferred on them. We shall further highlight in this context that while the designations held by each of these groups indicate for us the political dimension of the nature of stratification, their capacity to make grants is indicative of the economic hold that these groups had over their respective bases of power as owners of land and its resources. Finally, we converge to discuss that the consequent social power held by these groups is indicated to us through the mention of family names in the context of their description. On the basis of their description we intend to highlight the existence of several layers of relationships of domination and subordination existing within rural, local and supra local society. It is simultaneously our aim to focus on change particularly around the turn of the 12th century A.D. wherein several new terms of political ranking begin to emerge. This, we argue, is also indicative of the fact that more and more new social groups were being conferred political ranks as the expansion and consolidation of the state structure was taking place. Our next major theme of analysis in this chapter is to discuss how at the politico-religious levels of dominance we have such groups as the *brāhmaṇa* and the *mahājana,* and several individual non-*brāhmaṇa* ideologues who attained their economic power as a result of the state initiative in its attempt at legitimization by giving these groups land grants. It is chiefly in the context of the management of landed property by the above described dominant groups that we get to know about the existence of the subject groups whose mention in the sources is extremely limited. We next intend to discuss how their existence can be made on the basis of allusions made to them in the context of references to the land tenurial patterns or, the tax terms. Finally, in this chapter it is our intention to focus at the economic level, particularly from the beginning of the 12th century A.D., when a wide variety of social groups are mentioned in the inscriptions as participating in various types of economic activities. We describe these groups in relation to their activities in the agrarian, artisanal and the non-agrarian or mercantile arenas. Far from being homogenous, these social groups were highly stratified giving rise to complex social relations of interdependence between various groups as also within the dominant ones themselves.

Our next focus of attention is on analyzing the details of the **Economic Context in Chapter IV.** The chronological dimensions of social change when comprehended in relation to the spatial parameters of their location get crystallized in the form of economic change which is marked by a predominance of agrarian activity for a greater part of the 11th century A.D. Its gradual infiltration into an urban like economy by the turn of the 12th century A.D. can be clearly gauged through the change in the nature of grants made by various social groups. In the 11th century A.D. there is a predominant tendency to grant in lands which is slowly replaced, by the beginning of the 12th century A.D., with a majority of grants being made in commodities, cash and revenue. Social and economic change thus envisaged had wider implications for the growth in the rural settlement structures both in terms of their horizontal spread (broadening the productive sphere depending upon the fertility of soil and development and investment in irrigation) and vertical rise (socio-economic advancement from rural to urban) in their hierarchy.

In this chapter we also discuss the various ramifications of the land revenue structure and how investment of various types of grants led to the growth and importance of the *agrahāra* settlements and the temple institution. We have also proposed to underscore in this regard the variety of ways in which land tenurial patterns emerge and the significant changes that these undergo as a result of the initiative taken by various dominant social groups in making grants to religious institutions, namely, the temples. In the process, significant care was taken by these groups in improving the agrarian production by introducing various irrigation structures and employing labour which we also propose to take up for analysis. Further, the implications it had, in terms of a spurt in the non-agrarian activity, such as the artisanal and mercantile production, form an integral part of our discussion on the economic structure of our study.

In **Chapter IV : on the Spatial Context** we propose to give all details on the various types of place names and highlight their meaning in the context of the views of other scholars on the subject. A comprehension of the hierarchical nature of the settlement patterns can however be obtained by analyzing them in the context of the suffixes attached to individual settlements (*palli, vāḍa, ūr, grāma, paṭṭaṇa*) coupled with the contextual references made to them in terms of the socio-economic activity operating around them. We also intend in this context to comprehend the nature of the settlement space in relation to its physical location, wherein various terms such as *giri* (mountain), *kallu* (stone), *gere* (tank) and so on suffixed to some of these settlements signify the nature of their locales and further go to testify the complex nature of the settlement patterns during the period of study. In fact, the changing and the dynamic scenario of space has been focussed upon in this study. In this regard, our search for the questions on how certain categories of settlements emerged into prominence at a particular point in time leading to the formation of important nodes in the hierarchical pattern, is the central most strand of analysis.

To elaborate upon this phenomenon further one has to go beyond the spatial limits and search for the factors of change in the socio-political processes leading to the formation of local and supra local power structures which, we argue, were identified chiefly by the spatial context in which they were located. This we highlight, required among other things, improvement in the economic base by bringing more and more area into the vortex of the State structure at various levels through the improvement of techniques of crop production by augmenting the availability of water supply through the construction of tanks and so on. It also simultaneously needed legitimation of the politico-economic urges of local elites which began to be expressed through the creation of *agrahāra* and temple establishments. We discuss these points towards the end of **chapter V.** In essence, the emergence of certain settlements with a potential for the growth in the agrarian base from a physical into ideological space marked a crucial stage in the evolution of not just the settlement hierarchy, but importantly, it signified a socio-economic advancement of society achieved through the interaction of a host of historical factors. In such a transformation the role played by the temple institution as a tool of legitimation and integration in the hands of various social groups representing different levels of state structure was of particular significance. We turn to examine these two points in the last chapter.

Chapter VI is on the **Ideological Context** wherein we intend to explain how the political, economic and social spheres of activity conglomerate on the religious space represented by the temple institution. During the period of study the temple emerged as an important mechanism of redistribution of resources on the one hand, and on the other, into an overlord having the services of several social groups at its disposal. Importantly, the ideological attributes of the temple institution had wider implications in shaping the socio-political relations which we attempt to especially focus upon in this chapter. In this regard on the one hand, the temple helped in legitimizing the political power and status of various groups patronizing it and on the other, it helped in the spread of the state system to local levels through appropriation of the local cults and the consequent absorption of the local 'tribal' groups into its vortex at various levels. We intend to elaborate some of these issues as can be seen in the expansion of the settlements to new areas coupled with the rise in the number of temple institutions. Herein lies the importance of the role of temple as a mediator between the religious and secular space of the productive areas. Without large scale surplus production the temple would not have been able to rise in the first place. It is in these processes of mediation and integration that the temple became a popular platform for the fusion of local belief systems represented by various sects of Purāṇic Hinduism. In the present area of study we highlight the particular sects of Śaivism that grew in popularity during this period. It has been noted by us that Vaiṣṇavism and Jainism to a lesser extent were also patronized. However, the most popular and powerful ideological forces in this period and area of study was Kālāmukha Śaivism. In particular the latter find predominant mention in the inscriptional sources of our study wherein the ever increasing number and variety of deities coupled with various names of priests emerge as representing multiple belief systems of the local populace. That these had wider implications in terms of acculturating the new social groups into the mainstream of Brahmanism when their belief systems were integrated into the temple centred Bhakti movement by various levels of state structure form crucial manifestations of ideological dimensions of the period under consideration. The dominant ideology of the Brahmanism projected by the chiefs of the main ruling family in their attempts at legitimation also thrived and this has been discussed by us towards the end of this chapter. Importantly, the connecting threads of cultural integration between the dominant ideology operating at a pan Indian level and the local belief systems, at the regional level operating in a similar vein co-existed together. Sometimes exhibiting certain contradictions which were resolved only through the exertion of power.

The socio-economic processes of change when viewed from a regional perspective were intertwined into the complex processes of state formation which initiated several changes at the local level enabling an integration of various ideological forces which, in turn, combined to transform the socio-economic and cultural set up of early medieval south-western Deccan. The last part of the work, **Recaptulation and Conclusions** highlights major contributions of the present study. We have also suggested the possibility that for a study located in pre-modern India, the material and ideological forces have to be studied in relation to each other so as to theoretically see the inseparability of the secular and the religious. It shall not be out of place to state at the outset that this book hopes to present a fresh perspective on how the study of small regions in all their complexity can be done. The major conclusions are followed by a list of all the sources consulted by us while writing this book in the form of a consolidated **Bibliography.** This book is also accompanied by 4 sets of charts and 5 maps to help illustrate better the textual and spatial material incorporated by us in understanding **Rural Settlements and Stratification in South Western Deccan–1000 A.D.-1200 A.D.**

REFERENCES

1. Inaugural Address entitled, 'The Problems and Prospects of Regional History : Some Questions of Methodology, delivered by S. Bhattacharya at the ICHR zonal seminar *Elements of Transition in the History of the Deccan*, February 6-9, 1988, organized by the Department of History, University of Hyderabad (Cyclostyled), p. 1.
2. Alan R.H. Baker, 'Reflections on the Relations of Historical Geography and the Annales school of History', in Alan R.H. Baker and Derek Gregory (ed.), *Explorations*

in Historical Geography : Interpretative Essays, Cambridge University Press, 1988, pp. 4-5.

3. *Ibid.*, p. 4; p. 7.
4. That there has been transition from an ancient period marked by crucial changes in the socio-economic and political ideological set up during the early medieval period (normally associated with the period between 5th-13th centuries A.D.) has been well attested to in various historical works written with specific focus on this period of Indian history. Works in this direction have particularly been initiated by the Marxist historians who have studied these changes under the rubric of 'Indian Feudalism' as propounded by the pioneering work of R.S. Sharma's *Indian Feudalism* (A.D. 300-1200), Macmillan, Delhi, 1980. Without going into the historical debate surrounding the above characterization at this stage, we wish to emphasize on the notion of historical change initiated by these scholars for defining the early medieval period.
5. The historiographical bias for the early medieval period can be understood not just in relation to the availability of the large corpus of epigraphical data in the nuclear areas or river basins, but importantly, that this data has been edited and published in a systematic way in various journals and which had a considerable role to play in attracting a majority of scholars, including foreign scholars, to write on these regions.
6. B. Subbarao, *Personality of India : Pre and Proto Historic Foundation of India and Pakistan,* Baroda, 1958, pp. 85-140. In this work, the author introduces us to the concept of historical geography wherein different regions of India are divided into these categories of nuclear areas (with vast tracts of fertile land and therefore, possess the ability to support large empires), which are followed by the areas of relative isolation (regions of communications and migrations) and the areas of isolation (the blind alleys of civilization in India) which were supposed to have been inhabited by the tribal populace and therefore, remained backward. The above formulations based on geographical determinism do not, however, stand tenable for our research. Our intention was mainly to highlight the concept of nuclearity introduced by the author in comprehending the relationship of geography of historical developments.
7. G.R. Kuppuswamy, *Economic Conditions in Karnataka* (A.D. 973-A.D. 1336) Dharwar, 1975, p. 9.
8. S. Bhattacharya, *op. cit.*, 1988, p. 4.
9. B.D. Chattopadhyaya, *The Making of Early Medieval India,* OUP, Delhi, 1994, pp. 34-35.
10. To understand some of these we have taken special help from : Mr. Subrahmaniam (known popularly as Mysore Pandit), eminent epigraphist and also Dr. P.V.P. Sastry, Deputy Director (retired), Archaeology and Museums, Hyderabad.
11. When we enquired about the lack of information on Raichur taluq of the Raichur district during the early medieval period, Dr. K.V. Ramesh, former Director, Office of Epigraphy, Mysore expressed the possibility of it being a less settled area during this period as it was infested with thick jungles on the one hand and on the other, according to him, the constant wars fought in this area might have rendered any survival of the

epigraphical evidence extremely difficult. On the other hand, the authorities at the office of Archaeology and Museums at Hyderabad have expressed their inability to explicate the reasons for the less availability of the inscriptional data on Gadwal taluq and certain parts of Kurnool district relevant to our study during the early medieval period and have been extremely cooperative in extending whatever help they could in gaining access to the transcripts available with them. It is interesting to note that in these areas, inscriptional data for the Vijayanagara period is available in plenty.

12. To comprehend the historical significance of most of these terms, we have however, depended upon the secondary sources pertaining to our area of study.
13. P.V. Kane, *History of Dharmaśāstra* (Ancient and Medieval Religious and Civil Law), II, I, Bhandarkar Oriental Research Institute, Poona, 1974 (2nd ed.).
14. Velcheru Narayana Rao, David Shulman, Sanjay Subramanyam, *Symbols of Substance Court and State in Nayaka Period Tamil Nadu,* OUP, Delhi, 1992, p. 31.
15. R.S. Sharma has drawn our attention in this regard to the non-availability of archaeological evidence for rural sites during the early medieval period, which according to him, are attributable in a large measure to the neglect of archaeologists who have hitherto concentrated mainly on the urban sites of early India. See his *Urban Decay in India,* Delhi, 1987, p. 3.
16. B.D Chattopadhyaya, *Aspects of Rural Settlements and Rural Society in Early Medieval India,* Calcutta, 1990, p. 1.

1

HISTORIOGRAPHICAL CONTEXT

We are generally introduced to the discipline of history writing with the understanding that our endeavour in doing so should encompass all events, institutions, ideas and relationships between them to define the human past. Since many of the past societies and their practices cannot be retrieved through simple devises of acculmulating "given data", the interpretations of historians become seminal to our understanding of any aspect of the past. At the first level, as already delineated by us above in the **Introduction and Sources,** the historians analyze the relics and traces (is in the present case, inscriptions) left by past human action and therefore, must handle what scholars generally term as primary sources. In this chapter, however, we propose to focus on the second level of knowledge about the past, namely, in terms of what historians have interpreted and systematically analyzed in what Arthur Marwick in a recent article calls : "the human past as it is known from the *work of historians",*[1] (emphasis added). This body of knowledge thus generated becomes the historiographical context without which no informed historical writing can proceed. We also need to emphasize at the outset that historians, like other social scientists, have been influenced by various intellectual theories of explanation like Positivism, Marxism, Structuralism and so on. The modes of all types of epistemological analysis–'positivist', 'humanist', 'idealist', or 'materialist'–are different but, they share a common aim, namely, identifying a rational scientific method as opposed to the earlier, pre-modern concerns with the metaphysical explanations. We need to stress this here because an ancient society like India hardly presents us with texts that can be termed in the strict sense as 'historical'. Therefore, almost all of the above modes of historical explanation have had to grapple, with the problem of 'historical fact' in the context of India. Notwithstanding this basic problem, there have been several historiographical avenues that Indian historians have tread on. We next turn to closely focus on some of these as are relevant to the present study.

History has been defined as "a continuous process of interaction between the historian and his facts, an unending dialogue between the past and the present".[2]

This can be aptly applied to the study of the early Indian past wherein our comprehensions of it have undergone significant transformations; these being concomitant to changes in the interpretations and methodology that the scholars writing on it have adopted. In giving a brief review of the historical works pertaining to the region and period under study, we have classified these into three broad categories of historical writing. They are largely indicative of the major shifts in the methods of analysis in the writing of history and are, therefore, not chronologically exclusive. Importantly, one has attempted here to comprehend these approaches in methodology in their specific relation to the themes of analysis undertaken by scholars which correspond squarely to the dominant issues tackled by us in our research such as the different aspects of society, economy, rural set up and ideology of the early medieval period. We focus in this survey on writings pertaining to South India as a whole and the Deccan in particular.

In the conventional historical works on society, written within the positivistic methodological framework, we have two main strands in the approach to understanding various aspects of early social history. These are those works that deal with political/dynastic history perse and only make incidental references to the social set up of the period. Some of the writings that fall in this category are those of Nilakanta Sastri,[3] A.S. Altekar[4] and Venkataramanayya.[5] In the second category the focus shifts from the study of dynasties to a more focussed description of social and economic conditions. In this category we have the works of A.V. Krishnamurthy,[6] K. Sundaram,[7] S. Gururajachar,[8] Jyotsna Kamat[9] and others[10] who deal with specific groups in society that have direct and prolific mention in the inscriptional sources under study. We have clubbed all these works together chiefly because, while the latter's attention shifts from one aspect of the historical study to the other, their basic method of historical analysis remains 'conventional' in that positivism is still the guiding spirit with the essential aim being to accumulate empirical date on the subject rather than its analysis.

To begin, with, one finds that in all these writings the caste/*varṇa* division was accepted a prior as the basic determinant for understanding the division of the social classes in the early south Indian context. This is best articulated by K.A.N. Sastri in the words : "the institution of caste with all its social and economic implications was accepted almost universally and the upholding of the order organized on its basis was held to be the primary duty of the ruler".[11] This implies a view of history that perpetuates a static order of society based on textual delineations of the social structure which were considered by these historians as the social reality for all regions and period of history. On the other hand, A.S. Altekar, by taking into account the increase in the number of *vaṇas* and *jātis* during the medieval period in the western Deccan, delves into the problem of explaining the increase in untouchability. According to the author this resulted either due to the unclean profession followed by the untouchables or, due to their non-Aryan origin.[12] None of his explanations however, deal with the question of regional variations. Having relied heavily on the literary sources of study, one can discern in the above interpretations attempts made to approximate the *varṇa* categories of the North and impose them rigidly on various social groups of South India and the Deccan. Some attempts in this direction for the early medieval period have been made for particular regions. N. Venkataramanayya opines that while the *brāhmaṇa* held the highest position, the *kṣatriya varṇa* was placed second in the hierarchy in the Andhra country. He further goes on to write that the trading sections of the Telugu country can be equated to the *Vaiśya varṇa.* The *telikis* and other artisanal groups were included in the *śūdras* category but a large number of *sūdras* however were supposed to have indulged in agricultural activities in his opinion.[13] Till fairly recent time scholars have taken the stand that during the medieval period society was indeed organized only on the basis of a text book description of castes in which the *brāhmaṇa* stood at the top and the *chaṇḍāla* at the bottom of the social hierarchy with the *kṣatriya, vaiśya, śūdra* being located in between, A.V. Krishnamurthy, however, is cautious to inform us that the above division of society into fourfold caste divisions remained largely theoretical in nature and its practical importance was not very great.[14] In the discussion that follows in her book the author nonetheless describes the social structure as though it emanated only from caste differentiation and observes that the bulk of the population constituting agriculturists formed the *śūdra* category.[15]

It is pertinent to note that attempts were also made by some of the scholars to describe social groups in terms of their economic functioning such as those involved in the corporate activities of agricultural, artisanal and mercantile activity. In the works written with this emphasis one finds that historians have mostly written on those groups that have the most explicit mention in the inscriptional sources of the early medieval period. Thus prominent reference is made to the *mahājanas*[16] who were the residents of *agrahāras,* the *gāvuṇḍas*[17] who were the village headmen, the *okkalu*[18] who have been understood as the agriculturist guild and the various types of mercantile guilds.[19] According to K. Sundaram, the most conspicuous feature of the society of the early medieval period was the emergence of powerful self-regulating groups like the artisans *(pañchānaṃvāru)*, the oil mongers *(telikis)* and traders *(vaiśyas* and *balañjas).*[20] Further, those groups involved in offering various services to the temple institutions such as the dancers, singers, musicians and so on have also been taken into account in various historical works focussing on the early medieval period.[21] In these descriptions there was greater emphasis laid on the economic functioning of the above groups and very little mention is made of their caste/*varṇa* to which they belonged. This best exemplified in the way the secular functions of the *mahājanas* who were supposed to be *brāhmaṇas,* are described, as the land lords, administrators, bankers, tax collectors and so on in a detailed discussion by G.R. Kuppuswamy.[22]

On the whole we see that in some of the above studies there were sincere attempts made to comprehend the various elements of the social structure of early medieval period, but this was done either by adopting the bibliocentric view of caste categorization only, or, by a rigid compartmentalization of the data available from literary and the epigraphic sources on particular social classes. These studies therefore remain mere narratives of a description of social groups, their names and functions leaving an erroneous impression that there was hardly any change in their status. Further, the approximation of caste to class in order to comprehend the existence of regional social groups as though it was separate from the larger politico-economic background was serious limitation in these works in comprehending the totality of the social formation during of the early medieval period. This often resulted in them taking contradictory and position in characterizing the social structure of the period in terms of the importance attached to the *varṇa* framework on the one hand and on the other, in setting it aside as only a theoretical basis with little bearing on the social reality. Further, these scholars have taken the textual and inscriptional sources at their face value and therefore, focussed on the dominant sections of the society only. This has unconsciously led to an over emphasis on describing the upper castes *(brāhmaṇas* were greatly praised for their learning) and classes (the ruling and the professional guilds were given a lot of consideration) and their amusements, customs, education system, status of their women and so on. As a result, the criteria by which social history was defined and studies was thus curtailed.[23] The positivistic methodological framework adopted by these scholars handicapped them from looking beyond the available fact and also analyze the relationships of the dominant social groups with those that were subordinate even though they were not directly mentioned in the sources. These studies undoubtedly revealed information on aspects of social history but conditioned by a limited definition of it.

In contrast to the above, the Marxist scholars[24] introduced the class dimension to analyze the ancient Indian *varṇa* system and put forth the paradigm of studying the *varṇa* order in terms of abstractions of actual relations of production.[25] On this basic premise several issues related to the complex social formation of early medieval times have been dealt with extensively by these scholars. These historians have shown that there were significant changes in the traditional *varṇa* set up and attributed these to the changing economic scenario of the period marked by an increase in land grants, decline in the urban economy and the emergence of a closed rural set up.[26] The increase in the importance attached to the landed property in such an economic milieu, according to these scholars, had resulted in the emergence of unequal social relations studied under the label of feudal social formations. On the basis of their access to land and its resources, it is argued that groups in society came to be divided into two classes,[27] that of landlords who came to have titles to lands and villages and the other of the peasant producers who were oppressed by the former.[28] Several layers of hierarchy within the landowning social groups on the one hand, and various levels of stratification among the peasant producers on the other, have been highlighted in this context as characterizing the new class relations of the early medieval period which, in this view, cut across the ascriptive lines of the *varṇa* system as found embedded in the *Dharmaśāstra* texts. Thus, it has been argued by these scholars, that the depression of the older free peasantry to a dependant status, led to the lowering in the status of the *vaiśya varṇa* to be similar with that of the status given to members of that of *śūdra* category.[29] B.N.S. Yadava has exemplified this while explaining the term *kināsa*. It was earlier used to describe a free peasant of the *vaiśya varṇa* and once in the early medieval complex the *kināśa* attained the status of tenants, and their degradation to the status of the *śūdra varṇa* took place.[30] It has further been argued by the Marxist historians that the early medieval period also marked a significant social turn in terms of the increase in the number of *śūdra* and untouchable groups.[31] This, it is argued, was as a result of the spread in the agrarian economy to the outer areas and the subsequent assimilation of local tribal populace.[32] It is thus postulated that in the context of South India, the acculturated population were largely divided into two *varṇas*, namely, the *śūdra* and the *brāhmaṇa*. The absence of the *vaiśya* category in the period between the 6th-9th centuries A.D. has been attributed by Suvira Jaiswal to the decline in the trade and commerce with which *vaiśya* were traditionally associated during the early historical period.[33] On the other hand, the absence of the *kṣatriya varṇa* has been chiefly related to an absence of a traditionally powerful ruling lineage which could not establish horizontal marriage kinship relations as did the Rajputs in North India.[34] Thus, in this opinion, the creation of *sat kṣatriyas* and *sat śūdras*[35] as new categories for explaining the social reality of the status of the ruling elite in the early medieval period in South India are largely attributable to the rise in the politico-economic status of the non-*Brahmanical* groups.

Apart from emphasizing on the variations in the application of *Varṇa* categories in the regional context of South India, these new interpretations also underline the role of economic factors in understanding social change. Importantly, the relationship established between the artisanal groups, dependant peasantry with the landowning elements has been studied against the background of the closed village economy of the early medieval period. This, it is argued, led to the increasing immobility of professional groups and resulted in the proliferation of the concept of untouchability at this time.[36] In particular, these scholars have made significant contributions to our understanding of forced labour and the subjection of peasantry related to the wider politico-economic changes during this period. G.K. Rai has aptly highlighted the changing conception of the term *viṣṭi* (signifying forced labour) right from the Vedic period to its prevalence in the early medieval period, on the basis of both the epigraphic and the literary evidence.[37] Accordingly, the author has suggested that the term *viṣṭi* which in the Vedic times connoted only skilled labour, by the early centuries of Christian era came to signify forced labour[38] and its wide prevalence particularly between the 9th-10th centuries A.D. has been widely attested to with regard to various regions of India, including Karnataka.[39]

The significant contribution made by Marxist historiography in terms of providing a fresh perspective for our comprehension of the historical reality has raised several crucial issues regarding the understanding of rural societies and relationships within them. By over emphasizing the role played by the material conditions in determining social change in history, these scholars have tended to underplay, the role of ideology in shaping these relationships. In Marxist historiography, we find an absence of perspective to comprehend the tensions existing within the dominant groups on the one hand, and within the subject groups on the other[40] which must have also been present in defining the changing social scene. On the other hand, they have repeatedly given over emphasis to the *Dharmaśāstra* category of *varṇa* divisions as common reference point to comprehend the nature of social change during the early medieval period for various regions of India. It has been considered by their critics that this has been a major obstacle in the comprehension of the "problem of regional social stratification"[41] which according to B.D. Chattopadhyaya need not necessarily correspond to the normative divisions of society that had in effect originated in the north Indian context during the Vedic period.

Despite considerable number of historical works using the Marxist method have been devoted to the study of different regions of India such as Karnataka.[42] Andhra Pradesh,[43] Kerala[44] and Tamil Nadu[45], northern Deccan[46] and so on we find that their conscious attempts was to highlight upon uniform explanations of historical change in all these regions, commensurating largely with the north Indian situation. For example, in the works of R.N. Nandi growth of feudal classes in early medieval Karnataka have been explained on similar lines as those done by R.S. Sharma for north and central India which include, among other things, the growth in the surplus appropriating class and a corresponding servile labour force.[47] M.G.S. Narayanan, on the other hand has proposed to show how the historical developments in the early Tamilakam have eventually resulted in the formation of a "feudal society, state and culture" between the periods A.D. 1300–A.D. 1800 in his attempts to provide a board conceptual framework for the study of early medieval Tamil History.[48]

The analysis of complex social formations of the early medieval period in Marxist historiography has generated considerable debate in historical circles regarding the viability of the applicability of the feudal concept to other regions of India, in particular, to the south Indian context. In recent years there has been a spurt of historical literature written with approach using an interdisciplinary method but within a non-Marxist framework of analysis. Under this category of historical writings we have works of such scholars as Burton Stein,[49] N. Karashima[50], R. Champakalakshmi[51] and B. D. Chattopadhyaya.[52] By adopting different methods of historical analysis, these authors have brought out interesting data to comprehend various dimensions of social relationships during the early medieval period from a regional perspective. We wish to briefly summarise here the characterization of social formation in early medieval times formulated in these works which have a significant bearing on our understanding of the nature of regional specificity.

The works of Stein have brought forward the important role played by the ecological variables in shaping what he terms as the 'peasant society' of early medieval South India with specific emphasis on the Tamilakam region. The author has studied the peasant groups as having a symbiotic relationship with the land which they cultivated, the locality in which they resided, kin groups into which they were formed as located within specific spatial unit, namely, the *nāḍu* or the nuclear regions of early medieval Tamilakam, defined by the author as the peasant micro regions.[53] Going a bit deeper into the micro level analysis of the social stratification under the Chola rule in Tamilakam, N. Karashima has effectively brought out the crucial role played by the nature of settlement patterns and the economic dimension in defining the stratified nature of the rural social structure with the help of a statistical analysis of the inscriptional data. As such, his study focusses on highlighting differences in social relationships as they existed between the *brahmadeya* and the non-*brahmadeya* settlements marked by a peculiarity in the land tenurial patterns in each of these. In the former category, where individual ownership of land existed, the author has identified two distinct levels of social strata present in the form of land owners and cultivators and in the latter category, which is marked by communal land holding pattern, the landowners themselves were cultivators. The social set up of the latter villages however, underwent significant changes according to the author owing to the appearance of private land holdings, towards the end of the 10th century A.D. resulting in the stratification of the peasantry in the non-*brahmadeya* villages as well. The latter were now characterized, according to Karashima by the presence of influential land lords who began to be integrated in the Chota polity through conferring titles on them.[54] Karashima studies in essence constitute an analysis of the agrarian relationships established among the elite groups, at the local spatial level which, however, had a limited impact in the comprehension of various complex processes involved in defining the nature of regional state formation and its social basis during the early medieval period. This stands highlighted in the works of R. Champakalakshmi who has focussed on the same area and period of study as Stein and Karashima. According to her the Tamil society between the 7th-13th centuries A.D. witnessed the crystallization of the social structure into different castes marked by a sharp division into two main categories, that of the *brāhmaṇa* and the non-*brāhmaṇa (śūdra).*[55] These were basically considered to have resulted out of the various complex processes under operation over a long period of time (pre-7th century A.D.) marked chiefly by the acculturation of tribal groups consequent upon the expansion of the agrarian base of the *mārutam* ecological tracts. In such a social set up, "a regional version of the theoretical *varṇa* system developed with important modifications depending upon the specificities of the politico-economic system that emerged,"[56] represented at the political level chiefly through the claims made for *brahma-kṣatriya* status. At the economic level, the author has identified the presence of several professional groups such as the mercantile guilds (*nagaram, telikis, nānādeśi* and so on), the artisanal and agricultural workers divided into two social categories of *idaṅgai* (left hand) and *valaṅgai* (right hand)[57] and, finally, there were the *paraiya* groups. The last group has been understood as having been constituted of tribes that were being integrated slowly into the agrarian economy and owing to the growing economic disparity among the agricultural groups and the large scale dissemination of brahmanical ideas in the early medieval period they came to be characterized as untouchables.[58]

The regional dimension of social formation emerges most distinctly in the works, of B.D. Chattopadhyaya which have delved deeply into the problem of comprehension of social change from a regional perspective. In his study of the emergence of the Rajput clans during the early medieval period, the author has effectively demonstrated how the crystallization of a dominant socio-political group exhibits a close nexus in the operation of various structural phenomena such as the political, ideological, social and economic in bringing about the crucial social change. In this case study this has been represented by the concept of Rajputization that is said to indicate "a process of social mobility which in the wake of its formation into a structure, drew in such disparate groups as the Medas and the Hunas".[59] The proliferation of the Rajput clans and sub-clans during the early medieval period indicated, among other things, the complex processes of acculturation as a result of the agrarian expansion on the one hand, and on the other these demonstrated the phenomenon of "caste formation in the early medieval period in which the element of 'localism" was substantially involved".[60] Further, it had all the attendant aspects requisite for the emergence of a lineage group such as defined by the Kingship/familial ties which were strengthened through the marital relations established with other prominent lineages. It is thus argued in this view that the social formation during the early medieval period was a natural corollary to the spread in the local state system into outer lying areas and the hierarchical social relations emerging out of this need not always fit into the normative view of *varṇa* theory embedded in the *Dharmaśāstra* texts.[61] On the contrary Chattopadhyaya opines that one can get closer to historical reality if the social groups located in different regional contexts are studied against the background of the actual economic changes engulfing these regions which would be otherwise lost if studied under the framework of universal categories of their definition only in terms of the *varṇa* theory, particularly in terms of the fiction of *varṇa saṁkara*. It has been put forth by some scholars that it was the breakdown of *varṇa* that led to the emergence of several new elements in the social structure of the early medieval period. However, new social groups described in the inscriptional sources of the various regions of India are known through such terms as the *vellala, idaṅgai, valaṅgai* and *paraiya* in the context of Tamilakam, *gāvuṇḍa, prajāgāvuṇḍa, okkala, ugura* and so on in Karnataka rather than in terms of their *varṇa* affiliations. They in fact, refer to different categories of peasant and cultivating groups. In the light of the above views Chattopadhyaya concludes that the use of the generic category of *śūdra* becomes "entirely insufficient when explaining the composition and status of the peasantry and the agricultural labour which constituted the base of an internally and hierarchized society".[62] It is pertinent to note in the light of above alternative to understand regional social stratification that Nayanjot Lahiri, in the context of her study on early medieval Assam has arrived at certain relevant conclusions regarding the peculiar nature of the social set up of that region. The author has been able to actually divide the social groups of the period both professional (*kaivartas*) and administrative (*karaṇikas*) into various *jātis* or, occupational groups as against the broad *varṇa* framework in which the former were located.[63] It is interesting to note that the author concludes in her study that the scheme of *jāti* which can be reconstructed from the inscriptions of Assam is very different from the *varṇa* divisions of the *Dharmaśāstra* texts.[64] On the whole, her view suggests that the pattern of social divisions and stratification functioned on an economic basis made up of categories of people holding and enjoying land with well entrenched kin based relationships dominating the scene. This in effect formed the foundations for a comprehension of different dimensions of social relations during the early medieval period in Assam.[65] Thus to state in a nutshell, the earlier notions of an unchanging social structure have been effectively replaced by the Marxist historians who tried to comprehend social change in its relation to the wider politicio-economic changes during the early medieval period. But the generalizations that emerged in their conceptions of social stratification which were based on the traditional *varṇa* theory have however marred the comprehension of specific forms of social structure. For various regions of India during this period of transition. These limitations have however been sought to over come in the alternative paradigm put forth by B.D. Chattopadhyaya wherein local categories of hierarchical division based on occupational specialization studied in relation to their specific physical space have been shown to provide viable clues to comprehend the specific nature of social stratification. Relevance of such studio gets a heightened when adopted in relation to the context of the early medieval period, which witnessed a significant spurt in the growth of various regions in the Indian subcontinent. It is in this context of historical specificity that we wish to locate our regional study which has as its focus, the problem of social stratification.

Historical perceptions on economy of the early medieval period which is crucial for a comprehension of social change have undergone similar interpretative changes as they were dependent upon the method of approach adopted by the scholars over time. We wish to discuss some of the major issues raised about the interpretations of the economic structure under study. To begin with, among the conventional category of historical scholarship, we have works of G.R. Kuppuswamy,[66] S. Gururajachar,[67] K. Sundaram[68] and D.R. Das,[69] writtens with specific reference to various parts of the Deccan Peninsula. All these works have detailed discussions on the economic conditions of the early medieval period which cover both the agrarian and the urban environment prevalent at this time. In the discussion on the agrarian structure, focus has generally been on the description of various types of crops and their cultivation and irrigation system,[70] on various types of land tenurial patterns,[71] on the types of soils and so on. The description on the urban economy has generally involved such issues as the articles for trade, banking,[72] and artisanal industries such as mining, craft industry[73] and so on which were clubbed with a detailed discussion on aspects of finance and state revenue extracted from both the agrarian and the non-agrarian sectors.[74] Some of these scholars such as G. R. Kuppuswamy have even probed further into the legal aspects of the issues on land succession and ownership rights in land and so on.[75] It is significant to underscore here that on the one hand, the vast factual information recorded in these works covering even the minutest details of the economic structure during this period can be considered to form a solid data base for further research. On the other, study of economy totally divorced from the larger political[76] and social structure gives one an impression of its autonomous functioning. As a result of this even when there is an implicit recognition of change,[77] as the description of the urban economy normally follows the agrarian one, in these works, the interconnectedness between these two elements is not well established and therefore, the elements of change do not get clearly demarcated and revealed in these works, we have clubbed. This leaves the reader with an impression of the projection of a static and changeless economic structure in several of these histories which we have clubbed under the frame-work of conventional historiography.

The Marxist method of historical analysis has on the other hand, brought about a significant shift in terms of comprehending the changing nature of the economic milieu under the rubric of feudal economy by closely linking up the political initiative to the concept of economic change during this period of transition. In this view economic change in the early medieval period has been studied under two distinct phases. The early phase (300 A.D.-1000 A.D.) marked by the beginning and proliferation of land grants (following the decline in an earlier urban economy) is said to have led to the growth in the ruralization of the economic structure wherein a greater importance began to be attached to landed property and agriculture became the major source of wealth and revenue. In such an economic set up the generation of agrarian surplus through an increase in the agrarian base with the help of improvement in the methods of cultivation on the one hand, and on the other, through the usage of subject labour often with the use of extract economic coercion to extract revenue from peasants are considered to have formed the hall marks of the Indian feudal economy. It has further been suggested in this regard that the economic surplus thus generated was concentrated in the hands of a few landlords which enabled them to invest in non-agrarian activities leading to the revival of an urban phenomenon in the second stage (1000-1200 A.D.). This hypothesis worked out for the north Indian situation by R.S. Sharma[78] has been applied to various other regions of India too wherein the works of R.N. Nandi,[79] figure prominently in the context of our area of study. The Marxist scholarship marked a significant break from the conventional approach on studying the economic structure in that they correlated it to the larger political and social change under operation during the early medieval period for various parts of India. The over emphasis laid by these scholars on studying the economic change in terms of change to agrarian structure (from an earlier urban phenomenon) has however, generated the impression that the early medieval economy needs to be looked at in terms of its rural character per se. Further, the importance that these scholars have attached to foreign trade in bringing about this ruralization has meant that the external stimulus was given undue credence by them.

At this juncture studies conducted by the third category of scholars become significant as they provided a critique on the Marxist definitions of economy during this period. They have helped us in viewing the economic change during the early medieval period in terms of change brought about in the agrarian sector to an urban phenomenon through integration of various structural variables. Importantly, the urban growth has effectively been linked up to its agrarian nexus in defining the totality of economic change which is further seen as resulting out of the processes of local state formation for various regions of India by taking into consideration the ecological variable which is underlined as important for defining the economic structure. R. Champakalakshmi's works with particular focus on the Tamilakam region have made a significant dent in this direction. According to the author the urban like set up that evolved during the Chola rule (10th-12th centuries A.D.) in the Tamilakam region was largely a result of the expansion in the agrarian base around the *brahmadeya* and the temple centres that came into being as a result of the political initiative taken and acted as major integrative forces for various types of agrarian activities centred around them between the 7th-9th centuries A.D.[80] In a similar study, but related to a slightly later period, *i.e.*, of the Vijayanagara rule, Kathleen D. Morrison and Carla M. Sinopoli have identified chiefly three levels of integration which helped in bringing together agrarian zones of different ecological variations which thus facilitated a greater expansion in the agrarian base that was a prerequisite for the maintenance of the large scale urban activity during this period.[81] Among these, the economic mode of integration was supposed to have been effected through the collection of agricultural revenue by the Vijayanagara rulers. Secondly, a more direct and physical form of integration was involved in the construction of large scale reservoirs in which, at times, entire valleys were joined into a single watershed. The third mode of integration in the agrarian sector was effected through the temple institutions which attracted donations in land and commodities on a large scale.[82] Thus, economic change during the early medieval (and medieval) context when viewed from a regional perspective is essentially related to the positive processes of local state formation. The latter could have only resulted if, there was an expansion of productive spheres on a considerable scale by bringing into its vortex several new settlements located in fertile tracts through various elements of integration as has been seen in the above studies. Thus, the problematique of agrarian expansion and, the subsequent growth in the urban phenomenon, is closely related to the growth and spread in the rural settlements patterns of various types.

The rural set up of early India has also been subject to various definitions in terms of its characterizations and socio-economic and political set up in modern historical works. To comprehend the historical perceptions on the rural space one needs to go beyond the 20th century writings on it. This is so because the views expressed in the 19th century by the British administrator scholars on the rural settlements of India played a crucial role in essentialising certain notions about what they described as the Indian 'village community'. The utilization of the concept of 'village community' which was meant to encapsulate several characteristics of the nature of the Indian villages, has been traced back to the administrative report of Munroe written in 1806. In this he states that : "every village with its twelve *ayangadees* as they are called, is a kind of little republic with the *potall* (*patel*) at the head of it and India is a mass of such Republics...... while the village remains entire, they care not to what power it is transferred, wherever it goes, the internal management remains unaltered...... From the age of Manu until this day, the revenue settlements have been made either with or through the *potails.*"[83] This understanding expressed by Munro about the villages in India was commonly accepted by other scholars writing on India. Sir C.T. Metcalfe's famous minute written in 1830 comes out more clearly in his description of the village communities of India, that "the village communities are little Republics having nearly everything that they want within themselves, and almost independent of any foreign relations. They seem to last where nothing else lasts. Dynasty after dynasty tumbles down, revolution succeeds revolution...... but the village communities remain the same". In the continuing part of this minute he praises the role played by the village communities in the preservation of the Indian culture in the past.[84] Similar views on the villages can be seen in the writings of Mark Wilks[85], Mountstuart Elphinstone[86] and so on. These were all written in the early part of the 19th century for different parts of India. In the latter part of the 19th century the works of Karl Marx[87] and H. S. Maine[88] give a negative assessment of the role of village communities since it was thought that they contributed to the formation of a stagnant early Indian society. Taken as a whole, we find certain stereotypical notions about the early Indian socio-economic and political structure embedded in the usage of the term 'village communities' to describe the rural set up of India which can be listed as follows :

(a) First of all, on the political front, these village communities were considered as autonomous bodies functioning independent of the rule of the so called oriental despots.

(b) Secondly, the economic aspect of the village community was highlighted by emphasizing upon the communal ownership of the land in the villages along with the independent political status of the village communities which was said to have rendered them to be self sufficient units in all respects.

(c) Further, the above aspects of the rural set up were either, praised as the hallmarks of the Indian tradition or, were denounced as leading to the stagnant nature of the Indian society. These unchanging characteristics of the 'village communities' it was concluded in the above views, was, put an end to only with the advent of the British rule.

Henceforth, the definition and the concept of the term 'village communities' became common and was carried over into the later works written by both the Indian and the British scholars in the early part of the 20th century except in one aspect. The beginning of the 20th century saw a significant change in the way scholars began to explain the land holding patterns in the Indian villages. Baden Powell's work, *Origin and the Growth of village Communities in India* (1879), disproved of the earlier held notion of the existence of communal rights in land by providing evidence on the existence of individual ownership rights in the rural context.[89] On the other hand, the discovery of the *Arthaśāstra*, a text ascribed to the Mauryan period, opened up new insights into the understanding of local land holding patterns of early India. This text discussed not just one type of land holding pattern, but indicated the existence of a variety in this regard, such as the ownership of land by the king, by the community and by individuals.[90] This evidence therefore, indicated that by the early centuries A.D. there was a tremendous change in the land holding pattern of early India and this fact was clearly pointed out in the works written by Indian scholars from the beginning of the 20th century. A.S. Altekar's *A History of Village Communities in Western India* (1927) has been one of the first works that has directly focussed upon writing a history of village communities perse from ancient to modern times. Altekar wrote at a time when Nationalist writers were concerned about glorifying India's past. At the outset, Altekar sets out reason to express in the preface of his above work that : "the real history of India consists of the history of its village communities. Dynasties have come and dynasties have gone, but it is the village communities that have preserved intact the culture and tradition of old *Bhāratavarsha* through several revolutions".[91] This harks back to what Metcalfe had written earlier about the village communities being static, unchanging and politically autonomous units in ancient India.

The stereotypes of the changelessness of Indian villages and their self-sufficiency have been reflected in the historical works of other regions of India as well. These writings were a natural outcome of the expansion of regional histories written in the aftermath of the freedom movement. Prominent among these works for the southern part of India were those written on the subject of village communities by Nilakanta Sastri[92] and T.V. Mahalingam[93]. In his monumental work on South India, Nilakanta Sastri makes references to the village communities, which he considers were the "most stricking feature of the Chola period" due to the "unusual vigour and efficiency that characterized the functioning of the autonomous rural institutions."[94] In his work on village communities, T.V. Mahalingam, focusses his attention on the description of the village organizations, namely, the *sabha, ūr* and the *nāḍu.* He emphasizes that there was a sense of community feeling residing in each village, and he quotes Metcalfe approvingly in this regard. Mahalingam, however, sees a perceptible change in the local administration of the village bodies as a result of centralization under the Vijayanagara rulers.

One may discern that the issues tackled by the nationalist historians on defining the rural space revolved basically around three aspects. The first of these pertains to the emphasis in these writings on the local autonomy and the durability of the village administration which was supposed to have been based on democratic lines as understood in modern terms. In this regard the characterization of the 'village-communities' by the Western scholars as 'Little Republics' was widely accepted by the nationalists. Secondly, one sees an endeavour on the part of the nationalist scholars to prove the existence of private land holdings. Thirdly, the harmonious life of the people in these communities has been repeatedly stressed upon. In this context K.A.N. Sastri goes to the extent of writing "it was a wonderful social harmony based not on equality of classes or individuals but on a readiness to give and take, a mutual good will that had its roots deep down at the foundations of communal life."[95]

The views about the early south Indian villages as part of a harmonious social past expressed by these scholars have gained wide currency in the Indian historical scholarship on South India in general. It has resulted in the spurt of numerous works written within this conventional approach. Prominent among these writings are those of G.S. Dikshit,[96] A.V. Venkataratnam[97] for the Karnataka region and T. Venkateshwara Rao[98] for Andhra which best exemplify the historiographical thrust on defining the rural space for the area under study.[99] One can clearly gauge a replication of the earlier held notions and concepts of the 'village communities' in these works as for example in G.S. Dikshit's own words : "in ancient and medieval India, the dynastic were and wars of succession, the rebellions and usurpations, the rise and fall of empires had little bearing on the life of village communities".[100] A similar opinion is held by T. Venkateshwara Rao when he states that the "village communities were each an organisation borne out of the consciousness of kinship among the people. An interesting feature in these views is that the village communities remained unaffected by the political changes that swept over the country from time to time and have preserved to us intact the democratic traditions of the past."[101] These anachronistic understandings of the rural space only in terms of a projection of a pre-determined notion of the modern concept of a 'village community' which had no historical basis whatsoever. Even when the sources of the ancient, and in particular the early medieval period, refer to the existence of more than one category of rural settlements (such as the *grāma, ūr, palli, vāḍa* and so on),[102] notwithstanding the *agrahāra* and non-*agrahāra* types of villages which have been recognized in these writings in the sense of characterizing a *brāhmaṇa* or a non-*brāhmaṇa* settlements, they again have been subsumed under the concept of the village communities. In fact, the variability in the spatial terminology did not bring about any change in the way these conventional historians characterized rural space as they were totally preoccupied with the essentialized notion of an independent, unchanging and a totally self-sustained image of a village community which they sought to project in their works.[103] There was no correlation at all in the concept of space as a physical entity and the life of the people residing in it which were studied as two different insular entities. It has aptly been stated in this regard that, "creation of the ostensibly pure original Indian village of the past is thus a relatively new idea, but it has, with amazing ease, been incorporated into historical texts of both pre and post independent India to define village communities of the past as some kind of isolates unconnected to the larger fabric of society."[104]

By totally rejecting the idea of the postulations of unchanging and self-sufficient nature of village communities for the entire historical period in India, the Marxist scholars have brought out significant arguments to show that there were stages indicative of the major changes, in the development of villages in early India. They, however, studied the rural space as part of the larger political and economic developments under the framework of the concept of Indian feudalism.[105] The Prime postulates of studies made in this direction have been largely related to the spread in the village units during the early medieval period. This, it was argued, had resulted out of the decline in the urban centres (as a natural corollary of the decline in foreign trade and commerce) of the early historical phase on the one hand, and on the other, due to the increase in the grant of lands and villages to various political functionaries and the *brāhmaṇa* idealogues.[106] Importantly, consequent upon the above developments, it is further argued that there was the evolution of a stage in which socio-economic structure of the villages which tended to become virtually self-contained wherein the local needs were satisfied locally and in which, the scope for the functioning of the market system was extremely limited.[107] In this formulation thus, the village is essentially a closed entity, generating resources to the donee and although, prior to its transfer to the donee, it may have been inhabited by different social groups, its image is that of an undifferentiated community with no movement from within towards social mobility or, formation of inter-village networks.[108] Such a formulation was initially based on the data from north Indian inscriptions and was applied to other regions of India too. Thus, in the study of K.M. Shrimali on the Vākāṭaka economy of the northern Deccan, an interconnection between the absence in the mention of coins, the granting of lands and the growth in references to the small scale rural settlements, has been well established. According to the author this generated a milieu in which the beginnings of feudalism must have found their roots.[109] Similarly, R.N. Nandi's postulates for the Karnataka region have hinged upon the problem of the decay of towns and the dispersal of a section of urban population to the rural hinterland characterized by an agriculture based subsistence economy during the early medieval period.[110] The overemphasis on explaining the growth in ruralization during the early medieval complex and its adverse impact on the villages which were thus defined as self-sufficient led these scholars to unconsciously fall into the trap of the conventional historiography which they had denounced as unhistorical. This was so because firstly, they gave undue emphasis to the external stimulus of change, such as decline in foreign trade bringing about the above change of ruralization and secondly, unconsciously, emphasizing on political initiative as being the most important factor of generating the new land grant economy.[111] Such a handicap can be understood to have resulted out of the undue importance attached by these scholars to the decline in early historical urbanism and also of looking at this breakdown in terms of a pan-Indian phenomena. This was confined mostly to the northern, and a few pockets of the south Indian context, including parts of the Deccan region (north western Deccan). The comprehension of the spread in rural settlements to a large majority of hitherto unsettled areas of the Indian subcontinent required the problem to be studied from regional perspective. This was lacking in this strand of historical writing which, by and large, tried to explain a uniform pattern of developments for various regions during the early medieval period under the methodological umbrella of the concept of Indian Feudalism.

The regional dimension to the study of rural space during the early medieval period in India has been understood to a considerable degree in a recent spurt of historical works written with a non-Marxist approach. Works of Burton Stein,[112] N. Karashima,[113] Y. Subbarayulu,[114] R. Champakalakshmi[115] and B.D. Chattopadhyaya[116] figure prominently in this category. In Stein's work the elements of self-sufficiency and autonomy which were earlier applied to the single village unit can now be seen replicated at a supra-local level, namely, the *nāḍu.* Comprising of numerous distinctive localities, *nāḍu* is taken as the enduring and basic unit of south Indian peasant society[117] by Burton Stein to comprehend the socio-political structure of the Chola state in early medieval Tamilakam. The *nāḍu* segments in this context are viewed by him as ethnic-ecological units and considered totally independent of the control of the state which, according to the author, had only ritual control over the *nāḍus*.[118] Further, the hallmark of the social relations at the *nāḍu* level was said to be based on a harmonious *brāhmaṇa* and dominant peasant alliances thus leaving no room for conflicts.[119] Stein's formulations on the *nāḍu* segments have, however, been questioned by various scholars who have brought out evidence to indicate the exercise of administrative hold by the Chola state on the *nāḍu* units on the one hand,[120] and on the other, the existence of a variety of settlements such as the *brahmadeya, devadāna, nagaram* and so on within a single *nāḍu* unit have helped in refuting the concept of syncretism among social groups put forth by Stein.[121]

On the basis of a statistical analysis of various place names pertaining to different residential quarters, and the names of various social groups located within a single village, coupled with the evidence on the water facilities operating on an inter-village pattern, N. Karashima was able to conclude upon the fact that "the villages of the Cholamandalam in the middle of the Chola rule did not have so much of an independent nature as has been presumed".[122] The *brahmadeya* villages which stood in a minority, when compared to the non-*brahmadeya* ones, according to the author, played the crucial role of integrating and controlling the surrounding non-*brahmadeya,* villages at the time of the Chola rule.[123] Further, Karashima's formulations of the difference between the *brahmadeya* and non-*brahmadeya* villages on the basis of their tenurial patterns, *i.e.,* the former as having individual ownership rights and the latter representing communal ownership rights have been refuted by other scholars on the basic premise that non-mention of individual owners in the records (located in the temple institutions) does not warrant an absence in the individual land ownership itself.[124] Karashima's failure of taking into account the complex nature of the social set up of the non-*brahmadeya* villages have further been refuted by furnishing adequate data in this regard.[125]

Focussing his attention on the non-*brahmadeya (ūr)* villages of the Tamilakam region under the Cholas, Y. Subbarayulu, with the help of his analysis on the names of social groups, concludes upon the possibility of the existence of social relations beyond a single village.[126] Importantly, the author surmises that all these *ūr* villages which were basically agricultural settlements, clustered together to form the *nāḍu* unit which was thus, not a mere administrative sub-division imposed from above. Further, according to the author the State interacted with the *ūr* villages only through the *nāḍu* assembly which represented the interests of the rural settlements clustered in it.[127]

The concerns of the above scholars with only individual centres in settlements (such as the *brahmadeya* and the non-*brahmadeya* as separate entities), has, however, impeded a proper understanding of the interconnection between them and the agrarian expansion or, urban growth in a comprehensive manner.[128] In this regard R. Champakalakshmi's formulations with a focus on the settlements under the Chola rule set the right trend in our comprehension of the way various rural settlements, belonging to different ecological zones, were integrated through such institutional means as the *brahmadeya* and the temple networks, buttressed through the irrigation structures fostered under the royal initiative.[129] The author argues in this context that it is in these clusters of *brahmadeya* and the temple centres that became as the foci of urban expansion by the close of the 9th century A.D. where an initial search for the growth in the urban process in the Tamilakam region would be fruitful.[130]

Set in a similar vein, the works of B.D. Chattopadhyaya cover a broad spectrum of issues related to the problematique of the formation and proliferation of settlement patterns viewed from a regional perspective during the early medieval period. The complex processes involved in the growth and the spread of settlement structures into viable productive zones and their eventual crystallization into the *brahmadeya* and major temple settlements of urban growth have been considered by the author essentially a result of the socio-political processes of legitimation and integration operating in the context of the processes that led to local state formation.[131] Importantly, by relating all the above factors in relation to the physical location of the rural settlement, Chattopadhyaya has marked a considerable shift from earlier historical writings in characterizing the hitherto labelled early (medieval) Indian village in terms of its plurality of existence. According to the author, the variety of ways in which the suffixes (*vāḍa, palli, grāma* and so on) attached to the rural settlements figure in the epigraphic as well as literary sources of early India, when viewed against their geographical location significantly point to the underlying heterogenity of that characterizes the rural space at any given point of historical time.[132] It is against this background of ecological variability that marks the rural structures during the early medieval period that the growth in the *agrahāra* and the temple settlements have been comprehended.

This brings us to the question of how ideological parameters have been considered and defined by historians to comprehend various aspects of social structure and physical space of their location during the early medieval period. This period clearly saw the crystallization of several temple centred settlements and the massive popularity of the *Bhakti* ideology that added complexity to various issues of studying social change. Historical analysis on the role of ideology in this context has, however, varied in approach to the elaboration of this problem. We find that in the conventional category of historical writings, particularly those of K.A.N. Sastri[133] and A.V. Krishnamurthy,[134] considerable number of pages in their books are devoted to the description of religion and the temple building activity of the period. The emphasis is more on eulogizing the various forms of Hinduism and to discuss the spread of the *Purāṇic Bhakti* cults such as *Śaivism* and *Vaiṣṇavism*. These were supposed to have received large scale patronage from the ruling chiefs during the early medieval context. On account of the simultaneous growth in literary works devoted to the *Bhakti* ideology and philosophy, coupled with a great spurt in the temple building activity, and the royal patronage extended to these, K.A.N. Sastri considers the Chola period (850-1200) as the golden age of Tamil culture.[135] The author further goes on to view these developments in terms of a revival of the Hindu religion[136] which was said to be achieved in the main, through the spread of the *Purāṇic Bhakti* idiom in South India during the early medieval period. In particular the crystallization of *Puraṇism* in the form of local sectarian movement of the *Kālāmukhas*, with their specific location in the northern Karnataka region have also been focussed upon by some other scholars, on the basis of both epigraphic and literary sources available for the early medieval period.[137] Emphasis has, however, been laid on the philosophical under pinning of *Kālāmukha Śaivism*, wherein the differences it had with the Vedic school have been highlighted. P.B. Desai's monumental work on Jainism,[138] based entirely on the epigraphical sources, of which those of the Karnataka region form a crucial part has detailed descriptions on the Jaina Philosophy, the wide patronage it received from the rulers, the causes for its decline and so on. In the light of these studies, we have been able to pertinently note in this regard that such conventional historical works have invariably viewed the ideological moorings of the period purely in terms of religious beliefs and preachings which had an underlying moral purpose. This was totally unrelated to the social, economic and political contexts of the period when these religious beliefs spread and became popular. This is particularly interesting in the light of the fact that the temple institutions, in the same writings, have been praised a great deal for their secular functioning such as their role as bankers, as collectors of revenue, as landlords and so on as suggested in the work of K. Ismail.[139] These anomalies projected in the works of conventional scholars were largely a result of the compartmentalized approach they adopted in viewing various aspects of the historical phenomena as independent entities.

On the other hand, the Marxist historical works with their approach of equating ideology as essentially a product of the given material base, have tended to view various aspects of the ideological dimensions of the early medieval India in terms of depicting a feudal ethos keeping in tune with feudal socio-economic set up that they formulated for various parts of India.[140] Thus R.N. Nandi's conceptualizations on the role played by the *Bhakti* ideology during the early medieval period were rooted in defining the elements of subordination and domination which constituted the hallmark of the social relationships in interaction with the religion of the times. Nandi thus articulates "the effort to appropriate more of the increasing surplus during the feudal phase, is represented by a new ideology of social subordination, new rituals of gifts exchange and new centres of surplus appropriation"[141] Marxist comprehensions of *Bhakti* ideology for the South India have, however, been articulated in the writings of M.G.S. Narayanan and Kesavan Veluthat, wherein, the Tamil Bhakti cult has been studied as representing the agrarian feudal moorings and the Jaina and Buddhist establishments as products of trading class bias during the early medieval period.[142] Various other dimensions of the ideological manifestations present during the early medieval complex have been interpreted by R.S. Sharma also in relationship with social change such as those representing peasant discontent which was considered widespread during this period due to oppression unleashed by the landlords.[143] The crisis of the Kali age depicted in the religious texts of early centuries A.D. was supposed to have registered in reality the widespread protests of the productive groups through their refusal to pay taxes to the state, which according to R.S. Sharma ultimately led to the grant of lands alongwith various immunities and thus led to the creation of a new landed gentry.[144] At the same time, it is also argued that the *Bhakti* movement with its origins in the early medieval period, was a means to mainly to contain and channel the widespread peasant discontentment,[145] and therefore, several types of *saṃskāras*, vratas and the concept of *tīrtha yātra* and so on were introduced into the belief system during the early medieval times. These were all meant to have created only an illusion of equality between the peasant and the landlord by enabling them to partake in the rituals on an equal footing.[146] In reality, however, the feudal relations of production dominated and maintained the stubborn walls of inequality. By relating the element of change witnessed at the socio-economic base to the emergent ideological parameters during the early medieval period, the Marxist scholars marked a major shift in the interpretative context of how religion should be understood. This was a major departure from the hitherto common place understanding that it was something super-natural and ordained. However, by giving primacy to the material factors of change, these scholars tended to underplay the autonomous role played by ideology in bringing about the change at the social level. Importantly, it becomes crucial to underscore at this juncture that the paradigm of social protests and their projection in the Kali age crisis, viewed from a regional perspective would hold wholly untenable for several other parts of India which had hitherto not witnessed a dissemination of the Brahmanical ideas on a considerable scale. It is in the light of these limitations that one needs to look to alternate paradigms of ideological change in the context of the study of regional history.

In the writings of Hermann Kulke,[147] R. Champakalakshmi[148] and B.D. Chattopadhyaya[149] one sees that the ideology is mainly looked upon as an integrative factor playing a positive role in bringing about change. Therefore, they try to establish an interconnection between religion and the socio-economic base in the wider context of the political exigencies of local state formation during the early medieval period. In particular, the writings of Hermann Kulke have initiated a major stride in this direction by comprehending the effective use of ideological parameters made by the local polities in the context of state formation in early Orissa. In this regard the role of religious ideology, through the *Bhakti* medium and its institutional base in the temple, got totally transformed into a tool of acculturation, integration and legitimation in the hands of the local *rājas* who had in fact, originated from one of the tribes surrounding the nuclear areas located within Orissa.[150] In his analysis, it is pertinent to note that Kulke has made the tribes and their deities central to our comprehension of socio-economic and political changes initiated in his area of study. In such a context the cultural integration that operated through the appropriation and integration of several local and supra local deities and their crystallization in the form of the cult of Jagannātha as the regional deity, went hand in hand with the territorial integration of the local chiefs in the context of early medieval Orissa.[151] This provides one of the best examples of the role played by the regional idiom of integration operating at the local parameters of state formation which was achieved, in a large measure, through the crucial role played by ideology.

By situating ideological processes in the early medieval Tamilakam region, R. Champakalakshmi has projected in her analysis the crucial role played by temples and the monastic establishments for providing an institutional base to the several *Purāṇic* sects of Hinduism. This is seen as a mechanism of acculturation in integrating the extreme and non-conformist elements into the Tamil social organisation.[152] It is in these processes of social change, from tribal to peasant fostered through the increasing construction of the temples undertaken by the Chola rulers and the simultaneous process of broadening the productive base, that the complex role of ideology in transforming the material base can be seen operating her arguments. Importantly, the *Bhakti* ideology of the early medieval period is seen as representing the culmination of the process of acculturation through the assimilation of local folk cults into the pantheon of *Vaiṣṇavism* and *Śaivism.*[153] This is then interpreted as making a strong case of the crystallization of a regional culture through such a fusion.

A recognition in the integrative potential of the ideological forces in bringing about the socio-economic changes mark a significant shift from the earlier held historical perceptions. B.D. Chattopadhyaya has aptly highlighted in this context that when viewed from a regional perspective all the above discussed issues, social, economic, spatial and ideological cluster around the crucial element of local state formation which according to him, "mediated in the absorption of ideas and practices which had been taking shape as a wider temporal and ideological process. The taking root of these ideas and practices was not a simple fact of diffusion from some elusive centre. It was an indication essentially of where and in what forms state society was taking shape."[154]

Thus our comprehensions have indeed undergone significant transformations depending upon the changes in the methodology adopted by various scholars writing on it. We have seen in the above survey that the concerns of the conventional approach have been mainly with linear descriptions of the historical facts studied in a compartmentalized form. While the data recorded in their studied can be taken up for further research, their positivistic framework, of writing history has however failed to identify elements of change and complexity embedded in the historical formations characterizing the early medieval period. The Marxist method of historical writings have on the order hand marked a major shift from the above works by identifying various elements of change and transition for the early medieval complex by relating economic changes to the larger political and social set up. But their "pre-determined aim to adopt the feudalism theory",[155] to explain the historical developments for the entire Indian sub continent during the early medieval period, have however resulted in a tendency wherein the specific aspects of structural formations at the regional level got totally subsumed under the 'feudal' labels. This left an impression of uniform developments despite the fact that "serious problems are posed by the complexity of inscriptional evidence"[156] for the early medieval period which require new methods of analysis to arrive at the historical reality. The recent spurt of non-Marxist works, by not sticking to any particular framework of historical analysis have contributed significantly in terms of understanding the regional dimension of various aspects of historical change for the early medieval period. As such these studies have a significant bearing on our understanding of the specificities of the complex social relationships in early India which defy any rigid universalization at an all India level and further go to remind us of the need to bring to light specific structural formations at a regional level. At the outset we wish to posit our regional study in the context of these recent formulations on early medieval history, which have duly emphasized upon the necessity to first of all situate the resultant social formations of this period against their physiographic setting so as to arrive at the specific nature of historical change for any given region in India. We have therefore attempted to initiate our analysis of various issues of our study (social, economic, spatial and ideological) by locating these against their geographic setting which forms our main endeavour in following chapter. In the latter half of chapter II we highlight in detail various recent views on state formation in the early medieval period.

REFERENCES

1. Arthur Marwick, 'Two Approaches to Historical Study : The Metaphysical (Including 'Postmodernism') and the Historical', *Journal of Contemporary History,* Vol. 30, January, 1995, p. 12.
2. E.H. Carr, *What is History?,* Penguin, 1985 (rp.), p. 30.
3. K.A. Nilakanta Sastri,. *A History of South India,* OUP, Madras, 1987 (4th ed.), pp. 313-338.
4. A.S. Altekar, *The Rashtrakutas and Their Times,* Oriental Book Agency, Poona, 1934.
5. N. Venkataramanayya, *Eastern Chalukyas of Vengi,* Madras, 1950. pp. 278-294. In fact, here the author clubs the description of various aspects of the society under the heading of 'Eastern Chalukya Administration'.
6. Alladi Vaidehi Krishnamurthi, *Social and Economic Conditions of Eastern Deccan* (A.D. 1000-A.D. 1200), Secunderabad, 1970. pp. 30-50.
7. K. Sundaram, *Studies in Economic and Social Conditions of Medieval Andhra* (A.D. 1000-1600), Machilipatnam, 1968, pp. 25-84.

8. S. Gururajachar, *Some Aspects of Economic and Social Life in Karnataka* (A.D. 1000-A.D. 1300), Mysore, 1974, pp. 181-255. In this work, apart from the detailed description of the economic aspects, the author mainly focusses upon the educational system prevalent during his period of study and on the status of women and their role in the cultural, religious and administrative activities. These have been detailed as a part of his study on society.
9. Jyotsna Kamat, *Social Life in Medieval Karnataka,* New Delhi, 1980. This work stands apart from the above works as the entire book is dedicated to the description of such aspects of social life as the types of food and drinks prevalent during the period of study (pp. 1-21) coupled with such other aspects as vanity fair (pp. 22-67), leisure and pleasure (pp. 68-104) and the status of woman (pp. 105-130). In fact, studies of this nature belong to a category which believe in the oldest view of social history, that it was the history of manners, of leisure of a whole range of social activities which were conducted outside the arena of the political, economic, military and other institutions and which were all the concerns of specific kinds of history (Keith Hopkins, 'What is Social History' *History Today,* March, 1985, p. 39.)
10. In this category of historical work we have included the writings of such eminent scholars as G.S. Dikshit, G.R. Kuppuswamy and so on which have been published in various journals of the Karnataka University such as the *JKU* (Social Science) and *JHLU* (Humanities) from the 1950's to the 1970's and have concentrated chiefly on the description of various professional social groups such as the guild of agriculturists, mercantile groups and so on.
11. Sastri, *op. cit.,* 1987, p. 319.
12. Altekar, *op. cit.,* 1934 pp. 320-324.
13. Venkaramanayya, *op. cit.,* 1950. pp. 283-286.
14. Krishnamurthy, *op. cit.*, 1970, p. 30.
15. *Ibid.,* pp. 31-49.
16. For example, G.R. Kuppuswamy, 'Role of Mahajanas in the History of Medieval Karnataka', *JKU* (Social Sciences) VI, 1970, pp. 61-65.
17. For example, T. Venkateshwara Rao 'The Gaundas in Medieval Andhra', *Itihas,* Journal of A.P. State Archives, IV, Hyderabad, 1976, pp. 75-79.
18. G.S. Dikshit, 'Okkalu. A Corporate Body of Medieval Karnatak', *JKU* (Humanities), IV, June 1960, pp. 58-63.
19. G.S. Dikshit, 'Group Organization in Medieval Karnataka', *JKU* (Humanities) 1,2, June 1957, pp. 59-64.
20. K. Sundaram, *op. cit.,* 1968, p. iii.
21. K. Isamil, *Karnataka Temples.* Their Role in *Socio-Economic Life,* Delhi 1984, pp. 111-129.
22. G.R. Kuppuswamy, *op. cit.,* 1970, pp. 61-65.
23. For example, works of S. Gururajachar, *op. cit.,* 1974, pp. 181-255 and Jyotsna Karmat, *op. cit.,* 1980, (the entire text) best exemplity the type of writing history. In fact the latter claims to have initiated the study of various aspects of social history like

amusements, vanity, fair, dressing and ornaments and so on, for medieval Karnataka, with the prime intention of setting aside the importance given to political events as in her view in a democratic set up it is the people who matter more than those who govern or rule (p. xvii).

24. The Marxist method of analysis has brought about a significant change in our understanding of the early social formation in a historical perspective. Works of D.D. Kosambi (*An Introduction to the Study of Indian History,* Bombay, 1985 pp. 140-141) R.S. Sharma, *(Social Change in Early Medieval India)* (A.D. 500-A.D. 1200), the First Devraj Chanana Memorial Lecture, New Delhi, 1969, pp. 11-27, B.N.S. Yadava (Problem of the Interaction between Socio-Economic classes in the Early Medieval Complex', *IHR*, 3, 1, 1976, pp. 43-58), Vivekanand Jha ('Stages in the History of Untouchables' *IHR* 2, 1, 1975, pp. 14-31) and Suvira Jaiswal, ('Studies in Early Indian Social History; Trends and Possibilities, *IHR*, 6, 1-2, 1979-80, pp. 1-63) have attempted to analyse the dynamic nature of the *varṇa-jāti* system in the context of chiefly the northern part of India. The theoretical assumptions held by these scholars could, however, be applied to other regions of India as well.
25. Suvira Jaiswal, 'Caste in the Socio-Economic Framework of Early India', *PIHC,* 38th session, Bhuvaneswar, 1977, p. 25.
26. Sharma, *op. cit.,* 1969, pp. 6-11.
27. Yadava, *op. cit.,* 1976, pp. 45-46.
28. Sharma, 'Problems of Social Formations in Early India', Presidential Address, Sec 1, *PHIC*, 36th session, 1975, p. 8.
29. B.N.S. Yadava, 'Historical Investigation into Social Terminology in Literature : A Problem of the Study of Social Change', *PIHC,* Presidential Address, 53rd session, Warangal, 1993, p. 18.
30. Yadava, *op. cit.,* 1976, p. 51.
31. R.S. Sharma, *op. cit.,* 1969, pp. 22-23.
32. Vivekanand Jha, *op. cit.,* 1975, pp. 14-15.
33. Summarised from Suvira Jaiswal, *op. cit.,* 1979-80, pp. 40-41. In this context it is pertinent to highlight that R. Champakalakshmi, on the basis of her researches has shown the reemergence of the *vaisya varna* after the 10th century A.D. in Tamil Nadu. See her Presidential address, 'Urbanization in South India : the Role of ideology and Polity', *PIHC,* 47th session, Srinagar, 1986, pp. 17-18.
34. Suvira Jaiswal, *op, cit.,* 1979-80, pp. 33-34.
35. Altekar, *op. cit.,* 1930, pp. 318-325.
36. V.N. Jha, *op. cit.,* 1975, pp. 28-31.
37. G.K. Rai, 'Forced Labour in Ancient and Early Medieval India', *IHR*, 3, 1976-77, pp. 21-36.
38. *Ibid.,* p. 37.
39. *Ibid.,* p. 32.
40. In the Marxist methodology we have seen above that despite the fact that stratified relationships have been worked out at both levels, one can clearly discern an emphasis

being laid on the comprehension of tensions between the land lords as a dominant class on the one hand and the peasant groups as a dominated class on the other.

41. B.D. Chattopadhyaya, *The Making of Early Medieval India,* OUP, Delhi, 1994 p. 27.
42. R.N. Nandi, 'Growth of Rural Economy in Early Feudal India', Presidential Address, Section I, *PHIC,* 45th session, Annamali Nagar, 1984, pp. 5-7.
43. K. Satyanarayana, *Study of the History and Culture of the Andhras,* I, New Delhi, 1975. In this work the author literally borrows the concepts of 'feudalism from above' and 'feudalism from below' coined by D.D. Kosambi.
44. Kesavan Veluthat, *Brahmana Settlements in Kerala,* Calicut University, 1978, pp. 8-9.
45. M.G.S. Narayanan, 'A Critique of the History of South India and a Proposal for a New Conceptual Framework', *SIHC,* 7th session, Madras University, 1987, pp. 6-7.
46. K.M. Shrimali, *Agrarian Structure in Central India and the Northern Deccan* (A.D. 300-500), Delhi, 1987, pp, 26-30.
47. R.N. Nandi, *op.cit.,* 1984, p. 4. The author in effect initials the study to view the feudal problem in a regional perspective with the use of the incriptional data which according to him form the most reliable material for the study of feudal social formation in India, (p. 3).
48. M.G.S. Narayanan, *op. cit.,* 1987, pp. 6-7. In an earlier Presidential address presented, he had argued for the growth in the feudal social formations linked up closely to the system of making land grants and the corresponding growth in the *brāhmaṇa* settlements in the context of entire South India during the early medieval period. 'Trends and Prospects in Historiography', *PIHC,* 39th session, Hyderabad, 1978. p. 19.
49. Burton Stein, *Peasant State and Society in Medieval South India,* OUP, Delhi, 1980. The author has basically divided his study of peasant society into two parts. The first one characterized under the generic term of peasant society is clubbed with the study on the *nāḍu,* (peasant micro region) of the Tamilakam in the early medieval period (pp. 96-140) the second part takes into account the dual social divisions (*idangai, velangai*) rooted in the peasant localities for the same region and period of study (pp. 173-215).
50. N. Karashima, *South Indian History and Society,* Delhi 1984, pp. 37-64.
51. R. Champakalakshmi, 'Religion and Social Change in Tamil Nadu', in N.N. Bhattacharya (ed.), *Medieval Bhakti Movements in India,* Sri Caitanya Quin Centenary Commemoration Volume, New Delhi, 1989, pp. 162-173.
52. B.D. Chattopadhyaya, *Aspects of Rural Settlements and Rural Society in Early Medieval India,* Calcutta, 1985, pp. 1-13 and also his 'introduction' in B.D. Chattopadhyaya (ed) *op. cit.,* 1994. pp. 17-18.
53. Stein, *op. cit.,* 1980, pp. 17-19. Repeated emphasis laid by the author on the alliance between the *brāhmaṇas* and dominant peasantry (*vellalas* termed as *sat śūdras*) as the basis for the perpetuation of the dominance exercised by these groups located within the self sufficient nuclear areas of study have, however been held totally untenable for comprehending the historical reality. (D.N. Jha, Relevance of 'Peasant State and Society to Pallava–Cola Times', *IHR,* 8, 1-2, 1981-82, p. 79.)

54. N.Karashima, *op. cit.*, 1984, pp. 13-27.
55. R. Champakalakshmi, *op. cit.*, 1989, p. 162.
56. R. Champakalakshmi, *op. cit.*, 1986, pp. 17-18.
57. *Ibid.*, pp. 21-30.
58. *Ibid.*, p. 17.
59. B.D. Chattopadhyaya, 'Origin of Rajputs : The Political, Economic and Social Processes in Early Medieval Rajasthan', *IHR*, 3, 1, 1976, p. 81.
60. *Ibid.*, p. 81.
61. B.D. Chattopadhyaya, *op. cit.*, 1994, p. 25.
62. *Ibid.*, p. 27.
63. Nayanjot Lahiri, *Pre Ahom Assam* (Studies in the Inscriptions of Assam Between the 5th and the 13th centuries A.D.), New Delhi, 1991, pp. 115-116.
64. *Ibid.*, p. 117.
65. *Ibid.*, p. 118.
66. G.R. Kuppuswamy, *Economic Conditions in Karnataka,* (A.D. 973-A.D. 1336), Karnataka University, Dharwar, 1975. The entire work deals with various facets of the economy.
67. S. Gurajachar, *op. cit.*, 1974. His study purports to describe both the economic and social aspects of the early medieval period. Out of these he has devoted 4 chapters (3, 4, 5, 6) on the description of the economy.
68. K. Sundaram, *op. cit.*, 1968, Here the author focusses chiefly on the artisanal and mercantile productive activities.
69. Deepak Ranjan Das, *Economic History of the Deccan,* Delhi 1969. His study actually deals with an earlier period (1st-6th century A.D.) of history but because the author's focusses on the Deccan region, has elicited our interest in it.
70. S. Gururajachar, *op. cit.*, 1974. pp. 40-58.
71. G.R. Kuppuswamy, *op. cit.*, 1975, pp. 18-35.
72. *Ibid.*, pp. 51-69.
73. *Ibid.*, pp. 113-119.
74. K. Sundaram, *op. cit.*, 1968, pp. 17-36, S. Gururajachar, *op. cit.*, 1974, pp. 140-168 and so on.
75. G.R. Kuppuswamy, 'Land Succession in Medieval Karnataka', *JKU* (Social Sciences), IX, 1973, pp. 8-118. 'Dayavibhaga or System of Distribution of Heritage and Land Subdivision and Fragmentation in Medieval Karnataka', *JKU* (Social Sciences), XI, 1975, best exemplicity our contention.
76. Spurt in the historical works with focus on the social and economic aspects of history during the 1960's and 70's came into being mainly to provide a shift from an earlier emphasis laid on the political and dynastic history written under the nationalist/imperialist framework. This is clearly stated in the preface to the work of D.R. Das, *op. cit.*, 1969, p. vii.

77. Such a recognition is clearly depicted in the following words of G.R. Kuppuswamy, wherein he states that "One cannot but admit the extremely conventional nature of this economy, in which custom, tradition and implicit faith in scriptures or *śāṣtras* played a significant part, and this has led proper to underestimate, if not totally deny, the progressive and dynamic nature of the medieval economy in Karnataka". (G.R. Kuppuswamy, *op. cit.,* 1975, p. 1).
78. R.S. Sharma, *Indian Feudalism,* Delhi, 1980, pp. 213-226. The concluding part highlights for us the discussion centred around various dimensions of feudal developments detailed throughout the text.
79. Nandi, *op. cit.,* 1984, p. 3. According to the author, in the peninsular region as in other parts of India, the relapse of a market economy of towns into a subsistence economy of agriculture, which followed a widespread decay and desertion of towns from the 3rd century A.D., seems to be the key factor in our understanding of the origins of feudalism.
80. R. Champakalakshmi, *op. cit.,* 1986, pp. 13-15.
81. Kathleen D. Morrison and Carla M. Sinopoli, 'Economic Diversity and Integration in a Pre-colonial Empire', *World Archaeology,* 23, 3, February, 1992, p. 338.
82. *Ibid.*, pp. 338-339.
83. Louis Dumont, 'The village Community from Munro to Maine', in L. Dumont (ed.) *Religion, Politics and History in India,* Paris, 1970, p. 115.
84. N. Karashima, 'The Village Communities in Chola Times : the Myth or Reality' *Journal of the Epigraphical Society of India,* III, Dharwar, 1981, p. 5.
85. Mark Wilks, *Historical Sketches of South India in an Attempt to Trace the History of Mysore* (1810), ed. by Murray Hammick., Vol. I, Mysore, 1930.
86. M. Elphinstone, *Report on the Territories conquered from the Peshwa,* Delhi 1973 (first published in 1821) p. 21. It is significant to note here what the author has to say on the villages of the Deccan, "these communities contain in miniature all the materials of a State within themselves, and are almost sufficient to protect their members, if all other governments were withdrawn."
87. R.A.L.H. Gunawardana, 'The Analysis of Pre-Colonial Social Formulations in Asia in the Writings of Karl Marx', *IHR*, 2, 2, 1976, pp. 365-388.
88. H. Maine, *Village Communities in the East and the West,* Delhi, 1985 (rp) pp. 155-160.
89. However, the other aspects of the village community described by the earlier scholars were maintained by him. According to the author, "apart from the fact that the village is a geographical unit, the feeling of being a 'community' is maintained by the common interests and customs of the local group, by obedience to one hereditary headman, and its self contained life having its own staff of artisans and servants, the village does not need to look outside its own limits for the supply of its ordinary wants". B.H. Baden Powell, 'A Study of the Dakkan Villages, their Origin and Development', *JRAS, Gr. Britian and Ireland,* 1987. p. 239.
90. Irfan Habib, 'The Social Distribution of Landed Property in Pre-British India', in R.S. Sharma and V.N. Jha (ed.) *Indian Society Historical Probings,* New Delhi, 1984, pp. 264-316.

91. A.S. Altekar, *A History of Village Communities in Western India,* Bombay, 1972, p. ii.
92. Sastri, *op. cit.,* 1966 (first published in 1955) pp. 205-206.
93. T.V. Mahalingam, 'Village Communities in South India', in T.V. Mahalingam (ed.), *Readings in South Indian History*, Delhi, 1977, pp. 94-105 (This article was first published in *Transactions of the Archaeological Society of South India,* I, Madras, 1955).
94. Sastri, *op. cit.,* 1966, p. 205.
95. *Ibid.,* pp. 205-206.
96. G.S. Dikshit, *Local Self Government in Medieval Karnataka,* Dharwar, 1964. The entire work deals with various types of village activities, such as village administration, about the residents of the village, physical descriptions of it and so on.
97. A.V. Venkataratnam, *Local Government in the Vijayanagara Empire,* Mysore, 1972.
98. T. Venkateshwara Rao, 'Local Self Government in Medieval Andhra', *JAHRS,* XXXI, Rajahmundry, 1965-66, pp. 113-123.
99. In this context we have numerous works written during the 1960's and 70's not directly focussing on the rural history, but making definite references to various aspects of rural life in the same methodological framework as the works discussed above. Among such writings we have works of Sundaram, *op. cit.,* 1968, Kuppuswamy, *op.cit.,* 1975, S. Gururajachar, *op. cit.,* 1974 and so on.
100. Dikshit, *op. cit.,* 1964, p. 8.
101, Venkateshwars Rao, *op. cit.,* 1965-66, p. 113.
102. Chattopadhyaya, *op.cit.,* 1990. pp. 2-3.
103. K.A.N. Sastri, 'Grama'–An Examination of a New Interpretation', *JOR,* IV, iii, July-Sept., 1930, pp. 211-225. In this article the author takes note of differences that existed in the terminology of the *grāma* itself as a rural space when the furnished a list of such terms as *ekabhōga-grāma, kuṭika grāma* and so on (pp. 221-222), but its relationship with the socio-economic and political issues located within it is totally eluded in the discussion. In an earlier work written by V. A. Gadgil, there is a clear recognition of the differences between the terms *palli* and *grāma* as depicted in the literary texts of ancient India *Palli* has been considered to represent half of a *grāma* and the term *kuṃbha* has been equated to characterize half of a *palli.* But all these have been considered to indicate the differences in the physical sizes and it is ultimately concluded that "at the most what we can say is that *grāma* must have been the smallest unit consisting of cultivating owners, menials, *Brāhmaṇas, Kṣatriyas, Rathkāras* and Smiths, all alike politically subject to the kings". See the above author's 'The Village in Sanskrit Literature', *JBBRAS,* (New Series), II, London, 1926, p. 152.
104. Aloka Parasher Sen, 'The Village Given to Us', Intellectual Constructions of the Village Community in Historical Writing', in Alok Bhalla and Peter J. Bumke (ed.), *Images of Rural India in the 20th Century*, New Delhi, 1992 p. 25.
105. Prior to studies based on the Marxist method, social anthropological studies on India, initiated in the first half of the 20th century helped a great deal in exploding the myth of self sufficiency of rural India in the pre-British period. William H. Wiser's study

in the 1930's (The *Hindu Jajmani System,* 1936) pertaining to the social relationships of the rural milieu in terms of *jajmani* relations provided the main clue in this direction. According to Wiser, all the castes essential to form *jajmāni* relations cannot be found within a single community. This, would then mean that inter-village networks were exigent to cater to the needs of the *jajmani* relations at some point or the other. Thus, the notion of the self sufficiency of the village communities stands questioned. M.N. Srinivas has brought out various other factors such as the non-manufacturing of salt in all the villages, non availability of iron in every village, weekly markets and so on which might have, according to the author, fostered economic ties between various villages. See his, *Dominant Caste and Other Essays,* OUP, Delhi, 1987, p. 44. Social and anthropological insights need, however, to be tested in the light of historical aspects of change based on sources about village communities in the past.

106. Almost all historical works written under this methodology have similar discussions on the growth in the rural settlements during the early medieval context. Specialized in its context is the recent work of R.S. Sharma, *Urban Decay in India,* New Delhi, 1987.
107. R.S. Sharma, *op. cit.,* 1980, p. 214.
108. B.D. Chattopadhyaya, *op. cit.,* 1990, p. 9.
109. K.M. Shrimali, *op. cit.,* 1987, p. 30.
110. R.N. Nandi, *op. cit.,* 1984, p. 4.
111. Burton Stein, *op. cit.,* 1980, pp. 90-141.
112. D.N. Jha, 'Introduction' in D.N. Jha (ed.), Feudal Social Formations in Early India, Delhi, 1987, pp. 1-19.
113. N. Karashima, *op. cit.,* 1981, pp. 85-96.
114. Y. Subbarayalu 'The Place of Ur in the Economic and Social History of the Early Tamilnadu from A.D. 750-1350', in A.V. Narasimha Murthy and B.K. Gururaja Rao (ed.), *Rangavali : Recent Researches in Indology,* Delhi, 1983, pp. 171-176.
115. R. Champakalakshmi, 'The Study of Settlement Patterns in the Cola Period : Some Perspectives', *Man and Environment,* 14, 1, 1989, pp. 91-101.
116. B.D. Chattopadhyaya, *op. cit.,* 1990. This work deals with various aspects of rural settlements belonging to three different regions of India, such as Bengal, Rajasthan and South Karnataka.
117. Burton Stein, *op. cit.,* 1980. p. 90.
118. *Ibid.,* p. 23.
119. *Ibid.,* pp. 72-73.
120. N. Karashima, *op. cit.,* 1981, pp. xxv-xxvi.
121. D.N. Jha, *op. cit.,* 1981-82, pp. 86-87.
122. N. Karashima, *op. cit.,* 1981, pp. 85-96.
123. N. Karashima, *op. cit.,* 1984, pp. 37-38.
124. M.G.S. Narayanan, 'South Indian History and Society (Studies from Inscriptions, A.D. 850-1800) by Noboru Karashima : Review Article', *Tamil Civilization,* 3, 1, March, 1985, p. 68.

125. *Ibid.*, p. 69.
126. Y. Subbarayalu, *op. cit.*, 1983, p. 173.
127. *Ibid.*, p. 175.
128. R. Champakalakshmi, *op. cit.*, 1989, p. 91.
129. *Ibid.*, p. 92.
130. *Ibid.*, p. 99.
131. This has been summarized on the basis of various works written by B.D. Chattopadhyaya which throw significant light on understanding several crucial issues of state formation from a regional perspective in the context of early medieval period. In particular the author's 'Urban Centres in Early Medieval India : An Overview in S. Bhattacharya and Romila Thapar (ed.)'. *Situating Indian History*, OUP, Delhi, 1986, pp. 8-33 is a significant case in point.
132. Chattopadhyaya, *op. cit.*, 1990 pp. 2-9. In this work the authors has picked up three types of rural structures belonging to different ecological zones of early medieval India, which have enabled him to differentiate between the nature of each settlement unit on the basis of their physical/geographical location.
133. K.A.N. Sastri, *op. cit.*, 1966, pp. 422-441.
134. A.V. Krishnamurthy, *op. cit.*, 1970, pp. 192-229.
135. K.A.N. Sastri, *op. cit.*, 1966, p. 375.
136. *Ibid.*, p. 427.
137. David Lorenzen, 'Kalamukhas of the Sakti Parisad', ABORI, L II, Poona, 1972, pp. 97-138.
138. P.B. Desai, *Jainism in South India and Some Jaina Epigraphs*, Sholapur, 1957, pp. 96-174.
139. K. Ismail, *op. cit.*, 1984. As is suggested by its title, the entire work is devoted to the social and economic role played by the temple institutions during the early medieval period. These aspects are, however, studied totally divorced from the ideological dimension of the temple institution which has been totally idelined in this text. In fact, almost all the historical works in the conventional category (such as S. Gururajachar, G.R. Kuppuswamy, G.S. Dikshit and so on) can be seen taking cognizance of the secular functioning of the temple institution when they describe the temple as a major recipient of the grants of land, commodities, revenue made by various social groups. But their inability to go beyond the given historical source which normally describes seeking religious merit among the purposes of the grants, have led them to study various acts of the temple on separate planes.
140. D.D. Kosambi, *The Culture and Civilization of Ancient India in Historical Outline*, London, 1965, pp. 114-115. Material dimension to religious discourse in early India emerges for the first time in D.D. Kosambi's treatment of *Bhagavad Gīta*.
141. R.N. Nandi, *Social Roots of Religion in Ancient India*, Calcutta, 1986, p. 94.
142. M.G.S. Narayanan and Veluthat Kesavan, 'Bhakti Movement in South India', D.N. Jha (ed.), *Feudal Social Formations in Early India*, Delhi, 1987, pp. 358-372.

143. R.S. Sharma, 'Problems of Peasant Protest in Early Medieval India', *Social Scientist,* 16, 9, September, 1988, pp. 3-16.
144. *Ibid.,* pp. 4-5.
145. *Ibid.,* pp. 14-15.
146. *Ibid.,* p. 15.
147. Hermann Kulke, 'Fragmentation and Segmentation versus Integration? Reflections on the Concepts of Indian Feudalism and the Segmentary State in Indian History' *Studies in History,* IV, 2, 1982, (cyclostyled copy).
148. Champakalakshmi, *op. cit.,* 1989, pp. 162-173.
149. Chattopadhyaya, *op. cit.,* 1994, pp. 29-34.
150. Kulke, *op. cit.,* 1982, p. 28.
151. *Ibid.,* pp. 35-38.
152. Champakalakshmi, *op. cit.,* 1989, p. 167.
153. *Ibid.,* p. 163.
154. Chattopadhyaya, *op. cit.,* 1994, p. 35.
155. R. Champakalakshmi, 'A Framework for South Indian Polity', *The Book Review,* XVIII, 6, June, 1994, p. 4.
156. *Ibid.,* p. 4.

2

GEO-POLITICAL CONTEXT

The importance of comprehending the impact of the geographical factors on historical formations has been very aptly highlighted by Fernand Braudel when he states that "geographical space as a source of explanation affects all historical realities, all spacially defined phenomena; states, societies, cultures, economies."[1] Thus, for a comprehension of the socio-cultural evolution of human settlements it becomes imperative for us to discern, in the main, the impact of the physical surroundings on them. This is mainly because it is the interaction of human society with its natural surroundings, *i.e.,* the way it uses the natural resources within its reach *et. al.,* that motivate at large, the development of the economic and socio-cultural set up of any given human settlement at a particular period of time. The physical setting which surrounds and shapes the settlement patterns of humanity cannot, however, be viewed in terms of an uniform entity. In this context the geographers have identified for us the existence of diverse physiographical entities within a single geographical region. A 'region' in terms of geography may be defined as an area constituting broadly uniform features in its natural setting such as relief, climate, natural vegetation, geo-morphological formations, soils and so on.[2] This apparent uniformity of physiography at the regional level distinguishes each region from its neighbouring region. However, when viewed in closer proximity we find that these regions are replete with local diversities based chiefly on the local relief, climate and other such local topographical features that cannot be avoided as insignificant entities.

One finds that it is these local topographical entities having a distinct identity of their own, termed as 'sub-regions' or, regions of the second or third order, that go to define the specific nature of human settlements.[3] This makes it crucial for us to comprehend the geography of the region/sub-regions under study so as to arrive at sound conclusions over the specific structural formations and thus defy any universalization of this variable to analyse history. Our comprehension of the specificities of historical formations would then ultimately contribute to our perception of the totality of the historical phenomena at any given point of time.

One of the macro-regions of India, namely, the Deccan has come into focus often in the historical literature pertaining to early South India and the Maharashtra region. Our comprehensions of the historical geography of south western Deccan which is the main focus of our study, make it crucial for us to first of all get an understanding of what constitutes the Deccan peninsula as a whole and how it has been perceived by various scholars writing on it. This is mainly because the former was invariably treated as a part of the entire Deccan plateau. The expression 'Deccan' is a corruption of the Sanskrit word *dakshiṇa* or *dakshiṇāpatha* which means the 'right hand' or the South.[4] On this basis it has been considered that in a broad sense, the term 'Deccan' includes the whole of India between the southern sea and the Vindhyas. Perceptions on the physical boundaries of *'dakshiṇāpatha'* in the texts of early India have varied considerably. In this context, H.C. Ray Chaudhari has quoted works such as the Bharata's *Nāṭya Śāstra,* the Bhuvanakosha of the *Purāṇas,* the *Matsya Purāṇa* and the Pāli *Jātakas,* all of which include the Tamil country as the southern limit of what is referred to as *dakshiṇāpatha.*[5] On the other hand, we do not always have as its southern limit the Tamil country. Some of the early works like the Periplus equate, what is termed as Deccan today, to the region beyond Broach on the Narmada which by implication seems to be excluding the Tamil country from its definition.[6]

In drawing upon the works of the scholars situated in the context of modern India, we find a similar variance of opinion in their comprehension of what constitutes the 'Deccan' region. It has been observed through our survey of the secondary literature on the Deccan region that scholars are not agreed upon a single definition of the Deccan. Their perceptions of the Deccan as a historical entity have been largely shaped on the one hand, by their linguistic consideration and on the other hand, by the choice of their area and topic of interest. In this context we have been able to divide these works into two main types : (1) those that have dealt with the Deccan region perse and (2) those that have tackled the history of the Deccan as a part of their main concerns with the history of the southern peninsula as a whole. To the former category belong the works of R.G. Bhandarkar, J. Dubreuil, A.S. Altekar, G. Yazdani, D.R. Das, Sumati Mulay and so on. Works of K.A.N. Sastri, Sudhakar Chattopadhyaya and that of T.K. Ravindran, P.N. Chopra and N. Subrahmanian among many others best exemplify the latter category.

For R.G. Bhandarkar, who was mainly interested in the history of the Maratha region, the word 'Dekkan' in its specific sense denoted the region watered by the upper Godavari and that which lay between this river and the river Krishna. The word 'Deccan' is equated in its essential sense with the region of Maharashtra which forms the main focus of the author's attention.[7] In her recent study on historical geography Sumati Mulay also makes this kind of anachronistic reference to the Deccan region. In her own words, "*Dakshiṇāpatha,* or modern Deccan, in its widest meaning, was used for the whole of the Peninsula and in the narrower sense denoted the region now called Maharastra".[8] Both these writers were interested in writing the history of the Marathi speaking regions and therefore, they conformed the definition of the Deccan region to suit their linguistic interests. On the other hand, we find that A.S. Altekar has equated all the regions which were under the main control of the Rāshṭrakuta rulers to be the Deccan region. This definition has given primacy to the political configuration of an ancient dynasty at a particular point in time to define the region. He has thus included in his study, southern Gujarat, entire Maharashtra, parts of Karnataka and Andhra in his idea of the Deccan region.[9] Similarly, we find that G. Yazdani has approximated the Deccan with the region north of the Tungabhadra, stretching northwards as far as the borders of the Vidarbha country or the Berar.[10] This choice has been motivated by the fact that the primary concern of the editor of this volume on the history of Deccan was to write a comprehensive history of the erstwhile Hyderabad state.[11] Thus he had taken more recent political boundaries as his criteria for defining the Deccan. In other words, both these scholars have perceived the Deccan region in terms of the political boundaries which can be true of one period but not of all periods.

J. Dubreuil uses the word 'Deccan' to designate the entire area south of the Narmada which, according to him, is how it has been described in the earliest works on India.[12] His aim in this work had been to begin the ancient history of the Deccan with the time it had come under the influence of the Asokan rule as indicated by the location of his inscriptions. Therefore, the author, while considering the entire southern India as constituting the Deccan, avoids the regions ruled by the Cheras, Cholas and the Pandyas which, according to the him, "have always remained a little isolated".[13] We may find a more rational approach towards the definition of the Deccan region in the work of D.R. Das whose main interest of study was the economic aspects of it. The Deccan, according to the author included the southern part of Gujarat, the whole of Maharashtra, part of Andhra Pradesh, the northern part of Karnataka along with some adjoining tracks of Madhya Pradesh and Orissa, to the south of the river Mahanadi.[14] This definition is most expansive keeping in mind that his history was on economic aspects rather than on narrower political boundaries of dynasties. K.A. Nilakantha Sastri, on the other hand, equates the Deccan/Dakshina with all of South India, *i.e.,* the land lying south of the Vindhyas. The terms South India and the Deccan are considered interchangeable by the author.[15] A very similar approach can be seen in a recent work on South India. The author Sudhakar Chattopadhyaya has defined the land lying to the south of the Vindhyas as the Peninsular India which according to him was "known as Dakshiṇāpatha to the ancients".[16] In a text book definition of South India, the word 'Deccan' is considered to be an anglicised form of the Sanskrit–*dakshiṇāpatha* which means South India.[17] Authors of this work were concerned mainly with writing the history of the South India as a whole and in the process, they did not differentiate between the Deccan and the other parts of South India. By implication this would mean that the states of Maharashtra and Gujarat have been excluded by these authors from their definition of the Deccan region and thus they differ markedly from the scholars discussed earlier.

As can be seen from the above survey we would like to reiterate here that the changing perceptions of various scholars as to what constitutes the Deccan, have been largely a result of linguistic biases (Bhandarkar, Sumati Mulay), political or dynastic framework of study (Yazdani, Altekar) and regional interests (K.A.N. Sastri, Sudhakar Chattopadhyaya and P.N. Chopra and others). In current historical studies these interests have led the scholars to take into consideration the present day linguistic state boundaries for historical research. As such we find that the south western part of the Deccan region, which forms the main focus of our study, has been studied as a part of the history of the Karnataka state[18] on the one hand, and on the other, it has also been dealt with as a part of the history of the Andhra Pradesh state.[19] It has further been part of studies which are dynastic histories. These invariably include this region as it was always being contested for political supremacy.[20]

In terms of geography, the Deccan as a whole with a specific focus on the plateau area, alternately termed as the peninsular interior[21] or the vast peninsular upland, forms structurally the oldest land mass in the country. The peninsular consists of a great tabular block with a general slope to the east, bordering on the Indo-Gangetic plain in the north, to the tip of South India in the south, the western ghats in the west and the eastern ghats in the east. Its stretches constitute such broad physical features as the mountains, uplands, plateau, peneplains, river basins, troughs etc.[22] Climatically, today the entire area, except for the eastern hills, the western ghats and the rain shadow of the latter, could be described as tropical savannah with monsoon modifications, but such a description again conceals considerable variations.[23] Thus, having a wide latitudinal extent and consequently a variety of local climates giving rise to great variations in the soil and vegetation patterns, the Deccan has a higher degree of diversity than the northern plains.[24]

We have observed in our historiographical survey that as a result of the diverse physiographical structures of the Deccan plateau, all its sub-regions have not been subject to equal attention by historians working on its early history. The rule of the Śātavahanas in the Deccan during the early centuries A.D. was followed later by the rule of the Ikshvākus, Cutus and their successors such as the Vākatakas.[25] Studies on this period have been dealt with considerably by various scholars writing on the early history of the Deccan.[26] From the beginning of the Śātavahana period one sees an overall increase in the number of settlements in the fertile tracts of the upper Godavari and the upper Krishna valleys of the Deccan plateau.[27] While the western and eastern peninsula were strewn with thousands of rock-cut *caityas, lenas, vihāras, stūpas* and other religious establishments, the mid Deccan remained nearly barren during the early centuries A.D.[28] The lower Deccan emerged into focus particularly during the 6th-7th centuries A.D. under the rule of the Chālukyas of Bādami who also established their hold on the eastern Deccan region by establishing their rule in the Vengi region.[29] While the south western Deccan has figured intermittently in the political and art histories of the early medieval period beginning from the 6th century A.D.,[30] it is chiefly the eastern part of the plateau that seems to have gained greater prominence in terms of historical scholarship for defining this period.[31] Such a bias could be related to the prosperity of this region due to the fertility of the eastern part. Owing to the eastern tilt of the peninsular plateau it has the advantage of its rivers which rise in the western ghats to flow towards the eastern belt providing immense fertility to the soils of the eastern plains.[32] Such a strategic locale has necessarily meant its control by various dynasties of the lower Deccan and the extreme south during the early medieval period, which in turn, has naturally drawn the attention of the scholars of history. In the process one has observed that other parts of the Deccan region, particularly the south western part of it, constituting the area lying between the Krishna and the Tungabhadra rivers, has been given marginal attention in terms of discussing it only when it figured in the military conquests of the major powers that chiefly had their concerns in the eastern region of Vengi.[33] As much remains to be done in terms of analysing the nature and periods of change in this region we have chosen the south western part of the Deccan region **(Map I)** for our study with the hope of bringing to light the hitherto historically unresearched aspects of study at a specific micro level.

The area of our study roughly falls between longitudes 70° 30'–78° 18' E and latitudes 15° 0'–16° 34' N. The western boundary of this region comprises the plains or the maidan region of the western ghats. The river Krishna forms its northern boundary, the river Tungabhadra where river Varada meets it, forms its southern boundary and the eastern boundary is marked by the confluence of the rivers Krishna and Tungabhadra **(Map I)**. The region of our study, which could well be classified as the 'Krishna-Tungabhadra Doab,[34] has well defined local physiographical variations leading to the formation of distinctly demarcated sub-regions **(Map II)** each identified chiefly by one or more dominant characteristics. The region as a whole is constituted of the northern maidan region of the Karnataka plateau and bordering on its eastern and south eastern tips are the peneplains of the Telangana and Rayalaseema of the Andhra plateau.[35] The northern maidan (a terminology derived due to its relatively low and subdued relief), is a landscape of monotonous, seemingly endless plateau, covered with rich black cotton soil. The entire region of study is drained by several rivers, most significant among them being the Krishna to the north of the region under consideration and the Tungabhadra which forms the southern boundary. Others are the feeders to these rivers; important among these being the Varada, Hirahalla, Malaprabha and Ghataprabha. These rivers rise from the western ghats and flow towards the eastern belt of the Plateau.[36] They render, along with the local relief conditions, a diversified physiographic setting to the region under study which enables us to identify different 'sub-regions' of our area of study.

This region consists of such diverse local features of physiography as the hills, plains and peneplains. On the whole, three broad sub-regions or physiographic zones can be differentiated within the region of our study which, for the sake of convenience, have been classified by us into the categories of sub-region A, B and C **(Map II).** Sub-region A : The north western part of our area of study lying amidst the rivers Krishna, Malaprabha and Ghataprabha is marked on the north by the topography of Deccan trap which merges some what abruptly with that of granites towards its south. Beginning with the Sitamalai hills, this hilly landscape is typically that of gneiss and granite with irregular rock exposures separated by black soil. Wherever sand stones and quartzites outcrop, the topography consists of low lines of ridges. The valley widens out wherever the gneiss outcrops and gives agricultural land capable of local irrigation. The valley is well protected all round by the steep scarps of sand stone ridges and that must have been the principal reason for choice of this site by the early Chālukyan rulers as can be gauged by the existence of historical ruins in these parts.[37]

Sub-region B : Towards the south and the east of sub-region A lay the vast stretch of the plains region well supplied by rivers and streams. Beginning in the west with the river Malaprabha and its main tributary, the Bennihalla and several other seasonal streams,[38] the region is paralleled on either side by the rivers Krishna and Tungabhadra. The undulating topography of this northern maidan region is characterised today by dry beds of meandering streams and fissures due to intense soil erosion.[39] The monotony of the landscape is broken by an occasional isolated hill and is marked by scarps of the Manoli and Soundatti ranges. This region is considered to be extensively cultivated today representing the best developed tract of the area. It may however, be noted here that these plains were brought under cultivation gradually over a period of time and did not uniformly represent habitation in all historical periods. The soils of these plains are mainly of two types, namely, the black soil and the red soil.[40] While the western portion of this sub-region predominates in black soils, the eastern is characterized by a predominance of red soils. Both these soils show a variety both in texture and

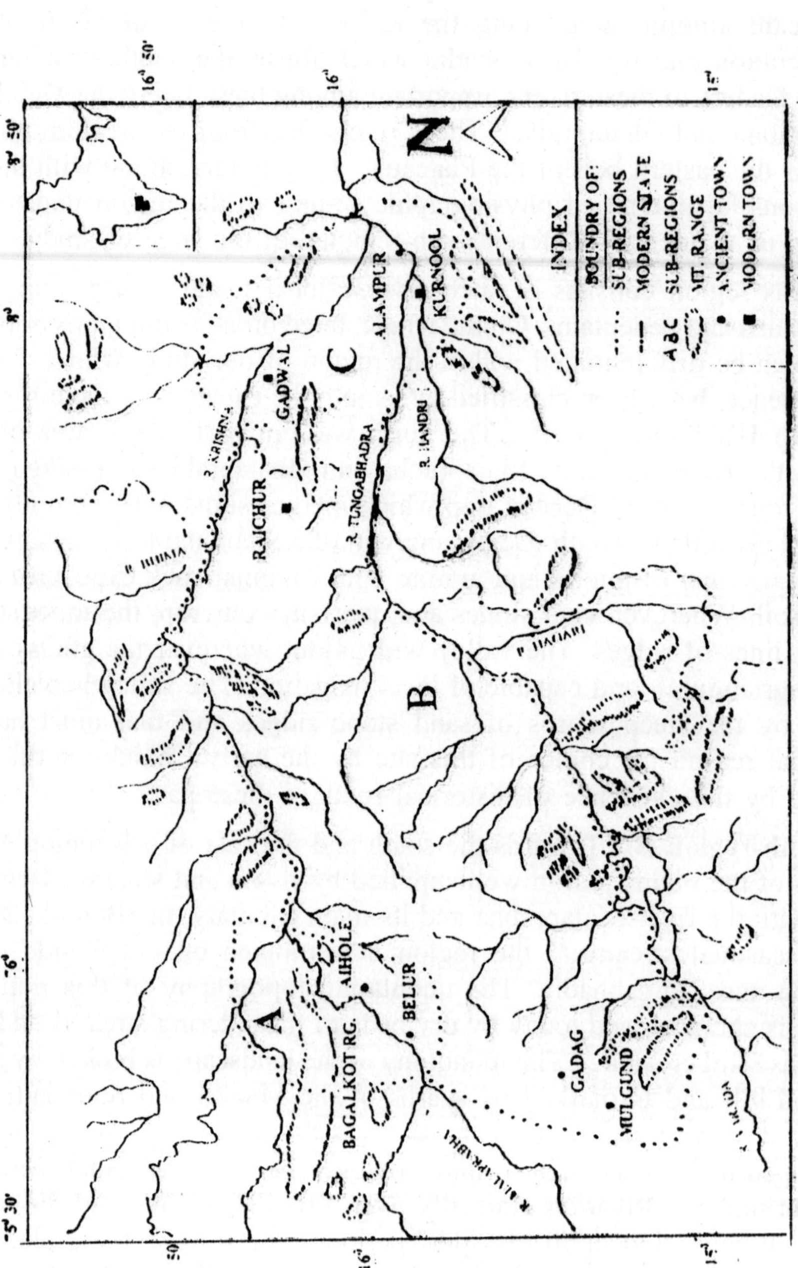

Map II : DELINEATION OF SUB REGIONS AND PHYSIOGRAPHY

appearance according to the nature of the underlying rocks and also exhibit a great deal of variation in thickness, consistency and colour.[41] The undulating black cotton soil strips, cut by numerous nalas characterize the region of Dharwar schists which is today practically denuded of trees and presents a monotonous land scape. While the gneissic region is generally more or less broken and covered with a thin mantle of red loamy soil, gneissic hills wherever they occur, form bold reliefs in the landscape.[42] The eastern half of the plains, leading to the confluence of the Krishna and the Tungabhadra rivers, is characterized by a few hillocks and scrub jungles and the sedimentary formations of this part of the region occupy more or less flat plateaus.[43] Characterized by low rainfall and general dryness, the Doab is richly endowed with major natural resources such as minerals and vast expanses of agricultural tracts.[44] The moisture retention capacity of the black soils of the west enables the crops to remain unaffected during the drought season.[45] The mighty river systems of the Krishna and the Tungabhadra consist of rich alluvial soils in the river basins. The eastern part of the plains constitute predominantly red soils, interspersed with regur or black soils. Today cotton and groundnuts grow well in this type of soil condition. Jawar, bajra, ragi, wheat and cereals are the other crops grown here.[46]

Sub-region C : The peneplains of the Andhra plateau have been divided into the Telangana and the Rayalaseema peneplains by having the Krishna river as their dividing line. This sub-region pertains chiefly to the south western part of Telangana and the north western parts of the Rayalaseema peneplains which lay continguous to the plains of the northern maidan. Its physical set up consists of a completely peneplained surface developed on the gneissic basement. In the southern part of the Telangana peneplain the surface is throughout an undulating plain.[47] The rivers Krishna and the Tungabhadra flow through this region towards the east forming a confluence at Alampur region. The Krishna-Tungabhadra (the middle Krishna valley) today represents a fertile level and highly populated tract with a predominance of the agrarian economy.[48] The major soil group is red earth. Black soils, mostly of clayed loams and deep clays, occur as narrow strips alongside the banks of the Krishna and Tungabhadra and the natural streams. The loamy sands are brown to red in colour and poor in fertility.[49] The river Tungabhadra forms the boundary between the Raichur Doab and the western Rayalaseema peneplain. The Rayalaseema plateau is a vast table land forming a northward extension of the Karnataka plateau. The amount of rainfall in Rayalaseema is much lower than in Telangana. This is because the region is located between two uplands–the Karnataka plateau on the west and the Andhra, or, eastern ghats in the east. Black cotton soils are predominant in the taluks of Nandikotkur and the adjoining areas. The availability of alluvial soils is quite small and is confined to a few villages near the confluence of Bhanavasi and the Krishna river.[50]

To put the above discussion in a nutshell, one has observed that the total region of our study, which forms a part of the macro-region of the Deccan peninsula, broadly constitutes the land lying between the Krishna and Tungabhadra rivers and has certain distinct physiographic variations. These can be highlighted firstly in terms of a predominance of a hilly terrain characterizing sub-region A. The Sitamani hills and the gneissic valleys located within them in this sub-region give a good agricultural land capable of local irrigation.[51] Sub-region B on the other hand, constituting a vast stretch of the plains, falls within the northern maidan region and has in its western part a predominance of the rich black soils and red soils in the east. The maidan region is considered to be extensively cultivated representing the best developed tract in its neighbourhood.[52] Finally, sub-region C constituting the peneplained surface of the Rayalaseema plateau, roughly includes the region around the confluence of the Krishna-Tungabhadra rivers. The major soil group here is red earth, comprising of clay loams[53] and black soils.[54] The undulating character of the terrain of this sub-region lends itself favourably to irrigation from tanks, wells and streams.[55]

In terms of the present day administrative boundaries which cut across the two linguistic states of Karnataka and Andhra Pradesh, our area of study comprises the south eastern portion of Bijapur district in sub-region A, eastern Dharwar and the entire Raichur district along with the southern tip of the Gulbarga district form sub-region B. Sub-region C can be said to constitute by the south-western and north-western parts of the Mahabubnagar and Kurnool districts respectively. Our emphasis on defining this area of study spanning over two administrative divisions of present day India, has been able to do away with an approach of viewing all historical changes within the rigid linguistic state boundaries which are purely a modern day creation.[56] Imposing these over the early past only means taking up an anachronistic view of historical reality which cannot be studied in its true sense within the purview of artificial boundaries of change for any given period of history. Deviation from such an approach has helped us in analysing the source material of our study in direct relation to the physical surroundings of its setting and thus arrive at sound conclusions over the socio-economic change of our period of study at a specific level.

Against the backdrop of the above geographical survey described by us we have been able to arrive at certain broad conclusions regarding the nature of historical geography of the area under study. A corresponding survey of the inscriptional data available for our study has enabled us to identify potential zones of fertile tracts for the early settlements. In this regard we have observed that sub-region A and the western part of sub-region B along with certain pockets of sub-region C stand out in terms of their richness in settlements. Chiefly, three clusters of temple sites **(Map VI)** largely indicative of the concentration of rural settlements to support them, have been identified as pertaining to the area and the period of our study.

These are :

I	Muddebihal–Bagalkot–Badami–Ilkal	–	sub-region A
II	Gadag–Naregal–Ron–Yelburga–Kopbal–Lingsugur–Shorapur	–	sub-region B
III	Alampur–Nandikotkur–Kurnool	–	sub-region C

Corresponding upon the above survey we have been able to identify an interesting pattern of historical and chronological evolution of the settlements belonging to each of these sub-regions at various points of time. Firstly, it was sub-region A and pockets of sub-region C, especially the Alampur region, that seem to have emerged to the forefront in terms of temple settlements much before the period taken up for the present study. In the context of sub-region A in particular, we see that most of its area formed the base for the early Chālukyan rulers (5th century A.D.–8th century A.D.) who had their capital at Badami in this sub-region **(Map III)**. It has been suggested that in fact, the sites chosen by the early Chālukyas for establishing their capitals and religious monuments had already attained importance in 'proto art history' known through the megalithic monuments located here. These, it is further suggested, became obscured by the Chālukyan temples of great artistic beauty, variety and vivacity.[57] In this respect places such as the Nandikeshwar–Mahakut section, Badami, Aihole and Pattadakal stand out in terms of their architectural remains for the early Chālukyan period. The Nandikeshwar–Mahakut section, locked in between two gorges, was in early Chālukyan days a flourishing tract as can be seen from extensive historical ruins at this place. The valley is well protected all round by the steep scarps of sand ridges which must have been the principal reason for the choice of this site by the Chālukyan rulers.[58] Other sites such as Pattadakal, Badami and Aihole are also found around the above discussed location. Of these, Aihole has been considered to be the birth place of the Chālukyan style of temple building. It is supposed to contain nearly seventy temples dating from A.D. 450 to A.D. 650.[59] Pattadakal, located on the left bank of Malaprabha, is supposed to represent the next stage in the development of Chālukyan art and is said to have the best temples of the early Chālukyan age which amount to about ten temples in number.[60] Badami on the other hand, is known for both the temples constructed in it by the early Chālukyas and its fortification by the Chālukyan ruler Pulakeśin I as early A.D. 543.[61]

In a similar way, one finds that sub-region C, particularly in the Alampur area, located near the confluence of the Krishna–Tungabhadra rivers, emerges into limelight in terms of its architectural splendour during the early Chālukyan period.

In fact, the temple-building activity in this sub-region seems to have started at a much earlier period. In this context it is stated that beginning in the Ikshvāku period, the art history of western Andhra seemingly had its chief centre at Alampur. This is so because as early as about A.D. 299, an inscription records the donations made by an individual to the God of Alampur.[62] The temples built by the early Chālukya rulers in this region however, reveal a distinct innovation in the temple architecture of Karnataka and Andhra.[63]

It is interesting to find that the next phase of evolution of the settlements, that is, during the rule of the Rāshṛakūṭa dynasty (8th-10th century A.D.), can be seen focussed chiefly upon the western part of sub-region B, which constituted primarily the eastern part of the Dharwar district **(Map III)**. Thus we find that in Gadag, the headquarters of Gadag taluka, altogether thirty four inscriptions have been found belonging to the reign of the Rāshṭrakūṭas and prior to the rule of the Vijayanagara dynasty. The earliest inscription is of the reign of Rāshṭrakūṭa Indra III, dated to A.D. 918.[64] Similarly, at another important temple site Hombala, nine inscriptions ranging between the periods 11th and the 16th centuries A.D., have been found.[65] Lakkundi, another renowned historical settlement has twenty nine inscriptions representing the later Chālukya, Kalāchuri, Yādava and Hoysala dynasties.[66] We have several such examples for this sub-region. The eastern part of sub-region B, particularly the western portion of the Raichur district, lying contiguous to the area just discussed, begins to figure actively in the inscriptional sources of mainly the western Chālukyas of Kalyāni, *i.e.,* from the latter half of the 10th century A.D. Several places such as Gabbur, Ittagi, Maski, Kallur, Kopbal, Kaknur, Lingsugur and so on, are mentioned as prominent centres in the inscriptions of the later Chalukyan rulers. It is however, significant to note that it is only during the period of the Vijayanagara rulers that Raichur including its eastern half, developed into a rich settlement zone.[67]

The aforesaid statements do not in any way mean that these tracts were not settled earlier to the dates mentioned above. We have conclusive evidences to show the occupation of sub-region B right from the pre-historic times. In this context the sites of Maski and Kallur from Raichur district stand out in terms of their richness in the availability of pre-historic sites.[68] Later, this sub-region seems to have been brought under the sway of the Mauryas and, just as in other parts of the Deccan, the edicts of Ashoka have been discovered at Maski and Kopbal.[69] From this period onwards we have concrete evidence of the rule over this region by various dynasties such as the Śātavāhanas, Vākāṭakas, early Chālukyas and so on who were controlling various parts of the Deccan region during different periods of time.[70] However, our intention in the main is to emphasize that from about 1000 A.D. there was an increase in the intensity with which settlements began to proliferate in sub-region B and this makes it stand out as different from both sub-regions A and C for the same period.

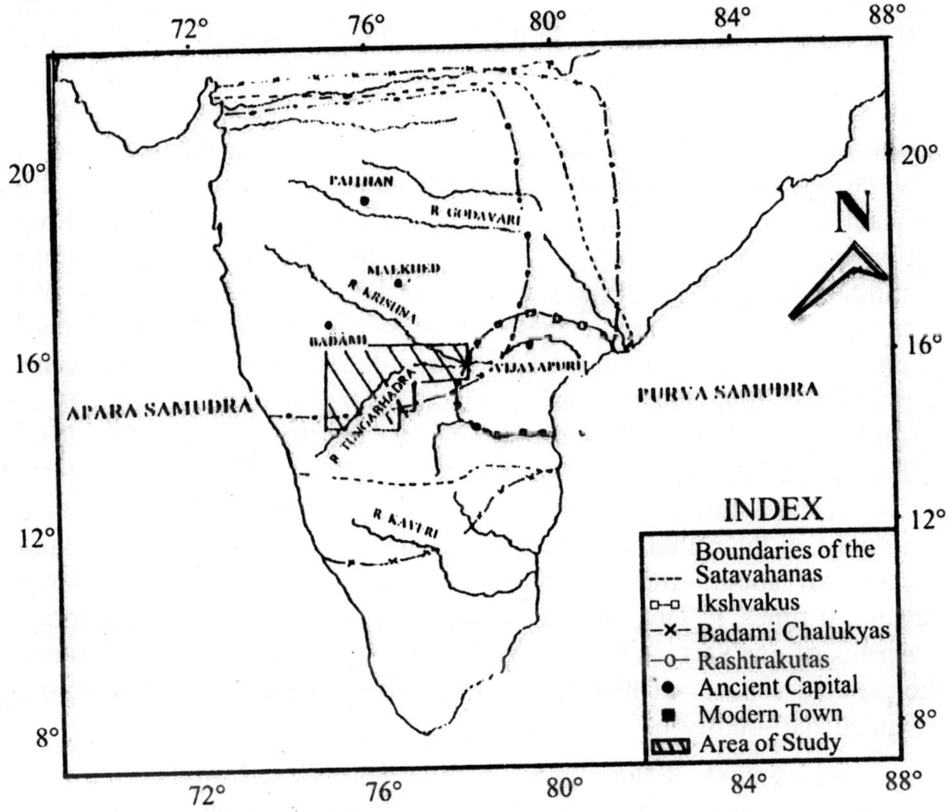

Map III : AREAS OF POLITICAL CONTROL IN THE PRE 10TH CENTURY A.D.

It is important to underscore at this juncture that whatever few historical works we have, on the history of pre-10th century A.D. south western Deccan as a whole, they have concentrated chiefly on writing the architectural and political history of the Chālukyas of Bādami with a focus on sub-regions A and C.[71] These two sub-regions have at large figured in a prominent way in historical writings of the south since the region of Vengi in the eastern Deccan had formed a bone of contention for various dynasties ruling over both the Deccan and the south during the pre-10th century A.D. period.[72] In this context we see a slow but distinct shift in the focus of historical writings for the period from 1000 A.D. onwards as now sub-region B begins to emerge as an area of brisk political activity. We have considerable number of works for this period highlighting the rule and wars fought by various major and minor dynasties located in this sub-region.[73] It may be significant to state at this juncture that the earlier politically contested region of Vengi begins to be slowly replaced by the Raichur Doab as the most coveted zone of military activity and figures as such in the historical scholarship of this period for the area of our study. In these works we begin to find that the physical description of the Doab as the most fertile area due to its location between two rivers Krishna and Tungabhadra, and its potential for generating revenue is given undue prominence.[74] Coupled with the above is the characterization of the Raichur area as the scene of perennial fighting beginning with the Chālukyas of Kalyāṇi and the Cholas and culminating with the Vijayanagara times.[75] The over emphasis on writing only on the military aspects has resulted in a neglect of understanding the potential of social and economic history of this area particularly in pre-Vijayanagar times. In fact, existing historiography has tended to underplay the crucial aspects of analysis such as the nature of social and economic formations and other related aspects of historical change which contribute significantly to comprehended the totality of the past.

It is in the context of the above historiographical survey that we wish to clarify our stand with regard to the study of the physiographic setting and its relation to understanding historical developments of the early medieval period for our area of study. We are here trying to comprehend not just an occupation of space by various ruling dynasties from outside, as has hitherto been done in the historical works of the region, but an evolution of well settled tracts as a result of the interaction between various human forces and the natural environ represented by the physiographic setting for different points of time and space. From the 10th century A.D. onwards the concentration of inscriptional sources in sub-region B and the increasing references made in them to various settlements and socio-economic and political aspects attest to the fact that this sub-region, unlike sub-region A and C was a centre of historical activity during this period. It is primarily for this reason that we have taken up sub-region B as the nuclear area of our analysis as it eventually displays a potential for comprehending various structural forces at work which have helped particularly in initiating the processes of regional state and social formation during the early medieval set up. We wish to then compare and contrast the historical developments of sub-region B with those of sub-regions A and C which represent a more developed phase of political activity visible in historical terms from the previous centuries. We wish to further highlight in this context that sub regions A and C which lie contiguously to the eastern and western borders of sub-region B seem to be at the same time, merging with it in terms of the development of its historical cultural pattern during the period under discussion. It is in this sense that sub-regions A and C can be organically linked up to the cultural evolution of sub-region B. At the same time it is pertinent to note here that local strands of such a fusion at a sub-regional level certainly exhibit subtle variations in terms of state formation and this owes much to the local topographical features which define each of these sub-regions.

The impact of the geographical configuration of the region under study can be seen considerably and most conspicuously in the nature of the political power structure that evolved during the period under study. However, before we discuss this we give a brief outline of the political history of the region and period of study. During this period south western Deccan witnessed the rise of numerous dynasties in different periods. Of these dynasties the most powerful between the period 1000-1200 A.D. had been the Western Chālukyas of Kalyāṇi (A.D. 973-A.D. 1200), the Kalāchuris of Kalyāṇi (A.D. 1156-A.D. 1183), Yādavas of Devagiri (A.D. 1175-A.D. 1312) and the Hoysalas of Dwarasamudra (A.D. 1022-A.D. 1348). Each of these ruled different parts of what we have described above as the south western Deccan and many of them naturally had control of territories outside this region as well **(Map IV)**.

It would be appropriate to state that the Chālukyas of Kalyāṇi emerged as the most powerful ruling dynasty for a major period of our study. This dynasty came to power in the western Deccan after overthrowing the Rāshṭrakūṭa dynasty in the second half of the 10th century A.D. (973 A.D.). At the time of accession, its first ruler Taila II was ruling over a small area at Bagewadi in the Bijapur district.[76] Taila II, before he actually became the sovereign king, was governing in these parts as a subordinate of the Rāshṭrakūṭas.[77] After establishing himself on the throne, with Manyakheta as his capital, Taila spent several years consolidating his sway in the western Deccan over the whole area between the rivers Narmada and the Tungabhadra.[78] Roughly speaking, the area under the rule of the later Chālukyas of Kalyāṇi comprised the whole of the Kannada speaking country, a considerable portion of that part of the Deccan which is now known as Maharashtra and the coastal Konkan tract called Goa.[79] The Chālukya rulers of Kalyāṇi, like their predecessors, were also involved in hard fought battles as a policy of aggrandize-

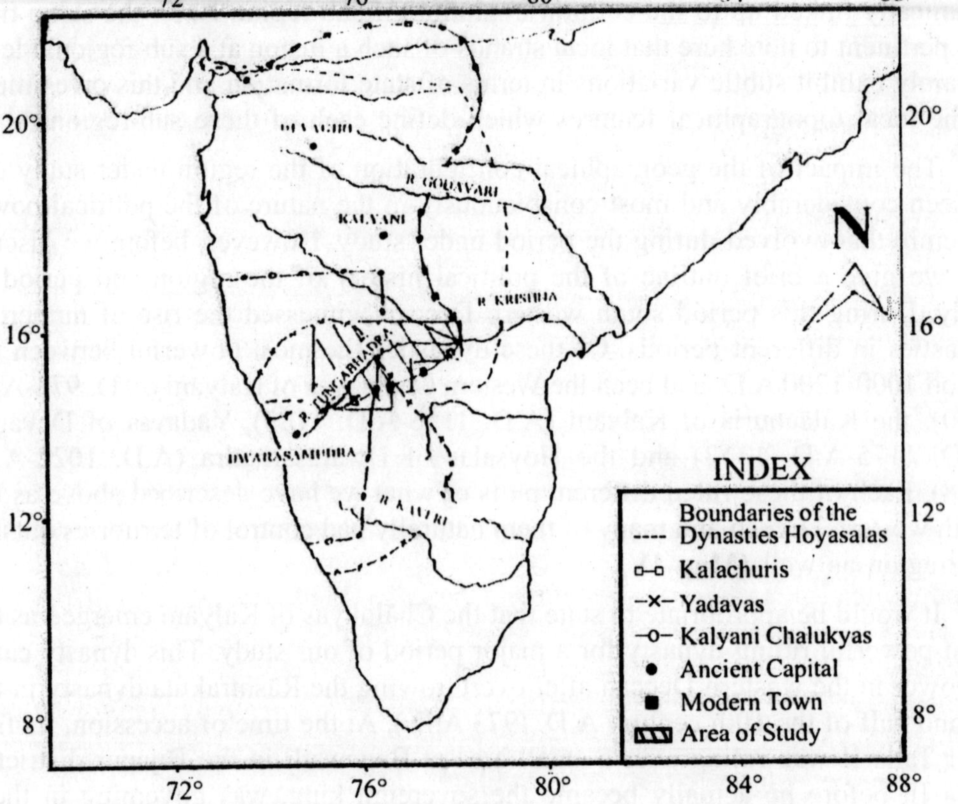

Map IV : AREAS OF POLITICAL CONTROL BY MAIN RULING FAMILIES (1000 A.D.–1200 A.D.)

ment over their neighbouring territories. This was with the Pāramaras in the northern Deccan and the Cholas in the extreme South India. In particular, their wars with the Chola rulers over the Vengi region have been considered the most fierce.[80] During this period, *i.e.,* from A.D. 973 to A.D. 1198, the Chālukya kingdom was ruled over by Taila II, Satyāśraya, Jayasiṁha II, Someśvara I, Someśvara II, Vikramāditya VI, Someśvara III, Jagadekamalla II, Taila III and Someśvara IV.[81] The capital of the Chālukyas was shifted from Manyakheta to Kalyāṇapura which is located in the present day Bidar district of Karnataka State during the reign of Someśvara I (A.D. 1044-A.D. 1068), and it continued to be a capital of all his successors.[82] It is important to underscore at this juncture that the capital city of the Chālukyas remained outside the present area of study delineated by us. During the rule of Someśvara IV, the last ruler of the Chālukyas, Kalyāṇi was captured by the Kalāchuri rulers around A.D. 1162 and the former shifted his capital to Jayantipura, *i.e.,* Banavasi[83] which was again located outside the area of study defined by us. Except for the southern area ruled by the Chālukyas (Kadur, Hassan, Bangalore, Mysore and Coorg districts), the Kalāchuris conquered the entire territory of the Chālukya rulers but ruled for only a brief period (A.D. 1157-A.D. 1183).[84]

Rulers of the Kalāchuri dynasty originally hailed from northern India. Having been dispossessed of their homeland due to the expansive activities of the Gūrjara-Pratihāras, some members of this family migrated towards the south and settled at Mangalivada in the Sholapur district around the beginning of the 9th century A.D.[85] This area continued to be their core area of political control when they functioned as subordinates to the rulers of the western Chālukyan dynasty.[86] One of the chiefs of this dynasty, Bijjala II assumed imperial titles by about 1157 A.D. and established his rule at Kalyāṇa.[87] His rule was, however, not recognized by other equally powerful rulers of such dynasties as the Yādavas of Devagiri and the Hoysalas of Dwārasamudra.[88] These dynasties eventually succeeded, in the latter half of the 12th century A.D., in partitioning the Chālukyan territories among themselves.[89] The Yādava chiefs, also known as the Seunas, originally belonged to the Nasik district in the present day Maharastra State.[90] These chiefs holding a subordinate status under the Chālukyas of Kalyāṇa were able to establish their independent rule by about A.D. 1185-86.[91] They were able to secure the northern territories of the Chālukya kingdom upto the river Krishna and established their capital at Devagiri,[92] which is also located in the present day Maharashtra State. The Hoysalas of Dwārasamudra, the chief rivals of the Yādavas discussed above, originally belonged to the Sahyadri mountain region below the Tungabhadra river, located in the present day Chikmagalur district of Karnataka.[93] These rulers, who were also the subordinates of the Chālukya rulers of Kalyāṇa, were able to declare their independence and consolidate their position in the Chālukyan territories south of the river Krishna by about A.D. 1190.[94] In fact, the river Malaprabha where it meets the river Krishna formed the boundary between the Hoysala and the Yādava territories of rule.[95]

The patterns of political control and the ensuing wars between various dynasties throughout the early medieval period that also affected our area of study, namely, the south western Deccan, were to a large extent shaped by the physiographical set up of the Deccan as a whole. In this context it would be pertinent to point out that S.M. Alam has brought out the existence of heterogeneous politico-geographical zones within the Deccan region by relating the nature of the political imperatives to the geography of the area.[96] Accordingly, the Deccan has been divided primarily into three zones. Firstly, he defines the 'marchland Deccan' or, the area of 'political assimilation' comprising chiefly the area between the Vindhyas and the Godavari. This has been defined as the region wherein its control was essential for the political powers in northern India to get access to the Deccan region for the ultimate invasion of South India. Then came the land lying between the rivers Godavari and the Krishna which has been defined by Alam as the 'heart land Deccan' or, the area of 'political control'. Due to it being a fertile region supporting a large population, Alam is of the opinion that it has served as a core or the nuclear area for the rise of powerful dynasties which also began to wield considerable influence over the area south of the river Krishna. The area south of the river Krishna according to the author constituted the 'peripheral Deccan' or, an 'area of political influence'. This was so because the area south of the Krishna river was in actual control of the local lords who owed allegiance to the imperial powers of the heartland region.[97]

One may accept the definition taken by Alam with regard to the area of our study which lies to the south of the river Krishna, to the extent that the political configuration of this region was subject largely to the influence exercised by various major dynasties whose actual base of political power remained essentially outside the south western Deccan. In this context all the three capitals of the Chālukyas of Kalyāṇi such as Mānyakheta, Kalyāṇi and Jayantipura were located outside the area taken up for the present study. Of these, Mānyakheta and Kalyāṇi were located north of the river Krishna. Other rulers of the region such as the Kalāchuris and Yādavas too had their bases of power north of the Krishna. While the former was based in the Sholapur region, the latter at Devagiri located in the Maharashtra State. On the other hand, the Hoysalas of Dwārasamudra had their core area of political control in the area south of the river Tungabhadra. It is significant to note in this context that it is chiefly those dynasties which were not native to the area between the rivers Krishna and Tungabhadra that have, during the period of our study, tried to control it, albeit from outside. Urges of various political powers to control the south western Deccan region could be effectively linked up to the presence of the fertile Raichur Doab in this region which had immense potential of generating agrarian surplus. In such a context, an examination of the processes of the exercise of political control which find an explicit expression in the form of military conquests undertaken by an outside power (in the period under consideration, it is chiefly the Kalyāṇi Chālukyas who emerge as the main rulers), would help us in comprehending the geo-political configuration peculiar to our area of study.

While basing themselves to the north of the Krishna river, with Kalyāṇi in the present day Bidar district as their capital, the Western Chālukyas (A.D. 973-A.D. 1198) tried to control the fertile tracts between the rivers Krishna and the Tungabhadra on the one hand, and on the other, the Vengi kingdom of the eastern Deccan. In the process they were engaged in constant wars with the Cholas and other smaller rules who owned allegiance to these rulers depending upon their strength. The frontier between the Chālukya and the Chola kingdom fluctuated about the line of the Tungabhadra as a result of many wars. It is commonly known that the Vengi and the Raichur Doab changed hands on several occasions.[98] Taila II's successor Chālukya Satyāśraya invaded Vengi in 1006 A.D. Around the same time the Chola ruler captured a good part of the Raichur Doab.[99] Later, Chālukya Jayasiṁha II wrested Raichur Doab and reached upto the Tungabhadra to annex some territory to its south.[100] On the whole the region lying between the Krishna and the Tungabhadra constituted the first line of defence in the north for the empires that were reared in the South. For the powers beyond the Krishna, the Tungabhadra was the boundary, and for the kingdoms south of the Tungabhadra, the Krishna was the ultimate limit.[101]

These urges of the rulers to gain vast fertile tracts can be linked up chiefly to the geographical configuration of the core area where the Chālukyas of Kalyāṇi ruled in the western Deccan, namely, the capital Kalyāṇa situated around the north of the river Krishna. This was largely a plateau area devoid of vast tracts of fertile land to enable a constant flow of agrarian surplus required to maintain the ruling strata. The Vengi region and the Raichur Doab on the other hand, being fertile regions, were frequently the bone of contention between the plateau kingdoms north of the river Krishna and the coastal kingdoms of South India who had the desire to control the entire water way.[102] In this context it is further significant to note that even later the Kalāchuris of Kalyāṇi and the Yādavas of Devagiri had their respective bases of power in the Deccan trap area of Sholapur and Bijapur districts respectively which were located north of the river Krishna and the Hoysalas of Dwārasamudra had their core area of control in the mountainous area south of the Tungabhadra river.[103] It is chiefly in the context of the conquests conducted by the Chālukyas of Kalyāṇi and in the subsequent establishment of their power over south western Deccan, particularly in the sub-region B, that we come across several locally entrenched powerful groups whose support the former required in maintaining their political hold to ensure a share for themselves in the agrarian surplus of the conquered area. Prominent among these local dynasties were the Sindas of Yalburga, Kadambas of Karāḍikallu and Haihayas of Raichur. These dynasties have been termed by eminent scholar B.R. Gopal as 'minor dynasties' in the sense that they never "ruled far beyond their own small areas on which soil they were born. As they were familiar with the topography of their regions, they could be of great military help to their overlords."[104] We next turn to take a closer look at these 'minor dynasties' **(Map V)** or chiefs who played a critical role in the polity of those times.

The Sindas of Yalburga (roughly A.D. 1033-A.D. 1194) had the hereditary right to rule over certain areas which were known separately as Kisukāḍ-70, Kelavadi-300, Bāgadage-70 and Nārāyaṁgal-12 and collectively known as the Sindavāḍināḍ. Of these places, the first three centred around Pattaḍakal, Badami and Bagalkot talukas of Bijapur district and the fourth was a small group of villages in Naregal of the Ron taluka in the Dharwar district. The capital of the members of this branch was at Erambarage, modern Yelburga of the Raichur district.[105] The Kadambas of Karāḍikallu (roughly A.D. 1066-A.D. 1215) had a hereditary right to rule over Karāḍikallu located in the Lingsugur taluka of the Raichur district. It was in the 11th-12th centuries A.D. that the headquarters of a small province called Karāḍikal-400 emerges into prominence. Records of these rulers are found mostly in Lingsugur taluka. One of their titles, *Krisṇānady-ubhaya-taṭa-rājahaṁsa* (the royal swan of both the banks of the river Krishna) clearly states that these Kadambas ruled over a region which spread over the river Krishna.[106] The Haihayas of Raichur[107] (roughly A.D. 1052-A.D. 1192) emerge as rulers of Ededore-2000 and the areas around it.[108] This area lay between the river Krishna on the north and the river Tungabhadra in the south constituting a large part of the present day Raichur district.[109] Records of these rulers are found mostly in the Manvi taluka of the above district.[110]

It is significant to note at this juncture that the rule of the local dynasties discussed above can be seen emerging in the inscriptional sources chiefly in the nuclear area of sub-region B and importantly, the period of rule by these groups coincides squarely with our period of analysis (A.D. 1000-A.D. 1200). In the context of the other sub-regions we have some areas of sub-region A controlled by the Sindas of Yalburga for a certain period of time, *i.e.,* in the latter half of the 11th century A.D. On the other hand, in sub-region C we have the Vaiḍumba and the Telugu Chola chiefs controlling the area from the middle of the 11th century A.D. onwards. We have been able to observe however, that these two dynasties did not have their core areas of political power located in sub-region C perse. The Vaiḍumbas claiming their descent from the western Gangas, were supposed to

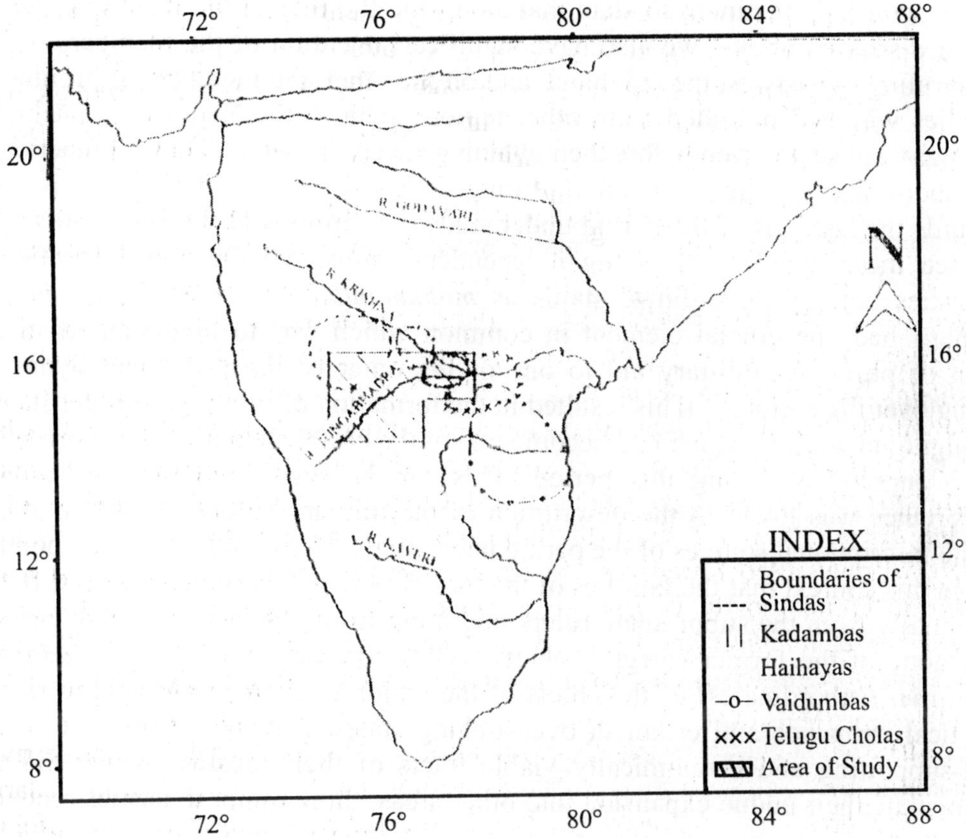

Map V : AREAS OF RULE BY MINOR DYNASTIES 1000 A.D.–1200 A.D.

have ruled over parts of North Arcot, Cuddapah, Nellore and the region south of Krishna from the 9th century A.D. onwards.[111] The Telugu Cholas on the other hand, appear to have ruled over different parts of Andhra right from the second half of the 10th and the first half of the 11th centuries A.D. onwards.[112]

It would be pertinent to state that alongside the rule of the local lineages of power discussed above, we also have significant mention of the members of the main ruling dynasty on the one hand, and on the other, the members of prominent families who had migrated from other regions such as the Yādavas, Kālāchuris, Hoysalas and so on, even before their attaining sovereign status. They all functioned as subordinates to the main rulers during different periods of study. It is only towards the last half of the period under study, *i.e.,* from A.D. 1170 onwards, that we see these dynasties attaining independent status. All the above mentioned dynasties holding subordinate status as *mahāmaṇḍaleśvaras* or *mahāsāmantādhipatis* had one crucial element in common which was to give support in the form of providing military aid to one or the other of the prominent dynasties ruling over the region.[113] This resulted in the formation of ruling groups constantly indulging in warfare which had become one of the established means of portraying one's supremacy during this period. This can be seen from the way utmost importance was given in the description of the military valour of various rulers in the inscriptional sources of the period under study. It should however be pointed out in this context that the families of the locally entrenched ruling groups differed essentially from the subordinate rulers migrating from outside. Thus, one can see that none of the former category chiefs styling themselves as the *'tadpādapadmōpajivi'* (subordinates) of the chiefs of the major dynasties were able to rise to political eminence and establish over-arching states. Having a firm base in the self-supporting and economically viable tracts of their locality, which did not necessitate their undue expansion into other areas, these minor dynasties rendered support to one or the other major dynasty contesting for power over the Raichur Doab. In such a situation, especially for the dynasties coming from outside these areas, marriage alliances with the powerful ruling families became a crucial means of integration with the already established families of the region. This effectively ensured for them a strong base to enhance their politico-economic control which otherwise may have been difficult to achieve by military conquest alone. In this context we have several instances of such marital alliances which were struck between different dynasties of the area of study during the period under consideration. Prominent among these were the marriage alliances between the families of Chālukyas of Kalyāṇi and the members of Nolamba Pallava rulers, with the Kadambas of Hangal[114] and the Kalāchuris of Kalyāṇi on the one hand,[115] and on the other, the marital relationships between the Kalāchuris of Kalyāṇi, when they attained an independent status in A.D. 1170, with the Sindas of Yalburga.[116] These can be considered to have formed one of the important social mechanisms of establishing hold for a longer duration of time by the respective dynastic powers in regions which they had newly conquered.

It is chiefly in these processes of exercising political control by both the major and the minor dynasties during the period under study that we see the south western Deccan emerge as an important enclave for the legitimation of political power. A comprehension of the nature of polity that emerged out of the geo-political exigencies we have discussed above has a significant bearing on our understanding of the socio-economic and cultural edifice that came into being during this crucial period of transition in the context of this specific region. Our comprehensions of the political power structure for the period under study are however, closely linked to the characterization of the nature of polity for the South India as a whole during the early medieval period. It is pertinent to underscore here that historical writings in this regard have focussed upon the comprehension of the nature of political authority as exercised by the main ruling dynasty over their respective areas of control. It is chiefly to analyse this assertion of authority that the perceptions of historical scholarship have undergone significant transformations in recent years. These have been necessarily dependent upon their respective themes of study and which were in turn crucially linked to the methodological approaches adopted by historians. In this regard one or the other elements, necessary for the formation of an effective polity, have been emphasized upon by the different scholars analysing the State structure for various regions of India during the early medieval period.

Serious attempts at such a study were first made by the Nationalist writers of India who had focussed chiefly on describing the administrative functioning of the State in terms of the paradigm of a centralized 'imperial' polity. In this context works of such scholars as A.S. Altekar, K.A.N. Sastri, G.S. Dikshit and K.R. Basavaraja would best exemplify our contention.[117] Altekar, whose main concerns were with the Rāshtrakuta dynasty of the Deccan region, describes their political power structure in terms of a centralized bureaucratic set up. The author states that "King in ministry was the normal form of government in the Rashtrakuta empire".[118] Speaking about the governance of the local bodies for the same region, Altekar defines them in terms of their existence on democratic lines.[119] K.A.N. Sastri, whose main concerns lay with the history of the deep south, details the centralized bureaucratic structure of the benevolent despotic rule of the Cholas in the Tamilakam region.[120] Speaking about the rule of the Cholas, the author says that the Chola monarchs "gave political unity to the whole of South India. For the first time they perfected a highly organized administrative system of central control and fostered the autonomy of village assemblies as none had done before".[121] A very similar approach can be seen in the characterization of the nature of polity in the context of the Kalyāṇi Chālukyan rule, too. While focussing his attention on the study of the local bodies during the early medieval period in Karnataka, G.S. Dikshit divides the study primarily under two headings, that of the 'central government' and 'provincial government'.[122] According to him the political power of the central government was of a limited nature as it could intervene in the matters of the local bodies only when something went wrong with the latter.[123] In a much later work of this nature K.R. Basavaraja, writing on the administrative set up of the Chālukyas of Kalyāṇi, articulates his aim as having "effectively drawn for us a picture of the pyramidal administrative set up in which power issued forth from the apex of imperial dispensation and percolated through several well conceived intermediary stages down to decentralized village level".[124] Thus, the modern concepts of a centralized governmental structure were sought to invariably explain the early medieval political structure of South India in this strand of historiographical writings.

In all the above works what stands out distinctly is that the authors were interested in defining the State structure as if it was imposed from above on the existing socio-economic and ideological base. It has aptly been stated in this context that "there is no effort in this conventional interpretation to demonstrate the manner in which the formal and concrete institution of the State is related to existing social arrangements and cultural features of south Indian society".[125] Resorting to the adoption of generalizations made at an all India level, these historians, dealing with regional history, have neglected the specificities of State formation which, among other factors, was dependent on geographical variations. Importantly, the contradictory stand taken by these scholars on the nature of polity of early South India is evident in their usage of such concepts as 'centralized' and 'imperial' rule on the one hand, and on the other, in highlighting the 'autonomous' and 'democratic' nature of the political structure at the village level. Inherent biases, *i.e.,* attempts at denigrating the Indian past by the Western scholars and attempts at eulogizing the south Indian past by some of the above mentioned scholars, were all written within a positivistic methodological framework. This impeded them from making a constructive analysis of the political structure at a regional level and its effective relationship with small localities or sub-regions that were integrated in to the so-called 'empire'.

The paradigm of a centralized 'imperial' polity of this period has, in recent times, been replaced in some quarters by the Marxist interpretation of polity in terms of decentralisation under the framework of the concept of 'Indian Feudalism'. This view has given primacy to the economic factors in comprehending the complex political power structure of the early medieval period in India as a whole.[126] The widespread prevalence of land grants attached with extensive administrative and economic immunities to various groups, both religious and secular, by the State leading to the creation of independent pockets of political power on the one hand,

and peasant subordination on the other, has been the basic premise on which the concept of feudal polity has been built for the various regions of India during the early medieval period. Thus, it is argued by R.S. Sharma that such a process of politico-economic change actually began with the decline of the Mauryan empire and by the 11th-12th centuries A.D., the whole of North India in this view was parcelled among various feudatory chiefs.[127] Empirical data indicating the above trends have been culled out for various regions of India and sought to be fit into the feudal framework of analysis. Armed with this interpretation, works of M.G.S. Narayanan, Kesavan Veluthat and R.N. Nandi are notable for highlighting the feudal characterizations of the south Indian polity for the early medieval period. In this regard, M.G.S. Narayanan makes use of terms such as 'temple-dominated feudalism'[128] and 'proto-feudalism'[129] to comprehend the nature of politico-economic relationships as they emerged in Cera-Chola times during the 9th-11th centuries A.D. in the regions of Kerala and Tamil Nadu. The co-existence in these kingdoms of the land-grants attached with extensive immunities to various religious institutions leading to the fragmentation of authority, and with an unusual proportion of foreign trade during this period (absence of such a feature had been considered to be a significant factor in the growth of feudal polity in the north Indian context), has led the author to conclude upon an early or a 'proto feudal' state for the early medieval south Indian context.[130] Kesavan Veluthat, also focussing on the Cera State, has highlighted its disintegration into many principalities[131] in the context of the proliferating *brāhmaṇa*-militia dominated settlements which had emerged into independent units entailing feudal privileges under the Cera rule (A.D. 800-A.D. 1124).[132] R.N. Nandi on the other hand, highlights the feudal developments in the context of early medieval Karnataka which, he argues, are organically linked to similar developments in other parts of country. The author refers to the feudalisation of the State in Karnataka in the context of a "system of government based on inseparable association of landholdership with the powers of government and numerous hierarchically structured private domains of governmental jurisdiction."[133] In this context he attributes the decline of 'monarchical centralization' which in his opinion was encouraged in the Śātavāhana period when a considerable measure of autonomy was granted to the provincial governors under them.[134]

The study of the nature of the polity in the above interpretations has been effectively analysed in relation to the socio-economic changes taking place during this period. However, discussion of the political power structure of the early medieval period merely in terms of a 'decentralized' polity, arising out of a hitherto centralized state, only means an over-simplification of the complex political relations of the period. In particular, this ignores the dynamics of State formation at a regional level.[135] The assumption of the Marxist scholars that there was always a centralized State before the emergence of a feudalized polity is untendable for the south Indian context as during the early medieval period this region saw a positive process of State formation in many of its sub-regions. On the other hand, by attempting to bring about a uniformity of developments in terms of emergence of feudal polity, in the context of the early medieval India as a whole, the Marxist scholars have failed to take into account the dynamics of the ecological variables and their impact on the subsequent nature of political relations at various levels of their formation. Related to this is the failure of the Marxian methodology in grasping the complex nature of the local agrarian relations which have led them to conclude erroneously that the existence of local landed magnates were created by State initiative; a basic premise of defining the feudal polity. This lacunae in their interpretation has been highlighted as a major handicap in comprehending the complexity of the political relationships for the south Indian context under the feudal model.[136] The existence of such writings did however, have an impact on the subsequent nature of studies on the early medieval State. It became a subject of serious scrutiny in the hands of various historians, who, by totally discarding the earlier held 'conventional' views, began to analyse State system in the light of fresh research on the subject. Indeed, the Marxist writings provided an effective critique of the earlier writings that had characterized the nature of early medieval polity as centralized.[137] Significantly, it is the limitations in the Marxist interpretations that have generated considerable debate over the validity of the generalizations of feudal state structure for various regions of India and have brought into focus the need for conducting fresh empirical studies with emphasis on historical geography to understand the regional variant. Such a thinking has stimulated serious studies at the regional level with particular focus on the Chola State of South India.

Foremost in this regard have been the works of Burton Stein, who by rejecting the earlier held concepts for State in South India in terms of 'centralized' or 'decentralized' forms, has put forth the model of a 'segmentary state' to comprehend the Chola State of medieval Tamilakam. In his characterization of south Indian polity, Stein has first of all laid emphasis on the ritual sovereignty as exercised by the Chola Kings on the ecological segments of political relations which were largely understood as belonging to varying physiographic zones, ranging from fertile tracts to the dry areas of cultivation. As such, the ritual sovereignty of the State was supposed to have had direct impact only on the 'nuclear' areas surrounding it and it is said to have shaded off as the distance increased to the periphery or the dry areas of cultivation. In such a situation it is suggested that the local segments, or, the *'nāḍu'* ecotypes exercised actual economic and political control over their respective regions having little to do with the centre of royal power.[138] Further, "the absence of links between local networks and the formal institutions of the State"[139] is the basic premise on which the author has rejected the idea of a centralized structure for the Chola period. Therefore, in this view it is logically assumed that there can be no 'decentralized' or 'feudalized' State structure prevalent in early medieval South India, as in the first place, there was no centre itself to initiate such a process.[140] The segmentary nature of Chola polity as propounded by Stein, while making a significant change from the generalized notions of the nature of polity at a regional level, has triggered off considerable debate over the empirical validity of such a categorization which has been considered by critics as being speculative in nature.[141] In this context, over emphasis laid by Stein on the importance of *nāḍu* territorial units and their independent nature on the one hand,[142] and on the other, the comprehension of Chola polity merely in terms of its ritual hold have been contested upon.[143] Stein's contribution to the study of south Indian polity can be stated to have been chiefly in terms of the conceptual frameworks that it has generated. He has also been one of the first scholars to emphasise on the question of geographical variations by using the path breaking work of Y. Subbarayulu on political geography of the Chola country.[144]

Studies on Chola polity in the various writings of N. Karashima occupy a significant place in the historiography of South India. By adopting the method of statistical analysis for the epigraphical data on the Cholas, the author has made an analysis of the land holding patterns of the region. This has helped him to arrive at sound conclusions over the nature of social stratification and the nature of polity of a particular region.[145] An analysis of the titles and the personal names mentioned in the inscriptions of the period has enabled Karashima to conclude that the Chola rule was centralized in nature as it indicated the existence of bureaucratic titles conferred on various officials. The latter part of the Chola rule he suggests came close to the concept of 'Indian Feudalism' as according to the author, the titles of the rulers during this time indicated the existence of locally powerful groups. The process of feudalization of the central rule of the early Chola state has been effectively linked to the changes taking place in the agrarian context such as the breakdown of the communally held land-holdings leading to a more complex tenurial system of individual landholdings during the 11th-12th centuries A.D. in the Tamilakam region. The above conclusions arrived at by the author have however, been aimed at providing an effective critique to the concept of segmentary state propounded by Stein with regard to Chola polity. In this context Karashima, relying heavily on the statistical analysis of empirical data, has furnished adequate evidence to substantiate his point about the exercise of actual political authority by the Chola kings in early medieval Tamilakam. It has been suggested in this regard that the above study, lacking in any significant conceptual analysis, still remains traditional in its interpretation[146] as it fails to provide any new framework of understanding for furthering fresh studies on the Chola State in the Tamilakam region. Karashima, it may be noted, by treading close to his data, while writing on the same region and period as Stein, however, gives a totally contrary picture to what the latter had suggested. Indeed, on the other hand, the solid foundation of his data has been used by scholars to build a theoretical framework that the Chola polity was feudal.[147]

It has aptly been stated in the context of the above studies that "it is the inadequate understanding of the links between centre and periphery—the intermediate zone that has marred a correct assessment of the nature of the State."[148] As a result of this realization we see in recent times more and more studies coming into being attempting to provide an effective perspective for comprehending the nature of the early medieval State chiefly in terms of identifying the links established between the centre and the periphery through the intermediaries located in varying ecological niches. In this context works of James Heitzman and R. Champakalakshmi for the Chola polity, Cynthia Talbot for the Kakatiya rule in Andhra, Hermann Kulke for Orissa and B.D. Chattopadhyaya for the northern and eastern India have a significant role to play.

Heitzman's studies on Chola polity have chiefly focussed upon comprehending the Chola state as an 'early state' in which the intermediate authorities representing the dominant groups at the "village level production relations could interact with the central state apparatus and weild effective power in their own right".[149] In such a study the ecological variable has been taken into serious consideration in shaping the nature of the intermediate authority and the consequent links established between the centre and the periphery. As such it is suggested that the nature and the degree of control exercised by the Chola rulers varied from the riverine tracts to the drier zones of their territory. In the former case he opines that the established lineage groups weilded power and in the latter, assemblies of local leaders asserted authority and it is these groups that are encountered in the process of their inclusion into the overarching State system.[150] The role played by ideology in integrating the intermediaries into the centre state of Chola rule has been studied as a crucial aspect of the Chola State structure during the early medieval period in the works of R. Champakalakshmi.[151] The author in this context has observed that the dominant ideology of the State emanated from various levels of social strata which was adopted and elaborated upon by the ruling sections of the State. This was then disseminated through various ideological apparatuses such as the *brāhmaṇas* and the brahmanical temples to reach the peripheries of the State as a means to expand and strengthen the State system. Such a process of the dissemination of the dominant ideology she argues was combined with the diversification of the "economic base and the restructuring of society".[152]

It is however, in the works of Hermann Kulke with focus on the medieval State of Orissa, that we get a comprehensive picture of the way various levels of State power were linked up to form an overarching State structure through the crucial role of ideological forces of legitimation in the context of the various manifestations of political power. The author has, in this regard, effectively emphasized upon the integrative aspects that enabled most of the early medieval Hindu kingdoms to operate at several levels, such as territorial, cultural, social and economic.[153] In the case of medieval Orissa, Kulke has effectively linked up the process of State formation to the dynasties controlling the nuclear tracts. They were the ones who had the capacity to rise to become sub-regional powers and then they tried to extend their sway into the outerlying tribal pockets of power.[154] He further argues that it is chiefly in the process of the exercise of control by the conquering chiefs over the conquered tracts that we see several factors of integration coming into operation in various forms of ideology manifest through the process of 'royalization' of the tribal deities at the tribal cult centres. Secondly, through a systematic and large scale establishment of *brāhmaṇas,* followed by the process of the construction of new imperial temples within the core region of kingdoms, Kulke significantly puts forth the view that these ideological apparatus acted as a counterbalance to the rise of local forces of tribal polity.[155] The author in this context has taken up various instances of such integrative mechanisms adopted by the rulers of Orissa right from ancient times. In the context of early medieval Orissa he writes : "it was the cult of Jagannatha which was acknowledged by the kings of Orissa since the 13th century A.D. as their overlord,"[156] and provides for us an excellent example of cultural integration through a regional tradition.

In the works of B.D. Chattopadhyaya one comes across the nature of early medieval Indian polity understood as essentially a problem in local State formation. On the other hand, the multidimensional processes involved in such a formation are also brought out in clear contours to get at the reality of the complex political relations during this period of transition for a given spatial context. In this context the author has identified three major processes of State formation under operation for the early medieval period. Accordingly, it has been proposed that the expansion of State society took place through local State formation resulting from a process of the peasantization of tribes along with the crucial process of cult appropriation and integration at various levels of its structure.[157] The nature of such a study of polity involves in the first place, taking into serious consideration several aspects of local State formation which involve such crucial issues as comprehension of the local and supra-local groups against the background of their geographical location on the one hand, and on the other, their expanding agrarian base expressed through land grants made to brahmanical ideologies on the other. Importantly, according to Chattopadhyaya the levels of power exercised by these groups are indicated to us through the feudatory titles and ranks conferred on them[158] by the overarching political authority. This represents one of the many dimensions of the early medieval State. Thus according to the author "the fact that political relations were regularly expressed as between the overlord and his feudatories suggests that the dominant mode in the formation of the structure was by encapsulation of the existing bases of power, the spearhead in the structure being the overlord."[159] In a much earlier study of his on the nature of early medieval State with focus on the Rajput polity, Chattopadhyaya had highlighted the crucial role played by the social variable in comprehending the emergence of various ruling lineages at the local level of the State structure. Thus, in this context the author had highlighted various processes involved in the transition from a tribal to State society in the early medieval context which, in its initial stage, was dependent on conquests and territorial expansion of the concerned clan.[160] Subsequently, he argued that there was an attempt at corresponding the rise in the political status through a rise in the social status which involved the processes of fabricating genealogies on the one hand, and on the other, strengthening the base of their power through maintaining kinship ties within one's own group and through the establishment of marital relationships with other powerful ruling groups.[161] The emergence of various sub-clans in the 12th century A.D. according to the author, can be looked upon as a "product of the mechanism of absorption of local elements"[162] and it is chiefly "the inter-clan relations governing the distribution of power that helped consolidate the structure of Rajput polity in the early medieval period."[163] In these processes of local State formation, Chattopadhyaya has aptly demonstrated the need to comprehend the ideological dimension of the early medieval polity as a crucial process in legitimizing the State system at the local level. This was achieved according to him through the appropriation and integration of local cults as representing heterogeneous beliefs and rituals[164] of disparate groups at the local level, which were then transformed into a regional idiom with a corresponding rise of the local power to a regional power.[165]

Taking cue from the continuing interest in regional studies few recent works have, by taking into account different regions of study located in the early medieval period, ably demonstrated the applicability of one or the other of above discussed variables in comprehending the nature of polity. In this context, Upinder Singh, in her analysis on the state structure of early medieval Orissa, has displayed the way various factors of integration such as the use of religious symbols conferring political titles on local bases of power and the land grants made to *brāhmaṇas* operated on parallel lines in the crytalization of state structure from an earlier tribal stage in her case study.[166] This very well corresponds to the hypothetical stand taken by B.D. Chattopadhyaya which we have discussed above. In a study of similar nature Nandini Sinha has focussed her attention on the rise of Guhilas of Mewar from a local base of polity into a regional power. She has effectively analysed here the intertwined processes of such a rise that involved among other things, territorial and agrarian expansion, political ranking and so on. She further points out that the crucial process of appropriation and integration of the local cult of *Ekalingāji* and *Pāśupatas* became a significant means of the legitimation of their rule at various levels of State formation.[167] On the other hand, we have the work of Cynthia Talbot who, by focussing her attention on the Kākatiya polity of the early medieval period, has brought out effectively the way in which a local political power, with its base in the dry-upland region could rise into a regional power. Importantly, by giving primacy to the ecological variable in comprehending the rise of Kākatiyan State, the author has emphasized upon the need to comprehend the crucial role played by military conquests and marital alliances established by the Kākatiya rulers with the powerful lineages of the conquered regions as a means of strengthening their socio-political hold over the conquered tracts.[168]

Thus the recent spurt of non-Marxist historical works have significantly demonstrated the viability of looking at out the nature of State structure during the early medieval period, from a regional dimension. It is pertinent to note in this context that by showing the positive processes of State formation as characterising the early medieval complex for different regions of India, these scholars have underlined the fact that one needs to look at State formation for this period as a movement from within rather than viewing it in terms of either a centralized or decentralized set up as imposed from above, totally unrelated to the changes below.

It is in the light of these views, particularly those of Kulke and Chattopadhyaya, that we wish to look at both the local and supra-local groups in the State structure as being a part of the dominant political and social elite operating within given economic relations of production. Viewing these groups merely in terms of representing a centralized or, a decentralized polity proves inadequate for our comprehension of the nature of power structure in our area of study as during this period we do not have any evidence for the existence of a single centralized State structure per se. On the other hand, we have the members of the main ruling family trying to wrest control of the fertile tracts in the south western Deccan from the locally entrenched powerful ruling groups. It is interesting to note in this context that the emergence of the latter and their importance in defining the polity of the times corresponds exactly to our period of study. It is chiefly in the processes of political control exercised by the above groups that one can see the main sub-region of our study, namely sub-region B, emerge as a zone of legitimation. This was achieved in the first place through the encapsulation of locally entrenched powerful social groups and their integration into the State structure by conferring titles of political status on the one hand, and on the other, through the creation of ideational apparatuses of legitimation. We wish to clarify at this stage that we are here focussing our attention on the vertical division of society in an area of study which was largely dependent on the physio-political and economic exigencies of their location. The ensuing political relations have been understood by us through an analysis of the stratified relations both at the local and supralocal levels of their functioning. Such a study would include in the first place, an analysis of both the administrative and the economic nature of terms used to describe various social groups, identification of the levels and the nature of stratification present among them and the mechanisms adopted by the powerful groups to keep up their dominance in relation to the less privileged groups. An understanding of these phenomena has been our main endeavour in the following chapters.

REFERENCES

1. Fernand Braudel, *Civilization and Capitalism 15th-18th Centuries : The Perspective of the World,* Vol. III, Gr. Britain, 1984, p. 21.
2. Moonis Raza and Aijaz Ahmed, *General Geography of India,* NCERT Publication, New Delhi, 1978, p. 73. There could be political or administrative regions as well. These, however, do not correspond to the natural divisions and therefore, naturally have overlapping features of physiographical setting.
3. *Ibid.,* pp. 74-76.
4. H.C. Ray Chaudhuri, 'The Geography of the Deccan' in G. Yazdani (ed.), *The Early History of the Deccan,* New Delhi, 1982 (1st Indian Edition) p. 3.
5. *Ibid.,* p. 3.
6. *Ibid.,* p. 4.
7. R.G. Bhandarkar, *Early History of the Dekkan* (Down to the Mahomedan conquest), New Delhi, 1985 (rp.) p. 2.
8. Sumati Mulay, *Studies in the Historical and Cultural Geography and Ethnography of the Deccan* (Based entirely on the Inscriptions of the Deccan from the 1st-13th centuries A.D.), Poona, 1972, p. 14.
9. A.S. Altekar, *Rashtrakutas and Their Times,* Poona, 1934, pp. 354-355. The author nowhere explicitly states in this work as to what, according to him constitutes the Deccan, and thus we can only deduce this from his work.
10. H.C. Ray Chaudhuri, *op. cit.,* 1982, p. 3.
11. G. Yazdani, *op. cit.,* 1982, pp. v-vii.
12. G. Jouveau Dubreuil, *Ancient History of the Deccan,* Pondichery, 1920, p. 5.
13. *Ibid.,* p. 5.
14. Deepak Ranjan Das, *Economic History of the Deccan,* (1st century A.D.-6th century A.D.), Delhi, 1969, pp. 4-5.
15. K.A.N. Sastri, *A History of South India,* Madras, 1976 (4th ed.), p. 1.
16. Sudhakar Chattopadhyaya, *Some Early Dynasties of South India,* Motilal Banarasi Das, Delhi, 1974 (1st ed.), p. 1.

17. P.N. Chopra, T.K. Ravindran, N. Subramaniam *History of South India,* New Delhi, 1979, pp. x-xii.
18. For example, P.B. Desai, *A History of Karnataka,* Dharwar 1970, B.R. Gopal, *Minor Dynasties of South India,* Karnataka, Vol. I, Madras, 1982, G.S. Dikshit, *Local Self-Government in Medieval Karnataka,* Dharwar, 1954 and so on.
19. For example, K. Sundaram, *Studies in Economic and Social Conditions of Medieval Andhra (A.D. 1000-A.D. 1600),* Triveni Publications, Machilipatnam, 1968. K. Satyanarayana, *A Study of the History and Culture of the Andhras.* Vol. I, People's Publishing House, New Delhi, 1982, V. Yashodadevi, 'The History of the Andhra Country-1000 A.D.-1500 A.D.,' *JAHRS,* Vol. XVIII, Rajahmundry, 1951, pp. 33-110 and so on.
20. For example, K.R. Basavaraja *Administration under the Chalukyas of Kalyana,* New Era Publications, Madras, 1983, Dinkar Desai, *The Mahamandalesvaras under the Chalukyas of Kalyani,* Bombay, 1964, D.P. Dikshit, *Political History of the Chalukyas of Badami,* Abhinav Publications, New Delhi, 1980 and so on.
21. O.H.K. Spate and A., T.A. Learmonth, *India and Pakistan : A General and Regional Geography,* New Delhi, 1984, p. 683.
22. Moonis Raza and Aijaz Ahmed, *op. cit.,* 1978, p. 77.
23. Spate & Learmonth, *op. cit.,* 1984, p. 685.
24. Moonis Raza and Aijaz Ahmed, *op. cit.,* p. 77.
25. S. Settar, 'Roots Relations and Relevance : The Chalukyan Backdrop', in Mulkraj Anand (ed.), *Marg,* XXII, 1, 1979, p. 10.
26. In this context, Himanshu Prabha Ray's *Monastery and Guild : Commerce Under the Satavahanas,* Delhi, OUP, 1986, K.M. Shrimali's, *Agrarian Structure in Central India and the Northern Deccan* (A.D. 300-A.D. 500), Munshiram Manoharlal, Delhi, 1987 figure prominently in terms of the analytical studies conducted for certain parts of the Deccan region.
27. Himanshu P. Ray, *op. cit.,* 1986, p. 37.
28. S. Settar, *op. cit.,* 1979, p. 10.
29. *Ibid.,* pp. 10-11.
30. For example, D.P. Dikshit, *op. cit.,* 1980; A.S. Altekar, *op. cit.,* 1934, B. Rajendra Prasad, *Chalukyan Temples of Andhradesa,* Abhinav Publications, 1983; Henry Cousens, *The Chalukyan Architecture of the Kanarese Districts,* A.S.I., New Imperial Series, No. 42, Calcutta, 1926 and so on.
31. In this context we have works of such scholars as A.V. Krishnamurthy, *Social and Economic Conditions of Eastern Deccan,* Secunderabad. 1970;' K. Sundaram, *Studies in Economic and Social Conditions of Medieval Andhra,* Machilipatnam, 1968, p. ii. and so on which lay stress on the social and economic conditions of the early medieval period of their respective regions of study when compared to several other historical works which write on the dynastic histories of the region.
32. Such a recognition is well attested by the historical scholarship pertaining to the eastern Deccan region. For example, A.V. Krishnamurthy, clearly states in her work

that her choice of the study of the eastern Deccan region has been motivated, among other reasons, by the fact that this area is more fertile and better developed than the central and western Deccan. *Op. cit.,* 1970, p. ix.

33. Several works written on South India and the Deccan region in general have references to the Krishna and the Tungabhadra rivers which have been considered to have played the role of frontiers between various kingdoms located in the Deccan and the deep south that fought for wresting control over the Vengi region. A vivid description of this is given in K.A.N. Sastri, *op. cit.,* 1966, pp. 6-7.
34. V. Yasoda Devi, 'The Krishna-Tungabhadra Doab (1000 A.D.-1335 A.D.)', *JAHRS,* vol. XXXII, 1971-72, p. 94.
35. The terminology for defining the main region of our study has been borrowed from R.L. Singh (ed.). *India : A Regional Geography,* Varanasi, 1989, p. 43.
36. Information gathered from, *Census of India* (Dharwar District) Series-9, Karnataka, 1981, p. 11.
37. *Gazetteer of India* (Bijapur district), Mysore State, Bangalore, 1966, pp. 15-16.
38. *Gazetteer of Bombay State* (Dharwar District), Bombay, 1959, pp. 6-9.
39. *Census of India* (Dharwar District), Series-9, Karnataka, 1981, p. 11.
40. *Ibid.,* p. 11.
41. *Ibid.,* p. 11.
42. *Gazetteer of India* (Raichur District), Bangalore, 1970, p. 9.
43. *Gazetteer of India* (Raichur District), Bangalore, 1970, p. 8.
44. *Census of India* (Raichur District), Series-9, Karnataka, 1981, p. 12.
45. B.S. Seshagiri Rao, *Bombay-Karnataka : A Geographical Survey,* Dharwar, 1941, p. 28.
46. *Census of India* (Raichur District), Series-9, Karnataka, 1981, p. 12.
47. R.L. Singh, *op. cit.,* 1989, p. 835.
48. *Ibid.,* p. 848.
49. *Census of India* (Mahboobnagar District), Series-2, Andhra Pradesh, 1981, p. 3.
50. Summarised from, R.L. Singh, *op. cit.,* 1989, pp. 847-849 and *Census of India* (Kurnool District), Series-2, Andhra Pradesh, 1981, p. 6.
51. *Gazetteer of India* (Bijapur District), Bangalore, 1966, p. 14-15.
52. *Census of India* (Dharwar District), Series-9, Karnataka, 1981, p. 11.
53. *Census of India* (Mahboobnagar District), Series-2, Andhra Pradesh, 1981, p. 3-4.
54. *Census of India* (Kurnool District), Series-2, Andhra Pradesh, 1981, p. 6.
55. *A.P. District Gazetteer* (Mahboobnagar) Hyderabad, 1974, p. 56 and for Kurnool District, p. 74.
56. In this context we have observed that our region has been studied by various scholars either as a part of the Karnataka State, or, as a part of the history of Andhra Pradesh during this period. For example, G.R. Kuppuswamy's *Economic Conditions in Karnataka* (A.D. 973-A.D. 1336), Dharwar, 1975, G.S. Dikshit, *Local Self Government*

in Medieval Karnataka, Dharwar, 1964, for the Karnataka State and K. Sundaram, *op. cit.,* 1976, for the Andhra region, best exemplify our contention. There are several other works written in this genre particularly for the early medieval period.

57. S. Settar, *op. cit.,* 1979, p. 9.
58. *Gazetteer of India* (Bijapur District), Bangalore, 1966, p. 15.
59. *Ibid.,* p. 95.
60. *Ibid.,* p. 98.
61. *Ibid.,* p. 97.
62. B. Rajendra Prasad, *op. cit.,* 1983, p. 77.
63. *Ibid.,* p. 11.
64. *Gazetteer of Bombay State* (Dharwar District), Bombay, 1959, p. 794.
65. *Ibid.,* p. 809.
66. *Ibid.,* p. 825.
67. Observations made from *Gazetter of India* (Raichur District), Bangalore, 1970, pp. 697-717.
68. *Ibid.,* pp. 30-32.
69. *Ibid.,* p. 37.
70. *Ibid.,* p. 4.
71. We have already highlighted these works in the context of our discussion on historiography. See ft. note. 30 above.
72. K.A.N. Sastri, *op. cit.,* 1966, pp. 176-177.
73. Most of the historical works written on the history of Chālukyas of Kalyāni and their feudatory chiefs have given primacy to these factors. Fleet's *Dynasties of Canarese Districts of the Bombay Presidency from the Earliest Times to the Musalman Conquest of A.D. 1318,* Bombay, 1896, pp. 426-583 has a discussion on various dynasties ruling this region, Dinkar Desai's *The Mahamandalesvaras Under the Chalukyas of Kalyani,* Bombay, 1951, pp. 67-111 describes the minor dynasties of sub-region B and so on.
74. P.M. Joshi, 'The Raichur Doab in Deccan History–Re-interpretation of a Struggle', *JIH,* XXXVI, iii, Dec. 1958, pp. 379-381. In this article the author highlights the strategic importance of the Raichur Doab in terms of the fertility of its land and the abundance of the mineral sources in it because of which it became the most coveted area in the hands of the Vijayanagara and the Bijapur rulers whose hostilities centred around the 'Raichur Doab' during the medieval period.
75. V. Yasoda Devi, *op. cit.,* 1971, pp. 94-101. In this the author has given a description of the military struggles that centred around the Raichur Doab, right from the 11th century A.D. to about the beginning of the Vijayanagara rule in the 14th century A.D.
76. A.S. Altekar, 'The Rashtrakuta Dynasty' in G. Yazdani (ed.), *op. cit.,* 1982, p. 259.
77. Sant Lall Katare, 'The Beginnings of the Chalukyas of Kalyani' *IHQ,* XIII, 1937, p. 252.
78. K.A. Nilakanta Sastri, *op. cit.,* 1976 (4th ed.), p. 181.

79. Dinkar Desai, *op. cit.*, 1951, p. 309.
80. Summarised from K.A.N. Sastri, *op. cit.*, 1976, pp. 173-190.
81. A.S. Altekar, *op. cit.*, 1982, p. 298.
82. J.F. Fleet, 1896, *op. cit.*, pp. 427-428.
83. P.B. Desai, *op. cit.*, 1970, p. 187.
84. *Ibid.*, p. 194.
85. P.B. Desai, *A Corpus of the Kannada Inscriptions in the Kannada Districts of Hyderabad State*, Hyderabad Archaeological Department, 1958, p. 9.
86. *Ibid.*, p. 10.
87. J.F. Fleet, *op. cit.*, 1896, p. 474.
88. K.A.N. Sastri, *op. cit.*, 1976, p. 198.
89. *Ibid.*, p. 6.
90. Sant Lal Katare, 'Early History of the Yadavas of Devagiri', JIH, XXX, Trivandrum, 1952, p. 119.
91. P.B. Desai, *op. cit.*, 1958, p. 12.
92. K.A.N. Sastri, *op. cit.*, 1976, p. 199.
93. P.B. Desai, *op. cit.*, 1970, pp. 249-250.
94. Summarised from *ibid.*, pp. 264-265.
95. J.F. Fleet, *op. cit.*, 1896, p. 519.
96. S.M. Alam, 'The Historic Deccan–A Geographical Appraisal' in V.K. Bawa (ed.), *Aspects of Deccan History*, Hyderabad, 1975, pp/ 16-29.
97. *Ibid.*, pp. 24-26. It would be pertinent to state here that Alam has based his characterization of the Deccan political zones chiefly on his studies on the emergence of various Muslim policies as a result of the influence of the Tughluq and Mughal rules in the Deccan, and importantly, these were not native to the area of their control.
98. Summarised from K.A.N. Sastri, *op. cit.*, 1976, p. 6.
99. *Ibid.*, p. 181.
100. V. Yasoda Devi, *op. cit.*, 1971-72, p. 96.
101. *Ibid.*, p. 94.
102. Romila Thapar, *A History of India*, Vol. I, Penguin, London, 1984, p. 168.
103. It is significant to note in this context that a majority of the major dynasties that have ruled various parts of the Deccan region during the early medieval period, such as the Chālukyas of Bādāmi, Rāshṭrakūṭas even much before our period of study, had their core areas in the dry upland regions and their attempts to control the fertile tracts such as Vengi in the eastern Deccan could be comprehended in the light of their geo-political base. Such a trend can however, be seen on the rise during the 12th and 13th centuries A.D. when more and more kingdoms, such as the Hoysalas, Kākatiyas and so on began to have their core areas in the dry upland regions and extended their sway over the fertile riverine and coastal tracts. See Çynthia Talbot, 'Political Intermediaries in Kakatiya Andhra, 1175-1325', *IESHR*, 31, 3, 1994, p. 262.

104. B.R. Gopal, *op. cit.*, 1982, p. 3.
105. Fleet, *op. cit.*, 1896, pp. 572-573.
106. B.R. Gopal, *op. cit.*, 1982, p. 70.
107. P.B. Desai, *op. cit.*, 1958, p. 16.
108. *Ibid.*, p. 16.
109. "Daddala Inscription of Chalukya Bhuvanaikamalla' EI, XXXVII, pp. 113-116.
110. A region wise survey of the Inscriptional data of our study has enabled us to come to this conclusion.
111. V. Yasodadevi, 'The History of Andhra Country : Subsidiary Dynasties (A.D. 1000-A.D. 1500), *JAHRS,* XXIII, 1954-1956, pp. 24-25.
112. *Ibid.*, p. 48.
113. Contemporary historical writings written on these dynasties are replete with evidence of such military support extended to the major dynasties of our period of study, See for example, J.F. Fleet, *op. cit.*, 189, pp. 535-584.
114. *Ibid.*, pp. 434-435.
115. S.L. Shantakumari, 'New Light on the Early Career of Bijjala II', *Journal of Epigraphical Society of India,* XVI, Mysore, 1990, p. 90.
116. 'Two Inscriptions from Ron' 'B', *EI,* XIX, pp. 226-236.
117. Other prominent works belonging to such category are those of C. Minakshi, *Administration and Social Life under the Pallavas,* Madras, 1939, T.V. Mahalingam, *Administration and Social Life under Vijayanagara,* Madras, 1975 (2nd. ed.), A.V. Venkataratnam, *Local Government in Vijayanagara Empire,* Mysore, 1972 and so on.
118. A.S. Altekar, *op. cit.*, 1934, p. 150.
119. *Ibid.*, pp. 198-199.
120. K.A.N. Sastri, *op. cit.*, 1976, pp. 202-205.
121. *Ibid.*, p. 6.
122. G.S. Dikshit, *op. cit.*, 1964, pp. 13-14.
123. *Ibid.*, p. 14.
124. K.R. Basavaraja, *Administration Under the Chalukyas of Kalyana,* Madras, 1983, p. ii.
125. Burton Stein, 'The State and the Agrarian Order in Medieval South India : A Historiographical Critique' in Burton Stein (ed.), *Essays on South India,* New Delhi, 1976, p. 67.
126. R.S. Sharma, *Indian Feudalism* (A.D. 300-A.D. 1200), New Delhi, 1980. Studies in this direction have been initiated by D.D. Kosambi, *An Introduction to the Study of Indian History,* Bombay, 1985 (2nd ed.). These scholars have primarily focussed on the historical developments of northern and central India.
127. R.S. Sharma, *op. cit.*, 1980, p. 4.
128. M.G.S. Narayanan, 'The Cera Kingdom of Makotai—Factual and Conceptual Problems Related to State Formation in Kerala', presented at *Seminar on the State in Pre-Colonial South India,* Centre for Historical Studies, JNU, (28th-30th March), 1989, p. 47.

129. M.G.S. Narayanan, 'South Indian History and Society (Studies from Inscriptions, A.D. 850-1800), by Noboru Karashima : Review Article', *Tamil Civilization*, 3, 1, March 1985, p. 67.
130. *Ibid.*, p. 67.
131. Kesavan, Veluthat, *Brahman Settlements in Kerala*, Calicut University, 1978, p. 86.
132. *Ibid.*, p. 5.
133. R.N. Nandi, 'Growth of Rural Economy in Early Feudal India' : Presidential Address, *PIHC*, 45th Session, Annamalai Nagar, 1984, p. 5.
134. *Ibid.*, p. 5.
135. B.D. Chattopadhyaya, *The Making of Early Medieval India*, OUP, Delhi, 1994, p. 24.
136. R. Champakalakshmi, 'A Framework for South Indian Polity' (Review Article), *The Book Review*, XVIII, 6, June, 1994, p. 6.
137. In his analysis of 'feudal' polity, Sharma repeatedly refers to the concept of decentralized political structure as characterising the post Mauryan period in the northern India. See R.S. Sharma, *op. cit.*, 180, pp. 1-26.
138. Burton Stein, *Peasant State and Society in Medieval South India*, Delhi, 1980, pp. 264-266.
139. Burton Stein, *op. cit.*, 1976, p. 65.
140. *Ibid.*, p. 88.
141. R. Champakalakshmi, 'Peasant State and Society in Medieval South India : A Review Article', *IESHR*, 18, 3-4, 1981, p. 426.
142. *Ibid.*, p. 424.
143. D.N. Jha, 'Relevance of "Peasant-State and Society" to Pallava-Cola Times' : A Review Article', *IHR*, 8, 1-2, 1981-82, pp. 88-91.
144. Y. Subbarayalu, *Political Geography of the Chola Country*, Dept. of Archaeology, Tamilnadu, 1973. In fact this work has been the basis for both Stein and Karashima's studies on Chola polity.
145. N. Karashima, *South Indian History and Society*, Madras, 1984, pp. 22-23. A very similar study has been conducted by Y. Subbarayulu for Tamilakam region–'the Chola State and the Agrarian Order–Some clarifications, presented at *Seminar on the State in Pre-colonial South India*, Centre for Historical Studies, JNU, (28th-30th March), 1989, pp. 1-21.
146. R. Champakalakshmi, 'Review Article' on N. Karashima's South Indian History and Society, in *SIH*, 2, 2, July-Dec., 1986, p. 283.
147. M.G.S. Narayanan, *op. cit.*, 1985, pp. 66-69.
148. R. Champakalakshmi, 'The State in Medieval South India : Emerging Perspectives', Presidential Address (Historiography Section), *PAPHC*, Srisailam, 1989, p. 270.
149. James Heitzman, 'State Formation in South India; 850 A.D.-1280 A.D.'. *IESHR*, Vol. XXIV, No. 1, January-March, 1987, p. 61.
150. *Ibid.*, pp. 59-60.

151. R. Champakalakshmi, 'Ideology and the State in South India, presented at *Seminar on the State in Pre-Colonial South India,* Central for Historical Studies, JHU, (28th-30th March) 1989, p. 2.

152. *Ibid.,* pp. 2-3.

153. Hermann Kulke, 'Fragmentation and Segmentation Versus Integration? Reflections on the Concepts of Indian Feudalism and the Segmentary State in Indian History' *Studies in History,* Vol. V, No. 2, 1982, p. 21.

154. Hermann Kulke, 'Royal Temple Policy and the Structure of Medieval Hindu Kingdoms,' in Kulke (ed.), *Kings and Cults : State Formation in India and South East Asia,* Manohar, Delhi, 1993, p. 2.

155. *Ibid.,* pp. 9-11.

156. Kulke, *op. cit.,* 1982, p. 28.

157. B.D. Chattopadhyaya, *op. cit.,* 1994, p. 16.

158. B.D. Chattopadhyaya, 'Political Processes and Structure of Polity in Early Medieval India; Problems of Perspective', Presidential Addresses, *PIHC,* Burdwan, 1983, pp. 25-83.

159. *Ibid.,* p. 44.

160. B.D. Chattopadhyaya, 'Origin of the Rajputs : The Political, Economic and Social Processes in Early Medieval Rajasthan', *IHR,* Vol. 3, No. 1, 1976, p. 62.

161. *Ibid.,* pp. 65-75.

162. *Ibid.,* p. 81.

163. *Ibid.,* p. 79.

164. B.D. Chattopadhyaya, *op. cit.,* 1994, p. 30.

165. *Ibid.,* p. 32.

166. Upinder Singh, *Kings, Brahmanas and Temples in Orissa–An Epigraphic Study. (A.D. 300-1147),* New Delhi, 1993, pp. 289-291.

167. Nandini Sinha, 'A Study of State and Cult : the Guhilas, Pasupatas and Ekalingaji in Mewar. 7th to 15th centuries A.D.', *SIH,* 9, 2, n.s., 1993, pp. 161-182.

168. Cynthia Talbot, *op. cit.,* 1994, pp. 270-271.

3

SOCIAL CONTEXT

In this chapter we focus upon the stratified nature of social groups as can be gauged through their mention in the inscriptional sources of study. One has attempted to define 'social stratification' as essentially referring itself to the fact that both the individuals and the groups of individuals are conceived of as constituting higher and lower differentiated strata or classes,[1] manifesting them- selves in relations of dominance and subordination.[2] Forms of dominance and subordination highlight the fact that just as the social formation cannot be viewed in terms of a mere uniform entity, simultaneously, these relations too cannot be comprehended in terms of autonomous phenomena functioning on exclusive planes of stratified relations. Societal processes encompassing various social groups and their actions, in effect, are a total outcome of the crucial role played by an interaction of the political, economic and ideological forces at a specific period in time and a particular space which have a significant bearing on the resultant social change. We wish to address ourselves to these aspects of social relations by situating them in the early medieval complex of south western Deccan. Such a study one hopes would afford us with enough scope to arrive at sound conclusions over various dimentions of 'social stratification' expressed chiefly through the concepts of 'class', 'power' and 'status'[3]. In early India these dimensions are further, webbed into the phenomena of a *varṇa-jāti* system. In historical studies of early India as whole, we have two basic historiographical strands of looking at social change. Among these, the traditional a point of view considers the political/administrative and or the ideological/ritual aspects of the social phenomenon as being the determinants of defining social status and social change in early India[4]. On the other hand, the politico-ideological aspects of social stratification are considered to be only surface manifestations of the existing relations of production by the Marxist historians[5]. We also have writings in recent times which emphasize upon the interactive nature of the above phenomena to comprehend the social set up of early India[6]. The historiographical aspects of understanding social history in early India have been discussed by us in detail in an earlier chapter[7].

We have initiated our analysis of the social structure of our study chiefly by discussing the dominant stratum among social groups who find direct mention in the inscriptional sources available to us. (See charts IA iv-x 1-30. IB iv-x 31-154. IC iv-x 155-170*). These social groups, described to us through the use of various terms such as family names, official designations, professional titles, official titles and also in a few instances, through their *varṇa* and *gotra* status, were an intrinsic part of the dominant socio-economic and politico-ideological structure of the times and therefore, had the means through which to articulate their views and actions. The level of stratification among these groups was in effect dependant largely upon the existing elite relationships that, in turn, revolved around the ownership, control and use of land as this was the major source of wealth in the agrarian economic set up of early medieval South Western Deccan.

Having divided our area of study into three sub-regions (A, B and C), we have observed that the variety and richness of the mention of social groups in the context of sub-region B (IB iv-x, 31-154) when compared to the sub-regions A (IA, iv-x, 1-30) and C (IC, iv-x, 155-170) affords us with tremendous potential to make an effective analysis of the various dimentions of stratified relationships as they emerged during this period. As has been observed by us in our earlier chapter, sub-region B stands focussed during this period in terms of a fruitful convergence of a host of historical factors such as the political, the economic and the ideological and which, coupled with its strategic physiographic setting, played a crucial role in characterizing the resultant social structure of this sub-region.[8] On the other hand, absence of the above stated dimentions on the same scale for sub-regions A and C marks these off as being peripheral during this period of our study. This does not in any way mean that they were not sought out for political control by the major and minor dynasties of this period but, the nature of politico-economic power vested in the elite and the subsequent effect this had on the social formation have revealed subtle variations which, in effect, afford us a comparative and contrastive study vis-a-vis sub-region B in the following analysis.

In the context of our study the dominant social groups are chiefly referred to in the inscriptions through the political ranks they held. We therefore, first take a detailed look at this dimension of social stratification. On the basis of their description we have been able to classify these groups into the functionaries who ruled at the local levels of power, the local potentates whose power corresponded to the supra local political base and lastly, the chiefs of the main ruling family who functioned from the apex of the political power structure during this period. An analysis of the terms used to describe these groups in terms of the sub-regional and chronological dimension of the land grants mentioned in inscriptions would enable us to comprehend effectively the nature and relative strength of dominance exercised by these groups.

To begin with, at the local level of polity which represents the exercise of the primary nexus of politico-economic dominance, we have the mention of the following terms used to denote the groups we have identified above as functionaries in the context of the various sub-regions of study. Thus, for sub-region A during the 11th century A.D. we have reference to such terms as *ūroḍeya* (IA, vi, 2) *heggaḍe* (IA, vi, 6) *karaṇa* (IA, vi, 13) and *suṅkavergaḍe* (IA, vi, 15). During the 12th century A.D. we have *hiriya heggaḍe* (IA, vi, 21) *prabhu* (IA, vi, 21), *gāvuṇḍas* (IA, vi, 22) *kulakaraṇi* (IA, vi, 22) *manneya* (IA, vi, 26) *pramukha karaṇa* (IA, vi, 26), *nāḍa suṅkavergaḍe* (IA, vi, 28) *mahāpradhāna heggaḍe* (IA, vi, 29) in addition to the continuation of the terms mentioned above for the previous century. All these terms basically signify the political and economic hold of various social groups over the rural society and have been interpreted in various ways by different scholars. In this context the term *ūroḍeya*[9] has been equated to mean a village headman[10], the term *gāvuṇḍa* has also been equated to mean a village headman[11] or, a chief farmer[12]. In this regard the latter has not been commonly applied in historical analysis but will be emphasized upon by us. Terms such as *prabhu, pergaḍe* and *heggaḍe* have been considered synonymous of *gāvuṇḍa.*[13] The term *karaṇa* has been interpreted to denote an accountant.[14] It has at the same time been understood as a supervisor who was appointed by the central authority to supervise the work of provincial governors.[15] The term *pasāyita* is on the one hand equated to a ministerial office at the centre[16] and on the other, it has also been interpreted to mean a fief holder.[17] *Suṅkavergaḍe* has been translated as being indicative of the rank of a superintendent of the income from tolls.[18] The term *kulakaraṇi* was supposed to have been one who did the work of accountants[19] and the term *manneya* signified the ruler of a group of villages.[20] He has also been considered to represent the immediate local authority who held the *manneya* or the headship of the place.[21]

In the context of sub-region B we have a greater more variety of social groups mentioned in the sources. For the 11th century A.D. we have reference to such terms as *manneya* (IB, vi, 33), *nal gāvuṇḍa* (IB, vi, 33) *gāvuṇḍa* (IB, vi, 35), *suṁkavergaḍe* (IB, vi, 35), *ūroḍeya* (IB, vi, 37), *mānevergaḍe* (IB, vi, 40) *soḍorevaḍiyara* (IB, vi, 45), *chulāyata* (IB, vi, 49) *joyisa* (IB, vi, 50), *pergaḍe* (IB, vi, 51), *senabova* (IB, vi, 52), *taṇtrapāla* (IB, vi, 53), *karaṇa* (IB, vi, 53), *nāḍa pergaḍe* (IB, vi, 53) *samasta pradhāna* (IB, vi, 56) *kulakaraṇi* (IB, vi, 59), collective mention of *rāṣṭrapati, viśayapati, grāmakūṭaka, āyuktaka, niyuktaka, adhikārika, mahattara* (IB, vi, 72). For the 12th century A.D. we have along with the continuation of most of the above terms, a further, list of terms like *mahāpradhāna karaṇa* (IB, vi, 93) *mahāpradhāna heggaḍe* (IB, vi, 110), *sarvādhikāri pergaḍe* (IB, vi, 113) *mahāpradhāna suṅkavergaḍe* (IB, vi, 116) *mahāprabhu* (IB, vi, 117) *nālprabhu* (IB, vi, 117), *mahāpradhāna taṁtrapāla* (IB, vi, 119) *sachiva* (IB, vi, 125), *pasāyita* (IB, vi, 125) *prabhu* (IB, vi, 147) and *arasu* (IB, vi, 148).

Among these terms such as *manneya, gāvuṇḍa, pergaḍe, heggaḍe, karaṇa, suṅkavergaḍe, prabhu, kulakaraṇi, pasāyita* and *ūroḍeya* have already been described by us above. We now take a closer look at some of the terms that have not been discussed so far. Terms such as *grāmakūṭa* have been considered synonymous of *gāvuṇḍa* or the village headman.[22] Those such as *nāḍa pergaḍe nāl gāvuṇḍa* or *nāḍa gāvuṇḍa* were supposed to have represented a slightly higher level of socio-political power as they have been equated to mean a district headman[23] or, to mean a non-official head of a sub-division.[24] At the same level of functioning we also have the terms *rāṣṭrapati* and *viśayapati* the former is generally understood to denote local chiefs and district officers[25] and the latter has also been interpreted to mean a district officer but according to scholars was also supposed to have, at the same time, enjoyed a feudatory status.[26] The term *mahattara* according to Altekar indicated heads of the families residing in a village and the elected members of the village council were supposed to have been selected from among this group.[27] On the other hand, the terms *āyuktaka, niyuktaka,* which often figure together, were indicative of clerical jobs such as those of accountants and sub accountants.[28] Similarly, the terms *senabova* was supposed to have been used for accountants.[29] The term *ahikārika* is equated to mean a minister, magistrate etc.[30] The term *chuḷāyata* has been equated to mean a herald or a messenger and the term *soḍorevaḍiyara, saudhare* has been equated with the modern term *chaudhary* signifying an office of some importance, namely, chief of the royal guard[31] and according to some scholars, also a tax collector.[32] The terms *tantrapāla* and *sachiva* have been equated to mean an officer in change of administration[33] and a councillor[34] while the term *arasu* has been understood as denoting the status of a king.[35] Further, the term *mahāpradhāna* generally equated to mean great minister, chief minister, chief administrator[36] when prefix to various terms such as *karaṇa, heggaḍe, pergaḍe* in the sources of the 12th century A.D. evidently indicated an enhancement in his political status during this period.

In the context of sub-region C we have reference to very few terms indicative of local level of political functionaries. Such terms as *pergaḍe* (IC, vi, 157), *mahāmātya suṅkavergaḍe* (IC, vi, 155), *saudhare* (IC, vi, 158) *gāvuṇḍas* (IC, vi, 158), and *janada prabhu* (IC, vi, 158) however, do figure during the 11th century A.D. For the 12th century A.D. we have no significant reference to any terms of the above type. The terms *gāvuṇḍa, saudhare, pergaḍe* and *suṅkavergaḍe* have already been discussed above and the new terms occurring in the context of sub-region C are few. *Mahāmātya* is considered interchangeable with the term *mahāpradhāna* and has ben equated to mean a chief minister or, an executive officer and when prefixed to the term *suṅkavergaḍe,* indicates an officer incharge of taxes.

The above description of the social groups mentioned in the inscriptions in their administrative capacity comes out as a mere list of officials in various capacities as can be directly seen in the sources. We have observed in this context that various scholars writing on the polity pertaining to our area of study have perceived these groups invariably is terms of the political ranks held by them. In particular, the ruling strata at the local level have been comprehended in terms of constituting a democratic polity. This is best exemplified in the context of the way in which the *gāvuṇḍa* and its equivalent ranks such as *heggaḍe, pergaḍe, prabhu* and so on, have been conceived of by the scholars writing on them. The *gāvuṇḍa* is considered to have been either appointed by the government[37] or, if he was not appointed by the government he had to be confirmed by it as a representative of the people to act as an agent of the government[38] and as an executive of the village *pañchāyat* (assembly).[39] Further, the other functionaries of the village, namely the *senabova, adhikāri, kulakaraṇi* and so on, are supposed to have been appointed by the village assembly.[40] In Marxist historiography with particular reference to such groups as the *grāmakūṭa, gāvuṇḍa, grāmabhōktṛ grāmapati, rāja, rājaputra, raṇaka* and so on, belonging to the various regions of India like southern Maharashtra and various parts of North India during the early medieval period, have been comprehended chiefly in terms of being intermediaries or vassals of the main ruling family. It is further suggested that they were created at the local level through the grant of lands which were attached with various administrative and economic immunities.[41]

On a closer analysis of the above discussed social groups located in the various contexts of their mention in the inscriptional sources, our study brings to the forefront a picture of a highly differentiated social structure which does not fit into any of the characterizations stated above. First, we find in this regard that the political ranks through which various social groups find mention in the inscriptions in fact, seem to have been an explicit attribute of the actual social and economic power wielded by most of the local chiefs. Related largely to the nature of the economy as it prevailed during this period that was characterised by a dominance of agriculture and the system of land grants, the mention of several official designations held by the ruling strata can be considered peculiar to such a set up. It significantly reflects the attachment and involvement of these groups to the ownership, management, and distribution of land which, in turn, defines their socio-political status in the rural society. Thus, one sees that reference to various groups have been made either, as donors of various measurements of land which was granted mostly to the religious establishments, or, as sellers of land granted, as protectors of grants, as builders of temples and, in rare instances, even as donees as can be seen below.

In the context of sub-region A during the 11th century A.D. (IA, xi, 1-17), the *ūroḍeya* figures in 2 instances a donor, *suṅkavergaḍe, karaṇa, pergaḍe, pasāyita* and the wife of a *heggaḍe* figure in one instance each as donors. We further, have, in this context, mention of 6 *gāvuṇḍas* as protectors of the land granted.[42] During the 12 century A.D. for the same sub-region (IA, xi, 18-30), the *pergaḍe* figures in 2 instances as a donor of land (IA, xi, 20, 23). Further, in another instance a grant of land was made on his request.[43] The term *heggaḍe* emerges 2 times in the capacity of a donor (IIA, xi, 26, 29). Futher, *prabhu* emerges as donor in 3 instances (IA, xi, 21, 30) and in one instance as the builder of a temple.[44] The *karaṇam* emerges as a donor in 2 (IA, xi, 23, 26) instances and the *nāḍa suṁkavergaḍe* in 1 instance (IA, xi, 28).

In the context of sub-region B however, the mention of various social groups belonging to the local level of exercising authority are more varied. During the 11th century A.D. in this sub-region (IB, xi, 31-85) we have reference to the *gāvuṇḍas* as donors in at least 4 instances (IB, xi, 33, 46, 59, 66). We further, have mention of this group in various other ways too such as in one case a grant of land was made on their request,[45] as witnesses to the grant,[46] as builders of a temple,[47] as protectors of the grants made,[48] as sellers of land,[49] and even as donees of land along with the *prabhus* in one instance.[50] The *nanneya* figures in 5 instances as donors of land or of *manneya* rights, (IB, xi, 33, 50, 57, 59, 62) and in one instance, as the seller of land.[51] The *pergaḍe* figures in 3 instances as a donor (IB, xi, 61, 74) and in one instance as the builder of a temple.[52] The *mānevergaḍe* figures in one instance as a donor (IB, xi, 50) and in another as a dones (IB, xii, 40), the *taṁtrapāla* and *karaṇa* figure in one instance each (IB, xi, 53, 70) in the capacity of donors. Terms such as *soḍorevaḍiyara* (IB, vi, 45, 49) appear as directing the land grants to be made in 2 instances and finally, the collective mention of various terms such as *mahattara, adhikārika, grāmakūṭaka, rāṣṭrapati viśayapati* and so on, figure once (IB, vi, 72) in the capacity of approvers of the grant of lands.

During the 12th century A.D. from sub-region B (IB, xi, 86-154) we have the *gāvuṇḍas* as donors in as many as 8 instances (IB, xi, 86, 89, 93, 113, 117, 121, 126, 130). The other ways in which they are mentioned is as sellers of land,[53] a grant of land was made on their request,[54] builders of temple[55] as protectors[56] as witnesses to the grants.[57] The *karaṇa* figures in 5 instances as a donor (IB, xi, 93, 94, 110, 125, 133), the term *heggaḍe* with various epithets prefixed to it figures as a donor in 5 instances (IB, xi, 110, 114, 119, 122, 126) and the *pergaḍe* in a similar way figures as donor in 4 instances (IB, xi, 114, 119, 122, 126). The term *prabhu* figures in 2 instances as a donor (IB, xi, 130, 134). On the other hand, we have the *manneya* and the *pasāyita* as donors in 1 instance each (IB, xi, 117, 125). Further, reference to such terms as *kulakaraṇi* and *senubova* is invariably made with reference to them being writers of charters. Finally, sub-region C during the 11th century A.D. (IC, xi, 155-168) out of a limited number of references made to the local level functionaries we have the *pergaḍe* emerging as a donor in 1 instance (IC, xi, 157) and the *saudhare, gāvuṇḍa* and *prabhu* figure in one instance together (IC, xi, 158) in the capacity of donors.

It is the light of the above nature of evidence wherein most of the local functionaries figure significantly as donors, rather than donees, of land to various religious institutions and beneficiaries on a considerable scale, that it becomes difficult for us to comprehend these groups merely in terms of representing a decentralized feudal polity created from above. One can, at the same time, clearly discern through the references cited above that these groups were not just political groups appointed by a centralized authority either. In this context the significant mention of terms such as *pergaḍe, heggaḍe, karaṇa, prabhu and gāvuṇḍa* as donors of various measurements of land pertinently highlights for us the strong possibility of them being land owners. Thus, while the designations held by each of these groups indicate for us the political dimension of the nature of stratification, their capacity to make grants is indicative of the economic hold that these groups had over their respective bases of power as owners of land and its resources. It is pertinent to underscore at this juncture that one cannot at the same time view all the social groups functioning at the local level in terms of having uniform status or relationships with each other. In this context terms indicating the roles of such functionaries as *kulakaraṇi, senabova, soḍorevaḍiyara* and so on, stand apart. While *kulakaraṇi*[58] and *senabova,*[59] figure in several instances as writers of charters the term *soḍorevaḍiyara*[60] figures in the context of directing a land grant made by a different donor. It is significant to note here that *senabova* also figures in a memory stone wherein he seems to have got killed in a fight along with his charioteers.[61] The nature of references to the social groups of this type effectively testify to the fact that they might have been appointed by a higher authority for the various functions performed by them. All the same time, their prominent position in the political hierarchy is highlighted by the fact that in an inscription dated to A.D. 1054 from sub-region B, *senabova* is included in the list of *pradhānas* (ministers) which has among others the *karaṇa* and the *nāḍapergaḍe* too.[62] Towards the end of the 12th century A.D. the *senabova's* functions seem to have undergone significant transformation as in an inscription dated to A.D. 1170 from sub-region B we have reference to the *senabova* as a donor and as the son of an *ūroḍeya.*[63] These above examples testify to the stratified nature of social groups as they emerge in terms of purely political ranking but which did not remain static in nature.

In a similar vein one cannot view the land owning chiefs such as the *heggaḍe, pergaḍe, prabhu, gāvuṇḍa* and so on, classified normally under a generic term of village headmen, in terms of having a uniform social placement in the hierarchy of groups in society. We have noted above that each of these groups figure in different contexts which effectively highlight for us the differential nature of their existence in the political hierarchy rooted at the local level of our study. In an inscription dated to A.D. 1033 from sub-region A, we have reference to the wife of a *heggaḍe* who makes the grant of land only after seeking the approval of a higher authority, namely the local potentate.[64] This evidently testifies to the limited nature of the politico-economic hold that this group had over the landed property. Further, the *pergaḍe* in an inscription dated to A.D. 1074 from sub-region A, is clubbed together with other political ranks such as *karaṇa* and *pasāyita* (which have been considered to be in the nature of supervisors) who were collectively termed as *pradhāna* and they all make a grant of land together.[65] It is however, significant to note that the *pergaḍe* emerges as a more powerful person in the context of sub-region B as here, he figures in the capacity of a builder of temples[66] and also, as a single donor in a couple of instances (IB, xi, 61, 74), particularly in the 11th century A.D. inscriptions. In the examples from sub-region C too the *pergaḍe* emerges significantly as a donor (IC, xi, 157, 167).

It is pertinent to underscore here that the context and the nature of references made to the *heggaḍe* and *pergaḍe* however, undergo significant change around the 12th century A.D. From now on we find that these two terms begin to be mostly prefixed with one or the other separate designations. As early as A.D. 1098 from sub-region B we have reference to a *hejjuṁka peggaḍe* who makes a grant of some taxes (IB, xi, 84). We have a significant reference in an inscription dated to A.D. 1145 from sub-region A, wherein we have the mention of *hiriya heggaḍe* who is also termed as *mahāpasāyitam* and *sarvādhikāri* of the local potentate (IB, vi, 21). In a similar reference in an inscription dated to A.D. 1144 from sub-region B, we have mention of the *sarvādhikāri pergaḍe* attached to a local potentate (IB, vi, 113). Thus, we find that during the 12th century these terms no longer merely indicate the land owning group perse and begin to signify the specific nature of the title to which they were attached. The spurt in commercial activity of the 12th century A.D. probably meant that several officers administering taxes (*suṅka*) and various other non-agrarian functions were needed and the earlier land owning communities began doing these tasks as well. Their importance in society naturally increased. In an inscription dated to A.D. 1148 from sub-region B we have reference to three types of *pergaḍes* such as *suṁkada pergaḍe, sādaḍa pergaḍe* and *pergaḍe vibhu,* who emerge as donors of taxes on an areca nut garden, on the mill and on mining respectively (IB, vi, xi, 117). This effectively attests to the specialized nature of the activity that the *pergaḍe* now came to be involved in. We thus have several other such examples like the *pergaḍe* of *pannāya suṁka* (IB, vi, 118), *hejjuṁka bīravanada heggaḍe* (IB, vi, 122), and so on. In the context of the above survey terms such as *pergaḍe, heggaḍe* and so on, clearly emerge as official designations which have no fixed connotation signifying a compartmentalized nature of their functions. Therefore, the meanings attached to understand these groups will have to be appreciated in the context in which they are mentioned as that helps to identify the changing economic background of the 12th century A.D. and this, in turn, helps to explain social change.

It is pertinent to further discuss that the terms *pergaḍe* and *heggaḍe* denote political ranks but their ability to make grants of land as observed above, effectively testifies to their economic power which in fact, enable them to be placed in a political hierarchy at the rural level. It is however, in the context of references made to the term *prabhu* which is mentioned on a significant scale in the inscriptions of the 12th century A.D. sources that we get a clear indication of how political ranking was conferred on the basis of the economic power held by its incumbants. The terms *prabhu* or *mahāprabhu* invariably figure as representing a ruler of a specific settlement or space with which they are associated. Thus, in one instance we have the mention of the *prabhus* of Bammalahala along with the *gāvuṇḍas* of the same place.[67] Both these groups figure as the donees of land in this inscription which is dated to A.D. 1096 from sub-region B. In A.D. 1103, in another inscription of the sub-region B we have reference to one Nāki *Gāvuṇḍa* as the *mahāprabhu* of Posavūra who emerges as the donor of some land (IB, vi, xi, 89). In an inscription of the same sub-region belonging to the period between A.D. 1076-A.D. 1124 we again have mention of *prabhus* as rulers of Naregal along with the *gāvuṇḍas* of the place.[68] In an inscription dated to A.D. 1178, the *prabhus* and *gāvuṇḍas* of Morata figure as donors in the sub-region B (IB, vi, xi, 130). For the same region in an inscription dated A.D. 1191 we have an interesting reference to the *prabhus* (IB, vi, 147) ruling over western and eastern streets of a place called Linga. In the above stated instances what clearly emerges is that the term *prabhu* was a political rank which was conferred evidently on the land owing groups as is indicated by the ability of the *prabhu* to invariably make grants of land. Importantly the association of the *prabhu* with the term *gāvuṇḍa* in several cases is significant to note because the *gāvuṇḍas* have also been distinctly mentioned as a land owning stratum from the beginning of the 11th century A.D.

The variety of references to the *gāvuṇḍa* in particular has had a significant bearing on our comprehension of the social, political and economic power wielded by the local functionaries. For the entire period of our study we have as many as 12 instances to the *gāvuṇḍas* as donors of various measurements of land. This stands out particularly in sub-region B. Apart from this the *gāvuṇḍas* also emerge as leasors[69] and sellers[70] of land, builders of temples,[71] witnesses to the grants made[72] and to sale purchase deeds.[73] They also figure as remitters[74] and donors of various taxes.[75] Association of the *gāvuṇḍas* with such varied economic and political activities during the 11th-12th centuries A.D. clearly testifies to the strong politico-economic power that this group commanded at the local level. That the term *gāvuṇḍa* strongly connotes a land holding stratum is further adduced by the references made to this group in several instances as owners of land which normally occur when boundaries to the land granted are demarcated in the inscriptions. As early as A.D. 1005, in sub-region B we have mention of the *hola* (field) of one Siri *Gāvuṇḍa* as bordering the grant made.[76] In an inscription dated to A.D. 1049 from sub-region A, we have reference to one Bhoga *Gāvuṇḍa,* amidst whose fields, the grant portion was located.[77] In an inscription dated to A.D. 1079 from the same sub-region we have reference to the fields of one Kovara *Gāvuṇḍa* which forms the boundary.[78] References of this nature increase during the 12th century A.D. wherein we find at least eight instances of this type from sub-region B.

Further, there are references to the *gāvuṇḍas* as a collective group of 4, 6, 8, and 12 in number in several instances. During the 11th century A.D. we have out of 12 references to the *gāvuṇḍa* as many as 10 of them figure in collective groups defined above (IB, vi, 58, 59, 60, 66, 70 and so on). G.S. Dikshit has put forth three types of explanations for such an occurrence. Firstly, he suggests that this was done because of the need to accommodate the claims of the numerous branches of the original family. Secondly, he suggests the *gāvuṇḍas* seem to have represented several hamlets that came together for administrative functioning and thirdly, according to the author the need to represent different parts of a big town might have led to the division of the *gāvuṇḍas* into various groups.[79] The above suggestions seem however, to be facile when we take into account the politico-economic nexus that the *gāvuṇḍa* group represented in the context of their locality and as such their formation into groups cannot be attributed to any one particular factor such as for political or administrative convenience only. Formation of the collective groups of the *gāvuṇḍas* seems to have been chiefly on the basis of landed interests which they evidently stood for as has been seen in the above discussion. We however, find that during the 12th century A.D. there are more references to individual *gāvuṇḍas* who probably rise from among the collective groups. Thus, out of about eleven instances to the *gāvuṇḍas* during the 12th century A.D. we have nearly seven instances (IB, vi, 85, 86, 89, 117, 120, 121, 152) of individual *gāvuṇḍas* from sub-region B, who now, begin figure as *prabhus* and *mahāprabhu* in certain cases. In an example from an inscription dated to A.D. 1103 is one *Nāki Gāvuṇḍa* is referred to as a *mahāprabhu* of Posavūr (IB, vi, 117) Dated to A.D. 1153 we have reference to one Holla *Gavuṇḍa* who is also referred to as *mahāprabhu* (IB, vi, 121). Evidently, *mahāprabhu* was a political title that was conferred on some of the prominent *gāvuṇḍas* acknowledging them as lords of their respective areas.

The rise of certain individual *gāvuṇḍa* families to the forefront can be largely attributed to their social standing as well which is indicated to us through the family names to which they traditionally claimed to have belonged. In an inscription dated to A.D. 1100 from sub-region B, we have reference to one Mārasinga

Gāvuṇḍa of Nārāyaṁgal, whose pedigree is furnished from three generations and he is stated to have belonged to the *murttage* family.[80] Reference to Nāki *gāvuṇḍa* in an inscription dated to A.D. 1103 (IB, vi, 89) figures in a more significant manner. He is supposed to have belonged to the *mōraka* family and was described to have administered Posavūru as an *ekabhōga.*[81] In fact, this family figures in another inscription dated to A.D. 1148 as again ruling over Hosavūra. In this case we have reference to the son and brother of Nāki *gāvuṇḍa* who emerge as builders of a temple and as donors of land (IB, vi, 117). The same family figures in yet another inscription which is dated to A.D. 1153 wherein Naki *Gāvuṇḍa's* son Holla *gāvuṇḍa* now figures as a *mahāprabhu* of Hosavūra. He is again referred to as belonging to the *mōraka kula* (family) and a detailed description of his ancestors is furnished in the inscription.[82] Thus, the significant role played by the social variable in enhancing the political status is pertinently underlined in the above instances. We have further observed in this regard that the socio-political relations of these groups at the local level of power did not remain static in nature. In such a context terms like *nāḍa-pergaḍe, nāl-prabhu, nāl-gāvuṇḍa* and *manneya,* which have been commonly understood to denote political authority exercised over several villages, in fact, are a significant pointer to the urges exhibited by the local functionaries to rise in the political hierarchy. They could aspire for this once they had galvanized economic resources and established the right social contacts.

A detailed understanding of the term *manneya* affords us ample scope to perceive the socio-economic nexus of political authority at a higher level than the *gāvuṇḍa.* It is pertinent to note here that a predominant mention of the term *manneya* is made in the context of the 11th century A.D. grants from sub-region B wherein this group emerges chiefly as donors of various measurements of land and of their *manneya* rights (IB, vi, 33, 43, 50, 57, 59 and so on), as sellers of land[83] and importantly, as belonging to such prominent families as that of the Sinda *kula* (IB, vi, 33) and the Kadamba *kula* (IB, vi, 62). Further the association of the *manneya* with a *gāvuṇḍa* family is significantly attested to in one of the above inscriptions wherein as early as A.D. 994, the *manneya* Koralaguṇḍa is also termed as a *nālgāvuṇḍa* (IB, vi, 33). Another much later inscription dated to A.D. 1148, refers to the *manneya* Bopparasa as belonging to the Sinda *kula* and Kunnula *vaṁśa* and this is made in association with the prominent gāvuṇḍa family of Hosavūra. In this context, Naki *Gāvuṇḍa,* the *mahāprabhu* of Hosavūra was supposed have been a brother of *manneya* Bopparasa thereby establishing kin relationship between the two families.[84]

It needs to be underscored at this juncture that it is chiefly in the context of the emergence of this group as supra local chiefs that we find sub-region B emerging as a zone for the legitimization of political power in the hands of the members of the main ruling family, who, in the process of expansion of their respective kingdoms tried to integrate various socially and economically powerful groups into the hierarchy of political ranking. It is in this context of their occurrence that we have attempted to comprehend the above described groups, namely, the local functionaries as constituting the essential fabric of a larger integrative polity. In such a situation we have observed that the *gāvuṇḍa* and the *manneya* representing the socio-economic and political nexus of power at the local base, provide the key to such an integration. In particular, the rise of the *manneya* holders to the level of supra local chiefs in exercising power over larger territorial units such as the *nāḍu,* represent a crucial stage in the process of political integration during the period under study. A study of the origin of these chieftaincies clearly indicates for us that conferring titles on various locally prominent families by the main ruling family was a way through which they could be brought in line with the vertical division of the socio-political structure. One of the earliest references of this nature can be traced back to A.D. 994 wherein *Koralaguṇḍa,* a member of the Sinda family figures as a manneya and *nāḷgāvuṇḍa* (IB.vi.33). It is interesting to note that at a much later period, *i.e.*, dated to A.D. 1062 Sindarasa of the same family has been referred to as holding the title of a *mahāsāmaṅta* (IB.vi.60). Further, in another instance of a similar nature, we have reference to one nāḍa pergaḍe dated to A.D. 1050 (IB.vi.53) who, by A.D. 1060 had risen to the rank of a *mahāsāmantādhipati* (IB.vi.59). In an inscription dated to A.D. 1022 we again have reference to the title of *manneya* held by a member of the Haihaya family of Raichur (IB.vi.43). By about A.D. 1052 we note that these family members begin be addressed as *mahāmaṇḍaleśvaras* (IB.vi.54). In a similar instance, one of the early members of the family of the *Kadambas* of *Karaḍikal* has been referred to as a *manneya* in an inscription dated to A.D. 1066[85]. The same person is referred to as a *mahāmaṇḍaleśvara* ten years later in a record dated to A.D. 1077 (IB.v.73). *Manneya* was a smaller office which has actually been conventionally translated to mean a chief, a respectable man and the ruler of a group of villages.[86] The rise of these chiefs to the position of a *mahāsāmanta, mahāsāmantādipati* and most importantly, to that of a *mahāmaṇḍaleśvara,* is a clear indication of the rise in their status. These titles have been basically interpreted to mean designations of feudatory chiefs, in a conventional sense. Thus, the title of *mahāsāmanta* is said to signify the status of a feudatory of a higher rank than that of the sāmaṅta.[87] The *mahāsāmantādhipati* on the other hand, is understood to have held a superior feudatory status than that of above stated titles with several subordinate chiefs under him.[88] The title of the *mahāmaṇḍaleśvara* which has been connoted to mean a governor of a district or a province, is supposed to have signified a far superior feudatory status.[89] According to R.S. Sharma the term *maha* attached to these designations shows that they were being brought in line with the feudal vassals.[90] It may be stated here that where as Sharma understands these terms in the light of a theoretical frame work defining 'Indian Feudalism'. Sircar has termed these relationships under the rubric of landlordism.[91]

The above discussion indicates that chiefs held a considerable social and economic power in the areas of their political control and this point is well attested in the inscriptional sources of study. Further, the above mentioned supralocal chiefs occur in the sources in terms of either donors of land or rulers over various provinces, or, invariably, in terms of the social status they commanded by virtue of belonging to a particular family that they represented in the sources. Thus, in an inscription dated to A.D. 1077 the *mahāmaṇḍaleśvara* Nāgavarmarasa is praised as the ornament of the Kadamba family (*kadambābharaṇa)* and figures as the donor of a village called Temgola over which he was supposed to have held hereditary rights of possession (IB.v.73). In an inscription dated to A.D. 1096, *mahāmaṇḍaleśvara* Ayyandeva is praised as belonging to the Haihaya lineage and emerges here as the donor of a village and some land (IB.v.83). These chiefs were supposed to have ruled over the tract of Eḍeḍore-2000 by about A.D. 1052.[92] Further, the Sinda chiefs of Yalburga who come to the forefront from the latter half of the 12th century A.D. claim to have ruled over the tracts of Bāgaḍage-70, Kisukāḍ-70, Kelāvāḍi-300 and Nārāyaṁgallu-12; together these units were termed as the Sindāvāḍi.[93] It is significant to note in this context that we have reference to nearly three branches of the Sinda family who claimed to have belonged to the Sinda *kula* and held the tigercrest (*vyāgraha lāñchana)* as their family banner.[94]

Among these, the Sindas of Bagadage were the first ones to rise on the political scale to the level of being *mahāmaṇḍaleśvaras* between the period A.D. 1069 to A.D. 1076.[95] During this period these chiefs emerge as donors of land and builders of temple signifying their economic basis of power.[96] The Sindas of Yalburga, it has been surmised were the descendants of the Sindas of Bāgaḍage.[97] Another branch of the Sinda family who claimed to have belonged to the *kunnula* vaṁśa rose to the level of being *mahāsāmanta* as mentioned in an inscription dated to A.D. 1062 (IB.v.60). Indeed they rose from an status of earlier status of *manneya nāḷgāvuṇḍa,* a position they held during the latter half of the 10th century A.D. (IB.vi.33). The area of control of these latter chiefs who also emerge as donors of land was, however, confined to a small tract, namely Mulguṇḍa-12. The above examples clearly state that the rise to political power of the various supra-local chiefs depended largely on their economic power as landlords and the corresponding rise in their social status by claiming strong familiar and matrimonial affiliations as has been seen in some of the cases discussed above. In the context of our study, particularly from the middle of the 11th century A.D. onwards for all the three sub-regions together, we come across nearly 18 families of supra local chiefs who held sway over different tracts of settlements. Among these, for sub-region A, we have the frequent mention of the Pallava (IA.v.4.12). Yādava

(IA.v.5.12). and Sinda chiefs (IA.v.15.28). For the sub-region B, we have prominent mention of such families as the Pallava (IB.v.37.73.76) and the Haihaya (IB.v.54, 63, 83, 108, 130, 145) the Sinda (IB.v.60, 97, 112, 122, 124, 126, 127, 128, 133, 135) and the Kadamba (IB.v.73, 104, 147, 154). Other names of families that figure in this sub-region are the Yādava (IB.v.57), Kaṭṭale (IB.v.65), Bappura (IB.v.98), Chola (IB.v.63), Kusuva (IB.v.101) and the Haṭṭagara (IB.v.113). For sub-region C there is prolific mention of the Chola (IC.v.155.158, 161, 162), and the Vaiḍumba (IC.V.165, 166) chiefs. There is only a single instance of the mention of the Pallava family (IC.v.168). In the above instances cited, one can clearly note the concentration of the families of supra-local chiefs from sub-region B and further, the emergence of these families can be seen only from the middle of the 11th century A.D. which coincides with the consolidation of the political hold by the Chālukya chiefs of the main ruling family. Such a correlation can be comprehended in a better light if we take into account the nature of the exercise of political control by various local potentates who invariably styled themselves as the subordinate *(tatpādapadmōpajivi)* of the main ruling family chiefs, in the context of the various sub-regions of study. On the basis of the nature of their reference in the sources, we have been able to classify these families into two main categories, namely, those that held hereditary titles of political hold over the territories they ruled and secondly, those that had acquired political eminence by virtue of their military valour. In the first category we have the families of the Haihaya chiefs (roughly A.D. 1052-A.D. 1191), Sinda chiefs (roughly A.D. 1077-A.D. 1215) and the Kadamba chiefs (roughly A.D. 1077-A.D. 1215) who have been described earlier as having a firm economic hold on the locality of their control. To the same category belong such families as those of the *Kaṭṭale* whose chief *Kaṭarasa* figures here in an inscription dated to A.D. 1071 as a donor of a piece of land out of his own *śivāta* (estate) (IB.v.65). The *Bappura* chiefs on the other hand, were supposed to have held hereditary rights over the Kisukāḍ-70 region and belonged to the *bali* vaṁsā and their chief Dāḍiga figures in this inscription dated to A.D. 1114 as the donor of a large measurement of land (IB.v.98). Similarly, the *mahāmaṇḍaleśvara* of the Kusuva family who was supposed have been governing Kisukāḍ-70 dated to A.D. 1121, is described as the donor of some land (IB.v.101) in an inscription dated to A.D. 1121.

On the other hand, in the second category delineated above we have several other supra local chiefs belonging to prominent families of rulers who actually hailed from outside the area defined for this study and tried to carve for themselves some political niche of control over various tracts from sub-regions A, B and C and thus emerge in the capacity of being chiefly the conquerors. We have in this context such families as that of the Nolamba Pallavas, the Telugu Cholas and the Vaiḍumbas that figure prominently in the inscriptional sources of study. As early as A.D. 1010 in the context of sub-region B, we come across one Iriva Nolambādhirāja who is described as the scion of the Pallava race of the Kañchi region (IB.v.37). The same chief referred to as Ghaṭiyaṅkakāra in an inscription dated to A.D. 1024 from sub-region A, figures as the Nolamba chief governing the tracts of Nolambavāḍi and Kariviḍi-30 divisions (IA.v.4). The above instances amply demonstrate the fact that this chief who also figures as a donor of land, seemed to have belonged to the family of Pallavas of Kañchi with a strong hold on the Nolambavāḍi tract. The Telugu Chola chiefs of the Eruva branch are mentioned prominently from the middle of the 11th century A.D as rulers of various tracts such as Kanne-300 Pedakal-800. Naravāḍi-500 and Aije-300 situated in sub-region C. These chiefs claim to belong to the family of Karikāla and bear the titles of Kāverivallabha.[98] In the inscriptions from sub-region C, it is these rulers who chiefly emerge as donors of villages and revenue accruing from various villages under their control (IC.v.xi.155, 158, 161, 162). In fact, several branches of the Telugu Chola chiefs were supposed to have ruled over various parts of Andhra deśa as subordinates of various main ruling families during the early medieval period.[99] By the latter part of the 11th century A.D. the Chola chiefs seemed to have been displaced by the Vaiḍumba family who begin to figure in the inscriptions of sub-region C from A.D. 1078 onward as rulers of Aije-300 (IC.v.165). According to V. Yasoda Devi, the Vaiḍumbas actually claimed descent from the Western Gangas and rose into prominence in various parts of the Andhra region during 10th-11th centuries A.D.[100]

The above evidence indicates that the concentration of these chiefs is well attested to particularly from sub-region C. In this context one finds that this sub-region emerges clearly as an area of conquest in which the supra local chiefs of the Andhra region ruling as the subordinates of the Chālukyas of Kalyāṇi wielded considerable influence. As discussed above this stands in contrast to sub-region B, wherein we find the locally entrenched land-owing hereditary groups emerging as the supra-local chiefs on a considerable scale. Further, such a phenomenon is witnessed only from the middle of the 11th century A.D. and it coincides effectively with the period of the consolidation of political hold by the Chālukya rulers. In such a situation one finds that the titles of *mahāmaṇḍaleśvara, mahāsāmanta* and so on, which signify intermediary stage of political power, emerge in clear contours as political ranks/designations that were conferred on the locally powerful groups by the members of the main ruling family. It is against this background that one can comprehend the proliferation and rise of several families at the supra local level. In the case of sub-region A, one finds that it exhibits strong influences of both types of supra-local authority. In this context sub-region A, which had a rich political history of direct control by the rulers of Badami Chālukyas and the Rāshṭrakūṭas during the pre 11th century A.D.

significantly differs from the other two sub-regions in the development of its political trajectory. We thus find that in this sub-region, we have an equally prominent role played by the Rāshtṛakūṭa chiefs, Pallava chiefs and the Sinda chiefs who dominate the scene for a major part of the 11th century A.D. on the one hand and on the other, one can clearly discern the impact of the rule of the main ruling family which was effected through various official functionaries installed by them. We next turn to examine this in the following analysis.

It is however, pertinent to note at this juncture that the *mahāmaṇḍaleśvaras,* who were supposed to have held semi-independent[101] status within their kingdoms,[102] tried at the same time to attain independent political power by claiming such titles as *mahārājādhirāja.* Among these, the most prominent during this period were the Kalāchuris of Kalyāṇi (IB.iii, 125), the Hoysalas of Dwarasamudra (IB.iii.148) and the Yādavas of Devagiri (IA, iii, 154) who had been able to attain sovereignty towards the end of the 12th century A.D. The fact that all thee families of rulers held subordinate titles of *mahāmaṇḍaleśvara* in the reign of the Kalyāṇi Chālukyas has been widely recognized. Thus, the Kalāchuris of Kalyāṇi who were supposed to have descended from some branch of the Kalāchuri stock originating in Central India, figure for the first time dated to A.D. 1128 as ruling over the Tardavāḍi district in sub-region A as the *mahāmaṇḍaleśvaras* of the Chālukyas of Kalyāni.[103] The Hoysala rulers have been considered as migrants from the northern India, settled among the hills of the western ghats slowly extended their territory in the east wherein they begin to rule as the subordinates of the Chālukyas of Kalyāṇi from about 11th century A.D.[104] The Yadavas of Devagiri on the other hand, were supposed to have remained in a subordinate status from the time of the Rāshtṛakūṭa rulers with firm political hold in the area around Nasik district[105] in Maharashtra. This status the Yādavas seem to have continued to maintain for a major part of the rule of the Chālukyas of Kalyani.[106] It is pertinent to note here that in fact. Taila II himself, the founder of the Chālukyan power in the latter half of the 10th century A.D. is referred to in A.D. 965 as the *mahāsāmantādhipati (pādapadmopajivin),* who at that time was governing a small tract of Tardavāḍi-1000 located from sub-region A.[107] The apex of political power structure in these hierarchical political relations is thus represented by the chiefs of the main ruling family bearing such high sounding titles as the *samastabhuvanāśraya, prithvīvallabha, mahārājādhirāja* and *chakravarti.*[108] These titles when interpreted in their literal sense would imply that the main ruler was eulogized as the refuge of the whole earth, favourite of fortune and earth, great emperor, supreme lord and supreme master.[109] By implication however, these terms would mean that the king was the supreme over lord, chiefs and princes owing allegiance to him.[110] Members of the main ruling family invariably figure in the eulogy section of the inscription wherein the family to which they belonged is praised a great deal. It is pertinent to underscore in this regard that the chiefs of the main ruling family figure more frequently as rulers of the various provinces under their control and in terms of the conquests conducted by them.

It is however, significant to mention here that references to the members of the main ruling family in terms of donors of grants seem to have reduced cosiderably during the period of our study when compared to the pre-11th century A.D., wherein the number of grants made by this section of the social groups had dominated the scene under the rule of the Chālukyas of Badami and that of the Rāshṭrakūṭas of Malkhed.[111] In the present study we have for the sub-region A, during the 11th century A.D. only 3 instances of the members of the main ruling family as donors (IA, xi, 3, 7, 14). In the context of sub-region B during the 11th century A.D. we have 14 instances of grants made by the main ruling family chiefs (IB, xi, 31, 40, 42, 45, 48, 49, 58, 59, 71, 72, 79, 81, 83), During the 12th century A.D. for the same sub-region their number dwindles down to only 2 instances (IB, xi, 137, 146). For sub-region C, on the other hand, we have during the 11th century A.D. only 3 instances of the main ruling family chiefs as donors (IC, xi, 156, 159, 160). During the 12th century A.D. one sees that for the sub-regions A and C there has been no reference to the members of the main ruling family as donors and as noted above, even in the context of sub-region B, we find that there are only two instances of donors who belong to main ruling families of the Kalāchuris of Kalyāṇi and the Yādavas of Devagiri for the latter half of the 12th century A.D. Since these main ruling families had their political hold over wider spatial parameters, it is understandable that they had established varying degrees of subordinate relationships with the local and the supra-local levels of power in particular sub-regions as discussed above. This is particularly highlighted by the fact that the local and supra-local chiefs invariably figure in relation to the mention of the main ruling family and as owing allegiance to them and even though in our earlier discussions we have indicated that they were prominent land owners in some cases, and in others, had emerged as powerful potentates controlling the economic resources of their respective areas. Only in very rare instances, during the latter half of the 12th century A.D. in particular, we find that the mention of the main rulers is often missing which substantially indicates the growing strength of the supra-local chiefs during this period. This is clearly apparent in the charts wherein the mention of the Sindas of Yalburga is made without reference to the main ruling family chief (IA, iv, 23, IB, iv, 133, 135). It is further, pertinent to underscore in this context that the exercise of dominance in the area of conquest by the main ruling family depended upon several factors such as the ability of these chiefs to pool resources (military and economic), striking marital relations with the supra-local chiefs, conferring titles and ranks on the locally entrenched powerful groups and employing members of their family at the local levels of governance. This intricate fabric of socio-economic and politico-military relations among the elite sections becomes crucial for understanding the nature of polity during this period.

Among various dimensions of political authority exercised by the main ruling family we find that the military dimension of their expansion into new territories finds most explicit mention the inscriptional sources. We thus find in this context that the chiefs of the main ruling family figure as paramount sovereigns camping at various fort settlements after having conducted victorious conquests which become one of the main reasons for the grants made by these chiefs. In an inscription dated to A.D. 1055 in sub-region B, we have reference to the Chālukya ruler Someśvara I as camping at Bannigola after quelling some disturbance at Kummaṭa which was then followed by a grant of land by the ruler.[112] In another inscription of the same sub-region dated to A.D. 1060, the same ruler is praised as the conqueror of the Cholas. The grant of a village was made by him on the occasion of his victorious expedition through the southern region and the subsequent conquest of the Cholas. The king was at this time camping at Puli.[113] In an inscription dated to A.D. 1068 from sub-region C, we have reference to the *digvijaya yatra* (victorious campaign) of the Chālukya Someśvara II against the Malavas of the North. The ruler was at this time camping at Berkkemoksha and makes a grant to mark the occasion.[114] We have during the 11th century A.D. at least 7 references of halting camps in the context of sub-region B and 2 instances in the context of sub-region C. In fact, a majority of these figure between the period A.D. 1050 and A.D. 1200. It is pertinent to note here that the maximum number grants made by the main rulers can be found during this period itself. Importantly, it was also during the latter half of the 11th century A.D. itself that we have discussed above an increasing mention of several supra-local chiefs as rising to prominence, this is further, substantiated by crucial references made to various supra local chiefs like the *mahāmaṇḍaleśvaras* as having aided various rulers in the expeditions undertaken by them. In his expeditions against the Malevas, the Chālukya Somesvara II was supposed to have been aided by the Hoysala chiefs.[115] Further, in an inscription dated to A.D. 1074 from sub-region C, we come across an Eruva Chola chief who was supposed to have supported, Somesvara II against the rebellion of his brother Vikramāditya VI who, on his side, was supposed to have been supported by the Yādava chiefs of Devagiri.[116] We have in a similar way references to the Sindas of Yalburga as having fought on side of the Chālukya Vikramāditya VI against the Hoysalas.[117] These are only a few of the several examples we have of such instances of military aid provided by the supra-local chiefs during the period of our study.[118]

Various military conquests conducted by the members of the main ruling family could not have been sustained without an effective system of controls implemented either, through the appointment of various official functionaries at the local and supra-local levels of political hierarchy or through the appointment of the members of the royal family at crucial positions. In this context the proliferation of such titles as *mahāmātya, nāyaka, tantrepāle, daṇḍanāyaka, mahāpradhāna, sandhivigrahi, mahāsāhaṇi* and so on, particularly from the middle of the 11th century A.D. from sub-regions A (IA, vi, 8-30) and B (IB, vi, 53-154) have a significant bearing on our comprehension of the political hold exercised by the chiefs of the main ruling family over those at the supra-local level. It is basically through a combination of these terms such as *mānevergaḍe daṇḍanāyaka, (IA, vi, 14) mahāpradhāna senādhipati* (IA, vi, 26), *mahāpradhāna senādhipati sandhivigrahi (IB, vi, 72)* and so on, that we have reference to various official designations in the context of sub-regions A and B in particular from the middle of the 11th century A.D. on a significant scale (IA, vi, 10-30, IB, vi, 53-154). The term *mahāpradhāna* has been equated to mean great minister, chief minister or administrator.[119] Alekar has equated it to the level of a prime minister.[120] The title nāyaka has been considered to indicate the status of a royal officer.[121] Further, the term *mānevergaḍe* has the connotation of being a superintendent of a royal house hold.[122] It is pertinent to note in these interpretations that the importance attached to these designations in terms of their close association with the apex power structure has been highlighted. It has further, been stated in this regard that while the terms *nāyaka* signified martial leadership.[123] the *mahāpradhāna* indicated basically an honorary rank conferred on all types of subordinates by an over lord.[124] On the other hand, the term *sandhivigrahi* has been interpreted to mean a minister for war and peace.[125] Such titles as *daṇḍanāyaka, daṇḍanātha* have been translated to mean the ranks of an army general; a military commander and so on.[126] The term *mahāsāhaṇi* has also been understood to mean a military officer.[127] Further, the term *senādhipati* has been considered in a similar way to imply a military rank held by the leader of forces or the military governor of a district and so on.[128] Differentiating the holders of above titles from the supra local chiefs (nobility) discussed above, Cynthia Talbot considers the former as purely official designations which had no power base of their own apart from the authority derived from their lord.[129] One can accept the view put forth by the author with regard to the nature of the official groups we have defined above only to the extent that they signify a specific function that the incumbents were supposed to have performed. In such a context one would expect that the *daṇḍanāyaka* or the *senādhipati* and so on, were to function only as the military chiefs or vice-versa. But when viewed from the point of view of the contextual refernces made to these designations, we find that they cannot be understood as signifying a uniform status even when two individuals held the same rank. As can be deducted from the following analysis, one can clearly discern the prominent role played by the social and economic factors, coupled with the ideological, that defined the political ranks conferred by the rulers both at the apex and at the supra local levels of the state structure. To underscore these aspects one has to first of all comprehend the various contexts in which different social groups were entitled to hold specific designations of political power. Firstly, the fact that all the above defined social groups held a position subordinate to the main rulers and the supra local chiefs is well attested in the inscriptional sources. Particularly in the context of the 11th century A.D. we find that these groups emerge primarily as donees or as appointed by some chief or the other. Further, it is noticed that they made grants only with the approval of their over lord.

As early as A.D. 1016, in an inscription from sub-region B, we have reference to one Chaṭṭapayya Nāyaka the *mānevergaḍe* who has been granted a village together with all the taxes by the main ruler (IB, v, xii, 40). The title *Nāyaka* attached to the name of this functionary signified that he might have hailed from among the martial community. In an inscription dated to A.D. 1052 from the same sub-region we have reference to one Gangara Chāvuṇḍamaya Nāyaka the *taṁtrapāla* as the subordinate *(tatpādapadmōpajivi)* of the Haihaya Chief and he emerges in the capacity of a donor in association with a mercantile body (IB, vi, 54). In an inscription dated to A.D. 1061 from sub-region A, we have reference to one Cheṭṭimayya, the *mahāpradhāna daṇḍanāyaka* (IA, vi, 10) who makes a grant only after seeking the approval of the main ruler. In an earlier inscription dated to A.D. 1056, from sub-region C, Lokamānikaseṭṭi, the *mahāmātya suṁka* vergaḍe (IB, vi, 155) is referred to as the subordinate of the supra local chief. We have several such instances in the context of 11th and 12th centuries A.D. for sub-regions A and B which attest to the fact that the above mentioned functionaries did not enjoy enough freedom as was done by the *gāvunḍas* and the *manneyas* who held hereditary titles of economic power as has been discussed earlier.

It is pertinent to underscore at this juncture that one cannot view above functionaries in terms of constituting a systematic bureaucratic set up as the titles held by these groups did not necessarily correspond to the actual function carried out by them. Further, these titles were often not used in an uniform manner either. This is highlighted by the fact that various designations figure as compound terms resulting out of several combinations and permutations of various titles depending upon the ability of the individual that held them. These trends can be discerned clearly in the references of the 12th century A.D.. We find in this context that in several instances, the *danḍanāyakas* also perform such functions as collecting various taxes such as the *vaḍḍarāvula* (IC, vi, 164), *achchupannāya* (IA, vi, 18) and were therefore, often clubbed with the title *suṁka vergaḍe* (IB, vi, 116). Further, we come across several designations being clubbed together to denote the political standing of a single individual and it is pertinent to note here that these often figure under different contextual situations. We thus have such combination of ranks as the *mahāpradhāna senādhipati* (IA, vi, 26), who emerges in the capacity of the ruler of a *nāḍu* and as a donor along with several others. *Mahāpradhāna deśiya daṇḍanāyaka hiriya heggaḍe* (IA, vi, 29) installs a deity. Further, the *mahāpradhāna karaṇa* and the *mahāpradhāna daṇḍanāyaka* (IB, vi, 93) figure significantly as donors of some land which was supposed to have belonged to some *gāvuṇḍas.* The *mahāpradhāna senādhipati manevergaḍe daṇḍanāyaka* emerges as holding a superior title over the *mahāpradhāna daṇḍanāyakam* (IB, vi, 99) who was supposed to be ruling at this time over three *nāḍus* under the command of the former. In another instance of such long titles we have the example of the *mahāpradhānam senādhipati karaṇam daṇḍanāyaka heggaḍe* who emerges as renewer of an earlier grant which was made on the request of the *pradhāna kannaḍa sandhivigrahi* who was the *heggaḍe* of Sripura (IB, vi, 110). Varied contexts in which the above titles emerge clearly indicate that the literal definition of the title did not always correspond to the function performed by its holder and further, the combinations of several titles held by each individual only go to substantiate the fact that these must have been honorific titles conferred on various locally prominent chiefs. In such a situation the mention of such titles as the *karaṇa* and the *heggaḍe* rather frequently in the context of refernces to a long line of designations is a significant pointer towards a considered direction of social change. The *karaṇa* and *heggaḍe* have been interpreted to imply the titles of the dominant ruler strata and their occurrence in the context of the above titles would signify an elevation in the political status of the above groups to the supra local level of functioning, primarily as the subordinates of the *mahāmaṇḍaleśvaras.* In this context we have in an inscription dated to A.D. 1154, from sub-region B, significant reference to one Joga *Gāvuṇḍa* who figures as the ruler of Rājūr and is described as the subordinate (*tatpādapadmōpajivi)* of the supra local chief. He was also supposed to have made a grant of land (IB, vi, 120). This further substantiates our contention that various official/administrative titles discussed above were conferred on the locally powerful groups particularly during the 12th century A.D. when we find that there was a definite change in the economic scenario many of the above functionaries then begin to figure as collectors of various types of taxes.

Importantly, in several instances, the mention of the *brāhmaṇas* and certain important families as holding the above designations has a considerable bearing on our comprehension of these titles in terms of the larger social and ideological setting. We have in this context an important example in an inscription dated to A.D. 1077 from sub-region B wherein we have the ancestral list of one of the distinguished *brāhmaṇa* functionaries who were conferred with various high sounding titles and grants of villages by the chiefs of main ruling family along with the insignia of royalty. One of the important members of this *brāhmaṇa* family held the titles of *mahāpradhāna heri lala saṅdhivigrahi daṇḍanāyaka chāmūpati* (IB, vi, 72). Further, we have among these functionaries significant references to some of the names of the families to which they belonged. We have in this context mention of a member of the Nolamba Pallava family who figures as the *mahāsāhaṇi* (IA, vi, 11) and we also come across a member of the Sahavāsi family who were supposed to have hailed from the Kashmira region and held the titles of *mahāpradhānam daṇḍanāyaka* (IB, vi, 133) under the main ruler. These instances strongly indicate the fact that the above defined designations cannot be viewed in terms of purely official ranks as has hither to been considered by various scholars.[130]

Simultaneous to the efforts made by the main rulers to enhance the political status of various local functionaries was the appointment of different members of the main ruling family such as the princes and queens in the various sub-regions of study as a means to ensure for themselves a strong base of support at the local levels. Thus, we have the famous example of Akkadevi, sister of Chālukya Jayasiṁha II (IA, vi, 3, 7, 9; IB, vi, 53). She is known to have ruled at the Kisukād-70 with Vikramapura as her capital for nearly 40 years (A.D. 1010-A.D. 1054).[131] Further, in A.D. 1014 we have reference to Chālukya Jayasiṁha II (IB, vi, 39) as the ruler of Eḍeḍore-2000. In fact, the heir apparent Someśvara II figures in A.D. 1053 as a *mahāmanḍaleśvara* (IB, v, 55) being the ruler of the Belvola and Puligere tracts. Earlier to this, in an inscription dated to A.D. 1046, we have reference to another Chālukya prince *kumāra* Jayasiṁha (IB, v, 52) as administering the village of Bannigola. It is significant to note that between A.D. 1055-A.D. 1124, we have references to 3 instances (IB, iv, 58, 71, 104) of the members of the ruling lineage administering various places in sub-region B. It is pertinent to note here that the concentration of these chiefs has invariably been in sub-region B particularly the eastern part of it which constitutes the fertile Raichur Doab. Further, greater incidence of these instances during the 11th century A.D. bears effective testimony to the fact that serious attempts were made by the main ruling family chiefs to gain a significant hold in this area through various processes of political control of which matrimonial alliances struck by the members of the main ruling families with various supra local chiefs also have a significant role to play. As early as A.D. 1010, we have reference to the Pallava chief Irivi Nolambādhirāja whose wife was supposed to have been the grand daughter of the Chālukya ruler Taila II. The Pallava chief is referred to here as ruling over the Nolambavāḍi-32,000. Kemgali-500, Ballakunḍe-300, Kukkanūr-30 and 5 towns within the Māsiyavāḍi province.[132] Further, the close association of the Kalāchūrya chiefs and those of the Chālukyas of Kalyāṇi has been highlighted in various secondary sources. In this context the famous Chālukya ruler Vikramāditya VI was supposed to have married the daughter of Jogama the Kalāchurya chief. It is interesting to note here that Jogama's son in turn marries the daughter of Vikramāditya VI.[133] When the Kalāchurya chiefs attain an independent status as the main rulers in the latter half of the 12th century A.D., they seem to have further, established matrimonial alliances with the supra local chiefs who held hereditary titles of power in the area delinated for our study. We thus have, in an inscription dated to A.D. 1179 from sub-region B an important reference to the mother of Sinda Vikramādityarasa who is described as the daughter of Bijjala, the Kalāchuri monarch.[134]

Political implications of the close association established between the above ruling families are highlighted by the fact that these gave an opportunity to the supra-local chiefs to rise in their socio-political status with their newly established royal links. On the other hand, it also helped in the significant process of the legitimization of the political actions of the members of the main ruling family at the local base of power. In this context we have a significant example of the chief of the Nolamba Pallava family who, in an inscription dated to A.D. 1077, figures as representing the Pallava family (he claims the titles of Pallava-*Pemāḍi)* on the one hand, and on the other hand, he identifies himself as a member of the Chālukya family through his usage of the title. Trailokyamalla, normally used by the Chālukyas rulers. He is mentioned in this inscription as the ruler of Karāḍikal-400 located in sub-region B.[135] In another inscription of the same sub-region during A.D. 1082, the same chief is addressed as *Yuvarāja* (prince) and is identified as the younger brother of the main ruler Vikramāditya VI. In this case the Pallava chief claims to rule over nearly four *nāḍus,* those of Puligere-300, Beluvala-300, Banavāsi-12,000 and Kundūr-1000.[136] It is effectively demonstrated in these instances that by virtue of his eminent family connections stated above, this Pallava chief who actually held hereditary titles of rule in the Nolambavāḍi region (a Pallava stronghold and lies outside our area of study)[137] now emerges as the ruler of Belvola-300 and Karāḍikal-400 which formed an integral part of sub-regions A and B. On the other hand, through their association with the Nolamba chiefs, the Chālukya monarchs may have got an effective leverage in the Nolambavāḍi region which they need for extending their sway South wars to conquer the fertile tracts that were under the control of the Cholas. It is essential to note here that the Nolamba Pallava chiefs do not claim any titles of political ranking as was claimed by the other supra-local chiefs discussed earlier.

Romila Thapar has pertinently pointed out in this regard that marriage alliances have an important role to play in the process or stratification and the building up of a hierarchy.[138] In fact, the social variable for the emergence of a distinct ruling strata can be comprehended through the processes of exogamous marriages which helped in assimilating new groups and at the same time, attempts at legitimation by these political groups only helped in increasing the distance between those of high status and commoners.[139] Importantly, the fact that the economic basis has a crucial role to play in these exogamous marriages needs to be significantly underscored. We have references for other regions of India during the early medieval period, wherein the marital alliances figure prominently in the horizontal spread of a distinct political stratum. In particular the crucial role played by the marriage alliances in the evolution of a distinct Rajput polity during the early medieval period in Rajasthan has been effectively highlighted by B.D. Chattopadhyaya[140] and this has a significant bearing on our comprehension of the complex political set up of the period under study.[141]

Attempts at legitimization of political hold by various levels of the state are, however, explicitly manifest in grants of villages and various measurements of land to religious groups, institutions and symbols which helped in generating an important community in the rural social sphere, namely the *brāhmaṇas* and their institutional bases. In this context we come across significant references to certain individual *brāhmaṇas* as donees of villages that were made to them invariably by the members of the main ruling family, particulary in the first half of the 11th century A.D. We thus have during this period reference to nearly 5 instances (IB, vii, 31, 32, 37, 38) of individual *brāhmaṇa* donees who have been granted various villages for performance of Vedic sacrifices by the main rulers. Among these as early as A.D. 973 we have the mention of one Revaya Dvedi Chattopādhyāya (IB, vii, 31), in A.D. 982 reference is made to one Vishṇu Bhaṭṭa (IB, vii, 32), in A.D. 1010 Amarāchārya Bhaṭṭāraka is named (IB, vii, 37) in A.D. 1012 Maunara Śridhara Bhaṭṭa finds mention (IB, vii, 38) and one Chauvedi Bhaṭṭa emerges as a donee in an inscription dated between A.D. 1044-A.D. 1068.[142] It is pertinent to note in these instances that the suffixes such as Chaṭṭophādhyāya, Baṭṭopādhyāya, Bhaṭ ṭa and so on, attached to the names of various *brāhmaṇas* clearly indicate that these groups were brought from outside and settled in the rural space of sub-region B in particular. Writing chiefly in the context of such references for Karnataka as a whole, Sister M. Liceria has concluded upon the possibility of these *brāhmaṇas* having migrated from such areas as Bengal, Karhad and even Tamilnadu to the Karnataka region to emerge ultimately as powerful landed intermediaries between the state and the peasantry by virtue of the grants of villages and lands made to them.[143] As the recipients of grants of villages these *brāhmaṇa* donees were, however, expected to help the main rulers in a variety of ways in exercising their administrative dominance at the political level, in increasing agrarian base at the economic level and by providing legitimization at the ideological level.[144] One sees in this context that the village granted to the above described individual *brāhmaṇas* were, in turn, granted invariably to groups of *brāhmaṇa* donees who figure in numbers of 20 (IB, vii, 31) 50 (IB, vii, 79) 104 (IB, vii, 38) and 200 (IB, vii, 80). It is significant to note that it is chiefly from among these groups of *brāhmaṇas* that an important section of the rural social sphere, namely, the *mahājanas* emerge in the context of our study.

The administrative role played by this group has been emphasized a great deal in various secondary sources pertaining to our study. According to G.R. Kuppuswamy the *mahājanas* representing the orthodox *brāhmaṇa* community, were constituted into different groups of assemblies for administrative functioning in various *agrahāra* villages.[145] But the author himself is bewildered over the range and variety in which the specific numbers of the *mahājana* groups figure in each village which according to him is any where between 12 and 32,000 in number.[146] Solution to his riddle can, however, be found when we view the *mahājanas* as basically a land owing elite having differential shares in the landed property within the *agrahāra* settlements. This is underlined by the fact that first and foremost the *mahājana* group comes into existence primarily as a donee. It is further, pertinent to note that the *mahājanas* were almost always identified with the place of their residence which might have been originally granted to them and are invariably referred to as led by an *ūroḍeya.* We thus come across the 200 *mahājanas* of Ālūr, 104 *mahājanas* of Roṇa, 1000 *mahājanas of Lokkiguṇdi*, 50 *mahājanas* of Kisuguṇḍi and so on (IB, vii, 37, 38, 51, 57). Further, it is common to find that they were eulogized for their learning. In fact, grants were often given to them ostensibly for the propagation of the Vedic learning in which they excelled. We have in this context significant reference to actual shares of various measurements of land allotted for the teaching of *nyāsa* and *prabhākara,* for *vyākaraṇa* (grammar) and so on.[147] It is, however, to be underscored here that it was chiefly in the cotext of references made to the *mahājanas* in their capacity of donors witnesses, trustees and protectors of the grants on the one hand, and on the other, as the administrators or in their association with various mercantile guilds by the turn of the 12th century A.D., that we get a comprehensive understanding of the multifacted roles performed by the *mahājana* group in the context of our study.

It has beenn noted by us that the *mahājanas* first occur in a majority of cases during the 11th century A.D. mainly in their capacity as donees. We thus have reference to 4 instances of *mahājanas* as donees in the sources of sub-region A (IA.xii.3, 9, 10, 17) and 5 instances of them in the context from sub-region B (IB.xii.31, 38, 50, 61, 81). From the latter half of the 11th century A.D. onwards one clearly discers a change in the role of the *mahājana* groups particularly in the context from sub-region B. Importantly, they now begin to emerge as donors, too (IB.xi.60, 64, 71, 75, 76, 78, 79, 84, 87). It was during this period again that the *mahājanas* are mentioned performing a variety of functions. In an inscription dated to A.D. 1054, reference is made to 50 *mahājanas* of Kisuguṇḍi as witness to the grants of land made by a local potentate.[148] In an inscription dated to A.D. 1082, 200 *mahājanas* of Kuritakuṁte emerge as the trustees of the grants made.[149] Between A.D. 1076-A.D. 1124, we have an interesting reference to the *mahājanas* wherein they issue a regulation stipulating taxes payable by the potters of the *agrahāra*. This significantly highlights the administrative role played by this group.[150] In another significant reference to the *mahājana* group in an inscription dated to A.D. 1106, they figure in the capacity of bankers. Here, the *mahājanas* were supposed to use the interest amount out of 6 *gadyānas* contributed by various individuals for the purpose of performing some festival.[151] In an inscription dated to A.D. 1144, the *mahājanas* emerge as sellers of land.[152]

From the middle of the 12th century A.D. onwards we can see a significant transformation in the nature of references to the *mahājana* groups who now begin to be associated with the mercantile guilds as witnesses to the grants made by them (IB, vii, viii, 123, 129, 131). Evidence of this nature tempts one to conclude upon the possibility of the *mahājanas* taking to trade at a time when the transition in the economy to one of commercial activity was taking place in the 12th century A.D. G.S. Dikshit has in fact, brought notice to the fact that the famous merchant guild Ayyāvoḷ-500 originated from the *agrahāra* Ayyāvole in Bijapur which had 500 *mahājanas* residing in it and later, it went on to become a famous trading centre.[153] It becomes difficult in this context for us to envisage the growth of the *agrahāras* into active trading centers without the active participation of the dominant social strata residing in it, namely, the *mahājana* groups. The fact that the *brāhmaṇas* took to commerce and trading during the early medieval times has been attested to for other regions of South India as well.[154] It is pertinent here to underscore the fact that the above instances of the mention of *brāhmaṇas* and the *mahājanas* in a variety of contexts can be surmised upon in the context of sub-region A as well wherein the *mahājanas* emerge as donees in majority of cases. Their association with the mercantile bodies is also referred to in an inscription dated to A.D. 1186 wherein they were to the protect the grants made by a local potentate (IA, vii, viii, 28). In the context of sub-region C, on the other hand, it is the temple as an important institution that invariably occurs as the beneficiary of various types of grants.

It is crucial to underscore at this juncture that despite the multifaceted role played by the *mahājana* as witnessed in the context of sub-region B, one sees that by the latter half of the 11th century A.D. itself the mention of the *mahājanas* as donees begins to be outnumbered by individual non-Brahmanical religious heads. The latter group now emerge as the most powerful section of the society owing to their proximity to the temple institution which, from the latter half of the 11th century A.D., emerges as the most crucial agent of legitimation in the hands of various social groups in all the three sub-regions of our study as can be gleaned through the charts (IA, xii, 11-30; IB, xii, 57-154; IC, xii, 155-170). As a result of the growth of the temple and its allied institution, the *maṭha* we in fact, witness during this period the emergence of a whole range of social groups such as the monks and nuns in the Jaina temples and ascetics catering to various types of religious teaching in the brahmanical temples. They were normally maintained by the temple institution out of the grants made to them but nonetheless emerge as a distinct stratum in the social structure of the period.[155] It is from among this section of the social stratum that the *āchāryas, sthānāpatis, mahāsthānādhipati* and so on, as emitters of religious power, dominate as the most formidable forces of society during the latter part of the 11th and during the 12th centuries A.D. These persons began to be closely involved in the maintenance, functioning and governance of the temples as they were major centres of political and economic power. In fact, a majority of the grants of villages and land were entrusted in the hands of these heads of the temples and *maṭhas.* It is also significant that they emerge as the donors and donees in their individual capacities and begin to claim a significant socio-political standing from the middle of the 12th century A.D. in all the three sub-regions of study. In an inscription dated to A.D. 1055 from sub-region C the *mahāsthānādhipati* of the temple of God Brahmeśvara emerges as a donor of some land.[156] In an inscription dated to A.D. 1100 from sub-region A we have reference to a *sthānāchārya* of the Siddeśvara temple who makes a grant of land.[157] In an earlier inscription dated to A.D. 1077, from sub-region B, we have an interesting reference to one Netra Śiva Paṇḍita in charge of the temple of Kirti Someśvara with the attributes of a ruler. He is described as skilled in the manifold lore of weapons and conversant with the intricacies of diplomacy.[158] In an inscription dated to A.D. 1106, from sub-region C, the *mahāsthānādhipati* of the temple of God Brahmeśvara claims himself to be the direct subordinate *(tatpādapadmōpajivi)* of the main ruler.[159] Further, from sub-region B in an inscription dated to A.D. 1178, we have reference to a *sthānāchārya* who is considered to be the king among monks and figures as the preceptor of several ruling chiefs.[160] These are only a few examples of several such instances mentioned in the context of our study which we shall discuss in detail in a separate chapter.[161] It suffices for us to state here that all the above discussed *sthānāpatis* belonged to the Kālāmukha sect of Śaivism who are found mentioned in a majority of cases as they had begun to wield considerable social and political power almost like that of the ruling chieftains.

Rise in the socio-political status of the dominant groups discussed above could not have been achieved without a sound economic base to sustain the extensive non-productive activity that these groups indulged in. Military conquests undertaken by a majority of the ruling groups had a significant role to play in the enhancement of their political status at various levels.[162] On the other hand, the description of these groups in the context of non-productive activity would logically imply the existence of a social stratum different from the above groups, which must have had a crucial role to play in generating the economic surplus by actually participating in various productive processes during the period of our study. The economic scenario for a major part of the period (throughout the 11th, and almost till the middle of the 12th century A.D.) was characterized by a predominance in agrarian activity. This was a period when genuine efforts were made by various groups of land lords to expand and extend cultivation to new areas through the grants of land and villages to various religious beneficiaries.[163] In such a scenario one sees that the peasant/peasant groups had an important role to play in generating surplus production from agriculture which formed an important source of revenue for the State. A peasant has been defined as a person who undertakes agriculture on his own, working with his own implements and using labour of his family.[164] In the context of our study we have prolific mention of groups of peasants/ cultivators who seem to conform to the above definition of peasantry furnished by us. Among these we have prominent reference, chiefly in the context of sub-region B, to such groups as *aruvat* (60) *okkalu* (IA, x, 23; IB, x, 35, 53, 61, 77, 93, 97, 99, 110 and so on), *meli-sāsivvaru* (IB, x, 77), *galeya*-300 (IB, x, 111), *toṁ ṭagalu* (IB, x, 84) and *ugura*-300 (IB, x, 84, 89, 112, 117, 127 and so on), which have all been interpreted to mean groups of agriculturists. The term *okkalu* originates from the root *okku* and basically meant an agricultural operation and thus *okkalu* has been accordingly translated to mean a cultivator.[165] However, since it has striking parallels with the Sanskrit words *kuṭumbin* and *grihapati,* it has, at the same time, been understood as a householder and therefore, the groups of 60 *okkalu* according to G.S. Dikshit basically signified an assembly of households.[166] We have reference to the term *aruvattokkalu* or, 60 *okkalu* in the inscriptional sources of our study in a variety of contexts which all point to the possibility of this group having been constituted basically of agriculturists/cultivators. Reference to the 60 *okkalu* is made in a majority of cases in the context of grants being made on their request (IB, x, 35, 97) and as protectors of land grants (IB, x, 124, 127).

In almost all these instances, it is pertinent to note their association with the *gāvuṇḍas* who figure as an important land owning community in the rural scenario. It is, however, in the context of grants made by these groups which begin to emerge only after the beginning of the 12th century A.D., that we get to know the actual nature of the functions performed by them. Thus, in an inscription dated to A.D. 1109, the 60 *okkalu* emerge as donors of one *paṇa* each on *menṭe* (plough) and *toṁṭa* (garden).[167] In another inscription dated to A.D. 1118, we have reference to the grant of one areca nut garden by the 60 *okkalu* in association with the *gāvuṇḍas* of the place.[168] These evidences indicate to us the strong possibility of the *okkalu* as holding some significant rights in the land which had superior rights of the *gāvuṇḍas.* As is indicated above in the first example, through their association with the plough, these groups must have owned cultivation rights. Further, a significant change can suggested in the status of the *okkalu* group towards the middle of the 12th century A.D. wherein they emerge as donors of land and taxes on a significant scale (IB, xi, 113, 120, 126, 127). This is of course invariably in association with the *gāvuṇḍas.* Towards the end of the 12th century A.D. the *okkalu* group are associated with another important agriculturist group namely the *ugura*-300 who figure as donors of taxes and income increasingly from the middle of the 12th century A.D. (IB, xi, 112, 117, 126, 127) *ugura* has been interpreted to mean an agriculturist and its close association with the term *uguruli* which implies an instrument used for harvesting betel leaves alludes strongly to the possibility of this group as representing a specialist kind of cultivators, in particular, its mention is made mostly in association with betel leaf sellers (*tāmbuliga seṭṭ is)* and it further, corroborates our above contention. In fact, one sees that during the 12th century A.D. there is a spurt in the agriculturists working in gardens of various types. References to the *toṁṭigalu (*gardeners) and the *galeya*-300 (another agricultural guild of gardeners)[169] can be understood in the light of above evidences. Further, that the term *mel-sasivvaru* indicates another group of agriculturist guild is attested through its association with the term *meli* which has been equated with the pillar attached to the middle of the threshing floor to which the oxen were tied.[170] The fact that this group was closely associated with cultivation is further adduced through the nature of the grant made by them which is constituted of cash income on each *meli*, the plough.[171] The variety of specialization in the cultivating groups and their increasing association during the 12th century A.D., with gardens of betel leaves and arecanuts, as has been seen above, can be clearly comprehended in the context of the emergence of the temple institution as a major consumer of these cash crops.

On a closer view of the nature of references made to the above groups of cultivators/peasants, one can clearly discern the fact that the *okkalu* and *ugura* stand apart from others by virtue of their capacity to make grants of land and importantly of taxes on a considerable scale. This gives us the impression that these groups might have enjoyed certain type of usufructary rights over land they cultivated and must have enjoyed some social standing too. On the other hand, the *toṁṭigalu, melsāsivvaru* and the *galeya*-300 only occur occasionally as donors. There is a single instance of one *paṇa/haṇa* charged on their *mente* (ploughs), as an item of donation. In a particular reference to the daily wages *(bhattamāṁ)* of *galeya*-300, a part of which forms the object of the grant made by them, leads us to conclude upon the possibility of them being hired labourers.

In the secondary sources of our study, particularly in the Marxist writings of scholars, there has been considerable stress on the nature of oppression that various peasant groups were subject to by the dominant politico-economic groups in society during the early medieval set-up. On the basis of the nature of their mention in the literary sources of early medieval period, B.N.S. Yadava has drawn our attention to the existence of an extremely stratified peasantry for the early medieval North India which cannot however, be studied under the blanket term of the peasant.[172] Accordingly, the author has brought to our notice an exhaustive list of terms indicative of various types of peasant groups, of which the *kuṭumbin, hālika* and *karṣaka* have been considered to be the most commonly used terms to denote the peasantry during the early medieval period. Among these, the term *kuṭumbin* (house holder) according to the author sometimes signified a free peasantry as owners of fields[173] and in certain contexts these emerge in the sense of sharecroppers.[174] It was however, in the usage of the terms such as *hālika* (plough weilder) and the *karṣaka* (agriculturist) that one gets an indication of an assortment of dependent agricultural workers who included such groups as share croppers, petty tenants, poor owner cultivators and so on.[175] B.N.S. Yadava has mainly focussed his attention on the way the earlier 'free peasant' attained a subject status due to the particular socio-economic set up of the early medieval period characterized in his view by a decline in the urban economy and an increase in the rural phenomenon. R.N. Nandi, focussing his attention on the Karnataka region has, in a similar way, argued that there was a growth of a servile labour linked to the early medieval socio-economic developments similar to those occurred in the North Indian context.

If we take into consideration the terminology furnished by B.N.S. Yadava on the peasant groups, one may view the *okkala* and the *ugura* groups as almost identical with the *kuṭumbin* in the sense tht they represent a certain level of freedom in carrying on agricultural operations and the possibility of them holding ownership of usufructary rights. Further, the *toṁṭagalu, mel sāsivvaru* and the *galeya*-300 can be considered akin to the *karṣakas* mentioned in North Indian context who represented a loose group of dependent agricultural workers. It is pertinent to state that due to the formation of these agriculturists into corporate groups peculiar to the socio-economic set up of the area under study during the early medieval period, one cannot, at the same time, surmise upon their subjection on par with the *karṣakas.* But their dependence on the dominant land owing strata is well attested particularly with regard to the *galeya*-300 when these are addressed to patronizingly in the inscription as the dear sons of the *mahājanas,* the land owners of their place.[176] It is significant to note here that we do have, in the context of our study, indications of the existence of certain servile sections of social groups who, however, have only a limited mention in the inscriptional sources and therefore, their existence can only be concluded upon on the basis of certain allusions made to these groups under various contexts.[177] We detail some of the examples below.

We have in an inscription dated to A.D. 1080 a reference to one individual named Rudramayya who was supposed to have been granted a *menti* (plough) by the *mahājanas* of the place.[178] In another inscription from the sub-region B dated to A.D. 1088, there is reference made to the *bhritya-dāsi varga (*man and woman servants) who were transferred along with the grants made by the *ūroḍeya* of the place.[179] In the same inscription we also have reference to the *devargge parichārikar* (God's servants) for whose maintenance 6 *gadyānas* annually had been set aside.[180] In the context of references of the above kind our attention is drawn to the prevalence of forced labour which was supposed to have been widespread during the early medieval period almost all over India.[181] In this regard R.S. Sharma [182] and G.K. Rai[183] have brought forth crucial evidence for the prevalence of forced labour in the context of North India. For the Karnataka region S.G. Ghatapanadi has furnished several instances on the basis of both literary and inscriptional data which attest to the prevalence of forced labour in this region during the early medieval period. The author has in this context highlighted the term *viṣṭi* as strongly representing the case of forced labour during this period.[184] In the context of our study we come across references to the term *biṭṭi (viṣṭi)* in two instances. In an inscription dated to A.D. 1109 from sub-region B, reference is made to the term *biṭṭi* in the context of it being equated to *kuli* (labour) which forms an object of the grant to a local God by a group of artisans *(savakaṭṭa kāraru sarvabiṭṭiyāgi chaitra pavitrakke aredalada kuli).*[185] In an inscription of a much later period, *i.e.*, dated to A.D. 1213, we again come across the term *biṭṭi* in the context of the service rendered by artisans *(kārukaruṁ biṭṭi besanam).*[186] On the basis of these few examples, it would, however, be far fetching to conclude upon the widespread prevalence of forced labour in the area taken for the present study.[187] They are, nevertheless, a significant pointer to the existence of different types of servile groups catering to the services of dominant social strata.

It is pertinent to note at this juncture that reference to the term *biṭṭi* made in the context of artisans, as has been noted above, can be attributed to the changing economic conditions between the 12th-13th centuries A.D. It is during this period that artisanal and mercantile activity begins to have considerable visibility in the inscriptional sources. Importantly, the growth in the construction of temples and their allied institutions during this period had a crucial role to play in engendering artisanal activity on a significant scale which eventually resulted in such artisians as blacksmiths, stone cutters, gold smiths and so on increasing as their services were crucial for the construction and maintenance of the temple institution. In fact, it is in the context of reference to these artisans that we get a clear idea of the nature of subjection prevalent in the productive activity, particularly during the 12th century A.D. We nonetheless wish to clarify at this stage, that in using the term 'subject' to describe the status of the artisans in the context of our study, we have basically taken it to mean the dependent state of a person to which he is relegated by virtue of the restrictions imposed on him by his socio-economic status.[188] We have several instances to indicate the subject nature of the artisans particularly when they figure as attached to various dominant elements in the society such as the temple institutions, political groups and mercantile groups. We have in this context reference to such terms as *kalkuṭiga* the stone cutter (IA, viii, 7, 14; IB, viii, 59, 130) *kammaṭa* the blacksmith (IB, viii, 94, 100, 125), *baḍagi* the carpenter (IB, viii, 130, 143) *akkasāli* the goldsmith (IB, viii, 84, 90, 118). They all figure prominently along with the names of certain artisans which normally have the suffix 'Oja'. As early as A.D. 1033 from sub-region A we have reference to one Malloja, the builder of a temple, who receives a grant of land as a maintenance gift out of the main grant made to the temple with which he was associated.[189] For the 11th century A.D. we have 3 more references of this kind in which the *kalkuṭiga* or, the stone masons figure as donees of various shares of land allotted mainly to the temple institution (IA, xii, 7, 14; IB, xii, 59). In fact, by the beginning of 12th century A.D. we begin to get explicit references to various artisans as belonging to some individuals and the temple institution. We thus have in an inscription dated to A.D. 1103 from sub-region B, wherein reference is made to one *akkasāle* (IB, viii, 90) who was supposed to have belonged to the main ruler. We further, have reference to the *akkasāles* of two *nāyakas.*[190] In an inscription dated to A.D. 1118 reference is made to the *kammaras* (IB, viii, 100) of the God. In the latter half of the 12th century A.D. (*i.e.*, between A.D. 1170 to A.D. 1186), we have at least 3 instances of the above type in which one kammaṭa (IB, viii, 125) is described as the dear son of the *mahājanas.* Further, there is reference to individual artisans called Dāsiseṭṭiya Bammoja and Ayiseṭṭiya Jinnoja (IB, viii, 141) and to Keśadevara Bammoja (IB, viii, 141). All the above instances adequately testify to the fact that the artisans had their existence tied to a dominant social authority.

It is pertinent to note that in the references made to artisans during the 12th century A.D., they invariably emerge as donors of various types of grants. In one case there are 2 instances of *kuli* (labour) (IB, xii, 94, 144), and 1 instance of the gift of rice that are granted out of the wages earned by one *baḍagi* (IB, xii, 143). We have another example of the *akkasālis* who make grant of some gold (IB, xii, 90). It is however, significant to note at this stage that apart from the above references to individual artisans, we also have notices of the emergence of various artisanal guilds particularly during the 12th century A.D. Of these, we have the most prominent mention of the *telligas* (oil mongers) who were normally referred to as *telligaraivattokkalu* (telliga-50) (IA, viii, 30, IB, viii, 60, 78, 84), followed by a few references to the *Kalkuṭiga gottali* (IB, viii, 95, 144), *baḍagi Kammarar* (IB, viii, 95, 141) *akkasāleyar* (IB, viii, 95), and *sālega*-5 (weavers guild) (IB, viii, 60). All these groups are mentioned chiefly as donors of various commodities such as oil, oil mills, lime, gold and money. Among these we find that the oil mongers emerge as the most powerful group, "who lived in their own streets and had their own tanks and temples."[191] These were followed by the weavers who began to be even termed as *seṭṭis* (IB, viii, 102), a suffix normally associated with the merchant groups. We have a similar development in the context of reference to goldsmiths (*akkasālis)* who, by the middle of the 12th century A.D. begin to have the suffix *nāyaka* (IB, viii, 118) and by the end of the 12th century even figure with the suffix of a seṭṭi (IB, viii, 138). In the latter context Aychi seṭṭi the *akkasāli* even figures as owning a gold mint *(hiriya akkasālada keniyalu)* and makes a grant of gold out of the income from his smithy.[192] It has however been suggested in this context that the guilds during the period under study emerged as superior artisanal groups *vis-a-vis* the individual artisans and craftsmen.[193] All the above instances significantly attest to the emergence of a distinct hierarchy in the context of the artisanal groups during the 12th century A.D.. We wish to clarify here that when we refer to the professional groups as subject social groups, we do not refer to the guilds into which these groups were formed, nor even to those individual artisans who seemed to have attained a significant social standing as has been seen above. We include in the category of subject groups those individual artisans and craftsmen, who functioned outside the guild organization and more importantly, were dependent on the land lords/mercantile groups for their existence. We have also observed in the context of our survey that it was in fact, the latter category of individual artisans that seemed to have outnumbered the former as is indicated through their prolific mention.

In fact, the context of socio-economic relationships established by a majority of the artisanal groups with the dominant strata in society enables us to conclude upon their status of social functioning in an atmosphere almost similar to that of *Jajmāni* relationships. In the sociological studies conducted by the modern scholars, the *jajmāni* relationships have been defined as a reciprocal social and economic arrangement between families of different groups within a village community.[194] These relations continue from one generation to another, and payment is normally made in the form of a fixed share in kind rather than in cash.[195] These relationships have been, according to Wiser, carefully elaborated to govern the distribution of labour in Indian villages[196] by which the exclusive properly right possessed by a member of an artisan or servant caste to serve a specific patron family is established for generations.[197] We have ventured here to take up such a definition which is basically a modern concept,[198] for the status enjoyed by the artisanal groups in the context of our study only to the extent that it signifies relations of interdependence on hereditary lines.[199] It is significant to note in this regard that we have mention of several artisans as sons/fathers, such as in an inscription dated to A.D. 1082 where engraver of the charter was located at Pombolal and his father belonged to a different place called, Purikārapura[200] in an instance dated to A.D. 1170, the engraver of the charter, Dāmoja is described as the son of the *kammaṭa* Chandoja, who was a favourite of the *mahājanas*.[201] In another significant reference for an earlier period *i.e*, in A.D. 1138 we have mention of one Gaṇapojana, the engraver of the charter at Śripura who was a son of Ojana who belonged to a temple of a different place namely Hosavūra.[202] These instances, while underscoring the hereditary nature of artisanal services, significantly attest to the fact that the artisans did not necessarily belong to the same place of residence for generations. It is pertinent to note at this juncture that it is chiefly the ties that the artisans established with their patrons such as the land lords, merchants and temples that we find greater emphasis in the sources of our study. Among all these patrons, it needs to be underscored that the temple institution seems to have had a major share in the extraction of labour from these groups, as has been seen by us in the above instances, wherein the grant of *kuli* (labour) by the artisans on the one hand, and on the other, the remuneration made by the temple in terms of maintenance grants had a significant role to play.

In fact, role of the temple as a major patron of various professional groups emerges more distinctly in the context of references made to various cultural groups who are invariably mentioned in relation to the temple institution in the inscriptional sources of study. Of these, we have prominent mention of groups such as the *sūḷe, pātra,* or the dancing girls (IA, ix, 1; IB, ix, 56, 59, 96), *pare-kara, pāḍuvargaiṁ* or the musicians (IC, ix, 157) and *vaṁśigam,* the flute players (IB, ix, 56, 59). While referring to all these groups in his study, A. Appadorai considers them as the employees in the services of the temple and the variety of interests represented by these groups make the position of the temple as an employer predominent.[203] While almost all these groups emerge as the recipients of the grants, we cannot attribute to them the status of being dominant as usually these were maintenance grants made for their services to the temples. Further, these groups cannot be considered to represent a homogeneous entity, since they got differential shares of the grants they were largely given in relation to the nature of their job in the temple as can be seen below. As early as A.D. 1004 from sub-region A, the drummers and the dancing girls are made a collective grant of 30 *mattars* out of the main grant of *200 mattars* made to the temple.[204] For the same sub-region in an inscription dated to A.D. 1047, the drummer Ketoja was granted 24 *mattars* of land for his maintenance.[205] In an inscription dated some where between A.D. 1044-A.D. 1068, in the context of sub-region A we have a significant reference to the different shares allotted to each of these groups. Of these Dhoroja who plays five great sounds, namely, the drummer had been allotted 40 *mattars* of land. The flute players received 10 *mattars,* the singers *(pāḍuvāri-baggam)* 30 *mattars,* the garland makers *(mālagāra)* received 13 *mattars.*[206] In the context of sub-region B in an inscription dated to A.D. 1012 the drummer figures as a recipient of 12 *mattars* of land[207] and in sub-region C a group of musicians were allotted 9 *mattars* of land which was further, to be shared with the students residing in the temple.[208] The above references made to cultural professional groups particularly in the context of the 11th century A.D. clearly present a case of hierarchical relations that existed in the temple precincts. Of these, the drummer is mentioned in a majority of cases by his name and he often receives a major share of the grant, and thus seems to have held a high status. The other groups such as the musicians are almost always referred to collectively as recipients and in one instance in an inscription dated to A.D. 1060, they are even made to share the 9 *mattars* of land that they received along with the students residing in the temple. The dancing girls on the other hand, emerge to the forefront only around the middle of the 11th century A.D. wherein they figure as major recipients of the grant made when compared to other cultural groups.

Speaking about the hierarchical relations present among the social groups in the temple, C.J. Fuller, who has conducted a sociological study of the present day Minakshi temple in Tamil Nadu, writes that the priests, more than any other group in the temple by virtue of their being closest to the God, occupy the highest place in the hierarchy after the deities themselves.[209] He further, goes on to state that the priests since they performed the most vital services for the deities, formed the principal servants of the temple and were superior to other servants of the temple, such as the chanters, musicians, dancing girls and so on; who performed subsidiary parts of worship.[210] In the context of our study however, we find that this was not the case always as we have observed that the priest who were actually involved in the worship of the deities did not figure prominently as donees. In fact, their maintenance formed a part of the larger services such as the repairs of the temples, feeding the ascetics and so on, for which the grant was directed. Thus, in an inscription dated to A.D. 1075, we have reference to a temple priest (*māṇi)* who was supposed to be maintained out of the interest incurred out of the gold and the contract produce of the land, which were granted for the main purpose of decorating the image, supply of flowers, and other worship in the temple.[211] In a similar reference in an inscription dated to A.D. 1088, we have mention of the worshipping priest (*pūjasiva āchārya)* at the temple for which the main grant of several *mattars* of land was made. Of this an amount of 6 *gadyānas* was set apart for maintaining the above priest.[212]. Further, in an inscription dated to A.D. 1095, reference to the priest (*pūjān)* is made in a similar way along with the other services in the temple for which the grant was actually made.[213] These evidences adequately testify to the fact tht priests in the temple did not necessarily represent the highest level in the hierarchy of temple servants.

On the other hand, as has been seen above, reference to various cultural services performed in the temple precincts were remunerated in a distinct fashion, often in terms of individual grants and large shares in maintenance grants. In these instances, even the names of the individuals, who belonged to the category of drummers and the dancing girls have been mentioned on a significant scale. In an inscription dated to A.D. 1054 from sub-region B, we have an interesting reference to several types of dancing girls which testify to their hierarchical set up. We have mention here of several types of fan bearing girls (*chāmarada sūḷe)* who were granted 11-12 *mattars* of land, dancing girls standing near the pillars of the temple (*kambhada sūḷe)* were allotted 13 *mattars* of land individually.[214] Further, in another inscription from the same place dated to A.D. 1060 we have significant reference to the dancing girls wherein we have even the mention of the specific functions they were assigned. We thus have reference to the woman meant for God's enjoyment, who is attached to the *piriyaravāḷa (devara-bhogakke naḍava piriyaravāḷa suḷege)* who was granted as much as 20 *mattars* of land. Further, those attached to the *pergaḍe* (*pergaḍe vāḷa sūḷe)* received 15 *mattars* of land. Four public women standing at the right and left columns (*bala-vakkada-eḍa-vakkada kambada sūḷe)* were assigned 48 *mattars* collectively. Similarly, four fan bearing public women of both the left and right pillars (*Chāmarada sūḷe)* were assigned 48 *mattars.* In another example, four dancing girls (*pātra)* were given 48 *mattars* and two public women meant for enjoyment (*bhogada sūḷe)* were given 24 *mattars* of land. In the same record the drummer was granted 24 *mattars* and the flute player was granted 12 *mattars* of land.[215]

Among the hierarchy of all these cultural groups it was again the drummer who seemed to have occupied the highest place. On the other hand, the hierarchized set up of the dancing/public women was based again on the specific nature of the function they were involved in. Of these, the dancing women attached to the *piriyaravāḷa* (keeper of the temple girls) and the one attached to the *pergaḍe* (village headman) were given preference over the others in terms of the payments made to them. The rest were given more or less an equal share. It is pertinent to bring to focus in this context another example of how there existed a hierarchy among the temple girls in an inscription dated between A.D. 1044-A.D. 1068. In this case they are basically divided into two groups such as the *pātram sūḷe* (dancing girls) who received only 48 *mattars* of land collectively as against the *bhogada sūḷe* (public women meant for enjoyment) who received nearly 76 *mattars* of land.[216] References of this type enable us to conclude upon a hierarchised set up within the temple institution which was however, denied not according to the ritual status or the proximity of the groups to the deity, but on the basis of the social significance attached to the functions performed in the temple precincts. In this context it has been aptly stated that the temple girls "not only performed their professional duties, but the very nature of their work implied their being used as objects of sexual gratification. In this context then, their access to wealth and other resources unconsciously depended very much on their social accessibility to the kings, chiefs and temple functionaries.[217] This explains the reason why specific group of temple girls *(pergaḍe sūḷe piriyaravāḷavala sūḷe* and *bhogada sūḷe)* enjoyed a preferential status.

By the beginning of the 12th century A.D. however, one sees a distinct change in the reference to cultural professional groups whose mention now in the inscriptional sources in extremely limited. Whatever mention we have of these groups does not in any way conform to their mention in the earlier period. Thus, in an inscription dated to A.D. 1112, a reference to *pātra,* the dancing girl, is made along with the attendants of the temple and they are made a collective grant.[218] In an inscription dated to A.D. 1178, we have reference to the *sūḷe-vala* or the dance master who was given 12 *mattars* of land and the drummer *(parekara)* who sounded the drum thrice a day before the God was given one house site.[219] These instances effectively testify to the change in the status of the cultural groups which seem to have fallen much below the level of status they had enjoyed during the 11th century A.D. Their non-mention in specific terms in a majority of sources of the 12th century A.D. has to be analyzed in the context of the increasing mention of rituals and other services which implied their existence. It has been suggested in this regard that during this period growth in the importance attached to the rituals and other temple services such as *aṅga-bhoga, raṅga-bhoga* which find frequent mention in the sources of 12th century A.D., had a significant implication for the nature of grants made. Now, the grants began to the directed to these rituals in the temples of which dancing and singing also formed a part. In a rare instance of its nature we have reference to a *sūḷevaḷa* (dancing master) who even emerges as a donor in an inscription dated to A.D. 1148.[220] All these attest to the fact that the dancing and singing activities might have been carried on, on a significant scale, even during the 12th century A.D. Further, it can perhaps be suggested that their non-mention in the sources of this period can be attributed to the increase in the powers of the priestly office who had a crucial role to play in the elaborate rituals of the period and the consequent degradation in the importance of the actual performers of various other professional services.[221]

It is pertinent to underscore here that the fortunes of these cultural groups were not just tied to the temples in which they functioned, but more importantly, to the nature of patrons too who had a great deal to do with the emergence of the temple institution. Despite the widespread growth of temples during the 12th century A.D. one notices a distinct decline in the mention of temple servants. According to K. Ismail, a majority of the temple servants were either, donated or, maintained by the donors.[222] It has further been stated in this regard that it was only when these servants coming from the other two sources were not adequate that the temple recruited necessary servants and maintained them on its own.[223] Thus, the temple servants were squarely dependent upon the dominant social strata who in the 11th century A.D. particularly in the context of sub-regions A and B constituted chiefly of the local functionaries as major patrons of temple institutions (IA, xi, 1-17, IB, xi, 31-85). We have observed in this context that the local functionaries do not have a major role to play as donors from sub-region C which accounts for a greater emphasis given in the region to the performance of rituals which importantly was mainly in the hands of the priestly groups and therefore, the possible reason for the non-mention of the cultural groups even during the 11th century A.D. on a significant scale. On the other hand, sub-regions A and B from the beginning of the 12th century A.D. witnessed a gradual shift in the nature of patrons to the temple. They now begin to be dominated by mercantile and artisanal groups whose grants of money and commodities were significantly directed towards the performance of specific rituals and festivals in the temple precincts which is another reason that seems to have subsumed the mention of individuals involved in their performance in the inscriptional data.[224]

One may gauge through the charts appended to the chapter that evidence of the mention of merchants and mercantile groups begins to emerge gradually from the beginning of the 11th century A.D. itself but, by the beginning of the 12th century A.D., their mention becomes so profuse that the predominant role of these groups in the gift giving network of temple institutions needs to be understood and reckoned with. We, however, note a sub-regional variation in the distribution of these mercantile groups. For the sub-region A during the 11th century A.D. we come across only a single reference to an individual with the suffix of a *seṭṭi* (IA, viii, 1). However, during the 12th century A.D. for the same sub-region we have several references to Ayyāvole-500 (IA, viii, 26, 29, 30) *mummurridaṇḍas* (IA, viii, 26, 30), *nāḍa-seṭṭi guṭṭa* (IA, viii, 26, 29, 30) *samasta nakara* (IA, viii, 28, 30). For the sub-region B during the 11th century A.D. itself we have a greater variety of groups emerge on the scene. We thus have reference to such terms as *nakara samūha* (IB, viii, 36), *tala samastha* (IB, viii, 36), *nagaram* (IB, viii, 54, 67, 72, 75), *nagara mahājana* (IB, viii, 55), the *samūha* (IB, viii, 74), *vaniga mahājana* (IB, viii, 75), *mahānagara* (IB, viii, 82), *nānādeśi* (IB, viii, 82), 500 *svāmis* (IB, viii, 85), 18 *paṭṭaṇas* (IB, viii, 85), 64 ghaṭikāsthānas (IB, viii, 85), 32 velpuras (IB, viii, 85), 64 yogapīṭhās (IB, viii, 85) along with the mention of several individuals (IB, viii, 36, 42, 51, 63, 66, 75, 82) and groups of *seṭṭis* such as 8 *seṭṭis* (IB, viii, 53, 59, 70), *seṭṭis* of a particular place (IB, viii, 60), *seṭṭis* of

2 *puras* (IB, viii, 74), *tāmbūliga setti* (IB, viii, 84) and several *settis* from various commercial centres (IB, viii, 85). During the 12th century A.D. for the same sub-region this tendency continues with greater intensity and we have reference to the *nakara* (IB, viii, 87, 92, 93, 94, 139, 144, 153) 500 *banajigas* (IB, viii, 87), *nānādeśi* (IB, viii, 92, 123, 154), *gātrigaru* (IB, viii, 92), *nakara samūha* (IB, viii, 93), *mahānakaraṁgalu* (IB, viii, 94, 136), *tāmbuliga*-1000 (IB, viii, 112, 114) *mummūridaṇḍas* (IB, viii, 116, 120, 123, 149, 153), 36 *bīḍu* (IB, viii, 116), *ubhaya nānādeśi* (IB, viii, 116, 136), *mahānāḍu* (IB, viii, 116), *gavares* (IB, viii, 120) 16 representatives of 8 *nāḍus* (IB, viii, 123), *prabhus* of 3 *paṭṭaṇas* (IB, viii, 123), *samasta nakaraṁgalu* (IB, viii, 129), *nagara mahājana* (IB, viii, 132, 150), the 500 (IB, viii, 132, 151), the *pura* (IB, viii, 132), *angaḍiya nakaraṁgalu* (IB, viii, 136), 500 *svāmis* of Ayyavoḷe (IB, viii, 152), *sthala samasta prabhu* (IB, viii, 154) along with reference to certain individual *seṭṭis* (IB, viii, 136, 142, 144) and groups such as 16 *seṭṭis* (IB, viii, 139). For the sub-region C on the other hand, during the 11th century A.D. we only have reference to an individual *seṭṭi* who also figures as a functionary (IC, vi, 155) and the group of 3 *seṭṭis* (IC, viii, 158) and during the 12th century A.D. we have reference to the *Ayyāvoḷe svāmi* (IC, viii, 170), *pramukha ubhayanānādeśi* (IC, viii, 170), Kannada-4000 (IC, viii, 170) and the chiefs of various business centres (IC, viii, 170).

The above terms clearly suggest that there was a definite increase in the nature and scale of the mention of mercantile groups particularly in the context of sub-region B from the latter half of the 11th century A.D. onwards. This can be largely attributed to the expansion of agrarian hinterland through the extensive grants of land and villages made in the above area right from the latter half of the 10th century A.D. In fact, the gradual emergence of the merchant groups representing trading activity can be discerned through their predominant mention in simple terms such as the mention of names of individuals with the suffix of *seṭṭi* along with an occasional mention of the *nakara/nagaraṁ* for a greater part of the 11th century A.D. By the turn of the 12th century A.D. we however, witness a distinct change in the mention of mercantile groups, who now begin to be represented through the usage of complex and varied terminology. Among these we have the prominent mention of the *nakara* in its varied forms such as *mahānagara, nagara, mahājana, nānādeśi/ubhaya nānādeśi,* 500 *svāmis* of Ayyāvoḷe, *mummūdaṇḍas, tāmbuliga seṭṭis* and so on, which represent various aspects of organized trading activity.

The suffix *seṭṭi* an equivalent of the Sanskrit term *śresthin* which signifies, according to D.C. Sircar, the leading member of a guild.[225] The context of references made to this suffix attests to the fact that association of it with the name of any individual signifies his involvement in some form of trading activity or the other. The *nagaraṁ (nakara)* in its conventional usage has been interpreted in the sense of an assembly of town or, a mercantile assembly similar to that of the *sabha* or *ūr* of the *agrahāra* and *non-agrahāra* settlements respectively.[226] According to R. Champakalakshmi the *nagaram* however, represented the merchant groups participating in local networks of trade[227] whereas, the 500 *svāmis* of Ayyāvoḷe was a supra local organization which had its origins in the *agrahāra* of Aihole in the Bijapur district of Karnataka as early as the 8th century A.D.[228] In fact, it is supposed to have become a much larger organization by the 11th-12th centuries A.D. drawing its members from various regions and communities. It is in this context that the term *nanadeśi* and *ubhaya nānādeśi* have been used interchangeably in the records of this period according to the author.[229] Thus, we have the division of the mercantile groups on the basis of the local and the supra-local interests represented by these and the *mummūridaṇḍas,* which have been interpreted as an advance guard of a caravan and the constituents of the 500 merchants,[230] were meant to protect these itinerant merchants from attacks of robbers and the like.

In the context of our study too one may discern certain similarities with the development of trade guilds of South India as a whole. In fact, it is in the emergence and the proliferation of the *nagaraṁ* group of merchants that we get certain crucial clues to the nature and the complexity which marked the organization of commercial groups during the 11th and 12th centuries A.D. particularly in sub-region B of our study. During the 11th century A.D. the *nakara/nagaraṁ* emerges at least in 5 instances (IB, viii, 36, 54, 67, 72, 75) of reference. Of these, as early as A.D. 1005, we have the *nakara samūha* in whose presence certain grants were made by an individual *seṭṭi* and the *tala samasta* of kukkanūr.[231] In A.D. 1052, *nagaraṁ* members are referred to as donors of some land along with a local functionary.[232] In an inscription dated to A.D. 1072 this group emerges in the form of donors of oil mills, land and a garden.[233] We have an interesting reference to the *nakaraṁ* in an inscription dated to A.D. 1077, wherein they were to punish the violators of celibacy in a local temple along with the rulers *(arasuṁ)* and people of the place *(ūruṁ)*.[234] In an inscription dated to A.D. 1080, the *nakaras* emerge as the donors of paddy.[235] In all these instances what one finds striking is the nature of grants made by the *nagaraṁ* which were mainly in the form of lands. Secondly, the association of these groups with the local functionaries and the people of their locality is significant to note. In one of the above instances the *nagaraṁ* even enjoyed the right to punish the violators of the temple which attests to their active involvement in the activities of their locality. These inferences are in a large measure suggestive of the possibility of the *nagaraṁ* as a representative of the local merchant groups who were basically agriculturists now taking to trade at the local level as is suggested by the nature of grants made by them. In fact, even out side the *nagaraṁ* the mention of individual and groups of *seṭṭis* who figure in a majority during the 11th century A.D. in sub-region B attests to the agrarian moorings of the mercantile groups at this time. In an inscription dated to A.D. 1010, we have reference to 8 *seṭṭis* of Suṇḍi who emerge as leasors of land in association with the *gāvuṇḍas* of the place.[236] In an inscription dated to A.D. 1037, we have reference to one Dāmodara Seṭṭi who was supposed to have been the son of a *pergaḍe* called Dhoyipayya.[237] Earlier, to this in an inscription dated to A.D. 1028, the wife of a *gāvuṇḍa* is described as the daughter of one Mada Nāgi Seṭṭi of Suṇḍi.[238] Further, we have a signifiant reference to 30 *seṭṭis* in an inscription dated to A.D. 1072, who are headed by one *Chāvuṇḍa Gāvuṇḍa* and they were granted leases of various lands by the temple establishment.[239] In an inscription dated to A.D. 1080, the *vaṇiga mahājana* emerge as donors of paddy and their close association with the dominant landowners owners of their place, *i.e.*, the *mahājanas* is well attested to.[240] In all these instances the fact that the trading groups during the period of our study, emerged out of a landowing stratum is firmly established through the nature of the grants made by them, as leasors of land and importantly, through their close association with the families of the *gāvuṇḍas* and the *mahājanas.* By the beginning of the 12th century A.D. one however, witnesses a gradual decline in the mention of traders in their individual capacity on the one hand, and on the other, as small groups of *seṭṭis* which had formed a dominant feature of the mercantile groups during the 11th century A.D.

Such a trend changes subsequently as is indicated in the growth of the variety of mercantile groups on an organized scale and the mention of individual *seṭṭis* mostly in terms of their professional association during the 12th century A.D. The latter had absorbed the individual merchants under various heads of mercantile activity depending upon the interests they represented. In such a context a variety of ways through which the *nagaraṁ* is referred to contributes significantly to our comprehension of the changing commercial scenario which was at this time wrought with diversification and specialization of mercantile activity on a significant scale. We wish to detail these aspects as they are mentioned in relation to the *nagaraṁ* group. In an inscription dated to A.D. 1095 we have for the first time a reference to *mahānagara (IB, viii, 82)* which was supposed to have been constituted to 16 *seṭṭis* referred to as the lords of Ayyāvoḷepura. These are mentioned in association with the *nānādeśi* and emerge as donors of land and gold. In an inscription dated to A.D. 1105 reference to the *nakaramu* (IB.viii.92) is made in association with the *nānādeśi* and *gātrigaru* who emerge as donors of an impost on sales of areca nuts. Further, in an inscription dated to A.D. 1109 we come across the *nakaraṅgaḷu* and the *mahānakaraṅgaḷu* (IB.viii.94) in the context of minting establishments, levies on which form the object of grants made by them. In a different inscription of the same period we have interesting reference to the *nakaras* in association with the 500 group *(ainnūrvāru)* (IB, viii, 93) and the *tāṁbuliga seṭṭis.* While the *nakara* emerge as donors of some cash income due to them from the transporters *(sāriga okkala)* and *aṅgaḍi okkala* (shop owners) and some salt, the *tāṁbuliga seṭṭis* emerge as donors of some taxes. In a much later inscription dated to A.D. 1175, reference is made to the *samasta nakaraṁgaḷu* of Balagānūr (IB, viii, 129) as donors of lands, the *nagara-mahājana* (IB, viii, 132) of Mulugunḍa figure in an inscription of A.D. 1178 along with the *pura* and the 500 as donors of land. We have a significant reference to the *mahānakaraṁgaḷu* (IB, viii, 136) in an inscription dated to A.D. 1179 in association with such groups as the *gandhavanadaṅgaḍiya nakara* and *bhaṭṭavattiyaṅgaḍiya nakaras.* In an inscription dated to A.D. 1184, reference is made to the 16 *seṭṭis* of Dharmapura along with the *nakaras* (IB, viii, 139) of the place who make a grant of land and were to protect the group. In A.D. 1189, the *nakaras* (IB, viii, 144) emerge as donors of arecanuts from shops. Further, the *nagara-mahājana* emerge as donors of land in inscriptions dated to A.D. 1196 and A.D. 1207 (IB, viii, 149, 150, 153).

We have been able to draw the following inferences from the above cited instances. Through the explicit references made to the *nagaraṁ/nakara* in relation to the shops, minting establishments and as donors of land and commodities such as salt, arecanuts and so on, they clearly emerge as purely a local group of merchants who had, during the 12th century A.D., diversified into various forms of local industrial and mercantile activities that had a strong nexus with the agrarian hinterland. This can be further attested by the fact that the *nakaras* can also be seen emerging as employers of various groups such as the *sāriga okkala,* (transporters) (IB, viii, 93) *angaḍi okkala* (shop keepers) (IB, viii, 93) and various workers in the minting establishments *(savakaṭṭu kāru, kammaṭi adhikāri)* (IB, viii, 94). On the other hand, the close association of the *nakara* (IB, viii, 136) with *aṅgaḍis* (shops) pertinently underscores the significant role played by the *nakaras* in the management of local networks of industry such as minting establishments and markets represented by shops during this period. Reference to such individual merchants as *banḍiya* Basava Seṭṭi (IB, viii, 142) whose association with transport is indicated in his title *banḍi* and the *mahāvaḍḍavyāvahari* the local money exchanger (IB, viii, 93) and reference to various *seṭṭis* and artisanal groups in the context of minting establishments and transactions can be comprehended in the light of above diversification witnessed in the local market network. We thus have mention of such diverse professional groups as the *kaṁchagāra* (braziers) (IB, viii, 144), *kumbāra* (potters) (IB, viii, 144), *seṇigaru* (weavers) (IB, viii, 144) *telliga* (oilmen) (IB, viii, 151), *kammaṭidalu nāḍvaanikāra* (ānikāra responsible for running the mint) (IB, viiii, 138), *kammaṭida hiriya senada bhōgaṁ* (IB, viii, 138), *keṇikaram* (IB, viii, 138) so on, and so forth. It is pertinent to note here that all these groups emerge as donors of small measurements of cash to various Gods and can be considered to have had an active role to play in the productive work of this period which seems to have been organized by the *nakara* (IB, viii, 136, 144). This significantly was a productive area of non-agrarian activity outside the direct control of the temple.

Another significant change in the context of references made to the *nagaraṁ* organization can be seen in its increasing association with the *mahānakaraṁgalu* (16 *seṭṭis* of *nāḍus* 8) (IB, viii, 94, 123) the 500 *svāmis* of Ayyāvoḷe (IB, viii, 154) nānādeśi (IB, viii, 92) *gātrigas* (IB, viii, 92) and the *mummūridaṇḍas* (IB, viii, 154) all of which have been understood as representing supra-local itinerant mercantile organizations with the Ayyāvoḷe guild as the focus of activity. This stands directly in contrast to the earlier predominant association of the *nagaraṁ* with the state functionaries. In fact, it is only from the beginning of the 12th century A.D. (A.D. 1109) that we find that the *nagaraṁ* group begins proclaiming for the first time to be the protectors of *vīra baṇañju dharma*[241] translated as the customary observances of the *balañja* group of merchants[242] or, the heroic creed of traders.[243] Attempts of the *nagaraṁ* to claim the status of a larger mercantile group on distinct lines is stated more clearly in an inscription dated to A.D. 1175 wherein the *samasta nakaraṁgalū* of Balagānūr are stated to have descended from the lineage of *kubera*. Further, their claim to take delight in making gifts of 1000 cows and food and so on,[244] only testifies to the agrarian moornings of the *nagaraṁ* group. According to R. Champakaslakshmi the process of urbanization witnessed during the 11th to 13th centuries A.D. in South India, owed a great deal to the organization of the local network of the *nagaraṁs,* coupled with the emergence of supra local mercantile groups to organize the long distance trade.[245]

The emergence of supra local organizations in the context of our study begins from around A.D. 1095 when we come across a group of 16 *seṭṭis* of Dharma Voḷal who claim to be the lords of Ayyāvoḷe pura and term themselves as constituting an assembly of *mahānagara*. It is significant to note here that members of this body are referred to as born to those who belonged to different countries *(nānādeśābhyantaradevargge puṭṭeyuṁ).* This is indicative of the fact that these 16 *seṭṭis* belonged to different areas and came together to form an assembly owing to their common professional interest. In the same inscription these *mahānagara* have been considered to be friends of another assembly of merchants namely, *nānādeśi,* and emerge in the capacity of donors of some land, gold and the tax of *aruvaṇa*.[246] In fact, we come across a wide variety of merchantile guilds along with the names of a number of individual *seṭṭis* who are referred to as hailing from different mercantile centers in an inscription dated to A.D. 1099 (IB, viii, 85). We thus have reference to the 500 *svāmis*, 18 *paṭṭanas* 32 *velpuras*, 64 *ghaṭikasthānas,* 64 *yogapiṭhas,* the 16 of the 8 *nāḍus, gavares gātrigas, bīras, bīravaṇigas,* and *tāmbuliga*-1000. The very nature and scale in which the various mercantile guilds figure in the above inscription is a significant pointer to the supra-local character exhibited by them when they are mentioned as belonging to so many places. Among these the *gavares* have been interpreted as either a guild of basket makers or a guild of corn merchants and are supposed to have constituted a significant part of the guild of 500 *svāmis* of Ayyāvoḷe along with the *gātrigas*.[247] The *biras* or the *bira* vaṇigas, as is indicated by the term *bīra* (bravery) probably constituted the group of protectors/soldiers of these itinerant group of merchants. It is significant to note here the absence in the mention of *mummūridaṇḍas* who are normally stated to have constituted this protective force. Further, the *tāṁbuliga-* 1000 constituted the betel leaf sellers.

All the above groups were supposed to have met in an assembly to bear witness to certain grants of commodities made by several individual *seṭṭis* hailing from at least 8 types of mercantile centers who probably belonged to the group of *tāṁbuliga*-1000, *gavares* and *gātrigas* who also participated in making the grants. In fact, the grant was directed towards one *gāvuṇḍa* who was supposed to have rendered significant services to the above groups.[248] It is pertinent to note that in this context, we come across nearly 7 instances to the supra local groups particularly during the 12th and early 13th centuries A.D. (IB, viii, 116, 120, 123, 149, 150, 154). We also have significant trends of the interaction of the *nakaraṁ* with the supra local groups during this period. For a major part of the 12th century A.D. one sees tht a few supra local groups such as the *tāmbuliga seṭṭi (IB, viii, 93), ubhayanānādeśi* (IB, viii, 136), *mahānakaraṁigalu* (IB, viii, 136) and so on, figure as interspersed between references predominated by mention of local mercantile and industrial guilds. This trend seems to have undergone a significant change in the context of references made to the *nakaram* towards the end of the 12th and the early 13th centuries A.D. In these instances we find that the *nakaraṁ* group is predominantly mentioned against the background of several references to the supra local groups (IB, viii, 149, 150, 153, 154). It is significant to underscore at this juncture that reference to the *nagaraṁ* is made in only one instance in the context of sub-region A (IB, viii, 28) which is outnumbered here by an important mention made to the supra local organizations during the 12th century A.D. (IA, viii, 19, 26, 29, 30). In sub-region C, wherein we have no mention of the *nagaraṁ* whatsoever the mention is only made to various supra local organizations towards the end of 12th century A.D. (IC, viii, 170). Earlier during the middle of the 11th century A.D. for sub-region C, too we only come across isolated references to a *seṭṭi* who was referred to as a functionary (IC, viii, 155). In the context of the above references to the supra local mercantile organizations, it is pertinent to note that they invariably claim to be protectors of *vīra-baṇañju dharma* and seemed to have come to the forefront by early 13th century A.D. through an interaction with the local assemblies of merchants as has been witnessed in the context of sub-region B. In so far as the grants made by all these bodies is concerned, they were predominantly made in various measurements of land towards the end of the 12th century A.D. Occassionally this was coupled with grant of taxes which signifies the political hold established by various mercantile groups (particularly the supra local ones such as the *tāmbuliga seṭṭis).* At the same time, it needs to be emphasized that the nature and composition of trade groups was still in a stage of transition from that of their formation at local levels to the emergence of the supra local organizations. In fact, it was the temple which provided focus to all these mercantile groups who invariably converage on this institution as donors of various types of grants so as to seek validation for their mercantile activities.

The emergence of the temple institution as the focus of political economic and ideological power had enabled it to draw support from a cross section of society bringing to light for us the existence of a variety of social strata during our period of study. It was chiefly in the context of the temple that we come across a wide variety of social groups interacting with the religious space in the capacity of either the donors, donees, sellers, executors, witnesses, protectors of land grants trying to seek legitimation at various levels of socio-economic structure. We have already noticed the role played by the dominant socio-political and economic groups. Apart from these we also come across significant references to certain women, playing the dominant role of donors and belonging to, various political and economic social groups. We have in this regard already noted the role played by the queens and various princesses from the royal life who emerge as both the rulers and as donors of various measurements of land to the temple institution.[249] These however, figure in the capacity of either daughters, wives, sisters or mothers of prominent men in society. We have on the other hand, certain crucial evidence in this regard which depict the fact that other women also held certain significant posts among the functionaries with titles similar to them. Thus in an inscription dated to A.D. 1148 we have reference to one *mahāprabhuvini* Lakmādevi who emerges as the donor of land.[250] In a similar reference dated to A.D. 1173, we have mention of one *gāuṇḍi* who emerges as the donor of certain taxes in association with the okkala and other local chiefs.[251] In an inscription dated to A.D. 1091 we have the significant reference to *telliga* (oil monger) Jakkiyabbe who made a grant of land after purchasing the same from the local *mahājanas.*[252] In a different type of reference we have mention of a woman called Revabbe *goravi* as a priest of a local temple who emerges as an independent donee.[253] Apart from these, we also come across references in a small measure to the existence of pastoral and hunting groups in the context of grants. Thus, in an inscription belonging to between the 11th-12th centuries A.D. we have mention made to a gift of 14 goats (*meṅkalu)* by the wife of a sāmañta Mailayya to the God.[254] We have in this context another interesting reference to one *kanna* the *kuriṁbana* (shepherd) whose stone formed one of the boundaries to the grants made.[255] In a significant reference from an inscription dated to A.D. 1184, we have mention of certain pastoral and hunting groups such as *kuṛiba-gāvunḍugaḷum (*chiefs of pastoralists) and *beḍaruṁ* (hunters) along with several others such as *huligajañguliya nāvikaru* and *mādagāra* whose chiefs grant the house tax to the God.[256]

Mention of various groups in the inscriptional sources is often made through the politico-economic status that these groups held in the functioning and governance of society. This does not in any way mean that their *varṇa* status was totally side lined. That *varṇa* was an implicit well recognized way of defining social status is most explicity stated by the importance given to the *brāhmaṇas.* Their caste status forms one of the basic criterion for the *brāhmaṇa* groups to emerge as most powerful donees during the period of our study. Here, it would be pertinent to point out that when we talk of the *brāhmaṇa varṇa* we cannot consider them as belonging to a homogeneous undifferentiated group. The land grant economy, as has been postulated by Suvira Jaiswal had brought about a stratified structure of this *varṇa.* She suggests that in early medieval times those *brāhmaṇas,* who made a living out of priesthood by accepting gifts and performing sacrifices for the people were considered lower in social status than those who were attached to high administrative or military posts. The latter tasks fell in the sphere of activities traditionally meant for the warrior class or, *kṣatriyas* and had in the ancient period been open to the *brāhmaṇas* only in times of distress.[257] In the context of our study, to the former category belonged those *brāhmaṇas* who performed worship in the temple (*devalaka brāhmaṇas)* and were allotted maintenance grants in terms of both cash and a small measurement of land. To the latter, we have reference to several of those *brāhmaṇas* who initially figured as donees of villages and large measurements of land owing to their knowledge in the Vedic sacrifices (*śrotriya brāhmaṇas).* This category of *brāhmaṇas* figure in a majority during the first half of the 11th century A.D. and some of these have even been identified on the basis of the *gotra* names used to describe them. We thus have references to Revaya Dvedi Chaṭṭopādhaya (IB, vii, 31) of the *kāśyapa gotra,* Vishṇu Bhaṭṭa (IB, vii, 32) of the *Viśwāmitra gotra* and so on. The theory of *gotra* appears to have evolved to support the claim of the *brāhmaṇas* to superior status by establishing their origins to the seven *ṛṣis* of the Vedic times.[258] *Brāhmaṇas* belonging to various superior *gotras* seem to have been selected by the main ruling family chiefs to provide ideological support at the local levels in the new areas of their conquest. Mention of *brāhmaṇas* as holding important positions in the ruling structure as *daṇḍanāyakas* has been well attested. One of these functionaries Venneyya Bhaṭṣṭa is stated to have belonged to the *kamma kula* and is praised at the same time as the warrior among the *brāhmaṇas.*[259] It is pertinent to note here that the *mahājanas* who emerge as major landlords during the period of our study are invariably praised for their Vedic learning on the one hand, and for their *brāhmaṇa varṇa* status in a majority of cases. In an inscription dated to A.D. 1049 reference is made to one *mahājana* Jakkimayya, who is supposed to have belonged to the *kaundinya gotra* and the *dhora kula* at the same time.[260] We further have an interesting reference to such groups as *goles* and go *brāhmaṇas* who, along with the *mahājanas* of their place emerge as protectors of grants made in their presence in an inscription dated to A.D. 1185.[261] All these evidence sufficiently go to prove that there were well defined stratified groups within the *brāhmaṇa* community that need to be comprehended against the family (*kula)* and the professional background they belonged to. Thus, reference to the *kamma kula* and the *dhora kula brāhmaṇas* indicates to us the importance attached to the regional and familial links of identification established within the *brāhmaṇa varṇa.*[262] The necessity to identify them as such probably arose to locate their original area of habitation or, the original family they belonged to which might have claimed a dominant social position in the area. In this context significant reference to the *goles* and the *go-brāhmaṇas* strongly attests to their pastoral moorings. Either, this alludes to the absorption of the priestly elements from among the pastoral groups of the area into the *brāhmaṇa varṇa* or, to those *brāhmaṇas* who had taken to the profession of pastoralists might have been termed as such. Simultaneously, in some areas the concept of land owning *brāhmaṇas* had got sufficiently well entrenched and their local affiliations (and the family to which they belonged) must have negated the necessity of having an identity on the basis of *gotra* status as we do not have any significant mention of *gotras* in the inscriptions during the 12th century A.D. Such a trend can also be attributed to the enormous growth in the temple institution as a major legitimizer of the social strata.

During the 12th century A.D. rather than individual *brāhmaṇ* families living in the village, it was the temple trustees and priests in the temple who had emerged as major land lords. They began to be depicted in inscriptions on the basis of their claim to affiliation either to the temple institution they belonged to or, to the identification with religious cult they represented rather than to the *brāhmaṇa varṇa.* On the other hand, we have already observed earlier that they made claims to the attributes of a warrior class which seemed to have gained greater credence during the early medieval set up. At the same time distinct references to the urges exhibited by the ruling groups to claim *kṣatriya* status can be seen emerging in the context of our study particularly among the supra local and the main ruling family chiefs from the latter half of the 11th century A.D. In an incription dated to A.D. 1080, the Pallava chief Permadi Jayasiṅgadeva is referred to as *kṣatriya pavitram.*[263] The Sinda Bopparasa, manneya of Mulugunḍa-12 who belongs to the *kunnula vaṁśa* claims himself to be Sinda *kṣatriya mahipa* dated to A.D. 1148.[264] In an inscription dated to A.D. 1183 reference is made to the Kalāchurya family as belonging to *kṣatriya varṇa*.[265] Further, reference to a Haihaya chieftain Allahulirasa as of the Haihaya *kula mahā kṣatriya vaṁśa* is made in an inscription dated to A.D. 1191-92.[266] All the above evidence cited belong to sub-region B and their claims to *kṣatriya* status significantly correspond to the rise in the political power of these chiefs during this period. We have already seen earlier that the Pallava rulers begin to rise to power in sub-region B in the context of our study right from the beginning of the 11th century A.D. Similar is the case with the Sinda chieftains of Mulugunḍa who appeared in the inscriptions from sub-region B as early as A.D. 994-95. The Haihayas on the other hand, are mentioned in the inscriptions first as *manneya* holders by A.D. 1022. The Kalāchuryas claim to the *kṣatriya* status corresponds squarely to their rise in the political status as main rulers. In the context of sub-region C too we come across similar evidence during the latter part of the 11th century A.D. wherein the Vaiḍumba chief Mallamahārāja claims to be a *kṣatriya pavitra*.[267] Earlier to the region of the Vaiḍumba chiefs, sub-region C was under the control of the Chola chiefs. The former's accession to power was thus marked by their claims to *kṣatriya* status by the Vaiḍumba chiefs. It has been aptly stated in this regard that close correspondence between the politico-economic status and social ranking is most pronounced among the claimants of the *kṣatriya varṇa* as even in theory their high status is derived from their possession of temporal power.[268]

We also have significant references to the *vaiśya varṇa* in the context of the inscriptions under study. Initially, the supra-local mercantile body such as the mention of the *mahānagara* in A.D. 1095 is referred as belonging to the *vaiśya kula kamala*.[269] Later on in an inscription dated to A.D. 1179, we have reference to one Aichaseṭṭi who claims to have belonged to the *vaiśya vaṁśa* and *nagara kula*.[270] Permeation of such a concept even to the level of *nagaraṁ* members can be significantly noted in this case as it hints at the spread of the *varṇa* ideology among several social classes. We further, have reference to *vaiśya kula* in the context of description of the mercantile organizations in an inscription dated to A.D. 1215.[271] An interchangeability is exhibited in the usage of the term, *vaiśya varṇa* sometimes as a *kula* (family) and sometimes expanded as corresponding to *vaṁśa* (lineage). This significantly attests to the fact that kinship ties where strongly emphasized along with the *varṇa* category. In fact, it has been postulated by following the Marxist scholars method that in the southern part of India, including the Deccan during the early medieval period, the spread of the *vaiśya varṇa* and the *kṣatriya varṇa* was limited. Instead, they argue that there was a particular trajectory in which there was the proliferation of the *brāhmaṇa* and the *śūdra varnas*. It has further been suggested that the latter *varṇa* now began to be equated with agriculturists, which was earlier considered to be the duty assigned to the *vaiśya varṇa.*[272] In the context of our study the only reference to the term *śūdra* which we come across has been made with regard to artisans who were supposed to have rendered *biṭṭi* (forced labour) as a grant to the God.[273] It is, however, with regard to the position of the *caṇḍāla* who is supposed to belong to the *pañcama varṇa,* that we have an idea of the lowest category in the social scale during the early medieval period.[274] In fact, the context of their mention in the sources of study clearly brings out, at least in theoretical terms the contempt attitude with which this group was looked upon. In an inscription dated to A.D. 1037, we have reference to the *caṇḍāla* whose birth is equated to that of a dog and an ass in the imprecatory verse.[275] In an inscription dated to A.D. 1071, we have repeated mention of the *caṇḍāla* in which the violators of the grant and the Chola conquerors are referred as such.[276] We again have reference to the *caṇḍāla* in an inscription dated to A.D. 1077 where they are compared to dogs and asses in the context of the mention of the punishments to be meted out in case of the violation of the grant.[277] Such references, it has been stated meant that "the *varṇa* ideology helped in securing the structured dependence of the land less labour in the form of untouchables or the so-called menial castes."[278]

Despite the references made to various *varṇa* categories in the context of our study it needs to be underscored that only taking into account the *varṇa* schema embedded in the *Dharmaśāstra* texts as a criteria for defining social stratification would preclude us from looking at the problem of regional specificity and fall into the trap of universalization of specific structural formation. This would then mean that a great majority of the social groups discussed by us earlier, both socio-political and socio-economic remained outside the *varṇa* categorization. This does not in any way mean that there was no principle of hierarchy present during this period defined on theoretical lines of stratification. We have a crucial reference in an inscription dated to A.D. 1012, which clearly attest to the presence of a clear conception of hierarchical social structure even out side the *varṇa* structure. Accordingly, it is stated that the fines for various crimes, were stipulated to be charged by taking into consideration the distinction of the *jāti* of the offender (*jāti bhedavaridu daṇḍavaṁ viśeshaṁ mālpa).* We further have the mention of the *gāvuṇḍas* as belonging to a higher *jāti (yikkuvarga gāvuṇḍārgaṁ)* and the chief men of the low *jāti (kīljātiya mukhyārgaṁ)* in this inscription.[279] It is significant to note that the above references have been made in the context of the conversion of a village into an *agrahāra* and the allotment of shares in the village to various groups. The donee had to obviously take into account the already existing hierarchical divisions in the village prior to its grant. References of this type enable us to realize upon the need to comprehend the social strata of any given region against the specific background of its social, economic and political setting rather than attribute universal categories such as *caṇḍāla* and *śūdra* which basically represent a normative view of the social structure propounded in relation to the specific nature of social relations of the North Indian context. Importantly, references made to various social strata in relation to the family *(kula)* to which they belonged coupled with the occupational status represented by them provide significant clues to comprehend the social variable of hierarchical relations at a specific level. We have already noted in this context the significant role played by the family names in representing the hierarchical relations present among them. Among these we have the prominent mention of the Sinda *kula,* Haihaya and kadamba lineages. The dominant land owing strata were referred to through such titles as *gāvuṇḍa, heggaḍe* and this clearly indicates that elite peasant groups were identificable most often by this nomenclature. The specified nature of hierarchical relations present among them would be precluded from analysis if we study these groups as only constituting a homogeneous *śūdra varṇa.* Similar is the case with the *okkala, mel-sāsivvaru, ugura* and so on, who emerge as groups representing various types of agrarian interests and who were involved actively in agricultural production and constituted a considerable part of rural social structure. We have various groups of artisans and mercantile guilds whose dominant interest in their occupation had enable them to carve out their own social symbols of identification with an accent on regional identification. In this context the mention of the term *kaṁchagārada kula* (represents the interests of braziers) for the longevity of which a grant was made by the artisans of this group.[280] The *nakaraṁ* of the merchants seems to have represented local mercantile interests similar to that of the *komaṭis* of Andhra[281] that can be separated from the *vīra baṇañjus* that characterized the supra local groups. The hereditary nature of these occupations is another significant pointer to the strong familial affiliations established by the above groups in relation to various professional activities based on hierarchical relations of production which were, however, rooted in the socio-economic ethos of their regional setting rather than on the nebulous structure of belief in the *varṇa* hierarchy only. We have evidence of claims made by various social groups as representing a specific *varṇa* category as has been seen above. But these were only attempts at the legitimization of the superior positions held by various groups which do not in any way signify the actual socio-economic status at a specific level. This is markedly brought to the forefront in the inscriptions as they refer to social groups, not so much by their *varṇa* affiliation, but more so, by their designations and occupational and professional status. This is basically the reason why one has essentially attempted the above analysis of various social groups as they are defined it their specific spatial context against the prevalent economic changes of this period. We next turn to elaborate upon the economic context that will enable us to sharply focus on rural society and its gradual transformation, in the following chapter.

REFERENCES

1. Bernard Barber, 'Introduction : Social Stratification' in David Sills (ed.), *International Encyclopedia of Social Sciences,* XV, pp. 288-289.
2. Andre Beteille, *Inequality and Social Change* (A. Ramaswamy Mudaliar Lectures), OUP, Delhi, 1988, p. 4.
3. Borrowed from *ibid.*, p. 5. These are widely used in sociological studies to understand the levels of stratification among various societies.
4. This could be best exemplified particularly for the Context of South India and the Deccan in the works of K.A.N. Sastri, *A History of South India* (from pre-Historic Times to the Fall of the Vijayanagara), OUP, 4th ed., Madras, 1966, A.S. Altekar, *The Rashtrakutas and their Times,* Oriental Book Agency, Poona, 1934, A.V. Krishna Murthy, *Social and Economic Conditions of Eastern Deccan* (A.D. 1000-1250), Secunderabad, 1970 and so on. Works of this kind have discussions on the rulers and their administrative set up functioning in a centralized/decentralized set up which is then followed by a brief discussion on the social conditions of the period, described invariably in terms of the caste system.
5. Works of such eminent scholars as R.S. Sharma, 'Social Change in Early Medieval India (A.D. 500-A.D. 1200), the *First Devraj Chanana Memorial Lectures,* Delhi, 1969, B.N.S. Yadava, *Society and Culture in Northern India in the 12th century A.D.*, Central Book Depot, Allahabad, 1973, Kesavan Veluthat, *Political Structure in Early Medieval South India,* Orient Longman, 1993, are only a few of the many works of this nature. These scholars have discussed the social relations of the early medieval complex in India as emerging out of the crucial role played by the economic set up of the period. According to them the land grant economy of the early medieval Indian complen engendered basically two types of social classes, that of the exploitative land lords and that of the exploited peasant groups.
6. Works of B.D. Chattopadhyaya in particular his 'Political Processes and Structure of Polity in Early Medieval India : Problems of Perspective'. *PIHC,* 44th session, Burdwan, 1983, pp. 25-63. Hermam Kulke, *Kshatriyaization and Social Change* (A Study Orissa Setting), Hiedelberg, 1977, have made a conceptual break through in this line of historical scholarship.
7. See Chapter I of the thesis on 'Historiographical Context', pp. 32-47.
8. See Chapter II of the thesis on Geo-political Context, pp. 107-108. It has aptly been stated in this regard that the "nuclearity of a region is related to how historical factors converge on it and not merely to its resource potential." See B.D. Chattopadhyaya, *op. cit.,* 1983, p. 41. That sub region B exhibits such crucial traits of historical phenomena is well attested through the profuse mention of various types of social, economic, political and ideological activity in the inscriptional sources of our study.
9. The term *ūroḍeya* has however been studied by us as a part of the *mahājana.* Social group which seems more appropriate as this term is invariably mentioned as representing the leader of the *mahājanas.* See pp. 195-197.
10. D.C. Sircar, *Indian Epigraphical Glossary,* Delhi, 1966, p. 354.
11. G.S. Dikshit, *Local Self Government in Medieval Karnataka,* Dharwar, 1964, p. 61.

12. D.C. Sircar, *op. cit.*, 1966, p. 109.
13. G.S. Dikshit, *op. cit.*, 1964, pp. 61-62.
14. D.C. Sircar, *op. cit.*, 1966, p. 145.
15. G.S. Dikshit, *op. cit.*, 1964, p. 18.
16. K.R. Basavaraja, *Administration under the Chalukyas of Kalyani,* Madras, 1983, p. 161.
17. R.S. Sharma, *op. cit.*, 1980, p. 78.
18. D.C. Sircar, *op. cit.*, 1966, p. 327.
19. G.S. Dikshit, *op. cit.*, 1964, p. 65.
20. D.C. Sircar, *op. cit.*, 1966, p. 198.
21. S. Gururajachar, *op. cit.*, 1974, p. 145.
22. G.S. Dikshit, *op. cit.*, 1966, pp. 61-62.
23. *Ibid.*, p. 116.
24. D.C. Sircar, *op. cit.*, 1966, p. 198.
25. *Ibid.*, p. 277.
26. A.S. Altekar, *op. cit.*, 1934, p. 177.
27. *Ibid.*, p. 205.
28. *Ibid.*, p. 197.
29. G.S. Dikshit, *op. cit.*, 1964, p. 65.
30. D.C. Sircar, *op. cit.*, 1966, p. 7.
31. P.B. Desai, *'Literature and Language'*. *HAS,* vol. 18, p. 34.
32. This understanding emerged out of a discussion with Dr. P.V.P. Sastry, former Dy. Director of Epigraphy, Department of Archaeology and Museums, Hyderabad.
33. D.C. Sircar, *op. cit.*, 1966, p. 337.
34. *Ibid.*, p. 283.
35. *Ibid.*, p. 183.
36. *Ibid.*, p. 181.
37. G.S. Dikshit, *op. cit.*, 1964, p. 61.
38. *Ibid.*, p. 63.
39. *Ibid.*, p. 59.
40. Dinkar Desai, *The Mahāmaṇḍaleśvaras under the Chālukyas of Kalyaṇi,* Bombay, 1951, pp. 346-348.
41. R.S. Sharma, *op. cit.*, 1980, pp. 69-71.
42. 'A Stone Inscription of the Sinda Family', *EI,* III. pp. 230-236.
43. 'Inscription on. XXXIII', *IA,* VI, pp. 139-142.
44. Inscription no. 58, *SII,* XV, pp. 78-82.
45. Inscription no. 50, *SII,* XI, pp. 36-38.

46. Inscription no. 65, *SII, XI,* pp. 55-57.
47. *Transcript,* A.R. no. B 342 of 1957-58.
48. Inscriptions of Sudi, G. *EI,* XV, pp. 94-96.
49. Inscriptions of Sudi, H. *EI,* XV, pp. 96-100.
50. Transcript. *A.R.* no. B. 530 of 1961-62.
51. *Transcript, A.R.* no. B. 534 of 1961-62.
52. 'Inscriptions From Yewur' B, *EI,* XII, pp. 269-291.
53. Inscriptions of Sudi, H, *EI,* XV, p. 97.
54. Inscription no. 163, *SII,* XI, pp. 209-211
55. Inscription no. 119, *SII,* XI, pp. 133-136.
56. Inscription no. 36, *SII,* XV, pp. 43-46.
57. Inscriptions of Sudi, H, *EI, XV,* p. 97.
58. Inscriptions no. 75, *SII,* XI, pp. 65-66.
59. 'Kilaratti Inscription', *EI,* XXXV, pp. 37-39.
60. Inscription no. 4, *HAS,* 18, pp. 43-44.
61. Inscription no. 57, *SII,* XI, pp. 47-48.
62. Inscriptions of Sudi, E, *EI,* XV, pp. 80-83.
63. Inscription no. 114, *SII,* XV, p. 145.
64. Inscription no. 68, *SII,* XI, pp. 58-59.
65. Inscription no. 113, *SII,* XI, pp. 111-112.
66. Gadag Inscription, *EI,* XIX, pp. 217-222.
67. Transcript. *A.R.* no. B 530 of 1961-62.
68. Inscription no. 119, *SII,* XI, pp. 133-136.
69. Inscriptions of Sudi, C, *EI,* XV, pp. 75-77.
70. Inscriptions of Sudi, H, *EI,* XV, pp. 96-100.
71. Transcript, *A.R.* no. B. 342 of 1957-58.
72. Inscription no. 65, *SII,* XI, pp. 55-57.
73. Inscriptions of Sudi, H, *EI,* XV, p. 97.
74. Inscription no. 75, *SII,* XI, pp. 65-66.
75. Inscription no. 25, *SII,* XV, p. 28.
76. Inscription no. 50, *SII,* XI, pp. 36-38.
77. Inscription no. 85, *SII,* XI, pp. 79-82.
78. Inscription no. 113, *SII,* XI, pp. 111-112.
79. G.S. Dikshit, *op. cit.,* 1964, p. 64.
80. Inscription no. 149, *SII,* XI, pp. 183-184.
81. Inscription no. 152, *SII,* XI, pp. 189-191.
82. Inscription no. 52, *SII,* XV, pp. 68-69.

83. Transcript, *A.R.* no. B. 534 of 1961-62.
84. Inscription no. 36, *SII,* XV, pp. 43-46.
85. B.R. Gopal, *Minor Dynasties of South-India : Karnataka,* I, Madras, 1982, p. 70.
86. D.C. Sircar, *op. cit.,* 1966, pp. 197-198.
87. *Ibid.,* p. 187.
88. *Ibid.,* pp. 187-188.
89. *Ibid.,* pp. 179-180.
90. R.S. Sharma, *op. cit.,* 1980, p. 78.
91. D.C. Sircar, *Landlordism and Tenancy in Ancient and Medieval India as Revealed by Epigraphical Records,* Lucknow, 1969.
92. Transcript, *A.R.* no. B. 256 of 1953-54.
93. Inscription no. 119, *SII,* XI, pp. 133-136.
94. B.R. Gopal, *op. cit.,* 1982, p. 85. Infact the author has identified for us four branches of the Sinda family belonging to different parts of Karnataka namely; the Sindas of Belaguṭṭi, of Bāgadage, of Kurgoḍu pratyanḍaka and of Renjeru having different foci of political control.
95. *Ibid.,* pp. 106-107.
96. 'A Stone Inscription of the Sinda family at Bhairanmatti', *EI,* III, pp. 230-236.
97. Dinkar Desai, *op. cit.,* 1951, p. 69.
98. 'Bichapalli Inscription', *EI,* XXXVI, pp. 69-74.
99. V. Yasodadevi, 'The History of the Andhra Country : Subsidiary Dynasties', *JAHRS,* XXIII, 1954-56, p. 48.
100. V. Yasodadevi, *op. cit.,* 1954-56, pp. 24-25.
101. B.R. Gopal, *op. cit.,* 1982, p. 5.
102. Dinkar Desai, *op. cit.,* 1951, p. iii.
103. J.F. Fleet, *Dynasties of Canarese Districts of the Bombay Presidency,* Bombay, 1896, p. 470.
104. B. Srikantaiya, 'The Hoysala Empire', *QJMS,* VII, 4, 1916-17, p. 292.
105. Sant Lal Katare, 'Early History of the Yadavas of Devagiri', *JIH,* XXX, pt. II, 1952, p. 119.
106. *Ibid.,* p. 124.
107. Sant Lal Katare, 'The Beginnings of the Chalukyas of Kalyani', *IHQ,* XIII, Calcutta, 1937, p. 253.
108. We find that these high sounding titles were claimed by almost all the main ruling family chiefs right from the Western Chālukyas of Kalyāni to the Yādavas of Devagiri and the Hoysalas of Dwarasamudra who, only towards the end of the 12th century A.D. emerge as sovereign rulers.
109. Lionel D. Barnett, *EI,* XII, p. 57.
110. R.S. Sharma, *op. cit.,* 1980, p. 77.

111. Tejaswini Yarlagadda, 'Social Groups and Economic Change (7th-13th century A.D.)', in Aloka Parasher Sen (ed.), *Social and Economic History of Early Deccan* (Some Interpretations), Manohar, New Delhi, 1993, p. 164.
112. Transcript, *A.R.* no. B342 of 1957-58.
113. Inscriptions of Sudi, F, *EI,* XV, pp. 85-94.
114. *'pañchalingala Inscription', EI,* XXXVI, p. 141.
115. *Ibid.,* p. 141.
116. 'Bichapalli Inscription', *EI,* XXXVI, pp. 69-74.
117. J.F. Fleet, *op. cit.,* 1896, p. 576.
118. Works of such scholars as B.R. Gopal, *op. cit.,* 1982, pp. 83-132, Dinkar Desai, *op. cit.,* 1951, pp. 67-111 are replete with descriptions of the above nature.
119. D.C. Sircar, *op. cit.,* 1966, p. 183.
120. Altekar, *op. cit.,* 1934, p. 165.
121. D.C. Sircar, *op. cit.,* 1966, p. 214.
122. *Ibid.,* p. 196.
123. Cynthia Talbot, 'Political Intermediaries in Kakatiya Andhra, 1175-1325', *IESHR,* XXXI, 3, July-September, 1994, p. 267.
124. *Ibid.,* p. 268.
125. D.C. Sircar, *op. cit.,* 1966, p. 295.
126. *Ibid.,* p. 80.
127. *Ibid.,* p. 187.
128. *Ibid.,* p. 309.
129. *Cynthia Talbot, op. cit.,* 1994, p. 267. The author here furnishes a long list of reasons for such a characterization of the official terms. According to her, first and foremost among these was the relative insignificance of the family background of the officers who only identified one or two preceding generations unlike the chiefs and princes who traced their descent back for numerous generations to the lineage founder. Further the absence in the hereditary nature of the official terms has been taken as the second most important cause. It is pertinent to note here the fact that the genealogies can as well as fabricated and need not point to the actual elevated status of the holder of political ranks at any level of the hierarchy has been overlooked by Cynthia Talbot who has taken into consideration the political variable as the primary determinant in defining the status of various social groups functioning in the hierarchical political structure of the early medieval set up.
130. Dinkar Desai, *op. cit.,* 1951, pp. 319-333. According to the author the designations discussed in the text by us represented basically the ranks of ministers whose duty was to limit the power of the main ruling chiefs.
131. As early as A.D. 1010 we have reference to Akkadevi's rule over the tract of Kisukad in 'Inscriptions of Sudi, C. *EI,* XV, pp. 75-77. From now on she figures in a series of records and figures for the last time in 'Inscriptions of Sudi', E(1), *EI,* XV, pp. 80-83 as ruling over the tracts of Kisuakad-70, Torugare-60 and Masiyavadi-140.

132. 'Alur Inscription', *EI,* XVI, pp. 27-31.
133. S.L. Shantakumari, 'New Light on the Early Career of Bijjala II' *JESI,* XVI, Mysore, 1990, p. 90.
134. Two inscriptions from Ron, B, *EI,* XIX, pp. 226-236.
135. Inscription no. 6, *HAS,* 18, pp. 46-49.
136. Inscription no. 127, *SII,* XV, pp. 146-149.
137. According to T.V. Mahalingam, the Nolamba pallavas, despite their claims to the lineage of pallavas of Kanchi their area of rule did not lie in the pallava dominion of the Tamil Country. On the other hand their actual area of control known as 'the Nolambapadi comprised portions of Anantpur district in Andhra Pradesh and Tumkur district in southern Karnataka, see his 'The Nolamba Pallavas : The Origin', *JIH,* XXXVI, I, Trivandrum, April 1958, p. 131.
138. R. Thapar, *From Lineage to State,* OUP, Bombay, 1984, p. 8.
139. *Ibid.,* p. 8.
140. B.D. Chattopadhyaya, 'Origin of the Rajputs : The Political, Economic and Social Processes in Early Medieval Rajasthan', *IHR,* 3, 1, 1986, pp. 73-75.
141. In the absence of any explicit references to the formation of a network of clan like those of Rajputs, we find it difficult to come to any such conclusion in the context of our study. Our intention in this discussion has been to basically highlight the marriage alliances as an important aspect of the social variable which operates as one of the means of integration of polity. In her recent article on Kākatiya polity Cynthia Talbot too has looked at the marriage alliances between the princely and chiefly lineages as central to the functioning of Kakatiya polity. But the author's over-emphasis on the political dimension of these relationships tends to sideline the social implications of such alliances. See Cynthia Talbot, *op. cit.,* 1994, p. 271.
142. 'Munirabad Stone Inscription', *HAS,* 5, p. 6.
143. Sister M. Liceria, 'Emergence of Brahmanas as Landed Intermediaries Karnataka, A.D. 1000-1300', *IHR,* 1. 1974, pp. 28-30.
144. We have detailed these dimensions of their functioning in separate chapters of our thesis, see chapter IV on Economic Context, pp. 333 and chapter VI on Ideological Context, pp. 637-639.
145. G.R. Kuppuswamy, 'Role of Mahājanas in the History of Medieval Karnataka', *JKU* (Social Sciences), VI, 1970, pp. 61-62.
146. *Ibid.,* p. 62.
147. 'Kotavumachgi Inscription', *EI,* XX, pp. 67-68.
148. Inscription no. 92, *SII,* XI, pp. 87-89.
149. Inscription no. 127, *SII,* XI, pp. 146-149.
150. Transcript, A.R. no. B529 of 1960-61.
151. Inscription no. 189, *SII, XI,* p. 246.
152. Inscription no. 131, SII, XV, pp. 167-168.

153. G.S. Dikshit, 'Constitution of the Trade Guilds in Medieval Karnataka', *JKU* (Humanities), 3, no. 2, June 1959, p. 56.

154. See K.R. Venkata Rama Ayyar, 'Medieval Trade, Craft and Merchant Guilds in South India', *JIH,* XXV, no. 3, Trivandrum, 1947, p. 269. Here the author has highlighted the Context of Tamil Nadu wherein he states that in a record from South Arcot district, the participation of *brahmins* in the trading activity is clearly attested to.

155. It becomes difficult for us to classify these under any particular social strata as has been done for other social groups. The fact that these groups were exclusive to the religious function they performed emerges distinctly. The Ideological dimension represented by these social groups has been detailed by us in chapter VI of our thesis on 'Ideological Context', see pp. 610-620.

156. Inscription no. 26, *A.P.G.A.S.,* 3, p. 120.

157. Inscription no. 183, *SII,* XI, pp. 242-243.

158. Inscription no. 6, *HAS,* 18, pp. 46-49.

159. Inscription no. 38, *APGAS,* 3, pp. 126-127.

160. Inscription no. 13, *HAS,* 18, pp. 63-74.

161. See Chapter VI, of the thesis on 'Ideological Context', pp. 618-621.

162. Various memory stones available for the period of our study, bear ample testimony to the fact that indulging in warfare was a normal feature even for the rural social groups. We have in this context reference to the death of one *talara-nāyaka* in A.D. 1018 who was supposed to have died in a battle of Channakalla Sime (Transcript, AR. no. B368 of 1963-64). In another instance of a similar nature in A.D. 1019, we have the commemoration of the death of a *senabova* along with his charioteers. (Inscription no. 57, *SII,* XI, pp. 47-48). Several references of this nature have been made in the context of our study of which the cattle raids form a significant feature.

163. We have detailed these aspects in chapter IV of the thesis on 'Economic Context', see pp. 313-315.

164. Irfan Habib, 'The Peasant in Indian History', General President's Address, *PIHC,* 43rd session, Kurukshetra, 1982, p. 3.

165. G.S. Dikshit, 'Okkalu—A Corporate Body of Medieval Karnataka', *JKU,* (Humanities), IV, June, 1960, p. 58.

166. *Ibid.,* p. 59.

167. Inscription no. 158, *SII,* XI, pp. 201-203.

168. Inscription no. 167, *SII,* XI, p. 214.

169. Inscription no. 5, *APGAS,* 9, pp. 29-30. In fact, the association of the term *galleya*-300 with the agriculturists has been largely based on the interpretation of the Kannada term *gale* which meant a plough. Further, the grant of this group to the deity Toṭigeśvara signifies its association with the class of gardeners.

170. M.D. Sampath, 'The Chitrameli', *Studies in History and Culture* (P.B. Desai Felicitation volume), Karnataka University, Dharwar, 1976, p. 315.

171. Transcript, *A.R.* no. B665 of 1958-59.

172. B.N.S. Yadava, 'Historical Investigation into Social Terminology in Literature' A Problem of the Study of social Change (Mainly in the Context of Early Medieval North India), Presidential Address, *PIHC,* 53rd session, 1993, Warangal, pp. 4-6.
173. *Ibid.,* p. 15.
174. *Ibid.,* p. 14.
175. *Ibid.,* p. 23.
176. Inscription no. 5, *APGAS,* 9, pp. 29-30.
177. In fact the tax terms and forms of land tenurial patterns which attest to the prevalance of a subject peasantry have been analysed by us in chapter IV of the thesis on Economic Context, see, pp. 337-342.
178. Inscription no. 10, *KI,* II, pp. 29-34.
179. 'Munirabad stone inscription', *HAS,* 5, p. 8.
180. *Ibid.,* p. 8.
181. Inscription no. 42, *SII,* XV, pp. 54-56.
182. R.S. Sharma, 'How Feudal was Indian Feudalism?', in D.N. Jha (ed.) *Feudal Social Formations in Early India,* Delhi, 1987, p. 168.
183. G.K. Rai, 'Forced Labour in Ancient and Early Medieval India', *IHR,* 3, 1976-77, pp. 16-42.
184. S.G. Ghatapanadi, 'Forced Labour in Ancient and Medieval Karnataka', *JKU,* (Social Sciences), 12, 1976, pp. 147-149.
185. Inscription no. 8, *HAS,* 18, pp. 51-52.
186. Inscription no. 159, *SII,* XV, pp. 203-205.
187. It is pertinent to note here that we have several references to the prevalence of *visṭi* in the agricultural production particularly during the Rāshṭrakuta period (*i.e.,* in the 9th-10th centuries A.D.) *see* Tejaswini Yarlagadda, *op. cit.,* 1993, p. 170.
188. We have been able to build up this definition on the basis of the etymological meaning attributed to the word 'subject' in A.S. Hornby, *Oxford Advanced Learners Dictionary of Current English,* Delhi, 1987, pp. 860-861. The word 'subject' which basically indicated lack of 'independence' can be contrasted with the term 'subordinate' which indicates the status of a person holding a junior rank or a position. *Ibid.,* p. 862.
189. Inscription no. 68, *SII,* XI, pp. 58-59.
190. Inscription no. 187, *SII,* XI, p. 245.
191. G.R. Kuppuswamy, *op. cit.,* 1975, pp. 103-105.
192. Inscription no. 62, *SII,* XV, pp. 87-88.
193. This has been deduced on the basis of a discussion with Dr. S. Nagaraju, professor, Department of History, University of Hyderabad, Hyderabad.
194. *Encyclopaedia Britannica,* Micropaedia, V. University of Chicago, 15th edition, 1974, p. 503.
195. *Ibid.,* p. 503.

196. Quoted in Bernard Kolver, 'On the Origins of the Jajmani System', *JESHO*, XXXI, 3, 1988 p. 265.
197. Peter Mayor, 'Inventing Village Tradition the late 19th Century Origins of the North Indian Jajmani System", *MAS*, 27, 2, 1993, p. 360.
198. *Ibid.*, p. 362.
199. Other aspects of the concept, which are considered crucial to the *jajmāni*, relations such as the caste factors, and a closed economic set up *et. al.*, do not get revealed in the data used for the present study.
200. Inscription no. 127, *SII*, XI, pp. 146-149.
201. Inscription no. 66, *A.P.G.A.S.* 3, pp. 73-77.
202. Inscription no. 50; *SII*, XI, pp. 36-38.
203. A. Appadorai, *Economic Conditions in South India* (A.D. 1000-A.D. 1500), Madras, 1936, p. 275.
204. 'Tumbagi Inscription' *EI*, XVII, pp. 7-10.
205. 'Arasibidi Inscription' *EI*, XVII, pp. 121-123.
206. Inscription no. 103, *SII*, XI, p. 101.
207. Kotavumachgi, Inscription, *EI*, XX, pp. 64-70.
208. Transcript, *AR*, no. B72 of 1960-61.
209. C.J. Fuller, *Servants of the Goddess : The Priests of a South Indian Temple*, London, 1984, p. 23.
210. *Ibid.*, p. 47.
211. Inscription no. 9; *KI*, II, pp. 25-28.
212. 'Munirabad Stone Inscription', *HAS*, 5, p. 8.
213. Inscription no. CXVI, *IA*, X, pp. 185-190.
214. Inscriptions of Sudi, E, *EI*, XV, pp. 80-83.
215. Inscriptions of Sudi, F, *EI*, XV, pp. 85-94.
216. Inscription no. 103, *SII*, XI, p. 101.
217. Aloka Parasher Sen, 'The Temple Girls and the Land Grant—Economy 8th-13th century A.D.', in Aloka Parasher Sen (ed.) *op. cit.*, 1993, pp. 254-255.
218. Inscriptions at Ittagi, A, *EI*, XII, pp. 37-38.
219. Inscription no. 13, *HAS*, 18, pp. 63-74.
220. Inscription no. 38, *SII*, XV, p. 48.
221. Aloka Parasher Sen, *op. cit.*, 1993, p. 251.
222. K. Ismail, *Karnataka Temples : Their Role in Socio-Economic Life*, Delhi, 1984, p. 112.
223. *Ibid.*, p. 112.
224. We have detailed these aspects in chapter VI of the thesis on 'Ideological Context', see pp. 587-604.

225. D.C. Sircar, *op. cit.,* 1966, p. 309.
226. K.R. Venkatnaramayana Ayyar, *op. cit.,* 1947, p. 269.
227. R. Champakalakshmi, "Urbanization in South India : The Role of Ideology and Polity", Presidential Address, Sec. I, Ancient India, *PIHC,* 47th session, Srinagar, 1986, p. 20.
228. *Ibid.,* p. 23.
229. *Ibid.,* p. 25.
230. T. Venkateshwara Rao, *Local Bodies in Pre-Vijayanagara Andhra,* Ph.D. Thesis, Karnataka University, Dharwar, 1975, p. 277.
231. As is indicated by its relation to the settlement the *talasamasta* might have represented a mercantile assembly extremely local in character. They were supposed to have met in an assembly at the time when the grant was made. Inscription no. 1, *HSA*, 18, pp. 39-40.
232. Inscription no. 5, *HAS,* 18, pp. 44-46.
233. Inscription no. 112, *SII,* XI, p. 110.
234. Inscriptions at Yewur, B, *EI,* XII, pp. 269-271.
235. Inscriptions no. 10, *KI,* II, pp. 29-34.
236. Inscriptions of Sudi, C, *EI,* XV, pp. 75-77.
237. 'Gadag Inscription' *EI,* XIX, pp. 217-222.
238. Inscription no. 65, *SII,* XI, pp. 55-57.
239. 'Two Inscription From Gawariwad, *EI,* XV, pp. 337-347.
240. Inscription no. 10, *KI,* II, pp. 29-34.
241. Inscription no. 158, *SII,* XI, pp. 201-203.
242. T. Venkateshwara Rao, *op. cit.,* 1975, p. 268.
243. S. Gururajachar 'the Vira-Baṇanjus of Karnataka' (1000-1300 A.D.) *Studies in History and Culture (*P.B. Desai Felicitation volume), Karnataka University, Dharwar, 1974, p. 307.
244. Inscription no. 12, *HAS,* 18, pp. 61-63.
245. R. Champakalakshmi, *op. cit.,* 1986, p. 22.
246. Inscription no. CXVI, IA, X, pp. 185-190.
247. T. Venkateswara Rao, *op. cit.,* 1975, p. 271.
248. Inscription no. 48, *SII,* XI, pp. 182-183.
249. See pp. 190-191.
250. Inscription no. 39, *SII,* XV, pp. 48-51.
251. Inscription no. 121, *SII,* XV, pp. 151-152.
252. Inscription no. 137, *SII,* XI pp. 151-152.
253. Inscription no. 50, *SII,* XI, pp. 36-38.
254. Inscription no. 9, *APGAS,* 3, p. 104.
255. 'Alur Inscription', *EI,* XVI, p. 27-31.

256. Inscription no. 58, *SII*, XV, pp. 78-82.
257. Suvira Jaiswal, *'Studies in Early Indian Social History : Trends and Possibilities'*, *IHR*, VI, July 1979-80, p. 24.
258. James Hastings (ed.), *Encyclopaedia of Religion and Ethics*, VI, New York, 1974, pp. 352-353. The seven *ṛṣis* enumerated as ancestors are Gautama, Bharadvāja, Viśvāmitra, Jamadagni, Vasiṣṭha, Kaśyapa and Atri with a later addition of Agastya. These rank as *gotrakarins*—the founders of the numerous brahmanical families and their descendents are the various *gotras* which are, however, not static in nature.
259. 'Alur inscription' *EI*, XVI, pp. 27-31.
260. Inscription no. 84, *SII*, XI, pp. 77-79.
261. Inscription no. 67, *SII*, XV, pp. 92-94.
262. This understanding emerged after discussion with Dr. S. Nagaraju, Professor, Department of History, University of Hyderabad.
263. Inscription no. 127, *SII*, XI, pp. 146-149.
264. Inscription no. 36, *SII*, XI, pp. 43-46.
265. Inscription no. 14, *HAS*, 18, pp. 74-79.
266. Inscription no. 15, *HAS*, 18, pp. 80-82.
267. Inscription no. 16, *APGAS*, 3, pp. 110-111.
268. Suvira Jaiswal, *op. cit.*, 1979-80, p. 33.
269. Inscription no. CXVI, *IA*, X, pp. 185-190.
270. Inscription no. 135, *SII*, XV, pp. 174-178.
271. Inscription no. 17, *HAS*, 18, pp. 89-93.
272. Summarised from Suvira Jaiswal, 'Changes in the Concept of the Sudra Varna in Early Middle Ages', *PIHC*, 41st session, Bombay, 1980, pp. 113-114.
273. Inscription no. 159, *SII*, XV, p. 205.
274. Vivekananda Jha, 'Stages in the History of Untouchables', *IHR*, II, no. 1, 1975, p. 28.
275. 'Gadag inscription', *EI*, IX, pp. 217-222.
276. 'Two inscriptions from Gawariwad', A, *EI*, XV, pp. 337-347.
277. Inscriptions at Yewur, B, *EI*, XII, pp. 269-291.
278. Suvira Jaiswal, 'Varna Ideology and Social Change', *Social Scientist*, 19, 3-4, March-April, 1991, p. 45.
279. Kotavumachgi Inscription, *EI*, XX, pp. 64-70.
280. Inscription no. 153, *SII*, XI, p. 192.
281. 'The Vaiśya Community of Medieval Andhra,' *JAHRS*, XXX, Rajahmundry, 1964-65, p. 11.

Chart – I : SOCIAL CONTEXT

Sub-Region A

i	ii	iii	iv	v	vi	vii	viii	ix	x	xi	xii	xiii
S.No.	*Name/Date Dynasty*	*Location*	*Main Ruler*	*Local Potentate*	*Functionaries*	*brāhmaṇa/ mahājana*	*Merchant/ Artisan*	*Cultural Groups*	*Peasants*	*Donor*	*Donee*	*Reference*
1.	Tumbagi Ins. Chalukyas of Kalyani AD 1004.	Muddebihal Tq. Bijapur Dt.	> Invabedaṇga Satyāśraya		@ Seṭṭi Brahmayya	* (led by the *ūroḍeya)*		&i *parekara* (drummers) &ii sūḷe (dancing girls)		@	Δ &i, &ii	*EI*, XVII, 7-10
2.	Ins. no. 524 Chalukyas of Kalyani AD 1014.	Muddebihal Tq. Bijapur Dt.			@ Nāgadevayya/ *ūroḍeya*	* 100				@	O	*SII*, XV, 355
3.	Belur Ins. Chalukyas of Kalyani AD 1022.	Badami Tq. Bijapur Dt.	> Jayasiṁha II sister of > Akkadevi			* 400				Sister of >	*	*IA*, XVIII, 270-275
4.	Ins. no. 61 Chalukyas of Kalyani AD 1024.	Hungund Tq. Bijapur Dt.	> Jayasiṁha II	# Ghate Yaṅkakāra (Nolanba Chief)						#	Δ	*SII*, XI, 50-51
5.	Ins. no. 66 Chalukyas of Kalyani AD 1032.	Muddebihal Tq. Bijapur Dt.	> Jayasiṁha II	# Nāgavarmaarsa (Yadāva Chief)	@ Vāvanayya Nāyaka (ūroḍeya)					#, @	Δ O	*SII*, XI, 57
6.	Ins. no. 68 Chalukyas of Kalayani AD 1053.	Muddebihal Tq. Bijapur Dt.	> Jayasiṁha II	# Gomarasa	@ Duggimayya (pasāyita and heggaḍe)		A Malloja (builder)			@	Δ &	*SII*, XI, 58-59
7.	Arasibidi Ins. Chalukyas of Kalyani AD 1047.	Hungund Tq. Bijapur Dt.	> Someśvara I aunt of > Akkadevi				A *kalkutiga* (stone mason)	& *parekara* (drummer)		Sister of >	Δ & A	*EI*, XVII, 121-123
8.	Kelawadi Ins. Chalukyas of Kalyani AD 1053.	Badami Tq. Bijapur Dt.	> Someśvara I	#Bhogadevarasa *(mahāsāmantādhipati)*	@ Supparasa *(mahāmatya)*					@	T	*EI*, IV, 259-262
9.	Ins. no. 88 Chalukyas of Kalyani AD 1053.	Hungund Tq. Bijapur Dt.	> Someśvara I aunt of Akkadevi			* 42				@	* 42	*SII*, XI, 84-85

Key to the Symbols : $: *brāhmaṇa*; > : Main Ruler; * : *mahājana*; < : Peasant; @ : Functionary; A : Artisan; ~ : merchant; O : maṭha; # : local potentate; Δ : Temple; & : Cultural groups; T : Tank.

Chart – I : SOCIAL CONTEXT

Sub-Region A

i	ii	iii	iv	v	vi	vii	viii	ix	x	xi	xii	xiii
S.No.	Name/Date Dynasty	Location	Main Ruler	Local Potentate	Function-aries	*brāhmaṇa/ mahājana*	Merchant/ Artisan	Cultural Groups	Peasants	Donor	Donee	Reference
10.	Ins. no. 96 Chalukyas of Kalyani AD 1061.	Hungund Tq. Bijapur Dt.	> Someśvara I		@ Chattimayya *(mahāpradhāna daṇḍanāyaka)*	* 42				@	* 42	*SII*, XI, 91
11.	Ins. no. 107 Chalukyas of Kalyani AD 1068.	Muddebihal Tq. Bijapur Dt.	> Someśvara II		@ Ballarasa *(mahasāhaṇi)*					@	Δ	*SII*, IV, 104-105
12.	Ins. no. 110 Chalukyas of Kalyani AD 1070.	Badami Tq. Bijapur Dt.	> Someśvara II	# Singanadeva (Pailava Chief)						#	Δ	*SII*, XI, 107
13.	Ins. no. 113 Chalukyas of Kalyani AD 1074.	Hungund Tq. Bijapur Dt.	> Someśvara II	# Lakshmarasa *(mahāmaṇḍaeś-vara).*	@ i.Devanayya Nayaka *(śrikarana)* @ii.Nākimayya *(pergaḍe)* @iii.Revanayya *(pergaḍe)* @iv.Aychap-ayya *(karaṇa)* @v.Kātimayya *(pasāyita)*					@ i, ii, iii, iv, v	Δ	*SII*, XI, 111-112
14.	Ins. no. 116 Chalukyas of Kalyani AD 1075.	Bagalkot Tq. Bijapur Dt.	> Someśvara II		@ Nimbanayya *(mānever-ggade daṇḍa-nāyaka)*		~ *angaḍi-dappa* (Shopkeepers) A Birojam & Surojam *(kalkutiga)* (Stone cutters)			> ~	Δ A Δ	*SII*, XI, 114-116
15.	Ins. no. 179 Chalukyas of Kalyani AD 1085.	Hungund Tq. Bijapur Dt.	> Vikramāditya VI	#Bammadēva rasa (Sinda Chief)	@ Mantara Barmanna *(suṅkavergaḍe)*					@	Δ	*SII*, XI, 239

Key to the Symbols : $: *brāhmaṇa*; * : *mahājana*; @ : Functionary; ~ : merchant; # : local potentate; & : Cultural groups; > : Main Ruler; < : Peasant; A : Artisan; O : maṭha; Δ : Temple; T : Tank.

Chart – I : SOCIAL CONTEXT

Sub-Region A

i	ii	iii	iv	v	vi	vii	viii	ix	x	xi	xii	xiii
S.No.	*Name/Date Dynasty*	*Location*	*Main Ruler*	*Local Potentate*	*Function-aries*	*brāhmaṇa/ mahājana*	*Merchant/ Artisan*	*Cultural Groups*	*Peasants*	*Donor*	*Donee*	*Reference*
16.	Ins. no. 132 Chalukyas of Kalyani AD 1086.	Muddebihal Tq. Bijapur Dt.	> Vikramāditya VI	#Nimbana *(mahāsāmanta dhioati)*						#	Δ	*SII*, XI, 153-154
17.	Ins. no. 135 Chalukyas of Kalyani AD 1087.	Hungund Tq. Bijapur Dt.	>Vikramāditya VI	#Avararasa *(mahāsāmanta dhioati)*		* 42				#	* 42	*SII*, XI, 160-161
18.	Ins. no. 5 Chalukyas of Kalyani AD 1106.	Hungund Tq. Bijapur Dt.	>Vikramāditya VI		@i.Anantapala *(daṇḍanāvaka)* @ii.Mādhava-bhaṭṭa *(mahā-pradhāna daṇḍanāyaka achchupannā-yada dhishtā-yaka*					@ii	Δ	*SII*, XV, 5
19.	Ins. no. 169 Chalukyas of Kalyani AD 1119.	Hungund Tq. Bijapur Dt.	>Vikramāditya VI				-Keśavayya Seṭṭi (of Ayy-avole-500)				Δ	*SI*, XI, 216-217
20.	Ins. no. XXXII Chalukyas of Kalyani AD 1139.	Badami Tq. Bijapur Dt.	> Jagadekamalla II	#Kalidasa *(mahāsāman-tādhi pati)*	@i.Mahādeva *(daṇḍanāyaka)* @ii.Pāladeva *(daṇḍanāyaka)* @iii. Rāma-devarasa *(pergaḍa)*					@i, @ii @iii	Δ	*A*, VI, 139-142
21.	Ins. no. 30 Chalukyas of Kalyani AD 1145.	Muddebihal Tq. Bijapur Dt.	> Jagadekamalla II	#Hemmadideva *mahāmaṇḍa-leśvara)* *(Yādava Chief)*	@i.Handeya Nāyaka *(hinya-heggaḍe)* @ii.Revarasa *(prabhu)*					@ii,~	Δ	*SII*, XV, 32-33

Key to the Symbols : $: *brāhmaṇa*; > : Main Ruler; * : *mahājana*; < : Peasant; @ : Functionary; A : Artisan; ~ : merchant; O : maṭha; # : local potentate; Δ : Temple; & : Cultural groups; T : Tank.

Chart – *I* : SOCIAL CONTEXT

Sub-Region A

i	*ii*	*iii*	*iv*	*v*	*vi*	*vii*	*viii*	*ix*	*x*	*xi*	*xii*	*xiii*
S.No.	*Name/Date Dynasty*	*Location*	*Main Ruler*	*Local Potentate*	*Function-aries*	*brāhmaṇa/ mahājana*	*Merchant/ Artisan*	*Cultural Groups*	*Peasants*	*Donor*	*Donee*	*Reference*
					@iii.8 *hiṭṭus*							
22.	Ins. no. 39 Chalukyas of Kalyani AD 1148.	Bagalkot Tq. Bijapur Dt.	> Jagadekamalla II		@i.Lakmādevi *(mahāprabhu yini)* @ii.12 *gāvuṇ-ḍas* @iii.Adiyanna *(kulakaraṇi)*					@i	Δ	*SII*, XV, 48-51
23.	Ins. no. 236 Chalukyas of Kalyani AD 1155.	Badami Tq. Bijapur Dt.		# Chāvuṇḍa (Sinda Chief)	@i.Somanātha Nāyaka *(pergaḍe)* @ii.Rayarasa *(karaṇam* @iii.8 *hiṭṭus*				< 6 O *okkalu*	@i, @ii	Δ Δ	*SII*, XV, 291-293
24.	Ins. no. 88 Chalukyas of Kalyani AD 1160.	Hungund Tq. Bijapur Dt.				*	~ Adiseṭṭi		< 50 *okkalu*	~, <	Δ	*SII*, XV, 114-115
25.	Ins. no. 126 Chalukyas of Kalyani AD 1174.	Muddebihal Tq. Bijapur Dt.	>Rayamuran Sovideva		@i.Bammade-vara *(mahapr-dhānam daṇḍ-anāyaka* @ii.Mahadeva Nāyaka *(Prabhu)*					@i	O	*SII*, XV, 159-160
26.	Ins. no. 58 Chalukyas of Kalyani AD 1184.	Middenojai Tq. Bijapur Dt.	>Someśvara IV		@i.Naranāra-simhadeva *(mahāpradhāna senādhipati)* @ii.Viththarasa *(daṇḍanāyaka* @iii.Machara-sayya *(prabhu)*		~i.Bammisetti *(nāda seṭṭi gutta)* ~ii.*mummūri-daṇḍa* A *mālagara*			@iv, v, vi, x ~i, ii	Δ Δ	*SII*, XV, 78-82

Key to the Symbols : $: *brāhmaṇa*; > : Main Ruler; * : *mahājana*; < : Peasant; @ : Functionary; A : Artisan; ~ : merchant; O : maṭha; # : local potentate; Δ : Temple; & : Cultural groups; T : Tank.

Chart – I : SOCIAL CONTEXT

Sub-Region A

i	ii	iii	iv	v	vi	vii	viii	ix	x	xi	xii	xiii
S.No.	Name/Date Dynasty	Location	Main Ruler	Local Potentate	Function-aries	brāhmaṇa/ mahājana	Merchant/ Artisan	Cultural Groups	Peasants	Donor	Donee	Reference
					@iv.Viruparasa *(manneya)* @v.Nannarasa *(deśiya daṇḍa-nāyaka* hiriya heggade) @vi.*pramukha-karana* @vii.Chikkaya nāyaka *(tantra-pāla)* @viii.Sankama-yya *(heggaḍe)* @ix.Somayya *(prabhu)* @ × 8 *hiṭṭus*							
27.	Ins. no. 56 Chalukyas of Kalyani AD 1184.	Muddebihal Tq. Bijapur Dt.	>Somesvara IV	#Virupeśvarad-eva *(mahā-maṇḍaleśvara)*						#	Δ	*SII*, XV, 73-74
28.	Ins. no. 242 Chalukyas of Kalyani AD 1186.	Hungund Tq. Bijapur Dt.		# Vira Bijjana and Vira Vikramāditya (Sinda Chiefs)	@i.Ayuktade-varasa *(nāḍasu-ṁkavergaḍe)* @ii.*pannāya dadhishṭāya*	*	~*samasta nakara*			# @i, @ii	Δ Δ	*SII*, XV, 301-302
29.	Ins. no. 147 Yadavas of Devagiri AD 1189.	Muddebihal Tq. Bijapur Dt.	>Bhillama	# Viruparasad-eva *(mahā-maṇḍaleśvara*	@i.Lakshmi-deva Nāyaka *(mahāpradhā-naṁ)* @ii.Nannarasa *(mahāpradhā-nam, deśiva daṇḍanāyaka hinya heggaḍe)*		~i.Machi Seṭṭi *(seṭṭigutta)* ~ii.Buri Seṭṭi iii.the 500 ~iv.Devarakati Seṭṭi			@i, @ii ~i, ~ii ~iii	Δ Δ	*SII*, XV, 189

Key to the Symbols : $: *brāhmaṇa*; > : Main Ruler; * : *mahājana*; < : Peasant; @ : Functionary; A : Artisan; ~ : merchant; O : maṭha; # : local potentate; Δ : Temple; & : Cultural groups; T : Tank.

Chart – I : SOCIAL CONTEXT

Sub-Region B

i	ii	iii	iv	v	vi	vii	viii	ix	x	xi	xii	xiii
S.No.	Name/Date Dynasty	Location	Main Ruler	Local Potentate	Function-aries	*brāhmaṇa/ mahājana*	Merchant/ Artisan	Cultural Groups	Peasants	Donor	Donee	Reference
30.	Ins. no. 156 Yadavas of Devagir AD 1207.	Hungund Tq. Bijapur Dt.	> Singhana		@ *prabhus*		A *telliga* (50 okkalu) ~i.*seṭṭi gutta* ~ii.the 1000 ~iii.500 *svāmis* of Ayyavole ~iv.*Mummu-ridaṇḍas* ~v.*nakaras*			@, ~A ~i, ~ii	Δ Δ	*SII*, XV, 20-21
31.	Ins. no. 11 Chalukyas of Kalyani AD 973.	Kopbal Tq. Raichur Dt.	> Taila II			$Revaya Dvedi Chaṭṭo-pādhyāya * 20				> $	$ *20	*IIAS*, 18, 57-60
32.	Nilgund Ins. Chalukyas of Kalyani AD 982.	Gadag Tq. Dharwar Dt.	> Taila II	# Sobhanarasa		$i. Vishṇu Bhaṭṭa $ii. 12				#	$i, $ii	*EI*, IV, 204-208
33.	Ins. no. 47 Chalukyas of Kalyani AD 994.	Gadag Tq. Dharwar Dt.	> Taila II	# Sobhanarasa (*mahāsāmanta-dhipati*	@i.Korala guṇḍa (*manneyanāl-gāyuṇḍa*) @ii.*gāvuṇḍas* @iii.Aycha-Gāvuṇḍa (head of above *gāvuṇḍas*)					@i, @ii @iii	Δ	*SII*, XI, 32-34
34.	Ins. no. 48 Chalukyas of Kalyani AD 1002.	Gadag Tq. Dharwar Dt.	> Irivabedanga Satyāśraya	# Sobhanarasa (*mahāsāmanta*)		$Kalajnani Vakkhanijiya.				#	$	*SII*, XI, 34-36
35.	Ins. no. 50 Chalukyas of Kalyani AD 1005.	Gadag Tq. Dharwar Dt.	> Irivabedanga Satyāśraya	# Sobhanarasa (*mahāsāmanta*)	@i.Benayya (*suṁka* (*vergaḍe*)				< 60 *okkalu*	#	0	*SII*, XI, 36-38

Key to the Symbols : $: *brāhmaṇa*; * : *mahājana*; @ : Functionary; ~ : merchant; # : local potentate; & : Cultural groups;
> : Main Ruler; < : Peasant; A : Artisan; O : *maṭha*; Δ : Temple; T : Tank.

Chart – I : SOCIAL CONTEXT

Sub-Region B

i	ii	iii	iv	v	vi	vii	viii	ix	x	xi	xii	xiii
S.No.	*Name/Date Dynasty*	*Location*	*Main Ruler*	*Local Potentate*	*Function-aries*	*brāhmaṇa/ mahājana*	*Merchant/ Artisan*	*Cultural Groups*	*Peasants*	*Donor*	*Donee*	*Reference*
36.	Ins. no. 1 Chalukyas of Kalyani AD 1005.	Yelburgi Tq. Raichur Dt.	> Irivabedanga Satyāśraya		@ii.Eight *gāvuṇḍas*		~i.Isvara Seṭṭi ~ii.*nakara samūha* ~iii.*tala samasta*			~i, ~iii	Δ Δ	*HAS*, 18, 39-40
37.	Alur Ins. Chalukyas of Kalyani AD 1010.	Gadag Tq. Dharwar Dt.	> Vikramāditya V	#Iriva Nolambādhi-raja. (Pallava Chief)	@i.Venneya Bhatta *(daṇḍa-nāyaka)* @ii.Chattiva-rayya *(ūroḍe-yam)*	* 200 $ Amarā-chārya Bhaṭṭāraka				*, @ii @i	@i $	*EI*, XVI, 27-31
38.	Kotavumachgi Ins. Chalukyas of Kalyani AD 1012.	Gadag Tq. Dharwar Dt.	> Vikramāditya V	#Kesavayya *(mahāsāmanta-dhipati*	@ *ūroḍeva*	$Sridhara-Bhaṭṭa * 104	A. *nāvida* (barber)	&.*parekara* (drummer)		# $	$ * @, &, A	*EI*, XX, 64-70
39	Ins. from Navali Chalukyas of Kalyani AD 1014.	Lingsugur Tq. Raichur Dt.	> Vikramāditya V	#Jayasimha II (Chālukya Chief)		$ Jogaśivā chārya				#	$	*EI*, XXXIV, 164-166
40	Transcript Chalukyas of Kalyani AD 1016.	Lingsugur Tq. Raichur Dt.	> Vikramāditya V	#Joyapayya *(mahāmandaleś-yara)*	@Chattapayya Nayaka *(mān-evergaḍe)*					> #	@ Δ	*A.R.* no. B 693 of 58-59
41	Two Ins. from Ron A. Chalukyas of Kalyani AD 1022.	Ron Tq. Dharwar Dt.	> Jayasimha II			* 104 $i. Machi-mayya $ii. A few				$i	$ii Δ	*EI*, XIX, 222-226

Key to the Symbols : $: *brāhmaṇa*; * : *mahājana*; @ : Functionary; ~ : merchant; # : local potentate; & : Cultural groups;
> : Main Ruler; < : Peasant; A : Artisan; O : maṭha; Δ : Temple; T : Tank.

Chart – *I* : SOCIAL CONTEXT

Sub-Region B

i	ii	iii	iv	v	vi	vii	viii	ix	x	xi	xii	xiii
S.No.	*Name/Date Dynasty*	*Location*	*Main Ruler*	*Local Potentate*	*Function-aries*	*brāhmaṇa/ mahājana*	*Merchant/ Artisan*	*Cultural Groups*	*Peasants*	*Donor*	*Donee*	*Reference*
42.	Ins. no. 58 Chalukyas of Kalyani AD 1022.	Mundargi Tq. Dharwar Dt.	> Jayasimha II	# Dasarasa *(mahāsāmanta)*	@ Nāgama Gāvuṇḍa		~ Dharma Seṭṭi			>, @	Δ	*SII*, XI, 48
43.	Transcript Chalukyas of Kalyani AD 1022.	Manvi Tq. Raichur Dt.	>i.Jayasimha II >ii.Mahādevi (above's queen)		@ Lokaditya *(manneya)*					>ii	Δ	*A.R.* no. B 534 of 1961-62
44.	Bannigol Ins. Chalukyas of Kalyani AD 1025.	Lingsugur Tq. Raichur Dt.	> Jayasimha II	# Vijayāditya (Eastern Chālukyan Chief)	@i.Maramayya ii.Sovayya iii.Namayya iv.Kalimayya *(ūroḍeyas)*					A Royal decree is used by # to @i, ii,iii,iv to collect revenue at specific rates		*EI*, XXXVI 118-120
45.	Ins. no. 3 Chalukyas of Kalyani AD 1027.	Lingsugur Tq. Raichur Dt.	> Jayasimha II		@i.Revanayya *(sodorevaḍi yara)* @ii.*samasta pradhānam*					daughter of the >	Δ	*IIAS*, 18, 42-43
46.	Ins. no. 65 Chalukyas of Kalyani AD 1028.	Gadag Tq. Dharwar Dt.	> Jayasimha II	#i.Vavanarasa *(mahāsāmanta)* #ii.Srpadarasa *(mahāsāmanta)*	@i.Sindarasa @ii.Aycha Gāvuṇḍa					@ii		*SII*, XI, 55-57
47.	Ins. no. 7 Chalukyas of Kalyani AD 1030.	Gadag Tq. Dharwar Dt.	> Jayasimha II	#i.Kundamarasa *(mahāmaṇḍaleśyara* #ii.Gollimayya		$				#ii	$	*KI*, III, 18-19
48.	Transcript Chalukyas of Kalyani AD 1031.	Manvi Tq. Raichur Dt.	> Jayasimha II			$ Madhusūdana Bhaṭṭa				Queen of >	$	*A.R.* no. B 545 of 1961-62

Key to the Symbols : $: *brāhmaṇa*; * : *mahājana*; @ : Functionary; ~ : merchant; # : local potentate; & : Cultural groups;
> : Main Ruler; < : Peasant; A : Artisan; O : maṭha; Δ : Temple; T : Tank.

Chart – I : SOCIAL CONTEXT

Sub-Region B

i	ii	iii	iv	v	vi	vii	viii	ix	x	xi	xii	xiii
S.No.	Name/Date Dynasty	Location	Main Ruler	Local Potentate	Functionaries	brāhmaṇa/ mahājana	Merchant/ Artisan	Cultural Groups	Peasants	Donor	Donee	Reference
49.	Ins. no. 4 Chalukyas of Kalyani AD 1032.	Lingsugur Tq. Raichur Dt.	> Jayasimha II		@i.*samasta pradhāna* @ii.Kālidasayya *(sodore yaḍiyara)* @iii.Revana *(chuḷāyata)*					>	Δ	*IIAS*. 18, 43-44
50.	Transcript Chalukyas of Kalyani AD 1033.	Lingsugur Tq. Raichur Dt.	> Jayasimha II		@i.Chavundamayya *(mānevergade)* @ii.Kalimayya *(daṇḍanāyaka)* @iii.Bacharasa *(manneya)* @iv.Kandapayya *(joyisa)*					@i, ii, iii, iv.	*	*A.R.* no. B 376 of 57-58
51.	Gadag Ins. Chalukyas of Kalyani AD 1037.	Gadag Tq. Dharwar Dt.	> Jayasimha II		@i.Madimayya Nayaka *(ūrodeya* @ii.Dhoyipayya *(pegaḍe)*	* 1000	~Dāmodarasetti				Δ	*EI*. XIX, 217-222
52.	Kalaratti Ins. Chalukyas of Kalyani AD 1046.	Lingsugur Tq. Raichur Dt.	> Someśvara I	# Kumāra Jayasimha (Chālukya Chief)	@i.Bammanayya *(senabova)* @ii.5 *ūroḍeyas*					#	Δ	*EI*. XXXV, 37-39
53.	Ins. of Sudi D Chalukyas of Kalyani AD 1050.	Ron Tq. Dharwar Dt.	>i.Someśvara I Aunt of > ii. Akkadevi		@i.Kalidasayya *(mānevergaḍe)* @ii.Milayya *(tantrapāla)* @iii.Chittimayya *(tantra-*		~ 8 *seṭṭis* of Suṇḍi		< 60 *okkalu*	@i.~ix along with Akkadevi of the main		*EI*. XV, 77-80

Key to the Symbols : $: *brāhmaṇa*; > : Main Ruler; * : *mahājana*; < : Peasant; @ : Functionary; A : Artisan; ~ : merchant; O : maṭha; # : local potentate; Δ : Temple; & : Cultural groups; T : Tank.

Chart – I : SOCIAL CONTEXT

Sub-Region B

i	ii	iii	iv	v	vi	vii	viii	ix	x	xi	xii	xiii
S.No.	Name/Date Dynasty	Location	Main Ruler	Local Potentate	Function-aries	brāhmaṇa/ mahājana	Merchant/ Artisan	Cultural Groups	Peasants	Donor	Donee	Reference
					pāla @iv.Demanna *(pradhāna)* @v.Chandi-mayya (aliyam) @vi.Chavunda-rayam *(aḍapa)* @vii.Dasimayya *(senabova)* @viii.Naga-devayya *(nāḍa pergade)* @ix.*pramukha karaṇaṁ*					ruling family granted a renewal of cor-porate regula-tions to ~, <.		
54.	Ins. no. 5 Chalukyas of Kalyani AD 1052.	Manvi Tq. Raichur Dt.	> Someśvara I	#Revarasa *(mahāmaṇḍa-leśvara)* (Haihaya Chief)	@ Chāvuṇḍa-ya Nāyaka *(tantrapāla)*		~ nagaran			@, ~	T	*IIAS*, 18 44-46
55.	Mulgund Ins. Chalukyas of Kalyani AD 1053.	Gadag Tq. Dharwar Dt.	> Someśvara I	#Somesvara II *(mahāmaṇḍa-leśvara)* (Chalukya Chief)	@i.Baldeva *(sandhivi-garahi)* @ii.Kancharasa *(nripa)*		~ *nagara mahājana*			@ii		*EI*, XVI, 53-57
56.	Ins. of Sudi, E(1) Chalukyas of Kalyani AD 1054.	Ron Tq. Dharwar Dt.	> Someśvara I		@i.*samasta pradhāna* @ii.Nagavar-mayya *(nāḍa-pergaḍe)* @iii.Revada-			&i.*vaṁsigam* &ii.*rayālayala* &iii.*chāmara-da sūḷe* &iv.*kambha-da sūḷe* &v.*pātraṁ*		@i-v, along with Akkadevi of the main ruling family issued a regulation for		*EI*, XV, 80-83

Key to the Symbols : $: *brāhmaṇa*; * : *mahājana*; @ : Functionary; ~ : merchant; # : local potentate; & : Cultural groups;
> : Main Ruler; < : Peasant; A : Artisan; O : maṭha; Δ : Temple; T : Tank.

Chart – I : SOCIAL CONTEXT

Sub-Region B

i	ii	iii	iv	v	vi	vii	viii	ix	x	xi	xii	xiii
S.No.	*Name/Date Dynasty*	*Location*	*Main Ruler*	*Local Potentate*	*Function-aries*	*brāhmaṇa/ mahājana*	*Merchant/ Artisan*	*Cultural Groups*	*Peasants*	*Donor*	*Donee*	*Reference*
					sayya *(senaboye)* @iv.Madha-vayya *(dharmā-dhyaksha)* @v.*pramukha karaṇaṁ*			*sūḷe*		disposing lands	the	
57.	Ins. no. 92 Chalukyas of Kalyani AD 1054.	Mundargi-petha Tq. Dharwar Dt.	> Someśvara I	#Mādhavarasa *(mahāsāmanta)* (Yadava Chief)	@ Dāsimayya *(manneya)*	* 50		.		@	Δ	*SII*, XI, 87-89
58.	Transcript Chalukyas of Kalyani AD 1055.	Lingasugur Tq. Raichur Dt.	> Someśvara I Queen of > Ketaladevi		@i.4 *gāvuṇḍas* @ii.Nāgavarma rasa *(Ūroḍeya)*					>	Δ @ii	*A.R.* no. B 342 of 57-58
59.	Ins. of Sudi, F Chalukyas of Kalyani AD 1060	Ron Tq. Dharwar Dt.	> Someśvara I	# Nagadeva *(mahāsāmanta-dhipati)*	@i.6 *gāvuṇḍas* @ii.Revapayya *(kulakarani)* @iii.3 *manne-vars*		~8 *seṭṭis* A Chandojam *(kalkutiga)* (stone cutter)	&i.*parekara* (drummer) &ii.*vamsigam* (flute player) @iii.several types of dancing girls		> # @iii	# Δ &i-iii A	*EI*, XV, 85-94
60.	Ins. no. 97 Chalukyas of Kalyani AD 1062.	Gadag Tq. Dharwar Dt.	> Someśvara I	#i.Permala Madarasa *(mahāmandale-śvara)* #ii.Aycharasa *(mahāsāmanta)* #iii.Bhimarasa *(mahāsāmanta)*	@i.*gāvuṇḍas* @ii.Ballala Soyimayya *(nagara-pergaḍe)*	* 120	~ *seṭṭis* of Mulugunda Ai.*sālega-5* (weavers) Aii.*telliga-50* (oilmen) Aiii.*mālagara-*			@i * 120 ~ Ai-iii	Δ Δ Δ	*SII*, XI, 91-94

Key to the Symbols : $: *brāhmaṇa*; > : Main Ruler; * : *mahājana*; < : Peasant; @ : Functionary; A : Artisan; ~ : merchant; O : maṭha; # : local potentate; Δ : Temple; & : Cultural groups; T : Tank.

Chart – I : SOCIAL CONTEXT

Sub-Region B

i	*ii*	*iii*	*iv*	*v*	*vi*	*vii*	*viii*	*ix*	*x*	*xi*	*xii*	*xiii*
S.No.	*Name/Date Dynasty*	*Location*	*Main Ruler*	*Local Potentate*	*Function-aries*	*brāhmaṇa/ mahājana*	*Merchant/ Artisan*	*Cultural Groups*	*Peasants*	*Donor*	*Donee*	*Reference*
				(Sindha Chief)			5 (garland makers)					
61.	Transcript Chalukyas of Kalyani AD 1065.	Lingsugur Tq. Raichur Dt.	> Somesvara I		@i.Kalimayya *(pergaḍe)* @ii.Chamundayya *(karaṇa)* @iii.Dannapayya *(adhyaksha)*	* 300			< 60 *okkalu*	@i-iii	* <	*A.R.* no. B 364 of 57-58
62.	Transcript Chalukyas of Kalyani AD 1066.	Lingsugur Tq. Raichur Dt.	>Somesvara I		@ Nagavarma rasa *(manneva)*					@	Δ	*A.R.* no. B 714 of 58-59
63.	Daddala Ins. Chalukyas of Kalyani AD 1069.	Manvi Tq. Raichur Dt.	> Somesvara II	#Jaṭachola Bhimamahāraja *(mahāmaṇḍaleśvara)* (Eruva Chola Chief) #Maleyammarasa *(mahāsāmanta)* (Haihaya Chief)			~ Maki Seṭṭi			~	Δ	*EI*, XXXVII 113-116
64.	Ins. no. 111 Chalukyas of Kalyani AD 1071.	Gadag Tq. Dharwar Dt.	>Somesvara II	# Baladevayya *(mahāsāmantadhipati)*		* 200				#, *	Δ	*SII*, XI. 107-110
65.	Two Ins. from Gawariwad A Chalukyas of Kalyani AD 1071.	Gadag Tq. Dharwar Dt.	> Somesvara II	#i.Lakshmarasa *(mahāmaṇḍaleśvara)* #ii.Kātarasa *(mahāsāmanta)*	@ Rechideva *(mahāprachaṇḍa) ḍaṇḍanāyaka)*		~ 30 seṭṭis headed by the *heggaḍe* Chāvuṇḍa Gāvuṇḍa			#i #ii @	Δ Δ Δ	*EI*, XV, 337-347

Key to the Symbols : $: *brāhmaṇa*; * : *mahājana*; @ : Functionary; ~ : merchant; # : local potentate; & : Cultural groups; > : Main Ruler; < : Peasant; A : Artisan; O : maṭha; Δ : Temple; T : Tank.

Chart – I : SOCIAL CONTEXT

Sub-Region B

i	ii	iii	iv	v	vi	vii	viii	ix	x	xi	xii	xiii
S.No.	*Name/Date Dynasty*	*Location*	*Main Ruler*	*Local Potentate*	*Functionaries*	*brāhmaṇa/ mahājana*	*Merchant/ Artisan*	*Cultural Groups*	*Peasants*	*Donor*	*Donee*	*Reference*
				(Kaṭṭale Chief)								
66.	Ins. no. 122 Chalukyas of Kalyani AD 1072.	Ron Tq. Dharwar Dt.	> Someśvara II		@ 4 *gāvuṇḍas*		~i.Kudiyama Seṭṭi ~ii.the 1000			@ ~i ~ii	Δ Δ	*SII*, XI, 141
67.	Ins. no. 112 Chalukyas of Kalyani AD 1072	Ron Tq. Dharwar Dt.	> Someśvara II		@ Venkapayya *(sumkavergaḍe)*		~ *nakaram*			@ ~	Δ	*SII*, XI, 110
68.	Ins. no. 2 Chalukyas of Kalyani AD 1074	Ron Tq. Dharwar Dt.	> Someśvara II		@ Jannamayya *(daṇḍanāyaka)*					@	Δ	*SII*, XV, 2-3
69.	Ins. no. 9 Chalukyas of Kalyani AD 1075.	Gadag Tq. Dharwar Dt.	> Someśvara II		@i.Mallideva *(daṇḍanāyaka)* @ii.*ūroḍeya*	* 1000				@i @ii	Δ Δ	*KI*, II, 25-28
70.	Ins. of Sudi, II Chalukyas of Kalyani AD 1075.	Ron Tq. Dharwar Dt.	> Someśvara II		@i.6 *gāvuṇḍas* @ii.Chakayya *(karaṇa)*		~i.8 *seṭṭis* of Suṇḍi ~ii.Maddisetti (maṇigāra) (jeweller)			@ii ~ii	Δ Δ	*EI*, XV, 96-100
71.	Ins. no. 117 Chalukyas of Kalyani AD 1076.	Ron Tq. Dharwar Dt.	> Someśvara II	#Singanna deva *(mahāmaṇḍaleśvara)*		* 400				sister of > # *	Δ Δ * (of other places)	*SII*, XI, 117-118
72.	Ins. at Yewur Chalukyas of Kalyani AD 1077.	Shorapur Tq. Gulbarga Dt.	> Vikramāditya VI		@i.Raviyana bhatt *(mahāpradhana*		~ *nakaramu*			> (earlier grant by	@	*EI*, XII, 269-271

Key to the Symbols : $: *brāhmaṇa*; > : Main Ruler; * : *mahājana*; < : Peasant; @ : Functionary; A : Artisan; ~ : merchant; O : maṭha; # : local potentate; Δ : Temple; & : Cultural groups; T : Tank.

Chart – I : SOCIAL CONTEXT

Sub-Region B

i	ii	iii	iv	v	vi	vii	viii	ix	x	xi	xii	xiii
S.No.	*Name/Date Dynasty*	*Location*	*Main Ruler*	*Local Potentate*	*Function-aries*	*brāhmaṇa/ mahājana*	*Merchant/ Artisan*	*Cultural Groups*	*Peasants*	*Donor*	*Donee*	*Reference*
					senadhipati, sandhivigrahi) @ii.Nāgavarma *(pergaḍa)* @iii.*rāṣṭrapati viśayapati grāmakutaka ayuktaka niyuktaka adhikārika mahattara*					Someś-vara I) @i	Δ	
73.	Ins. no. 6 Chalukyas of Kalyani AD 1077.	Lingsugur Tq. Raichur Dt.	> Vikramāditya VI	#i.Nolamba Pallava Permādi (Pallava Chief) #ii.Nāgavarma-rasa *(mahā-maṇḍaleśyara)* (Kadamba Chief)						#i. #ii	Δ Δ	*HAS*, 18, 46-49
74.	Ins. no. 7 Chalukyas of Kalyani AD 1079.	Lingsugur Tq. Raichur Dt.	> Vikarmāditya VI		@i.Sūkshma-siva Bhalāra *(pergaḍa)* @ii.3 *ūroḍevas*		~i.the *samūha* ~ii.*seṭṭis* of two *puras*			@i-ii, ~i~ii	Δ $	*HAS*, 18, 49-51
75.	Ins. no. 10 Chalukyas of Kalyani AD 1080.	Gadag Tq. Dharwar Dt.	> Vikaramāditya VI		@.*ūroḍeva*	* 1000	~i.*vaniga mahājana* ~ii.Revanayya Seṭṭi ~iii.*nakara*			@, * ~i, ii, iii	Δ Δ	*KI*, II, 29-34
76.	Ins. no. 127	Gadag Tq.	> Vikaramāditya	#i.Jayasimga-	@i.Mabalayya	* 200				#ii	T	*SII*, XI,

Key to the Symbols : $: *brāhmaṇa*; > : Main Ruler; * : *mahājana*; < : Peasant; @ : Functionary; A : Artisan; ~ : merchant; O : maṭha; # : local potentate; Δ : Temple; & : Cultural groups; T : Tank.

Chart – I : SOCIAL CONTEXT

Sub-Region B

i	ii	iii	iv	v	vi	vii	viii	ix	x	xi	xii	xiii
S.No.	Name/Date Dynasty	Location	Main Ruler	Local Potentate	Function-aries	brāhmaṇa/ mahājana	Merchant/ Artisan	Cultural Groups	Peasants	Donor	Donee	Reference
	Chalukyas of Kalyani AD 1082.	Dharwar Dt.	VI	deva (Younger Brother of >) (Pallava Chief) #ii.Vamadevayya (*mahāsāmanta*)	(*kulakaraṇi*)					*, @ii	T	154-157
77.	Transcript Chalukyas of Kalyani AD 1087.	Deodurg Tq. Raichur Dt.	> Vikramāditya VI						<i.*mel-sāsivara* <ii.*māl-agara* 60 *okkalu*	<i <ii	Δ Δ	*A.R.* no. B 665 of 58-59
78.	Ins. no. 133 Chalukyas of Kalyani AD 1087.	Gadag Tq. Dharwar Dt.	> Vikramāditya VI			* 200	Ai.*jaragana-doni* 1000 Aii.*telliga*-50	& Dasa (*nāvida*) (*barber*)		* & Ai-ii	Δ Δ Δ	*SII*, XI, 154-157
79.	Munirabad Stone Ins. Chalukyas of Kalyani AD 1088.	Koppal Tq. Raichur Dt.	> Vikramāditya VI		@ Someśvara bhatta (*ūroḍeya*)	* 50				> * 50	$ Δ	*IIAS*, 5, 1-12
80.	Ins. no. 137 Chalukyas of Kalyani AD 1091.	Gadag Tq. Dharwar Dt.	> Vikramāditya VI			* 200	A.Jakkiyabbe (*telliga*) ~ Chattiyanna (*tambuliga*)			A	Δ	*SII*, XI, 165-166
81.	Transcript Chalukyas of Kalyani AD 1095.	Deodurg Tq. Raichur Dt.	> Vikramāditya VI			$ sarva kratu *Somayaji* * 200				> $	$ *	*A.R.* no. B 661 of 58-59
82.	Ins. no. CXVI Chalukyas of	Gadag Tq. Dharwar Dt.	> Vikramāditya VI				~i the 16 Seṭṭis (*mahā-*			~i~iii	Δ	*IA*, X, 185-190

Key to the Symbols : $: *brāhmaṇa*; > : Main Ruler; * : *mahājana*; < : Peasant; @ : Functionary; A : Artisan; ~ : merchant; O : maṭha; # : local potentate; Δ : Temple; & : Cultural groups; T : Tank.

Chart – I : SOCIAL CONTEXT

Sub-Region B

i	ii	iii	iv	v	vi	vii	viii	ix	x	xi	xii	xiii
S.No.	*Name/Date Dynasty*	*Location*	*Main Ruler*	*Local Potentate*	*Function-aries*	*brāhmaṇa/ mahājana*	*Merchant/ Artisan*	*Cultural Groups*	*Peasants*	*Donor*	*Donee*	*Reference*
	Kalyani AD 1095.						*nagara)* ~ii *nanadesi* ~iii Setti Sangavayya *(mahā vadda-vvavahān)* ~iv Ayyavole pura					
83.	Transcript Chalukyas of Kalyani AD 1096.	Manvi Tq. Raichur Dt.	> Vikramāditya VI	# Chandarasa *(mahāmaṇḍale-śvara)* (Haihaya Chief)		$i.sarvakratu Somayaji $ii.some				> $, # #	$i $ii Δ	*A.R.* no. B 556 of 61-62
84.	Ins. no. 145 Chalukyas of Kalyani AD 1098.	Gadag Tq. Dharwar Dt.	> Vikramāditya VI		@i.*karaṇam-galu* @ii.*hejjumka peggaḍe* @iii.*ūroḍeva*	* 200	~*tambūliga-setti* Ai Khavojana *(akkasāli)* (gold smith) Aii.*telliga* 50		<i.*torhta* galu (garde- <ii. *ugura* 300 <iii.*me-ntevalu*	@i,ii @iii, * <i-iii Ai-ii	Δ Δ Δ Δ	*SII*, XI, 176
85.	Ins. no. 148 Chalukyas of Kalyani AD 1099.	Ron Tq. Dharwar Dt.	> Vikramāditya VI		@ Simga Gāvuṇḍa		~i. 500 *svāmis* ~ii. 18 *pattaṇas* ~iii. 64 *ghati-kasthānas* ~iv. 32 *vel-puras* ~v. 64 *yoga-pithas* ~vi. the 16 of 8 *nāḍus*			~i~xii	@	*SII*, XI, 182-183

Key to the Symbols : $: *brāhmaṇa*; * : *mahājana*; @ : Functionary; ~ : merchant; # : local potentate; & : Cultural groups;
> : Main Ruler; < : Peasant; A : Artisan; O : maṭha; Δ : Temple; T : Tank.

Chart – I : SOCIAL CONTEXT

Sub-Region B

i	ii	iii	iv	v	vi	vii	viii	ix	x	xi	xii	xiii
S.No.	Name/Date Dynasty	Location	Main Ruler	Local Potentate	Function-aries	brāhmaṇa/ mahājana	Merchant/ Artisan	Cultural Groups	Peasants	Donor	Donee	Reference
							~vii. *gavares* ~viii. *gātrigas* ~ix. *biras* ~x. *bīravaṇi-gas* ~xi. *tambuliga* 1000 ~xii. several *Seṭṭis* from various commercial towns					
86.	Ins no. 149 Chalukyas of Kalyani AD 1100.	Ron Tq. Dharwar Dt.	>Vikramāditya VI	# Anantapāla-yya *(mahāsāmanta)*	@ Marasinga Gāvuṇḍa					@	Δ	*SII*, XI, 183-184
87.	Transcript Chalukyas of Kalyani AD 1100.	Sholapur Tq. Gulbarga Dt.	> Vikramāditya VI		@ Srikanṭa svāmi *(daṇḍanāyaka)*		~i. *nakaras* ~ii. 500 *banajigas*			* ~i, ~ii	Δ Δ	*A.R.* no. B 520 of 1960-61
88.	Ins no. 150 Chalukyas of Kalyani AD 1102.	Gadag Tq. Dharwar Dt.	> Vikramāditya VI	# Bhivanayya *(mahāsāmanta)*	@ Madhava-bhatta *(mahāpradhāna daṇḍanāyaka)*					@	Δ	*SII*, XI, 185-187
89.	Ins no. 152 Chalukyas of Kalyani AD 1103.	Gadag Tq. Dharwar Dt.	> Vikramāditya VI		@i.Naki Gāvu-ṇḍa *(mahāpra-bhu)* @ii.Sarvadeva-yya Nāyaka & Devapayya Nāyaka (incharge of *hejjuṁka*)				< *ugura* 300	@i @ii < A	Δ Δ Δ	*SII*, XI, PP 189-191

Key to the Symbols : $: *brāhmaṇa*; * : *mahājana*; @ : Functionary; ~ : merchant; # : local potentate; & : Cultural groups;
> : Main Ruler; < : Peasant; A : Artisan; O : maṭha; Δ : Temple; T : Tank.

Chart – I : SOCIAL CONTEXT

Sub-Region B

i	ii	iii	iv	v	vi	vii	viii	ix	x	xi	xii	xiii
S.No.	*Name/Date Dynasty*	*Location*	*Main Ruler*	*Local Potentate*	*Function-aries*	*brāhmaṇa/ mahājana*	*Merchant/ Artisan*	*Cultural Groups*	*Peasants*	*Donor*	*Donee*	*Reference*
90.	Ins. no. 153 Chalukyas of Kalyani AD 1103.	Ron Tq. Dharwar Dt.	> Vikramāditya VI				A Uttavoja *(akkasāle)* (gold smith)			A	Δ	*SII*, XI, 192
91.	Ins. no. 155 Chalukyas of Kalyani AD 1104.	Ron Tq. Dharwar Dt.	> Vikramāditya VI	#Bammarasa *(mahāmaṇḍa-leśvara)*						#	Δ	*SII*, XI, 194-197
92.	Ins. from Yewur Chalukyas of Kalyani AD 1105.	Shorapur Tq. Gulbarga Dt.	> Vikramāditya VI	@ Raviyāna-bhaṭṭa *(daṇḍanāyaka)*			~i. *nakaramu* ~ii. *nānādeśi* ~iii.*gātrigaru*			~i~iii	Δ	*EI*, XII, 324-331
93.	Ins. no. 158 Chalukyas of Kalyani AD 1109.	Gadag Tq. Dharwar Dt.	> Vikramāditya VI		@i.8 *gāvuṇḍas* @ii.Sāmipayya *(mahāpradhā-nam daṇḍanā-yaka)* @iii.Nāgavarma Nāyaka *(Mahā-pradhānam Karaṇa)* @iv.*hejjuṁkada pergaḍe karaṇa-ṁgaḷu*		~i.*nakara samūha* ~ii. 500 *nakara* ~iii.*tambūliga seṭṭi gaḷu* ~iv. Chāvunda Setti *(mahā-vaḍḍavyava-nān)* ~v. *angaḍi okkalu* Ai. *doni* 1000 Aii. *sāṅga okkalu*		< 60 *okkalu*	~@i-iv ~i-vi Ai-ii <	Δ Δ Δ Δ	*SII*, XI, 201-203
94.	Ins. no. 8 Chalukyas of Kalyani AD 1109.	Devadurg Tq. Raichur Dt.	> Vikramāditya VI				~i. *nakaraṁ gaḷu* ~ii. *mahāna-*			~i~iii Ai-iii	Δ	*IIAS*, 18, 51-52

Key to the Symbols : $: *brāhmaṇa*; * : *mahājana*; @ : Functionary; ~ : merchant; # : local potentate; & : Cultural groups; > : Main Ruler; < : Peasant; A : Artisan; O : *maṭha*; Δ : Temple; T : Tank.

Chart – I : SOCIAL CONTEXT

Sub-Region B

i	ii	iii	iv	v	vi	vii	viii	ix	x	xi	xii	xiii
S.No.	*Name/Date Dynasty*	*Location*	*Main Ruler*	*Local Potentate*	*Function-aries*	*brāhmaṇa/ mahājana*	*Merchant/ Artisan*	*Cultural Groups*	*Peasants*	*Donor*	*Donee*	*Reference*
							karaṁgalu ~iii. 1000 Ai. *kammati da adhikāṅ* Aii. *kammati-karu* Aiii. *savaka-ttukaru*					
95.	Ins. from Yewur D Chalukyas of Kalyani AD 1110.	Shorapur Tq. Gulbarga Dt.	> Vikramāditya VI				Ai. *kalkutiga gottali* Aii. *kamcha-gara gottali* Aiii. *badagi kammarar* Aiv. *akkasa-leyar* Av. *berattum-bar*			Ai-v	Δ	*EI* XII, 332-333
96.	Ins. Attagi A Chalukyas of Kalyani AD 1112.	Yalburg Tq. Raichur Dt.	> Vikramāditya VI	# Mahādeva-yya *(mahāsāmanta)*	@ *ūroḍeva*	* 40C		& *pātrapāvuta* (dancing girls)		#	Δ &	*EI*, XIII, 37-38
97.	Ins. no. 163 Chalukyas of Kalyani AD 1113.	Ron Tq Dharwar Dt.	> Vikramāditya VI	# Ācharasa *(mahāmaṇḍa-leśvara)* (Sinda Chief)	@i.*pergaḍe* @ii.8 *gāvuṇḍas*	$ 3			< 60 *okkalu*	#	T $3	*SII*, XI, 209-211
98.	Ins. of Sudi K Chalukyas of Kalyani AD 1114.	Ron Tq. Dharwar Dt.	> Vikramāditya VI	# Dādiga *(mahāmaṇḍa-leśvara)* (Bappura Chief)						#	O	*EI*, XV, 105-108

Key to the Symbols : $: *brāhmaṇa*; > : Main Ruler; * : *mahājana*; < : Peasant; @ : Functionary; A : Artisan; ~ : merchant; O : *maṭha*; # : local potentate; Δ : Temple; & : Cultural groups; T : Tank.

Chart – I : SOCIAL CONTEXT

Sub-Region B

i	ii	iii	iv	v	vi	vii	viii	ix	x	xi	xii	xiii
S.No.	Name/Date Dynasty	Location	Main Ruler	Local Potentate	Function-aries	*brāhmaṇa/ mahājana*	Merchant/ Artisan	Cultural Groups	Peasants	Donor	Donee	Reference
99.	Ins. no. 167 Chalukyas of Kalyani AD 1118.	Gadag Tq. Dharwar Dt.	> Vikramāditya VI		@i.Sayipayya *(mahāpradhā-naṁ senādhi-pati mānever-gaḍe daṇḍanā-yaka)* @ii.Nāgavarma Nāyaka *(mahāpradhā-naṁ daṇḍanā-vakaṁ)*				< 60 *okkalu*	@iii, <	Δ	*SII*, XI, 214
100.	Ins. no. 193 Chalukyas of Kalyani AD 1118.	Gadag Tq. Dharwar Dt.					A Ketoja and Gangayya *(kammari)*			A	Δ	*SII*, XI, 250
101.	Ins. no. 170 Chalukyas of Kalyani AD 1121.	Ron Tq. Dharwar Dt.	> Vikramāditya VI	#Ācharasa *(mahāmandale-śvara)* (Kusuva family)						#	Δ	*SII*, XI, 217-218
102.	Transcript Chalukyas of Kalyani AD 1121.	Lingsugur Tq. Raichur Dt.	> Vikramāditya VI				A Muddisetti *(pramukha of pattasā liga kula)*			A	Δ	*A.R.* no. B 512 of 1959-60
103.	Transcript Chalukyas of Kalyani AD 1122.	Manvi Tq. Raichur Dt.			@ Nimbanayya *(daṇḍanāyaka)*					@	Δ	*A.R.* no. B 572 of 1961-62
104.	Ins. no. 9 Chalukyas of Kalyani AD 1124.	Lingsugur Tq. Raichur Dt.	> Vikramāditya VI	#Madhavattiar-asa *(mahāma-ṇḍeleśvara* (Kadamba Chief)	@ 6 *oḍeyas*					# @	Δ	*HAS*, 18, 52-54

Key to the Symbols : $: *brāhmaṇa*; * : *mahājana*; @ : Functionary; ~ : merchant; # : local potentate; & : Cultural groups; > : Main Ruler; < : Peasant; A : Artisan; O : *maṭha*; Δ : Temple; T : Tank.

Chart – I : SOCIAL CONTEXT

Sub-Region B

i	ii	iii	iv	v	vi	vii	viii	ix	x	xi	xii	xiii
S.No.	Name/Date Dynasty	Location	Main Ruler	Local Potentate	Functionaries	brāhmaṇa/ mahājana	Merchant/ Artisan	Cultural Groups	Peasants	Donor	Donee	Reference
105.	Ins. no. 198 Chalukyas of Kalyani AD 1124.	Gadag Tq. Dharwar Dt.							< 50 *okkalu*	<	Δ	*SII*, XI, 253-254
106.	Ins. no. 200 Chalukyas of Kalayani AD 1126.	Gadag Tq. Dharwar Dt.			@i.Sellapayya *(dandanayaka)* @ii.Kesiraja *(sandhivigrahin)*	*	A *doni* 1000			@ii	Δ	*SII*, XI, 255-256
107.	Ins. no. 13 Chalukyas of Kalyani AD 1130.	Ron Tq. Dharwar Dt.				* i 84 *ii 42				*i, *ii	Δ	*SII*, XV, 11-12
108.	Transcript Chalukyas of Kalyani AD 1134.	Manvi Tq. Raichur Dt.	> Someśvara III	#Buchidevarasa *(mahāmaṇḍaleśvara) (Haihaya* family)						#	Δ	*A.R.* no. B 565 of 61-62
109.	Ins. no. 11 Chalukyas of Kalyani AD 1136.	Koppal Tq. Raichur Dt.	> Someśvara III			* 20				*	Δ	*HAS*, 18 57-60
110.	Ins. no. 50 Chalukyas of Kalyani AD 1138.	Gadag Tq. Dharwar Dt.	> Someśvara III		@i.Mahadevayya *(mahāpradhāna senādhipati, karaṇaṁ heggaḍe dandanāyakam)* @ii.Padmarasa *(heggade, pradhāna kannaḍa sandhivigrahi)* @iii.6 *gāyuṇḍas*				< 60 *okkalu*	@i	Δ	*SII*, XI, 36-38

Key to the Symbols : $: *brāhmaṇa*; * : *mahājana*; @ : Functionary; ~ : merchant; # : local potentate; & : Cultural groups;
> : Main Ruler; < : Peasant; A : Artisan; O : *maṭha*; Δ : Temple; T : Tank.

Chart – I : SOCIAL CONTEXT

Sub-Region B

i	ii	iii	iv	v	vi	vii	viii	ix	x	xi	xii	xiii
S.No.	Name/Date Dynasty	Location	Main Ruler	Local Potentate	Function-aries	brāhmaṇa/ mahājana	Merchant/ Artisan	Cultural Groups	Peasants	Donor	Donee	Reference
111.	Ins. no. 5 Chalukyas of Kalyani AD 1143.	Yalburgi Tq. Raichur Dt.	< Jagadekamalla II			* 1000			< gale-ya 300 (guild of agri-cultur-ists)	<	Δ	*APGAS*, no. 9 29-30
112.	Ins. no. 28 Chalukyas of Kalyani AD 1144.	Ron Tq. Dharwar Dt.	< Jagadekamalla II	# Jagadekam-alla Permadi *(mahāmaṇḍle-śvara)* (Sinda Chief)	@ *ūroḍeva*	*	~ *tambūliga-* 1000 ~ii.*maleya-bolangara*-504 ~iii.Bammana *(maleya)*		<*ugura-* 300	~i~iii <	Δ Δ	*SII*, XV, 30-31
113.	Ins. no. 25 Chalukyas of Kalyani AD 1144.	Gadag Tq. Dharwar Dt.	< Jagadekamalla II	#Hemm-adideva *(mahāmaṇḍ-aleśvara)* (Hattagāra family)	@i.Namiyanna *(sarvādhikari pergaḍe)* @ii.8 *gavuṇḍas*				< 60 *okkalu*	@i @ii, <	Δ Δ	*SII*, IV, 28
114.	Ins. no. 27 Chalukyas of Kalyani AD 1144.	Ron Tq. Dharwar Dt.	< Jagadekamalla II	#Bamma-nayya *(mahāsāmanta)*	@i.Ananda-devarasa *(daṇḍanāyaka)* @ii.Bachayya *(achuoannāya dadhisṭāyaka)* @iii.Chanda-paya Nayaka *(pannāvada kenikara beggaḍe)*		~ *tambūliga* 1000			@iii	Δ	*SII*, XV, 29-30
115.	Transcript Chalukyas of Kalyani AD 1144.	Devadurg Tq. Raichur Dt.	< Jagadekamalla II						<i.*male-gara*-60 *okkalu*	<i <ii	Δ Δ	*A.R.* no. B 664 of 58-59

Key to the Symbols : $: *brāhmaṇa*; > : Main Ruler; * : *mahājana*; < : Peasant; @ : Functionary; A : Artisan; ~ : merchant; O : *maṭha*; # : local potentate; Δ : Temple; & : Cultural groups; T : Tank.

Chart – I : SOCIAL CONTEXT

Sub-Region B

i	ii	iii	iv	v	vi	vii	viii	ix	x	xi	xii	xiii
S.No.	Name/Date Dynasty	Location	Main Ruler	Local Potentate	Function-aries	brāhmaṇa/ mahājana	Merchant/ Artisan	Cultural Groups	Peasants	Donor	Donee	Reference
116.	Transcript Chalukyas of Kalyani AD 1145.	Sherapur Tq. Gulbarga Dt.	< Jagadekamalla II		@ Gayadhara Daṇḍanāyaka *(mahāpradhāna* suṁka vergaḍe)		~i. *mummūr-idaṇḍas* ~ii.*mūvattā rubidu* ~iii.*ubhaya nānādeśi* ~iv.*mahānāḍu*		<ii *billa* 300	@	Δ	*A.R.* no. B 521 of 1960-61
117.	Ins. no. 36 Chalukyas of Kalyani AD 1148.	Gadag Tq. Dharwar Dt.	< Jagadekamalla II	# Vira-Chāvuṇḍa rasa *(mahāmaṇ-ḍaleśvara)*	@i.Bopparasa *(manneya)* @ii.Naki-Gavunda *(mahāprabhu)* @iii.Holla-Gāvuṇḍa *(nālprabhu)* @iv.*sumika-pergadalu* @v.*sādada-pergaḍe* @vi.*pergaḍe vibhus* @vii.*gāyuṇḍas* @viii.Basava mayya Nāyaka *(bhandārada)* @ix.Kalideva Nayaka *(adhikāri pergaḍe)*		A *doni*-1000		<*ugura*-300	@ii-vi <, A	Δ Δ	*SII*, XV, 43-46

Key to the Symbols : $: *brāhmaṇa*; * : *mahājana*; @ : Functionary; ~ : merchant; # : local potentate; & : Cultural groups;
> : Main Ruler; < : Peasant; A : Artisan; O : maṭha; Δ : Temple; T : Tank.

Chart – I : SOCIAL CONTEXT

Sub-Region B

i	ii	iii	iv	v	vi	vii	viii	ix	x	xi	xii	xiii
S.No.	Name/Date Dynasty	Location	Main Ruler	Local Potentate	Function-aries	brāhmaṇa/ mahājana	Merchant/ Artisan	Cultural Groups	Peasants	Donor	Donee	Reference
118.	Ins. no. 10 Chalukyas of Kalyani AD 1149.	Yalburgi Tq. Raichur Dt.	< Jagadekamalla II		@i.Revarasa *(mahāpra-dhāna, daṇḍa-nāyaka)* @ii.Sāranga-pani Nāyaka *(pergaḍe* of *pannāya suṁka)* @iii.Aneyakesi-mayya *(mahā-pradhāna daṇḍādhinātha)* @iv.Mamma-rasa *(daṇḍādhinātha)* @v.Mādirāja nāyakam *(daṇḍanāyakaṁ suṁka dhikān)*		~Bāchimayya-Nāyaka *(angaḍiya)* A Nagimayya Nayaka *(akkasāḷi)*			@ii @v ~ A	Δ Δ Δ Δ	*IIAS*, 18, 54-57
119.	Transcript Chalukyas of Kalyani AD 1153.	Manvi Tq. Raichur Dt.		# Buchi devarasa *(mahāmaṇḍa-leśvara*	@i.Chāvuṇḍana *(heggaḍe)* @ii.*mahāpra-dhāna taṁtra pāla*		~ *hannvaṇa-* 1000	& *haḍapa* (of God)		@i, ii ~	& &	*AR*. no. B 568 of 61-62
120.	Ins. no. 43 Chalukyas of Kalyani AD 1154.	Ron Tq. Dharwar Dt.			@ Joga-Gāvuṇḍa		~i. *gavare* ~ii. *mummun-daṇḍas*		< 60 *okkalu*	@, < ~i, iii	Δ Δ	*SII*, XV, 56-57
121.	Ins. no. 52 Chalukyas of Kalyani AD 1155.	Gadag Tq. Dharwar Dt.	>Taila II		@i.Bopparasa *(manneva)*					@i-ii	Δ	*SII*, XV, 68-69

Key to the Symbols : $: *brāhmaṇa*; > : Main Ruler; * : *mahājana*; < : Peasant; @ : Functionary; A : Artisan; ~ : merchant; O : maṭha; # : local potentate; Δ : Temple; & : Cultural groups; T : Tank.

Chart – I : SOCIAL CONTEXT

Sub-Region B

i	*ii*	*iii*	*iv*	*v*	*vi*	*vii*	*viii*	*ix*	*x*	*xi*	*xii*	*xiii*
S.No.	*Nεme/Dεte Dynastγ*	*Location*	*Main Ruler*	*Local Potentate*	*Function-aries*	*brāhmaṇa/ mahājana*	*Merchant/ Artisan*	*Cultural Groups*	*Peasants*	*Donor*	*Donee*	*Reference*
					@ii.Holla-Gavunda (*mahāprabhu*)							
122.	Ins. no. 237 Chalukyas o Kalyani AD 1165.	Ron Tc. Dharwar Dist.		# Chanvunda rasadeva (*mahāmaṇḍa-leśvara* (Sinda Chief)	@ Isvarayya (*hejjuṁka-biravaṇada beggaḍe)*					@	Δ	*SII*, XV, 293
123.	Ins. no. 106 AD 1 66.	Gadag Tq. Dharwar Dt.			@ *ūroḍeva*	* 120	~i. 16 representatives of 8 *nāḍus* ~ii. *prabhus* of three *pattaṇas* ~iii.*mummu-ri daṇḍas* ~iv.*nānādeśi*			~i-iv	Δ	*SII*, XV, 136-137
124.	Ins. no. 238 AD 1 69.			#Chāvuṇḍa-rasadeva (*mahāmaṇḍa-leśvara)* (Sinda Chief)	@i.*ūroḍeva* @ii.*sarva-gāvuṇḍagalum* @iii.*adhikā-rigalum*				< 60 *okkalu*	$	T	*SII*, XV, 293-296
125.	Ins. no. 66 Kalachuryas of Kalyani AD 1174.	Yelburgi Tq. Raichur Dt.	>Rāyamuran Sovideva		@i.Tejiraja (*daṇḍanāyaka)* @ii.Boppana Nayaka (*pradhāna-karaṇa)* @iii.Maha-deva Nāyaka	* 1000	A Chandoja (*kammaṭa)*			@i-vi	Δ	*APGAS* no. 3 73-77

Key to the Symbols : $ *brāhmaṇa*; * : *mahājana*; @ : Functionary; ~ : merchant; # : local potentate; & : Cultural groups;
> Main Ruler; < : Peasant; A : Artisan; O : maṭha; Δ : Temple; T : Tank.

Chart – I : SOCIAL CONTEXT

Sub-Region B

i	ii	iii	iv	v	vi	vii	viii	ix	x	xi	xii	xiii
S.No.	Name/Date Dynasty	Location	Main Ruler	Local Potentate	Function-aries	*brāhmaṇa/ mahājana*	Merchant/ Artisan	Cultural Groups	Peasants	Donor	Donee	Reference
					(sachiva) @iv.Kalimayya nāyaka *(Śri karaṇa)* @v.Bommideva *(pasāyita)* @vi.*sthala karaṇas*							
126.	Ins. no. 240 AD 1173.	Gadag Tq. Dharwar Dt.		# Vira-bijjala *(mahāmaṇḍa-leśvara)* (Sinda Chief)	@i.12 *gāvuṇ-ḍas* @ii.Remmarasa *(beggaḍe)*		~the 1000		<i 60 *okkalu* <ii ugura-300	@i, ii <, <ii ~	Δ Δ	*SII*, XV, 296-297
127.	Ins. no. 121 Kalachuryas of Kalyani AD 1173.	Gadag Tq. Dharwar Dt.	> Rāyamuraṅ Sovideva	#Virabi-jjarasa *(mahāmaṇḍa-leśvara)* (Sinda Chief)	@i.*gauṇḍi* @ii.Chandi-maya Nāyaka @iii.Madhava Daṇḍanāyaka @iv.Dāsima-rasam *(mahāprabhu)*		~the 1000		<i 60 *okkalu* <ii *ugura-*300	@i-ii ~ <i, <ii @iv	Δ Δ Δ Δ	*SII*, XV, 151-152
128.	Ins. no. 241 AD 1174.	Ron Tq. Dharwar Dt.		# Virabi-jjala (SindaChief)	@ Mahadeva Dandanayaka *(mahāpra-dhānaṁ)*	* 140			< 50 *okkalu*	@ <	Δ Δ	*SII*, XV, 297-301
129.	Ins. no. 12 Kalachuris of Kalyani AD 1175.	Sindhnur Tq. Raichur Dt.	> Rāyamuraṅ Sovindeva			*	*~samasta naka raṁgalu*			~	Δ	*HAS*, 18, 61-63

Key to the Symbols : $: *brāhmaṇa*; > : Main Ruler; * : *mahājana*; < : Peasant; @ : Functionary; A : Artisan; ~ : merchant; O : maṭha; # : local potentate; Δ : Temple; & : Cultural groups; T : Tank.

Chart – I : SOCIAL CONTEXT

Sub-Region B

i	ii	iii	iv	v	vi	vii	viii	ix	x	xi	xii	xiii
S.No	*Name/Date Dynasty*	*Location*	*Main Ruler*	*Local Potentate*	*Function-aries*	*brāhmaṇa/ mahājana*	*Merchant/ Artisan*	*Cultural Groups*	*Peasants*	*Donor*	*Donee*	*Reference*
130.	Transcript Kalachuris of Kalyani AD 1178.	Manvi Tq. Raichur Dt.	>Sankamadeva	# Maili-devarasa *(mahāmaṇḍa-leśvara)* (Haihaya Chief)	@i.*prabhus* @ii.*gāvuṇḍas*		Ai.Timmoja (mason) Aii.malloja (carpenter)		< *billa* 300	# @i-ii <	Δ Δ Δ Ai-ii	*A.R.* no. B 556 of 60-61
131.	Ins. at Ittagi B Kalachuris of Kalyani AD 1178.	Yalburgi Tq. Raichur Dt.	>Sankamadeva		@ *ūroḍeya*	* 400	~ Nagade-vayya nayaka *(mahāvaḍḍa-vvayahāri)*				Δ	*EI*, XIII, 59-61
132.	Ins. no. 131 Kalachuris of Kalyani AD 1178.	Gadag Tq. Dharwar Dt.	>Sankamadeva				~i.*nagara-mahājana* ~ii.*pura* ~iii.the 500			~i~ii	Δ	*SII*, XV, 167-168
133.	Ins. no. 13 AD 1178.	Yalburgi Tq. Raichur Dt.		#i.Permandi *(mahāmaṇḍa-leśvara)* (Sinda Chief) #ii.Chamu-ndaraja *(mahāmaṇḍa-leśvara)*	@i.Dhannugi *(daṇḍanātha)* @ii.Lakshmi deva *(mahāpra-dhāna, dan-ḍanāyaka)* @iii.*karaṇam galu*			&i.Basavana *(sūlevala)* (dance master) &ii.*parekara* (drummer)		@i-iii	Δ &i-ii	*HAS*, 18, 63-74
134.	Ins. from Yewur G Kalachuris of Kalyani AD 1179.	Shorapur Tq. Gulbarga Dt.	>Sankamadeva		@ Tripura ntakadevarasa *(mahāprabhu)*					@	Δ	*EI*, XII, 336-340
135.	Two Ins. from Ron B AD 1179.	Ron Tq. Dharwar Dt.		#Vikramā-dityarasa (Sinda Chief)	@i.Bachayya sahani *(mahāpra-*	* 104			< 60 *okkalu*	#, <, @	Δ	*EI*, XIX, 226-236

Key to the Symbols - $: *brāhmaṇa*; * : *mahājana*; @ : Functionary; ~ : merchant; # : local potentate; & : Cultural groups;
> : Main Ruler; < : Peasant; A : Artisan; O : maṭha; Δ : Temple; T : Tank.

Chart – I : SOCIAL CONTEXT

Sub-Region B

i	ii	iii	iv	v	vi	vii	viii	ix	x	xi	xii	xiii
S.No.	*Name/Date Dynasty*	*Location*	*Main Ruler*	*Local Potentate*	*Function-aries*	*brāhmaṇa/ mahājana*	*Merchant/ Artisan*	*Cultural Groups*	*Peasants*	*Donor*	*Donee*	*Reference*
					dhānam) @ii.*ūroḍeya*							
136.	Ins. no. 135 Kalachuris of Kalyani AD 1179.	Gadag Tq. Dharwar Dt.					~i. Aycha-seṭṭi ~ii.*mahāna-karaṁgalu* ~iii.*angaḍiya nakaramgalu* ~iv.*ubhaya-nānādeśi* Ai.*kamma-tidalu* Aii.*bhaṇḍa-sāleya* Aiii.*tala-bhoga-kenikaram* Aiv.various types of *kenikaram*			~i~iv Ai-iv	Δ Δ	*SII*, XV, 174-178
137.	Ins no. 14 Kalachuris of Kalyani AD 1183.	Yalburgi Tq. Raichur Dt.	>Singana-deva		@ Divakara Daṇḍanāyaka	$ 1000	A *kāruka* (barber)			> @	$ 1000 Δ	*HAS*, 18, 7-79
138.	Ins. no. 62 Chalukyas of Kalyani AD 1184.	Gadag Tq. Dharwar Dt.	>Somesvara IV				Ai.Aychi-Seṭṭi Aii.Mahādeva Setti (*kammati dalu nādvā-ṇikara)* Aiii.*kammaṭi daḷu putha grahaka*			Ai-vii	Δ	*SII*, XV, 87-88

Key to the Symbols : $: *brāhmaṇa*; > : Main Ruler; * : *mahājana*; < : Peasant; @ : Functionary; A : Artisan; ~ : merchant; O : maṭha; # : local potentate; Δ : Temple; & : Cultural groups; T : Tank.

Chart – I : SOCIAL CONTEXT

Sub-Region B

i	ii	iii	iv	v	vi	vii	viii	ix	x	xi	xii	xiii
S.No.	*Name/Date Dynasty*	*Location*	*Main Ruler*	*Local Potentate*	*Function-aries*	*brāhmaṇa/ mahājana*	*Merchant/ Artisan*	*Cultural Groups*	*Peasants*	*Donor*	*Donee*	*Reference*
							Aiv.Madha vadevam *(kammaṭida-hiriyasena bhogam)* Av.*hiriya-akkasāle* Avi.*kenikaram* Avii.*kammaṭi danikaraṇa*					
139.	Ins. no. 57 Chalukyas of Kalyani AD 1184.	Mundargi Tq. Dharwar Dt.	>Somesvara IV		@i.Tejimayya *(mahāpra-dhāna senādhi-pati)* @ii.Bakana *(daṇḍanāyaka)* @iii.Revarasa (holding *pannāya suṁka)*		~i. 16 *seṭṭis* ~ii. *nakaras*			@i-iii ~i-ii	Δ Δ	*SII*, XV, 74-78
140.	Ins. no. 61 Chalukyas of Kalyani AD 1184.	Gadag Tq. Dharwar Dt.	>Somesvara IV				Ai.Achiseṭṭi Aii.Maha-devasetti *āṇikara)*			Ai-ii	Δ	*SII*, XV, 87
141.	Ins. no. 67 Chalukyas of Kalyani AD 1135.	Gadag Tq. Dharwar Dt.	>Somesvara IV			* 1000	Ai.Vishnu setti *(maleya-āṇikara)* Aii.*kamma-tikka* Aiii.*baḍagi kammarār*			Ai-v	Δ	*SII*, XV, 92-94

Key to the Symbols : $: *brāhmaṇa*; > : Main Ruler; * : *mahājana*; < : Peasant; @ : Functionary; A : Artisan; ~ : merchant; O : maṭha; # : local potentate; Δ : Temple; & : Cultural groups; T : Tank.

Chart – I : SOCIAL CONTEXT

Sub-Region B

i	ii	iii	iv	v	vi	vii	viii	ix	x	xi	xii	xiii
S.No.	*Name/Date Dynasty*	*Location*	*Main Ruler*	*Local Potentate*	*Function-aries*	*brāhmaṇa/ mahājana*	*Merchant/ Artisan*	*Cultural Groups*	*Peasants*	*Donor*	*Donee*	*Reference*
							Aiv.several artisans Av.*seṭṭi garu*					
142.	Ins. no. 70 Chalukyas of Kalyani AD 1186.	Gadag Tq. Dharwar Dt.	>Somesvara IV				Ai.Śankara Seṭṭi *(anikara)* Aii.Basava Seṭṭi *(baṇḍiya)*			Ai	Δ	*SII*, XV, 95-96
143.	Ins. no. 69 Chalukyas of Kalyani AD 1186.	Gadag Tq. Dharwar Dt.	>Somesvara IV				A kalloja *(baḍagi)*			A	Δ	*SII*, XV, 95
144.	Ins. no. 73 Chalukyas of Kalyani AD 1189.	Gadag Tq. Dharwar Dt.	>Somesvara IV		@ *ūru tala-vāranāyaka*	* 120	~i. Chandi Seṭṭi ~ii. *naka-ramgalu* Ai.Marana *(mālara)* Aii.*hamna-vanagaru* Aiii.*kamcha gāra* Aiv.*kumbāra* Av.*seṇigaru*		< 60 *okkalu*	@ ~i-ii Ai-v <	Δ Δ Δ Δ	*SII*, XV, 99-104
145.	Ins. no. 15 AD 1191.	Sindhnur Tq. Raichur Dt.		#3 Haihaya Chiefs *mahāmaṇḍa-leśvara*			~ 3 *seṭṭis*			#		*HAS*, 18, 80-82
146.	Gadag Ins. Yadavas of Devagiri AD 1191.	Gadag Tq. Dharwar Dt.	> Bhillama-deva	@ Jaitasimha *(mantn)*						>		*EI*, III, 217-220

Key to the Symbols : $: *brāhmaṇa*; * : *mahājana*; @ : Functionary; ~ : merchant; # : local potentate; & : Cultural groups;
\> : Main Ruler; < : Peasant; A : Artisan; O : maṭha; Δ : Temple; T : Tank.

Chart – I : SOCIAL CONTEXT

Sub-Region B

i	ii	iii	iv	v	vi	vii	viii	ix	x	xi	xii	xiii
S.No.	*Name/Date Dynasty*	*Location*	*Main Ruler*	*Local Potentate*	*Function-aries*	*brāhmaṇa/ mahājana*	*Merchant/ Artisan*	*Cultural Groups*	*Peasants*	*Donor*	*Donee*	*Reference*
147	Ins. no. 16 Yadavas of Devagiri AD 1030.	Lingsugur Tq. Dharwar Dt.	> Bhillama-deva	# Bajjarasa *mahāmaṇḍa-leśvara* (Kadamba Chief)	@i.Aneya-maleyanāyaka *(mahāpradhāna)* @ii.Revarasa Sankayya. Mallaya, *(prabhus)* @iii.Echarasa Dhananjaya Samkayya *(prabhus)*					#, @i		*HAS*, 18, 83-89
148.	Ins. no. 207 Hoysalas of Dwara-samudra AD 1192.	Gadag Tq. Dharwar Dt.	>Viraballala II		@i.Bicharasa *(hejjuṁkada adhikari)* @ii.Mahābala Gāvuṇḍa @iii.*arasus* and *suṁka-vergaḍes*					@i	Δ	*SII*, XV, 250-251
149.	Ins. no. 211 Hoysalas of Dwarasamudra AD 1196.	Mundargi Tq. Dharwar Dt.	Vira Ballala II				~i. *dakṣina* Ayyavole ~ii. *mahānādu* ~iii. *nakara mahālana* ~iv.*mummuri-daṇḍas*			~i-iv	Δ	*SII*, XV, 253-254
150.	Ins. no. 210 Hoysalas of Dwara-samudra AD 1196.	Mundargi Tq. Dharwar Dt.	Vira Ballala II				~i. *nakara mahājana* ~ii. *mummu-ridaṇḍas* ~iii. 9 *puras*			~i-iii	Δ	*SII*, XV, 252-253

Key to the Symbols : $: *brāmaṇa*; > : Main Ruler; * : *mahājana*; < : Peasant; @ : Functionary; A : Artisan; ~ : merchant; O : maṭha; # : local potentate; Δ : Temple; & : Cultural groups; T : Tank.

Chart – I : SOCIAL CONTEXT

Sub-Region B

i	ii	iii	iv	v	vi	vii	viii	ix	x	xi	xii	xiii
S.No.	*Name/Date Dynasty*	*Location*	*Main Ruler*	*Local Potentate*	*Function-aries*	*brāhmaṇa/ mahājana*	*Merchant/ Artisan*	*Cultural Groups*	*Peasants*	*Donor*	*Donee*	*Reference*
151.	Ins. no. 215 Hoysalas of Dwara-samudra AD 1199.	Gadag Tq. Dharwar Dt.	>Viraballala II					Ai.Kesavana *(telliga)* Aii.Machana *(tuppakka)* Aiii.Keti Setti *telliga)*	< 50 *okkalu*	Ai-iii <	Δ Δ	*SII*, XV, 258-260
152.	Hosur Ins. Hoysalas of Dwara-samudra AD 1207.	Gadag Tq. Dharwar Dt.	>Viraballala II		@i.Chikka Narasimgayya *(mahapra-dhānam-sarvādhikari)* @ii.Mahābala Gāvuṇḍa					@	Δ	*EI*, XXXII, 171-174
153.	Ins. no. 220 Hoysalas of Dwara-samudra AD 1207.	Gadag Tq. Dharwar Dt.	>Viraballala II				~i.*nagara mahājana* ~ii.the 500 ~iii.*sthala samasta* ~iv.*mummū-ridaṇḍas* Ai.*telliga*-50			~i-iv Ai	Δ Δ	*SII*, XV, 267-269
154.	Ins. no. 17 Yadavas of Devagiri AD 1215.	Lingsugur Tq. Raichur Dt.	> Singaṇa-deva	#Bajjarasa *(mahāmaṇḍa-leśvara)* (Kadamba Chief)	@i.Damodara (general of >) @ii.Parasura-ma (above's sub-ordinate) @iii.*ūroḍeya* @iv.Parasa-yya Daṇḍanā-yaka *(mahā-pradhānaṁ)*		~i.500 *svāmis* of Ayyavole ~ii.*nakaras* ~iii.*seṭṭi gutta* ~iv.*mummu-ndaṇḍa* ~v.*nānādeśi* ~vi.*sthala samasta*			@i-iv ~i-vi	Δ Δ	*HAS*, 18, 89-93

Key to the Symbols : $: *brāhmaṇa*; * : *mahājana*; @ : Functionary; ~ : merchant; # : local potentate; & : Cultural groups; > : Main Ruler; < : Peasant; A : Artisan; O : maṭha; Δ : Temple; T : Tank.

Chart – I : SOCIAL CONTEXT

Sub-Region C

i	ii	iii	iv	v	vi	vii	viii	ix	x	xi	xii	xiii
S.No.	Name/Date Dynasty	Location	Main Ruler	Local Potentate	Function-aries	*brāhmaṇa/ mahājana*	Merchant/ Artisan	Cultural Groups	Peasants	Donor	Donee	Reference
155.	Ins. no 4 Chalukyas of Kalyan AD 1056.	Alampur Tq. Mahaboobnagar Dt.	>Someśvara I	# Irugana Chola Maharaja *(mahāmaṇḍa-leśvara)* (Chola Chief)	@ Lokamani-ka setti *(mahāmatya suṁkavergaḍe)*		*prabhu*			@	Δ	*Telangana sasanalu* II 20-21
156.	Transcript Chalukyas of Kalyani AD 1058.	Nandikotkur Tq. Kurnool Dt.	>Someśvara I							>	Δ	453/68 of Hyd. Archaeolo-gy and Museums Office
157.	Transcript Chalukyas of Kalyani AD 1060.	Alampur Tq. Mahaboobnagar Dt.	>Someśvara I		@ Davapayya *(pergaḍe)*			& *pāduvar-gam* (musicians)		@	Δ &	*A.R.* no. B 72 of 1960-61
158.	Ins. no. 11 Chalukyas of Kalyani AD 1067.	Alampur Tq. Mahaboobnagar Dt	>Someśvara I	# Chiddana Cholamaha-raja *(mahāmaṇḍa-leśvara)* (Chola Chieftain)	@i.Kosanaya Pergaḍe *(saudhare)* @ii.6 *gāvuṇḍas* @iii.*janada prabhuṁgalu*		~3 *settis*			@i-iii	Δ Δ	*APGAS*, 3 105-106
159.	Panchalingala Ins. Chalukyas of Kalyani AD 1068.	Kurnool Tq. Kurnool Dt.	>Someśvara II							>	Δ	*EI*, XXXVI 139-143
160.	Transcript Chalukyas of Kalyani AD 1069.	Nandikotkur Tq. Kurnool Dt.	>Someśvara II							>	Δ	337/68 of Hyd. Archaeolo-

Key to the Symbols : $: *brāhmaṇa*; * : *mahājana*; @ : Functionary; ~ : merchant; # : local potentate; & : Cultural groups;
> : Main Ruler; < : Peasant; A : Artisan; O : maṭha; Δ : Temple; T : Tank.

Chart – *I* : SOCIAL CONTEXT

Sub-Region C

i	ii	iii	iv	v	vi	vii	viii	ix	x	xi	xii	xiii
S.No.	*Name/Date Dynasty*	*Location*	*Main Ruler*	*Local Potentate*	*Function-aries*	*brāhmaṇa/ mahājana*	*Merchant/ Artisan*	*Cultural Groups*	*Peasants*	*Donor*	*Donee*	*Reference*
												gy and Museums Office
161.	Ins. no. 22 Chalukyas of Kalyani AD 1073.	Alampur Tq. Mahaboobnagar Dt.	>Someśvara II	# Chidda-nachola mahāraja (Chola chieftain)						#	Δ	*APGAS*, 3, 117-118
162.	Bichapalli Ins. Chalukyas of Kalyani AD 1074.	Alampur Tq. Mahaboobnagar Dt.	>Someśvara II	# Chidda-nachola mahāraja (Chola chieftain						#	Δ	*EI*, XXXVI 69-74
163.	Transcript Chalukyas of Kalyani AD 1075.	Nandikotkur Tq. Kurnool Dt.	>Someśvara II	#Satyarasa *mahāmaṇḍa-*leśvara)						#	Δ	*A.R.* no. 317 of 37-38
164.	Ins. no. 8 Chalukyas of Kalyani AD 1076.	Alampur Tq. Mahaboobnagar Dt.	>Someśvara II		@ Naranama-yya *(yaḍḍarā-vula daṇḍanā-yaka)*					@	Δ	*APGAS*, 3 103-104
165.	Ins. no. 16 Chalukyas of Kalyani AD 1078.	Alampur Tq. Mahaboobnagar Dt.	> Vikramāditya VI	#Mallamahā-raja (Vaidumba Chief)						#	Δ	*APGAS*, 3, 110-111
166.	Ins. no. 14 Chalukyas of Kalyani AD 1080.	Alampur Tq. Mahaboobnagar Dt.	> Vikramāditya VI	#Mallamaha-raja (Vaidumba Chief)						#	Δ	*APGAS*, 3, 107-108
167.	Ins. no. 18 Chalukyas of Kalyani AD 1082.	Alampur Tq. Mahaboobnagar Dt.	> Vikramāditya VI	@Malla-payya (pergaḍe)						@	Δ	*APGAS*, 3, 113-114

Key to the Symbols : $: *brāhmaṇa*; * : *mahājana*; @ : Functionary; ~ : merchant; # : local potentate; & : Cultural groups;
> : Main Ruler; < : Peasant; A : Artisan; O : maṭha; Δ : Temple; T : Tank.

Chart – I : SOCIAL CONTEXT

Sub-Region C

i	ii	iii	iv	v	vi	vii	viii	ix	x	xi	xii	xiii
S.No.	*Name/Date Dynasty*	*Location*	*Main Ruler*	*Local Potentate*	*Function-aries*	*brāhmaṇa/ mahājana*	*Merchant/ Artisan*	*Cultural Groups*	*Peasants*	*Donor*	*Donee*	*Reference*
168.	Ins. no. 33 Chalukyas of Kalyani AD 1087.	Gadwar Tq. Mahaboobnagar Dt.	> Vikramāditya VI	# Hallava-rasa (Pallava Chief)						#	Δ	*APGAS*, 3, 40-41
169.	Ins. no. 37 Chalukyas of Kalyani AD 1107.	Alampur Tq. Mahaboobnagar Dt.		#Mallarasa (*mahāmaṇḍa-*leśvara)						#	Δ	*APGAS*, 3, 125-126
170.	Ins. no. 32 Chalukyas of Kalyani AD 1151.	Alampur Tq. Mahaboobnagar Dt.					~i.Ayyavole *svami* ~ii.*pramukha ubhaya-nānādesi* ~v.kannaḍa-4000 ~vi.Chief men of various business centres			~i-vi	Δ	*APGAS*, 3, 123

Key to the Symbols : $: *brāhmaṇa*; * : *mahājana*; @ : Functionary; ~ : merchant; # : local potentate; & : Cultural groups;
> : Main Ruler; < : Peasant; A : Artisan; O : maṭha; Δ : Temple; T : Tank.

4

ECONOMIC CONTEXT

Our comprehension of the social groups and their changing relations delineated in the previous chapter can be heightened by placing them in their economic context; an analysis of which forms the focus of our attention in this chapter. Evolution of an economy peculiar to the system of granting lands in lieu of cash payments to functionaries of State and religious beneficiaries becomes the dominant feature of the early medieval period almost all over the Indian subcontinent. Chief characteristics of such an economy have been identified as the relapse of market economy of towns into a subsistence economy of agriculture based largely on rural settlements, the emergence of landed intermediaries who were granted economic privileges and a large mass of subject peasantry who were dependent on the former.[1] Without going into the polemics of the applicability of the term 'Indian feudalism' for our study we wish to reiterate here our intention to focus primarily upon the dynamics of economic change brought about by a host of interactive factors at a specific spatial level during the early medieval period. As explicitly manifest in the inscriptional sources, the region under study was marked by a predominance of the mention of land grants particularly for a major part of the 11th century A.D., and this was followed by an increasing mention of the grants of various commodities and taxes from the 12th century A.D. onwards (see Charts II A, B, C appended to the chapter). It is chiefly with regard to aspects of economic change both in the agrarian and non-agrarian spheres that we wish to associate ourselves in the following analysis.

The system of making land grants to religious beneficiaries along with various immunities had actually been started by the Śātavahana rulers in the western Deccan from the early centuries A.D. This practice was carried with vigour under the Vākaṭaka rulers of the central Deccan after the decline of the Śātavahanas, and by 6th-7th Centuries A.D., land grants to religious beneficiaries became a common phenomenon.[2] The data thus available to us from the inscriptions of this time begin to give us extensive information on various facets of the land grant economy. In the inscriptional sources pertaining to our area and period of study, as indicated in the charts appended (II A, B, C), the economic transactions that have been referred to were inextricably related to various types of grants made to different kinds of beneficiaries. A large majority of these were religious in nature. In this context it becomes crucial for us to comprehend the nature of the grants made ranging from villages and various measurements of land to those of various commodities. It is chiefly in the context of the gradual shift in the nature of grants made, *i.e.,* from a predominance of grants of land in the first phase of our study (11th century A.D.) to those of various commodities and coins in the second phase (12th century A.D.), that we can discern a subtle change in the econon.ic set up. The dialectics of such a change can then be broadly visualized in terms of a significant shift from the dominant agrarian activity to one in which non-agrarian activity too begins to have a considerable share in the economic scenario, marking a definite stage characterised by elements of a 'rural-urban' continuum.

Having divided our area of study into three sub-regions (A, B and C), we have taken up sub-region B as the nuclear area of our analysis. We have observed in this context that a study of the 'Raichur Doab' or, the 'Krishna-Tungabhadra Doab' which occupies a major part of sub-region B, has hitherto mainly been viewed in terms of a military or warring zone, while in terms of a study of the economic aspects it still remains a desideratum. Further, with a majority of our information in this period focussed on sub-region B, it affords us with the potential to comprehend the changing contours of the economic space at a micro-level in an effective way.[3] Such an analysis is then compared and contrasted with the information from sub-regions A and C, the economic contexts of which however, figure in a limited manner when compared to sub-region B. It is significant to note here that we find considerable variance in the nature of the economic activity described in the inscriptional sources of all the three sub-regions particularly with reference to the nature of grants made as will follow in the descriptions below. A chronological study of these aspects of the economic structure of the time would help us a great deal in comprehending the economic basis for the changing social relations of the period under study.

Since it is the nature of rights held in land and their transformation affected through the grants to various beneficiaries that acted as the prime forces in the change of the economic scenario, it becomes pertinent for us to initiate our discussion with the question of land rights. Importance of land as the chief source of wealth and the association of the surplus appropriating class with it during our period of study is well attested by the land transactions described in the inscriptional data. These land transactions indicate to us the mechanisms of surplus appropriation and distribution adopted by the richer sections of the society of the period and thus form the prime factors in defining the nature of the economy as it prevailed. Transfer of land of various sizes was in fact made among a minority of the social groups. It nonetheless led to a significant change in the land holding pattern when compared to earlier times. The very fact that certain sections of the society had the ability to grant land raises the pertinent question of the nature of rights in land that these groups traditionally held.

There has been considerable controversy between the Western scholars of the late 19th and early 20th centuries on the one hand, and the Nationalist historians of India on the other, over the nature of rights in land in pre-British India. Writings of the former, represented by such scholars as Karl Marx and later, Vincent Smith, negated the existence of privately owned land in early India as in those times, according to these scholars, all land was owned by the despotic ruler.[4] On the other hand, nationalist scholars such as U.N. Ghoshal, K.P. Jayaswal etc. have argued for the existence of a clear notion of the concept of private ownership of land in early India.[5] The attitude of the nationalist writers on the nature of rights in land in early India, can however, be best exemplified in the works of A.S. Altekar. As the author of the *History of Village Communities in Western India,* he completely rules out the possibility of any communal holding of land in early India and even goes to the extent of characterizing the early Indian land tenures as those of individual peasant proprietorship with the principles of Ryotwari system present in them.[6]

It is from the middle of the 20th century that the writings on early India begin to be written from a different perspective by such scholars as D.D. Kosambi[7] and R.S. Sharma.[8] These scholars adopting the tool of historical materialism have studied the material basis of property relations for various periods of early India. Their studies have brought out the fact that not only is there evidence to prove the existence of private property in land, but also that there were changes in the nature of property relations over the centuries.[9] Thus for instance, they point out that the rights held in land in the early medieval period were not the same as they were earlier in the Vedic and the post Vedic ages.[10] This was because the nature of rights held in the landed property began to take shape according to the imperatives imposed by the prevalent economic structure of the time. D.D. Kosambi and R.S. Sharma have dealt largely with the economic structure of the Indo-Gangetic plains. In recent times we have significant contributions being made in terms of understanding the specific nature of property relations for various regions of India. Among these, relevant to our study are the works of such eminent scholars as R.N. Nandi, N. Karashima and Dharma Kumar who have brought out valuable information regarding the nature of rights held in land in the early medieval period, particularly in peninsular India. While Dharma Kumar[11] and N. Karashima[12] have focussed chiefly on the extreme South, the work of Nandi[13] focusses chiefly on the Karnataka region. All these scholars attest to the growth of private property in land in the early medieval period at the cost of previously held communal holdings. Through their respective areas of studies, R.S. Sharma[14] and Dharma Kumar[15] have brought out the possibility of the existence of a multiplexity[16] of rights on a single land holding during the early medieval period. The specific nature of these rights however, varied in its content and terminology from region to region.

To comprehend the nature of rights held in landed property one has to analyse the nature of land transactions made. It has been shown for other regions of India such as the southern peninsula, that during this period there were two principal categories of land holdings, namely, beneficial and non-beneficial holdings. While the former were held by the *brāhmaṇas (brahmadeyas)* and the temples (devadāna), the latter were held by the rich peasant communities.[17] While the former category of land rights have been considered private in nature,[18] it has been suggested that the latter, or the non-beneficial holdings, paid full taxes and had customary communal rights over the land they cultivated.[19] In the inscriptional sources of our study beneficial tenures give frequent references to various privileges and immunities attached to the donee. These are largely indicative of the nature of land rights held by different social groups.

From the 11th century A.D. onwards we find that on the whole, grants of small measurements of land or field made by lesser chiefs out number those of the grants of villages made by the main ruling family chiefs and the local potentates (see charts IIA, B, C, Columns iv, v, vi).[20] When viewed in terms of chronological and sub-regional dimensions, we have for sub-region A during the 11th century A.D. out of about 17 inscriptions charted, only 2 instances of grants of villages, 7 instances of grant of large measurements of land[21] and 6 instances of grants of small measurements of land in all (IIA, vi, 1-17). For the same sub-region during the 12th century A.D. we have out of 15 instances, only one reference to the grant of a village, 2 instances of the grant of large measurements of land and 10 instances of small measurements of land as objects of grants made (IIA, vi, 18-32). In sub-region B during the 11th century A.D., out of 46 inscriptions charted, we have 12 references to the grant of villages, 18 instances of a grant of large measurements of land and 15 instances of a grant of small measurements of land (IIb, vi, 33-80). For the 12th century A.D. in sub-region B, we have out of about 64 instances, only 9 references to the grant of villages, 12 instances of a grant of large measurements of land and nearly 22 instances of grant of small measurements of land (IIB, vi, 81-145). For sub-region C during the 11th century A.D., out of 16 inscriptions charted by us, we have nearly 7 instances of grants of villages, 2 instances of a grant of large measurements of land and one instance of a grant of a small measurement of land granted (IIC, vi, 146-161). For the 12th century A.D. of the same sub-region, out of about 4 inscriptions charted, we have one instance of the grant of a village and one instance of the grant of a large measurement of land (IIC, vi, 162-165).

The above description of the chronological and sub-regional trends in the context of grants of land and villages indicates to us that firstly, there is a visible decline in the number of villages granted during the 12th century A.D., when compared to the data of the previous century. We have also observed in this context that while small measurements of land predominate the scene in sub-region A (IIA, vi, 1-32), sub-region B constitutes grants of both large and small measurements of land (IIB, vi, 33-145) and on the other hand, sub-region C has a majority of large measurement of land and villages (IIC, vi, 146-165). These trends can however, be comprehended in a better light when viewed in the context of the nature of the donors making grants during various periods and sub-regions of study. As we have already noticed in the previous chapter,[22] in the context of sub-region A, functionaries figure in a majority as donors (IIA, iv, 1-32), in sub-region B we however, have the members of the main ruling family and the local potentates dominating the scene during the 11th century A.D. (IIB, iv, 33-80) and the functionaries figure as a majority in the 12th century grants (IIB, iv, 81-145). On the other hand, in sub-region C we have the local potentates and the main rulers participating actively throughout the period of our study in a majority of the cases (IIC, iv, 146-165).[23] What emerges significantly in the above survey is that it is chiefly with regard to the grants made by the local potentates and the main ruling family chiefs, as has been seen in the case of the grants of the 11th century A.D. in sub-regions B and C as a whole, that we have the predominance of village grants and grants of large measurements of land. On the other hand, with regard to the grants made largely by the functionaries as witnessed in the contexts of sub-region A as a whole and during the 12th century A.D. in sub-region B, that we find the predominance of small measurements of land grants. It is significant to underscore at the same time that we also have few instances of grant villages made by functionaries but in a majority of these cases they seemed to have required the permission of the main ruling family in this regard. Thus, in an inscription of A.D. 1170 of sub-region B, a functionary granted a village only with the approval of the main ruler.[24] In another inscription of the same sub-region, dated A.D. 1178, the grant of a village by the functionary is recorded to have been made in a similar fashion.[25] What remains prominent in the above survey is that the privilege of making grants of villages rested mostly with the main ruling family chiefs followed by the local potentates who figure in relatively large numbers during the 11th century A.D. and it is this which accounts for a greater number of villages and large measurements of land granted during this century.

The very fact that certain powerful ruling families had the capacity to grant large number of villages and large measurements of land, goes to indicate the extensive rights that these groups enjoyed in their territory.[26] It has held by earlier scholars such as U.N. Ghoshal that what was usually granted by the king was his own fiscal and semi-fiscal claims over the villages granted. It has further been stated that the land of the grants was often waste land which thus helped in the extension of cultivation.[27] In the legal texts of early India we however, find that on the one hand, there is staunch support for the existence of royal ownership of land and on the other, these texts also encourage the growth in the private ownership of landed property.[28] This apparent contradiction in the attitude of the legal writers of the early medieval period, it has been argued, only helped in the growth of private property in land of both the king and the dominant land holding peasants.[29] The theory supporting the royal ownership of land also tended to legalise the grants made by the main ruling family chiefs to the brahmanical ideologues thus leading to the growth of private ownership over land held by the *brāhmaṇas* and temple trustees. In the context of our study too, we find that it was chiefly in the grants made to the *brāhmaṇas* and the brahmanical temples that extensive economic and juridical immunities were attached. These immunities indicate the transfer to various rights that the donor had over the grant, to the donee. As shall be illustrated in the following description the immunities granted to the donee were not necessarily in the form of usufructury rights but rather, they tended to confer different kinds of proprietory rights over to the donce through the grants that were made.

We have in this context the use of various terms to indicate the specific nature of the economic privileges granted. We have terms such as *sarvanamasya* (IIA, xi, 6) *agrahāra* (IIB, xi, 33) *mānya* (IIB, xi, 75) *sarvabādhaparihāraṁ* (IIA, xi, 12), *śulka-kara-vādha-parihāraḥ* (IIB, xi, 140) to indicate revenue free land tenures. *Sarvanamasya* holding indicates a holding fully exempt from all taxes.[30] *Agrahāra* or the *brahmadeya* tenures have been understood as the right to enjoy the grant in the form of a rent free land given to the *brāhmaṇa.*[31] *Mānya* land also is indicative of a tax free tenure.[32] Further, *sarvabādhaparihāram* has been interpreted to mean a complete exemption from taxes.[33] The term *śulka-kara-vādha-parihāraḥ* is indicative of the freedom of the donee from the obligation of the payment of the tolls or customs[34] and the dues to be realised by the king.[35]

Terms such as *abhyantarasiddhi* (IIB, xi, 41), *tribhogābhyantarasiddhi* (IIB, xi, 64), *samstādeyasahitaṁ* (IIB, xi, 140), *nidhi-nikṣepa-jala-pāṣāṇādisahitaṁ* (IIB, xi, 131) *śulkadaṇḍādisahitaṁ* (IIB, xi, 131) have been used to describe the various economic rights transferred to the donee for the usage of various kinds of property of the grant. The term *abhyantarasiddhisahitaṁ* is indicative of the rights conferred on the donee over the internal income, revenue or taxes payable to the village authorities as against those payable to the king.[36] The term *tribhogābhyantarasiddhi* has been interpreted to mean the right to enjoy one-third of the revenue, the other two parts going in equal shares to Gods and the *brāhmaṇa.*[37] The term *samastādeyasahitaṁ* has been interpreted as a grant made with the rights over every kind of income.[38] *Nidhi-nikṣepajala-pāṣāṇādisahitaṁ* are the terms used to indicate the rights conferred on the donee over the hidden property, namely the rock and the water resources mentioned in the grant.[39] Further, while the term *suṁka* has been interpreted in the general sense of a tax, the term *daṇḍa* is indicative of the income derived from fines.[40]

Apart from the above mentioned economic rights conferred on the donees in major grants cited above, we also have certain juridical immunities attached to them which can be considered tantamount to transferring almost all proprietory rights over to the donees. These are conveyed to us through the use of such terms as *tejaḥsvāmya* (IIC, xi, 163, 164). This has been explained to denote the rights of ownership endowed with full authority which resulted from *aṣṭabhōga* (IIC, xi, 163, 164) or the eight kinds of enjoyment.[41]

It would be pertinent to state here that in the context of our study, among the recipients of beneficial tenures, it is the brahmanical temples that out number the individual *brāhmaṇa* donees[42] throughout our period and sub-regions of study as can be gauged from the charts appended to the chapter (IIA, B, C, v). During this period out of the 164 inscriptions charted by us, we have only 25 instances of individual *brāhmaṇa* donees. Further, in the grants which were made predominantly to the temples very rarely have all the extensive immunities cited above. Out of 144 instances of grants made to the temples, we have only 38 grants of villages, and of these, as few as 2 inscriptions have all the immunities cited above (IIB, xi, 140, 142). It is significant to note here that both these grants are made towards the end of the 12th century A.D. and that too, by the newly emerging, main ruling families such as the Yādavas of Devagiri and the Hoyasalas of Dwārasamudra. Prior to this, we have another instance of the grant of a village to a *brāhmaṇa* with extensive immunities (IIB, xi, 131), by another newly emerging main ruling family, namely, the Kalāchuris of Kalyāni, It would be pertinent to state here that even towards the beginning of the 11th century A.D., when for instance, the village Ummachige of sub-region B, was converted into a *sarvanamasya agrahāra* with 104 *mahājanas,* the shares of land allotted in it were however, directed in majority to the temple establishment located in that settlement.[43] It is interesting to note here that nearly 300 *mattars* of land was set apart along with several house sites for the upkeep of the temples and the ascetics and their pupils. On the other hand, the *ūroḍeya* of the village was given 200 *mattars* as *mānya* land along with the grant of certain taxes and further, one house-site each was set apart for the *gāvuṇḍas* and the chief men of the lowcaste.[44] This typical example of the creation of an *agrahāra* settlement is on the one hand, indicative of the differential nature of land holding patterns within the *brāhmaṇa* villages and on the other, of the growing importance of the temple institutions with a viable economic base even within the *agrahāra* settlements.

It is however, pertinent to note at this juncture that not all the beneficial land holdings granted to the *brāhmaṇas* and the temple institutions were always exempt from the payment of revenue to the state. We have, in this context, numerous examples indicative of the payment of certain dues by these beneficiaries at some point or the other. As early as A.D. 995 in an inscription from the sub-region B three *mattars* of garden land and red soil land were granted to the temple of Mūlasthāna for which *aruvaṇa* of 12 *gadyānas* was to be paid.[45] The *aruvaṇa* is considered to be in the nature of a quit rent payable to the authorities at a concessional rate.[46] Further, we have an interesting reference to the imposition of *kara,*[47] ranging from 7 *paṇas* to 2 *gadyānas* depending upon the amount of the land granted to certain temples. This grant dated to A.D. 1049 belonged to the sub-region A.[48] Similarly, in an inscription from sub-region B of A.D. 1123, 500 *brāhmaṇa* donees were to pay the owner of the land which was granted four hundred gold pieces in the form of quit-rent.[49] In an inscription of A.D. 1155 of the sub-region B we have reference to a certain *suṁka* (tax) levied on God's garden.[50] We again have in the same sub-region reference to a certain tax termed *bīravaṇa* which was levied on the garden of one particular temple and was granted to another temple by the local functionaries in an inscription of A.D. 1173.[51]

It is, however, to be underscored that we get to know about various revenue impositions and their nature chiefly in the context of the grants being made in the beneficial tenures. It is in the context of their study that we come across an important section of the land holding pattern, namely, the non-beneficial tenures held by a majority of the donors making grants of land and revenues to the temples and their allied institutions such as the *maṭhas,* tanks and ascetics, sometimes inclusive of the *brāhmaṇas.* Among the donors of this category, we have various groups in society consisting of the lesser chiefs and functionaries of the state, professional groups such as artisanal bodies and other such groups such as *teligas* (oil mongers), *sālega* (weavers), *mālegāra* (garland makers), *okkaḷus* (agriculturists), *kumbāra* (potters), *nāviḍa* (barbers), and so on which are cited occasionally. Lastly, merchants and merchant guilds figure prominently in the grants of various measurements of land made predominantly to the temple institutions during our period of study.[52] It is in the context of the non-beneficial tenures held by the above groups prior to their donation to beneficiaries that it has been stated that these people "enjoyed just customary rights and privileges and were subject to normal governmental revenue assessment".[53] It has been further contended that "those persons liable to the payment of land revenue had extensive property rights and that the term land owner could be applied to them".[54] These authors have made these conclusions chiefly on the basis of a study of non-*brahmadeya* tenures under the Chola rulers. One may argue here that the assumptions that non-*brahmadeya* or non-beneficial holdings were subject to normal governmental assessment can be shown to be equally relevant to the tenures of the region under consideration.

As is indicated in the charts (IIA, B, C, xi) we find that a majority of the grants made by the lesser chiefs and other dominant social groups were transformed to being revenue free *(sarvanamasya, sarvabādhaparihāraṁ)* after they were granted to the temples. This would then entail the assumption that these tenures, before their donation, were subject to the payment of revenue. We have in this context mention of such revenue terms as *siddhāya* (IIB, x, 52), *aruvaṇa* (IIB, x, 62), *pannāya* (IIA, x, 19) *banniga-dere* (IIB, x, 126), *bīravaṇa* (IIA, x, 29), *manneyadere* (IIA, x, 15), *uṁbali* (IIB, x, 78) which are made prominently in the records under study. The *siddhāya* has been interpreted to mean fixed or previously settled *(siddha)* revenue *(āya)* of the state, generally deemed to be permanent in nature and levied on land, houses, shops *etc.*[55] *Pannāya* is equated to the revenue derived from an estate that is granted.[56] While *banniga-dere* was probably a tax levied on gardens and *bira-vana* is equated by scholars to the cess on betel leaves.[57] Further, *manneyadere* is considered a form of tax collected for a chieftain or ruler of a group of villages *(manneya)*.[58] *Uṁbalam* has been equated on the one hand, to internal properties and gifts of free allotments[59] on the other, it is equated to a tax paid towards meeting the expenditure of the service rendered by higher officials.[60] Apart from these taxes on land, we also have prominent mention of *suṁka* (IIC, x, 162) *daṇḍa* (IIB, x, 71), *hejjuṁka* (IIB, x, 86) and *vaḍḍarāvula* (IIC, x, 155) in the inscriptions of our study. *Suṁka,* understood in the general sense of a levy or a tax and figures in the inscriptions with other combinations such as *manneya-suṁka* (IIA, x, 15) which is charged by the immediate local authority,[61] *kuliya-suṁka* (IIB, x, 88) is equated to mean tolls charged per tree.[62] Another popular combination of *suṁka* is *pannāyada suṁka* (IIB, x, 109) and this is clubbed mostly with the term *daṇḍa* or revenue accruing from fines in the immunities of the grants (IIB, x, 131). *Hejjuṁka* described as a great toll or, a general levy[63] is supposed to be received by the intermediary between the king and the local chief.[64] Definition of *vaḍḍarāvula* tax has been understood as a toll on superior quality goods[65] but this does not hold good on all occassions as it is mentioned in various contexts of our study. We have an interesting example of it being levied on 18,000 *mattars* of land along with the *hejjuṁka* in an inscription belonging to sub-region B dated to 1146 A.D.[66] It is significant to note here that these latter taxes figure more prominently from the first quarter of the 12th century A.D. and often figure in the form of grants to the temples and their services.

While direct mention of the revenue terms is largely indicative of the nature of surplus appropriation by various levels of state, we however, get to know about the nature, or to be more specific, the stratified nature of rights held in the landed property in the context of the non-beneficial tenures chiefly through an analysis of the capacity with which various social groups figure in the tax structure and the tenurial pattern of the land grant economy.

In the context of our study the granting capacity and the contextual nature of the mention of the various social groups enables us to conclude upon the existence of different types of land rights in the non-beneficial tenures of the period of study. First of all, references to the *manneyas* as holders of *manneya sāmya* of villages,[67] sellers[68] and donors[69] of various measurements of land conclusively proves their superior hold over the landed property. The *gāvuṇḍas, heggaḍes* and the *pergaḍes* figure prominently as donors,[70] leasors[71] sellers[72] and protectors[73] of land grants. In particular, the *gāvuṇḍas* figure as a collective group of normally six persons, participating in various deeds.[74] They also emerge as the prominent owners of land and fields and their properties often formed distinct boundaries of the grants made.[75] Next to the chiefs, we have the mention of the *okkalus* who are referred to invariably as a corporate body of 50, 60, and 80 *okkalus*. The term *okkalus* has been equated to mean a cultivator.[76] They often figure in combination with the *gāvuṇḍas* as protectors of grants[77] and the grants were often being made at their request.[78] In this context we have interesting examples of both the *gāvuṇḍas* and the *okkalu* groups emerging as the tax or revenue payers. In an inscription of 1138 A.D. belonging to the sub-region B the *aruvaṇa* of one of the gardens of a *gāvuṇḍa* becomes the object of a grant to the temple.[79] In an earlier inscription of A.D. 1096 of the same sub-region, the *prabhus* and the *gāvuṇḍas* are granted several *mattars* of land by the local potentate and they are exempt from the payment of the taxes such as *mūligadere* and *uṁbali*.[80] In an inscription of A.D. 1050 in sub-region B, a body of 80 *okkalu* was exempted from the payment of *siddhāya* for a period of two years on account of the wreckage caused due to war.[81]

Individual ownership of landed property during this period is repeatedly attested to in recent historical works with regard to mainly the non-beneficial tenures. It is popularly opined in this regard that while the *agrahāra* holdings were held in common in other cases private ownership of land was in vogue.[82] That there existed private ownership of landed property during the period under study is well documented in the inscriptional sources of our study as well. In this context we have a variety of land owners mentioned throughout our study. Their ownership rights over land cannot however, be studies under a uniform heading. In such a situation one sees that first of all it is chiefly the main rulers and their family members that emerge as holders of extensive rights over land and villages under their control. Thus, we find that the grant of villages and large measurements of land was often made either by the main rulers or, their kith and kin. In an inscription of A.D. 1027, belonging to sub-region B, we have a royal princess granting about 100 *mattars* of land to a Jaina temple.[83] In an earlier inscription of A.D. 1022 belonging to sub-region A, the royal princess Akkādevi, converts a village into a *sarva-namasya agrahāra.*[84] At a much later date in A.D. 1107, of sub-region C the queen of the main ruler seems to have granted four villages to a local temple. Some shares of this land in these villages were also allotted to the *āchāryas* of the temple by the queen separately.[85] These and several other grants made by the main rulers themselves, a few of which were attached with extensive immunities,[86] give us the impression that this category of social groups, despite their small numbers, had a firm hold over landed property both in administrative and economic terms. It is significant to underscore here that we have at the same time a few instances of grants of villages made by the main rulers, wherein the nature of rights granted highlight for us the limited nature of their enjoyment in terms of absolute ownership rights. We have in this context an interesting example of A.D. 1060 from sub-region B in which, after the grant of a village was made over by the main ruler to a local temple with its title deed, we have mention to the grant of the *manneya* (revenue) of the same village by a different group, namely the *manneyars* of the village. The latter seem to have had hereditary rights of revenue collection over the village granted which they relinquished in this case after its grant by the main ruler.[87] We have a similar instance in sub-region A from an inscription dated to A.D. 1075, wherein a village was granted by the main ruler to one temple and its *manneya sāmya* (revenue rights) were granted to a different temple by one Chandarasa who might have held the title of a *manneyar.*[88]

It is in the context of the landed rights held by the *manneyars* who, in most cases, emerge as the local potentates with the titles of *mahāmaṇḍaleśvaras* and *mahāsāmantādhipatis,*[89] that we come across a clear stratum of a land owning group at a supra-local level. In about A.D. 1053, in an inscription belonging to sub-region B we find that a Sinda prince made a grant of a field of 12 *mattars* out of his own *śivāta.*[90] In another inscription of the same sub-region, dated to A.D. 1077, we have the mention of the hereditary ownership of a particular region *(tamma kadambānvaya vaṁśada teṁgolida manneya sāmyaṁ)*, which was granted to a temple by the Kadamba chieftain.[91] At a much later date *i.e.,* in A.D. 1114, also in sub-region B, we have another instance of a grant of 1000 *mattars* of land to a local temple granted by the local potentate out of *mānya* holding belonging to his *śivāta.*[92] It is significant to note here that this group emerges more actively in the context of the grants made in sub-region B (IIB, iv, 33-80) and C (IIC, iv, 146-161), particularly during the 11th century A.D. We find in this context that while the ownership rights of the local potentates in sub-region B in certain instances at least are stated clearly, those of the sub-region C are not defined in a similar way. This could be chiefly because the local potentates of the sub-region C, unlike this group in sub-region B, did not have their origins in that area but had come to it from elsewhere, namely, in the Andhra region.[93] The grants of villages and large measurements of land that some of these groups made in sub-region C, at times, were attached with extensive immunities (IIC, xi, 153, 156, 157, 160, 161) and this therefore is clearly indicative of the firm economic hold that the local potentates had in this area which they came to settle in.

In the context of sub-region A (IIA, iv, 1-32) throughout the period of study we find that the local functionaries and lesser chiefs predominate the scene as land owners in their respective localities. In the context of sub-region B they emerge into prominence during the 12th century A.D. (IIB, iv, 81-145). It is among these social groups that we find the third strata of the land owning group emerge in the form of *gāvuṇḍas, heggaḍes, pergaḍes, prabhus, nāyakas* and so on. It is characteristic of grants made by these groups to the temple institution that they can make these grants in a majority of instances in terms of small measurements of lands and gardens. In this context we have distinct references being made to various functionaries as owners of land whose fields frequently form the boundaries of the grants made. In an inscription of A.D. 1049 from sub-region A the fields of one Bhoga-Gāvuṇḍa surround the land granted to a local temple.[94] In another inscription of the same sub-region belonging to A.D. 1079, we have the mention of the fields of one Kovara Gāvuṇḍa which form one of the boundaries for grant made.[95] In the context of sub-region B in an inscription of A.D. 1005, we have reference to the grant of a garden made out of the fields of one Siri Gāvuṇḍa.[96] It is however, from the beginning of the 12th century A.D. mainly in sub-region B that we find increasing references being made to the landed properties of the *gāvuṇḍas* and the *nāyakas* either, as boundaries or, as a part of it being the object of the grants made. Thus, in an inscription of A.D. 1103, the *hejjuṁka* tax of the *toṁṭa* (garden) of two *nāyakas* forms the object of the grant.[97] In A.D. 1104 in an inscription of the same sub-region, we have several instances of landed properties of various *gāvuṇḍas (gāvuṇḍa volada),* that formed boundaries to the grants made.[98] Apart from the above functionaries who figure as landowners (known in inscriptions through their designations and/or titles), we also come across certain significant references to landowners who figure collectively, and at times, even individually, but hold no designation or title. In the former category of a landowning group we have an interesting instance in an inscription of A.D. 1022 from sub-region A in which reference is made to a flower garden which was supposed to have belonged to 500 houses.[99] In a much later inscription of A.D. 1174 from sub-region B we have reference to the fields of the *prabhus* and *praja* (people) of a particular village which form the object of the grant.[100] Among the individual landowners we have reference in an inscription of A.D. 1080 from sub-region B to one Mābalayya, whose 12 *mattars* of wet land was made exempt from payment of the *benniṛke* tax.[101] In another inscription of the same sub-region dated to A.D. 1088, we have an interesting example of a person named Alva, who figures as the owner of some pasture land. Further, in another example the landed property of a certain individual was acquired by him as the share having been given to him as the eldest son *(jesṭhāṁśada bhūmi)* formed one of the boundaries of the land grant made in the inscription.[102] Between the period A.D. 1139 to A.D. 1149, in an inscription from sub-region B, we have reference to the field of the son of one Tippaya Nāyaka which forms the boundary of the grant made.[103]

Evidence of the latter kind namely, ownership rights as an individual, pertinently raise the question of the rights of inheritence that an individual had within his family structure. In the patriarchal system of inheritence for which the guidelines laid by the Mitākshara are followed for a major part of our country, the ownership rights were supposed to belong to all males descended lineally from a common ancestor upto four generations.[104] In such a system, the sons and the grandsons acquired the rights of ownership at the time of birth itself and it became difficult to partition the property without the consent of the parents.[105] It was only in sitution where the person died without any male issue that, the women come into the picture of inheriting property as wives and daughters of the deceased.[106] In the context of our study while, the evidence for the male ownership of property overwhelms us as has been observed in the above survey, we also have considerable allusions to the proprietory rights held by women over various shares of land. In this context we have reference to a variety of women such as the queens, wives of local potentates, wives of the functionaries and the temple girls. Interestingly, we find here that while the former three categories figure in the capacity of donors, the fourth group emerges chiefly in the form of donees.

The queens of the main ruling family outnumber the other women in the capacity of donors. In this regard for sub-region A, we have two instances of the sister of the main ruler (IIA, iv, 3, 9) who makes grants of a village and some land to temples and *brāhmaṇas* during the 11th century A.D. For sub-region B we again have two instances of the grants of land made by the daughter of the main ruler (IIB, iv, 46) and by the queen (IIB, iv, 48) during the 11th century A.D. In the context of sub-region C too we have come across in the first quarter of the 12th century A.D. two instances of grants of villages and land by the queens of the main ruling family (IIC, iv, 163, 164). We have only one instance of the mention of the wife of a local potentate in the capacity of the donor. In this case, the inscription belonging to sub-region B and dated to A.D. 1171, refers to one Siriyadevi, wife of a Sinda chief renewing the grant of a village made to a local temple along with her minor princes.[107] We have a couple of instances of wives of the functionaries as donors for various sub-regions and periods of study. In A.D. 1033 in sub-region A we have reference to one Bālikabbe Gauḍi, the wife of a *heggaḍe* who makes the grant of some land and a house site to a local temple.[108] For sub-region B in an inscription dated to A.D. 1102 we have reference to the wife of one Chāvuṇḍamayya who makes the grant of some land along with her husband to a local tank.[109] We further have references to women who belong to different social backgrounds and figure in the capacity of donors. In this context, we have reference to one *telliga* (oil monger) Jakiyabbe who makes a grant of some land to a *satra* in A.D. 1091 in an inscription from sub-region B.[110] In the same sub-region reference is made to one *gauṇḍi,* who along with some professional groups, grants some taxes to a temple in A.D. 1173.[111] In sub-region C Chākamma, the wife of a doorkeeper of a local potentate makes the grant of some land to a local God in A.D. 1151.[112]

At the other end of a the economic structure, namely, those women who figure as donees, we have the prominent mention of the temple girls. The temple girls are almost always referred to in the context of the temples in which they were appointed and it was in this capacity that this group emerges as the donees of a part of the main grant made to the temple institution. It is significant to note here that we have the mention of the temple girls in the inscriptional sources of our study chiefly in the context of the grants made during the 11th century A.D. located in sub-regions A and B. In an inscription of A.D. 1004 in sub-region A the *sūḷeya,* or the dancing girls, were given about 30 *mattars* of land along with the drummers of the temple.[113] In an inscription of sub-region B dated to A.D. 1054, we have interesting reference to the differential shares allotted to various types of dancing girls belonging to the temple by several functionaries of the place. We have here particular references made to dancing girls such as those who belonged to the *pergaḍe* the fan bearing dancing girls and those standing near the pillars of the temple and so on. It is significant to note here that while the first category in this instance were granted the maximum share, 14 *mattars,* the second group received 13 *mattars* and the third received the least, 12 *mattars* individually.[114] Thus the differential shares allotted to these groups depended upon the level of their hierarchical position in the temple establishment. It is significant to note in this regard that the few references to temple that we have, were almost always patronised by the functionaries. This must have been one of the reasons for their absence in the inscriptions of sub-region C. Further, the complete disappearance of this group from the inscriptions of the 12th century A.D., even in sub-regions A and B has been attributed to the increasing powers of priestly office and rituals in the temple precincts.[115] This marginalised the direct mention of the temple girls in the inscriptions as now their role was subsumed by their mention through a ritual or performance they were expected to do. Nevertheless, the shares of land allotted to the dancing girls as a part of the temple institution enables us to conclude upon the nature of rights held by them. Landed property owned by them was extremely limited and most commonly they shared in maintenance grants that were given to the temple or to the dancing and singing party as a whole.

In contrast to the temple girls who were mainly donees, men and women as donors of various shares in land, emerge as owners of land with distinct rights of private ownership, which, among others, included the right to sale, purchase and, gift[116] the landed property. We have considerable references to the sale-purchase deeds of land particularly in the context of sub-region B. As early as 994 A.D. in this sub-region, the *nalgāvuṇḍa* purchases a *tomṭa* (garden) for the purpose of granting.[117] In another early inscription of A.D. 1022 belonging to the same sub-region, the royal queen is supposed to have obtained land from one Lokāditya, the *manneyar,* for the purpose of making a grant.[118] It is however, only towards the beginning of the 12th century A.D., in sub-region B, that we find an accentuation of the mention of sale deeds in the context of the land of the *gāvuṇḍas.* In an inscription of A.D. 1100, a Śaiva priest is supposed to have obtained some land from one Molleya Saṁka Gāvuṇḍa.[119] In another inscription of the sub-region B in A.D. 1109, we have an important reference to the purchase of some land *(bhōgabhūmiyiṁ ponnum koṭṭumāru-koṇḍu)* from two *gāvuṇḍas* by paying gold coins.[120] In an inscription of A.D. 1191 for the same sub-region, a land of 100 *mattars* was purchased from the *prabhus* by the *mahāmaṇḍaleśvara* for the purpose of making a grant.[121]

The growth in the individual's share of landed property among the rich peasantry *(gāvuṇḍas, prabhus, heggaḍes,* and so on) can be easily discerned in the transformation of this social group, who up to the middle of the 12th century A.D. particularly in sub-region B, figured predominently as donors in a collective and official capacity, but later, emerged in an individual capacity as donors of relatively smaller measurements of land.[122] For instance, in the grants of the 11th century A.D. it was mostly the grants made by groups of six gāvuṇḍas which found frequent mention. We have in this early period very few references to individual *gāvuṇḍas* who figure as donors. In A.D. 1100 we have reference to one Mārasinga Gāvuṇḍa who makes a grant of 24 *mattars* of land.[123] We have another such instance in A.D. 1103, wherein one Nāki Gāvuṇḍa figures as a donor of two gardens and two fields.[124] From the period A.D. 1109 to about A.D. 1125, we have three instances of grants made by groups of 8 *gāvuṇḍas*[125] and 6 *prabhus.*[126] From about A.D. 1148 we have nearly four instances of individual *gāvuṇḍas* as donors. In an inscription of A.D. 1148, one Hollagāvuṇḍa renews an earlier grant of land.[127] In A.D. 1153, we have one Joga Gāvuṇḍa who makes a grant of 5 *mattars* of land.[128] In A.D. 1155 we again have one Hollagāvuṇḍa granting one *mattar* of land income from a garden.[129] In another instance from an inscription of A.D. 1156, we have a Joga Gāvuṇḍa as the donor of one *mattar* and 350 *kamma* (less than a mattar)[130] of land.[131] Most of these donations and grants were made to the temple. It is pertinent to note here that impingement over earlier held communal rights of property in land can be easily discerned in the growing fragmentary nature of the grants and the increase in individual donors particularly towards the middle of the 12th century A.D. Coupled with the above evidence, the fact that the legal texts of the period such as the writings of the commentator, Vigñānesvara have laid elaborate rules of inheritance and sub-division of landed property,[132] establishes the case of rights of private individuals over land.

In contrast to the non-beneficial tenures and their privatization, it is commonly believed that the lands were held in common in brahmanical villages or *agrahāras* where the scope for sub-division is supposed to have been limited.[133] In the context of the above statement it is significant to note here that the *brāhmaṇas* themselves (who figured in the pre-11th century A.D. as the major donees) begin to make extensive grants of large measurements of land to the temple institutions which were built in their *agrahāra* settlements. We have as many as 17 instances (IIA, iv, 7, 18 and so on, IIB, iv, 59, 61, 70, 71, 73, 74 and so on) of the grants made by them often as a collective group of *mahājanas,* as recorded in the charts and we notice that they are on the increase towards the end of the 11th century A.D. For instance, in an inscription of sub-region B dated to A.D. 1077, a grant of villages was made to a *brāhmaṇa* belonging to the *kaśyapa gotra* by the main ruler. This donee then allotted large measurements of land within these settlements to the God Svayambhu.[134] In another inscription of A.D. 1088, large measurements of land were made over by a *brāhmaṇa* out of the village presented earlier to his grand father to the temple of God Someśvara established by him.[135] Between the period A.D. 1080-1100 itself we have as many as 6 instances of grants that were made by the *mahājanas* and *brāhmaṇas* (IIB, iv, 70, 71, 73, 74, 75, 83). According to Heitzman, as a result of this trend, "over time, the resources of the *brahmadeya* tended to move slowly into the deities in important local temples",[136] the process of which "occured through the progressive alienation of shares by individual *brāhmaṇas* as personal acts of piety... through sales to secular donors who then bestowed the land on the temples".[137] We also have several instances of sales of land by *mahājanas* for the purpose of making grants. As early as A.D. 1037, in an inscription of sub-region B, we have reference to the sale of 56 *mattars* of land by the *ūroḍeya* (head of the *mahājanas*) from the fields of the *ūroḍeya (ūrodeya volada*) for granting to a temple.[138] We however, have increasing references to the sales of the land by the *mahājanas* towards the end of the 11th century A.D., particularly in the context of sub-region B. Thus, we have an important reference to the donor, a *mahājana* himself purchasing land from his group of *mahājanas* for the purpose of granting it to a temple in an inscription dated to A.D. 1087.[139] This effectively indicates to us the collective hold that the *mahājanas* had over the landed property of their *agrahāras*. Between the period A.D. 1091 to about A.d. 1189, we have nearly four instances of sale and purchase deeds between the *mahājanas* and secular donors to the temples and in almost all these cases the *mahājanas* are referred to in groups. The nature of evidence furnished by us with regard to the land holding pattern in the *agrahāra* settlements however, stand directly in contrast to the conclusions arrived at by N. Karashima for early medieval Tamilakam wherein the author observes that the *brahmadeyas* were characterized by private land holdings, while the non-*brahmadeyas* by communal land holding pattern.[140]

One of the major implications of the land grants made throughout the period in various sub-regions of our study by different social groups discussed above, is the enormous growth in the politico-economic power of the temple institution. It emerges as a major donee (IIA, B, C, 1-165) during our period of study and consequently, as a landlord wielding tremendous economic power through the control it exercised over the economic resources at its disposal. In this context the role of the temple gradually began to be that of the State too, in that it began to assign taxes, collect revenues, get land cultivated and so on. It is pertinent to underscore in this regard that we have no data on the actual collection perse of revenue by the temple institution in the inscriptional sources of our study. But we have, on the other hand, considerable references to the grants of various types of revenue to the temple particularly from the latter half of the 11th century A.D. onwards (IIA, x, 10-32, IIB, x, 58-145, IIC, x, 146-165) which must have armed them with wide powers to collect revenue and redistribute resources. It is chiefly in the realm of the management of temple establishments in the form of *sthānāpatis, mahāsthānādhipatis* and *āchāryas* as the major trustees of the grants made to the temples, that the *brāhmaṇas* now begin to wield extensive power. In this regard, we have a few instances of the rights exercised by this group over the land donated to temple for various sub-regions of our study. In an inscription of A.D. 1014, we have reference to the sale of 10 *mattars* of land by the *sthānāchāryas* of a temple for the purpose of granting it to the temple.[141] In A.D. 1055 of sub-region C, a grant of 100 *mattars* of land of land was made by a *mahāsthānādhi*/ *pati* of a temple to an individual donee.[142] In A.D. 1100 in sub-region A, an inscription registers a grant of 4 *mattars* of land made by the *āchārya* of a temple for the upkeep of a tank.[143] Extensive economic hold that all the above land lords (social groups as donors and temples as donees) had, also placed them in a position to command advantages over the productive processes.

Primarily, control and use of labour for effective cultivation of land and other productive purposes becomes a crucial factor in the exercise of dominance by the different types of landowners. In the absence of any direct references made to the groups actually involved in the productive processes, it leaves us to conclude upon their implied existence and their status on the basis of allusions made to them in the context of the way agricultural production was carried and also from an analysis of the tax terms and various rights conferred on the beneficiaries. First of all, we have instances of land being leased out by the religious establishments and functionaries to non-cultivating groups for managing the agricultural production. As early as A.D. 1010, in sub-region B, six *gāvuṇḍas* and eight *seṭṭis* of Suṇḍi leased out 114 *mattars* of land to the *mahājanas* on the condition of the payment of quit rent.[144] Further, at the payment of a quit rent of four *gadyānas,* certain land were leased out by a Jaina establishment to thirty *seṭṭis* in an inscription belonging to the same sub-region in A.D. 1071.[145] We further have an interesting reference to the grant of a village along with its hamlets, to about 500 *brāhmaṇas* in A.D. 1123 who, it was stipulated, had to pay a quit rent in the form of *piṇḍadāna,* of an amount of 400 gold pieces to the owner of the land.[146] The term *piṇḍadāna,* has been equated to mean lumpsum payment from tenants.[147] According to Kuppuswamy leasing helped in extensive cultivation as the tenants were bound by the agreement to keep the land continuously under a state of cultivation.[148] The lessees of land discussed above, were definitely not responsible for the direct cultivation of crops as is indicated by their social standing. This naturally implied the use of labour that was subjected to them for various tasks of cultivation.

In this context Kuppuswamy gives us enough evidence for 13th century A.D. southern Karnataka that attests to the fact that the cultivation was carried out by the *brāhmaṇas* with the help of tenant cultivators.[149] According to him, the latter were attached to one block or group of land and were not normally allowed to leave and migrate to other areas as this would upset the condition and practices that normally governed the lease.[150] In the context of our study too we have a few instances of references to the existence of a variety of labouring groups, particularly for sub-region B, who functioned under the control of different land owning conditions. In an inscription of A.D. 1075, mention is made of 'contract produce' (guttage) of wet land, the interest amount of which was stipulated to go for the services of the God.[151] This effectively indicates for us the employment of 'contract labour' for the cultivation of crops during the period of our study. Further, Gururajachar has brought notice to the term *kammaṭa,* which means an estate cultivated by land owners with his farming stock, but by the labour of others.[152] The author here surmises this as the positive evidence of the existence of hired labour during the early medieval period in Karnataka as a whole.[153] In a significant example of hired labour in an inscription of A.D. 1143, we have mention of a guild of gardeners/cultivators, *guleyu-300*, who make a grant of their wages (*bhattamāṁ*) to a local God.[154] This evidence strongly alludes to the existence of hired labour during the period of our study who seem to have been employed on the basis of daily wages for undertaking crop production.

It is significant to note here that on the basis of the nature of references made to the cultivating groups in our sources, their subject status has been interpreted considerably in the secondary sources of the period under study. In particular, the term *viṣṭi,* equated to mean forced labour or unpaid labour,[155] has been given considerable attention in these works. It is pertinent to note here that in the context of our study itself we have come across only a single reference to the term *biṭṭi (viṣṭi)* in an inscription of A.D. 1213 from sub-region B.[156] According to S.G. Ghatapanadi the mention of *viṣṭi* in the form of labour is not wanting in the sources of Karnataka.[157] His study focusses on the ancient and medieval contexts of the northern Karnataka region. In the works of G.K. Rai, we have several references to the prolific mention of the term *viṣṭi* in the literary texts right from the ancient times for India as a whole. According to the author the widespread prevalence of *viṣṭi* in the form of forced labour however got family entrenched only from the early medieval period.[158] The subject and servile status of the cultivating peasant groups located in the northern and western India during the early medieval period forms a topic of scrutiny in the works of B.N.S. Yadava. The author, in his work, cites several examples from both the literary and the epigraphic sources of the period that attest to the prevalence of dependant labour to work in the fields of rich peasants during the period under study.[159] R.S. Sharma in this regard has highlighted for us the issue of the transfer of cultivating groups along with the land granted by the donor to the donee in the context of particularly the northern and eastern India during the early medieval period itself.[160] It is pertinent to state here that Sharma's emphasis on the nature of the subjection of peasantry and the question of 'serfdom' which have been considered as essential traits of the 'Indian Feudalism' concept, were based chiefly on Chinese travellers account and to some extent on the epigraphic evidence of the transfer of people along with the land granted.[161] It is pertinent to bring here a couple of direct references to the existence of servile groups in an inscription dated to A.D. 1080 in the context of sub-region B of our study which attests to the prevalence of servile groups attached to the land granted. In this instance there is mention of *bhritya-dāsivargga* (man and women servants) who were granted along with the land to a temple by a *mahājana.*[162] In the same inscription we also have the mention of the *devargge parichārika* (servants of the God). In the absence of any prolific evidence of above type, one cannot definitely conclude upon the existence of the notion of 'serfdom' perse as one of the forms of dependant peasantry in the context of our study. What one has been trying to drive at, with the help of examples cited above is however, that we have considerable proof to show that there did exist different types of dependent peasant groups who provided labour for production purposes to the non-cultivating groups in region and period of our study. In particular, it has been aptly observed in this context, that the subject and the servile status of the labour generally got accentuated as a result of the growth in the private land holdings at this time.[163] We have already discussed earlier that an increase in private land holdings and their fragmentation had taken place in south-western Deccan as well.

During this period, one has, already discussed the fact that the system of making grants led to the creation of a new landed elite who began to claim a considerable share in the surplus appropriation of the produce. Further, the granting of various politico-economic immunities along with several tax benefits to these beneficiaries, armed them with sufficient power to exercise considerable authority over the use of dependent labour. It is significant to note in such a context that all the above cited examples of the cultivating and labouring groups belong to the grants that refer to beneficial tenures attached with immunities of particular tax benefits. It becomes pertinent to state here that it is chiefly in relation to the imposition of the taxes and revenue extractions from the peasant cultivators that various secondary works have highlighted the subject nature of the peasantry during the early medieval period. In Sharma's own words "subjection of peasantry in early medieval times, ... can be explained by several factors, the most important of which was increase in the burden of taxation on the villagers".[164] The system of taxation during the early medieval complex has been considered to be most oppressive in nature with its long list of taxes mentioned in the sources of the period. As articulated by Gururajachar, with regard to early medieval Karnataka, "the outstanding feature which has bewildered students of history and still bewilders us in the study of these documents, is the formidable list of taxes.[165] In the context of our study too, we have a considerably long list of tax terms as a subject of donation in the inscriptions. Among these, the more frequently mentioned, are such terms as *aruvaṇa* (IIB, x, 62, 82, 102 and so on), *manneya* (IIA, x, 13, 15, IIB, x, 58, 112 and so on), *pannāya* (IIA, x, 15, 19, 29, IIB, x, 106, 109 and so on), *siddhāya* (IIA, x, 21, IIB, x, 52), *hejjuṁka* (IIB, x, 86, 106, 110) and *vaḍḍarāvula* (IIB, x, 108, IIC, x, 155). All these tax terms indicated various shares in revenue collection as can be judged from the meanings attributed to each of these terms. The term *aruvaṇa* signified a tax levied on *mānya* land amounting to about six *paṇas* in share.[166] *Manneya,* is normally suffixed with the term *suṅka* and has been equated to mean a tax collected by a local chieftain.[167] The term *pannāya* could be understood in the sense of revenue derived from the land granted[168] which is equated to about fifty percent in share to produce.[169] *Siddhāya* is understood in the general sense of a fixed land revenue.[170] The terms *vaḍḍarāvula* and *hejjuṁka* on the other hand, have been understood in the general sense of revenue and, when attached to land or garden, only meant income derived from them.[171] Apart from the above, we have several more tax terms that figure in the inscriptional sources of our study and have specific meanings attached to them. Among these we have the prominent mention of such taxes as those imposed on labour such as *biṭṭi (viṣṭi)*, on haystack such as the *bannigadere* (IIB, x, 126), on the plough such as *meṅṭe* (IIB, x, 88), on the harvest such as *kuliyasuṅka* (IIB, x, 88) along with other terms such as *sugapana* (IIB, x, 104), *bīrapana* (IIB, x, 104) and *mūligadere* (IIB, x, 78). Of these *bīrapaṇa* is translated either as soldier's tax or, as tax on betel leaves, *mūligadere* could be interpreted as the tax levied on the original owner or occupant of some property. According to G.S. Dikshit the term *mūliga* denoted the original owner of some land[172] and the term *'dere'* is equated to mean a tax.[173] In the context of sub-region C we do not have any significant reference to specific terms of taxes except the term *vaḍḍarāvula.* But significantly there is prolific mention of the grant of cash income accruing from the villages along with a mention of extensive immunities granted to the donees. These instances effectively attest to the extractions of surplus in the context of sub-region C (IIC, x, 146-165) the pattern of which is different from that described above for sub-regions A and B. The detailed list of taxes enumerated were oppressive in nature in the sense that they left hardly any arena of agricultural production untouched. There was further, little scope for the peasant cultivators to function in an atmosphere free of landlords or lease holders control. In particular, it is significant to note here, that one sees a relative growth in the number of taxes from the end of 11th century A.D. in the context of sub-region A (IIA, x, 15-32) and B (IIB, x, 77-165). This trend seems to be corresponding to the grant of smaller measurements of land consequent upon the growth in private land holdings. Apart from the above discussed tax terms, the rights conferred on the donee over the collection of the *daṇḍa* (IIB, x, 41, 67, 71) or fines, must have armed him with considerable authority over the extraction of labour and other resources. The extensive immunities granted to the temple institutions in particular, bestowed full proprietory rights to the elite groups enabling them to command the advantages of the production processes of the time to their optimum level. In such conditions, one can conclude that a category of peasants probably possessed land but were compelled to pay rent in cash, kind or labour to the land lords and function in response only to the needs of the land lord.[174]

Apart from the use of labour and its management for increasing the productivity by the landlords, important economic measures were adopted by them to improve the techniques of production which led to a very significant change in socio-economic set up of the period, especially from the early part of the 12th century A.D. onwards. Growth in the knowledge of irrigation techniques, types of soils and the consequent growth in crop production, form significant features of the changing agrarian scenario of the period under consideration.

First of all, one can easily gauge from the inscriptional sources available, that there was serious concern to expand and improve agricultural production during our period of study. These efforts were expressed primarily in the care taken for classifying the available land under different heads depending upon the nature of soil and the attempts to reclaim waste land for agricultural purposes through the grants. In the context of our study we find that the concept of taking into consideration the nature and types of soil formed a dominant feature in all the three sub-regions throughout the period. In the context of sub-region A we have frequent mention of the cultivated area in the sense that reference is often made to rice land *(sālyakshetra),*[175] and *gadde* (wet) land,[176] which alluded to the existence of a tank or river in its neighbourhood. Reference is also made to the waste land under reclamation in a couple of instances located from inscriptions dated to the middle of the 11th century A.D. In an inscription of A.D. 1047 waste land forms part of the grants made.[177] Further, in another inscription of A.D. 1049 we again have the mention of *vyudhabhūmi* (waste land) which is made as a grant.[178] In the latter case it is interesting to note that we have the imposition of a certain amount of *kara* (tax) on the land granted which differed for different types of land. Thus, while one *gadyāna* was charged on the waste land granted, two *gadyānas* were charged for the land located above a river. It is however, in the context of the sub-region B that we get introduced to a variety of soil types among the granted land. We have here significant references to *kariyanela* (black soil),[179] *gadde* (wet) land,[180] *kisukāḍu* (red soil),[181] *pasalu* (pasture land)[182] and *takkilu* (un-ploughed land)[183] as objects of grants. It is pertinent to note here that it were chiefly the red and black soils that dominated the scene in sub-region B. In an inscription of A.D. 1178 of the same sub-region, we have a detailed description of the nature of soil *kemmanna kuṇi* (red soil site) which is praised a great deal for its long lasting fertility. It is stated accordingly that however much the earth is removed from that spot of the soil, by digging pits, it maintains its ground level.[184] In a much earlier inscription dated to A.D. 1025, the revenue amount was fixed according to the nature of the soil. In this context, while one *mattar* of black soil *(kariya keyi)* land was to yield five *paṇas* of revenue, one *mattar* of red soil *(kisukaḍ)* was to pay one *paṇa.*[185] This particular instance exemplified the superior nature of the quality of black soil over the others. It has however been suggested that the fertility of the red and the black soil land depended in a large measure on the nature of the underlying rocks.[186] The moisture retention capacity of the black soil is supposed to be quite high but on the upland regions the soil remains shallow and is not very productive.[187] On the other hand, the fertility of the red soils depended upon its lime content and, except for the presence of this, they are supposed to be poor in fertility.[188] Efforts made by the rulers to extend cultivation into new areas enabled them to cover waste land too. This can be gauged from an inscription dated to A.D. 1178, wherein the grant of a village was made along with its waste area to the donee.[189] In a similar way, in the context of sub-region C too, we come across a variety of soil types as objects of the grants made. We have significant mention of such soil types as wet land *(regaḍy)*[190] *(galduge),*[191] dry land (*valgaḍlu),*[192] black soil *(kare nela)*[193] and red soil *(kisu mattar).*[194] In the context of the descriptions of various types of soils mentioned in the inscriptional sources of early medieval Karnataka, Kuppuswamy has aptly highlighted the fact that while the wet land were granted in small measurements, the drier ones were made over in larger measurements.[195]

Coupled with the attempts to categorize soil types and reclaim waste land, were the sincere efforts made by the landowning groups to provide irrigational facilities by building and maintaining tanks and wells in some cases to suit the dry climatic conditions of the area under study which was characterised in general by low rain fall.[196] Tanks, defined as hollow spaces in the ground partly or wholly artificial, created to hold the rain water throughout the year, seem to have emerged as principal means of irrigation during this period almost all over the southern Peninsula.[197] Ashok Shettar's work focussing on the early medieval southern Karnataka has attested to the increase in the references to tanks from the middle of the 11th century A.D. onwards in the inscriptional sources of his area of study.[198] In one of the significant works on a description of irrigation system of South India, with particular focus on the Tamilakam region, attention has been paid to the construction of wells as well along with the tanks which were supposed to have been initiated, from the Pallava period itself *i.e.,* from the 9th century A.D. onwards.[199] In the context of our study we find that the mention of tanks begins to gain momentum particularly in sub-region A (IIA, xii, 7-29) and B (IIB, xii, 53-127) from the middle of the 11th century A.D. It is significant to note here that we have at the same time no reference to any irrigation activity in the context of sub-region C. This could have been primarily due to the fact that the grants made in sub-region C were mostly made either by the local potentates who did not belong to that place or, by the members of the main ruling family without any great involvement of the locally entrenched functionaries in these matters. In fact, it were the local functionaries, as has been observed by us above, that played a prominent role in the grants that were made in sub-region A and B and as will be seen below they were also largely responsible for the construction and maintenance of irrigation structures in these sub-regions. It has been aptly suggested by Ramudu that these groups, "developed in the soils which were drained by the tanks... Tank irrigation in such situation became not only the source of power, but also symbol of authority.[200] The absence of the mention of tank building activity during the period of our study in sub-region C has been observed by other scholars as well. One such opinion refers to the fact that it was only from the time of the Kākatiya rulers, *i.e.,* from the 13th century A.D. onwards, that we find that construction of a considerable number of irrigation works picking up momentum in the Telangana region.[201] As a result of this tendency sub-region C seems to have emerged into largescale agrarian production, exhibiting tremendous potential to sustain large scale politico-economic activity, only from the post 12th century A.D. period.[202]

In the context of our study we find that the tanks (*gere*) and other irrigation sources *(bāvi, kāluva, samudra)* are mentioned either in terms of them forming boundaries to the lands granted or, they themselves emerge as objects of donation of the various grants in the context of their construction undertaken by various landowning groups. In an inscription of A.D. 1049 in sub-region A a river and a tank *(gaura-kere)* figure as boundaries to the lands granted.[203] In another inscription of the same sub-region in A.D. 1053, we have the grant of 20 *mattars* of land for the upkeep of a tank called *kelawāḍi* by a local functionary.[204] Again in sub-region A, a tank name *Sindāra-gere* formed a boundary to the grants made and recorded in an inscription of A.D. 1075.[205] In this way, between the period A.D. 1075 and 1187 for sub-region A we have as many as five instances of tanks either, as boundaries or, as objects of donation (IIA, xii, 13, 17, 18, 25, 29). In an inscription of A.D. 1119, for sub-region A, we have an interesting reference to the construction of a well *(bāvi)* by one *seṭṭi*.[206] In the sources of sub-region B we however, have reference to the construction and maintenance of irrigation works in a variety of contexts. As early as A.D. 1012, income accruing from various fines are directed towards the upkeep of a tank called 'deyimgere' after the formation of an *agrahāra*.[207] In A.D. 1022, we have reference to a well being constructed by a functionary.[208] We further have the mention of a local tank for the unkeep of which a grant of 13 *mattars* of black soil was granted by a functionary.[209] In an inscription of A.D. 1069, the queen herself gave some land for digging a well at her *bhaṭṭagrāma*.[210] In A.D. 1077, we have an interesting reference to one Annama Gavuṇḍa's tank, named after a functionary, which borders on the grants of the land made.[211] This attests to the fact that tanks were also privately owned. Thus, we have in the context of sub-region B between A.D. 1082 and 1184, reference to as many as 15 instances (IIB, xii, 71-133) of tanks and wells in the inscriptional sources of our study. Out of these, we have one very interesting reference made in a record dated to A.D. 1088, wherein after receiving the grant of a village, the *brāhmaṇa* donee founded a canal from the Tungabhadra river and planted and grew many trees alongside it. In this context we also have mention of several low level and high level canals *(Kāluva)* in this settlement.[212] This best exemplifies for us the amount of care that was taken for increasing land productivity with the help of important irrigation facilities and networks. For a primarily dry-region like south-western Deccan, these were essentially focussed on small scale irrigation works and these have been a continued means of sustaining agriculture in these parts till today.

Extensive use of irrigation methods and the knowledge of the effective use of various soils discussed above, naturally yielded good results in the form of an increase in the crop production and also diversification in cash crops. This can be deduced from examples, in particular towards the latter half of 11th century A.D., wherein surplus generation is clearly indicated in that people began giving various types of produce for purposes of religious consumption. In the inscriptional sources of the period we have increasing references to the betel leaves (IIB, viii, 80, 109) and areca nuts (IIA, viii, 10, 28) forming the objects of grants. These are cash crops necessary for use in the temple precincts and for popular consumption by the different classes of people. Apart from these, rice (IIB, viii, 137), wheat (IIB, viii, 88), paddy (IIB, viii, 70, 107) and other grains (IIB, viii, 121, 135) mentioned as items of donations, are only a few essential crops of the many names of crops mentioned during this period. The fact that there was an increase in the crop production of the period is attested by various scholars writing on the Karnataka region. Several types of rice both superior *(gaṇdhasāli)* and inferior *(khar)* have been described along with the mention of the availability of various spices such as cloves, camphor, pepper, turmeric, cardamoms during this period for Karnataka as a whole.[213] Apart from these, we further have references to the availability of various millets and pulses, ragi, jowar and sugarcane on the one hand and on the other, availability of coconuts and oranges as prominent fruit crops.[214] It is significant to note here that some of these items, particularly, betel leaves, areca nuts and coconuts gained great ritual significance and their wide prevalence during this period can be attributed to the increase in the patronage extended to the temple institution where many of the major rituals were performed.

One of the significant consequences of the extensive patronage given to the brahmanical temples by the landowning groups was the emergence of the temple itself into a major landlord with its efficient management of agricultural production and its appropriation. Alongside the temple institution, we have also seen that the period under study witnessed a marked growth in the private ownership of landed property. It is in the context of these positive initiatives exhibited by various land owning groups such as the rulers, rich peasantry, *brāhmaṇas* and the temple institution to extend and improve cultivation that we find that land grants became a means to reclaim new lands through the introduction of irrigation facilities on the one hand, and on the other, through the intensive use of labour which was often in the relation of subjection to the former. All these factors in turn had a significant bearing on changing the economic set up of the period. Firstly, these resulted in the generation of agrarian surplus on a considerable scale. Secondly, the appropriation and concentration of the above surplus in the hands of the landed elite enabled these groups to invest in commercial activity thus bringing about the tremendous economic change resulting in an urban like environment peculiar to the early medieval period. Changes in the economic setup can be comprehended chiefly through identifying a shift in the nature of the grants made to various sub-regions institutions particularly from the 12th century A.D. onwards for various religious of our study. A perusal through the inscriptions of the 11th century A.D. for sub-region A (IIA, vii, 1-18), sub-region B (IIB, vi, 33-83) and sub-region C (IIC, vi, 146-161) gives us an impression of a largely rural setting in which various measurements of land and villages were granted. On the other hand, one can easily discern a shift in the nature of the grants made particularly during the 12th century A.D. which significantly indicates a preponderance of grants in commodities and coins in sub-regions A (IIA, viii, ix, 19-32), B (IIB, viii, ix, 84-145) and C (IIC, viii, ix, 162-165). During the 11th century A.D. we have only occasional references to the grant of commodities, coins and merchants dealing with these, and as discussed below the mention of all these three aspects gained greater momentum only during the 12th century. Now, there is also an increased mention of mercantile guilds indicating the existence of *organised* trade, commercial taxes and metallic money along with the mention of the grants of commodities. In this context we would like to point out that we have reference to as few as only 11 instances of merchants and their activity during the 11th century A.D. This stands in contrast to their prolific mention in the 12th century A.D. during which the number goes upto about 42 instances. These merchants and their activities are mentioned extensively in terms of their formation into corporate guilds. They are often described in terms of 500 *svāmis,*[215] 18 *paṭṭaṇas,*[216] 8 *nāḍus,*[217] *ubhaya nānādeśi,*[218] *nānādeśi,*[219] *mummū ridaṇḍas,*[220] *mahānāḍu,*[221] 36 *bīḍus,*[222] and so on and as belonging to various *sthalas* such as Tumbula, Gabbūr, Maddūr, Ālampur and so on. The context of their mention strongly alludes to the latter being commercial centres as these are almost always associated with the merchant groups.

Most pertinently, we wish to highlight below that it is in the nature of the grants made by the above mentioned commercial groups that one can discern a significant change in the economy. This was expressed in the grant of various articles, levies and coins pertaining to trading activity. For instance, in an inscription of A.D. 1080 from sub-region B, trade guilds of the jowar shops were supposed to have granted various measurements of paddy levied from each shop to the local deity.[223] In an inscription from sub-region C dated to A.D. 1088, we have the merchant guilds granting income *(āya)* out of sales-purchases *(koṇḍalli-koṭṭalli)* along with a shop *(aṇgaḍi)* to a temple.[224] In another inscription from sub-region B in an inscription of A.D. 1105, we have reference to grants of levies of 5 areca nuts on sales of areca nuts and 25 betel leaves on each load.[225] In an inscription of A.D. 1207 from sub-region A, a grant of income from the sale purchase deeds is recorded.[226] Further, mention of grants of specific commercial tolls and taxes are also quite prolific in the context of our study (IIA, x, 28, 29, 32, IIB, x, 80, 84, 85, 88, 89 and so on). As early as A.D. 1056, in the context of sub-region C we have reference to the grant of specific tolls *(suṅka)* to a deity on various items of merchandise such as *karpūraṁ* (camphor), *paṭṭa-sūtraṁ* (silk thread), *śri khaṇḍakke, sakara* (sugar), *patti* (cotton) and so on. All these were levied on each unit of weight.[227] In an inscription of A.D. 1109 from sub-region B we have an interesting reference to various kinds of levies charged from the shopkeepers, transporters, miners, betel leaf sellers and so on who were to pay it mostly in terms of a *paṇa* (unit of money) on every specific measurement of their merchandise.[228] Further, in the same sub-region in an inscription of A.D. 1153, we get reference to the grant of taxes *(suṅka)* obtained on sales of certain commodities by various mercantile groups.[229] In the context of sub-region C in an inscription dated to A.D. 1182 we have a major reference to the grant of income derived from tolls on various transactions of sales and purchase *(koṭṭalli-koṇḍalli)* of such items as grains *(dhānya)*, areca nuts *(aḍake)* and so on.[230] Pertinently, the significant mention of transporters such as *sāriga okkala*[231] and *baṇḍiyaseṭṭi*[232] during this period which attests to the use of a certain organised means of transportation to move the articles of merchandise from one place to the other.

It is significant to note in this context that alongside the reference to commercial activity that can be deduced from the above examples, we have considerable number of direct references to the grant of metallic currency *(gadyāna, paṇa)* at least from the latter half of the 11th century A.D. for sub-region A (IIA, ix, x, 10 onwards), sub-region B (IIB, ix, x, 55, onwards) and sub-region C (IIB, ix, x, 150 onwards). B.D. Chattopadhyaya has aptly stated in this context that the epigraphic evidence for the coins in the Deccan region for the period which roughly starts with the consolidation of the western Chalukyan power in the Deccan and ends again with the restoration of the Chālukyan power by the rulers of Kalyāṇa is not as profuse as it is from the later Chālukyan period onwards.[233] In the context of our study we have ample evidence to substantiate the above statement. As early as A.D. 1005 in the sub-region B, we have a reference to the grant of 100 *gadyānas* of gold.[234] Such a trend can however, be seen on an increase particularly towards the close of the 11th century A.D. and the beginning of the 12tth century A.D. For sub-region B in an inscription of A.D. 1106, we have reference to a grant of the interest amount of 12 *paṇas* on 6 *gadyānas.*[235] In a similar reference from an inscription dated to A.D. 1112 for the same sub-region, one *paṇe* of interest amount was taken on 120 *gadyānas* and this was to be granted.[236] It is significant to note here that we have also increasing evidence for the collection of taxes and revenue in terms of cash from around the 12th century A.D. For instance, in an inscription dated to A.D. 1082 for sub-region C we have reference to the grant of 60 *gadyānas* out of the income due from a village (IIC, x, 158). In the context of sub-region A in A.D. 1085, we have reference to the grant of 5 *paṇas* out of the taxes *manneya suṅka* and *pannāya suṅka* (IIA, x, 15). In an inscription of the period between A.D. 1076-A.D. 1125, from sub-region B, we have reference to the levy of various taxes such as *gātuka, kiru kulaya* (petty toll) and so on over the potters, which were to be collected in terms of *gadyānas* and *paṇas.*[237] In an inscription dated to A.D. 1139 from sub-region A, the *siddhāya* of 10 *gadyānas* forms the object of the grant (IIA, x, 21). References made to the above instances of the use of coins in the context of various transactions cited, allude significantly to the prevalence of a monetized economic set up atleast from the 12th century A.D. onwards. In this regard, the mention of various minting establishments in our inscriptions sources further strengthen our contention. In an inscription of A.D. 1109 from sub-region B, we have mention of a minting establishment, *kammaṭa* along with its workers and officers to carry on the minting operations.[238] Care was supposed to have been taken to regulate the quality and standards of coins minted under different licenses.[239] In A.D. 1186, in the same sub-region reference is made to the grant of 5 *paṇas* out of the income from minting operations.[240] In this context our attention has been drawn by R.N. Nandi to the minting establishment at *Lokkuṇḍi* of the Dharwar district which issued coins known as *Lokkigadyāna, lokkipon, Lokkiya-visa.*[241]

Commercial activity described above by us has figured in the context of all the three sub-regions of our study. It is however, pertinent to underscore at this juncture that one has observed the commercial phenomenon as more marked in its nature and scale in the context of sub-region B. Variations of this nature in the sub-regional context can be linked up again to the agrarian scenario wherein the grant of various measurements of land and villages was found in a majority in the context of sub-region B. This sub-region had also witnessed a significant spurt in the creation of *agrahāras* and the temple institutions that played a crucial role in enhancing the agrarian produce from a mere subsistence level. Importantly, the strategic location of this tract amidst several streams provided an economically viable base to generate the surplus in agriculture which was a necessary prerequisite for the subsequent commercial and urban economic change.

The underlying economic change visible in the above description closely hinges upon the question of the nature of commercial growth during the later period of our study from predominantly agrarian activity during the earlier period. It is pertinent to note in this context that during the 11th and 12th centuries A.D. similar changes in the economic scenario have been witnessed for various other regions of India as well. For instance, R.S. Sharma speaks in terms of the revival of urban phenomenon from its earlier decadent state in the western and central India during this period.[242] Tarafdar on the other hand, has detailed for us the urban growth in the context of early medieval Bengal. He has, in this regard, described the monetized economic set up of the region which was supported by an elaborate currency system, prosperous urban centres with well developed commercial links.[243] R. Champakalakshmi's works have focussed on the commercial activity of the Tamilakam region during the Chola rule, *i.e.,* 11th and 12th centuries A.D.[244] What is significant to analyse in this context is whether one can consider the commercial spurt of the early medieval period with particular reference to our area of study, on par with the urban phenomenon witnessed in the Gangetic basin and the Deccan during the early historical period. Early historical urbanism was marked by a brisk trading activity on a sub-continental scale with a viable agrarian hinterland that enabled the commercial transactions to reach a certain level of complexity both in the internal and sea borne trade, as evidenced by the hoards of Roman coins and well developed sea routes connecting the early historic sites.[245] On the basis of the epigraphic evidence available for the commercial activity of the period under study for the various regions of India it has, however, been suggested by B.D. Chattopadhyaya that early medieval urbanism significantly differs from its early historical counterpart in the sense that unlike the earlier times the exchange networks of this period could not rise above its regional context. During early historical times, he argues, the commercial transactions took place on a subcontinental level and on a considerable scale.[246] Through a close scrutiny of commercial activity in the context of our study we have found that it betrays a limited nature of the urban phenomenon in the sense that the trading activity of the period was still in an incipient state with the agrarian features juxtaposed closely with the commercial transactions. Kuppuswamy has aptly observed in this regard that "it is futile to attempt a clear-cut classification of medieval economy of Karnataka into different sectors, namely urban and rural... the distinction was only one of degree and not of kind".[247] In such a situation one has attempted to characterize the commercial spurt in our area of study in terms of a stage in 'rural urban continuum'[248] which is discussed below.

Accordingly, one has observed in this context that there is strong evidence to suggest a close nexus between the trading groups and the articles of their trade with the agrarian scenario. At least in the beginning of our period of study, the individual merchants *(seṭṭis)* emerge as closely associated with landed property.[249] As early as A.D. 1004, in an inscription from sub-region A, we have the mention of a *seṭṭi* who grants a field of 200 *mattar.*[250] In an inscription dated to A.D. 1010, in the context of sub-region B, reference is made to 8 *seṭṭis* who figure as leasors of lands.[251] In another inscription of the same sub-region dated to A.D. 1071 we have reference to 30 *seṭṭis* who were granted certain leases of lands.[252] These merchants who figure in the inscriptional sources of 11th century A.D. mostly as individuals, emerge significantly in terms of organised trading groups in the sources of the 12th century A.D. Among these we have the frequent mention of such guilds as 500 *svāmis* of *Ayyāvole, nānādeśi, nakaraṁ* and the *mummūridaṇḍas.* Local character of the *nakaramu (nagaraṁ)* has been significantly highlighted in various secondary sources in the sense of it being equated to mean a local assembly.[253] The nānādeśis and the *mummūridaṇḍas* were supposed to have been organised on a provincial basis.[254] It is mainly in the context of Ayyāvole 500 that supra local character is attributed to as it has been considered to represent a vast organisation of associated traders.[255] In this context the agrarian character of the *nagaraṁ* which figures frequently in the inscriptional sources of our study, has been aptly highlighted by R. Champakalakshmi when she states that the status of the members of this guild "was hardly different from that of the agricultural groups for they were agriculturists now taking to trade".[256] In this regard we have an interesting example in an inscription dated to A.D. 1075 from sub-region B, wherein mention is made of Sunday markets *(āditya vāradol nereva santheya)* The tolls collected at these markets were the subject of a grant,[257] and this evidently testifies to the existence of a local net work of markets. We further have frequent references to shops *(angaḍi)* which were sometimes granted (IIA, viii, 27, 28, IIB, viii, 83, 110) and shopkeepers *(aṅgaḍidappa*[258]*, aṅgaḍi-okkalu).*[259] Even the nature of articles of merchandise such as grain, paddy, wheat, sugar, jaggery, betel leaves, salt, bamboos and areca nuts that dominated the trading scene seem to have catered largely to the needs of a local market. Further, the nature of tolls *(suṅka)* levied during this period again go to testify the agrarian nexus of the commercial set up of the period of study. Two frequently mentioned toll *(suṅka)* terms such as *pejjuṁka* or *hejjuṁka* (IIB, x, 86) and *vaḍḍarāvula* (IIB, x, 108) have been equated to signify heavy customs dues.[260] It is however significant to note here that these were levied in the beginning on land paddy.[261] In the context of our study we have an interesting reference to the levy of *hejjuṁka* and *vḍḍarāvula suṅka* on 18000 mattars of land in an inscription dated to A.D. 1146 from sub-region B.[262] Then the very nature of certain commercial taxes as above becomes a crucial pointer towards the problematique of defining the early medieval urbanism in clear contours as the very contexts of their reference do not clearly tell us about their exact purpose. The increasing availability of coins and the minting operations described by us above no doubt testify to the prevalence of monetized economy during this period. Further, it has been acknowledged by other scholars too that it is only from the 10th century A.D. onwards that references to the indigenous coins in circulation become meaningfully profuse in the epigraphs of Karnataka.[263] The coinage of this period however, differed distinctly from that of the early historical phase, when the coins were chiefly discovered in the flourishing entrepots and along the trading routes of the period.[264] On the other hand, during our period of study the inscriptional data shed light on the consistent and regular use of coined money in all major areas of economic life.[265] We have already seen in this context that even revenue payments begin to be paid in terms of cash on a large scale. Thus, we see that the gold coins and other forms of currency such as *paṇa* were not used for commercial transactions alone and their existence need not be attributed to the prevalence of large scale trade and commerce perse in the context of our study.[266] Rather, it can be suggested that the circulation of money remained very much defined by local consideration and imperative inhibiting a development of a market economy in its fullest sense.

It is significant to note at this juncture that in all the three sub-regions of our study, whatever mention of the commercial activity is made, it figures in the context of the temple institution. The brahmanical temple in particular as a major beneficiary of the gifts made by several wealthy social groups emerges by the 12 century A.D. picture as an overarching organization of economic integration and redistribution of sources. We have already discussed above the patronage extended to the temple by the land owning groups which resulted in the temple itself becoming a major land lord with its efficient management of land resources and as the appropriator of agricultural revenue. With the gradual shift in the economic scenario marked by a limited commercial growth, the temple also emerges as a major consumer of various articles of mechandise which we have just described above. Coupled with these, the temple further begins to play the role of an employer for various artisanal and professional services performed in the temple precincts. Thus, with the growth in the importance of the temple institution various types of economic activity begin to be clustered around the temple. It becomes the focal point for the agrarian, commercial and artisanal production during this period. With the particular patronage extended by the commercial and the artisanal groups in the form of land, money and articles it "meant that non-landed persons could have gained acceptance (and commercial contacts) in a community of worship that encompassed various segments of society and a considerable territorial expense."[267]

Concomitant with the increase in the trading activity therefore, one sees here a significant growth in the number of artisanal and other professional groups who initially figure as rendering service in the temples and later emerge as donors of grants, in the form of articles and money to the temple. Spurt in the activity of artisanal and professional groups thus mentioned chiefly occurs in the context of sub-regions A (IIA, viii, 20-32) and B (IIB, viii, 84-145). This can be attributed primarily to the nature of the services involved in the construction and worship in temples. As a result of this we find that we have reference to a variety of economic activities that emerge and which were dependent squarely on the nature of services rendered in the temples. First of all, we have observed that in the grants made to the temple, frequent reference is made either, to the construction or, repairs and restoration of the temple structure for which considerable number of grants were directed. This, along with other services such as engraving charts on the walls and stones in the temple precincts, making of idols for worship, clothes and gold ornaments to be adorned on the deities, offerings of oil and ghee for burning the lamps in the temple and so on rendered artisanal services crucial for the temple institution. In such a context one comes across reference to a variety of specialized groups mentioned in the inscriptions catering to various services of the temple particularly from the beginning of the 12th century A.D.

onwards. Thus, we have the mention of stone cutter *(kalkuṭiga)*, carpenter *(baḍagi)*, *oil monger* (telliga), ghee seller *(tuppakka)*, gold smith *(akkasāle)*, weaver (*sālega)*, brazier and black smith *(kamchagāra)*, basket maker (gavares), garland maker *(mālagāra)*, barber *(nāviḍa)*, potter *(kumbāra)* and so on figure in a variety of contexts. It is chiefly in the context of the mention of the above groups performing various acts in the temple precincts that we get to know about the various kinds of artisanal activity prevalent during our period of study.

In such a situation we have the mention of particularly the individual artisans such as carpenters, stone masons and barbers in a majority during the 11th century A.D. in sub-regions A and B.[268] This bears ample evidence to the limited nature of artisanal production during this period. It is significant to note here that the mention of these individuals is made in the context of them being donees of various shares in the grants made to the temple. The shares were primarily given to them for their maintenance. Speaking about the artisanal groups in the context of medieval Andhra, K. Sundaram states that the artisan community usually attached themselves to the temples of the locality in which they resided and without the services of these people, the temple could not have been maintained.[269] At this stage, *i.e.,* during the 11th century A.D. in the context of our study artisanal activity was connected directly to the temple services and more importantly, these artisans figure as the employees of the temples. We have in this context significant references to these groups performing various acts in the temple and, as indicated above were remunerated through shares in lands by the temple institution. As early as A.D. 1012 in an inscription from sub-region B reference is made to a barber *(nāviḍa)* who is granted 12 *mattars* of land.[270] In the context of sub-region A we have in an inscription dated to A.D. 1033, mention of an artisan who is supposed to have constructed a temple, and was remunerated through the grant of 6 *mattars* of land.[271] Similarly, in the context of sub-region C too we have reference to an artisan who is remunerated by the temple with a grant of 100 *mattars* of land in A.D. 1055.[272] In the context of sub-region A we come across two more instances of grants of land being made to individual artisans *i.e.,* to the stone cutters[273] and in sub-region B, we have reference to a carpenter *(baḍagi)* as the donee[274] in an inscription of 11th century A.D. It is pertient to note in the above stated examples that there is a predominance in the mention of masons involved in the construction activity of the temples which was taking place on a large scale during the 11th century A.D. It is only around the 12th century A.D. that one sees a significant shift in terms of the mention of artisans who now begin to figure in a majority cases through the formation of guilds. One sees the mention to such guilds as those of the stone cutters *(kalkuṭtiga goṭṭali)*, braziers (*kaṁchagara goṭṭali)*, carpenters, blacksmiths and goldsmiths *(baḍagi, kammara, akkasāl yaru)* in an inscription of A.D. 1110 from sub-region B.[275] We further have a reference to the guild of oil mongers[276] *(telliga*-50) who are mentioned frequently in the context of inscriptions of sub-region B and miners [277] *(jaragina doni)* in the same sub-region. Towards the end of the 12th century A.D. we have profuse references to the carpenters guild *(baḍagitānakkaru* [278] *baḍagi kammara)*[279] braziers *(kaṁcha-gāra).*[280] and that of garland makers *(mālagāra*-50).[281] The above cited references effectively allude to the organized nature of artisanal activity which seemed to have emerged as a result of the proliferation in these services in catering to the needs of the bourgeoning temple institutions and the commercial groups particularly during the 12th century A.D. In such a context one can effectively attribute the proliferation of individual artisans, particularly stone masons who now begin to emerge as donors in the form of artisanal guilds, to the increasing temple construction activity and for such activities as the engraving of charters on the temple walls. Further, the frequent mention of oil mongers and their corporate groups of 50 and 500 can be chiefly attributed to the importance attached to the burning of lamps in the temples for which oil was a must. As can be gauged from the column on commodities in the charts appended to the chapter (IIA, viii, 20, 24, 28, 30, IIB, viii, 60, 61, 63, 66 and so on), the grant of oil *(soṅṭe)* and oil mills *(gāṇa)* becomes an important object of grant from the latter half of the 11th century A.D. In this context it is significant to note that we have reference to *gāṇada tere* (tax on oil mill) which figures as an object of the grant (IIB, x, 109). It is pertinent to note here that we also have mention of the taxes levied on mining *(jaragina tere),*[282] potters *(kumbāra)*[283] and artisans *(kāruka)*[284] which significantly indicate for us the active participation of these groups in the economy of the 12th century A.D. south western Deccan. The particularly organized nature of mining activity expressed through its association with such corporate groups as *doni*-1000 can be attributed to the growth in the importance of agricultural implements, weapons and similar requirements in the temple such as making to idols and for other decorations in the temple.

We have further noticed in our discussions and descriptions of artisanal activity that the role of weaving and metal working is well attested to in the inscriptional sources through the mention of various groups involved in the above mentioned professions. Thus, we have the frequent mention of the terms *paṭṭa sālega*[285] and *seṇigaru*[286] to describe various types of weavers who also figure in corporate groups of five *(sālega* 5) in some of the sources.[287] On the other hand, in the context of the metal working activity we have the significant mention of the goldsmiths *(akkasāle)* in the inscriptions of 12th century A.D. particularly in the context of sub-region B. Prolific mention of the groups associated with gold smithy is made through the use of such terms as *akkasāle,*[288] *hiriya-akkasāle*[289] in various contexts. Some of these specialist craftsmen can be described below. For instance, in an inscription dated to A.D. 1103 from sub-region B, we have reference to one *akkasāle* as belonging to the king.[290] In another inscription of the same sub-region of A.D. 1104, reference is made to the *akkasāles* of local chiefs.[291] These and other references made to the gold smiths as donors of gold to the temple institutions, highlights their crucial role in the economic set up of the period. The role of the black smiths particularly, in the inscriptional sources of the latter half of the 12th century A.D., is actively represented in the context of the mention of minting establishments kammāṭa). A variety of black smiths *(kammaras)* in this context as occupying various ranks of management in the mints, such as *kammaṭida adhikāri* (mint officers), *kammaṭi kāru* (mint owners)[292] and so on figure in the sources of our study from the beginning of the 12th century A.D. and their mention can be seen to increase towards the end of the 12th century A.D.[293] It is significant to note in this context the mention of certain types of artisans such as *keṇikara* whose contextual reference is largely indicative of the fact that they were involved in various artisanal activities on a contract basis. In this context the term *keṇi* has been equated to mean contract amount.[294] Their mention particularly in the latter half of the 12th century A.D. significantly coincides with the growth in the artisanal production for which large scale artisanal labour is probably required. It has been aptly stated in this context that 'while some of the artisans such as the potter, the tanner, the black smith remained largely a part of the agrarian subsistence economy, the weavers, most metal workers, oil men and even masons and carpenters participated in the process of urbanization especially the emergence of temple towns in the medieval period.[295]

Coupled with the economic activities of the groups discussed above, we also have significant mention of a different type of professional activity which was largely non-productive in nature and was focussed entirely on the nature of religious services to be offered in the temple institution. Represented in the form of the functions performed by these cultural professional groups such as musicians, barbers, flute players, drummers, dancing girls, these groups had a significant cultural and ideological role to play in the temple institution as gleaned from inscriptions of the 11th century A.D. It is pertinent to note in this context that professional groups centred in the temple complex were totally dependent upon the temples for their remuneration and it is in the context of these groups that the role of the temple as an employer becomes all the more significant. However, in the grants of the 12th century A.D. we find a significant decline in the mention of these groups in the inscriptional sources of our study. Such a trend can largely be attributed to the economic change we have discussed above which led to a significant shift in the nature of patronage to the temple from the earlier predominance of the land owning groups as patrons of the temples was overwhilemed by the commercial and artisanal groups. Whereas the former had extended support to individuals performing certain roles in the temple through immovable property like land. The latter extended patronage mostly in terms of cash, commodities and gold and these had to be necessarily given to the rituals or functions to be performed in the temple like various festivals, to burning lamps, to the constructions of pillars and so on. This does not mean that the temple ceased to employ the professional groups, but they are now not directly mentioned in the inscriptions. Thus, the nature of patronage to the temple institution by the commercial groups was closely connected to their economic means and interests.

It is pertient to state here that all the above discussed economic activities figure largely in the context of the temple institution in the form of either objects of the grants made or, as representing various services in the temple. The nature of source material available for the early medieval period, which has its location itself in the temple premises, makes it difficult for us to conclude upon the existence of any other economic activity outside the purview of the temple. We however, have allusions to the existence of certain hunting[296] and pastroal[297] groups in exceptional cases but these are also referred to in the context of them patronizing the temple institution. We are not trying to suggest here that all the economic activity took place only in the temple precincts but that we get know about the existence of it, when the groups participating in the activity get associated with the temple institution. Naturally, the productive area in terms of the total economic activity was larger than the single sites of the temple or temples. With the aforesaid limitations of the epigraphic sources, unless systematic excavations are conducted around major temple sites, it would be difficult to assess the nature of productive relations between the various village communities and the temple or the state to the fullest extent.[298]

The change in the economic structure witnessed in such a situation can however be attributed to the changes in the patterns reinforced through the political and ideological thrust expressed in the grants of land and villages made to the religious symbols. Gradually the dominant social groups began to interest themselves in the changed economic activity of the time, namely commercial activities. The agrarian nexus of the commercial setup was however, never lost as it remained the chief source of surplus appropriation. Importantly, the scale and nature of economic activity which was witnessed more markedly in the context of sub-region B when compared to sub-region A and C, can be effectively linked up to the creation of new settlements in the fertile tracts of the sub-region B. In particular, with almost all the groups involved in various economic activities trying to seek validation by participating in the gift giving and temple management functions, the temple emerges as a major complex at the centre of nucleated settlements. It is chiefly in the context of the emergence of settlements on a large scale with temple as a legitimizing factor at the centre, that one can effectively comprehend the changing economic scenario between the 11th to 12th century A.D. In our next chapter we focus on the spatial dimension of the socio-economic change discussed above.

REFERENCES

1. B.N.S. Yadava, 'Problem of the Interaction Between Socio-Economic Classes in Early Medieval Complex', *IHR*, 3, 1976-77, pp. 43-44. These characteristics attributed to the early medieval Indian complex by the school of scholars proposing the concept of 'Indian Feudalism', have however, not been accepted by all scholars. See Harbans Mukhia, 'Was there Feudalism in Indian History?', Presidential Address (Medieval India Section), *PIHC*, 40th session, Andhra University, Waltair, 1979, pp. 229-280, B.D. Chattopadhyaya, 'Trade and Urban centres in Early Medieval North India', *IHR*, 1, 2, 1974, pp. 203-219. While the former has pointed to the concept of free peasantry to characterise the early medieval socio-economic set up in India, the latter work has effectively refuted the concept of urban decline as characteristic of the post-Gupta North Indian context.
2. R.S. Sharma, *Indian Feudalism*, Delhi, 1980, pp. 2-3.
3. We have made an indepth analysis of the geographical delineation and the historical factors for the variations existing in each of the sub-regions of our study in Chapter II of our thesis on 'Geo-Political Context'. See pp. 96-101.
4. D.N. Jha, *Studies in Early Indian Economic History*, Delhi, 1980, pp. 2-3.
5. *Ibid.*, p. 10.
6. A.S. Altekar, *A History of Village Communities in Western India*, Bombay, 1927, pp. 80-81.
7. D.D. Kosambi, *An Introduction to the Study of Indian History*, Bombay, 1985 (rp.), pp. 113-114.
8. R.S. Sharma, *op. cit*, 1980, pp. 110-126.
9. Irfan Habib, 'The Social Distribution of Landed Property in Pre-British India', in R.S. Sharma, V.N. Jha (ed.), *Indian Society : Historical Probings*, New Delhi, 1974, pp. 265-287.
10. R.S. Sharma, *Perspectives in Social and Economic History of Early India*, Delhi, 1983, pp. 26-34.
11. Dharma Kumar, 'Private Property in Asia? The Case of Medieval South India', *CSSH*, 2, April, 1985, p. 343.
12. N. Karashima, *South Indian History and Society (Studies from Inscriptions, A.D. 850-1800)*, New Delhi, 1984, p. XVII.
13. R.N. Nandi, 'Growth of Rural Economy in Early Feudal India', Presidential Address, Sec. *I*, *PIHC*, 45th Session, Annamalai Nagar, 1984, p. 3.
14. Sharma, *op. cit.*, 1980, pp. 10-26. In this the author has highlighted with the help of the legal texts of the period, the existence of superior rights held by the *brahmanas* on the one hand, and also of the inferior rights held by the cultivators.

15. Dharma Kumar, *op. cit.*, 1985, pp. 351-355. In this work the author has highlighted the existence of multiple rights over the lands of early medieval South India in the form of both communal ownership of land and joint family ownership.
16. *Ibid.*, p. 351.
17. *Ibid.*, p. 345.
18. N. Karashima, *op. cit.*, 1984, p. XXI.
19. Dharma Kumar, *op. cit.*, 1984, p. 348.
20. Tejaswini Yarlagadda, 'Social Groups and Economic Change (7th-13th centuries A.D.)', in Aloka Parasher Sen (ed.), *Social and Economic History of Early Deccan*, Manohar, New Delhi, 1993, p. 164. We have observed that during the pre-10th century A.D. (The early Chalukyan and the Rashtrakuta periods), the grants of villages by the main ruling family chiefs outnumbered those given by the lesser chiefs.
21. By this we mean land measure exceeding 20 *mattars* in extent. According to S. Gururajachar, *mattaru* or the land measurement popularly used during the early medieval period in Karnataka varied considerably in its measurement. As for instance some times 900 *kammas* went to make one *mattar* and some times 100 *kammas* made up to a single *mattar* see 'Weights and Measures in Karnataka (up to 1300 A.D.)', *Studies in Indian Epigraphy II*, Mysore, 1975, p. 81.
22. See Chapter III, above on 'Social Context', pp. 158-164.
23. We have observed in chapter II above on the 'Geo-Political context that the local potentates representing local linkages of power had stronger holds in sub-regions B and C. Particularly in sub-region C the ruling dynasties of the Andhra region had a prominent role to play. On the other hand sub-region A can be seen to have influences of both *i.e.*, the members of the main ruling family and those of the local dynasties of the sub-region B at different points of time. See pp. 117-120.
24. 'Inscription no. 66', *APGAS*, no. 3. pp. 73-77.
25. 'Inscription no. 13', *HAS*, 18, pp. 63-74.
26. The kinship ties and the lineages linkages that the local potentates held with the members of the main ruling family which have been discussed in the chapter, on 'Social Context', must have armed them with extensive powers to grant villages. See pp. 189-191.
27. Summarised from Irfan Habib, *op. cit.*, 1974, p. 281.
28. Sharma, *op. cit.*, 1980, p. 124.
29. *Ibid.*, p. 124.
30. D.C. Sircar, *Indian Epigraphical Glossary*, Delhi, 1966, p. 303.
31. *Ibid.*, p. 60.
32. G.R. Kuppuswamy, *Economic Conditions in Karnataka (A.D. 975-A.D. 1336)*. Karnataka University, Dharwar, 1976, p. 20.
33. D.C. Sircar, *op. cit.*, 1966, p. 402.
34. *Ibid.*, *(śulka)* p. 327.
35. *Ibid.*, *(kara)* p. 144.

36. *Ibid.*, p. 3.
37. *Ibid.*, p. 343.
38. 'Gadag Inscription of the Yadava Bhillama (A.D. 1191)', *EI,* Vol. III. p. 220.
39. Sircar *op. cit.*, 1966, p. 216.
40. S. Gururajachar, *Some Aspects of Economic and Social Life in Karnataka (A.D. 1000-A.D. 1300)*, Parasanga, University of Mysore, Mysore, 1974, p. 145.
41. Sircar, *op. cit.*, 1966, p. 339.
42. Tejaswini Yarlagadda, *op. cit.*, 1993, p. 164. Here we have observed that in direct contrast to the period under study, the *brāhmaṇa* donees dominated the scene during the period from the 7th century A.D. to the middle of the 10th century A.D. They were invariably given grants of villages with extensive immunities.
43. 'Kotavumachgi Inscription of Vikramaditya V', *EI,* XX, pp. 64-70.
44. *Ibid.*, p. 68.
45. 'Inscription no. 47', *SII,* XI, pp. 32-34.
46. S. Gururajachar, *op. cit.*, 1974, pp. 24-25.
47. The term *kara* has already been explained earlier in this chapter.
48. 'Inscription no. 85', *SII,* XI, pp. 79-82.
49. 'Nilgunda Plates of Vikaramaditya VI' *EI,* XII, p. 154.
50. 'Inscription no. 52', *SII,* xv, pp. 68-69.
51. 'Inscription no. 121', *SII,* xv, pp. 151-152.
52. Sub-regional distribution of these groups has been discussed in detail in the chapter II on 'Social Context', See pp. 220-223.
53. Y. Subbarayulu, 'The Place of Ur in the Economic and Social History of the Early Tamil Nadu from A.D. 750 to A.D. 1350', in A.V. Narasimha Murthy and B.K. Guruaja Rao (ed.), *Rangavali : Recent Researches in Indology*, Delhi, 1983, p. 172.
54. Dharmakumar, *op. cit.*, 1985, p. 348.
55. S. Gururajachar, *op. cit.*, 1974, p. 143.
56. *Ibid.*, p. 144.
57. *Ibid.*, p. 162.
58. *Ibid.*, p. 162.
59. Lionel D. Barnett, 'Two Inscriptions from Gawariwad–'A', *EI,* XV, p. 346.
60. This understanding emerged after discussion with Dr. P.V. Parabrahma Sastry, Retired Dy. Director in Epigraphy, Department of Archaeology and Museums, Hyderabad.
61. S. Gururajachar, *op. cit.*, 1974, p. 145.
62. G.R. Kuppuswamy, *op. cit.*, 1976, p. 211.
63. *Ibid.*, p. 214.
64. S. Gururjachar, *op. cit.*, 1974, p. 145.
65. G.R. Kuppuswamy, *op. cit.*, 1976, p. 217.

66. Transcript, *A.R.* no. B 521 of 1960-61.
67. 'Inscription no. 116', *SII,* XI, pp. 114-116.
68. 'Transcript' *A.R.* no. B 534 of 1961-62.
69. 'Inscription no. 47', *SII,* XI, pp. 32-34.
70. 'Inscription no. 65', *SII,* XI, pp. 55-57.
71. Inscriptions of Sudi 'C', *EI,* XV, pp. 75-77.
72. Inscriptions of Sudi 'H' *EI,* XV, pp. 96-100.
73. *Ibid.,* pp. 96-100.
74. For instance, 'A Stone Inscription of the Sinda family at Bhairanmatti', *EI,* vol. III, pp. 230-236. Here the *gāvuṇḍas* figure as a group of 6 *gāvuṇḍas.*
75. One of the typical examples, 'Inscription no. 155', XI, pp. 144-147. Here we have the mention of the fields and the tank of various *gāvuṇḍas.*
76. G.S. Dikshit, 'Okkalu—A Corporate Body of Medieval Karnataka', *JKU* (Humanities) IV, June, 1960, p. 58.
77. 'Inscription no, 119', *SII,* XI, pp. 135-136.
78. 'Inscription no. 163', *SII,* XI, pp. 209-211.
79. 'Inscription no. 50', *SII,* XI, pp. 36-38.
80. 'Transcript' *A.R.* no. B 530 of 1961-62.
81. 'Inscriptions of Sudi' 'D', *EI,* XV, pp. 77-80.
82. S. Gururajachar, *op. cit.,* 1974, pp. 21-25.
83. 'Inscription no. 3', *HAS,* 18, pp. 42-43.
84. 'Belur Inscription' *IA,* XVIII, pp. 270-275.
85. 'Inscription no. 15', *APGAS,* no. 3, pp. 108-110.
86. We have already referred to these in detail in the beginning of this chapter. See pp. 316-318.
87. 'Inscriptions of Sudi', 'F', *EI,* XV, pp. 85-94.
88. 'Inscription no. 116', *SII,* XI, pp. 114-116.
89. Rise of *manneyas* into local potentates has been discussed in detail in chapter III of our book on 'Social Context'. See pp. 169-174.
90. 'Mulgund Inscription' *EI,* XVI, pp. 53-57, We have no definite meaning attributed to this term. It's contextual reference however leads us on to conclude upon its meaning as an 'estate'.
91. Inscription no. 6, *HAS,* 18, pp. 46-49.
92. 'Inscriptions of Sudi', 'K', *EI,* XV, pp. 105-108.
93. This issue had been tackled in a greater detail in chapter II of our book on 'Geo-Political Context', See pp. 119-120.
94. 'Inscription no. 85', *SII,* XI, pp. 79-82.
95. 'Inscription no. 113', *SII,* XI, pp. 111-112.

96. 'Inscription no. 50', *SII,* XI, pp. 36-38.
97. 'Inscription no. 152', *SII,* XI, pp. 189-191.
98. 'Inscription no. 155', *SII,* XI, pp. 144-147.
99. 'Belur Inscription', *IA,* XVIII, pp. 270-275.
100. 'Inscription no. 241', *SII,* XV, pp. 297-301.
101. 'Inscription no. 10', *KI,* II, pp. 29-34.
102. 'Munirabad Stone Inscription', *HAS,* no. 5, p. 7.
103. 'Inscription no. 42', *SII,* XV, pp. 34-35.
104. Dharmakumar, *op. cit.,* 1985, p. 355.
105. G.R. Kuppuswamy, 'Dayavibhaga or System of Distribution of Heritage and Land Sub-division and Fragmentation in Medieval Karnataka', *JKU* (Social Sciences), XI, 1975, p. 97.
106. G.R. Kuppuswamy, 'Land Succession in Medieval Karnataka', *JKU* (Social Sciences), IX, 1973, p. 113.
107. 'Inscription no. 117', *SII,* XV, pp. 147-148.
108. 'Inscription no. 68', *SII,* XI, pp. 58-59.
109. 'Inscription no. 151', *SII,* XI, pp. 187-188.
110. 'Inscription no. 137', *SII,* XI, pp. 165-166.
111. 'Inscription no. 121', *SII,* XV, pp. 151-152.
112. 'Inscription no. 28', *APGAS,* no. 3, pp. 121-122.
113. 'Tumbige Inscription', *EI,* XVII, p. 7-10.
114. 'Inscriptions of Sudi', E(1), *EI,* XV, pp. 80-83.
115. Aloka Parasher Sen, 'Temple Girls and the Land Grant Economy (8th-13th centuries A.D.) in Aloka Parasher Sen (ed.) *op. cit.,* 1993, p. 251.
116. Dharmakumar, *op. cit.,* 1985, p. 349.
117. Inscription no. 47, *SII,* XI, pp. 32-34.
118. 'Transcript' *A.R.* no. B 534 of 1961-62.
119. 'Inscriptions of Sudi' 'H', *EI,* XV, p. 97.
120. Inscription no. 158, *SII,* XI, pp. 201-203.
121. Inscription no. 16, *HAS,* 18, pp. 83-89.
122. For sub-region A we have found that the *gāvuṇḍas* very rarely figured as donors of lands and on the other hand, we have the mention of those groups who had purely official designations conferred on them such as the *daṇḍanāyaka, suṅkavergaḍe* and so on, who make grants along with the others such as the local potentates and royal members. In the context of sub-region C too almost a similar situation prevailed in the sense that among the category of donors we mostly have the local potentates, royal family members, and those holding other official designations such as the *sunkavergaḍe* and so on. With regard to these two sub-regions one finds it difficult to arrive at any solid conclusion over the nature of hereditary rights held in land by the peasant groups.

123. 'Inscription no. 149', *SII,* XI, pp. 183-184.
124. 'Inscription no. 152', *SII,* XI, pp. 189-191.
125. 'Inscription no. 158', *SII,* XI, pp. 201-203.
126. 'Inscription no. 9', *HAS,* 18, pp. 52-54.
127. 'Inscription no. 36', *SII,* XI, pp. 43-46.
128. 'Inscription no. 43', *SII,* XV, pp. 56-57.
129. 'Inscription no. 52' (B.K. no. 115 'A' of 1926-27), *SII,* XV, pp. 68-69.
130. S. Gururajachar, *op. cit.,* 1975, p. 81.
131. 'Inscription no. 53', *SII,* XV, pp. 69-71.
132. G.R. Kuppuswamy, *op. cit.,* 1975, pp. 94-101.
133. *Ibid.,* p. 101.
134. 'Inscriptions from Yewur', B, *EI,* XIII, pp. 269-291.
135. 'Munirabad Stone Inscription', *HAS,* 5, pp. 1-12.
136. James Heitzman, 'Temple Urbanisation in Medieval South India', *The Journal of Asian Studies,* 46, 4, Nov. 1987, p. 815.
137. *Ibid.,* p. 815.
138. 'Gadag Inscription' *EI,* XIX, pp. 217-222.
139. 'Inscription no. 134', *SII,* XI, pp. 157-160.
140. N. Karashima, *op. cit.,* 1984, p. xxi.
141. 'Inscription from Navali', *EI,* XXXIV, pp. 164-166.
142. 'Inscription no. 26', *APGAS,* 3, p. 120.
143. 'Inscription no. 183', *SII,* pp. 242-243.
144. 'Inscriptions of Sudi' 'C', *EI,* XV, pp. 75-77.
145. Two Inscriptions from Gawariwad, A *EI,* XV, pp. 337-347.
146. 'Nilgunda Plates', *EI,* XII, pp. 142-155.
147. G.R. Kuppuswamy, *op. cit.,* 1975, p. 214.
148. G.R. Kuppuswamy, 'Land Leases in Medieval Karnataka', *JKU* (Social Sciences), X, 1974, p. 73.
149. *Ibid.,* pp. 64-69.
150. Ibid., p. 70.
151. 'Inscription no, 9', KI, II, pp. 25-28.
152. S. Gururajachar, *op. cit.,* 1974, p. 37.
153. *Ibid.,* p. 40.
154. 'Inscription no. 5', *APGAS,* no. 9. pp. 29-30.
155. Sircar, *op. cit.,* 1966, p. 379.
156. Inscription no. 159, (B.K. no. 9 of 1926-27), *SII,* XV, I. 48, p. 205. We have on the other hand, observed that for the pre-11th century A.D., *i.e.,* during the Rāshṭrakūṭa

rule, we have considerable evidences of the mention of *viṣṭi* in the inscriptional sources for the region under study. See Tejaswini Yarlagadda, *op. cit.*, 1993, pp. 170-171.

157. S.G. Ghatapanadi, 'Forced Labour in Ancient and Medieval Karnataka', *JKU* (Social Sciences), 12, 1976, p. 148.

158. G.K. Rai, 'Forced Labour in Ancient and Early Medieval India', *IHR* 3, 1976-77, p. 32.

159. B.N.S. Yadava, 'Immobility and Subjection of Indian Peasantry in Early Medieval Complex', *IHR*, 1, 1974, pp. 18-23.

160. R.S. Sharma, *op. cit.*, 1980, pp. 187-190.

161. R.S. Sharma, How Feudal was Indian Feudalism?, *The Journal of Peasant Studies*, 12, nos 2 and 3, January-April, 1985, p. 21.

162. 'Munirabad Stone Inscription', *HAS*, no. 5. 1922, pp. 1-12.

163. R.N. Nandi, *op. cit.*, 1984, p. 23.

164. R.S. Sharma, *op. cit.*, 1980, p. 217.

165. Gururajachar, *op. cit.*, 1874, p. 141.

166. Sircar, *op. cit.*, 1960, p. 29.

167. Gururajachar, *op. cit.*, 1944, p. 162.

168. *Ibid.*, p. 144.

169. Sircar, *op. cit.*, 1960, p. 234.

170. G.R. Kuppuswamy, *op. cit.*, 1975, p. 215.

171. Gururajachar, *op. cit.*, 1974, p. 145.

172. G.S. Dikshit, *op. cit.*, 1964, p. 62.

173. G.S. Gai, *Historical Grammar of Old Kanada*, Poona, 1946, p. 195.

174. R.S. Sharma, *op. cit.*, 1980, p. 213.

175. 'Inscription no. 85', *SII*, XI, pp. 79-82.

176. 'Inscription no. 116', *SII*, XI, pp. 114-116.

177. Arasibidi Inscription, *EI*, XVII, pp. 121-123.

178. Inscription no. 85, *SII*, XI, pp. 79-82.

179. 'Inscriptions from Navali', *EI*, XXXIV, pp. 164-166.

180. Inscription no. 4, *HAS*, 18, pp. 43-44.

181. Kilaratti Inscription *EI*, XXXV, pp. 37-39.

182 'Munirabad Stone Inscription', *HAS*, no. 5, p. 8.

183. 'Inscriptions at Ittagi' A. *EI*, XIII, pp. 37-38.

184. 'Inscription no. 13', *HAS*, 18, pp. 63-74. According to the editor, it is interesting to note that an open site of red soil outside the locality of Kukkanur (where the soil is located), is still known as Kemmana Kuni. The belief that the soil maintains its ground level despite digging is still current among the people of place, p. 71.

185. Bannigol Inscription, *EI*, XXXVI, pp. 118-120.
186. *Gazetteer of Bombay State* (Dharwar District), Bombay, 1959, p. 15.
187. B.S. Seshagiri, *Bombay–Karnataka–A Geographical Survey*, Dharwar, 1941, p. 28.
188. *Ibid.*, p. 29.
189. Inscription no. 13, *HAS*, 18, pp. 63-74.
190. 'Transcript', no. 175/72 of office of the *Archaeology and Museums*, Hyderabad.
191. 'Transcript', *AR*, no. B 73 of 1960-61.
192. 'Transcript', no. 175/72 of office of the *Archaeology and Museums*, Hyderabad.
193. 'Transcript', *AR*, no. B 73 of 1960-61.
194. Inscription no. 33, *APGAS*, no. 3, pp. 40-41.
195. G.R. Kuppuswamy, *op. cit.*, 1975, p. 50.
196. We have been able to arrive at this conclusion on the basis of a survey of the district gazetteers for various sub-regions of our study. A detailed description of the physiography of the area under study has however, been given in chapter II on 'Geo-political Context', See pp. 96-101.
197. B.N. Chaturvedi, 'The Origin and Development of Tank Irrigation in Penninsular India', *Deccan Geographer*, 6, 2, (July-December, 1968), p. 62.
198. Ashok Sheltar, 'Aspects of Agricultural Expansion in Early Medieval Southern Karnataka', in K. Veerathappa (ed.), *Studies in Karnataka History and Culture* (Proceedings vol. II of the Karnataka History Congress), Mysore, 1987, p. 71.
199. V.R.R. Dikshitar, 'A History of Irrigation in South-India', *Indian Culture*, XII, 2, Calcutta, 1945, pp. 71-74.
200. M. Ramudu, 'Tank Irrigation under the Rayas of Vijayanagara–Some Theoretical Considerations', *APHC*, Section II, 13th session, Srisailam, 1989, p. 78.
201. K. Pramila, *Economic and Social Conditions in Medieval Telangana* (A.D. 1000-1323, unpublished Ph.D. thesis, Department of History, Nagarjuna University, 1988, pp. 93-94.
202. J.F. Richards, *Mughal Administration in Golconda*, Clarendon Press, Oxford, 1975, pp. 3-4.
203. Inscription no. 85, *SII*, XI, pp. 79-82.
204. 'Kelawadi Inscription, *EI*, IV, pp. 259-262.
205. Inscription no. 116, *SII*, XI, pp. 114-116.
206. Inscription no. 169, *SII*, XII, pp. 216-217.
207. 'Kotavumachgi Inscription, *EI*, XX, pp. 64-70.
208. 'Inscription from Ron', 'A', *EI*, XIX, pp. 222-226.
209. Inscription no. 5, *HAS*, 18, pp. 44-46.
210. 'Transcript', *A.R.* no. B 570 of 1961-62.
211. 'Inscriptions at Yewur', 'B', *EI*, XII, pp. 269-291.
212. 'Munirabad Stone Inscription', *HAS* 5, pp. 1-12.

213. G.R. Kuppuswamy, *op. cit.*, 1975, pp. 62-63.
214. R.N. Nandi, *op. cit.*, 1984, pp. 40-48.
215. Inscription no. 148, *SII*, XI, pp. 182-183.
216. *Ibid.*, pp. 182-183.
217. *Ibid.*, pp. 182-183.
218. 'Transcript', *A.R.* no. B 521 of 1960-61.
219. 'Inscriptions at Yewur' C, *EI*, XIII, pp. 329-331.
220. Inscription no. 32, *APGAS*, 3, p. 123.
221. 'Transcript', *A.R.* no. B 521 of 1960-61.
222. Inscription no. 32, *APGAS*, 3, p. 123.
223. inscription no. 10, *KI*, II, pp. 29-34.
224. 'Transcript', *A.R.* no. B 82 of 1960-61.
225. 'Inscription at Yewur', C, *EI*, XII, pp. 329-331.
226. Inscription no. 156, *SII*, XV, pp. 200-201.
227. Inscription no. 4, *Telangana Sasanalu*, II, pp. 20-21.
228. Inscription no. 158, *SII*, XI, pp. 201-203.
229. Inscription no. 43, *SII*, XV, pp. 56-57.
230. Inscription no. 32, *APGAS*, 3, p. 123.
231. Inscription no. 158, *SII*, XI, pp. 201-203.
232. Inscription no. 70, *SII*, XV, pp. 95-96.
233. B.D. Chattopadhyaha, *Coins and Currency Systems in South India* (A.D. 225-A.D. 1300), New Delhi, 1977, p. 118.
234. Inscription no. 1, *HAS*, 18, pp. 39-40.
235. Inscription no. 189, *SII*, XI, pp. 37-38.
236. 'Inscriptions at Ittagi', *EI*, XIII, pp. 37-38.
237. 'Transcript', *A.R.* no. B 529 of 1960-61.
238. 'Inscription no. 8', *HAS*, 18, pp. 51-52.
239. P.B. Desai, 'Minting Establishments', *HAS*, 18, p. 31.
240. 'Inscription no. 70', *SII*, XV, pp. 95-96.
241. R.N. Nandi, *op. cit.*, 1984, p. 55.
242. R.S. Sharma, *op. cit.*, 1980, p. 226.
243. M.R. Tarafdar, 'Trade and Society in early Medieval Bengal', *IHR*, IV, 2, pp. 274-284.
244. See for example R. Champakalakshmi, 'Urbanization in South India : The Role of Ideology and Polity' Presidential Address, Sec.1, *PIHC*, 47th session, Srinagar, 1986, pp. 18-30.
245. Himanshy Prabha Ray, *Monastery and Guild (Commerce under the Satavahanas)*, OUP, Delhi, 1986, p. 158.

246. B.D. Chattopadhyaya, 'Urban Centres in Early Medieval India'. An Overview, in Sabyasachi Bhattacharya and Romila Thapar (eds.), *Situating Indian History*, OUP, Delhi, 1986, p. 31.
247. G.R. Kuppuswamy, *op. cit.*, 1975, p. 95.
248. This term has been borrowed from R. Champakalakshmi who uses it to characterize the commercial growth in the context of the Chola regime during the early medieval period in her article, 'Urbanization in Medieval Tamil Nadu', in S. Bhattacharya and Romila Thapar (eds.), *op. cit.*, 1986, p. 39.
249. We have detailed in chapter III on 'Social Context' the social aspects of the agrarian moorings of the merchants. See pp. 225-226.
250. 'Tumbagi Inscription', *EI*, XVII, pp. 7-10.
251. 'Inscriptions of Sudi', C, *EI*, XV, pp. 75-77.
252. 'Two Inscriptions from Gawariwad' A, *EI*, XV, pp. 337-347.
253. K.R. Venkatarama Ayyar, 'Medieval Trade, Craft and Merchant Guilds in South India', *JIH*, vol. XXV, no. 3, Trivandrum, 1947, p. 269.
254. G.S. Dikshit, 'Constitution of Trade Guilds in Medieval Karnataka', *JKU* (Humanities), vol. 2, June, 1959, p. 53.
255. *Ibid.*, p. 53.
256. R. Champakalakshmi, *op. cit.*, 1986, p. 20.
257. 'Inscriptions of Sudi', H. *EI*, XV, pp. 96-100.
258. 'Inscription no. 158', *SII*, XI, pp. 201-203.
259. 'Inscription no. 116', *SII*, XI, pp. 114-116.
260. Gururajachar, *op. cit.*, 19, p. 145.
261. R.N. Nandi, *op. cit.*, 1984, p. 56.
262. 'Transcript', *A.R.* no. B 521 of 1960-61.
263. B.D. Chattopadhyaya, 'Coinage in Early Medieval Andhra'. A Note on Chronology and Distribution', *JAHRS*, vol. XXXV, Hyderabad, 1976, p. 246.
264. *Ibid.*, p. 249.
265. R. Nandi, *op. cit.*, 1984, p. 51.
266. In his study of coins during the early medieval period in the context of Silahara rulers of Western India, K.M. Shrimali has similar observations on the types and denominations of coins which according to the author remained extremely localized. But the author goes on to conclude that the coins could not, at the same time, penetrate deep into the economic ethos. See K.M. Shrimali, 'Cash Nexus on Western Coast A.D. 850-1250 : A Study of the Silacharas' in Amalkumar Jha (ed.) *Coinage, Trade and Economy*, 3rd International Colloquium, Nasik, (January 8th-11th), 1991, p. 189.
267. Cynthia Talbot, 'Temples, Donors and Gifts : Patterns of Patronage in 13th century South India', *Journal of Asian Studies*, vol. 50, no. 2, May, 1991, p. 327.
268. We have made a detailed analysis of all these groups in chapter II on 'Social Context', See pp. 207-213.

269. K. Sundaram, 'The Artisan Community of Medieval Andhra (A.D. 1000-A.D. 1600), *JIH*, XVIII, pt. 11, Trivandrum, 1965, p. 906.
270. Kotavumachgi 'Inscription', *EI*, XX, pp. 64-70.
271. 'Inscription no. 68', *SII*, XI, pp. 58-59.
272. 'Inscription no. 26', *APGAS*, 3, p. 120.
273. 'Inscription no. 116', *SII*, XI, pp. 114-116, 'Arasibidi Inscription', *EI*, XVII, p. 121-123.
274. 'Transcript', *A.R.* no. B 255 of 1953-54.
275. 'Inscriptions from Yewur', D, *EI*, XII, pp. 332-333.
276. 'Inscription no. 145', *SII*, XI, p. 176.
277. 'Inscription no. 158', *SII*, XI, pp. 201-203.
278. 'Inscription no. 69', *SII*, XV, p. 95.
279. 'Inscription no. 67', *SII*, XV, pp. 92-94.
280. 'Inscription no. 73', *SII*, XI, pp. 99-104.
281. Transcript, *A.R.* no. B 664 of 1958-59.
282. 'Inscription no. 158', *SII*, XI, pp. 201-203.
283. Transcript, *A.R.* no. B 529 of 1960-61.
284. 'Inscription no. 14', *HAS*, 18, pp. 74-79.
285. Transcript, *A.R.* no. B 512 of 1959-60.
286. 'Inscription no. 73', *SII*, XV, pp. 99-104.
287. 'Inscription no. 97', *SII*, XI, pp. 91-94.
288. 'Inscription no. 145', *SII*, XI, p. 176.
289. 'Inscription no. 62', *SII*, XV, pp. 87-88.
290. 'Inscription no. 153', *SII*, XI, p. 192.
291. 'Inscription no. 187', *SII*, XI, p. 245.
292. 'Inscription no. 8', *HAS*, pp. 51-52.
293. 'Inscription no. 62', *SII*, XV, pp. 87-88, 'Inscription no. 67', *SII*, XV, pp. 92-94.
294. 'Inscription no. 135', *SII*, XV, pp. 174-178.
295. Vijaya Ramaswamy, 'Artisans in Vijayanagar Society', *IESHR*, vol. 22, no. 4, 1985, p. 419.
296. 'Inscription of no. 58', SII, XV, pp. 78-82.
297. 'Inscription no. 9', *APGAS*, 3, p. 104.
298. Carla M. Sinopoli Kathleen D. Morrison, 'Dimension of Imperial Control. The Vijayanagara Capital', *American Anthropologist*, 97, 1, March 1995, pp. 83-96.

Chart – II : ECONOMIC CONTEXT

Sub Region A

i	ii	iii	iv	v	vi	vii	viii	ix	x	xi	xii	xiii
S.No.	Name/Date Dynasty	Location	Donor	Donee	Types of Grants					Immunities	Irrigation	Reference
					Lands	Village	Commod-dities	Cash	Revenue			
1.	Tumbagi Ins. Chalukyas of Kalyani AD 1004.	Muddebihal Tq. Bijapur Dt.	@	Δ & O	-120m 30m -50m							*EI*, XVII. 7-10
2.	Ins. no. 524 Chalukyas of Kalyani AD 1014.	Muddebihal Tq. Bijapur Dt.	@	O	30m							*SII*, XV. 355
3.	Belur Ins. Chalukyas of Kalyani AD 1022.	Badami Tq. Bijapur Dt.	sister of >	*		¼				*sarvanamasya agrahāra*		*IA*, XVIII. 270-275
4.	Ins. no. 66 Chalukyas of Kalyani AD 1032.	Muddebihal Tq. Bijapur Dt.	#, @	Δ O	12m +1m		1 oil mill					*SII*, XI.57.
5.	Ins. no. 68 Chalukyas of Kalyani AD 1033.	Muddebihal Tq. Bijapur Dt.	@	Δ	36m +1m					*sarvanamasya*		*SII*, XI. 58-59
6.	Arasibidi Ins. Chalukyas of Kalayani AD 1047.	Hungund Tq. Bijapur Dt.	@	Δ $ &	+1m 12m 24m +1m					*sarvanamasya* *sarvanamasya* *sarvanamasya*		*EI*, XVII. 121-123
7.	Ins. no. 85 Chalukyas of Kalyani AD 1049.	Bagalkot Tq. Bijapur Dt.	$	Δ	various measure-ments of land belon-ging to different places						T ~~~ ~~~ ~~~	*SII*, XI. 79-82
8.	Kelawadi Ins. Chalukyas of Kalyani AD 1053.	Badami Tq. Bijapur Dt.	@	T	20m						T	*EI*, IV, 259-262

Key to the Symbols :
+ : Gardens; : Fields; # : Local Potentate; $: *brāhmaṇa*; * : *mahājana*; ~ : Merchant; > : Main Ruler;
@ : Functionary; < : Peasant; & : Cultural Professional Group; ~~~ : Stream; ¼ : Village; Δ : Temple;
A : Artisan; m : *maṭṭar*; K : *Kamma*; n = *nivaratana*; T : Tank; O : *maṭha*; Ins. : Inscription

Chart – II : ECONOMIC CONTEXT

Sub Region A

i	ii	iii	iv	v	vi	vii	viii	ix	x	xi	xii	xiii
S.No.	Name/Date Dynasty	Location	Donor	Donee	Types of Grants					Immunities	Irrigation	Reference
					Lands	Village	Commod-dities	Cash	Revenue			
9.	Ins. no. 88 Chalukyas of Kalyani AD 1058.	Hungund Tq. Bijapur Dt.	sister of of < >	*	108m +1m					*sarvanamasva*		*SII*, XI, 84-85
10.	Ins. no. 96 Chalukyas of Kalyani AD 1061.	Hungund Tq. Bijapur Dt.	@	*			100 areca nuts		1 *pana* on every areca garden			*SII*, XI, 91
11.	Ins. no. 107 Chalukyas of Kalyani AD 1068.	Muddebihal Tq. Bijapur Dt.	@	Δ	some land							*SII*, XI, 104-105
12.	Ins. no. 110 Chalukyas of Kalyani AD 1070.	Badami Tq. Bijapur Dt.	#	Δ	12m					*sarvabādha-parihāram sarvanamasya*		*SII*, XI, 107
13.	Ins. no. 116 Chalukyas of Kalyani AD 1075.	Bagalkot Tq. Bijapur Dt.	>	Δ &	12m +2m	¼				*talavritti*	T	*SII*, XI, 114-116
			#	Δ					*mannev-asāmva*	*sarvabādha-parihāram*		
14.	Ins. no. 113 Chalukyas of Kalyani AD 1079.	Hungund Tq. Bijapur Dt.	@	Δ	60m					*sarvabādha-parihāram*		*SII*, XI, 111-112
15.	Ins. no. 179 Chalukyas of Kalyani AD 1085.	Hungund Tq. Bijapur Dt.	@	Δ					5 *paṇas* out of *manneva suṅka* & *pannāya suṅka*			*SII*, XI, 239
16.	Ins. no. 132 Chalukyas of Kalyani AD 1086.	Muddebihal Tq. Bijapur Dt.	#	Δ	12m							*SII*, XI, 153-154

Key to the Symbols :
+ : Gardens; : Fields; # : Local Potentate; $: *brāhmaṇa*; * : *mahājana*; ~ : Merchant; > : Main Ruler;
@ : Functionary; < : Peasant; & : Cultural Professional Group; ~~~ : Stream; ¼ : Village; Δ : Temple;
A : Artisan; m : *mattar*; K : *Kamma*; n = *nivaratana*; T : Tank; O : *matha*; Ins. : Inscription

Chart – II : ECONOMIC CONTEXT

Sub Region A

i	ii	iii	iv	v	vi	vii	viii	ix	x	xi	xii	xiii
S.No.	Name/Date Dynasty	Location	Donor	Donee	Types of Grants					Immunities	Irrigation	Reference
					Lands	Village	Commod-dities	Cash	Revenue			
17.	Ins. no. 135 Chalukyas of Kalyani AD 1087.	Hungund Tq. Bijapur Dt.	#	*	12m 450k					*sarvanamasya*	T	*SII*. XI, 160-161
18.	Ins. no. 183 Chalukyas of Kalyani AD 1100.	Bagalkot Tq. Bijapur Dt.	$	T	4m						T	*SII*. XI, 242-243
19.	Ins. no. 5 Chalukyas of Kalyani AD 1106.	Hungund Tq. Bijapur Dt.	@	Δ					fixed shares in the income from the *pannāva* tax			*SII*. XV, 5
20.	Ins. no. 169 Chalukyas of Kalyani AD 1119.	Hungund Tq. Bijapur Dt.	~	Δ	12m		1 oil mill					*SII*. XI, 216-217
21.	Ins. no. XXXIII Chalukyas of Kalyani AD 1139.	Badami Tq. Bijapur Dt.	@	Δ					10 *gadvānas* of gold out of *siddhāva* income			*IA*. VI, 139-142
22.	Ins. no. 30 Chalukyas of Kalyani AD 1145.	Muddebihal Tq. Bijapur Dt.	@, ~	Δ	18m							*SII*. XV, 32-33
23.	Ins. no. 236 Chalukyas of Kalyani AD 1155.	Badami Tq. Bijapur Dt.	@	Δ	11m							*SII*. XV, 291-293
24.	Ins. no. 88 Chalukyas of Kalyani AD 1160.	Hungund Tq. Bijapur Dt.	~, <	Δ	+1		1 *angadi* (shop) 1 *gāṇa* (oil mill)					*SII*. XV, 114-115
25.	Ins. no. 126 Chalukyas of Kalyani AD 1174.	Muddebihal Tq. Bijapur Dt.	@	Δ	12m					*sarvanamasya*	T	*SII*. XV, 159-160

Key to the Symbols : + : Gardens; : Fields; # : Local Potentate; $: *brāhmaṇa*; * : *mahājana*; ~ : Merchant; > : Main Ruler;
@ : Functionary; < : Peasant; & : Cultural Professional Group; ~~~ : Stream; ¼ : Village; Δ : Temple;
A : Artisan; m : *maṭṭar*; K : *Kamma*; n = *nivaratana*; T : Tank; O : *maṭha*; Ins. : Inscription

Chart – II : ECONOMIC CONTEXT

Sub Region A

i	ii	iii	iv	v	vi	vii	viii	ix	x	xi	xii	xiii
S.No.	Name/Date Dynasty	Location	Donor	Donee	Types of Grants					Immunities	Irrigation	Reference
					Lands	Village	Commod-dities	Cash	Revenue			
26.	Ins. no. 134 Chalukyas of Kalyani AD 1178.	Badami Tq. Bijapur Dt.	@	*		¼				parameśvaradatti		SII, XV, 170-174
27.	Ins. no. 58 Chalukyas of Kalyani AD 1184.	Muddebihal Tq. Bijapur Dt.	@ ~	Δ	25m		1 *angaḍi* (shop) 1 *gāṇa* (oil mill)					SII, XV, 78-82
28.	Ins. no. 56 Chalukyas of Kalyani AD 1184.	Muddebihal Tq. Bijapur Dt.	#	Δ	100m +2		1 *angaḍi* (shop) 1 *gāṇa* (oil mill) 5 arecanuts		1 *gadvāna* out of income from each village of Hag-arittage-300			SII, XV, 73-74
29.	Ins. no. 242 AD 1186.	Hungund Tq. Bijapur Dt.	# @	T Δ	500k				*bīravana, pan-nāya* income		T	SII, XV, 301-302
30.	Ins. no. 147 Yadavas of Devagiri AD 1189.	Muddebihal Tq. Bijapur Dt.	@ ~	Δ Δ	12m		1 *mana* of oil on pur-chase and sale			sarvanamasya		SII, XV, 189
31	Ins. no. 148 Yadavas of Devagiri AD 1190.	Muddebihal Tq. Bijapur Dt.	@ ~	Δ Δ	6m		oil			sarvanamasya		SII, XV, 190
32	Ins. no. 156 Yadavas of Devagiri AD 1207.	Hungund Tq. Bijapur Dt.	@ ~ <	Δ Δ Δ	some land		oil		cash income derived out of tolls from each village of kara-			SII, XV, 200-201

Key to the Symbols :

+ : Gardens;	– : Fields;	# : Local Potentate; $: *brāhmaṇa*;	* : *mahājana*;	~ : Merchant;	> : Main Ruler;
@ : Functionary;	< : Peasant;	& : Cultural Professional Group;	~~~ : Stream;	¼ : Village;	Δ : Temple;
A : Artisan;	m : *mattar*;	K : *Kamma*; n = *nivaratena*;	T : Tank;	O : *maṭha*;	Ins. : Inscription

Chart – II : ECONOMIC CONTEXT

Sub Region B

i	ii	iii	iv	v	vi	vii	viii	ix	x	xi	xii	xiii
S.No.	Name/Date Dynasty	Location	Donor	Donee	Types of Grants					Immunities	Irrigation	Reference
					Lands	Village	Commod-dities	Cash	Revenue			
									dikal-300 levies on oil mills			
33.	Ins. no. 11 Chalukyas of Kalyani AD 973.	Kopbal Tq. Raichur Dt.	> $	$ *						*sarvanamasya* *agrahāra*		*IIAS*, 18, 57-60
34.	Nilgund Ins. Chalukyas of Kalyani AD 982.	Gadag Tq. Dharwar Dt.	#	$	30n							*EI*, IV, 204-208
35.	Ins. no. 47 Chalukyas of Kalyani AD 994.	Gadag Tq. Dharwar Dt.	@	Δ	+3m 3m							*SII*, XI, 32-34
36.	Ins. no. 48 Chalukyas of Kalyani AD 1002.	Gadag Tq. Dharwar Dt.	@	$	100m					*sarvabādha-parihāram sarvanamasya*		*SII*, XI, 34-36
37.	Ins. no. 1 Chalukyas of Kalyani AD 1005.	Yalburgi Tq. Raichur Dt.	~	Δ				100 *gad-vānas*				*HAS*, 18, 39-40
38.	Ins. no. 50 Chalukyas of Kalyani AD 1005.	Gadag Tq. Dharwar Dt.	#	O	+2 6m							*SII*, XI, 36-38
39.	Alur Ins. Chalukyas of Kalyani AD 1010.	Gadag Tq. Dharwar Dt.	* @	@ $	100m 100m					*sarvabādha-parihāram sarvanamasya*		*EI*, XVI, 27-31
40.	Ins. of Sudi C Chalukyas of Kalyani AD 1010.	Ron Tq. Dharwar Dt.	@ , ~	leased to *	114m							*EI*, XV, 75-77
41.	Kotavumachgi Ins.	Gadag Tq.	@	$						*sarvābhyan-*	T	*EI*, XX,

Key to the Symbols :
+ : Gardens; : Fields; # : Local Potentate; $: *brāhmaṇa*; * : *mahājana*; ~ : Merchant; > : Main Ruler;
@ : Functionary; < : Peasant; & : Cultural Professional Group; ~~~ : Stream; ¼ : Village; Δ : Temple;
A : Artisan; m : *mattar*; K : *Kamma*; n = *nivaratana*; T : Tank; O : *maṭha*; Ins. : Inscription

Chart – II : ECONOMIC CONTEXT

Sub Region B

i	ii	iii	iv	v	vi	vii	viii	ix	x	xi	xii	xiii
S.No.	Name/Date Dynasty	Location	Donor	Donee	Types of Grants					Immunities	Irrigation	Reference
					Lands	Village	Commod-dities	Cash	Revenue			
	Chalukyas of Kalyani AD 1012.	Dharwar Dt.	$	Δ & @	62m 20m 200m				*suṁka* (taxes) *daṇḍa* (fines) T	*tarasiddhi sarvanamasya-agrahāra*		64-70
42.	Ins. from Navali Chalukyas of Kalyani AD 1014.	Lingsugur Tq. Raichur Dt.	#	$	10m					*sarvanamasya saryabādha-parihāraṁ*		*EI*, XXXIV, 164-166
43.	Ins. from Ron A Chalukyas of Kalyani AD 1022.	Ron Tq. Dharwar Dt.	$	Δ	-50m +335k		1 oil mill	50 gold *gadyānas*		*sarvabādha-parihāraṁ*	T	*EI*, XIX, 222-226
44.	Ins. no. 58 Chalukyas of Kalyani AD 1022	Mundargi Tq. Dharwar Dt.	> , @	Δ	6m							*SII*, XI, 48
45.	Bannigol Ins. Chalukyas of Kalyani AD 1025.	Lingsugur Tq. Raichur Dt.	A royal decree is issued by # to @						to collect revenue at specified rates on various fields			*EI*, XXXVI, 118-120
46.	Ins. no. 3 Chalukyas of Kalyani AD 1027.	Lingsugur Tq. Raichur Dt.	Daughter of >	Δ	100m +1m		1 oil mill					*IIAS*, 18, 42-43
47.	Ins. no. 65 Chalukyas of Kalyani AD 1028.	Gadag Tq. Dharwar Dt.	@	Δ	+1m 4m							*SII*, XI, 55-57
48.	Transcript Chalukyas of Kalyani AD 1031.	Manvi Tq. Raichur Dt.	Queen of >	$	100m							*A.R.* no. B545 of 1961-62

Key to the Symbols : – : Gardens; : Fields; # : Local Potentate; $: *brāhmaṇa*; * : *mahājana*; ~ : Merchant; > : Main Ruler; @ : Functionary; < : Peasant; & : Cultural Professional Group; ~~~ : Stream; ¼ : Village; Δ : Temple; A : Artisan; m : *mattar*; K : *Kamma*; n = *nivartana*; T : Tank; O : *maṭha*; Ins. : Inscription

Chart – II : ECONOMIC CONTEXT

Sub Region B

i	ii	iii	iv	v	vi	vii	viii	ix	x	xi	xii	xiii
S.No.	*Name/Date Dynasty*	*Location*	*Donor*	*Donee*	*Types of Grants*					*Immunities*	*Irrigation*	*Reference*
					Lands	*Village*	*Commod-dities*	*Cash*	*Revenue*			
49.	Ins. no. 4 Chalukyas of Kalyani AD 1032.	Lingsugur Tq. Raichur Dt.	>	Δ	102m +1m		1 oil mill					*IIAS*, 18, 43-44
50.	Gadag Ins. Chalukyas of Kalyani AD 1037.	Gadag Tq. Dharwar Dt.	~	Δ	56m							*EI*, XIX. 217-222
51.	Kilaratti Ins. Chalukyas of Kalyani AD 1046.	Lingsugur Tq. Raichur Dt.	@	Δ	10m							*EI*, XXXV, 37-39
52.	Ins. of Sudi D Chalukyas of Kalyani AD 1050.	Ron Tq. Dharwar Dt.	A renewal of corporate regulations made by various @ to ~, < is issued.						exempt from *siddhāya* levied on shops, houses and lands for a period of 2 years.	*sarvabādha-parihāraṁ*		*EI*, XV, 77-80
53.	Ins. no. 5 Chalukyas of Kalyani AD 1052.	Manvi Tq. Raichur Dt.	@ , ~	T	13m						T	*IIAS*, 18, 44-46
54.	Mulgund Ins. Chalukyas of Kalyani AD 1053.	Gadag Tq. Dharwar Dt.	#	Δ	12m					*sarvabādha-parihārah*		*EI*, XVI, 53-57
55.	Ins. no. 92 Chalukyas of Kalyani AD 1054.	Mundargi Tq. Dharwar Dt.	@	Δ				47*gad-vānas*				*SII*, XI, 87-89
56.	Transcript Chalukyas of Kalyani AD 1055.	Lingsugur Tq. Raichur Dt.	>	Δ	13m							*A.R.* no. B342 of 57-58

Key to the Symbols : + : Gardens; - : Fields; # : Local Potentate; $: *brāhmaṇa*; * : *mahājana*; ~ : Merchant; > : Main Ruler; @ : Functionary; < : Peasant; & : Cultural Professional Group; ~~~ : Stream; ¼ : Village; Δ : Temple; A : Artisan; m : *mattar*; K : *Kamma*; n = *nivaratana*; T : Tank; O : *matha*; Ins. : Inscription

Chart – II : ECONOMIC CONTEXT

Sub Region B

i	ii	iii	iv	v	vi	vii	viii	ix	x	xi	xii	xiii
S.No.	Name/Date Dynasty	Location	Donor	Donee	Types of Grants					Immunities	Irrigation	Reference
					Lands	Village	Commod-dities	Cash	Revenue			
57.	Ins. no. 94 Chalukyas of Kalyani AD 1059.	Mundargi Tq. Dharwar Dt.	~	Δ				35 gold gad-vānas				*SII*. XI, 89-90
58.	Ins. of Sudi E Chalukyas of Kalyani AD 1060.	Ron Tq. Dharwar Dt.	>	#						*sarvanamasya* with all *parihāras*	T	*EI*. XV, 85-94
			#	& T	36m 120m							
			@						revenue of the *manneya*	*sarvabādha-parihāraṁ*		
59.	Ins. no. 97 Chalukyas of Kalyani AD 1062.	Gadag Tq. Dharwar Dt.	@, * ~, A	Δ	15m							*SII*. XI, 91-94
60.	Daddala Ins. Chalukyas of Kalyani AD 1069.	Manvi Tq. Raichur Dt.	~		24m +1m		1 oil mill					*EI*. XXXVI, 113-116
61.	Ins. no. 111 Chalukyas of Kalyani AD 1071.	Gadag Tq. Dharwar Dt.	#	Δ	36m					*sarvabādha-parihāram*		*SII*. XI, 107-110
			*	Δ	10m		1 oil mill					
62.	Gawariwad Ins. A Chalukyas of Kalyani AD 1072.	Gadag Tq. Dharwar Dt.	# # #	Δ Δ Δ	50m				*(aruvaga)* quitrent of 62 gold pieces	*sarvanamasya*		*EI*. XV, 337-347
			@	Δ	12m					*sarvabādha-parihāram*		
63.	Ins. no. 112 Chalukyas of Kalyani AD 1072	Ron Tq. Dharwar Dt.	@	Δ			1 oil mill			*sarvanamasya*		*SII*. XI, 110
			~	Δ	+45k		3 oil mills			*sarvanamasya*		

Key to the Symbols – : Gardens; @ : Functionary; A : Artisan; : Fields; < : Peasant; m : *mattar*; # : Local Potentate; & : Cultural Professional Group; K : *Kamma*; $: *brāhmaṇa*; n = *nivartana*; * : *mahājana*; ~~~ : Stream; T : Tank; ~ : Merchant; ¼ : Village; () : *matha*; > : Main Ruler; Δ : Temple; Ins. : Inscription

Chart – II : ECONOMIC CONTEXT

Sub Region B

i	ii	iii	iv	v	vi	vii	viii	ix	x	xi	xii	xiii
S.No.	Name/Date Dynasty	Location	Donor	Donee	Types of Grants					Immunities	Irrigation	Reference
					Lands	Village	Commod-dities	Cash	Revenue			
64.	Ins. no. 2 Chalukyas of Kalyani AD 1074.	Ron Tq. Dharwar Dt.	@	Δ		¼				*tribhōgabhya-ntarasiddhi, sarvanamasya*		*SII*, XV. 2-3
65.	Ins. of Sudi H Chalukyas of Kalyani AD 1075.	Ron Tq. Dharwar Dt.	>	Δ		¼				*sarvanamasya astabhogam sarvābhyanta-rasiddhi*		*EI*, XV, 96-100
			@	&	some land							
66.	Ins. no. 117 Chalukyas of Kalyani AD 1076.	Ron Tq. Dharwar Dt.	sister of >	Δ			oil mill	some cash 10 gad-*vānas*				*SII*, XI, 117-118
			#	Δ								
67.	Ins. at Yewur B Chalukyas of Kalyani AD 1077.	Shorapur Tq. Gulbarga Dt.	>	@		3 ¼				*sarvabādha-parihāram*		*EI*, XII, 269-291
			@	Δ	412 m				*suṁka* (taxes) *daṇḍa* (fines)	*teia-svāmya-sarvabādha-parihāram, sarvanamasyam, tribhogābhya-ntarasiddhi*		
68.	Ins. no. 6 Chalukyas of Kalyani AD 1078.	Lingsugur Tq. Raichur Dt.	#	Δ						*sarvabādha-parihāraṁ sāmvaṁ*		*IIAS*, 18, 46-49
69.	Ins. no. 7 Chalukyas of Kalyani AD 1079.	Lingsugur Tq. Raichur Dt.	@, ~	Δ	26m							*IIAS*, 18, 49-51
				$	20m							

Key to the Symbols : + : Gardens; : Fields; # : Local Potentate; $: *brāhmaṇa*; * : *mahājana*; ~ : Merchant; > : Main Ruler; @ : Functionary; < : Peasant; & : Cultural Professional Group; ~~ : Stream; ¼ : Village; Δ : Temple; A : Artisan; m : *maṭṭar*; K : *Kamma*; n = *nivaratana*; T : Tank; O : *maṭha*; Ins. : Inscription

Chart – II : ECONOMIC CONTEXT

Sub Region B

i	ii	iii	iv	v	vi	vii	viii	ix	x	xi	xii	xiii
S.No.	Name/Date Dynasty	Location	Donor	Donee	Types of Grants					Immunities	Irrigation	Reference
					Lands	Village	Commod-dities	Cash	Revenue			
70.	Ins. no. 10 Chalukyas of Kalyani AD 1080.	Gadag Tq. Dharwar Dt.	~	Δ				one sattuga of paddy from each shop				KI, II, 29-34
			*	Δ	3m					sarvabādha-parihāraṁ		
71.	Ins. no. 127 Chalukyas of Kalyani AD 1082.	Gadag Tq. Dharwar Dt.	#	T					danda (fines)	sarvanamasya	T	SII, xi, 146-149
			*	T	16m 9m					sarvanamasya	T	
72.	Ins. of Sudi I Chalukyas of Kalyani AD 1084.	Ron Tq. Dharwar Dt.	queen of >	Δ		¼				sarvanamasya		EI, XV, 100-102
73.	Ins. no. 134 Chalukyas of Kalyani AD 1087.	Gadag Tq. Dharwar Dt.	*	Δ	20m					sarvabādha-parihāram		SII, IX, 157-160
					4m					sarvanamasyam	T	
74.	Ins. no. 133 Chalukyas of Kalyani AD 1087.	Gadag Tq. Dharwar Dt.	*	Δ	5m					sarvabādha-parihāram		SII, XI, 154-157
			A	Δ	2m		oil	1 paṇa		sarvanamasyam		
75.	Munirabad Stone Ins. Chalukyas of Kalyani AD 1088.	Koppal Tq. Raichur Dt.	>	$							T, ~~~	IIAS, 5, 1-12
			@	Δ	+80k 20m					sarvabādha-parihāram mānyabhritya-dāsi vargga sahitam sarva svāmam		
			*	Δ	200k 4m					sarvabādha-parihāraṁ		

Key to the Symbols :
+ : Gardens; .. : Fields; # : Local Potentate; $: *brāhmaṇa*; * : *mahājana*; ~ : Merchant; > : Main Ruler;
@ : Functionary; < : Peasant; & : Cultural Professional Group; ~~~ : Stream; ¼ : Village; Δ : Temple;
A : Artisan; m : *mattar*; K : *Kamma*; n = *nivaratana*; T : Tank; O : *matha*; Ins. : Inscription

Chart – II : ECONOMIC CONTEXT

Sub Region B

i	ii	iii	iv	v	vi	vii	viii	ix	x	xi	xii	xiii
S.No.	Name/Date Dynasty	Location	Donor	Donee	Types of Grants					Immunities	Irrigation	Reference
					Lands	Village	Commod-dities	Cash	Revenue			
76.	Ins. no. 137 Chalukyas of Kalyani AD 1091.	Gadag Tq. Dharwar Dt.	A	o	6m					*sarvanamasya sarvabādha-parihāraṁ*		*SII.* XI, 165-166
77.	Transcript Chalukyas of Kalyani AD 1096.	Deodurg Tq. Raichur Dt.	>	$		¼						*A.R.* no. B661 of 58-59
			$	*		¼				*agrahāra*		
78.	Transcript Chalukyas of Kalyani AD 1096.	Manvi Tq. Raichur Dt.	#	@	75m				exemption from the payment of taxes of *mūliqadera* & *umbali*			*A.R.* no. B530 of 1961-62
79.	Transcript Chalukyas of Kalyani AD 1099.	Manvi Tq. Raichur Dt.	>	$								*A.R.* no. B566 of 1961-62
			#	Δ	100m							
80.	Ins. no. 148 Chalukyas of Kalyani AD 1099.	Ron Tq. Dharwar Dt.	~	@					income on sale of betel leaves			*SII.* XI, 182-183
81.	Ins. no. 149 Chalukyas of Kalyani AD 1100.	Ron Tq. Dharwar Dt.	@	Δ	24m +3		1 oil mill					*SII.* XI, 183-184
82.	Ins. of Sudi H Chalukyas of Kalyani AD 1100.	Ron Tq. Dharwar Dt.	>	$					*aruvaṇa* tax			*EI.* XV, 97
83.	Transcript Chalukyas of Kalyani AD 1100.	Shorapur Tq. Gulbarga Dt.	*	Δ	450k +1		1 oil mill 1 *angaḍi*					*A.R.* no. B520 of 60-61
			*, ~	Δ	4m							

Key to the Symbols : + : Gardens; : Fields; # : Local Potentate; $: *brāhmaṇa*; * : *mahājana*; ~ : Merchant; > : Main Ruler;
@ : Functionary; < : Peasant; & : Cultural Professional Group; ~~~ : Stream; ¼ : Village; Δ : Temple;
A : Artisan; m : *maṭṭar*; K : *Kamma*; n = *nivaratana*; T : Tank; O : *maṭha*; Ins. : Inscription

Chart – II : ECONOMIC CONTEXT

Sub Region B

i	ii	iii	iv	v	vi	vii	viii	ix	x	xi	xii	xiii
S.No.	Name/Date Dynasty	Location	Donor	Donee	Types of Grants					Immunities	Irrigation	Reference
					Lands	Village	Commodities	Cash	Revenue			
84.	Ins. no. 150 Chalukyas of Kalyani AD 1102.	Gadag Tq. Dharwar Dt.	@	Δ				gold income				SII, XI, 185-187
85.	Ins. no. 153 Chalukyas of Kalyani AD 1103.	Ron Tq. Dharwar Dt.	A	Δ				some gold				SII, XI, 192
86.	Ins. no. 152 Chalukyas of Kalyani AD 1103.	Gadag Tq. Dharwar Dt.	@	Δ	+2 2m					*sarvanamasya sarvabādha-parihāraṁ*		SII, XI, 189-191
			@	Δ					*hejjuṁka* of their gardens	*sarvanamasya*		
			A	Δ				1 *paṇa*	part of their *bhatta* (wages)			
87.	Ins. no. 155 Chalukyas of Kalyani AD 1104.	Ron Tq. Dharwar Dt.	#	Δ	some land		1 oil mill			*aṣṭabhoga-sāṁya sarvanamasya*		SII, XI, 144-147
88.	Ins. no. 158 Chalukyas of Kalyani AD 1109.	Gadag Tq. Dharwar Dt.	@	Δ	+1					*sarvabādha-*parihāraṁ		SII, XI, 201-203
			~	Δ			2 *ballas* of sal. & wheat		1 *paṇa* over one unit of oil			
			<	Δ					1 *paṇa* on *mente* 1 *paṇa* on *toṁṭa*			
			A	Δ					1 *paṇa* on *doni*	*sarvabādha-parihāraṁ*		
			@	Δ	12m				*kulivasuṁka* (garden)	*sarvabādha-parihāraṁ*		
			~	Δ					*bīrapaṇa*	*sarvabādha*		

Key to the Symbols :

+ : Gardens; : Fields; # : Local Potentate; $: *brāhmaṇa*; * : *mahājana*; ~ : Merchant; > : Main Ruler;
@ : Functionary; < : Peasant; & : Cultural Professional Group; ~~~ : Stream; ¼ : Village; Δ : Temple;
A : Artisan; m : *mattar*; K : *Kamma*; n = *nivaratana*; T : Tank; O : *maṭha*; Ins. : Inscription

Chart – *II* : ECONOMIC CONTEXT

Sub Region B

i	ii	iii	iv	v	vi	vii	viii	ix	x	xi	xii	xiii
S.No.	*Name/Date Dynasty*	*Location*	*Donor*	*Donee*	*Types of Grants*					*Immunities*	*Irrigation*	*Reference*
					Lands	*Village*	*Commod-dities*	*Cash*	*Revenue*			
										parihāraṁ		
89.	Ins. no. 18 Chalukyas of Kalyani AD 1109.	Deodurg Tq. Raichur Dt.	~	Δ					incomes derived from whole sale levies on the minting esta-bilishments & sale of commodities			*IIAS*, 18. 51-52
90.	Ins. from Yewur Chalukyas of Kalyani AD 1110.	Shorapur Tq. Gulbarga Dt.	A	Δ			lime	1/4 gold piece	*Anada* on each residence			*EI*, XII, 332-333
91.	Ins. at Ittagi A Chalukyas of Kalyani AD 1112.	Yalburgi Tq. Raichur Dt.	>	Δ						*tribhogābhva-ntarasiddhi, sarvanamasya*		*EI*, XIII, 37-38
			#	Δ	-500					*sarvanamasya sarvabādha-pariharaṁ*	T	
			#	*				12 *gad-vānas* of gold		*sarvanamasya sarvabādha-parihāraṁ*		
92.	Ins. no. 163 Chalukyas of Kalyani AD 1113.	Ron Tq. Dharwar Dt.	#	T	24m					*sarvabādha-parihāraṁ*	T	*SII*, XI, 209-212
				$	12m							
				$	12m							
				$	6m							
93.	Ins. Sudi K Chalukyas of Kalyani AD 1114.	Ron Tq. Dharwar Dt.	#	o	1000m					*sarvabādha-parihāraṁ*		*EI*, XV, 105-108

Key to the Symbols : + : Gardens; : Fields; # : Local Potentate; $: *brāhmaṇa*; * : *mahājana*; ~ : Merchant; > : Main Ruler; @ : Functionary; < : Peasant; & : Cultural Professional Group; ~~~ : Stream; ¼ : Village; Δ : Temple; A : Artisan; m : *maṭṭar*; K : *Kamma*; n = *nivaratana*; T : Tank; O : *maṭha*; Ins. : Inscription

Chart – II : ECONOMIC CONTEXT

Sub Region B

i	ii	iii	iv	v	vi	vii	viii	ix	x	xi	xii	xiii
S.No.	Name/Date Dynasty	Location	Donor	Donee	Types of Grants					Immunities	Irrigation	Reference
					Lands	Village	Commod-dities	Cash	Revenue			
94.	Ins. no. 167 Chalukyas of Kalyani AD 1118.	Gadag Tq. Dharwar Dt.	@, <	Δ	+1					*sarvabādha-parihāraṁ*		*SII*, XI, 214
95.	Ins. no. 193 Chalukyas of Kalyani AD 1118.	Gadag Tq. Dharwar Dt.	&	Δ				5 *gad-yānas*				*SII*, XI, 250
96.	Transcript Chalukyas of Kalyani AD 1120	Lingsugur Tq. Raichur Dt.	#	Δ								*A.R.* no. B711 of 1958-59
97.	Ins. no. 170 Chalukyas of Kalyani AD 1121.	Ron Tq. Dharwar Dt.	#	Δ	12m							*SII*, XI, 217-218
98.	Transcript Chalukyas of Kalyani AD 1122	Manvi Tq. Raichur Dt.	@	Δ	some land							*A.R.* no. B572 of 1961-62
99.	Ins. no. 9 Chalukyas of Kalyani AD 1124.	Lingsugur Tq. Raichur Dt.	#, @	Δ	3m							*IIAS*, 18, 52-54
100.	Transcript Chalukyas of Kalyani AD 1134.	Manvi Tq. Raichur Dt.	#	Δ	32m							*A.R.* no. B565 of 61-62
101.	Ins. no. 11 Chalukyas of Kalyani AD 1138.	Koppal Tq. Raichur Dt.	*	Δ				2 *gad-yānas* annually				*IIAS*, 18, 57-60
102	Ins. no. 50 Chalukyas of Kalyani AD 1136.	Gadag Tq. Dharwar Dt.	@	Δ	4m +1				*aruvaṇa* of a garden	*sarvabādha-parihāram sarvanamasyam*		*SII*, XI, 36-38

Key to the Symbols :

+ : Gardens; : Fields; # : Local Potentate; S : *brāhmaṇa*; * : *mahājana*; ~ : Merchant; > : Main Ruler;
@ : Functionary; < : Peasant; & : Cultural Professional Group; ~~~ : Stream; ¼ : Village; Δ : Temple;
A : Artisan; m : *mattar*; K : *Kamma*; n = *nivaratana*; T : Tank; O : *maṭha*; Ins. : Inscription

Chart – II : ECONOMIC CONTEXT

Sub Region B

i	ii	iii	iv	v	vi	vii	viii	ix	x	xi	xii	xiii
S.No.	Name/Date Dynasty	Location	Donor	Donee	Types of Grants					Immunities	Irrigation	Reference
					Lands	Village	Commod-dities	Cash	Revenue			
103.	Ins. no. 5 Chalukyas of Kalyani AD 1143.	Yalburgi Tq. Raichur Dt.	<	Δ		¼			A portion of annual wages earned by the <			*apgas*, 9, 29-30
104.	Ins. no. 25 Chalukyas of Kalyani AD 1144.	Gadag Tq. Dharwar Dt.	@	Δ					*bira paṇa*			*SII*, XV, 28
			@, <	Δ					*suga paṇa*			
105.	Ins. no. 28 Chalukyas of Kalyani AD 1144.	Ron Tq. Dharwar Dt.	~	Δ			1 oil mill			*sarvanamasya*		*SII*, XV, 30-31
			~	Δ				1 pana				
106.	Ins. no. 27 Chalukyas of Kalyani AD 1144.	Ron Tq. Dharwar Dt.	@	Δ					income from *pannāya cess*			*SII*, XV, 29-30
107.	Transcript Chalukyas of Kalyani AD 1144.	Deodurg Tq. Raichur Dt.	A	Δ			paddy		levies on different articles of merchandise			*A.R.* no. B664 of 58-59
108.	Transcript Chalukyas of Kalyani AD 1146.	Shorapur Tq. Raichur Dt.	@	Δ					*hejjuṁka* and *vaḍḍarāvula* taxes on 18,000 *mattars* of land			*A.R.* no. B521 of 1960-61
109.	Ins. no. 36 Chalukyas of Kalyani AD 1148.	Gadag Tq. Dharwar Dt.	@	Δ	+3m 7m					*sarvabādha-parihāraṁ sarvanamasvaṁ*		*SII*, XV, 43-46
			@	Δ					cess on betel leaves	*sarvanamasya*		
			~	Δ				1 pana				
			~	Δ					Tax on oil mill (*gāṇadatere*)			

Key to the Symbols : + : Gardens; : Fields; # : Local Potentate; $: *brāhmaṇa*; * : *mahājana*; ~ : Merchant; > : Main Ruler; @ : Functionary; < : Peasant; & : Cultural Professional Group; ~~ : Stream; ¼ : Village; Δ : Temple; A : Artisan; m : *mattar*; K : *Kamma*; n = *nivaratana*; T : Tank; O : *maṭha*; Ins. : Inscription

Chart – II : ECONOMIC CONTEXT

Sub Region B

i	*ii*	*iii*	*iv*	*v*	*vi*	*vii*	*viii*	*ix*	*x*	*xi*	*xii*	*xiii*
S.No.	*Name/Date Dynasty*	*Location*	*Donor*	*Donee*	*Types of Grants*					*Immunities*	*Irrigation*	*Reference*
					Lands	*Village*	*Commod-dities*	*Cash*	*Revenue*			
			@	Δ					*pannāvasṁka* of God's garden	*sarvabādha-parihāraṁ*		
110.	Ins. no. 10 Chalukyas of Kalyani AD 1149	Yalburgi Tq. Raichur Dt.	$	Δ	4m							
			$	Δ	300k							
			A	Δ				10 gold pieces				*IIAS*, 18, 54-57
			~	Δ			One shop (*angadi*)					
			@	Δ					*hejjuṁka* tax			
111.	Ins. no. 43 Chalukyas of Kalyani AD 1153.	Ron Tq. Dharwar Dt.	@, <	Δ	5m							*SII*, XV, 56-57
			~	Δ	some land		*hāga* oil 1 oil mill					
112.	Ins. no. 52 Chalukyas of Kalyani AD 1155.	Gadag Tq. Dharwar Dt.	@	Δ					*manneya suṅka dasavanda* income of garden			*SII*, XV, 68-69
			@	Δ	1m							
113.	Ins. no. 53 Chalukyas of Kalyani AD 1155.	Ron Tq. Dharwar Dt.	@	T	1m 350k					*sarvanamasya*	T	*SII*, XV, 69-71
114.	Ins. no. 106 Chalukyas of Kalyani AD 1166.	Gadag Tq. Dharwar Dt.	~	Δ					levies on various merchandise			*SII*, XV, 136-137
115.	Ins. no. 238 Chalukyas of Kalyani AD 1169.	Ron Tq. Dharwar Dt.	#	T	6m					*sarvabādha-parihāram sarvanamasya*	T	*SII*, XV, 293-296

Key to the Symbols : + : Gardens; @ : Functionary; A : Artisan; : Fields; < : Peasant; m : *mattar*; # : Local Potentate; $: *brāhmaṇa*; & : Cultural Professional Group; K : *Kamma*; n = *nivartana*; * : *mahājana*; ~~~ : Stream; T : Tank; ~ : Merchant; ¼ : Village; O : *maṭha*; > : Main Ruler; Δ : Temple; Ins. : Inscription

Chart – II : ECONOMIC CONTEXT

Sub Region B

i	ii	iii	iv	v	vi	vii	viii	ix	x	xi	xii	xiii
S.No.	Name/Date Dynasty	Location	Donor	Donee	Types of Grants					Immunities	Irrigation	Reference
					Lands	Village	Commod-dities	Cash	Revenue			
116.	Ins. no. 66 Kalachuris of Kalyani AD 1170.	Yalburgi Tq. Raichur Dt.	@	Δ		¼				*sarvabādha-parihāram sarvanamasya nidhinikshepa sahitaṁ*		*APGAS*, 3 73-77
117.	Ins. no. 114 Kalachuris of Kalyani AD 1170.	Ron Tq. Dharwar Dt.	@	Δ				30 *gad-yānas*				*SII*, XV, 145
118.	Ins. no. 117 Kalachuris of Kalyani AD 1171.	Ron Tq. Dharwar Dt.	#	Δ								*SII*, XV, 147-148
119.	Ins. from Yewur F Kalachuris of Kalyani AD 1173.	Shorapur Tq. Gulbarga Dt.	@	Δ	1m +1/4m					*sarvanamasya*		*EI*, XII, 335-336
120.	Ins. no. 121 Kalachuris of Kalyani AD 1173.	Gadag Tq Dharwar Dt.	<, ~ @	Δ					*Pannāya* tax	*sarvanamasya*		*SII*, XV, 151-152
121.	Ins. no. 241 Kalachuris of Kalyani AD 1174.	Ron Tq. Dharwar Dt.	@ <	Δ Δ	10m 26m		2 *balla* grains oil	50 *gad-yānas*		*sarvabādha-parihāraṁ sarvanamasya*		*SII*, XV, 297-301
122.	Ins. no. 12 Kalachuris of Kalyani AD 1175.	Sindhunur Tq. Raichur Dt.	~	Δ	*ardhavritti of land*				*bali, teru, suli kolli, talāra pārikaya* taxes	*sarvabādha-parihāraṁ samastateio-pabhoga*		*IIAS*, 18, 61-63
123.	Transcript Kalachuris of Kalyani AD 1178.	Manvi Tq. Raichur Dt.	#	Δ		¼						*A.R.* no. B556 of 1960-61

Key to the Symbols : + : Gardens; : Fields; # : Local Potentate; $: *brāhmaṇa*; * : *mahājana*; ~ : Merchant; > : Main Ruler;
@ : Functionary; < : Peasant; & : Cultural Professional Group; ~~~ : Stream; ¼ : Village; Δ : Temple;
A : Artisan; m : *mattar*; K : *Kamma*; n = *nivaratana*; T : Tank; O : *maṭha*; Ins. : Inscription

Chart – II : ECONOMIC CONTEXT

Sub Region B

i	ii	iii	iv	v	vi	vii	viii	ix	x	xi	xii	xiii
S.No.	Name/Date Dynasty	Location	Donor	Donee	Types of Grants					Immunities	Irrigation	Reference
					Lands	Village	Commod-dities	Cash	Revenue			
124.	Ins. at Ittagi B Kalachuris of Kalyani AD 1178.	Yalburgi Tq. Raichur Dt.	~	Δ	35m					*sarvanamasya sarvabādha-parihāram*		*EI*, XII, 59-61
125.	Ins. no. 13 Kalachuris of Kalyani AD 1178.	Yalburgi Tq. Raichur Dt.	@	Δ						*sarvabādha-parihāraṁ sarvanamasya*		*HAS*, 18, 63-74
126.	Ins. no. 132 Kalachuris of Kalyani AD 1178.	Gadag Tq. Dharwar Dt.	@	T					*bannigadera* tax		T	*SII*, XV, 168
127.	Two Ins.from Ron B Kalachuris of Kalyani AD 1179.	Ron Tq. Dharwar Dt.	#	Δ T O	20m 2m 2m					 *sarvanamasya*	T	*EI*, XIX, 226-236
128.	Ins. from Yewur B Kalachuris of Kalyani AD 1179.	Shorapur Tq. Gulbarga Dt.	@	$	10m							*EI*, XII, 336-340
129.	Ins. no. 135 Kalachuris of Kalyani AD 1179.	Gadag Tq. Dharwar Dt.	~	Δ				cash income	levies on merchandise			*SII*, XV, 174-178
130.	Ins. no. 10 Kalachuris of Kalyani AD 1181.	Gadag Tq. Dharwar Dt.	@	Δ			3 oil presses 1 *mana* of oil					*KI*, II, 29-34
131.	Ins. no. 14 Chalukyas of Kalyani AD 1183.	Yalburgi Tq. Raichur Dt.	>	$		¼				*nidhiniksepa pasānārāmādi sahitaṁ tribhogā bhyantara siddhi asta bhoga*		*HAS*, 18, 74-79

Key to the Symbols : + : Gardens; : Fields; # : Local Potentate; $: *brāhmaṇa*; * : *mahājana*; ~ : Merchant; > : Main Ruler; @ : Functionary; < : Peasant; & : Cultural Professional Group; ~~~ : Stream; ¼ : Village; Δ : Temple; A : Artisan; m : *mattar*; K : *Kamma*; n = *nivaratana*; T : Tank; O : *matha*; Ins. : Inscription

Chart – *II* : ECONOMIC CONTEXT

Sub Region B

i	ii	iii	iv	v	vi	vii	viii	ix	x	xi	xii	xiii
S.No.	*Name/Date Dynasty*	*Location*	*Donor*	*Donee*	*Types of Grants*					*Immunities*	*Irrigation*	*Reference*
					Lands	*Village*	*Commod-dities*	*Cash*	*Revenue*			
										teiasvāmyah yuktaṁ sulka-daṇḍa sāda-kāruka kara-mauli kāṁanādi sakala dravyopana nopetam		
132.	Ins. no. 62 Chalukyas of Kalyani AD 1184.	Gadag Tq. Dharwar Dt.	A	Δ				some gold. 1 *paṇa* 4 *haṇa*				*SII*, XV, 87-88
133.	Ins. no. 57 Chalukyas of Kalyani AD 1184.	Mundargi Tq. Dharwar Dt.	#, @ ~	T T	24m 450k				*pannāyasuṁka*		T	*SII*, XV, 74-78
134.	Ins. no. 64 Chalukyas of Kalyani AD 1185.	Gadag Tq. Dharwar Dt.	@ *	Δ Δ	6m * 4m					*sarvabādha-parihāraṁ sarvanamasya*		*SII*, XV, 89-90
135.	Ins. no. 67 Chalukyas of Kalyani AD 1185.	Gadag Tq. Dharwar Dt.	A A	Δ Δ			some oil 1 *balla dhānya*	5 *hana*				*SII*, XV, 92-94
136.	Ins. no. 70 Chalukyas of Kalyani AD 1186.	Gadag Tq. Dharwar Dt.	~	Δ				5 *paṇas* out of minting opera-tions				*SII*, XV, 95-96
137.	Ins. no. 69 Chalukyas of	Gadag Tq. Dharwar Dt.	A	Δ			rice					*SII*, XV, 95

Key to the Symbols : + : Gardens; – : Fields; # : Local Potentate; $: *brāhmaṇa*; * : *mahājana*; ~ : Merchant; > : Main Ruler; @ : Functionary; < : Peasant; & : Cultural Professional Group; ~~~ : Stream; ¼ : Village; Δ : Temple; A : Artisan; m : *maṭṭar*; K : *Kamma*; n = *nivaratana*; T : Tank; O : *maṭha*; Ins. : Inscription

Chart – II : ECONOMIC CONTEXT

Sub Region B

i	ii	iii	iv	v	vi	vii	viii	ix	x	xi	xii	xiii
S.No.	Name/Date Dynasty	Location	Donor	Donee	Types of Grants: Lands	Village	Commod-dities	Cash	Revenue	Immunities	Irrigation	Reference
	Kalyani AD 1186.											
138.	Ins. no. 73 Chalukyas of Kalyani AD 1189.	Gadag Tq. Dharwar Dt.	$	Δ	24m					sarvabādha-parihāram sarvanamasya		SII, XV, 99-104
			~	Δ	some land		some articles from each shop					
139.	Ins. no. 16 Chalukyas of Kalyani AD 1191.	Lingsugur Tq. Raichur Dt.	#, @	Δ	100m					aruvaṇavilla sarvabādha-parihāraṁ		HAS, 18, 83-89
140.	Gadag Ins. Yadavas of Devagiri AD 1191.	Gadag Tq. Dharwar Dt.	>	Δ						sā-śulka kara-bādha parihāra samastādeya-sahita tribhogayuktam sarvanamasya		EI, III, 217-220
141.	Ins. no 15 AD 1191.	Sindhnur Tq. Raichur Dt.	#	Δ	12m					sarvabādha-parihāraṁ		HAS, 18, 80-82
			#	Δ	21m							
			#	Δ	18m							
142.	Gadag Ins. Hoysalas of Dwarasamudra AD 1192.	Gadag Tq. Dharwar Dt.	>	Δ						nidhinikṣepa jala-pāsa nāramadi sahitaṁ tribhogā bhyantaraṁ aṣṭabhoga teja-svāmya yuktam śulka daṇḍa sakala		EI, VI, 89-97

Key to the Symbols : + : Gardens; · : Fields; # : Local Potentate; $: *brāhmaṇa*; * : *mahājana*; ~ : Merchant; > : Main Ruler; @ : Functionary; < : Peasant; & : Cultural Professional Group; ~~~ : Stream; ¼ : Village; Δ : Temple; A : Artisan; m : *maṭṭar*; K : *Kamma*; n = *nivartana*; T : Tank; O : *maṭha*; Ins. : Inscription

Chart – II : ECONOMIC CONTEXT

Sub Region C

i	ii	iii	iv	v	vi	vii	viii	ix	x	xi	xii	xiii
S.No.	Name/Date Dynasty	Location	Donor	Donee	Types of Grants					Immunities	Irrigation	Reference
					Lands	Village	Commod-dities	Cash	Revenue			
143.	Ins. no. 74 Chalukyas of Kalyani AD 1194.	Ron Tq. Dharwar Dt.	#	Δ	16m					*dravyopārjjanopetam*		*SII*. XV, 104-105
144.	Hosur Ins. Hoysalas of Dwarasamudra AD 1207.	Gadag Tq. Dharwar Dt.	* @	@ Δ	1m 1m					*sarvabādha-parihāram*		*EI*. XXXII, 171-174
145.	Ins. no. 7 Yadavas of Devagiri AD 1215.	Lingsugur Tq. Raichur Dt.	~ @	Δ	20m +1m		1 *gāna* (oil mill)		income derived from the fees collected on the transactions of money, sales of commodities, minting operations marriages and other ceremonies of merchants.	*sarvanamasya sarvabādha-parihāraṁ*		*IIAS*. 18, 89-93
146.	Ins. no. 4 Chalukyas of Kalyani AD 1056.	Alampur Tq. Mahbubnagar Dt.	@	Δ					taxes *(suṁkaṁ)* of 4 nadus			*Telangana Inscriptions*, 2, 20-21
147.	Transcript Chalukyas of Kalyani AD 1058.	Nandikotkur Tq. Kurnool Dt.	>	Δ		¼				*tribhogābyantarasiddhi*		453/68 of office of Archeology & Museums, Hyderabad

Key to the Symbols : + : Gardens; @ : Functionary; A : Artisan; — : Fields; < : Peasant; m : *maṭṭar;* # : Local Potentate; $: *brāhmaṇa;* & : Cultural Professional Group; K : *Kamma;* n = *nivaratana;* * : *mahājana;* ~~~ : Stream; T : Tank; ~ : Merchant; ¼ : Village; O : *maṭha;* > : Main Ruler; Δ : Temple; Ins. : Inscription

Chart – II : ECONOMIC CONTEXT

Sub Region C

i	*ii*	*iii*	*iv*	*v*	*vi*	*vii*	*viii*	*ix*	*x*	*xi*	*xii*	*xiii*
S.No.	*Name/Date Dynasty*	*Location*	*Donor*	*Donee*	*Types of Grants*					*Immunities*	*Irrigation*	*Reference*
					Lands	*Village*	*Commodities*	*Cash*	*Revenue*			
148.	Transcript Chalukyas of Kalyani AD 1060.	Alampur Tq. Mahbubnagar Dt.	@	Δ &	11m 9m							*A.R.* no. B72 of 1960-61
149.	Ins. no. 42 Chalukyas of Kalyani AD 1060.	Alampur Tq. Mahbubnagar Dt.	@	$	47m							*APGAS*, 3 131-132
150.	Ins. no. 11 Chalukyas of Kalyani AD 1067.	Alampur Tq. Mahbubnagar Dt.	@	Δ					cash income from each village of Aija-300			*APGAS*, 3 105-106
151.	Panchalingala Ins. Chalukyas of Kalyani AD 1068.	Kurnool Tq. Kurnool Dt.	>	Δ		¼				*tribhogābhyantarasiddhi nidhinidhāna nikṣepam*		*EI*, XXXVI, 139-143
152.	Transcript Chalukyas of Kalyani AD 1069.	Nandikotkur Tq. Kurnool Dt.	>	$		¼				*tribhogābhyantarasiddhi*		337/68 of office of Archeology & Museums, Hyderabad
153.	Ins. no. 22 Chalukyas of Kalyani AD 1072.	Alampur Tq. Mahbubnagar Dt.	#	Δ	some land					*tribhogābhyantarasiddhi*		*APGAS*, 3 117-118
154.	Bichapaili Ins. Chalukyas of Kalyani AD 1074.	Alampur Tq. Mahbubnagar Dt.	#	Δ		¼				*sarvābhyantarasiddhi*		*EI*, XXXVI, 69-74
155.	Ins. no. 8 Chalukyas of Kalyani AD 1076.	Alampur Tq. Mahbubnagar Dt.	@	Δ					*vaddarvula* tax from 4 *nadus*			*APGAS*, 3 103-104

Key to the Symbols : + : Gardens; @ : Functionary; A : Artisan; : Fields; < : Peasant; m : *mattar*; # : Local Potentate; $: *brāhmaṇa*; & : Cultural Professional Group; K : *Kamma*; n = *nivaratana*; * : *mahājana*; ~~~ : Stream; T : Tank; ~ : Merchant; ¼ : Village; O : *maṭha*; > : Main Ruler; Δ : Temple; Ins. : Inscription

Chart – II : ECONOMIC CONTEXT

Sub Region C

i	ii	iii	iv	v	vi	vii	viii	ix	x	xi	xii	xiii
S.No.	Name/Date Dynasty	Location	Donor	Donee	Types of Grants					Immunities	Irrigation	Reference
					Lands	Village	Commod-dities	Cash	Revenue			
156.	Ins. no. 16 Chalukyas of Kalyani AD 1078.	Alampur Tq. Mahbubnagar Dt.	#	Δ		¼				*paramesvara-datti*		*APGAS*, 3 110-111
157.	Ins. no. 14 Chalukyas of Kalyani AD 1080.	Alampur Tq. Mahbubnagar Dt.	#	Δ		¼				*tribhogābhva-ntarasiddhi*		*APGAS*, 3 107-108
158.	Ins. no. 18 Chalukyas of Kalyani AD 1082.	Alampur Tq. Mahbubnagar Dt.	@	Δ		¼			60 *gadyānas* out of the income of a village	*sarvabādha-parihāraṁ*		*APGAS*, 3 113-114
159.	Ins. no. 33 Chalukyas of Kalyani AD 1087.	Gadwal Tq. Mahbubnagar Dt.	#	Δ	151m 2m		2 oil mills 160 areca nuts		2 *paṇas* from every village in Aije-300			*APGAS*, 3 40-41
160.	Ins. no. 33 Chalukyas of Kalyani AD 1095.	Alampur Tq. Mahbubnagar Dt.	#	Δ		¼				*tribhogā-bhyantara siddhi sarvanamasya*		*Telangana Inscriptions* 2, 63-64
161.	Ins. no. 23 Chalukyas of Kalyani AD 1097.	Alampur Tq. Mahbubnagar Dt.	#	Δ	some land					*tribhogā-bhyantara siddhi sarvanamasya*		*APGAS*, 3 118-119
162.	Ins. no. 37 Chalukyas of Kalyani AD 1107.	Alampur Tq. Mahbubnagar Dt.	#	Δ					income accru-ing from the *suṅka* and *daṇḍa* of a village			*APGAS*, 3 125-126
163.	Ins. no. 15 Chalukyas of Kalyani AD 1107.	Alampur Tq. Mahbubnagar Dt.	queen of >	Δ						*tribhogā bhyantara siddhi aṣṭabhoga teja*		*APGAS*, 3 108-110

Key to the Symbols : + : Gardens; – : Fields; # : Local Potentate; $: *brāhmaṇa*; * : *mahājana*; ~ : Merchant; > : Main Ruler; @ : Functionary; < : Peasant; & : Cultural Professional Group; ~~~ : Stream; ¼ : Village; Δ : Temple; A : Artisan; m : *maṭṭar*; K : *Kamma*; n = *nivaratana*; T : Tank; O : *maṭha*; Ins. : Inscription

Chart – II : ECONOMIC CONTEXT

Sub Region C

i	ii	iii	iv	v	vi	vii	viii	ix	x	xi	xii	xiii
S.No.	Name/Date Dynasty	Location	Donor	Donee	Types of Grants					Immunities	Irrigation	Reference
					Lands	Village	Commod-dities	Cash	Revenue			
164.	Ins. no. 26 Chalukyas of Kalyani AD 1109.	Alampur Tq. Mahbubnagar Dt.	queen of >	Δ	101 m + 12 m					*sāmya* *sarvanamasya tribhogā bhyantara siddhi aṣṭabhoga teja sāmya*		*Telangana Inscriptions* 2. 50-51
165.	Ins. no. 32 Chalukyas of Kalyani AD 1182.	Alampur Tq. Mahbubnagar Dt.	~	Δ					income derived from tolls on various transactions			*APGAS*. 3 123.

Key to the Symbols : + : Gardens; : Fields; # : Local Potentate; $: *brāhmaṇa*; * : *mahājana*; ~ : Merchant; > : Main Ruler; @ : Functionary; < : Peasant; & : Cultural Professional Group; ~~~ : Stream; ¼ : Village; Δ : Temple; A : Artisan; m : *mattar*; K : *Kamma*; n = *nivaraṭana*; T : Tank; () : *maṭha*; Ins. : Inscription

5

SPATIAL CONTEXT

The concept of settlement and the use of the term in descriptions of prehistoric cultures has been made ever since the 19th century to distinguish archaeological sites which contained habitation debris (settlement sites) from non-occupation sites (including burial, ritual sites etc.).[1] Such a study has been further extended to comprehend these sites in terms of the manner in which communities belonging to a society or culture distribute themselves over the landscape.[2] A comprehensive analysis of the dynamics of such settlement patterns in historical periods entails a study of not just the geographical dimension, but more crucially an analysis of a host of factors such as economic, social, political and ideological that have converged to form the settlement structure in a particular way. It affords us with a dimension to comprehend the resultant social relationships at various levels, such as the rural and the non-rural on the one hand, and on the other, the local and supra-local, encompassing a thorough analysis of the formation of hierarchies both at the spatial and social contexts for various types of settlements.

An analysis of the individual structures and the lay out of the communities[3] is chiefly focussed upon in the studies of prehistoric and early historic settlement patterns due to the abundance of archaeological data available for these periods. The study of the archeological sites of the Harappan civilization which have helped a great deal in the construction of the social, economic, political and ideological structures best exemplifies our contention. In the absence of any such archaeological evidence such a study is however, precluded for the period of our research, particularly with reference to the availability of evidence on individual structures of the habitation areas. Dearth of archaeological data for the settlement sites of the early medieval period can be largely related to the preoccupation of the archaeologists with digging the early historical urban sites resulting in minimum attention being paid to the rural sites lying in their periphery.[4] In such a situation, the rural settlements found in predominance during the early medieval period have remained largely neglected in archaeological studies. In this context the inscriptional records located in the extant temple sites of the early medieval period form a crucial source of information to comprehend the spatial context of the area of our study.

We get to know about the settlement patterns during this period chiefly through an examination of the various names of places mentioned in the inscriptional sources of our period in the context of the grants made. *Analysis* of *place* names found in the inscriptional and literary sources have been taken as crucial factors in the comprehension of settlements during this period for various regions in India. A.K. Choudhary has made use of the literary texts such as the *Purāṇas, Smṛitis, Kāvyas,* foreign accounts and so on, and supplemented these with the epigraphic material, to comprehend the rural settlements of North Eastern India during the early medieval period.[5] He has been able to account for the existence of different types of village settlements in his region of study by identifying and various contexts in which terms describing the rural scenario have been used.[6] In this context, the use of terms such as *palli, pallika, ghoṣe, ghoṣaka,* and those of *kheta, khetaka, kharvāta,* and so on have been shown to be indicative of various stages in the growth of a rural settlement from an earlier hunting and pastoral state.[7] Rural settlements of the central Deccan have been studied in a similar way by R.N. Mishra in the light of the Vākāṭaka inscriptions.[8] In his study the author has primarily focussed upon an analysis of the suffixes attached to place names such as *khetaka, palli, vāṭaka* and sc on. According to him these are indicative of the hierarchical position of the settlements and this hierarchy was dependent upon the density of population.[9] By taking up a linguistic analysis of the place names available for the same period and region as above, K.M. Shrimali has arrived at the conclusion that, in contrast to the suffixes denoting urban settlements indicated through the use of *pura* and *nagara,* suffixes denoting varieties of rural settlements which are indicated through the use of such terms as *palli, kheta, grāma,* and so on, are far more numerous.[10] An analysis of the suffixes attached to various place names found in the inscriptional sources is again emphasized as an important criterion to comprehend the settlement patterns of early Maharashtra in the works of Malati Mahajan.[11] In this context, the author has focussed upon the comprehension of the evolutionary stages of various settlements as indicated by the changes in the names of suffixes attached to the place names. Thus, according to her double suffixes such as *palligrāma, wāḍigrāma* attached to names of places indicate the fact that the original habitation was developed into *grāma* in a later period; the suffix *palli* and *wāḍi* in this context indicating forms of early human settlements.[12] Further, suffixes such as *giri, koṇḍa* and others denoting the names of streams, tanks and so on have also been taken into account by scholars as important indicators of the topography of the region.[13] Considering every place name as a fossilized philological fact, A.S. Thyagaraju has made an extensive linguistic analysis of the suffixes and prefixes attached to early places in the *context* of the Andhra region.[14] On the basis of his study of Telugu place names, the author has been able to differentiate between tribal villages *(gūḍem)*, villages emerging out of migration (*valasa)* and encampment areas *(paliyam)*.[15]

All the above studies have contributed significantly to our comprehension of various meanings attached to place names which were purported to correspond to different stages in the development of settlements right from early historic times. In this sense these works indicate to us the fact that "space was differentiated and perceived as corresponding to different social spheres."[16] On the other hand, one sees in these works an over emphasis being laid on the meanings of suffixes of the place names perse, which are seen as located within very broad frameworks of time studies in relation to the modern linguistic boundaries of space.[17] As a result of this one sees that works of this nature, best exemplified by those of Malati Mahajan and A.D. Thyagaraju,[18] tend to universalize the settlement terminology which remains totally divorced from an analysis of the actual historical processes made in relation to the elements of human geography that had a crucial role to play in the very emergence of settlement structures. In effect, these studies emerge as basically place name studies and the viability of their interpretations attributed to various suffixes of the names of places need, however, to be tested further for their applicability in relation to specific time and spatial parameters of historical change.

Unlike a majority of the above studies, we have focussed in this chapter primarily upon an analysis of the settlement structures as they emerged during the period A.D. 1000- A.D. 1200 against the backdrop of the larger social, economic and political changes located within the specific region of South Western Deccan. The area of our study has further been divided into three sub-regions (A, B, and C) depending upon the local topographical diversities which have a significant bearing on the resultant spatial structures. On the basic of the richness of the data available in the context of sub-region B for the growth of settlements of various types, we have considered this sub-region as a nuclear area of analysis. We have already seen in the earlier chapters that the politico-economic and the social dimensions of change emerge in clear contours in sub-region B owing chiefly to the strategic location of the area. In fact, it was chiefly through an interaction of the above factors that the sub-region B emerges as a productive area of political legitimation. An index to the proliferation of settlements here is provided through the *agrahāra* and the temple settlements, particularly the latter ones, that begin to emerge actively in the context of the period of our study. On the other hand, sub-regions A and C had witnessed an active construction of temple building activity much earlier to our period and therefore, the nature of settlements in these areas represent a mature phase in the development of settlements and provide an effective contrast to those of sub-region B. Even in the secondary sources of our study, we have observed that the sub-regions A and C have figured actively in the cultural and political histories pertaining to the period prior to the 10th century A.D. in particular.[19] The sub-region B, on the other hand, particularly its eastern half, which mainly constitutes the fertile Raichur Doab, has often been represented as a warring zone giving us an impression that normal settlements were absent in this area.[20] It is in the light of above views that we wish to analyze the settlements of our period as essentially representing a particular phase in the emergence of settlements which were dependent as much upon their physiographic location as on the human agents responsible for their growth in the context of a specific historical time, namely, the early medieval complex.

To comprehend various dimensions of settlement patterns, it is pertinent note at his juncture, that one needs to take into account the crucial role played by the context in which a particular settlement is mentioned in the inscriptional sources. In fact, it is a correlation of the contextual reference of space with the terminology used to define it, that goes a long a way in defining the nature of any given settlement. We have therefore, attempted to depict these aspects of settlements in the charts appended to this chapter (IIIA, 1-23, IIIB 24-130, IIIC 131-143), wherein columns v, vi, vii, viii, x and xi give us an idea about the suffixes of place names (Column iii and Columns ix and xiv, signify the context [rural or urban]) in which these are described coupled with the representation of the location of the temple structure (column xiii) which had a crucial role to play in defining the nature of the settlements. In the inscriptional sources of our study we have various contexts in which the settlements are mentioned. Primarily, their mention is in the context of the grants made and this brings out the economic context of the physical space which then conglomerates on the religious space to which grants are directed. It is in relation to the above two aspects of the settlements that we find a variety of social groups filling the picture and defining the social space or the habitat. While at times, some of the settlements themselves form objects of grants, they are mostly described to us either, in the form of boundaries to the land grants made or, as the location for the grants of land and other commodities made. This enables us to comprehend the physical features of the settlements of the period which have various types of nomenclature used to describe them in the inscriptional sources of our study. In this context, terms such as *palli, vāḍa, ūr, grāma, pura* and *paṭṭaṇa* figure prominently as located in a larger spatial unit called the *nādu*. We now turn to understand these in terms of the chronological parameters and sub-regional distribution in the following analysis.

The nāḍu was a broad area, or unit, where all the above mentioned settlements were located. According to G.S. Dikshit, the term was used for all divisions above the village.[21] According to S.J. Mangalam, in the Tamil language, the *nāḍu* originally meant the cultivated or, settled area. It later on came to be designated for a large political division and also figured as a state revenue unit.[22] In the context of the Tamilakam region, however, *nāḍu* has been interpreted to mean a cluster, or grouping of peasant settlements, formed around the nucleus of a common irrigation source and strengthened by kinship ties.[23] In this context Burton Stein has repeatedly stressed upon the ethnic coherence of the *nāḍu* which he considered as the nuclear areas of the Chola territory representing the control of the dominant peasantry.[24] In all the above discussions, *nāḍu* emerges as a broad territorial area comprising within its fold several smaller settlement units. In the context of our study, the *nāḍu* was represented chiefly through the numerical suffixes attached to it.[25] Names of territorial divisions such as Nolambavadi-32,000 (IIIB, iv, 32), Banavāsi 1000 (IIIB, iv, 25), Belvola-300 (IIIB, iv, 27, 28, 29), Aija-300 (IIIC, iv, 132, 134, 135), Eḍeḍore-2000 (IIIB, iv, 35, 44) are only a few examples of several names used for the *nāḍu* or territorial units in our period of study. That the numerical suffixes represented the number of settlement units in each *nāḍu* has been generally agreed upon by various scholars.[26] For the bigger numerical suffixes such as Nolaṁbavāḍi- 32,000, it has been suggested that they might refer to *nāḍus* which represented each thousand.[27] This would then mean that the above territorial unit consisted of 32 *nāḍus*. Without going into the details of the controversy centred around the viability of the large numbers attached to various names of places, it would suffice here to state that, the large numbers attached to various names of places, representing *nāḍus*, indicated a higher level in the territorial structure. Inversely, the smaller number such as Kisukāḍ-70 (IIIA, iv, 20, IIIB, iv, 33, 49), Bāgaḍage-70 (IIIB, iv, 49), Toragare-60 (IIIB, iv, 52) and so on represented an intermediate stage in the growth of settlement clusters, from a local single unit of settlement to a supra-local, and ultimately, leading to the formation of a region, termed mostly in this context, as the Kuntala *deśa* (country).

It has been shown for the Chola rule in the Tamilakam region during the early medieval period that *nāḍu* was not an artificially created political unit but basically represented a peasant micro region and an economic as well as an ethnic territory.[28] In the context of our study we have an almost similar situation in the sense that various *nāḍus* do not represent political divisions made for administrative purposes, but emerge basically in association with the rise in the political power of a particular ruling family. Thus, the Nolambavāḍi nāḍu represents the Pallava hold, Banavāsi is associated with the rise of Kadambas who had ruled earlier to the period of our study. We find with reference to our area of study that the *nāḍu* or, even smaller territorial units bearing the name of one or the other smaller settlements located within them, (Karāḍikal (IIIB, ix, 123) from Karāḍikal-400), Kukkanūr (IIIB, ix, 85) from Kukkanūr-30 indicate to us basically the emergence of a particular settlement structure into a node in the cluster of several settlements surrounding it in a hierarchical pattern. It is pertinent to note at this juncture the emergence of a few *nāḍus* that grew into prominence during the period of our study. Among these for sub-region A during the 11th century A.D., Kisukāḍ-70 (IIIA, iv, 2, 5, 8, 11, 12) figures prominently and we have Hagariṭṭage-300 (IIIA, iv, 14, 16, 18, 19) for the 12th century A.D. for the same sub-region. For sub-region B during the 11th century A.D., we again have Kisukāḍ-70 (IIIB, iv, 33, 49, 50, 52, 55, 61) along with Belvola-300 and Puligere-300 (IIIV, iv, 25, 26, 27, 28, 29, 34, 48) Eḍeḍore-2000 (IIIB, iv, 35, 44, 58, 66) and Karāḍikal-300/400 (IIIB, iv, 46, 53, 57) and during the 12th century A.D. for sub-region B we have, along with the continuation of all the above tracts (excepts Puligere), emergence of Kelavāḍi-300 (IIIB, iv, 95, 98, 106) and Bāgaḍage *nāḍu* (IIIB, iv, 98, 105, 106). For sub-region C during the 11th century A.D., Aija-300 (IIIC, iv, 132, 134, 135, 136, 139) and Naravāḍināḍ (IIIC, iv, 133, 135, 141) figure prominently. The rise to prominence of only a few of these tracts over several other *nāḍu* territorial units mentioned in the sources, has wider implications in our comprehension of the complexity of the settlement structures located in them not only in terms of their physical setting, but importantly, in terms of understanding various historical processes such as economic, political, social and ideological forces under operation in bringing about the particular settlement into particular focus.

A comprehension of the hierarchical nature of the settlement patterns could, however, be obtained by analyzing them in terms of the suffixes attached to individual settlement, coupled with the contextual references made to these in terms of socio-economic activity operating in them. Suffixes such as *palli, vāḍa, ūr, grāma,* and *paṭṭaṇa* figure prominently in the context of settlement names during the period of our study. Names of places such as Sānḍiyanahalli (IIIA, v, 9), Puvvaravalli (IIIB, v, 37), Būruvalli (IIIC, v, 139) exemplify the *palli* suffixes. Nālvatumbāḍa (IIIA, vi, 4), Maltiyavāḍa (IIIB, vi, 28) exemplify the *vāḍa* settlements. Perūr (IIIA, vii, 2), Eleya Posavūr (IIB, vii, 27), Pulinūru (IIIC, vii, 140) are only a few of the numerous instances cited in the inscriptions indicating the ūr settlements. Further, places such as Miṇiṅjige (IIIA, viii, 19), Lokkiguṇḍi (IIIB, viii, 31), Pañchaliṅga (IIIC, viii, 133) and so on are described in terms of grāma settlements. Vikramapura (IIIA, x, 11), Śivapura (IIIB, x, 66), Hatampura (IIIC, x, 132), bear the *pura* suffixes and we have Erambarage (IIIA, xi, 15), Huligola (IIIB, xi, 105) and so on which are described as *paṭṭaṇas*.

According to G.S. Dikshit, *grāma, ūr, palli, vaḍa* are equivalent terms which could be considered as indicative of a village settlement.[29] However, we have different meanings attached to each of these terms given by various scholars. In one view, palli is equated to be pastoral or cowherd settlement.[30] In the context of north eastern India, *palli* has been interpreted to mean a hamlet where hunters and forest or hill dwellers lived in huts and a small *palli* has been termed as *pallika*.[31] These settlements, considered to be the settlements of wandering people, it is suggested, were smaller than the *grāma.*[32] Place names ending with *valli* are considered to be inter-changeable with *palli* (or the *halli)* suffix and therefore, they too indicate smaller settlement units than the *grāma.*[33] *Vāḍa* has been interpreted to mean an enclosure, a piece of enclosed ground, or enclosure of a village or town and so on.[34] Further, *vāḍa* is also equated to a settlement space constituted of ten or more huts and almost always with a small village set up.[35] *Ūr* on the other hand, has been connoted completely and therefore, it could be used in the sense of the planting of new places.[36] This ending added to settlements can thus emphasize the growth of new settlements in the form of full fledged villages in agriculturally viable areas. In the context of the early Tamilakam region this term has been used by some scholars to signify peasant or non-*brahmadeya* villages, as opposed to the *brahmadeya* villages of the place.[37]

The term *grāma* has been equated to a village settlement[38] perse, which in turn, is defined as referring to a consolidated agricultural community, distinguished from such other types of settlement patterns as tribal groups, dispersed hamlets, suburbs and towns.[39] On the other hand, S.J. Mangalam, rejecting the interpretation of *grāma*, in the sense of a village, has defined it as indicating a piece of land, the area of which is a *krośa* or a land yielding a yield of 1000 karshas.[40] Further, *grāma* is regularly contrasted with the term *araṇya* in Vedic literature.[41] *Grāma* has also been connoted to mean an 'estate' owned by an individual or group of persons.[42] The term *pura* has been equated to mean a fortified settlement[43] on the one hand, and on the other, it is equated to a town[44] and therefore, could also mean a city.[45] *Paṭṭaṇa* has a definite equation to a market place, a prosperous city and when it is suffixed to *rājadhāṇi* it would mean a large town containing a seat of political authority. Further, when suffixed to *baṇañju,* it would mean a large urban settlement inhabited and controlled by groups of merchants.[46] Apart from the above suffixes attached to spatial terminology which largely indicate to us the various ways in which settlement structures could be characterized, we also have in this context usage of certain suffixes which primarily connote the physical features of the locality or the area in which they were located.

Thus, for instance, we have such suffixes as *guṇḍa* in Niruguṇḍa (IIIB, iii, 25), *giri* in Eṭagiri (IIIB, iii, 41), *gere* in Hoṭṭalakere (IIIA, iii, 4), *vāvi* in Langanavāvi (IIIC, iii, 138), *gola* in Bannigola (IIIB, iii, 38), and *kallu* in Polukallu (IIIC, iii, 142) which figure prominently and consistently in the inscriptional records. The term *guṇḍa* as a transformed form of the term *koṇḍa* is equated to mean a hill or a mountain.[47] Similarly, the term *giri* has also been interpreted to mean a hill.[48] These indicate for us the possibility that the settlement must have originated around hills and therefore they acquired this particular suffix. In the inscriptions of our study, we have as many as 5 instances of such places. Of these we have Ponnugoṇḍa (IIIA, iii, 10), Nirugoṇḍa (IIIB, iii, 25), Muluguṇḍa (IIIA, iii, 27), Eṭagiri (IIIB, iii, 41) during the 11th century A.D. and Muḍiguṇḍūru (IIIB, iii, 94) figures in inscriptions of the 12th century A.D. The term *kere* (*gere*) has been equated to mean a tank,[49] denoting the emergence of the settlement due to its location near a tank. Similarly, the suffix *vāvi* denoting a well,[50] could be understood in the same way as above wherein a settlement was noted by the existence of a well which was crucial for its survival. Further, the suffix *gola (kola)* has been interpreted to convey the sense of villages built near ponds.[51] In the context of sub-region A during 11th century A.D. we have 1 instance of the *kere* suffix as it is used in the place named Hoṭṭalakere (IIIA, iii, 4) and for the 12th century A.D. in the same sub-region we have another single instance of it in the name of Kaḍakere (IIIA, iii, 17). In the context of sub-region B during the 11th century A.D. We come across nearly 8 instances of *kere* suffixes, Huligere (IIIB, iii, 29), Bayḍumbagere (IIIB, iii, 48) Kappaḍigere (IIIB, iii, 48), Torugere (IIIB, iii, 50), Kereyūr (IIIB, iii, 58), Annigere (IIIB, iii, 60), Musiyagere (IIIB, iii, 62), Ālamgere (IIIB, iii, 77), 1 instance of *vāvi* suffix, Tanakavāvi (III, iii, 43) and 23 instances of *gola* suffixes, Bannigola (IIIB, iii, 46), gummuṅgola (IIIB, iii, 60) and Teṁgola (IIIB, iii, 65). During the 12th century A.D. for the sub-region B we have 2 instances of the *kere* suffix Mūlavalligere (IIIB, iii, 96), and Oḍegere and 1 instance of the *gola* suffix for the place home Huligola (IIIB, iii, 105). In the context of sub-region C we have only one instance of the *vāvi* suffix (IIIC, iii, 138) during the 11th century A.D. On the other hand, the use of the suffix *kallu,* denoting a stone for place names, is largely indicative of the stony or rocky nature of the place to which it was attached.[52] We have 5 instances of the usage of *kallu* in the context of sub-region B. Of these, Mosalikallu (IIIB, iii, 44) Karāḍikal (IIIB, iii, 46) and Gorikallu (IIIB, iii, 58) figure during the 11th century A.D. and Bennekallu (IIIB, iii, 85), Kallūru (IIIB, iii, 94) figure in the 12th century A.D. It is interesting to note that in the context of sub-region C we come across nearly 3 instances of this type in the place names Pedakal (IIIC, iii, 135) which figures in 11th century A.D. and Polukallu (IIC, iii, 142) and Nāyakallu (IIIC, iii, 143) which are mentioned in the inscriptions of the 12th century A.D.

The above survey clearly indicates a concentration of these suffixes in sub-region B. It is significant to note in this context that the suffix *kallu* figures most prominently in place names found in the eastern part of sub-region B which constitutes the Raichur Doab and lies contiguous to sub-region C which also accounts for a majority of these suffixes. The above suffixes denote the physical locales of the early settlements and thereby signify the nature of the ancient landscapes as they originally stood. More importantly, we get to know through these terms that these landscapes and its environment have undergone significant changes overtime as a result of the exploitation of these natural landscapes in the hands of men setling here. Above all, these have a significant bearing on our comprehension of the proliferation of the settlement structures as is indicated by the existence of a large number of settlements mentioned above and found centered around tanks, wells, and ponds which could not have come into being without human effort.

The above discussion on the variety of suffixes available in inscriptions, indicates for us the complexities to understand any given historical space. It further underscores the fact that the normal settlement is much too complex to be encapsulated by the most commonly used generic terms *grāma* or *paṭṭaṇa*. Further, apart from showing the dynamic nature of how a settlement undergoes a change, these terms also indicate for us various nodes in the formation of a settlement structure at various levels. While the lines of demarcation between all these settlements cannot always be drawn with unequivocal sharpness, [53] these suffixes could, however, suggest to us in broad terms, the potentiality of a settlement to evolve certain typical characteristics at a given point of time as a result of the influence of a host of historical factors as can be seen below.

The contextual reference made to various settlements in the inscriptional sources help us to a large extent in the analysis of space during our period of study. Thus, we have the mention of *halli/palli/valli* suffixed place names mentioned under different contextual situations. In the context of sub-region A, by about A.D. 1049, we have an interesting reference to a place called Mūlavalligrāma (IIIA, v, 6) which formed the location point for some of the grants made in the record. Further, in about A.D. 1070, certain land was granted from Sāṇḍiyanahalli (IIIA, v, 9). For sub-region B, as early as A.D. 1022, Puvvaravalli (IIIB, v, 37) has been described as the camping place where the queen came to reside at the time of the grant. On the other hand, Kallamanapalli (IIIB, v, 61) forms an object of the grant made to a temple in A.D. 1074. While Gulugavalli (IIIB, v, 62) is mentioned among the boundaries of the grant made in an inscription dated to A.D. 1075, Kalasavalli (IIIB, v, 68) in an inscription dated to A.D. 1082 is referred to in the context of the purchase of land by the *mahājanas* which was located here. By about A.D. 1113, Puvvaravalli (IIIB, v, 86) is referred to as an *agrahāra* settlement. While Haḍalagere (IIIB, v, 108) described as *halli,* forms the object of the grant in A.D. 1170, Poṭṭūra (IIIB, v, 108) and Managlūra (IIIB, v, 108) *hallia* mentioned in the same record, figure as boundaries to the above mentioned settlement. The mention of Kallavanahalli (IIIB, v, 109) is again made in A.D. 1171, wherein the renewal of its earlier grant to a temple is issued. About A.D. 1178, we have the mention of Huniseyanahalli (IIIB, v, 117) as the object of the grant. In an earlier inscription dated to A.D. 1173, we have reference to Kanlyahalli (IIIB, v, 110) as a temple settlement along with the mention of various professional groups residing here. By about A.D. 1196, we have the mention of a donor, who is a *gauḍa* and has his residence at Kūṛalahalli (IIIB, v, 127) and in A.D. 1207,

Tuppadahalli (IIIB, v, 128) is mentioned among the boundaries of the grant made in this inscription. For sub-region C in A.D. 1068, Kālpalli (IIIC, v, 133) figures as a larger settlement when compared to Guḍigeri (IIIC, v, 133) and which formed an object of the grant. In fact, the latter has been termed as a hamlet of Kālpalli. Further, in an inscription dated to A.D. 1078, specific amounts of land granted from Būṛuvalli (IIIC, v, 139) and from Ballunḍavalli (IIIC, v, 139) are mentioned.

Several crucial issues emerge in the context of the above survey regarding the nature of *palli* suffixed settlements during the period of our study. Firstly, a majority of the instances, cited above go to indicate to us that the generally ascribed definitions attributed to it discussed earlier do not always hold good for defining all settlements mentioned above during this period. Most of these settlements seem to have undergone a change and were already established in a full fledged manner. In other words, they had, by the 11th century A.D., evolved from smaller settlements to be centres of the agrarian hinterland. In this context references to such places as Mūlavalligrāma (IIIA, v, 6) in 1049 A.D. and Sāṇḍiyanahalli (IIIA, v, 9) in A.D. 1070 as location points for the lands granted on the one hand, and on the other hand, Puvvaravalli (IIIB, v, 37) which figures as a camping place as early as 1022 A.D. and the emergence of Kālpalli (IIIC, v, 133) by A.D. 1068 as a larger settlement unit best exemplify our contention that most of the *palli* suffixed settlements had emerged by 11th century A.D. into well settled rural units. However, we do have a few exceptions in this regard which help us in comprehending an important dimension of the rural settlements, namely, the hierarchical patterning of space in the context of the *palli* suffixed settlements. In this context we have such settlements as Haḍalagere (IIIB, v, 108) which forms the object of the grant and is described as a *halli*, Poṭṭūr (IIIB, v, 108) and Mangulūra (IIIB, v, 108) form the boundaries for the above settlement and the emergence of Kālpalli (IIIC, v, 133) by A.D. 1068. It has been suggested that the profuse mention of boundary stones bordering these settlements are largely indicative of the fact that these *hallis* were newly demarcated, mostly belonging to the *polimera* or pasture lands of the established villages, mentioned in the grant.[54] In this context it is interesting to note that these settlements do not however have the suffix of *halli* attached to their names but are addressed as *hallis* in the text of the inscription.[55] While *palli* suffixed places of this type stand at the lowest stratum in the hierarchy of the settlements, places such as Kalasavalli (IIIB, v, 139), Būruvalli (IIIC, v, 139), Baliunḍavalli (IIIC, c, 139) and so on, wherein the lands granted are located could be considered as representing an intermediate stage in the hierarchy of settled villages.

In the case of Kalasavalli, it is the *mahājanas* of the Kuṛitakumte *agrahāra* who make a purchase of the land from one Sankimayya of this place[56] and in another case, specific amounts of land, belonging to Baliunḍavalli and Būruvalli were granted by the queen to a temple.[57] These two contexts of the mention of this place exemplify that the *halli* or *palli* ending places could be clearly understood as well settled villages with a strong agrarian base. We, however, have a more complex settlement structure emerging from the beginning of the 12th century A.D. in the case of *palli* suffixed settlements, which could be considered as representing a higher level in the hierarchy of *palli* settlements. In this context we have two interesting examples such as Puvvaravalli (IIIB, v, 86) which emerges as an *agrahāra* by about A.D. 1113 and Kaniyahalli (IIIB, v, 110) which in an inscription dated to A.D. 1173 is referred to as a temple settlement along with the mention of various professional groups residing here. In these two settlements one can clearly discern the complex web of the physical, economic, social and political forces conglomerating on a religious space. This critically absent in the earlier contextual references to *pallis*. These examples then provide us with a crucial dimention to comprehend the nature of change in a settlement pattern from a simple spatial structure to an advanced stage in the agrarian milieu represented by a well developed hinterland with a dynamic socio-economic and political base.

Contextual references to *vāḍa* suffixes too can be seen in a variety of cases during the present period of study. In sub-region A in an inscription dated to A.D. 1047, Gānada Halūr (IIIA, vi, 5) biṭṭa-(small *vāḍe)* of Kisukāḍ-70 formed an object of the grant. In A.D. 1145 from the same sub-region, Belūr (IIIA, vi, 14) the *vāḍa* is referred to as a temple settlement. Further, Gottakhaṇḍike (IIIA, vi, 16) in an inscription dated to A.D. 1174, described as a *baliya vāḍa* of Hagari-ṭtage-300, is referred to as a temple settlement. By A.D. 1184 Miṇinjige (IIIA, vi, 19), described as a *mahāgrāma* and *baliya-vāḍa* of Hagariṭṭage-300, emerges as an important temple settlement.

For the sub-region B we have, as early as A.D. 1002, reference to Maltiyavāḍa (IIIB, vi, 28) as the location of the land granted. In A.D. 1071, Muḍageri (IIIB, vi, 60), Gummuṁgola (IIIB, vi, 60), Iṭṭage (IIIB, vi, 60) and Gavarivāḍa (IIIB, vi, 60) have all been described as *vāḍa* and figure as the objects of the grant made. In A.D. 1075, Musiyagerey (IIIB, vi, 62) described as the *baliya vāḍa* forms an object of the grant. In A.D. 1084, we again, come across a *vāḍa* settlement. Poṁgari (IIIB, vi, 69) which forms an object of the grant. In an inscription of A.D. 1103, Posavūra (IIIB, vi, 81), described as the *baliya vāḍa,* is referred to as the property of the local God. Further, in A.D. 1121, Nārāyaṅgal (IIIB, vi, 90) known as a temple settlement, is referred to as a *vāḍa.* In A.D. 1148, Hosavūra (IIIB, vi, 100) is described for its beauty and the ruling family of the place find significant mention in this inscription. By A.D. 1178 we again have reference to a *baliya vāḍa* Selagara (IIIB, vi, 115) which has been granted to a local temple along with its waste area. Another *baliya vāḍa* in an inscription dated to A.D. 1179, Hiriya Maniyūr (IIIB, vi, 120), is mentioned amidst reference to an agriculturist guild 60 *okkalas*. In the context of sub-region C, we have reference in an inscription dated to A.D. 1058 to Jyāmaṭūru (IIIC, vi, 131) which is described as a *praviṣṭa vāḍa* called a hamlet by the editor of the inscription and this forms the object of the grant. Further, Kandanavolal (IIIC, vi, 141), described as a *vāḍa* in A.D. 1107, also forms the object of a grant.

In the context of above description of *vāḍa* settlements we can see two distinct trends emerging during this period. Firstly, for a major part of the 11th Century A.D. we find that there is a predominance in *vāḍas* as objects of grants made to the temples. By about the beginning of the 12th Century A.D. we see a distinct change in this trend as most of the settlements emerge as temple settlements. At this juncture it would be pertinent to note the change in the suffixes attached to the *vāḍa* settlements particularly in the context of sub-region B during the 12th century A.D. from those that existed in the 11th century A.D. During the 11th Century A.D. we have a predominance of such suffixes as *vāḍa* in Malteyavāḍa (A.D. 1002) geri in Mudageri (A.D. 1071), *gola* in Gummuṁgola (A.D. 1071), gere in Musiyagere (A.D. 1075) and kallu in Nārāyaṅgal (A.D. 1121). On the other hand, the *vāḍa* settlements are found attached with ūr suffixes for a major part of the 12th Century A.D. in the same sub-region such as Mudinūr (A.D. 1100), Posavūr (A.D. 1103), Hosavūr (A.D. 1148) and Hiriya Maniyr (A.D. 1179). This aptly signifies the fact that the *vāḍa* settlements at least, in the initial period of our study emerge basically as newly settled spatial units that were being brought into the vortex of the agrarian hinterland through them being granted to the religious institutions. Their emergence as *ūr* settlements with temples located in their centres in a majority of cases during the 12th Century A.D. however, brings to the forefront the extension of a well cultivated tract which begin to form an integral part of productive sphere. It is pertinent to note here that the term *vāḍa* was not usually suffixed to the majority of place names and was instead used to define a particular spatial unit either, as big *(baliya)* or, small (*biṭṭa*) *vāḍa* and this was not specific to any one type of settlement. We have further observed in this regard that the term *baliya vāḍa* was applied to both the settlements that formed objects of grants (such as Jyāmatūru, Selagara) and to those that were temple settlements (such as Hosavūr), Miṇiṅjige). In such cases it was chiefly the context of its occurrence and not the terminology of its definition that determined the actual status of space in the hierarchical pattern of the settlement structure. The latter attributes could, however, be distinctly noticed in context of *ūr* suffixes attached to the settlements under study. We wish to highlight below some of the important *ūr* settlements that figure in our sources.

For sub-region A in an inscription dated to A.D. 1022, we have the mention of Perūr (IIIA, vii, 2) as an *agrahāra* settlement. In A.D. 1047, Gānada Halūr (IIIA, vii, 5) is referred to as the object of a grant. In A.D. 1075, Bāḍubbeyapālu

(IIIA, vii, 11) during A.D. 1178, is referred to as the capital of the main ruler. In an inscription dated to A.D. 1184 Karaganūru (IIIA, vii, 18) figures among the boundaries of the land granted. For sub-region B we have, as early as A.D. 973, the mention of Moḍeyanūr (IIIB, vii, 24) as a newly created *agrahāra* and temple settlement. In A.D. 994 Eleya Posavūru (IIIB, vii, 27) is mentioned as a temple settlement. In an inscription dated to A.D. 1005, Sirivūra (IIB, vii, 29) and Saratavūra (IIIB, vii, 29) are mentioned in the context of governance of their taxes. In the same year Kukkanūr's (IIIB, vii, 30) assembly of merchants are mentioned in the context of grants made by them. In A.D. 1060 Śivanūr (IIIB, vii, 55) forms an object of the grant. In A.D. 1071 Soratavūr (IIIB, vii. 59) emerges into an *agrahāra* settlement. Kallamanūr (IIIB, vii, 62) during A.D. 1075, figures as a boundary. In A.D. 1077 Ehūr (IIIB, vii, 66) figures as an object of the grant. At Ermaganūr (IIIB, vii, 72) in A.D. 1087 a big well and a tank are referred to have been constructed here. Gabbūr (IIIB, vii, 75) in A.D. 1095, is mentioned as an *agrahāra*. From the beginning of the 12 Century A.D. we, however, find that new settlements having *ūr* suffixes are relatively small in number in this sub-region. It is chiefly the earlier mentioned *ūr* settlements that emerge at this time as a complex of settlement units and some of these even attain an urban like character. In this context, we have reference to Hiriya Gabbūr (IIIB, vii, 83) in A.D. 1109 showing characteristics of an urban like settlement with references here to minting establishments, assembly of merchants, mint officers and so on.[58] In the context of sub-region C we have reference to Guḍiyūru (IIIC, vii, 139) and Kadambūru (IIIC, vii, 139) as location of grants of land made. *Pulinūru* during A.D. 1095 (IIIC, vii, 140) figures as an object of the grant. One important feature of most of these settlements is their mention either, as *agrahāras* or, as places with an existence of temples. Some of them are further identified with a particular physical location as in this case of Mālad Ālūr (IIIB, vii, 32) or as Ālur of the plain.[59]

All the above factors indicate that the *ūr* settlements were well established rural areas with substantial areas of cultivable land for them to be made into *agrahāras* and temple settlements. This can be contrasted with the earlier discussed *palli* and *vāḍa* suffixed settlements which cannot be equated with the *ūr* settlements in terms of their complexity and richness. In this sense the *palli* and *vāḍa* suffixed settlements, in majority of the cases, could be considered to represent a stage lower than the *ūr* settlements in the hierarchical spatial contours. On the whole, the *ūr* suffixed settlements emerge as revenue paying settlement units such as in the case of Śivanūr (IIIB, vii, 55) wherein, with the grant of this place, the *manneya* (revenue) obtained from here was also transferred to the donee. In this context, we have an interesting example in an inscription dated to A.D. 1067 which refers to a term *Aijamunnūralūralu* which meant *ūrs* located in Aije-300. The gold income obtained from these villages was granted to a temple in this case.[60] We have observed that our earlier definition of the *ūr* as indicative of a newly emerging settlement structure holds good with regard to our data for these *ūr* suffixes and this is brought out clearly in the context of their distribution in various sub-regions of our study. We have seen that in sub-region 'A' only two *ūr* suffixed settlements are mentioned and out of these one of them Perūr (IIA, vii, 2), is an *agrahāra* and the other Gānadahalūr (IIIA, vii, 5) is an object of the grant. Similarly, in the context of sub-region C we have three instances of *ūr* settlements. Among these, 2, Jyamatūru (IIIC, vii, 131) and Pulinūru (IIIC, vii, 140) are objects of grants. It is chiefly in the context of settlements of sub-region B that we find *ūr* settlements have an active role to play particularly during the 11th century A.D. wherein several new names emerge in the context of the creation of either, the *agrahāra* or, to a large extent, the temple centred spatial milieus which provide the key to our comprehension of the growing complexity of the rural space.

It is, however, the *grāma* suffixed settlements that seem to stand out in their complex settlement structure as can be gauged from contextual references in which they are mentioned. In sub-region A during the later part of 12th century A.D., *i.e.,* in A.D. 1184, we have reference to Miṇiṅjige (IIIA, viii, 19) as *mahāgrāma.* For sub-region B we come across a large variety of such references for both the 11th and 12th centuries A.D. As early as A.D. 982 we have mention of Nirugunḍa (IIIB, viii, 25) wherein a plot of land located in the *antar-grāma* (inner village) of this place forms an object of the grant.[61] In A.D. 1007, Lokkigunḍi (IIIB, viii, 31) mentioned as *mahāgrāma* (big *grāma*), is referred to in the context of the construction of a Jaina temple at that place.[62] In an inscription dated to A.D. 1031, Ballaniṭṭage (IIIB, viii, 37) is referred to as a *bhaṭṭagrāma* which has been translated to mean a village owned by *brāhmaṇas* as a rent free holding and similar to an *agrahāra* village.[63] It is significant to note that in the context of this settlement a grant of land and a house site was made by the queen to one *brāhmaṇa.* In an earlier inscription dated to A.D. 1022 the same settlement Ballaniṭṭage, is mentioned in the context of the installation of a deity by the queen at this place.[64] In A.D. 1060 we have reference to Puli (IIIB, viii 55) as the *appayanavīḍu* (halting camp) of the main ruler and is described as a *baliyagrāma* (big *grāma*).[65] In the same inscription we have reference to several *bhaṭṭa-grāmas* such as Kariṭṭage (IIIB, viii, 55) and Bālguli (IIIB, viii, 55) which were ruled by a local chief.

In an inscription dated to A.D. 1069 Kappakallu (IIIB, viii, 58) emerges as a *bhaṭṭa-grāma* and a temple settlement.[66] The Niḍgunḍi grāma (IIIB, viii, 61) is described as a *baliya agrahāra* in an inscription dated to A.D. 1074 and is also referred to as an important temple settlement.[67] In an inscription dated to A.D. 1077, Mukkunḍe (IIIB, viii, 66) has been given the status of a *vipra-grāma.*[68]

According to Sircar, the term *vipra* indicates a class of *brāhamaṇas* who were adept in juggelery and magical practices.[69] In this inscription the settlement of Mukkuṇḍe along with two other settlements form the object of the grant made to a *brāhmaṇa* chief. Mukkuṇḍe in particular is glorified as an ornament to the tract in which it is located. Similar status, that of *vipra-grāma* is attributed to Pombolal (IIIB, viii, 68) in an inscription dated to A.D. 1082. Interestingly, in the same inscription, we have reference to Kuṛitakūṁte (IIIB, viii, 68) as an *agrahāra* settlement. Between A.D. 1084 to 1088 we have mention of as many as 3 *grāmas* as *agrahāra* settlements (IIIB, viii, 71, 72, 73). In A.D. 1124 we have reference to the place Liṅga (IIIB, viii, 91), as a *bhaṭṭa-grāma* which was being administered by the queen as her *bhṭṭa-grāma.*[70] Kukkanūr (IIIB, viii, 108) in an inscription dated to A.D. 1170 figures as a *grāma* and *agrahāra*. We have in A.D. 1191 Hiriya Haṇḍigola (IIIB, viii, 124) *nāmaḥ grāmaḥ* forming an object of the grant. We have another such instance in an inscription dated to A.D. 1192 where in Hoṁbalalu (IIIB, viii, 126) and was described as *abhidhāne grāma.*[71] This term could be interpreted as extension of protection to the settlement from danger and its safety was guaranteed.[72] It is significant to note that the period in which these two *grāmas* figure as objects of grants corresponds to the emergence of new families of main rulers, namely, the Yadavas of Devagiri and the Hoysaḷas of Dwāra Samudra. In the context of sub-region C, in A.D. 1068, Pañchaliṅga *grāma* (IIIC, viii, 133) emerges as consisting of the *sthalavritti* of 1400 *mattars* of land in extent spreading over two groups of 6 *bāḍas* of *sthalavritti* has been explained as a tenure in which payment of tax was made in kind from the produce.

The above examples cited by us with regard to the *grāma* settlements have helped us in arriving at certain crucial conclusions. Firstly, the term *grāma* very rarely is suffixed to the names of the places mentioned and it is only in the context of their description that we get to know them as *grāmas.* In this context, the complex and compound terminology attributed to these places indicates to us to the existence of a hierarchy within the *grāma* settlements. Thus, the mention of such terms as *mahāgrāma* in the context of certain settlements such as Lokkiguṇḍi, Nidgundi and Miṇiṅjige and its non-mention for others such as Hiriya-Haṇḍigola and Hombalalu, certainly indicates that the former held prominence over the latter due to various historical factors. Further, the characterization of the *grāma* settlements into *bhaṭṭa-grāma, agrahāra, vipra grāma* has a significant bearing on our comprehension of the variety of *brāhmaṇa* settlements during this period. On the other hand, the status of *abhidāne grāma* conferred on one of these settlements along with the *brāhmaṇa* villages bears ample evidence to the elevation of certain settlements into prominence through political intervention which was of course due to the potentiality exhibited by these settlements to generate surplus and thus maintain a host of *brāhmaṇas* and temple institutions which are profusely mentioned as located in them. All these factors definitely imply that the *grāma* settlements had an edge over the other settlements such as *palli, vāḍa,* and *ūr* in the hierarchy of the settlement structure during the period of study as these represent through the variety in which they are mentioned, an advanced stage of the rural milieu.

All these settlements, however, cannot be treated as mutually exclusive categories since the spatial terminology indicate that they were placed in a vertical division of hierarchy which nonetheless interacted with each other. We have instances in which these terminologies and suffixes tend to overlap in their description of settlements. Thus, for example Modeyanūr (IIIB, viii, 24) having the *ūr* suffix is also referred to as Modita *grāma.* Miṇinjige (IIIA, viii, 19) is described both as a *vāḍa* and a *grāma.* It is interesting to note that the *sthala vritti* of the Pañchaliṅga *grāma* (IIIC, viii, 133) was spread over two groups of six *bāḍas.* Despite the existence of hierarchies, which largely depended upon the extent of advancement made in terms of their economic, social and political configuration, all the above discussed terms could be corresponded to defining broadly a rural spatial category.

The usage of *pura* or its Kannada equivalent *volāl,*[73] are suffixes which have been used to denote more than one type of settlement pattern in our records. They have a significant bearing on our comprehension of these settlements only in terms of how they are actually described rather than from the name which may define its character or status in the context of our study. In an inscription dated to A.D. 1010, we have mention of the place Suṇḍi (IIIB, x, 33) as a *pura,* wherein we have reference to both *gāvuṇḍas* and the merchants of the place mentioned in the context of leasing of lands.[74] In A.D. 1047, we have the mention of Vikramapura along with Jaina temple located there.[75] In an inscription dated to A.D. 1049 we have reference to one Śripura (IIIA, x, 16) described as a *grāma.* In this settlement, as many as six temples have been mentioned as located here and we also have interesting references to hills, tanks and rivers bordering on this place.[76] In A.D. 1032, Bharatapura (IIIB, x, 42) is referred to as an *agrahāra* wherein we have reference to 200 *mahājanas* of the place.[77] In A.D. 1059, we have reference to Dharmavola (IIIB, x, 54) which mentions a *nagara jinālaya* and the assembly of merchants *(nagara samudāya).*[78] By 1060 A.D., Suṇḍi (IIIB, x, 55), which was earlier referred to as only a pura is now called a *rājadhāni* (capital) *pura* and we have reference here of a temple and a tank constructed during this period.[79] In an earlier inscription dated to A.D. 1054, we have reference to the *pola* (fields) of Suṇḍi.[80] In an inscription dated A.D. 1062, reference to Mulguṇḍapura (IIIB, x, 56) is made along with several mercantile bodies and a major temple.[81] In an inscription dated to A.D. 1075 Vikramapura (IIIA, x, 11) emerges as a major temple settlement with frequent mention of fertile lands, garden lands and shops located in it.[82] In another inscription dated to the same year, Vikramapura (IIIB, x, 62) emerges as the residing place of the chief of the main ruling family at the time the grant was made. Further, in the same inscription, we have reference to markets meeting on Sundays at Suṇḍi (IIIB, x, 62) which is called a *rājadhāni pura.*[83] In an inscription dated to A.D. 1077, we have reference to a place called Śivapura (IIIB, x, 66) which figures as a small settlement mentioned in the context of some people working for God residing here.[84] In an inscription dated to A.D. 1079, the name of the settlement is not mentioned and instead we have reference to the *seṭṭis* of two *puras.*[85] In an earlier inscription dated to A.D. 1058, another settlement named Śivapura (IIIC, x, 131) forms an object of the grant.[86] The frequent mention of Hatampura (IIIC, x, 132, 138, 139, 140) is made in the context of it being a major temple settlement.[87] Pombolal (IIIB, x, 68) in A.D. 1082, is referred to as *vipra grāma.*[88] In an inscription dated to A.D. 1109 we have reference to Eleya-Śripura (IIIB, x, 84), wherein we have mention of several agricultural and mercantile guilds and a major temple as located here.[89] It is interesting to note here that the same place is referred to ten years later in an inscription dated to A.D. 1118, as Eleya-Śripura (IIIB, x, 88) and here we have reference to *gāvuṇḍas* and agricultural groups and a temple.[90] In an earlier inscription dated to A.D. 1107, Kandanavolal (IIIC, x, 141) forms an object of the grant.[91] In A.D. 1114, we have mention of the place Achalapura (IIIB, x, 87) which according to the editor of this record, could probably be the residential quarter connected with sanctuary of God Achaleśvara which is located within its precincts.[92]

The variety of ways in which the *pura* suffixes emerge in the records of our period render it difficult for us to accept the traditional definition attributed to *pura* in terms of a city, a town or any other urban space the meaning of which we had discussed earlier. A great flexibility has to be adopted to understand the urban milieu of their mention with regard to the (in relation to the) context in which they are mentioned. Particularly significant in this regard are such settlements as Śivapura (IIIB, x, 66, IIIC, x, 131), Achalapura (IIIB, x, 87), Kandanavolal (IIIC, x, 141) and so on which largely emerge as small settlement units having no specific attributes described with regard to their socio-economic and political advancement and figure chiefly in terms of objects of grants. On the other hand, we, however, find that a majority of the *pura* suffixed settlements emerge in terms of their complexity as major temple settlements as in the case of Vikramapura (IIIA, x, 12) which also rises to the status of a *rājadhāni.* Similar is the case of the settlement called Suṇḍi (IIIB, x, 52). Poṁbolal (IIIB, x, 68) in an inscription dated to A.D. 1082 is referred to as a *vipra-grāma,* which by A.D. 1189 (IIIB, x, 152) is described as a *mahāgrahāra* and a major temple settlement.[93] Importantly, the *pura* settlements in a majority of the cases could be identified as depicting an urban like character as we see that as early as A.D. 1010, in Suṇḍi (IIIB, x, 33) the existence of merchants was mentioned : In an earlier inscription dated to A.D. 1059 at Dharmavolal (IIIB, x, 54) there is reference to a *nagara* Jinālaya and a *nagara samudāya.* It is interesting to note that by A.D. 1184, this place is referred to as Dharmapura and 16 *seṭṭis* and *nakaras* of the place are mentioned along with the mention of two temples located here. This place is also addressed to as an *ūr* at some point of its reference in the inscription.[94] Further, in A.D. 1062, reference to Mulguṇḍapura (IIIB, x, 56) is made along with mercantile bodies located here and in another inscription dated to A.D. 1079, we have reference to the *seṭṭis* of two puras and so on.[95]

Writing about the conception of the early medieval urban phenomenon, B.D. Chattopadhyaya has drawn our attention to certain important clues to cull out such information from the inscriptional sources. Among these the nature of the grants made, mention of mercantile and industrial groups coupled with the suffixes of places have been considered an important indicators of differentiate between a rural and non-rural space. Accordingly, if the major object of the grant, instead of lands/fields by contrast, relates to industrial/commercial items, mention of mercantile groups and so on it may be said to represent an urban like set up.[96] While some of the just discussed feature are evidence for a non-rural character of the settlement, we cannot, at the same time, attempt a clear cut classification of these into urban and the earlier mentioned ones as rural. The distinction was only one of degree and not of kind as, in actual practice, the villages exhibited more the features of a rural or agricultural economy while the towns or cities betrayed more of an urban or industrial and commercial economy.[97] Such a distinction was particularly nebulous for the *pura* suffixes mentioned during the period of the present study. We have seen in the case of Suṇḍi in an inscription dated to A.D. 1010, the merchants are mentioned as leasing lands and, as late as A.D. 1109, in the case of Eleya-Śripura, we have mention of agricultural groups and mercantile guilds emerging as donors for a temple located at this place. In such a context, if we take the presence of merchants and their guilds functioning in the non-agrarian activities such as trade and other commercial activities as any indications of an urban phenomenon, then these settlements could at best be considered to exhibit such traits only in part.

On the other hand we find that *paṭṭaṇa* suffix, only gradually begins to get mentioned in the inscriptions towards the end of 11th century A.D. This gives a definite shape to our understanding of what the urban space during the early medieval context should be understood as. In an inscription dated to A.D. 1124 we have reference to Muluguṇḍa (IIIB, xi, 92) as *ādivaṭṭaṇa* (*ādi* here is translated as time immemorial).[98] We have reference here to *seṭṭis* and the *telliga*-50 of the place.[99] In A.D. 1151, Eṛambarage (IIIA, xi, 15) is referred to as *paṭṭaṇa* and we have reference here to Jaina monks.[100] In A.D. 1166 we have the mention of

Huligola (IIIB, xi, 105) described as an *agrahāra* and *balañjadādi paṭṭaṇa* (immemorial *paṭṭaṇa* of the merchants), and to the *mahānāḍu* assembly of merchants who met here to make grants. In this inscription we further have the mention of various other *paṭṭaṇas* located in Belvola-300 whose prabhus were supposed to have attended *mahānāḍu* along with several other merchants.[101] Further, in an inscription dated to A.D. 1178 Mulugunda (IIIB, xi, 114) is again referred to as *anādipaṭṭaṇa* and the *nagara mahājana* of the place are referred to a donors to a temple.[102] In A.D. 1191 Karāḍikal (IIIB, xi, 123) is described as *anādi paṭ ṭaṇa* and this place is praised for its ponds which were said to be full of water, fields and gardens rich with crops, thriving inhabitants and flourishing temples of Gods. In the same inscription Mudugal (IIIB, xi, 123) is referred to as a *rājadhāni* and *paṭṭana* and is mentioned in the context of it being described as a seat of political power for a local chieftan.[103] Mulugunḍa (IIIB, xi, 129) in an inscription dated to 1207 is referred to as a *rājadhāni paṭṭana* and the mercantile bodies of the place are eulogized a great deal here as they emerge as donors of land and money to the God Telligeśvara of the place.[104]

The above examples cited by us definitely indicate a trend towards the growth of an urban-like environment at least from the beginning of the 12th century A.D. wherein we find that the *paṭṭaṇa* settlements emerge clearly as commercial centres with various mercantile bodies like *nakara, nānādeśi mummuri-daṇḍas, seṭṭis* and so on operating actively in these places. The presence of these bodies definitely stands in contrast to the earlier described settlements wherein the agrarian activity dominated the scene. In this sense equation of *paṭṭaṇa* as a market place and as a large and prosperous city can be accepted.[105] In this context we have basically two types of *paṭṭaṇa* that are described in sources, namely, the *rājadhāni paṭṭaṇa* defined as dynastic quarters superimposed on a *paṭṭaṇa* and the *banañjuvaṭṭaṇa,* a town dominated by merchant colonies.[106] We wish to highlight here notice to certain settlement names which end with the suffix *sthala* found in all the three sub-regions of the present study. In the context of sub-region A we have the mention of Hagariṭṭiya *sthala* (IIIA, iii, 21) Karaganura *sthala* (IIIA, iii, 21) Kandagale *sthala* (IIIA, iii, 22) towards the end of the 12th and early 13th centuries A.D. In sub-region B we have an isolated reference to Kukkanūr *sthala* (IIIB, iii, 30) as early as A.D. 1005. In sub-region C we again come across several *sthala* suffixes attached to such places as Tuṁbula (IIIC, iii, 143), Gabbūr (IIIC, iii, 143), Ālampur (IIIC, iii, 143) and so on towards the end of 12th century A.D. The association of these settlements invariably with several mercantile guilds and the commodities of trade enables us to surmise upon the fact that these represent important trading centres. Even in the early 11th century A.D. with reference to the *sthala* at Kukkanūr we have the mention of a merchant (*seṭṭi*) who makes some grant of gold and the *nakaraṁ* or merchant assembly.[107] In view of above evidence the period under study has been largely considered by various scholars as the beginning of a new phase of urban activity.[108] In the area under study we cannot however, witness a full fledged urban growth under operation in the sense that we still have a large majority of rural settlements dominating the scene and the pockets of commercial activity that emerged at this time could at best be seen as organically related to the agrarian hinterland and very much dependent on it. Therefore, revival of an urban phenomenon in terms of its earliest breakdown at the end of the early historical period holds untenable for the present study. The overwhelming evidence available during this period for the expansion of agrarian settlements had a crucial economic implication in defining the form of the productive base that provided the surplus necessary for the incipient growth of an urban-like phenomenon at this point in time. In this context our analysis of various suffixes attached to the settlements of the region under study becomes a significant pointer to two basic trends. Firstly, our tabulation has shown large majority of rural settlements during this period which are mentioned in the sources. Of these only some gradually lead towards an urban like environment by the beginning of 12th century A.D. Secondly, it is important to note that one can clearly discern a certain hierarchical pattern of settlements but, at the same time, all of them were in a process of change.

In the light of above study on the general terminology used to define settlements in the medieval period it becomes pertinent for us to understand the difference between a settlement attached with a suffix defining its status perse, and the description of the settlement in the inscription with attributes different from the meaning of the suffix. This point can be clarified further through the examples given below. Not all the settlement units with *palli* suffixes can be understood in the sense of small tribal or pastoral unit as is indicated in the meaning of the suffix *palli* given by us above. In this regard we have the mention Puvvaravalli (A.D. 1022) which, at the point in time when the grant was being made, was described as the camping place for the queen. Later, in A.D. 1113 Puvvaravalli emerges as an *agrahāra* settlement. This clearly indicates its rise to prosperity as an agrarian village will enough surplus so that it could be marked out for a grant as an *agrahāra.* Among the settlements with the *vāḍa* as the suffix, we have the mention of Nālvathumbāḍa (A.D. 1033) which was an important well established place being ruled over by a local potentate. Therefore, this enables us to conclude that *vāḍas* cannot merely, be understood as military camps of a temporary nature as is often generalized by the scholars. In another example to a village *(grāma)* in an inscription dated to A.D. 1068, two groups of six baḍas come together to constitute the *sthala-vritti* of Pañchliṅgagrāma. Among the *ūr* suffixed settlements, we see a lot of variation. While some of these have the status of a *vāḍa* as Posavūra (A.D. 1103) which is described as a big *vāḍa* in the inscription, some are described as *halli* as in the case of Mangalūra and Poṭṭūr (A.D. 1170) and interestingly, most of these are described as *grāmas*. In the case of Modeyanūr it is also termed as Moditagrāma (A.D. 973). The variability of *ūr* settlements from its allusion to being *palli* type on the one hand, and grāma on the other, could be because they were continuously growing and therefore, those that were already established held features akin to the *grāma*, while those that were in incipient stages of growth were similar of *pallis* or *vāḍas*.

In view of the above description we have tried to understand various suffixes attached to the settlements as indicating the nature of the space and the contextual reference to it as enabling us to comprehend the changing nature of a settlement pattern at a given point of time. These also help us in comprehending the hierarchical patterning of the space understood chiefly to their description from one stage to other. We wish to state here that by the 12th century A.D. new names begin to be mentioned in the sources to describe settlements which do not necessarily fit into the designation of the suffixes discussed by us above. Some of these are *gere, geri, kallu, vāvi, guṇḍa* and *gola* which are used as suffixes and described in various contexts of their reference. They nonetheless, significantly indicate to us the spread in the agrarian economy to new hitherto uncultivated areas of the region under study.

At this juncture it would be pertinent to elaborate upon the sub-regional pattern of the spatial suffixes used to describe settlements as this would help us in analyzing their spread in the context of their physiographic setting. Out of the various instances of settlements mentioned in sub-region A (IIIA, iii, 1-23) we have reference to only two instances of *palli* settlements (IIIA, v, 6, 9), 6 instances of the *vāḍa* type of settlements (IIIA, vi, 4, 5, 10, 11, 17, 19), four instances of the *ūr* type (IIIA, vii, 2, 5, 17, 18) and two instances of the *grāma* (IIIA, viii, 6, 19) settlements all defining of rural scenario. The instance of *pura* suffix mentioned here is in the context of Vikramapura (IIIA, x, 5, 8, 11) which is mentioned three times and this indicates its importance. Similarly the *paṭṭaṇa* suffix is mentioned once with regard to the place of Erambarage (IIIA, xi, 15). On the other hand, in the context of sub-region B (IIIB, iii, 24-130) we find that a variety of settlements emerge throughout the present period of study. It is chiefly in this sub-region that the usage of various suffixes defining the nature of settlements is made substantially. This again stands in contrast to the settlements of sub-region C wherein we find that out of various settlements charted out by us (IIIC, iii, 131-143), we have mention of 3 *pallis* (IIIC, v, 133, 139), 2, *vāḍa* (IIIC, vi, 131, 141) 3 *ūr* (IIIC, vi, 139, 140) and 1 *grāma* (IIIC, vi, 133) settlement and the *pura* suffixed settlement Hatampura finds frequent mention as a major temple settlement (IIIC, x, 132, 138, 139). The suffix *paṭṭaṇa* is conspicuous by its absence in this sub-region.

Against the background of the above survey our observations regarding the nature of settlements made in the chapter on physiography[109] become pertinent to comprehend the spatial spread of the settlements for the various sub-regions. We are well aware of the fact that the disproportionate quantification of data furnished above nowhere points towards absolute trends in the patterns of settlement growth. However, when analysed closely, we wish to emphasize that dearth of data for sub-regions A and C by itself is a significant pointer to comprehend that sub-region B must have been seen as an actively considered areas for the proliferation of various settlements during the period of the present study. This is further effectively indicated to us by the creation of several *agrahāra* and temple settlements in the fertile areas of sub-region B right from the beginning of the period of this study. It has already been observed by us that sub-regions A and C had come into focus in terms of emergence of several temple settlements as early as the 7th to 9th centuries A.D. Therefore subsequently, during the 10th-13th centuries A.D., they represent a certain level of development in terms of the settlement patterns. It is significant to note here that in sub-region A a large number of names of settlements such as Tuṁbige (IIIA, iii, 1), Gokage (IIIA, iii, 5), Bāgadage (IIIA, iii, 6) Paṅgaragi (IIIA, iii, 7) Taṅgodage (IIIA, iii, 11), Hagariṭ ṭage (IIIA, iii, 14) and so on end in the *ge* and *gi* suffixes. These terms have been interpreted to represent the word '*key*' which in Kannada meant cultivable land and therefore, the underlying meaning in the above place names, developed to mean a habitat.[110] In this sense, the settlements of sub-region A during the period 11th-13th century A.D. cannot be understood as new settlements but those that had previous antecedents of habitation. On the other hand, in sub-region C it is only Hatampura and Alampur which emerge as major temple settlements and all the other smaller settlements figure only in terms of being either, objects of grants made to the temple of Alampur or, as the location site of the grants made. It is, however, references to *tīrthas* or, religious settlements such as Pariyāla *tīrtha* (IIIC, iii, 136), Elaramatirtha (IIIC, iii, 136), by about A.D. 1074, that marks a significant growth in the settlements of this sub-region. It is mainly in sub-region B that we see the greatest potential for the development of a variety of settlements indicating clearly that there was agrarian expansion in this area in the post 10th century A.D. period. It is for this reason that the study of settlement patterns in sub-region B becomes important to highlight further.

The changing and dynamic picture of historical space can be elaborated upon and better understood if we ask the question as to how only certain categories of settlements emerged into limelight at a certain point of time in a particular micro-region leading to the formation of important nodes in the hierarchical pattern. To understand this phenomenon one has to go beyond mere spatial limits and search for the factors of change in the socio-political processes leading to the formation of the local and supra-local power structures. The latter it may be emphasized were chiefly identified by the spatial context in which they were located. This formation requires among other things, improvement in the economic base involving the integration of more and more areas into the vortex of political power and the simultaneous legitimation of their politico-economic urges through the creation of the economically powerful *agrahāra* and temple establishments. It is in this context of socio-political change that one can explain the description of various settlement units such as *agrahāras, rājadhāni, nelevīḍu, bhaṭṭta grāma, mahāgrāma* and so on.

Among these the most explicitly characterized settlements in the inscriptional sources of our period of study are the *agrahāra* settlements (indicated through + sign in the charts). Literally, the term *agrahāra* connotes a village, or land assigned to the priestly class for their maintenance.[111] It is also interpreted to mean a tax free village granted by the kings or, their subordinates to the *brāhmaṇas* for purposes of the pursuit of their knowledge.[112] We have several examples of the creation of *agrahāra* settlements out of the existing *ūr*, *vāḍa* and *grāma* settlements particularly during the 11th century A.D. As early as A.D. 973, we have reference to the grant of Modeyanūr (IIIB, iii, 24) by the Chālukya ruler to a *brāhmaṇa* named Revaya-Dvedi Chaṭṭopādhyāya who then bestowed it upon 20 *mahājanas* thus making it into an *agrahāra* settlement.[113] In A.D. 1012, we have another reference to the grant of village Ummachige (IIIB, iii, 34) to a *brāhmaṇa* named Śridhara Bhaṭṭa by a local potentate who then transferred the settlements into the hands of 104 *mahājanas* resulting in the formation of an *agrahāra*.[114] Saratavūra (IIIB, iii, 29) and Kukkanūr (IIIB, iii, 30) which do not figure as *agrahāras* in A.D. 1005, emerge as such by A.D. 1071 (IIIB, ii, 59) and A.D. 1143 (IIIB, iii, 97) respectively. On the whole, in the context of the present study we have as many as 47 instances of the mention of *agrahāra* settlements. Apart from these, we also come across references to *vipra-grāma* (*brāhmaṇa* village) which were granted to individual *brāhmaṇa* families. Among these, there is the prominent mention of Mukkuṇḍa (IIIB, iii, 66) in A.D. 1077 and Pombolal (IIIB, iii, 68) in A.D. 1082. It is pertinent to note here that a majority of the above settlements were located in the fertile tracts of the Krishna and Tungabhadra rivers (MAP VI) as is indicated either, through the mention of location points of some of the settlements or, through references to various types of soils which were found around these settlements. In an inscription dated to A.D. 1077 Mukkuṇḍe the *vipra grāma* is mentioned as located on the bank of Tungabhadra river and is glorified as an ornament to the tract in which it was located.[115] Further, in another inscription dated to A.D. 1088 we have reference to Puilge *grāma* as an *agrahāra* which is also stated to have been located on the bank of Tungabhadra river. We further have several references to various types of canals as located in the village.[116]

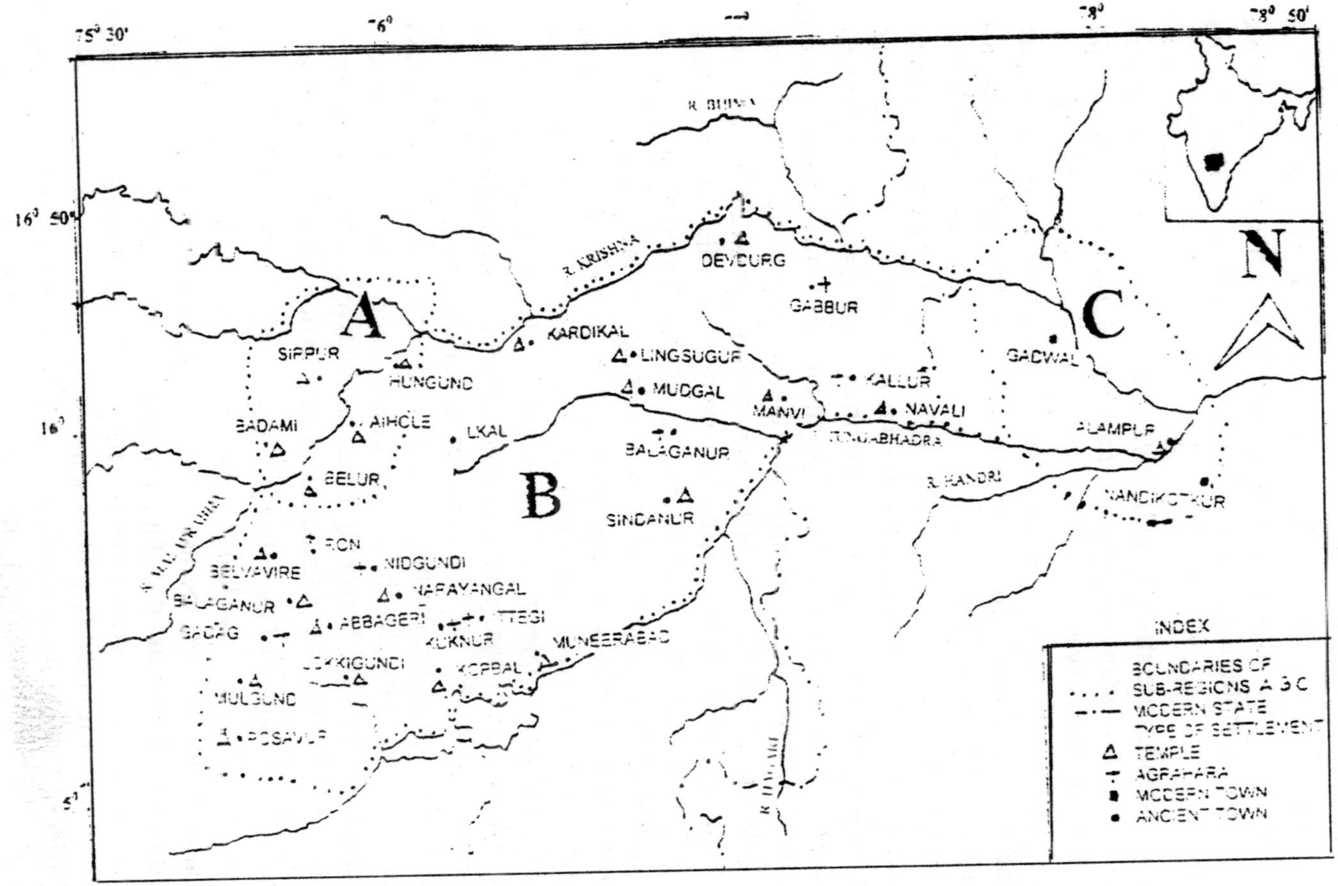

Map VI : MAJOR SETTLEMENTS (1000 A.D.–1200 A.D.)

In an inscription dated to A.D. 1025, reference is made to various types of soil such as *kariya keyye* (black soil fields) *kisukāḍ* (red soil land) and so on[117] which strongly indicate the fertile nature of the soils at this place.[118] In a much later inscription dated to A.D. 1178, we have reference to the Kukkanūr *agrahāra* wherein we have a detailed description of the fertile red soil site at this place. It is stated in these descriptions that it never looses its fertility despite digging it several times.[119]

All these instances are strongly indicative of the fact that in creating various *agrahāra* and other *brāhmaṇa* settlements, fertile locales were focussed upon by the donors. Special status was confirmed upon the above settlements by State intervention. This had far reaching implications both at the economic and social levels. At the economic level, great care was taken by the *agrahāra* donees to improve the productive base of their settlements by introducing various methods of artificial irrigation such as the construction of tanks and wells on a large scale. We have several instances to this effect in the inscriptional sources of the present study. We wish to detail here some of the important ones. In an inscription dated to A.D. 1012, we have reference to the creation of an *agrahāra* settlement wherein shares of certain incomes were set apart for the maintenance of a tank called Deyimgere.[120] In one of the most significant evidences of this nature we have in an inscription dated to A.D. 1088, where there are details on the way an irrigation network was planned out in the *agrahāra* Pulige. Thus, we are told that there was the construction of an irrigation canal from the Tungabhadra river with a mesh work of sub-channels. We have several references in this inscription to various types of minor irrigation works like low level canals, high level canals, and streams. Paddy land and irrigated gardens as well as the irrigation networks are given as the boundaries of the grants of lands made.[121] In another significant mention of irrigation sources we have references to the construction of a tank *(devigere)* at the *mahāgrahāra* of Iṭṭage in A.D. 1112.[122] It is in these processes of the economic change brought about by political intervention that we see the physical space of the 'village' becoming more productive enabling it to produce agrarian surplus with the ultimate potential to invest it in non-agrarian activities too.

It is chiefly in the context of these transformations that we find that a hierarchy of *agrahāra* settlements emerge at least by the latter half of the 11th century A.D. This is indicative to us through the use of various adjectives being used in the inscriptions to define the status of different *agrahāras*. Most of these adjectives explain the level of complexity exhibited by the concerned *agrahāra* settlement. In this context we have observed that while some of the *agrahāras* were mentioned simply as *agrahāras,* some find mention as *mahāgrahāras* (great *agrahāras*). Thus, for instance in A.D. 1098, Lokkiguṇḍi is described through several epithets such as *agrahāra tilakam, agrahāra chūḍāmaṇi, mahāgrahāra* and so on (ornament to *agrahāras,* great *agrahāra*) and is praised a great deal as the place of wealth and fortune, as a place where temples, shops and merchants abounded.[123] We have seen above that Iṭṭagi in A.D. 1112 was also termed as a *mahāgrahāra.* It is further praised as a locate for the rise of several temples and tanks indicative of the prosperity of the place. Kukkanūr as an abode of innumerable temples and several fields has been mentioned a number of times as a *mahāgrahāra.* One of the most important features of all the above *agrahāra* settlements was the location of temples in them; the construction of which normally followed the creation of an *agrahāra* as in the case of *Muḍiyanūr, Ummachige, Pulige* and so on. Naturally it was the *agrahāra* villages which had the necessary surplus to support the temple institutions which were among the first to witness temple building activity. This began to attract patronage from a host of social groups in and around the *agrahāra* villages. We shall focus on this point in an elaborate manner in the next chapter notwith- standing the emphasis here that the control of these *agrahāras* by the *brāhmaṇa* donees cannot be sidelined.

In the context of the *agrahāra* settlements in this study, we see that the *mahājanas* more than individual *brāhmaṇas* by name, figure as an important section of the social group residing in them. These groups emerge collectively as landlords exercising their rights to sell, purchase and get the lands cultivated, they become trustees of the temples located in their respective settlements. They are witness to the grants made, and towards the end of our period of study, they can also be seen in close association with the trading community.[124] We further have observed from the data that the *mahājanas* had separate localities to reside within the *agrahāras*. Thus, as early as 1010 A.D., we have reference to the *mahājanas* of *Suṇḍi* residing in the local *brāhmapuri* area and to them certain lands were leased out.[125] In a much later inscription dated to A.D. 1170, we have the mention of several names of *brāhmaṇas* residing at *brahmapuri* who were to equally divide the land among themselves in the *agrahāra* of *Kukkanūr.*[126] This would then imply that there must have been a considerable section of population living outside the *brāhmaṇa* localities constituting the original inhabitants of the *agrahāras*. In this context we have the mention of a variety of social groups such as gardeners, potters, artisans, barbers as residing in the *agrahāra* settlements catering to the services of the *mahājanas.* In A.D. 1012, we have an unique reference to *kīl-jātiya* (low caste) *gāvuṇḍas* and *ekku varge* (high caste) *gāvuṇḍas* along with the pastoral groups at the time of the creation of the *agrahāra* of Ummachige. They were also allotted a percentage (albeit little) of the share in the lands of these settlements.[127] In an undated inscription of the reign of Vikramāditya VI (A.D. 1076-1124), we have reference to the potters *(Kumbāra)* of the *agrahāra Muḍinūr,* who were issued a stipulation of tax impositions by the *mahājaṇas* of the place.[128] It is interesting to note that in an inscription dated to A.D. 1126, a barber (*nāviḍa*) emerges as a donor and a builder of a temple in the *agrahāra* of Kuritakuṁte. Interestingly, he is described as the dear son (*priya putra*) of the *mahājanas* of the place.[129] In an inscription dated to A.D. 1143, we have reference to a guild of gardeners (*galeya*-500) who are also described as the dear sons (*priya putra*) of the *mahājanas* of Kukkanūr and figure as donors to a temple.[130] These examples cited by us provide ample evidence to the existence of both the *brāhmaṇa* and the non-*brāhmaṇa* groups in *agrahāra* settlements.

It is further surmised by us through the nature of the functions performed in the *agrahāras* that their existence proved crucial for surplus for productive activities of both the agrarian and non-*agrarian* kind in these villages. The nature of politico-economic control exercise by the *mahājanas* over these non-*brāhmaṇa* productive groups can be discerned in the way, they had imposed taxes over the potters residing in their settlements.[131] It is significant to note at this juncture that we do not come across any formal political body through which the *mahājanas* functioned as has been discussed in the case of the Tamilakam region, wherein the *brāhmaṇas* of the *brahmadeya* villages were supposed to have formed into an assembly called *sabha* for the purpose of village administration.[132] In the context of our study we have the mention of *mahājanas* forming various groups that were denoted by the numerical prefixes such as 50 *mahājanas* of Kisuvāvi, 1000 *mahājanas* of Lokkiguṇḍi and so on. These were invariably led by an *ūroḍeya* or headman.[133] Further, the nature of political power exercised by the *mahājanas* does not seem to have been absolute. We have an interesting references to various levels of political power outside the *agrahāra* settlement having their hold on these places. Thus for instance, in an inscription dated to A.D. 1025, *ūroḍeyas* of the Bannigola *agrahāra* were issued a decree to implement the revenue collection at specified rates by the younger brother of the Western Chālukya ruler who held *tribhoga* rights over this *agrahāra*.[134] Further, Bannigola in A.D. 1046, is mentioned as *kuṭumbiṭṭi agrahāra* or one administered by the members of the Chālukya family.[135] A little later in A.D. 1055, Bannigola is described in the same way and now, the *tribhoga* rights are described to be held by the queen of the Chālukya ruler.[136] The term *tribhoga* has been interpreted 'to mean to enjoy one third of the revenue', the other two parts going in equal shares to the Gods and *brāhmaṇas*.[137] The term *kuṭumbiṭṭi* has been understood as a corrupt form of *kuṭumba-vritti* and therefore, indicating a holding given for the maintenance of one's family.[138] It is clear from the above that the Bannigola *agrahāra* was earlier assigned to one of the members of the main ruling family and was later made into an *agrahāra* settlement with various levels of politico-economic shares created in it.[139] In an inscription dated to A.D. 1054, we have reference to an individual named Dāsimayya, who held the *manneyasvāmya* of the *agrahāra* Kisuguṇḍi with the rights of *sarvābhyan-tarasiddhi*. While *manneya svāmya* meant that he held a tenure as a chief,[140] the *sarvabhyantarasiddhi* has been interpreted to mean the rights held over the entire internal revenue income in this *agrahāra*.[141] These are clearly indicative of the superior rights held by the chieftain on the *agrahāra* granted to 50 *mahājanas*. In another inscriptions dated to A.D. 1076, we have reference to as many as three types of rights held over the *agrahāra* settlement of Niḍguṇḍi which is incidentally also called a *baliya* or big *agrahāra* with 400 *mahājanas* living in it. The younger sister of the Chālukya ruler is referred to as holding the *tribhoga* rights over it and a local chief ruling over Kisukāḍ-70, where the *agrahāra* is located, was said to have the right over the income of the *mahājanas* set apart for performing a festival, and a part out of the latter income was granted by him for the same festival.[142] Exercise of politico-economic power by the non-*brāhmaṇa* groups over the *agrahāras* is a clear indication of the actual nature of political and economic control originally exercised in these areas which began to be shared subsequently with the *mahājana* groups after the creation of the *agrahāra*.

It is, however, in the context of the non-*agrahāra* settlements that the rights held by a majority of the ruling chiefs can be clearly discerned. It has been suggested in the historical studies on early Tamilakam that the study of non-*brahmadeya* or non-*agrahāra* villages is indispensable for an elucidation of the South Indian village community as they are thought to be older than the *brahmadeya* villages.[143] In our study the non-*agrahāra* settlements figure as objects of grants to the *agrahāras* and the temple or, as the temple settlements themselves or, as the locations for lands granted to the above institutions and as boundaries to the lands/villages granted. During the 11th century A.D., we find that these villages as objects of grants figure in a majority of cases. Among these, we have reference to Śivanūr (IIIB, iii, 55) Musiyagere (IIIB, iii, 62), Teṁgola (IIIB, iii, 65) Muḍiyanūr (IIIB, iii, 70) Poṁgari (IIIB, iii, 69) Kallamanapalli (IIIB, iii, 61) and so on as objects of grants to various temples. Among other non-*agrahāra* settlements during 11th century A.D., we have the prominent mention of Eleya-Posavūr which figures as an abode of God Mūlasthānadeva as early as A.D. 994.[144] In A.D. 1005 Sirivūra and Saratavūra have been mentioned in the context of governance of their *suṅka*.[145] Further, the settlement of Nāvile figures in A.D. 1066 in the context of the grant of its *manneya* (revenue) to a temple.[146] Even among the settlements granted to the temples, we have specific reference to the *manneya* of those places which were included in the grant of the settlement. Thus, in A.D. 1060, Śivanūr, which was made an object of the grant, was given along with its *manneya*.[147] Similarly, in A.D. 1077, we come across Teṁgola which was granted to a temple along with its *manneya* income.[148] The references made to the non-*agrahāra* villages during the 11th century A.D. was not prolific and this points significantly to the fact that the variety and the complexity which characterized the *agrahāra* settlements made the mention of the former diminutive. Importantly, references to the temple establishments in the non-*agrahāra* villages are conspicuous by their absence in a majority of the cases. However, mention of some of these villages as locations for the grants of gardens and lands is indicative of the fact that some of these had by the beginning of the 11th century A.D. formed an integral part of the agrarian hinter land. This is further adduced through the mention of the *manneya* (revenue) and *suṅka* (taxes) from these places which had formed a significant part of the grants made. On the basis of evidences of this nature we have further been able to surmise on the clear possibility that these settlements were full revenue paying units. This can be contrasted with *agrahāra* settlements which were exempt from any such payment in a majority cases.[149] On the other hand, through the grant of actual villages themselves several smaller settlements were gradually being brought in line with the mainstream of the agrarian productive base in this region.

By the turn of the 12th century A.D., one, however, sees a significant transformation in the nature of the non-*agrahāra* settlements wherein, some of these begin to emerge as major temple centered spatial units characterized by a certain level of complexity in their socio-economic and political make-up. Among these, names of places such as Posavūra (IIIB, iii, 81) Eleya Śrīpura (IIIB, iii, 84) Abbeyagere (IIIB, iii, 90) Rājavūr (IIIB, iii, 99) Yewūr (IIIB, iii, 119) figure prominently for a major part of the 12th century A.D. Places such as Hiriya Maniyūr (IIIB, iii, 120) and Liṅga (IIIB, iii, 123) emerge to the forefront only towards the end of the 12th century A.D. On the other hand, we have reference to several other rural settlements during this period which begin to figure in large numbers either among the boundaries of the grants made such as, Kaniyahallu (IIIB, iii, 85) Mangalūra *halli* (IIIB, iii, 108) and Poṭṭūr *halli* (IIIB, iii, 108) or, as the locations for various grants of lands such as Kuḍaganūr (IIIB, iii, 111) Benatūra (IIIB, iii, 105) Oḍagere (IIIB, iii, 119) Kūṛalahalli (IIIB, iii, 127) and so on. Further, some figure as objects of grants to the temples such as Bennekallu (IIIB, iii, 85) Muttage (IIIB, iii, 89) Haḍala-Gera (IIIB, iii, 108) Kallavanahalli (IIIB, iii, 115) Hiriya Hanḍigola (IIIB, iii, 124) and Hombalalu (IIIB, iii, 126). The hierarchical levels which can be discerned in the above instances of non-*agrahāra* settlements point to two basic trends. Firstly, an increase in the names of various types of rural settlements is strongly suggestive of a significant expansion in the rural agrarian base on the one hand, and on the other, some of these were able to emerge to the forefront as important centres of temple settlements underscoring the fact that there was a significant improvement and increase in the agrarian production in these settlements which enabled them to maintain various religious establishments on a significant scale. It is pertinent to underline at this juncture that we have, at the same time, considerable growth in the references made to the incidence of the usage of artificial irrigation techniques such as tanks and wells. In certain cases the nature of soil has also been taken into account to describe the settlements. In an inscription dated to A.D. 1104, we have references to *kara bhūmi* (black soil land) and *gāvuṇḍa gere* (tank owned by a *gāvuṇḍa*) which were located at Nārāyaṅgal.[150] In an inscription dated to A.D. 1105 we come across the significant mention of *gadde* (rice) land which was supposed to have been located below Annama Gāvuṇḍa's tank and some garden land lying towards the north of a stream in the non-*agrahāra* settlement of Yewār.[151] By about A.D. 1113, we have reference to the actual grant of land made to a tank called Devimgere located in a settlement called Abbeyagere.[152] In an undated record pertaining to the rule of king Chālukya Vikramāditya VI, we come across repeated references to *kara bhūmi* (black soil land) as bordering those fields that were granted.[153] Towards the end of the 12th century A.D. we have references to at least 3 instances of the mention of tanks which were granted various measurements of land for their upkeep in such settlements as Hiriya Maniyūr (1169 A.D. and 1179 A.D.) and Belühaḍe (1178 A.D.). We further have reference to the grant of a village Benaṭūra along with its waste area.[154] All these examples have a significant bearing on our comprehension of the concerns shown by the residents of non-*agrahāra* villages to extend and improve agrarian production on a considerable scale. By about the middle of the 12th century A.D. places such as Muluguṇḍa and Posavūra begin to be eulogized for the fertility of their lands (*uttama bhoga bhūmi)* and for their beauty *(saurabhaṁ*).[155]

Hierarchical relationships thus formed between various settlement units have an explicit expression in the form of usage of such prefixes as *kiru* (small) and *hiriya* (big) attached to the names of certain places which begin to appear prominently from the first quarter of the 12th century A.D. Among these we have significant mention of such places as Kiru Nārāyaṁgal (IIIB, iii, 90) and Hiriya Nārāyaṁgal (IIIB, iii, 90) which form a part of Nārāyaṁgal (IIB, iii, 90) which in turn is an integral unit of the numerical sub-division of Nārāyaṁgal-12 (IIIB, iii, 90). We further have, in the latter half of the 12th century A.D., reference to such places as Hiriya Maṇiyūr (IIIB, iii, 120) and Chikka (small)-Maṇiyūr (IIIB, iii, 120). All these instances exemplify the growth in the complexity of the settlement terminology used to describe settlement patterns of the 12th century A.D. This was owing largely to the expansion of the rural space through either, the grants of villages or, lands on a large scale to various temple establishments, located in different spatial units. In fact, we get crucial clues in this direction in the references made to the above settlements in the inscriptional sources themselves. The mention of various types of the settlements called Nārāyaṁgal cited above is made in the context of a gift of land which was basically directed towards the benefit of a temple located in Kiru Nārāyaṁgal (small Nārāyaṁgal) but attached to a bigger temple at Hiriya Nārāyaṁgal (big Nārāyaṁgal).[156] This is strongly suggestive of the possibility that Kiru Nārāyaṁgal got attached to the bigger settlements as an outcome of the grant of the same to one of the temples located in Nārāyaṁgal, which now began to be termed with the suffix *hiriya* so as to be identified on the basis of its higher level of socio-economic advancement as against its later addition. In an inscription dated to A.D. 1179 we have another significant reference to names of such places as Hiriya Maniyūr which is described as the *baliya bāḍam* (big *vāḍa*) and to Chikka Maniyūr (small Maniyūr) which figures among the boundaries of the fields granted from the former.[157] It is pertinent to note here that in an earlier reference to Hiriya Maniyūr in an inscription dated to A.D. 1169, we have mention of the location of a tank and a Jaina establishment and the grants were directed towards the tank.[158] These evidences effectively indicate a level of control enjoyed by Hiriya Maniyūr over Chikka-Maniyūr which might have been attached to the former at some historical point in time. This is what probably gave rise to such differences in their nomenclature which leave an impression that they were two different parts of a single settlement unit and were thus divided, according to some scholars for the sake of convenience of administration.[159] It needs to be underscored at this juncture that on one hand, the location of a temple institution within a given spatial unit, marked a significant turn in the economic advancement of the rural settlement in terms of the generation of agrarian surplus, on the other hand, subsequent rise in the socio-political groups within the rural scenario added another important dimension to our comprehension of the degree of complexity that typified the rural space during the early medieval period.

The nature of political control exercised over the non-*agrahāra* rural settlements was in the main dependent upon the level of economic advancement achieved in them but was, nonetheless, crucially linked to the political initiative taken by various ruling groups who constituted an integral part of the rural social structure during the period of our study. Thus, it was basically a nexus of the social and economic power that was sought to be projected politically and it is in the process of political control exercised by various ruling strata at the local level, that one sees the growth and proliferation in the rural settlements of south western Deccan during the early medieval period. This we highlighted above with particular emphasis on those settlements that were located in the fertile plains of the Krishna and Tungabhadra rivers (sub-region B of our study) (MAP VI). During the 11th century A.D., as has been observed by us earlier, we have only limited number of references to the non-*agrahāra* settlement units and out of these, a majority had formed objects of grants and the remaining few were the location points for the grants made with the exception of Eleya Posavūru which emerges as an independent temple settlement as early as A.D. 994 itself. We therefore, have to look for crucial clues on non-*agrahāra* settlements from the nature of socio-political authority exercised in the contextual references made to the nature of the grants made coupled with information on the major participants in these transactions.

As early as A.D. 994 we have reference to the *manneya* and *nāl gāvuṇḍa* of Eleya Posavūr who emerges as a major donor of land made to the temple establishment of the same place along with the *gāvuṇḍas* of Muluguṇḍa-12 of which Eleya-Posavūr had formed a part.[160] Further, in A.D. 1005 we come across mention of the governor of the *suṅka* (taxes) of Sirivūra and Saraṭavūr, who made a grant of the same to a temple on the request of 8 *gāvuṇḍas* of the place, who also figure as the protectors of the grant.[161] In an inscription dated to A.D. 1022, we come across a place called Aragilvāla situated on the bank of the river Tungabhadra wherein grants of land were made by one Nāgama *Gāvuṇḍa* to a temple built by a *seṭṭi* (merchant).[162] We have reference to Posavūru again in an inscription dated to A.D. 1028 wherein Sindarasa of the Sinda family was supposed to have been ruling under the command of the wife of a local potentate who had control over the Kisukāḍ *nāḍu* in which Posavūru was located.[163] We have an interesting reference to Sirivura in A.D. 1042, wherein one Kuṁchavāḍuga Dāsayya of the Sinda *Kula* constructed the main gate of *siri vāgilu* (gate of fortune) and was therefore given remission of taxes by the *gāvuṇḍas* of the place.[164] We come across reference to Śivanūr in A.D. 1060 which was granted by the local potentate, with the permission of the main ruler, to a local temple. It is pertinent to note here that the *manneya* (revenue) rights over this village which were held by the *manneyars* were relinquished separately by them and this was to apply to the future generations too.[165] Further, reference to another settlement, Nāvile which is supposed to be located on the bank of river Krishna, is made in a similar way in an inscription dated to A.D. 1066, wherein the grant of the *manneya* of the place is directed to a temple located at that place by a *manneya* (chief of several villages) of the Kadamba family.[166] In another example, the village of Kallamanapalli in A.D. 1074 was granted to a temple by a *daṇḍanāyaka* with the permission of the main ruler.[167] In A.D. 1075, we have reference to Musiyagere as an object of the grant made by the main ruler.[168] In an inscription dated to A.D. 1077, we have an interesting reference to the village of Teṁgola which was granted by the Nolaṁba Pallava chief (ruler of several larger territorial divisions) but the *manneya* rights of which were granted separately by the Kadamba chief who had hereditary claims over it.[169]

The above survey has enabled us to conclude upon the existence of basically three levels of political authority exercised over the non-*agrahāra* rural settlements under study. At the primary level we have groups of *gāvuṇḍas* who had displayed their ability to donate land, remit taxes and bear witness to grants of lands made in their localities. At the secondary level we have the *manneyar* (chief of several villages) who claim to belong to such prominent families as the Sindas and Kadambas and who held hereditary titles of possession of revenue in the areas of their control which has been well attested in the above instances cited by us. In fact, it is from this group of local chiefs that we see a significant emergence of the supra local political authority particularly from the beginning of the 12th century A.D. onwards. During the 11th century A.D. the supra local authority had, however, been exercised by the appointees of the main ruling family such as the *mahāprachaṇḍa daṇḍanāyakas* or individuals belonging to earlier prominent ruling families such as the Nolamba Pallavas. These ruling chiefs who represent a third level of the exercise of political authority had control over more than one large territorial unit such as Belvoḷa-300, Kisukāḍ-70 and so on and seemed to have held limited political rights in relation to the specific spatial unit of settlement. For example, as mentioned above when the grant of Teṁgola was proposed to be made by the Nolamba chief in A.D. 1077, intervention of the Kadamba *manneya* was required to grant the rights of revenue over the concerned settlement. Similar was the case with Śivanūr granted in A.D. 1060 by another supra local chief who held the title of *mahāprachaṇḍa daṇḍanāyaka.* On the one hand, the *manneya* rights over this were separately granted by the *manneyars* of the place and on the other, he had to seek the permission of the main ruler to grant the village to a local temple. It is, however, pertinent to note here that the supra local chiefs attempted to establish their hold over certain areas of governance within the rural settlements. In the reference made to the governor of *suṅka* (taxes) in A.D. 1005 over the villages of Soratavūra and Sirivūra, he claims to be a subordinate of the supra local chief. Interestingly, in one of the unusual references of its kind we find the mention of the Sinda chief as ruling over Posavūr under the command of the wife of a supra local chief in A.D. 1028. Instances of this nature basically represent adjustments made between the supra local and local authority in sharing the political power over the rural space in which the latter definitely had an edge over the former owing chiefly to their hereditary claims of economic power rooted at the local base. In a similar way, one can discern significant attempts made by the chiefs of the main ruling family who represent the exercise of political authority at the apex of power structure. Actual rights of politico-economic authority exercised by this group seemed to have also been severely limited by the rights of the *manneyar* as has been seen by us in the case of the grant of Śivanūr. Further, the grant of other villages such as Musiyagere and Kallamanapalli which has been referred to by us above did not carry the grant of *manneya* rights along with them. We also come across a couple of instances referring to the members of the royal family as holding camps at certain villages. Thus, in an inscription dated to A.D. 1022, the queen of the royal family makes a grant of land at Ballaniṭṭage after obtaining the same from the *manneya* of the Haihaya family, when she was actually camping at a place called Puvvaravalli.[170] These evidently testify to the limited nature of actual politico-economic rights held by the main rulers at the local base of power.[171]

Among the social groups residing in the non-*agrahāra* villages during the 11th century A.D., the local functionaries themselves constituted an important group of dominant peasantry as they emerge, in a majority of cases, as owners of land within their locality. These land owners are often mentioned along with groups of *okkalas* who figure in numbers of 60, and seemed to have represented the class of agriculturists taking to actual cultivation.[172] It is, however, from the first quarter of the 12th century A.D. that we begin to witness a significant change in the nature of the pattern of rural settlements which were characterized by a higher degree of complexity in their spatial, social, economic and political configuration. We have already discussed above the nature of economic advancement made through the introduction of irrigation techniques which led to the growth in the temple centred settlements on the one hand, and on the other, to the proliferation of several new settlements in the context of various grants made to the temple institutions. We wish to exemplify further only a few of such temple centred settlements which signify various dimensions of the changing trends of the period of their optimum level. As early as A.D. 1109, Eleya Sirivūra emerges as a major temple settlement wherein we have reference to several types of socio-economic and political groups such as the *gāvuṇḍas,* who figure along with the 60 *okkalas* (these were the major groups that had figured in an earlier inscription too) coupled with the mention of the *mahāpradhānas* who figure for the first time along with several mercantile and professional groups such as the *doni*-1000, *ugura*-300 and the *nakara samūha.*[173] By A.D. 1138, we come across several more few groups in the same settlement in the form of the *heggaḍe* of the place who also held the titles of *pradhāna* and *saṅdhivigrahi* and another chief termed as *pattale karaṇa* and *senādhipati* and so on. Importantly, now the *gāvuṇḍas* no more figure simply as *gāvuṇḍas* of *Śrīpura,* they begin to be identified chiefly through the names of the localities in which they resided within the settlement. Thus, we come across such terms as *gāvuṇḍas* belonging to *hiriya keri* (big street) of Śrīpura, *gāvuṇḍas* and 60 *Okkalus* belonging to a locality called Mulavalageri of the same place.[174]

These examples clearly testify to a definite change taking place in the direction of increasing hierarchical relations even within the spatial set up corresponding significantly to the growth in the complexity of the socio-political relations. Similar trends can be discerned in various other non-*agrahāra* settlements too which begin to emerge in this manner at an increasing pace around the middle of the 12th century A.D. (IIIB, iii, 99, 100, 102, 109, 110). Among these, reference can be made to the settlement of Posavūra in an inscription dated to A.D. 1148 which represents another significant land mark in the growing complexity of the settlement patterns. In this instance, the Sinda family chief is termed as the *manneya* of Mulguṇḍa-12 and Posavūru is now headed by one Nāki *Gāvuṇḍa,* the *mahāprabhu* and his son Holla *Gāvuṇḍa* is termed as the *nāḷprabhu*. Apart from these we have mention of several functionaries such as *suṅkada pergaḍe, sādada pergaḍe, vibhu, gāvuṇḍas,* a subordinate of the supra local chief ruling over Belvola-300 and *adhikāri pergaḍe* holding the governance of *pannāya.*[175] It is significant to note in the light of above evidences that the *gāvuṇḍas* were still an important socio-economic and political force to be reckoned with at the primary level of the exercise of political power in the rural settlements. However, references made to the *manneya* are reduced considerably and we begin to see these groups functioning in the form of supra-local chiefs through several intermediary levels of functionaries located in the rural space as the *mahāpradhānas* of various types who begin to hold a long line of titles. All these newly emerging functionaries with high sounding titles begin to address themselves invariably as the subordinates of the supra-local authority.

Against the above background, the role played by the members of the main ruling family in controlling the local areas is seen through the creation of their spheres of influence in the form of *nelevīdu* (permanent capital)[176] *rājadhāni* (captial)[177], *appayanavīḍu* (halting place)[178] and so on. It is pertinent to note here that the main ruling family chiefs had their *nelevīdu* for a major part of their rule in the capital city of Kalyāṇapura while their temporary capitals (*appayanavīḍu*) were shifting from place to place. For the most part we have observed that the establishment of military camps, temporary capitals of members of the main ruling family had been established, on the fertile areas of particularly the Raichur Doab with a higher degree of incidence during the 11th century A.D. when the concerns of the rulers were chiefly with the consolidation of their political rule over south western Deccan. We have been able to identify nearly 5 instances of military camps set up by the members of the royal family in this area. They are: Puvvaravalli in A.D. 1022 (IIIB, iii, 37), Pulipoduru in A.D. 1027 (III, iii, 39), Etagiri in A.D. 1031 (IIIB, iii, 41) Kereyūr in A.D. 1069 (IIIB, iii, 58). In the inscriptions they have been described as the halting camps of various queens of the royal house hold. Further, in an inscription dated to A.D. 1071, the main ruler Someśvara II himself was holding *appayanavīḍu* at Kakkaragola which was located on the banks of the Kirudore (Tungabhadra) river.[179] Apart from this, attempts were also made by the members of the main ruling family to establish their rule over certain areas located in the fertile tracts of sub-region B. Of these, the *Bannigola agrahāra* emerges prominently as being administered by the younger brother of the main ruler. In another case the famous *Akkādevi,* a royal princess held control over the Kisukāḍ-70 region till the middle of the 11th century A.D. and so on.[180] All these examples point significantly to the fact that sub-region B emerges as a sphere of political influence in the hands of various ruling families who begin to share the politico-economic power in these areas through adjustments of their areas of control both spatially and politically with the local elements of power.

In fact, it is in the above processes of political control, *i.e.,* in the urges exhibited by rulers at various levels in the exercise of their political authority and to carve for themselves their spheres of politico-economic influence, that we find answers to the hierarchical growth in the pattern of settlements which we witnessed in our descriptions given above for this period of study. It needs to be underscored at this juncture that the emergence of a particular settlement into either, an *agrahāra* or a temple settlement and its consequent rise into prominence depended, in a large measure, on the political initiative taken in this direction which often tended to coincide with the rise in the status of the particular chief extending his patronage. We give below a few examples to substantiate this point. As early as A.D. 973, the creation of the *agrahāra* Modeyanur coincided with the attempts at the stabilization of his newly founded kingdom by the Chālukya ruler Taila II.[181] We have already observed that the Chālukya rulers indulged in granting a maximum number of villages during the 11th century A.D. which included in a majority of cases the temple as the donee. Towards the end of the 12th century A.D., which witnessed the rise of several new families of main rulers, the incidence of the grant of villages to *brāhmaṇas* and the temples was on the increase. Thus, in an inscription dated to A.D. 1170 which coincides with the rise into power of the Kalāchūryas, the creation of Kukkanūr into an *agrahāra* is recorded.[182] It is interesting to note that Kukkanūr is again claimed to have been converted into an *agrahāra* settlement in another inscription dated to A.D. 1183,[183] by the rulers of the *Yādava* family whose rule as main rulers significantly coincides with this period. Repeated interest shown by various rulers over this attests to the fact that it was increasingly recognized as an economically powerful settlement.

It is chiefly after identifying the above kinds of processes we find that owing to convergence of different historical factors, some *grāmas* or, for that matter any physical space, could emerge as a node in a cluster of rural settlements. We are thus able to illustrate the process of the formation of rural settlement hierarchy.[184] We have in this context first the identification of several small territorial units which significally represent the establishment of such nodes in the settlements. Among these, Mulugunḍa-12, Nārāyangal-12 and Kukkanūr-30 emerge prominently representing various stages in the growth of rural space perse. The association of the above groups of villages with the rise in the political power of certain prominent locally powerful chiefs is well attested to in the inscriptional sources of this study. Thus, Mulugunḍa-12 has been closely associated with the strengthening of their hold on this tract by the Sinda chiefs of *Kunnūla vaṁśa* right from the beginning of our period of study. It is in fact through the close association of the ruling families of Posavura and Mulugunḍa-12, who were supposed to have belonged to the same kin groups, that these two settlements which are recorded as important temple settlements right from the beginning of this study, emerge to the forefront by the middle of the 12th century A.D. with significant economic advancement achieved in them. In an inscription dated to A.D. 1148, these two settlements are eulogized as having the best land meant for enjoyment (*uttama bhoga bhūmi*) and for their beauty. This is coupled with the mention of several ruling professional and trading groups residing in them who participate as donors of a variety of grants. By now it is clearly stated that the rule of a branch of the Sinda family belonging to the Mōṛaka *kula* is firmly established over Posavūra with Nāki *Gāvuṇḍa* as the *mahāprabhu* and his son *Holla Gāvuṇḍa* as the *nāḷ prabhu.* Further, the uncle of Nāki *Gāvuṇḍa, Bopparasa* held the *manneya* rights of Mulguṇḍa-12.[185] In its relationship with Mulguṇḍa-12, it is all along stated in the inscriptional sources, that Posavūra formed the property of the temple at Mulguṇḍa-12.

It is, however, in the emergence of the Sinda chiefs of Erambarage to prominence that we get a comprehensive understanding of the correspondence of the rise in political power with a significant growth in the settlements ruled by them. By the early 12th century A.D. the Sinda *mahāmaṇḍaleśvaras* emerge as ruling over the tract of Nārāyaṅgal-12 which coincides significantly to the coming to the forefront of *Abbeyageri* located in Nārāyaṅgal-12 in an inscription dated to A.D. 1113.[186] In A.D. 1121 we have the emergence of other new settlements such as *Kiru*-Nārāyaṅgal and *Hiriya* Nārāyaṅgal as important temple settlements.[187] All these have been referred to as ruled by the Sinda chiefs of the Kusuva family. Another important settlement, namely, kukkanūr-30 known for the fertility of its soil in several inscriptions is recorded to have been held by various ruling chiefs right from the beginning of the 11th century A.D. By A.D. 1002 it was under the control of a *mahāsāmanta* who is referred to as ruling by the favour of the main ruler.[188] By A.D. 1010, we have reference to the Nolamba chief who was closely related to the Chālukyas of Kalyāṇi as having control over kukkanūr-30.[189] Towards the latter half of the 12th century A.D. we have seen above that several rulers of newly emerging dynasties begin to stake claim to it by repeatedly granting it to *brāhmaṇas.* This significantly explains the reasons why even as early as A.D. 1005, Kukkanūr is referred to as a *sthala* in the context of the mention of merchant guilds located at this place.[190] By the latter half of the 12th century A.D. Kukkanūr is chiefly eulogized as a major temple settlement.[191]

It is significant to note at this juncture that the above cluster of villages come together to form larger territorial units such as the *nāḍus.* In the context of our study we have the prominent mention of the Kisukāḍ-70 (IIA, iv, 2, 5, IIIB, iv, 33, 50) Bāgaḍage nāḍu (IIIB, iv, 98, 105, 106) which formed a part of the Belvola *nāḍu* (IIIB, iv, 25, 27, 28, 29) on the one hand, and on the other the Karāḍikal *nādu* (IIIB, iv, 46, 53, 57) and Kelavāḍi *nāḍu* (IIIB, iv, 95, 98) which formed part of the Eḍeḍore *nāḍu* (IIIB, iv, 35, 44). The rise into prominence of all these *nāḍus* is again related to the strategic location of various settlements which were constituted in them and the subsequent political attention received by these at various periods of time. Kisukāḍ *nāḍu* and Bāgaḍage *nāḍus* constituted chiefly of the western and the north western most part of the present area of study. The other two tracts such as Karāḍikal and Kelavāḍi constituted the eastern tract of sub-region B delineated in the present study which forms a major part of Raichur Doab. We have observed that at this stage of historical development it is chiefly the *Belvola* nāḍu which emerges to the forefront as the most settled tract constituting such important sub-divisions as Kisukāḍ-70 and Bāgaḍage-70, which in their turn, contained several clusters of groups of villages such as Nārāyaṅgal-12, Kukkanūr-30 and Mulugunḍa-12. Members of the main ruling family seemed to have exercised greater control over Belvola-300, particularly in the tract of Kisuk□āḍ-70, which constituted the north-western part of our study spanning over sub-region A and a part of sub-region B. We have seen several times that the Kisukāḍ-70 tract was under the control of the royal princess *Akkādevi* for many years between A.D. 1022- A.D. 1055 who had her capital at *Vikramapura*. After Akkādevi, Kisukāḍ-70, in A.D. 1070, came under the control of the Pallava chief who held family ties with the Chālukyas of Kalyani.[192] By the latter half of the 11th century A.D., the Sindas of Erambarage began to have control over Kisukāḍ-70 along with other tracts of Belvola-300, such as Nārāyaṅgal-12 and Bāgaḍage-70 with their capital at Erambarage. All these areas, coupled with the political hold exercised by the Sinda chieftains over *Kelavāḍi*-300, that formed a part of Ededore-2000 began to be termed as the *Sindavāḍināḍ*.[193]

Eḍeḍore-2000 constituting the eastern part of sub-region B and the sub-region C of present area of study consisted chiefly of Karāḍikal-400, *Kelavāḍi*-300, Aije-300, which figure prominently in the inscriptional sources of this period. In an inscription dated to A.D. 1004, Eḍeḍore-2000 is referred to have been ruled over by the crown prince of the Chālukyan family.[194] By about A.D. 1046, another member of the Chālukyan family figures as governing over one of the villages of Karāḍikal-300.[195] It is however, only in association with the locally entrenched ruling families of the Haihayas and the *Kadambas* that various tracts of Eḍeḍore-2000 emerge into prominence. In particular, the Kadambas of Karāḍikal emerge as the *manneya* holders of various settlements located in Karāḍikal-400 by about A.D. 1077,[196] and by A.D. 1124, they emerge as firmly established over the Karāḍikal-400 tract with the titles of *mahāmaṇḍaleśvara*.[197] Towards the end of 12th century A.D. this tract emerges into considerable focus as a well developed *nāḍu* with major temple settlements established in it. In an inscription dated to A.D. 1191, Karaḍikal *nāḍu* is praised a great deal as being filled with fertile fields and groves of tree wealth, rivers and villages. In the same inscription, the chief settlement of the above tract, namely, Karādikal is even referred to as an important urban centre.[198] On the other hand, the Kelavāḍi tract of Eḍeḍore-2000 emerges into prominence through its association with the Sinda chiefs of Erambarage. Aije-300 on the other, figures as being ruled over by various families of the supra local chiefs such as the Telugu Chola chiefs and the Vaiḍumbas who basically had their roots in various parts of Andhra. It is significant to note in the above survey that *Belvola nāḍu* emerges into limelight as a well settled tract right from the beginning our study. Eḍeḍore-2000 on the other hand, begins to emerge as such only by the end of the 12th century A.D. with only pockets of it such as Karāḍikal, Kelavāḍi and Aije *nāḍus* showing signs of significant growth in terms of a proliferation of settlements.

Such a spurt in the growth of settlements, we wish to argue, was basically an outcome of the local processes of state formation which got precipitated through an interaction of various locally entrenched socio-economic forces with those of the dominant state system represented by the Chālukyan State. The absence of any large scale irrigation structure being imposed from above pertinently underscores the fact that the local control of technology and resources had a significant role to play in bringing about the necessary change in which small scale irrigation networks and building of temple structures had a major role to play. In this sense the socio-political configuration of the present area of study essentially differs from those of the Chola State wherein it is argued that the sub-regions (*nāḍus*) "were systematically integrated and organized through institutional means *i.e.,* the *brahmadeyas* and the temples".[199] In such an integration, the large scale irrigation structures built by Chola rulers seemed to have played an important role in the case of Tamilnadu.[200] On the other hand, in the context of our study it was basically individual rural settlements controlled by locally dominant peasant groups that had been integrated through various institutional means such as the *brahmadeya* and the temple. Importantly such an integration was first projected in the minor clusters of villages represented through smaller numerical suffixes which then, went on to constitute a *nāḍu* territorial unit and this, which did not, by any means, represent an artificially created unit imposed from above for administrative purpose alone.

In the light of above analysis comprehending various settlement units as "closed and insulated from the outside world until the emergence of market towns,"[201] has no historical basis whatsoever. The emergence of *agrahāra* settlements in the initial stages of the period of our study, coupled with the enormous growth in the temple institutions by the middle of the 12th century A.D., had significant implications for the integration of rural settlements by providing them a focal point of convergence which enabled these to interact with each other on a considerable scale and thus, establish crucial links of communication, both socially and spatially. As early as A.D. 1010, we have reference to the rural settlements of Sirivūra and Ittage in which the road going from Sirivūra to Iṭṭage formed the boundary to grants of land made in the *agrahāra* of Mālad Ālūra.[202] In an inscription dated to A.D. 1049, land granted to a temple located in the *agrahāra* of Pombulcha was located in the non-*agrahāra* settlements of Bāyḍumbagere and Kappaḍigere.[203] In another significant reference from an inscription dated to A.D. 1077, we have mention of grant of land belonging to the places of Kiriya Bellumbaṭṭi and Piriya Bellumbaṭṭi to the God at Ehūr.[204] In an inscription dated to A.D. 1112, we have reference to the grant of a village located in Kukkanūr-30 which was made to the temple at the *agrahāra* of Iṭṭage. In the same inscription among the boundaries of the land granted to the temple, the road going from Kukkanūr to Talkallu figures. The settlements of Kaniyahallu and Muḍiyanūr also figure among the boundaries of the granted land.[205] References of above kind significantly indicate the fact that space was always viewed in relation to its neighbouring settlements which by itself is a significant pointer towards the interactive nature of various spatial units which gets reflected considerably at the level of social relationships established between them as well. There are several such references to explain this point. In an inscription dated to A.D. 1028, one Aycha Gāvuṇḍa of Posavūra is referred to as having married the daughter of a *seṭṭi* from Suṇḍi.[206] In an inscription dated to A.D. 1076, we have reference to the term *parasthāna da mahājana* (*mahajanas* of other places) for whose *pūja* the *mahājanas* of Niḍguṇḍi seem to have kept aside a certain amount of money.[207] We have, in A.D. 1082, reference to the purchase of land made by the *mahājanas* of Kuṛitakuṁte from one Saṅkimayya of Kalasavalli.[208] In almost all these cases we find that it was either, the *agrahāra* or more importantly, the temple that acted as agents of integration of various settlements enabling them to come closer and establish a network of functioning.

Such as coming together of social groups between settlements can be seen on an increasing pace by the turn of the 12th century A.D. This was owing chiefly to the gradual transformation taking place in the economy of the rural space, leading on to a spurt in the commercial set up at some of these settlements. Various mercantile groups and guilds, including artisanal groups, belonging to different places of origin came together owing to the common professional interests shared by them.[209] Among these we have identified groups such as *taṁbuliga*-1000, *mummūridaṇḍas, gavares* and *nānādeśis* who associated themselves with the Ayyāvoḷe-500 group of merchants as itinerant group of traders having their organization at a supra local level, as against the *nagaraṁ* group which basically represented a local level agrarian based mercantile community whose network of trading activities were confined to specific localities of their function. The *nagaraṁ* groups figure in a majority and one such type can be identified with the rural settlement of Eleya Śripura in A.D. 1109 where they figure along with the *gāvuṇḍas* and *okkalu* of the place.[210] In an earlier inscription dated to A.D. 1080, the Lokkiguṇḍi *agrahāra,* the *nagaraṁ* figure basically as owning several shops.[211] Towards the end of the 12th century A.D. the local mercantile groups figure prominently in such settlements as of Kaniyahallu (IIIB, iii, 110) the *gāvuṇḍas, ugura* and the *okkalas* also have special mention. In the latter half of the 12th century A.D. we get prolific references to the term *paṭṭaṇa* (city) which figures in association with various supra local and local mercantile bodies and therefore it represents a higher level in the hierarchy of settlements which is urban in character during this period of study. Among these we have the mention of *agrahāra* Huligola that is significantly termed as *baḷañjadādi paṭṭaṇa* (meaning foremost trading centre). There are references here to several merchants hailing from different places and many mercantile bodies of the *prabhus* of various *paṭṭaṇas* belonging to places located in Belvola-300, Kisukāḍ-70 and Bāgadage-70 who, along with *grāmānugrāmada sthala samasta* (trading bodies of various villages), met in a *mahānādu* to make certain grants.[212] We thus have between the period A.D. 1178-A.D. 1215, mention of nearly 4 instances of *paṭṭanas* such as Mulguṇḍa, termed in A.D. 1178, as *anādi paṭṭaṇa* (IIIB, xiv, 114) Karāḍikal figures in A.D. 1191 also as *anādi paṭṭaṇa* (IIIB, xiv, 123) Mulguṇḍa figures in A.D. 1207 as a *rājadhāni paṭṭaṇa* (IIIB, xiv, 129) and Mudugal, in A.D. 1215 is referred to as a *rājadhāni paṭṭaṇa* (IIIB, xiv, 130). Despite such prolific references as the cities towards the end of the twelfth century, we cannot view these settlements as depicting full fledged urban phenomenon perse for various reasons as underlined below. First of all, the very nature of description given with regard to a majority of the above settlements betrays certain agrarian moorings in their character. Thus, Karāḍikal *paṭṭana* in A.D. 1191 is prised for its ponds full of water, fields and gardens rich with crops, thriving inhabitants and flourishing temples of Gods.[213] Similarly, Mudugal the *rājadhāni pattana* is praised for its gardens, tanks and temples in A.D. 1214.[214] On the other hand, it is the *nakara* group of merchants who figure prominently in the Muluguṇḍa *paṭṭana* both in A.D. 1178[215] and A.D. 1207[216] along with other mercantile bodies as donors of land and money. The growth of urban centres during this period of our study can at best be viewed as representing an advanced stage in the economic growth of the local productive spheres which enjoyed extensive patronage from various ruling groups of the period. Thus Mudugal figures as the capital of the Kalāchuris, Muluguṇḍa was a strong hold of the Sinda chiefs, Karāḍikal was the base for the Kadamba chiefs indicates that they all had political significance attached to them while at the same time their rise as prominent trading centres underscores the economic development in the hinterland surrounding them. These however, represent only certain pockets of commercial activity when a majority of the settlements, as can be gauged through the charts, have to be depicted and characterized as rural settlements. In such a context, the growth of urban centres peculiar to the early medieval set up can be considered to represent an outcome of the proliferation and expansion of agrarian settlements which was taking place on a considerable scale throughout the period of the present study. This was made possible through grants of land and villages chiefly to the temple institutions, which emerge as major centres of politico-economic power in both the *agrahāra* and the non-*agrahāra* settlements. Thus the emergence of the rural settlements of our study with potential for the growth in the agrarian base from physical space into ideological space marked a crucial phase in the evolution of settlement structures, namely the temple settlements. To comprehend this phenomenon in totality one needs to take into account the crucial aspect of ideological parameters of change which form our main theme of analysis in the following chapter.

REFERENCES

1. Ruth Tringham, 'Introduction : Settlement Patterns and Urbanization' in P.J. Ucko, R. Tringham and D.W. Dimbley (eds.), *Man, Settlement and Urbanism*, London, Duckworth, 1972, p. xix.
2. Bruce Trigger (ed.), *Time and Traditions* (Essay in Archaeological Interpretations), Edinburgh University, Edinburgh, 1978, p. 193.
3. *Ibid.*, p. 193.
4. R.S. Sharma, *Urban Decay in India* (A.D. 300-A.D. 1000), Munshiram Manoharlal, New Delhi, 1987, p. 3. In this context, the author has brought out significantly the problems faced by an archaeologist while excavating a pre-industrial town.
5. A.D. Chaudhary, *Early Medieval Village in North-Eastern India* (A.D. 600-A.D. 1200) Punthi Pustak, Calcutta, 1971, pp. 1-14.
6. *Ibid.*, pp. 33-52.
7. *Ibid.*, pp. 43-44.
8. R.N. Misra, 'Village Life and Settlements in the Light of Vakataka Inscriptions' in B.M. Pande, B.D. Chattopadhyaya (ed.), *Archaeology and History* (essays in Memory of A. Ghosh) Vol. II, Agam Kala Prakshan, Delhi, 1987, pp. 643-646.
9. *Ibid.*, p. 644.
10. K.M. Shrimali, *Agrarian Structure in Central India and the Northern Deccan* (A.D. 300-500), Munshiram Manoharlal, Delhi, 1987, p. 23.
11. Malati Mahajan, *A Cultural History of Maharashtra and Goa* (From Place-Name Inscriptions), Sundeep Prakashan, Delhi, 1989, pp. 17-33.
12. *Ibid.*, p. 17.
13. *Ibid.*, pp. 34-48.
14. A.S. Thyagaraju, 'A Study of Telugu Place Names' *JAHRS*, Vol. XIV, July 1943, p. 51.

15. *Ibid.*, pp. 57-58.
16. B.D. Chattopadhaya, *Aspects of Rural Settlements and Rural Society in Early Medieval India,* Centre for Studies in Social Sciences, Calcutta, 1990, p. 2.
17. Most of these works claim to trace the place name history within very broad frameworks of time, the upper limit being the 1st century A.D. and the lower limited varies between the early medieval to late medieval times (1200 A.D.-1600 A.D.) See for example, Malati Mahajan, 'Glimpses of Topography by Place Names Found in Inscriptions From Maharashtra in *Studies in Indian Place Names,* VI, Mysore, 1984, p. 38. Another good example would be of A.S. Thyagaraju, 'A Study of Telugu Place Names', *JAHRS,* XXIII, 1954-56, pp. 133-137. His study of place names of Andhra has in fact appeared in several issues of the above journal (XIV-XXIII) in a serialized form. In this particular volume the author has furnished a detailed list of the suffixed along with their meanings for the periods between the 1st to the 17th century A.D.
18. In fact, studies of this nature have been initiated by eminent archaeologist-H.D. Sankalla whose work, *Studies in the Historical and Cultural Geography and Ethnography of Gujarat* (Places and Peoples in Inscriptions of Gujarat-300 B.C.-1300 A.D.), Poona, 1949 has set the trend in place name studies. This was followed by Sumathi Mulay's *Studies in the Historical and Cultural Geography and Ethnography of the Deccan* (Based Entirely on the Inscriptions of the Deccan first 1st-13th century A.D.) Deccan College Dissertation Series, Deccan College, Poona, 1972.
19. We have detailed these aspects in Chapter II of the thesis on 'Geo Political Context' See pp. 102-104. We have seen in this study that the growth of settlements was concentrated in the pre-10th century A.D. period chiefly in the Aihole-Bādāmi-Pattaḍakal areas which corresponds to the sub-region A of our study as the Chālukyas of Bādāmi had their nuclear area of control in this tract. In a similar way, Ālampur area of sub-region C had actively been considered for constructing the temple structures by the Chālukyas of Bādāmi who had aimed at acquiring the Vengi region of the Eastern Deccan during their rule. During the Rāshtrakuṭa Period (9th-10th century A.D.) we observe a gradual spread towards the Southern Deccan wherein Dharwar district-(which forms the western portion of Sub-region B) comes into considerable focus with the emergence of *agrahāra* and temple settlements in this part. We have further noticed that it was however, only under the Chālukya rulers of Kalyāṇi (11th-13th centuries A.D.) that we see the land lying between the Krishna and the Tungabhadra rivers, including the eastern part of it (Raichur Doab) rise to the forefront in terms of richness in settlement patterns and socio-economic life.
20. G.R. Kuppuswamy, *Economic Conditions in Karnataka,* (A.D. 973-A.D. 1336). Karnataka University, Dharwar, 1975. The author here considers Raichur district (Eḍedorenāḍ) as a geographically unprotected area with vast stretches of fertile land due to which it was, during the early medieval period, "often drenched in blood as a result of violent rivalry", p. 9. It is pertinent to note the author's remarks as he was writing on the economic history of the Karnataka region which narrowly corresponds to our period of study.
21. G.S. Dikshit, *Local Self Government in Medieval Karnataka,* Karnataka University, Dharwar, 1964, p. 22.

22. S.J. Mangalam, *Historical Geography and Toponomy of Andhra Pradesh,* Sundeep Prakashan, New Delhi, 1986, p. 10.
23. Y. Subbarayalu, 'The Place of Ur in the Economic and Social History of the Early Tamilnadu from A.D. 750-1350', A.V. Narasimha Murthy and B.K. Gururaja Rao (ed.), *Rangavali : Recent Researches in Indology,* Delhi, 1983, p. 175.
24. Burton Stein, *Peasant State and Society in Medieval South India,* OUP, Delhi, 1980, pp. 109-111.
25. In fact the list of *nāḍu* territorial units in the inscriptional sources of our study is quite exhaustive as can be seen from the chart (IIIA, B, C, iv, 1-143). We have observed that many of these names such as Nolambavadi, Banavasi, Purigere and so on do not even correspond to the present area of study and have been mentioned in the context of reference to rulers who seem to have had political control over more than one tract. We have, therefore, focussed our attention only on those *nāḍus* which figure frequently and correspond squarely to the present area of study.
26. G.S. Dikshit, *op. cit.,* 1964, pp. 24-28.
27. *Ibid.,* p. 26.
28. R. Champakalaksmi, 'The Study of Settlement Patterns in the Chola Period Some Perspectives' *Man and Environment,* 14, 1, 1989, p. 193.
29. G.S. Dikshit, *op. cit.,* 1964, pp. 21-22.
30. R.N. Misra, *op. cit.,* 1987, p. 644.
31. A.K. Choudhary, *op. cit.,* 1971, p. 45.
32. Malati Mahajan, *op. cit.,* 1989, p. 19.
33. *Ibid.,* p. 20.
34. R.C. Hiremath, 'Linguistic Investigation of Some Place Names in Karnataka', *JIH, XXXI,* i, 1953, p. 84.
35. S.C. Joshi, 'Etymology of Place Names Patti-Hatti', *ABORI, XXXIII,* Poona, 1952, p. 49.
36. R.C. Hiremath, *op. cit.,* 1953, p. 84.
37. Y. Subbarayulu, *op. cit.,* 1983, pp. 171-172.
38. G.R. Kuppuswamy, *op. cit.,* 1975, p. 15.
39. Geertz Clifford, 'Village' in David Sills (ed.), *International Encyclopedia of Social Sciences,* 16, p. 318.
40. S.J. Mangalam, *op. cit.,* 1986, p. 13. The author has taken this definition from the *Sukraniti* (Chapter 1 : 385-86).
41. V.A. Gadgil, 'The Village in Sanskrit Literature', *JABBRAS,* (New Series), II, London, 1926, p. 151.
42. K.A. Nilakanta Sastri, 'Grama—An Examination of a New Interpretation', *JOR,* IV, pt. III, July-September, 1930, Madras, pp. 211-215.
43. Om Prakash Prasad, *Decay and Revival of Urban Centres in Medieval South India* (A.D. 600-A.D. 1200), Common Wealth Publishers, New Delhi, 1989, p. 73.

44. B.B. Rajapurohit, 'Distribution of Halli and Pura Suffixes in Karnataka', *Studies in Indian Place Names,* IV, Mysore, 1984, p. 119.
45. D.C. Sircar, *Indian Epigraphical Grossary*, Motilal Banarasidas, Delhi, 1966, p. 266. This meaning is mainly indicated through the translation of such terms as *purapati, pura-pradhāna* and so on, as the mayor of the city and so on.
46. Om Prakash Prasad, *op. cit.,* 1989, p. 73. Similar opinion is held by G.R. Kuppuswamy, *op. cit.,* 1975, pp. 95-96.
47. K.M. Bhadri, 'Some interesting Place Names in Karnataka', *Studies in Indian Place Names,* III, Mysore, 1982, p. 74.
48. Malati Maharajan, *op. cit.,* 1984, p. 38.
49. *Ibid.,* p. 48.
50. *Ibid.,* p. 50.
51. R.C. Hiremath, *op. cit.,* 1953, p. 83. In D.C. Sircar, *op. cit.,* 1966, we have the mention of the term *golla* translated as a cowherd. p. 117. If we take *gola* to be a derivative of the above term, then the settlement to which *gola* is attached could be understood in the sense of a pastoral settlement.
52. Malati Maharajan, *op. cit.,* 1984, p. 54.
53. *Geertz, op. cit.,* vol. 16, p. 318.
54. We have been able to arrive at such a conclusion on the basis of inferences made by Sri P.V.P. Sastry, eminent epigraphist who has now retired from the Department of Archeology, Hyderabad, regarding the nature of settlements mentioned in this record. It is his interpretation given to me while explaining this terminology that is mentioned here.
55. Inscription no. 12, *APGAS,* no. 3, p. 76.
56. Inscription no. 127, *SII,* pp. 146-149.
57. Inscription no. 15, *APGAS,* no. 3, pp. 108-110.
58. Inscription no. 8, *HAS,* 18, pp. 51-52.
59. Lionel D. Barnett, *EI,* XVI, p. 27.
60. Inscription no. 11, *APGAS,* 3, pp. 105-106.
61. Nilgund Inscription *EI,* IV, pp. 204-208.
62, Inscription no. 52, *SII,* XI, pp. 34-43.
63. Transcript, *AR* no. B 545 of 1961-62.
64. Transcript, *AR* no. B 534 of 1961-62.
65. Inscriptions of Sudi, F, *EI,* XV, pp. 85-94.
66. Transcript, *AR.* no. B 570 of 161-62.
67. Inscription no. 117, *SII,* XI, pp. 117-118.
68. Inscriptions at Yewur, B, *EI,* XII, pp. 269-291.
69. D.C. Sircar, *op. cit.,* 1966, p. 375.
70. Transcript, *AR.* no. B 241 of 1953-54.

71. 'Gadag Inscription', *EI,* VI, pp. 89-97.
72. K. Iswara Dutt, *Inscriptional Glossary of Andhra Pradesh,* A.P. Sahitya Academy, Hyderabad, 1967, p. 14.
73. K.M. Bhadri, *op. cit.,* 1982, p. 75. In this context the author has exemplified the Place Name '*Kisuvolal*' which in its Sanskritized form meant Raktapura or red town.
74. Inscriptions of Sudi, C, *EI,* XV, pp. 75-77.
75. Arasibidi Inscription, *EI,* XVII, pp. 121-123.
76. Inscription no. 85, *SII,* XI, pp. 79-82.
77. Inscription no. 538, *SII,* XI, p. 358.
78. Inscription no. 94, *SII,* XI, pp. 89-90.
79. Inscriptions of Sudi, F, *EI,* XV, pp. 85-94.
80. Inscriptions of Sudi, E, *EI,* XV, pp. 80-83.
81. Inscription no. 97, *SII,* XI, pp. 91-94.
82. Inscription no. 116, *SII,* XI, pp. 114-116.
83. Inscriptions of Sudi, *EI,* XV, pp. 96-100.
84. Inscriptions at Yewur, B, *EI,* pp. 269-291.
85. Inscription no. 7, *HAS,* 18, pp. 49-51.
86. Transcript, 458/68 of *Archaeology and Museums* Office, Hyderabad.
87. See for example, Inscription no. 33, Telangāṇa Śāsanālu, II, pp. 63-64.
88. Inscription no. 127, *SII,* XI, pp 146-149.
89. Inscription no. 158, *SII,* XI, pp. 201-203.
90. Inscription no. 167, *SII,* XI, p. 214.
91. Inscription no. 37, *APGAS,* 3, pp. 125-126.
92. Lionel D. Barnett, *EI,* XV, p. 108.
93. Inscription no. 73, *SII,* XV, pp. 99-104.
94. Inscription no. 57, *SII,* XI, pp. 74-78.
95. Inscription no. 97, *SII,* XI, pp. 91-94.
96. B.D. Chattopadhyaya, 'Urban Centres in Early Medieval India : An Overview', in Sabyasachi Bhattacharya and Romila Thapar (eds.), *Situating Indian History* OUP, Delhi, 1986, pp. 16-18.
97. G.R. Kuppuswamy, *op. cit.,* 1975, p. 95.
98. *Ibid.,* p. 205.
99. Inscription no. 198, *SII,* XI, pp. 253-254.
100. Inscription no. 47, *SII,* XV, p. 63.
101. Inscription no. 106, *SII,* XV, pp. 136-137.
102. Inscription no. 131, *SII,* XV, pp. 167-168.
103. Inscription no. 16, *HAS,* no. 8. pp. 83-89.

104. Inscription no. 20, *SII*, XV, pp. 267-269.
105. O.P. Prasad, *op. cit.*, 189, p. 73.
106. R.N. Nandi, 'Growth of Rural Economy in Early Feudal India', Presidential Address, Ancient India Section, *PIHC*, 45th Session, Annamalai Nagar, 1984, p. 63.
107. Inscription no. 1, *HAS*, 18, pp. 39-40. It is pertinent to note that the term *sthala* has nowhere been translated upon. Even in the work of O.P. Prasad, *op. cit.*, 1989, which gives an exhaustive list of various terms dealing with urban centres, it is interesting that any reference to *sthala* has been eluded pp. 185-189.
108. Particularly significant for our study are the works of O.P. Prasad, *op. cit.*, 1989, pp. 12-13. The author has furnished extensive data with regard to the growth of the urban centres during 1000 A.D.-1300 A.D., with concentration in the northern and north western Karnataka which overlaps with our area of study in part (pp. 75-77). But the period preceding (600-1000) has been considered as one of urban decay by this author due to the absence of commercial activity in this phase and R.N. Nandi, *op. cit.*, 1984, pp. 61-65. He too has a similar opinion as above in viewing the urban centres of 11th to 13th centuries A.D. as emerging out of their initial decay in the period preceding it.
109. See, chapter II of the book of '*Geo-Political Context*', pp. 102-107.
110. Jayavant Kulli, '*Some Place Names of Bijapur and Gulbarga Area*', *Studies in Indian Place Names,* III, Mysore, 1982, pp. 48-49.
111. K.R. Basavaraja, Agraharas in Medieval Karnataka, *JKU* (Humanities), IV, June, 1960, p. 106.
112. A.V. Krishnamurthy, 'Agraharas in Andhra', *APHC,* Kakinada, 1984, p. 45.
113. Inscription no. 11, *HAS*, 18, pp. 57-60.
114. 'Kotavumachgi Inscription', B, *EI,* XX, pp. 64-70.
115. 'Inscription at Yewur', B, *EI,* II, pp. 269-291.
116. 'Munirabad Stone Inscription' *HAS*, 5, pp. 1-12.
117. 'Bannigol Inscription', *EI*, XXXVI, pp. 118-120.
118. We have detailed various soil types in chapter IV of the book on Economic Context', see pp. 342-346.
119. Inscriptions no. 13, *HAS*, 18, pp. 63-74.
120. 'Kotavumachgi Inscription', *EI*, XX, pp. 64-70.
121. 'Munirabad Stone Inscription', *HAS*, 5, pp. 1-12.
122. 'Inscriptions at Ittagi', A, *EI*, XIII, pp. 37-38.
123. 'Gadag Inscription' *EI,* XV, pp. 348-363.
124. We have detailed these aspects in chapter III of the thesis on 'Social Context'. See pp. 195-198.
125. Inscription of Sudi C, *EI*, XV, pp. 75-77.
126. Inscription no. 66, *APGAS*, 3, pp. 73-77.
127. Kotavamuchgi Inscription, *EI*, XX, pp. 64-70.
128. Transcript, *A.R.* no B. 524 of 1960-61.

129. Inscription no. 200, *SII*, XI, pp. 255-256.
130. Inscription no. 5, *APGAS*, 9, p. 30.
131. This aspect has been detailed in an earlier chapter III of the book on Social Context, pp. 205-206.
132. N. Karashima, *South Indian History and Society* (A.D. 850-1800), Delhi, 1984, p. 3.
133. See chapter III of the book on the 'Social Context' pp. 194-196.
134. 'Bannigol Inscription', *EI*, XXXVI, pp. 118-120.
135. 'Kilaratti Inscription', *EI*, XXXV, pp. 37-39.
136. Transcript, *AR*, no. B. 342 of 1957-58.
137. D.C. Sircar, *op. cit.*, 1966, p. 343.
138. S. Ritti, *EI*, XXXV, p. 38.
139. Inscription no. 92, *SII*, XI, pp. 87-89.
140. D.C. Sircar, *op. cit.*, 1966, pp. 197-198.
141. *Ibid.*, p. 402.
142. Inscription no. 117, *SII*, XI, pp. 117-118.
143. Karihima, *op. cit.*, 1984, p. 3.
144. Inscription no. 47, *SII*, XI, pp. 32-34.
145. Inscription no. 50, *SII*, XI, pp. 36-38.
146. Transcript *AR*. no. B. 714 of 1958-59.
147. Inscriptions of Sudi, F, *EI*, XV, pp. 85-94.
148. Inscription no. 6, *HAS*, 18, pp. 46-49.
149. We have discussed this aspect in detail in chapter IV of the book on 'Economic Context', see pp. 316-319.
150. Inscription no. 155, *SII*, XI, pp. 194-197.
151. Inscription from Yewur C, *EI*, XI, XII, pp. 329-331.
152. Inscription no. 163, *SII*, XI, pp. 209-211.
153. Inscription no. 119, *SII*, XI, pp. 133-136.
154. Inscription no. 13, *HAS*, 18, pp. 63-74.
155. Inscription no. 36, *SII*, XV, p. 44.
156. Inscription no. 170, *SII*, XI, pp. 217-218.
157. Two Inscriptions from Ron, B, *EI*, XIX, pp. 226-236.
158. Inscription no. 238, *SII*, XV, pp. 293-296.
159. G.S. Dikshit, *op. cit.*, 1964, p. 64. Of course the author does not state it directly but one can infer this through the suggestions given by him for the existence of more than one gavundra (village headman) within a single settlement unit.
160. Inscription no. 47, *SII*, IX, pp. 32-34.
161. Inscription no. 50, *SII*, XI, pp. 36-38.

162. Inscription no. 58, *SII*, XI, p. 48.
163. Inscription no. 65, *SII*, XI, pp. 55-57.
164. Inscription no. 75, *SII*, XI, pp. 65-66.
165. Inscription of Sudi, F, *EI*, XV, pp. 85-94.
166. Transcript, *A.R.* No. B. 714 of 1958-59.
167. Inscription no. 2, *SII*, XI, pp. 2-3.
168. Inscription of Sudi, H, *EI*, XV, pp. 96-100.
169. Inscription no. 6, *HAS*, 18, pp. 46-49.
170. Transcript, *A.R.* no. 534 of 1961-62.
171. We have made a detailed discussion of the socio-political standing enjoyed by each of these groups in chapter III of the book on 'Social Context', see pp. 177-179.
172. *Ibid.*, pp. 200-206.
173. Inscription no. 158, *SII*, XI, pp. 201-203.
174. Inscription no. 50, *SII*, XI, pp. 36-38.
175. Inscription no. 36, *SII*, XV, pp. 43-46.
176. B.R. Gopal, *EI*, XXXVI, p. 139.
177. D.C. Sircar, *op. cit.*, 1966, p. 270. According to the author sometimes it is also used to indicate the head quarters of a chief or a governor.
178. B.R. Gopal, *EI*, XXXVI, p. 139, this term actually indicates a temporary camping place as opposed to *nele-vidu*.
179. Inscription no. 8, *APGAS*, 9, p. 36.
180. We have discussed these in chapter III on '*Social Context*' see pp. 189-191.
181. Inscription no. 11, *HAS*, 18, pp. 57-60.
182. Inscription no. 12, *APGAS* 3, pp. 73-77. Infact, this place had figured as an *agrahāra* even prior to this period. If we take into account the economic significance attached to the settlement considering the fertile nature of the soil existing here which has been subject to a great deal of praise in the context of its references in other inscriptional sources as well, it would not be surprising that various rulers wanted to proclaim their control over this area which had formed a part of the larger tract of Kukkanur-36.
183. Inscription no. 14, *HAS*, 18, pp. 74-79.
184. B.D. Chattopadhyaya, *op. cit.*, 1990, p. 4.
185. Inscription no. 36, *SII*, XI, pp. 43-46.
186. Inscription no. 163, *SII*, XI, pp. 209-211.
187. Inscription no. 170, *SII*, XI, pp. 217-218.
188. Inscription no. 48, *SII*, XI, pp. 34-36.
189. 'Alur Inscription', *EI*, XVI, pp. 27-31.
190. Inscription no. 1, *HAS*, 18, pp. 39-40.
191. Inscription no. 14, *HAS*, 18, pp. 74-79.

192. Inscription of Sudi, G, *EI*, SV, pp. 94-96.
193. B.R. Gopal, *Minor Dynasties of South India : Karnataka,* I, Madras, 1982, p. 107.
194. Inscription from Navali, *EI*, XXXIV, pp. 164-166.
195. Kilaratti Inscription, *EI*, XXXV, pp. 37-39.
196. Inscription no. 6, *HAS*, 18, pp. 46-49.
197. Inscription no. 9, *HAS*, 18, pp. 52-54.
198. Inscription no. 16, *HAS,* 18, pp. 83-89.
199. R. Champakalakshmi, *op. cit.,* 1989, p. 92.
200. *Ibid.,* p. 100.
201. R.N. Nandi, *op. cit.,* 1984, p. 63.
202. 'Alur Inscription', *EI*, XVI, pp. 27-31.
203. Inscription no. 84, *SII*, XI, pp. 77-79.
204. Inscriptions at Yewur, B, *EI*, XII, pp. 269-291.
205. Inscriptions at Ittagi, A, *EI*, XIII, pp. 37-38.
206. Inscription no. 65, *SII*, XI, pp. 55-57.
207. Inscription no. 117, *SII*, XI, pp. 117-118.
208. Inscription no. 127, *SII*, XI, pp. 146-149.
209. We have discussed all these groups in detail in chapter III of the thesis on 'Social Context' pp. 220-233 and also see chapter IV on 'Economic Context'.
210. Inscription no. 158, *SII*, XI, pp. 201-203.
211. Inscription no. 10, *KI,* II, pp. 29-34.
212. Inscription no. 106, *SII*, XV, pp. 136-137.
213. Inscription no. 16, *HAS*, 18, pp. 83-89.
214. Inscription no. 17, *HAS,* 18, pp. 89-93.
215. Inscription no. 131, *SII*, XV, pp. 167-168.
216. Inscription no. 220, *SII*, XV, pp. 267-269.

Chart – III : SPATIAL CONTEXT

Sub Region A

i	ii	iii	iv	v	vi	vii	viii	ix	x	xi	xii	xiii	xiv	xv
S.No.	Date & Location	Name of the Settlement	nāḍu	palli	vāḍa	ūr	grāma	Context (Rural)	pura	paṭṭaṇa	Capital	Temple Settlement	Context (Urban)	Reference
1.	Tumbagi Ins. AD 1004.	Tumbige						❑, +				Δ		*EI*, XVII,
	Muddebihal Tq. Bijapur Dt.	Pagalaṭṭi-300												7-10
2.	Belur Ins. AD 1022.	Perūr						❑, +				Δ		*IA*, XVIII,
	Badami Tq.													270-275
	Bijapur Dt.	Kisukāḍ-70	♣											
3.	Ins. no. 61 AD 1024.	Maravolal						❑				Δ		*SII*, XI,
	Hungund Tq.	Nolambavāḍi	♣											50-51
	Bijapur Dt.	Kariviḍi-30						❑ GV						
4.	Ins. no. 68 AD 1033.	Nālvatumbāḍa			♠			❑						*SII*, XI,
	Muddebihal Tq.	Tambedhaḍe						❑				Δ		58-59
	Bijapur Dt.	Hoṭṭalakere									⌘			
5.	Arasibidi Ins. AD 1047.	Gānada				●		❑						*EI*, VII,
	Hungund Tq.	Halūr												121-123
	Bijapur Dt.	Vikramapura							◆			Δ		
		Gokage						❑						
		Kisukad-70	♣											
6.	Ins. no. 85 AD 1049	Śripura							◆			Δ		*SII*, XI,
	Bagalkot Tq.	Mūlavalli grāma					#							79-82
	Bijapur Dt.	Penugoṇḍa-30						❑ GV						
		Bāgadage-70	♣											
7.	Kelawadi Ins. AD 1053.	Kelavādi						❑						*EI*, IV,
	Badami Tq.	Pangaragi-12						❑ GV						259-262

Key to the Symbols : ♣ : nāḍu; * : palli; ♠ : vāḍa; ● : ūr; # : grāma; ❑ : Context (Urban); ⌘ : Capital
Δ : Temple Settlement; ◆ : pura; ❖ : paṭṭana; ☒ : Context (Urban); + : agrahāra GV : Group of Villages

Chart – III : SPATIAL CONTEXT

Sub Region A

i	ii	iii	iv	v	vi	vii	viii	ix	x	xi	xii	xiii	xiv	xv
S.No.	*Date & Location*	*Name of the Settlement*	*nāḍu*	*palli*	*vāḍa*	*ūr*	*grāma*	*Context (Rural)*	*pura*	*paṭṭana*	*Capital*	*Temple Settlement*	*Context (Urban)*	*Reference*
	Bijapur Dt.	Kelawādi-300	♣											
8.	Ins. no. 88	Vikramapura							♦		⌘			*SII*, XI,
	AD 1058.													
	Hungund Tq.	Pampeyatirtha						❑						84-85
	Bijapur Dt.	Kisuknd-70	♣											
9.	Ins. no. 110	Sāṛḍiyanahalli		*				❑						*SII*, XI,
	AD 1070.													
	Badami Tq.													107
	Bijapur Dt.	Kisuvolal										Δ	❑	
10.	Ins. no. 113	Ponnuguṇḍa			♠						⌘	Δ		*SII*, XI,
	AD 1074.													
	Hungund Tq.	Ponnugunda-30						❑						111-112
	Bijapur Dt.													
11.	Ins. no. 116	Bādubbeyapalu				●		❑						*SII*, XI,
	AD 1075.													
	Bagalkot Tq.	Targodage						❑						114-116
	Bijapur Dt.	Vikramapura							♦			Δ		
		Karakuruva-40						❑ GV						
		Kisukad-70	♣											
		Tardavādināḍ	♣											
12.	Ins. no. 135.	Vikramapura							♦		⌘	Δ		*SII*, XI,
	AD 1087.													
	Hungund Tq.	Karividi-30						❑ GV						160-161
	Bijapur Dt.	Kisukād-70	♣											
13.	Ins. no. 169	Ayyavole											⊠ +	*SII*, XI,
	AD 1119.													
	Hungund Tq.													216-217
	Bijapur Dt.													
14.	Ins. no. 30.	Belūr				●						Δ		*SII*, XV,
	AD 1145.													
	Muddebihal Tq.													32-33

Key to the Symbols : ♣ : nāḍu; * : palli; ♠ : vāḍa; ● : ūr; # : grāma; ❑ : Context (Urban); ⌘ : Capital
Δ : Temple Settlement; ♦ : pura; ❖ : paṭṭana; ⊠ : Context (Urban); + : agrahāra; GV : Group of Villages

Chart – III : SPATIAL CONTEXT

Sub Region A

i	ii	iii	iv	v	vi	vii	viii	ix	x	xi	xii	xiii	xiv	xv
S.No.	*Date & Location*	*Name of the Settlement*	*nāḍu*	*palli*	*vāḍa*	*ūr*	*grāma*	*Context (Rural)*	*pura*	*paṭṭaṇa*	*Capital*	*Temple Settlement*	*Context (Urban)*	*Reference*
	Bijapur Dt.	Hagarittage-300	♣											
15.	Ins. no. 47. AD 1151. Hungund Tq. Bijapur Dt.	Erambarage								❖		Δ		*SII*, XV, 63
16.	Ins. no. 126. AD 1174. Muddebihal Tq. Bijapur Dt.	Gottakhandike			♠			❑				Δ		*SII*, XV, 159-160
		Hagarittage-300	♣											
17.	Ins. no. 134 AD 1178. Badami Tq. Bijapur Dt.	Nuggivāda			♠			❑			⌘	Δ		*SII*, XV, 73-74
		Kadakere						❑						
		Modeganūr				•		❑ +						
		Hangarage-12						❑ GV						
18.	Ins. no. 56 AD 1184. Muddebihal Tq. Bijapur Dt.	Karaganūru				•		❑						*SII*, XV, 73-74
		Bammanahalli		*										
		Tāliyakūti						❑						
		Hagarittage - 300	♣											
19.	Ins. no. 58. AD 1184. Muddebihal Tq. Bijapur Dt.	Mininjige			♠		#	❑				Δ		*SII*, XV, 78-82
		Hagarittage	♣											
20.	Ins. no. 242. AD 1186. Hungund Tq. Bijapur Dt.	Kisukādunāḍu	♣											*SII*, XV, 301-302
21.	Ins. no. 147. AD 1189. Muddebihal Tq. Bijapur Dt.	Hagarattiya sthala											⊠	*SII*, XV, 189
		sthala Karaganūra sthala											⊠	

Key to the Symbols : ♣ : nāḍu; * : palli; ♠ : vāḍa; • : ūr; # : grāma; ❑ : Context (Urban); ⌘ : Capital
Δ : Temple Settlement; ◆ : pura; ❖ : paṭṭana; ⊠ : Context (Urban); + : agrahāra GV : Group of Villages

Chart – III : SPATIAL CONTEXT

Sub Region B

i	ii	iii	iv	v	vi	vii	viii	ix	x	xi	xii	xiii	xiv	xv
S.No.	Date & Location	Name of the Settlement	nāḍu	palli	vāḍa	ūr	grāma	Context (Rural)	pura	paṭṭaṇa	Capital	Temple Settlement	Context (Urban)	Reference
22.	Ins. no. 156. AD 1207. Hungund Tq. Bijapur Dt.	Kandagale sthala Karādikal-300	♣									Δ	☒	SII, XV, 200-201
23.	Ins. no. 164. AD 1220. Hungund Tq. Bijapur Dt.	Kandegale										Δ	☒	SII, XV, 208-210
24.	Ins. no. 11. AD 973. Kobal Tq. Raichur Dt.	Modeyanūr				● +						Δ		HAS, 18, 57-60
25.	Nilgund Ins. AD 982 Gadag Tq. Dharwar Dt.	Nirugunḍa Belvola-300 Purigere-300 Kogali-500 Banavāsi	 ♣ ♣ ♣ ♣				#							EI, IV, 204-208
26.	Transcript AD 991 YalburgaTq. Raichur Dt.	Kukkanūr-30 Purigare-300 Belvola-300 Banavāsi-1000	 ♣ ♣ ♣					□ GV						A.R. no. B 221 of 1955-56
27.	Ins. no. 47. AD 994. Gadag Tq. Dharwar Dt.	Eleya Posavūr Mulugunḍa Mulugunḍa-12 Belvola-300 Purigere-300	 ♣ ♣			●		□ □ □ GV						SII, XI, 32-34
28.	Ins. no. 48. AD 1002.	Kardugu						□ +						SII, XI,

Key to the Symbols : ♣ : nāḍu; Δ : Temple Settlement; * : palli; ♦ : pura; ♠ : vāḍa; ❖ : paṭṭana; ● : ūr; ☒ : Context (Urban); # : grāma; + : agrahāra; □ : Context (Urban); GV : Group of Villages; ⌘ : Capital

Chart – *III* : SPATIAL CONTEXT

Sub Region B

i	*ii*	*iii*	*iv*	*v*	*vi*	*vii*	*viii*	*ix*	*x*	*xi*	*xii*	*xiii*	*xiv*	*xv*
S.No.	*Date & Location*	*Name of the Settlement*	*nāḍu*	*palli*	*vāḍa*	*ūr*	*grāma*	*Context (Rural)*	*pura*	*paṭṭaṇa*	*Capital*	*Temple Settlement*	*Context (Urban)*	*Reference*
	Gadag Tq. Dharwar Dt.	Maiteyavāda			♠			❑						34-36
		Kukkanūr-30						❑ GV						
		Belvola-300	♣											
		Purigere-300	♣											
		Kundūru-500	♣											
29.	Ins. no. 50. AD 1005. Gadag Tq. Dharwar Dt.	Sirivūra				●		❑						*SII*, XI, 36-38
		Saratavūra				●		❑						
		Sabbi-30						❑ GV						
		Huligere-300	♣											
		Beluvola-300	♣											
		Halasige-12,000	♣											
30.	Ins. no. 1. AD 1005. Yalburg Tq. Raichur Dt.	Kukkanūru				●						Δ	⊠	*IIAS*, 18, 39-40
		sthala												
31.	Ins. no. 52 AD 1007. Gadag Tq. Dharwar Dt.	Lokkiguṇḍi					#	❑ +				Δ		*SII*, XI, 39-43
		Māsavādi-400	♣											
32.	Alur Ins. AD 1010. Gadag Tq. Dharwar Dt.	panchabāḍa			♠			❑						*EI*, XVI, 27-31
		Saptagrāma					#	❑						
		Ālūra				●		❑						
		Sirivūra				●		❑						
		Ittage						❑						
		Kukkanūr-30						❑						
		Ballkunde-300	♣											
		Kemgali-500	♣											
		Māsiyavādinādu	♣											
		Nolambavādi-32,000	♣											

Key to the Symbols : ♣ : nāḍu; Δ : Temple Settlement; * : palli; ♦ : pura; ♠ : vāḍa; ❖ : paṭṭana; ● : ūr; ⊠ : Context (Urban); # : grāma; + : agrahāra; ❑ : Context (Urban); GV : Group of Villages; ⌘ : Capital

Chart – III : SPATIAL CONTEXT

Sub Region B

i	ii	iii	iv	v	vi	vii	viii	ix	x	xi	xii	xiii	xiv	xv
S.No.	Date & Location	Name of the Settlement	nāḍu	palli	vāḍa	ūr	grāma	Context (Rural)	pura	paṭṭaṇa	Capital	Temple Settlement	Context (Urban)	Reference
33.	Ins. of Sudi C	Surdi							◆			Δ	⊠	EI, XV,
	AD 1010.	Siriguppe						❑						
	Ron Tq.	Sarnka ūr				●								75-77
	Dharwar Dt.	Kisukād-70	♣											
34.	Kotavumachgi Ins.	Unumachige						❑ +				Δ		EI, XIX,
	AD 1012.	Nārāyamgal-12						❑ GV						
	Gadag Tq.	Belvola-300	♣											64-70
	Dharwar Dt.	Puligere-300	♣											
35.	Ins. from Naval	Ededore-2000	♣											EI, XXXIV
	AD 1014													
	Lingsugur Tq.													164-166
	Raichur Dt.													
36.	Ins. no. 58	Āragilvala						❑				Δ		SII, XI,
	AD 1022													
	Mundargi Tq.													48
	Dharwar Dt.	Māsevavādi-140	♣											
37.	Transcript	Ballanittage						❑				Δ		A.R.
	AD 1022.													no. B 534
	Manvi Tq.	Puvveravalli		*				❑						of 1961-62
	Raichur Dt.	Aryamavādi-300	♣											
38.	Bannigol Ins.	Bannigola						❑						EI, XXXVI
	AD 1025.	Moraganūr				●					⌘			
	Lingsugur Tq.	Kandurage-70	♣											118-120
	Raichur Dt.													
39.	Ins. no. 3.	Mosangi						❑			⌘	Δ		HAS, 18,
	AD 1027.													
	Lingsugur Tq.	Palipodara												42-43
	Raichur Dt.													
40.	Ins. no. 65.	Posavūr				●						Δ		SII, XI,
	AD 1023.													
	Gadag Tq.													55-57

Key to the Symbols : ♣ : nāḍu; Δ : Temple Settlement; * : palli; ◆ : pura; ♠ : vāḍa; ❖ : paṭṭana; ● : ūr; ⊠ : Context (Urban); # : grāma, + : agrahāra; ❑ : Context (Urban); GV : Group of Villages; ⌘ : Capital

Chart – III : SPATIAL CONTEXT

Sub Region B

i	ii	iii	iv	v	vi	vii	viii	ix	x	xi	xii	xiii	xiv	xv
S.No.	Date & Location	Name of the Settlement	nāḍu	palli	vāḍa	ūr	grāma	Context (Rural)	pura	paṭṭaṇa	Capital	Temple Settlement	Context (Urban)	Reference
	Dharwar Dt.	Mulugunḍa-12						❑ GV						
41.	Transcript.	Ballanittage					#							*A.R.*
	AD 1031.													no. B 545
	Manvi Tq.													of 1961-62
	Raichur Dt.	Etagiri									⌘			
42.	Ins. no. 528.	Bhāratapura						❑ +	◆			Δ		*SII*, XI,
	AD 1032.													
	Mundargi Tq.													358
	Dharwar Dt.													
43.	Transcript	Tanakavāvi						❑ +						*A.R.*
	AD 1033.													no. B 376
	Lingsugur Tq.													of 57-58
	Raichur Dt.	Kelavādi-300	♣											
44.	Transcript	Ballanittage					#	❑				Δ		*A.R.*
	AD 1036.													no. B 536
	Manvi Tq.	Mosalikal-300	♣											of 61-62
	Raichur Dt.	Ededore-2000	♣											
45.	Ins. no. 75.	Siriūra				●		❑						*SII*, XI,
	AD 1042.													
	Mundargi Tq.	Pañchagrāma					#	❑						65-66
	Dharwar Dt.	Masiyavadi-140	♣					❑ +						
46.	Kilaratti Ins.	Bannigola												*EI*, XXXV,
	AD 1046.													
	Lingsugur Tq.	Pannāleyakota									⌘			37-39
	Raichur Dt.	Karādikal-300	♣											
47.	Ins. no. 81.	Benatūr				●		❑ +						*SII*, XI,
	AD 1049.													
	GadagTq.	Ittage						❑						74
	Dharwar Dt.	Kuṛitakuntiya						❑						

Key to the Symbols : ♣ : nāḍu; * : palli; ♠ : vāḍa; ● : ūr; # : grāma; ❑ : Context (Urban); ⌘ : Capital
Δ : Temple Settlement; ◆ : pura; ❖ : paṭṭana; ☒ : Context (Urban); + : agrahāra GV : Group of Villages

Chart – III : SPATIAL CONTEXT

Sub Region B

i	ii	iii	iv	v	vi	vii	viii	ix	x	xi	xii	xiii	xiv	xv
S.No.	Date & Location	Name of the Settlement	nāḍu	palli	vāḍa	ūr	grāma	Context (Rural)	pura	paṭṭaṇa	Capital	Temple Settlement	Context (Urban)	Reference
48.	Ins. no. 84 AD 1049. Gadag Tq. Dharwar Dt.	Pombulcha						❑				Δ		SII, XI, 77-79
		Bāydumbagere						❑						
		Kappādigere						❑						
		Belvola-300	♣											
		Purigere-300	♣											
49.	Ins. no. 86 AD 1050. Mundargi Tq. Dharwar Dt.	Pannāvaleya Kote									⌘			SII, XI, 82-84
		Kisukad-70	♣											
		Bāgadage-70	♣											
		Māsiyavādi-140	♣											
50.	Ins. of Suci 'D' AD 1050. RonTq. Dharwar Dt.	Torugare-60	♣											EI, XV, 77-80
		Kisukād-70	♣											
		Māsavadi-140	♣											
51.	Ins. no. 92 AD 1054. Mundargi Tq. Dharwar Dt.	Kisuguṇḍi						❑				Δ		SII, XI, 87-89
52.	Ins. of Sudi 'E' AD 1054. RonTq. Dharwar Dt.	Suṇḍi							♦			Δ		EI, XV, 80-83
		Torugere-60	♣											
		Kisukād-70	♣											
		Māsiyavadi-140	♣											
53.	Transcript AD 1055. Lingsugur Tq. Raichur Dt.	Bannigola						❑ +				Δ		A.R. no. B 342 of 1957-58
		Karādikai-300	♣											
54.	Ins. no. 94. AD 1059. Munargi Tq. Dharwar Dt.	Dharmavolal										Δ	☒	SII, XI, 89-90

Key to the Symbols : ♣ : nāḍu; * : palli; ♠ : vāḍa; ● : ūr; # : grāma; ❑ : Context (Urban); ⌘ : Capital
Δ : Temple Settlement; ♦ : pura; ❖ : paṭṭana; ☒ : Context (Urban); + : agrahāra; GV : Group of Villages

Chart – III : SPATIAL CONTEXT

Sub Region B

i	ii	iii	iv	v	vi	vii	viii	ix	x	xi	xii	xiii	xiv	xv
S.No.	Date & Location	Name of the Settlement	nāḍu	palli	vāḍa	ūr	grāma	Context (Rural)	pura	paṭṭaṇa	Capital	Temple Settlement	Context (Urban)	Reference
55.	Ins. of Sudi	Śivanūr				●		□						*EI*, XV,
	AD 1060.													
	RonTq.	Balguli						□						85-94
	Dharwar Dt.	Karittage						□						
		Sundi							♦		⌘	Δ		
		Puli					#							
		Torugere-60	♣											
		Kisukād-70	♣											
		Sindavādinadu	♣											
56.	Ins. no. 97	Mulguṇḍapura							♦			Δ	⊠	*SII*, XI,
	AD 1062.													
	Gadag Tq.	Mulguṇḍa-12						□ GV						
	Dharwar Dt.	Belvola-300	♣											91-94
		Purigere-300	♣											
57.	Transcript	Nāvile						□				Δ		*A.R.*
	AD 1066.													no. B 714
	Lingsugur Tq.													of 1958-59
	Raichur Dt.	Karādikal-300	♣											
58.	Transcript	Kappakallu					#	□				Δ		*A.R.*
	AD 1069.													no. B 570
	Manvi Tq.	Kereyūru				●		□						of 1961-62
	Raichur Dt.	Gorikallu-12						□ GV						
		Mosailkallu-300	♣											
		Ededore-2000	♣											
59.	Ins. no. 111.	Soratavūr				●						Δ		*SII*, XI,
	AD 1071.													
	GadagTq.													107-110
	Dharwar Dt.													
60.	Gawariwad Ins.	Mudageri			♠			□						*EI*, XV,
	AD 1071	Gummuṁgola			♠			□						
	Gadag Tq.	Ittage			♠			□						337-346
	Dharwar Dt.	Gavarivāda			♠			□						

Key to the Symbols : ♣ : nāḍu; * : palli; ♠ : vāḍa; ● : ūr; # : grāma; □ : Context (Urban); ⌘ : Capital
Δ : Temple Settlement; ♦ : pura; ❖ : paṭṭaṇa; ⊠ : Context (Urban); + : agrahāra; GV : Group of Villages

Chart – III : SPATIAL CONTEXT

Sub Region B

i	ii	iii	iv	v	vi	vii	viii	ix	x	xi	xii	xiii	xiv	xv
S.No.	Date & Location	Name of the Settlement	nāḍu	palli	vāḍa	ūr	grāma	Context (Rural)	pura	paṭṭana	Capital	Temple Settlement	Context (Urban)	Reference
		Annigere						❑				Δ		
		Belvola-300	♣											
		Pulgere-300	♣											
61.	Ins. no.2.	Kallamanaplli						❑						*SII*, XV,
	AD 1074.													
	Ron Tq.	Nicguṇḍi						❑				Δ		2-3
	Dharwar Dt.	Kisukād-70	♣											
62.	Ins. of Sudi H	Musiyagerey			♠			❑						*EI*, XV,
	AD 1075.	Kallamanūr				●		❑						
	Ron Tq.	Gulugavalli		*				❑						96-100
	Dharwar Dt.	Vikramapura							♦					
		Suṇḍi							♦		⌘	Δ		
		Kisukād-70	♣											
63.	Ins. of Sudi G (2)	Suṇḍi							♦			Δ	❑	*EI*, XV,
	AD 1076.													
	Ron Tq.	Vikrampura							♦		⌘			94-96
	Dharwar Dt.													
64	Ins. no. 117	Nidgundi					#	❑				Δ		*SII*, XI,
	AD 1076.													
	RonTq.	Avagevādi									⌘			117-118
	Dharwar Dt.	Kisukad-70	♣											
65.	Ins. no. 6	Temgola						❑						*IIAS*, 18,
	AD 1077.													
	Lingsugur Tq.													46-49
	Raichur Dt.	Karādikal-400	♣											
66.	Ins. at Yewur 'B'	Mukkunde				●	#	❑						*EI*, XII,
	AD 1077.	Ehūr				●		❑				Δ		
	ShoranpurTq.	Gangapoor				●		❑						269-291
	Gulbarga Dt.	Śivapura						❑	♦					
		Kiriya Bellumbatti						❑						
		Piriya Bellumbatti						❑						

Key to the Symbols : ♣ : nāḍu; Δ : Temple Settlement; * : palli; ♦ : pura; ♠ : vāḍa; ❖ : paṭṭana; ● : ūr; ⊠ : Context (Urban); # : grāma; + : agrahāra; ❑ : Context (Urban); GV : Group of Villages; ⌘ : Capital

Chart – III : SPATIAL CONTEXT

Sub Region B

i	*ii*	*iii*	*iv*	*v*	*vi*	*vii*	*viii*	*ix*	*x*	*xi*	*xii*	*xiii*	*xiv*	*xv*
S.No.	*Date & Location*	*Name of the Settlement*	*nāḍu*	*palli*	*vāḍa*	*ūr*	*grāma*	*Context (Rural)*	*pura*	*paṭṭaṇa*	*Capital*	*Temple Settlement*	*Context (Urban)*	*Reference*
		Nārāyambole-70	♣											
		Sāgara-300	♣											
		Ededorenad	♣											
67.	Ins. no. 19	Lokkiguṇḍi					#					Δ	⊠	*KI.* II,
	AD 1080.													
	Gadag Tq.													29-34
	Dharwar Dt.													
68.	Ins. no. 127.	Pombolal					#	❑						*SII.* XI,
	AD 1082.													
	Gadag Tq.	Kuritakente					#	❑ +				Δ		146-149
	Dharwar Dt.	Kalasavalli		≅										
		Purigere-300	♣											
		Belvola-300	♣											
		Kundūr-1000	♣											
69.	Ins. of Sudi 'I'	Pomgari			♠			❑				Δ		*EI.* XV,
	AD 1084.	Suldi							♦		⌘	Δ		
	Ron Tq.	Kisukād-70	♣											100-102
	Dharwar Dt.													
70.	Ins. of Sudi 'J'	Mudiyanūru				●		❑						*EI.* XV,
	AD 1084.	Suṇḍi							♦		⌘			
	Ron Tq.	Kisukād-70	♣											103-105
	Dharwar Dt.													
71.	Transcript	Hiriya Gabbūr					#	❑				Δ		*A.R.*
	AD 1084.													no. B 565
	Deodurg Tq.													of 58-59
	Raichur Dt.													
72.	Ins. no. 134	Kurita Kumtiya					#	❑ +						*SII.* XI,
	AD 1087.													
	Gadag Tq.	Ermeganūr				●		❑				Δ		157-160
	Dharwar Dt.	Siriguppe						❑						

Key to the Symbols : ♣ : nāḍu; * : palli; ♠ : vāḍa; ● : ūr; # : grāma; ❑ : Context (Urban); ⌘ : Capital
Δ : Temple Settlement; ♦ : pura; ❖ : paṭṭana; ⊠ : Context (Urban); + : agrahāra GV : Group of Villages

Chart – *III* : SPATIAL CONTEXT

Sub Region B

i	ii	iii	iv	v	vi	vii	viii	ix	x	xi	xii	xiii	xiv	xv
S.No.	*Date & Location*	*Name of the Settlement*	*nāḍu*	*palli*	*vāḍa*	*ūr*	*grāma*	*Context (Rural)*	*pura*	*paṭṭaṇa*	*Capital*	*Temple Settlement*	*Context (Urban)*	*Reference*
73	Munirabad Stone Ins AD 1088. KoppalTq. Raichur Dt.	Pulige					#	□ +				Δ		*IIAS*, 5, 1--12
74.	Ins. no. 137 AD 1091. Gadag Tq. Dharwar Dt.	Soratavūra				●		□ +				Δ		*SII*, XI, 165-166
75.	Transcript AD 1095. Devadurg Tq. Raichur Dt.	Havihalu						□ □						*A.R.* no. B 661 of 58-59
		Kalmale												
		Kabbūr				●								
76.	Gadag Ins. AD 1098. Gadag Tq. Dharwar Dt.	Lokkigundi					#	□ –				Δ	⊠ +	*EI*, XV, 348-368
		Belvolanād	♣											
77.	Ins. no. 148 AD 1099. Ron Tq. Dharwar Dt.	Alamgere						□						*SII*, XI, 182-183
		Kisukād-70	♣											
78.	Transcript AD 1100 Shorapur Tq. Gulbarga Dt.	Mudinūr				●		□ +						*A.R.* no. B 520 of 60-61
		Hagarittage						□				Δ		
79.	Ins. no. 150. AD 1102. GadagTq Dharwar Dt.	Galdugu						□ +				Δ		*SII*, XI, 185-187
		Belovlanād	♣											
		Palasige-12000	♣											
80.	Ins. no. 151 AD 1102 Ron Tq.	Beluvaniga						□				Δ		*SII*, XI, 187-188

Key to the Symbols : ♣ : nāḍu; Δ : Temple Settlement; * : palli; ♦ : pura; ♠ : vāḍa; ❖ : paṭṭana; ● : ūr; ⊠ : Context (Urban); # : grāma; + : agrahāra; □ : Context (Urban); GV : Group of Villages; ⌘ : Capital

Chart – *III* : SPATIAL CONTEXT

Sub Region B

i	*ii*	*iii*	*iv*	*v*	*vi*	*vii*	*viii*	*ix*	*x*	*xi*	*xii*	*xiii*	*xiv*	*xv*
S.No.	*Date & Location*	*Name of the Settlement*	*nāḍu*	*palli*	*vāḍa*	*ūr*	*grāma*	*Context (Rural)*	*pura*	*paṭṭaṇa*	*Capital*	*Temple Settlement*	*Context (Urban)*	*Reference*
	Dharwar Dt.													
81.	Ins. no. 152	Posavūru			♠			❑						*SII.* XI,
	AD 1103.													
	Gadag Tq.													
	Dharwar Dt.	Muluguṇḍa-12						❑ GV				Δ		189-191
82.	Ins. no. 189	Nidguṇḍi						❑ +				Δ		*SII.* XI,
	AD 1106.													
	Ron Tq.													
	Dharwar Dt.													246
83.	Ins. no. 8	HiriyaGabbūr				●						Δ	⊠	*HAS,* 18,
	AD 1109.													
	DevadurgTq.													
	Raichur Dt.													51-52
84.	Ins. no. 158	Eleya										Δ	⊠	*SII.* XI,
	AD 1109. No. 158	Śiripura							♦					
	GadagTq.													
	Dharwar Dt.													210-203
85.	Ins. at Ittagi	Ittage						❑ +				Δ		*EI.* XIII,
	AD 1112.													
	Yalburgi Tq.	Bennekallu						❑						37-58
	Raichur Dt.	Kukkanūru				●								
		Kaniyahallu						❑						
		Mudiyanūr				●		❑						
		Nārāyamgal-12						❑ GV						
		Kukkanūr-30						❑ GV						
		Belvolanāḍ	♣											
86.	Ins. no. 163	Abbeyageri						❑						*SII.* XI,
	AD 1113.													
	RonTq.	Puvvaravalli		*				❑ +						209-211
	Dharwar Dt.	Nārāyaṁgal-12						❑ GV						
		Kisukāḍnāḍu	♣											

Key to the Symbols : ♣ : nāḍu; Δ : Temple Settlement; * : palli; ♦ : pura; ♠ : vāḍa; ❖ : paṭṭana; ● : ūr; ⊠ : Context (Urban); # : grāma; + : agrahāra; ❑ : Context (Urban); GV : Group of Villages; ⌘ : Capital

Chart – III : SPATIAL CONTEXT

Sub Region B

i	ii	iii	iv	v	vi	vii	viii	ix	x	xi	xii	xiii	xiv	xv
S.No.	Date & Location	Name of the Settlement	nāḍu	palli	vāḍa	ūr	grāma	Context (Rural)	pura	paṭṭana	Capital	Temple Settlement	Context (Urban)	Reference
		Belvola-300	♣											
87.	Ins of Suci K	Sundi							◆		⌘	Δ		EI, XV,
	AD 1114.	Achatapura						❑	◆					
	Ron Tq.	Kisukād-70	♣											105-108
	Dharwar Dt.													
88.	Ins. no. 167.	ElayaSirivūra				●		❑				Δ		SII, XI,
	AD 1118.													
	Gadag Tq.													214
	Dharwar Dt.													
89.	Transcript	Nāvile						❑				Δ		A.R.
	AD 1120.													no. B 711
	Lingsugur Tq.	Muttage						❑						of 58-59
	Raichur Dt.	Karadikal-300	♣											
90.	Ins. no. 170	Kiru Nārāyaṁgal						❑				Δ		SII, XI,
	AD 1121.													
	Ron Tq.	Hiriya Nārāyaṁga						❑				Δ		217-218
	Dharwar Dt.	Abbegere						❑						
		Nārāyaṁgal			♠			❑						
		Nārāyaṁgal-12						❑ GV						
		Kisukād-70	♣											
		Belvola-300	♣											
91.	Ins. no. 9	Liṅga					#	❑				Δ		HAS, 18,
	AD 1124													
	Lingsugur Tq.													52-54
	Raichur Dt.	Karādikal-400	♣											
92	Ins. no. 198	Mulugunda								❖		Δ	⊠	SII, XI,
	AD 1124													
	Gadag Tq.													253-254
	Dharwar Dt.													
93.	Ins. no. 13	Kisuvāvi						❑ +						SII, XV,
	AD 1130													

Key to the Symbols : ♣ : nāḍu; * : palli; ♠ : vāḍa; ● : ūr; # : grāma; ❑ : Context (Urban); ⌘ : Capital
Δ : Temple Settlement; ◆ : pura; ❖ : paṭṭana; ⊠ : Context (Urban); + : agrahāra; GV : Group of Villages

Chart – *III* : SPATIAL CONTEXT

Sub Region B

i	*ii*	*iii*	*iv*	*v*	*vi*	*vii*	*viii*	*ix*	*x*	*xi*	*xii*	*xiii*	*xiv*	*xv*
S.No.	*Date & Location*	*Name of the Settlement*	*nāḍu*	*palli*	*vāḍa*	*ūr*	*grāma*	*Context (Rural)*	*pura*	*paṭṭaṇa*	*Capital*	*Temple Settlement*	*Context (Urban)*	*Reference*
	Ron Tq.													11-12
	Dharwar Dt.	Honneyanūr						❑ +						
94.	Transcript	Kallūru				●		❑ +				Δ		*A.R.*
	AD 1134.													no. B 512
	Manvi Tq.	Mudigundūru-300	♣											of 1961-62
	Raichur Dt.													
95.	Ins. no. 11	Modeyanūr				●		❑ +						*IIAS*, 18,
	AD 1136													
	Kopbal Tq.	Kelavādi-300	♣											57-60
	Raichur Dt.	Ededore-2000	♣											
96.	Ins. no. 50.	Sripura						❑	♦					*SII*, XI,
	AD 1138.													
	Gadag Tq.	Mūlavalagere						❑						36-38
	Dharwar Dt.	Muddigere						❑						
		Hosavūr				●		❑				Δ		
97.	Ins. no. 3.	Kukkanūr				●		❑				Δ		*APGAS*, 9,
	AD 1143.													
	YalburgiTq.													30
	Raichur Dt.													
98.	Ins. no. 28	Kiru Nārāyaṁgal						❑				Δ		*SII*, XV,
	AD 1144.													
	RonTq.	Nārāyamgallu						❑						30-31
	Dharwar Dt.	Kisukādunāḍu	♣											
		Bāgadagenāḍu	♣											
		Kelavādināḍu	♣											
99.	Ins. no. 27	Rājavūr				●		❑				Δ		*SII*, XV,
	AD 1144.													
	Ron Tq.													29-30
	Dharwar Dt.	Kuṁtige												
100.	Ins. no. 36.	Hosavra				●		❑				Δ		*SII*, XV,
	AD 1148.													

Key to the Symbols : ♣ : nāḍu; * : palli; ♠ : vāḍa; ● : ūr; # : grāma; ❑ : Context (Urban); ⌘ : Capital
Δ : Temple Settlement; ♦ : pura; ❖ : paṭṭana; ⊠ : Context (Urban); + : agrahāra GV : Group of Villages

Chart – III : SPATIAL CONTEXT

Sub Region B

i	ii	iii	iv	v	vi	vii	viii	ix	x	xi	xii	xiii	xiv	xv
S.No.	Date & Location	Name of the Settlement	nāḍu	palli	vāḍa	ūr	grāma	Context (Rural)	pura	paṭṭaṇa	Capital	Temple Settlement	Context (Urban)	Reference
	Gadag Tq. Dharwar Dt.	Mulugunda-12						❑ GV						43-46
101.	Ins. no. 10. AD 1149. Yalburgi Tq. Raichur Dt.	Kukkanūr Belvola-300	 ♣			●		❑ +				Δ		*IIAS*, 18, 54-57
102.	Ins. no. 43. AD 1153. Ron Tq. Dharwar Dt.	Rājūr sthala				●		❑				Δ	☒	*SII*, XV, 56-57
103.	Transcript AD 1155. Deodurg Tq. Raichur Dt.	Piriyagabbūr				●						Δ	☒	*A.R.* no. B 668 of 58-59
104.	Ins. no. 53 AD 1155. Ron Tq. Dharwar Dt.	Beluvaniga Nāvilage Belvola	 ♣					❑ + ❑ +						*SII*, XV, 69-71
105.	Ins. no. 106 AD 1166. Gadag Tq. Dharwar Dt.	Huligola Bāgadage-70 Kisukād-70 Belvola-300	 ♣ ♣ ♣						♦	❖			☒ +	*SII*, XV, 136-137
106.	Ins. no. 238. AD 1169. Ron Tq Dharwar Dt.	Hiriyamaniyūr Nārāyamgal-12 Kisukād-70 Bāgadage-70 Eḷavādi-300	 ♣ ♣ ♣			●		❑ ❑ GV				Δ		*SII*, XV, 293-296
107.	Ins. no. 114. AD 1170.	Kundūr				●		❑				Δ		*SII*, XV,

Key to the Symbols : ♣ : nāḍu; * : palli; ♠ : vāḍa; ● : ūr; # : grāma; ❑ : Context (Urban); ⌘ : Capital
Δ : Temple Settlement; ♦ : pura; ❖ : paṭṭana; ☒ : Context (Urban); + : agrahāra; GV : Group of Villages

Chart – III : SPATIAL CONTEXT

Sub Region B

i	ii	iii	iv	v	vi	vii	viii	ix	x	xi	xii	xiii	xiv	xv
S.No.	*Date & Location*	*Name of the Settlement*	*nāḍu*	*palli*	*vāḍa*	*ūr*	*grāma*	*Context (Rural)*	*pura*	*paṭṭaṇa*	*Capital*	*Temple Settlement*	*Context (Urban)*	*Reference*
	Ron Tq.													145
	Dharwar Dt.													
108.	Ins. no. 12	Hadalagere						❑						*APGAS*, 3,
	AD 1170.											Δ		
	Yalburgi Tq.	Kukkanūr				●		❑ +						73-77
	Raichur Dt.	Mangalūrahalli		*		●		❑						
		Pottūrnalli		*		●		❑						
		Modenūr				●					⌘			
		Kukkanūr-36						❑ GV						
109.	Ins. no. 117	Kallavanahaili		*				❑						*SII*, XV,
	AD 1171.													
	Ron Tq.											Δ		147-148
	Dharwar Dt.	Nidguṇḍi						❑ +						
110.	Ins. no. 121.	Kaniyahalli		*				❑						*SII*, XV,
	AD 1173.													
	Gadag Tq.													151-152
	Dharwar Dt.	Soratūr				●						Δ		
111.	Ins. no. 241	Nidguṇḍi						❑ +				Δ		*SII*, XV,
	AD 1174.	Jakkiligeri						❑						
														297-301
	Dharwar Dt.	Kudaganūr				●								
		Beluvinaka									⌘			
		Kisukād-70	♣											
112.	Ins. no. 12	Hiryabalagaranūr				●		❑ +						*IIAS*, 18,
	AD 1175.													
	Sindhnur Tq.													61-63
	Raichur Dt.													
113.	Ins. at Ittagi	Ittagi						❑ +				Δ		*EI*, XIII,
	AD 1178.													
	YelburgiTq.													59-61
	Raichur Dt.													

Key to the Symbols : ♣ : nāḍu; * : palli; ♠ : vāḍa; ● : ūr; # : grāma; ❑ : Context (Urban); ⌘ : Capital
Δ : Temple Settlement; ◆ : pura; ❖ : paṭṭana; ⊠ : Context (Urban); + : agrahāra GV : Group of Villages

Chart – III : SPATIAL CONTEXT

Sub Region B

i	ii	iii	iv	v	vi	vii	viii	ix	x	xi	xii	xiii	xiv	xv
S.No.	*Date & Location*	*Name of the Settlement*	*nāḍu*	*palli*	*vāḍa*	*ūr*	*grāma*	*Context (Rural)*	*pura*	*paṭṭaṇa*	*Capital*	*Temple Settlement*	*Context (Urban)*	*Reference*
114.	Ins. no. 131	Mulgunda								❖		Δ	⊠	*SII*, XV,
	AD 1173.													
	Gadag Tq.													167-168
	Dharwar Dt.	Muddumāmbalapura							◆				⊠	
115.	Ins. no. 13.	Selagara			♠			☐						*IIAS*, 18,
	AD 1173													
	Yelburgi Tq.	Benatūra				●		☐						63-74
	Raichur Dt.	Kukkanūr				●		☐ +				Δ		
		Kukkanūr-30						☐ GV						
		Beluvolanāḍu	♣											
116.	Ins. no. 73.	Pombolal						☐ +				Δ		*SII*, XV,
	AD 1189.													
	Gadag Tq.													99-104
	Dharwar Dt.													
117.	Ins. no. 16	Limga						☐						*IIAS*, 18,
	AD 1191.													
	Lingsugur Tq.	Karāḍikal								❖		Δ		83-89
	Raichur Dt.	Mudugal								❖	⌘			
		Belvola-300	♣											
		Karāḍikainād	♣											
		Ededorenād	♣											
118.	Gadag Ins. of Yadava	Hiriya.					#	☐						*EI*, III,
	Bhillama AD 1191.	Handigola												
	Gadag Tq.	Erātaka					#	☐				Δ		217-220
	Dharwar Dt.	Belvola-300	♣											
119.	Ins. no. 15	Hiriya				●		☐				Δ		*IIAS*, 18,
	AD 1192.													
	Sindhanur Tq.	Balaganūr												80-82
	Raichur Dt.	Madanasirūr				●					⌘			
120.	Gadag Ins. of	Eratuka					#	☐				Δ		*EI*, VI,
	Viraballala II AD 1192	Hombalalu					#	☐						

Key to the Symbols : ♣ : nāḍu; Δ : Temple Settlement; * : palli; ◆ : pura; ♠ : vāḍa; ❖ : paṭṭana; ● : ūr; ⊠ : Context (Urban); # : grāma; + : agrahāra; ☐ : Context (Urban); GV : Group of Villages; ⌘ : Capital

Chart – III : SPATIAL CONTEXT

Sub Region B

i	ii	iii	iv	v	vi	vii	viii	ix	x	xi	xii	xiii	xiv	xv
S.No.	Date & Location	Name of the Settlement	nāḍu	palli	vāḍa	ūr	grāma	Context (Rural)	pura	paṭṭaṇa	Capital	Temple Settlement	Context (Urban)	Reference
	GadagTq. Dharwar Dt.	Belvola-300												89-97
121.	Ins. no. 210. AD 1196. Mundargipetha Tq. Dharwar Dt.	Dehutageri						❑				Δ		SII, XV, 252-253
		Kūralahalli		*										
122.	Hosur Ins. of Viraballala AD 1207 GadagTq. Dharwar Dt.	Hosavūr				●		❑						EI, XXXII, 171-174
		Tuppadahalli		*				❑						
		Mulugunḍa-12						❑ GV						
123.	Ins. no. 220 AD 1207. Gadag Tq. Dharwar Dt.	Mulugunda								❖	⌘	Δ	⊠	SII, XV, 267-269
		Belvolanādu	♣											
124.	Ins. no. 17. AD 1215. Lingsugur Tq. Raichur Dt.	Mudugal								❖	⌘	Δ	⊠	HAS, 18, 89-93
		Karādikalnāḍu	♣											
		Ededorenāḍu	♣											
125.	Transcript AD 1058. Nandikotkur Tq. Kurnool Dt.	Śivapura						❑	Pu*					458/68 of Archaeology and Museums Office, Hyd.
		Jyāmatūru			♠	●		❑	◆					
		Mosagi						❑				Δ		
126.	Ins. no. 11 AD 1067. Alampur Tq. Mahbubnagar Dt.	Hatampura						❑				Δ		APGAS, 3 105-106
		Aija-300	♣											
127.	Panchalingala Ins. AD 1068. Kurnool Tq.	Gudigeri						❑						EI, XXXVI 139-143
		Kālpalli		*				❑						
		Pañchalingagrāma					#	❑				Δ		

Key to the Symbols : ♣ : nāḍu; Δ : Temple Settlement; * : palli; ◆ : pura; ♠ : vāḍa; ❖ : paṭṭana; ● : ūr; ⊠ : Context (Urban); # : grāma; + : agrahāra; ❑ : Context (Urban); GV : Group of Villages; ⌘ : Capital

Chart – III : SPATIAL CONTEXT

Sub Region C

i	ii	iii	iv	v	vi	vii	viii	ix	x	xi	xii	xiii	xiv	xv
S.No.	Date & Location	Name of the Settlement	nāḍu	palli	vāḍa	ūr	grāma	Context (Rural)	pura	paṭṭaṇa	Capital	Temple Settlement	Context (Urban)	Reference
	Kurnool Dt	Bekkemoksha						❑						
		Kandūrnad	♣											
		Nalavādināḍ	♣											
128.	Transcript AD 1069. Nandikotkur Tq. Kurnool Dt	Pacikareyapa						❑						No. 337 of Archacology and Museums Office Hyd.
		Mosagi						❑				Δ		
		Aije-300	♣					❑						
129.	Ins. no 22 AD 1073. Alampur Tq. Mahbubnagar Dt.	Kanne-300	♣											APGAS, 3, 117-118
		Aije-300	♣											
		Naravadi-500	♣											
		Paeckal-800	♣											
130.	Bichapalli Ins. AD 1074. Alampur Tq. Mahabubnagar Dt.	Pariyalatirtha						❑				Δ		EI, XXXVI 69-74
		Eramatirtha						❑						
		Aije-300	♣											
131.	Transcript AD 1075. Nandikotkur Tq. Kurnool Dt.	Edeyamatha						❑				Δ		A.R. no. B 317 of 1937-38
132.	Ins. no. 16 AD 1078. Alampur Tq. Mahabubnagar Dt.	Langanavāvi						❑						APGAS, 110-111
		Harampura						❑	◆			Δ		
133.	Ins. no. 15 AD 1078. Alampur Tq. Mahabubnagar Dt.	Baliundavalli		*				❑						APGAS, 108-110
		Biruvalli		*				❑						
		Gudiyūru				●		❑						
		Kadambūru				●								
		Harampura							◆			Δ		

Key to the Symbols ♣ : nāḍu; Δ : Temple Settlement; * : palli; ◆ : pura; ♠ : vāḍa; ❖ : paṭṭana; ● : ūr; ⊠ : Context (Urban); # : grāma; + : agrahāra; ❑ : Context (Urban); GV : Group of Villages; ⌘ : Capital

Chart – III : SPATIAL CONTEXT

Sub Region C

i	ii	iii	iv	v	vi	vii	viii	ix	x	xi	xii	xiii	xiv	xv
S.No.	Date & Location	Name of the Settlement	nāḍu	palli	vāḍa	ūr	grāma	Context (Rural)	pura	paṭṭaṇa	Capital	Temple Settlement	Context (Urban)	Reference
		Aija-300	♣											
134.	Ins. no. 33 AD 1095. Alampur Tq. Mahabubnagar Dt.	Pulinūru					#	❑						Telangana Inscriptions II, 63-64
		Hatampura							♦			Δ		
135.	Ins. no. 37 AD 1007. Alampur Tq. Mahabubnagar Dt.	Kandanavolal			♠			❑						APGAS, 3, 125-126
		Hatampura							♦			Δ		
		Naravādi-500	♣											
136.	Transcript AD 1127. Kurnool Tq. Kurnool Dt.	Polukallu						❑						A.R. no. 107 of 59-60
137.	Ins. no. 32 AD 1182. Alampur Tq. Mahabubnagar Dt.	Tumbula sthala											⊠	APGAS, 3, 123
		Gobbūr sthala											⊠	
		Maddūr sthala											⊠	
		Alampūr sthala											⊠	
		Ajiyasthala											⊠	
		Nāyakallu sthala											⊠	

Key to the Symbols : ♣ : nāḍu; Δ : Temple Settlement; * : palli; ♦ : pura; ♠ : vāḍa; ❖ : paṭṭana; ● : ūr; ⊠ : Context (Urban); # : grāma; + : agrahāra; ❑ : Context (Urban); GV : Group of Villages; ⌘ : Capital

6

IDEOLOGICAL CONTEXT

The emergence of various types of settlements (both *agrahāra* and non-*agrahāra*) into major temple settlements during the period under study is a phenomenon which encompasses in its fold an analysis of not just the physical descriptions of the temple institution and its role in the political and economic domains, but more importantly, the ideology that was conserved in this institution. This has far reaching implications in terms of our comprehension of a crucial process involved in the formation of local and supra local regions. Such a study involves various issues relating to both the legitimizing and the acculturating role of the temple institution[1] at various levels of state and social structure. Interrelated aspects of an analysis of this nature would then include a comprehensive understanding of the complex dimensions of the ideological manifestations operating at such diverse levels as the religious, social, political and economic phenomena, expressed in the form of Purāṇic complications juxtaposed with Vedic rituals and *varṇa* ideology on the one hand, and on the other, through the descriptions of genealogies embodied in the *praśastis* of dominant social groups coupled with the imprecatory verses at the end of grants which provide another crucial dimension of the ideological process during this period.[2] We wish to address ourselves to these complexities of the ideological processes with particular emphasis on the role played by the temple institution which, as has been seen in our earlier chapters, had emerged into the most powerful legitimizing instrument in the hands of almost all types of rich and well placed social groups and therefore, emerges as central to the formation of the ideological structure at various levels during the period under study.

The first foundation of Hindu temple architecture in the Deccan is supposed to have been laid by the Ikṣvāku rulers who succeeded the Śātavahanas in south eastern India in about the first quarter of the third century A.D.[3] Such a phenomenon seems to have gained considerable momentum in South India as a whole, and the Deccan region in particular, around the 5th-6th centuries A.D. This was when temple constructions began to be made in brick and some were also excavated in rock.[4] In the western Deccan region, building of religious monuments can be traced back to the proto-historic period itself wherein, structures of the megalith times began to be erected to serve ritualistic or religious requirements of simple pastoral and agricultural groups. In some cases these were made out of the sand stone cut into enormous blocks from the outcrops of the Kaladgi hill chains.[5] Later, the western peninsula under the Śātavāhana dynasty and the Buddhist influence, began to be strewn with thousands of rock-cut *caityas, vihāras* and *stūpas* and other religious monuments.[6] It has been suggested in this context that the temples of the Chālukyan dynasty datable to the 5th-6th centuries A.D. became heirs to the combined achievements of both the megalith and the Śātavāhana structures in the western Deccan, as the sites of the brahmanical temples often coincided with the sites of the religious monuments of the earlier times.[7] It is said that particularly in the lower Deccan, which coincides with the present day Karnataka area, the Chālukyan temples became direct heirs to the distant and dormant cultures of the megalithic and early historic times.[8]

The numerical growth of the temples during the early Chālukyan period went hand in hand with the structural evolution of the temples. This can be seen in the Aihole group of temples of the 5th-6th centuries A.D. which began to have important additions such as the spire (*śikhara*), the circumambulatory passage *(pradakṣiṇa)* and the pillared assembly hall *(maṇḍapa)*. These attributes of the temple structure, while distinguishing it from the secular buildings, catered to a variety of forms of worship.[9] The temple building activity under the aegis of the early Chālukyas was concentrated chiefly only in a few regions of the Deccan such as Aihole, Badami, Pattadakal and Ālampur. It however, began to gain greater momentum between the 8th and the 9th centuries A.D. under the rule of the Rāshṭrakūṭas who began to build temples in new regions of the Deccan. Inscriptions from the Nasik District of Maharashtra, the Rewa district of Madhya Pradesh, Mysore, Kolar, Dharwar and Tumkur districts of Karnataka etc., begin to give prolific information about the emerging temples of this period.[10] The most famous monuments of the Rāshṭrakūṭa period are those around Ajanta and Ellora.[11] During this period, the emergence of *maṭhas* or, the educational foundations attached to the temple institution, marked a significant turn in the growth of the complex nature of the temple structure and its appendages from an earlier simple form. This phase, namely, from the 8th century A.D. onwards marked an important turn in the growth of the temple as an economic institution as the granting of villages to these institutions was initiated which transformed them into rich landlords around this time.[12] Such a process reached its climax during the 10th century A.D., when a large number of Vaiṣṇavite and Śaivite temples begin to be constructed and endowed with land grants and benefices almost all over the Deccan.[13] In fact, during this period we find that the temple building activity witnessed a significant spurt in various other regions of India, too. It is important to emphasize as suggested by Devangana Desai that numerous local centres of art grew up in the period between A.D. 650- A.D. 900, in terms of the varied local ethnic-cultural background in which local themes and visions predominated. The author has here cited the examples of the temples at Bhubaneswar in Orissa, Osia in Rajasthan, Aihole and Pattadakal in Karnataka which indicate new experiments in the ground plans, *śikhara* designs and so on.[14] Technical skills in the construction of temple building activity began to be excelled in the context of Tamilakam under the Chola rule during the 12th-13th centuries A.D.[15] According to R. Champakalakshmi, during this period, a significant variation in temple architecture was introduced with emphasis on the additional structures leading to a horizontal magnification of the temple, *i.e.,* structural expansion through a complex of shrines, pillared halls within the enclosures, each marking a further stage in the participation of diverse groups in temple building and gift giving activities.[16] Nearer home, in the eastern Deccan, namely Coastal Andhra, we find that the temple architecture took a definite shape under the aegis of the eastern Chālukyas of Vengi.[17]

In the context of our study, we find that the temple building activity was largely concentrated in sub-region B (Map VI) between the 11th-13th centuries A.D. Among some of the important extant temples of this sub-region we have the Navalinga group of temples and the Kalleśwara temple of Kuknūr in the Raichur district.[18] These temples are supposed to represent the fine architecture of the Chālukyas of kalyaṇi. Further, the temple of Mahadeva at Iṭṭagi of the same district is considered to be one of the best specimens of the later Chālukyan architecture.[19] It has an open hall added in front of its covered *maṇḍapa.* Its delicate filigree and scroll work, and varieties of lathe-turned pillars of deepest moulding, have been considered as the marvels of craftsmanship.[20] It is interesting to note that Lakkundi of the Dharwar district is supposed to contain ruins of as many as 50 temples of the later Chālukyan rule.[21] Among these, the temple of Kāśi-Viśveśvara is supposed to represent a high water mark in decorative architecture of the later Chālukyan times.[22] While we witness the emergence of new temples in sub-region B, sub-regions A and C have origins of temple building activity much earlier, *i.e.,* during the time of Chālukyas of Bedami itself. Temples of Meguti, Ladkhan and Koutagudi at Aihole are traced back to the 6th century A.D. and among these the temple of Meguti is supposed to be the only extant temple in India which preserves the changes through which a Buddhist cave-temple passed on to become a Jaina and then a Brāhmaṇical structural temple.[23] In the Badami taluk of Bijapur district, we have the remains of four richly ornamented and well preserved caves and temples of Malegatti Śivālaya, Teggina Irappa, Yogeśvara and so on which date back to the early Chālukyan period.[24] The temples of Pattadakal, in sub-region A are considered the best to exemplify the

Dravidian or Southern style of architecture. Among these, the temple of Virūpākshesvara is renowned for its architectural magnificance of the early Chālukyan period and even today, it is used for daily worship.[25] The temples of sub-region C, particularly those belonging to the Ālampur region, were built under the direct patronage of the Chālukyas of Bādami.[26] The principal temple (still extant) is a cluster of shrines dedicated to the Nava Brahmas. It is situated in the fortress and bears a striking resemblance to the Pāpanātha temple at Pattadakal. The *śikharas* of these shrines are supposed to have a curvilinear form outwardly decorated with a network of miniature architectural devices such as *amalakas* that give a beautiful effect.[27] Apart from the Brahmeśvara temple described above, this place is also noted for the temples at Pāpanātha and Ganika Siddeśvara.[28] Other prominent places in sub-region C, associated with the early Chālukyan experiments in temple construction, are the sites of Satyavolu and Pāpanāśanam which had apsidal structures which closely linked them to the form of the early Buddhist structures.[29] The above survey of the emergence and growth of temple settlements for various sub-regions of our study, largely indicates the fact that sub-region B, with its newly emergent temple structures during the period of our study (1000 A.D.-1200 A.D.) provides us with immense potential to tackle the problem of the formation of a local state structure in its early stage *vis-a-vis* the ideological parameters of the growing temple. This could then be compared and contrasted with changes of a similar kind in sub-regions A and C which seem to represent a more mature phase of temple building activity in its nature and context during this period.

Temple building activity and the consequent growth in the temple ideology pre-supposes a surplus producing economy and a certain level of social hierarchy which is crucial for patronizing and sustaining the institution as a whole. We have already observed earlier that several social groups belonging to various levels of social hierarchy had extended patronage to the temple building activity of the period under study.[30] Gifts made by these people ranged from grants of small pieces of land and house sites to large measurements of land, fields, gardens and villages and also the grant of various types of commodities such as oil, grains, areca nuts and so on. These were made, some times, along with cash and various types of taxes.[31] As a result of large scale patronage extended to the temple, they ultimately emerged as over-arching institutions with wide range of economic and political powers at their bestowal. Economic benefits (Charts II, A, B, C) bestowed on the temples enabled them to emerge as major land lords owning several villages and large amounts of land. This necessitated the temple to employ labour for production on its lands on the one hand, and on the other, it was able to employ various professional groups involved in daily ritual and artisanal services of the temple. Further, the temple began to play the role of the state too, as it was given grants of various taxes (Chart II, A, B, C, 1-165) and was thus, naturally empowered to collect revenue. The role of the temple as a financier and banker have also been highlighted in the context of its economic activities during the period under study with particular reference to the Karnataka region.[32] Thus, the transformation of the temple into a mechanism of the redistribution of resources on the one hand, and on the other, into an overiord having the services of several social groups at its disposal, marked a significant change in the nature of the temple institution perse, and therefore it cannot be looked at merely as a religious institution catering to the devotional urges of the people in an autonomous manner. While the very purpose of the existence of the temple was for worship and performance of rituals, its multi faceted role transformed it into an all powerful socio-economic legitimizer for all categories of society during this period. In turn, the ideological attributes of the temple institution of the period, had far wider implications in shaping the socio-political relationships in the region taken up for the present study. It has been aptly stated in this context that "what the temple achieved through being a landed magnate and an efficient organizer of production and distribution was further reinforced by an ideology propagated by the *bhakti* movement."[33]

The proliferation of temple structures outlined above had a significant role to play in the spread of the *bhakti* ideology represented chiefly through the forms of Śaivism and Vaiṣṇavism embedded in what has commonly come to be called Purāṇic Hinduism. The temple provided an institutional base to the spread of these sectarian cults on an organized and an unprecedented scale during the period under study. This particular form of Vaiṣṇavism can be traced back to the period between the 7th-9th centuries A.D. when literary expression to it was found in the composition of the *Nalayira Prabandhaṁ* in the Tamilnadu region.[34] Due to its close association with the Vedānta philosophy on the one hand, and on the other, at a later stage due to the influence of the Vedic-educated Śrirangaṁ priesthood on the course of the movement, it eventually remained elitist in character[35] and could not gain a firm ground during the period under study in various parts of the Deccan as well as the extreme South.[36] On the other hand, the Śaiva *Siddhānta* philosophy based on the *āgamas* which had their origins in the 9th century A.D., openly expressed the dislike for the Vedānta.[37] During the early medieval period it had evoked tremendous response from a cross section of the social strata, prominent among them in its initial stages, were the ruling chiefs and the landed elite in the Deccan as well as the South. In fact, the first definite formulation of the philosophy of the Tamil Śaiva *Siddhānta* has been attributed to the work of a *vellala* (land lord) who lived in the early 13th century in the Tamilakam region.[38]

In the context of the present study the key to such an expansion in the Śaivite ideology can be obtained in the first place through a survey of the names of various deities mentioned as located in the temple establishments for various sub-regions during the period under consideration. For sub-region A during the 11th century A.D., out of 12 inscriptions charted by us (IVA, v, 1-12) we find that 3 inscriptions have reference to Jaina affiliations (IVA, v, 2, 9, 11) and the rest are described through various names such as God Kalideva (IVA, v, 1), Śivālaya (IVA, v, 3) God Bāleśvara (IVA, v, 4), God Mallikārjuna (IVA, v, 5), God Siddeśvara (IVA, v, 6) and so on and these can be chiefly identified with God Śiva. For the same sub-region during the 12th century A.D., out of 13 inscriptions charted by us (IVA, v, 13-25) we have 1 instance of the mention of God Viṣṇu (IVA, v, 13) and in the rest we find the mention of the name of God Śiva described in various forms. It is significant to note that there are none of the Jaina affiliated structures mentioned during this period, *i.e.,* during the 12th century. Further, the increase in the variety of names for God Śiva in the form of God Mahāliṅga (IVA, v, 19), God Gaṅgeśvara (IVA, v, 20), Trikūṭa (IVA, v, 21), Vīra Bayseśvara (IVA, v, 22), Nanneśvara (IVA, v, 23), Siriyameśvara (IVA, v, 24), Telligeśvara (IVA, v, 25) are indicative of the proliferation of Śaivite worship in its diverse forms. For the sub-region B we have been able to chart out on the whole, about 104 inscriptions (IVB, v, 26-135) out of which nearly 40 (IVB, v, 26-67) belong to the 11th century A.D. It is the of some significance to note here that we have a great variety in the names of the deities mentioned here right from an early stage. Firstly, we have 2 records that mention the Jaina sect (IVB, v, 44, 45) and 2 that mention the Buddhist (IVB, v, 62, 66). There are further 2 of God Viṣṇu (IVB, v, 59, 63) and 1 each of Saraswati (IVB, v, 59) and Mahālakshmi (IVB, v, 61), 4 belong to the Traipuruṣa Gods (IVB, v, 26, 32, 33, 36), and the remaining 29 belong to various forms of God Śiva, mentioned through a variety of names such as Mūlasthānadeva (IVB, v, 27, 29), Gavareśvara (IV, v, 28), Dharmeśvara (IVB, v, 31), Bhogeśvara (IVB, v, 37), Nāgeśvara (IVB, v, 41), Nāgareśvara (IVB, v, 42, 46), Achaleśvara (IVB, v, 43, 57), Pañchalingadeva (IVB, v, 48, 55), Maruleśvara (IVB, v, 49), Svayambhu Śiva (IVB, v, 52) and so on. For the same sub-region during the 12th century A.D. out of about 68 inscriptions charted out a (IVB, v, 68-135), 3 mention their affiliation to the Jaina faith (IVB, v, 79, 108, 125), 1 to Goddess Saraswati (IVB, v, 78) 2 to God Viṣṇu (IVB, v, 75, 81), 2 to the Traipuruṣas (IVB, v, 89, 106) and 1 to the Kālika Goddess (IVB, v, 116). The remaining references mention various forms of God Śiva. Here we have several new names emerging as appellations for Śiva such as Kammaṭeśvara (IVB, v, 80) Totigeśvara (IVB, v, 92), Kavataleśvara (IVB, v, 98), Morakeśvara (IVB, v, 100), Goyideśvara (IVB, v, 107), Vidireśvara (IVB, v, 115), Chāmeśvara (IVB, v, 118), Bonteśvara (IVB, v, 128), Kalakaleśvara (IVB, v, 131) and Billeśvara (IVB, v, 132). For the sub-region C, during the 11th century A.D. out of 13 records (IVC, v, 136-148) charted out by us, 2 mention the Jaina sect (IVC, v, 147, 148) and the remaining mention the forms of God Śiva, of which a particular form in the name of God

Brahmeśvara, figures prominently (IVC, v, 137, 142, 144, 146) along with the such other names as God Kukkuṭeśvara (IVC, v, 138), Pañchaliṅgadeva (IVC, v, 140), Mallikārjunadeva (IVC, v, 141), Bikkeśvara (IVC, v, 145) and so on. For the 12th century A.D. in this sub-region, we have 1 instance of God Viṣṇu (IVC, v, 150) and the rest mention God Śiva in the form of Brahmeśvara (IVC, v, 149, 151, 152), Someśvara (IVC, v, 153) and Gavareśvara (IVC, v, 154).

The list of names of various deities furnished above for the different periods and sub-regions highlight the predominant mention of God Śiva in his several forms and this clearly establishes the fact that the cult of Śiva was on the ascendency during this period in the area of our study. Importantly, the large variety of names used to address God Śiva, particularly in the context of sub-region B, along with a protracted increase in them during the 12th century A.D., has a significant bearing on our comprehension of the territorial spread[39] in the temple establishment on the one hand, and on the other, the expanding social base in the patronage network owing to the changing economic scenario.[40] It is pertinent to note and reiterate here what we have already observed in an earlier chapter, that for a major part of the 11th century A.D. in all the three sub-regions of study, we had witnessed a predominance in the grant of lands and villages made by various levels of state power who also formed an integral part of the land owning group. On the other hand, we had also witnessed that by the turn of the 12th century A.D., there was a significant shift in the social base, wherein various professional groups such as the artisans and their guilds coupled with different types of mercantile guilds and individual merchants began to have a considerable share in patronizing the temple through giving a variety of donations to it. It is further interesting to note here that names of some of these temples began to represent the names of the donors/builders which some`times coincided either, with the rise in the status of the concerned chief seeking legitimation or, more importantly, these indicate a new trend in the socio-economic transformation that marked the 12th century A.D. In the former case we have reference to such temples as Nāgeśvara at Suṇdi built by one Nāgadeva who acquired the status of a *mahāsāmantādhipati* in the year A.D. 1060.[41] Similarly, we have the temple of Sindeśvara named in connection with the Sinda chieftains (A.D. 1069-1076).[42] The Akkeśvara temple at Suṇḍi was installed with a deity by Akkadevi,[43] the royal princess of the Chālukyas of Kalyāni. At even local levels we have a *karaṇa* called Chākimayya who built the temple of Chākeśvara.[44] In another inscription dated to A.D. 1075, we have reference to one Mārulimayya who belonged to the family of the *pergaḍe,* and who installed the God Māruleśvara.[45] In another example God Morakeśvara was named after the family name *(Morakakula)* of one Naki Gāvuṇḍa in A.D. 1104.[46] Similarly, the temple of God Brahmeśvara was named after the Sinda *mahāmaṇḍaleśvara* Bammarasa in A.D. 1104.[47]

The other type of patrons were essentially elites who were involved in mercantile and artisanal activity. Thus we find an increasing reference to such Gods as Kammaṭesvara (IVB, v, 72, 80) associated with the *kammaṭa* or the artisan groups, the God Nakareśvara (IVB, v, 46, 114) with the *nakara* or the mercantile groups, God Telligeśvara (IVA, v, 25; IVB, v, 135) with the *telligas* or the oil mongers, and so on. Their mention can be seen on the rise towards the end of the 11th century A.D. In fact, the association of the latter with the Jaina establishments can also be seen on a considerable scale. In this context such names given to the Jaina establishments as Nagara Jinālaya (IVB, v, 39, 79) and Kammaṭida Jinālaya (IVB, v, 125) bear testimony to the close association of the merchant and professional groups with these non-brahmanical establishments. Isolated references made to the Bauddha *vihāras* (IVB, v, 62, 66) and the mention of mercantile groups in association with them further bears testimony to the existence of a multiplicity of belief systems during the period under study particularly in the context of sub-region B, which was in a state of transformation on all fronts (social, political, economic). P.B. Desai has furnished a detailed sketch of the prevalence of certain flourishing Jaina centres under the rule of the Chālukyas of Kalyāni[48] with their particular concentration only in certain pockets in the present area of study such as the Hungund taluq of sub-region A and Kopbal taluq of sub-region B. Royal patronage to some of these institutions is attested to a certain extent through such names given to the *Jinālayas* as Guṇada Beḍāngi Jinālaya (IVA, v, 11), named after the royal princess Akkādevi who bore the title of *guṇada beḍangi* (woman of virtue). We further have reference to *arasara basadi* (king's basadi) (IVA, v, 9) which, as the name suggests, might have been built by some ruling chief. In the context of sub-region B we come across Jagadekamalla Jinālaya (IVB, v, 35) which was patronized by the main ruler Jagadekamalla Jayasiṁha II. Further, Girigotemalla Jinālaya (IVB, v, 44) although built by *seṭṭi* was named after *mahāsāmanta* who made certain grants to it.[49] It is pertinent to note here that the above examples cited particularly in association with the patronage of the ruling groups have their mention chiefly in the context of the 11th century A.D. Loss in the patronage to the Jaina institutions by the rulers during the latter part of the 11th, and for a major part of the 12 century A.D., can be clearly discerned in the fact that the couple of instances (IVB, v, 79, 125) referring to these religious establishments emerge purely in association with the mercantile and professional groups. Nilakanta Sastri has drawn our attention to the fact that the early medieval period for a major part of South India, including the Deccan region, was marked by a growth on the one hand, of an intense emotional *bhakti* to Śiva or Viṣṇu and on the other, of an out spoken hatred for Buddhists and Jains.[50] In this context we have an interesting reference in an inscription dated to A.D. 1184 from sub-region A, wherein a Śaiva priest claims to have established the cult of Śiva at several places after having destroyed the Jaina and the Buddhist creeds.[51] According to

Romila Thapar, the bitter rivalry between various sects during this period might have resulted more out of "competition for commercial power and patronage" than for purely religious purposes.[52] The ascendancy of Śaivism over other sects is, however, clearly established in the case of our study as can be gauged through the numerous instances of Śaivite temples cited by us above.

The dominance exercised by the Śaivite sectarianism expressed through its organized monastic establishments attached to the temple institutions has been considered the hall mark of the religious ideological base in the Deccan region.[53] Through its various phases of growth (beginning in the 8th-9th centuries A.D.), the monastic movement of Śaivism spread both territorially and doctrinally through the establishment of Śaiva temples in various parts of the Deccan and the South.[54] By the 10th-11th centuries A.D. one may witness the fulfilment and maturity of the process wherein, a symbiotic relationship can be seen to have been established between the temple institution and the monastic establishment attached to it. In this arrangement, the intellectual bias of the monastic movement represented by the Śaiva *Agamas* provided a much needed legitimation to the temple centred cults[55] which were interpreted by the temple priesthood. On the other hand, the temple institution provided an institutional base for their physical expansion on a considerable scale. During the period under study, the emergence of the Pāśupata and Lākula ascetics of the Kālāmukha doctrine, which emerges as a major sect of Śaivite monasticism,[56] had a significant bearing on our comprehension of the local forms of the operation of Śaivite ideology. The dominance exercised by this form of Śaivite philosophy has been attested for various areas of the Deccan region which includes parts of Central India, Maharashtra, Karnataka and Andhra Pradesh.[57] In the inscriptional sources of present study too we can clearly discern the dominant hold of the Kālāmukha doctrine in the temple institutions of various sub-regions which is well represented in the prolific mention of various priests belonging either, to the *Pāśupata* or the *Lākula* sects and who emerge as the major trustees to the temple grants (IVA, vii, 1-25, IVB, vii, 26-135, IIVC, vii, 136-154). On the basis of the role performed by the *Kālāmukhas* and the *Pāśupatas* in the early medieval Tamilnadu, it has been suggested that these represented more a group of non-conformists who were brought into the system, claimed *brāhmaṇa* status, and came to occupy a position of authority through the headship of the *maṭhas* in the 9th-10th centuries A.D. and later as priests and royal preceptors.[58] In fact, the practices and way of life led by the followers of the Kālāmukha sects have been considered to significantly "represent an expression of radical protest against the norms and values of Brāhmaṇical society."[59] Importantly, we also come across, during this period, prominent mention of various other manifestations of Śaivite sects which are essentially non-brahmanical in their form and content.

Among these, the *Kāpālikas* and the worshippers of female deities located in various *śakti piṭhas* have been identified on a significant scale as representing the *tāntric* practices of worship during the period under study. According to P.B. Desai the *tantric* practices seem to have spread in many parts of Maharashtra and Karnataka between the periods 10th-12th centuries A.D. as attested by the epigraphic evidences.[60] It is pertinent to note that Alampur an important temple site in sub-region C was regarded as a *śākta pīṭha* with Yogeśvari as the presiding deity right from the 10th century A.D. onwards.[61] Further the milieu of tāntricism was, according to R.R. Sharma, laid down in numerous magical rituals to achieve liberation *(mukti)* and enjoyment *(bhukti)* and in fact, to fulfil all kinds of the material desires *(kāmyani)* of the people.[62] As a result of the above witnessed growth in the spread of *bhakti* ideology, both in terms of its spatial and philosophical dimensions, during the early medieval period, the conventional school of historical scholarship has comprehended these developments in terms of representing a 'revival' in the Hindu/Brahmaṇical religious order as against the Buddhist/Jain dominance exercised in the pre 6th century A.D. period over a major part of the Deccan and South India.[63] On the other hand, the Marxist scholarship and advocates of the 'Indian Feudalism' school consider the *bhakti* movement of the early medieval period as a clear cut manifestation of the exploitative tendencies of feudal mode of production. According to them in such an ideological set up the new jargon of *bhakti* literature come to be considered as suggestive of the new feudal case relationships with a corresponding ideology.[64] In particular, their perception of the existence of various deities in the temple in terms of, each deity occupying the position of the lord for his devotee, was as much recognized in the *bhakti* movement as the plurality and co-existence of the lords, each lord singularly commanding loyalty from his immediate vassal.[65] This, according to them, clearly indicates the projection of the politico-economic relations of the feudal model in to the 'feudal bhakti' concept.

We have attempted to essentially argue in this regard that all the above discussed manifestations of religious developments represent a crucial level in the integrative role performed by the ideological forces during this period. In such a situation, the ascendency of Śaivism over the other Purāṇic sects such as Vaiṣṇavism, exhibit the capacity of the former to integrate its extreme forms like the *Kālāmukha, Pāśupata,* the *Kāpālika* and also the most outspoken non-conformists like the Siddhās.[66] Herein lies the success of Śaivism expressed through its easy adaptability to various local situations which was a necessary prerequisite to suit the early medieval context which saw a positive expansion in the settlement patterns and a corresponding increase in deities in the form of God Śiva. The mediating space in such an integration has, however, been the temple institution with its ability to legitimize the power and status of its patrons on the one hand,

and on other, through the appropriation of the local cults and the consequent absorption of the tribal and other marginal groups at various levels of the social structure. To comprehend the operation of the above phenomena, one has to make an analysis of the ideational apparatuses involved in first and foremost, the patronage network, the centre of which does not in any way exclude the creation of *agrahāras* as one of the mechanisms of integration. The role of the *agrahāra* was ostensibly created for the perpetuation of Vedic learning but this was, over a period of time, undoubtedly taken over by the temple institution. However, patronage extended to the *agrahāras* in the first place coupled with the occasional performance of Vedic rituals (IVA, vi, 1-25, IVB, 26-135, IVC, vi, 136-154) on the one hand, and on the other, claims made by various ruling families to the higher *varṇa* status[67] significantly attest to another dimension in ideological integration which was under operation during the period under study. The residents of the *agrahāra,* namely, the *mahājanas* themselves as major patrons of various temple institutions, both in the *agrahāra* and the non-*agrahāra*, was a significant initial step in the complex process that operated through a combination of various ideological dimentions of integration. However, as has been aptly pointed out "repeated references to branches of Vedic and affiliated learning and to impressive Purāṇic compilations point to the general dominance of brahmanism. Yet, movements against the norms and the order which brahmanism stood for, as well as tensions within brahmanism are evident."[68] This complexity of ideological issues get reflected in our study as well. We now turn to examine these issues in detail.

To comprehend the way both the dominent Vedic and Purāṇic ideology and the local belief systems interacted with each other in bringing about the complex cultural milieu, one needs to first of all look at the actual content of worship housed in the temple institution in the form of deities and the *mathas* attached to these temples. It, however, needs to be emphasized at this juncture that the key to our understanding of the sectarian religious activity of this period does not lie only in our comprehension of the names of various deities and their symbolism which form only one part (albeit central) of the temple institution. More importantly, a combined analysis of the entire temple establishment that houses deities on the one hand, and on the other, the *maṭhas* attached to these which housed the priests representing various sects form crucial aspects of analysis to understand the totality of the ideological space and its significant role in shaping the cultural milieu of the period under study. Such an analysis entails a description of not just the various symbols of worship, but also the nature and forms of patronage with respect to their corresponding social base and this needs to be taken into serious consideration so as to arrive at firm conclusions over the legitimizing role of religion during the early medieval period in the context of a regional study.

To comprehend various levels of ideological legitimation under operation, one needs to first of all analyse the specific forms of patronage directed towards various aspects of the temple establishment vis-a-vis the nature of the social group making the grant. For this purpose we have attempted a classification of patronage network in the temple institution into three categories. Under the first category we have grouped together the patronage extended towards the temple building, additions made to its structure such as pillars, *maṇṭapa* (halls), and repairs involved in it, installation of the deity and so on (IVA, viii, 1-25, IVB, viii, 26-135, IVC, viii, 136-154) as these represent support given to develop the physical attributes of the temple. Under the second category, various modes of worship of the deity have been taken into account which include *pūja* performance, burning lamps (*nandādivi*), food offerings *(naivedya),* various festivals *(caitra, pavitra, sankrānti)* conducted at the temples and different rituals covered under the services of *aṅga bhōga* and *raṅga bhōga* (IVA, ix, 1-25, IVB, ix, 26-135, IVC, ix, 136-154). The *aṅga bhoga* ceremony is supposed to have included the provision of all princely comforts and luxuries to the deity such as bathing with scented water, anointing the body with milk or ghee, sandal wood powder, and also providing food, clothes, garlands and so on.[69] On the other hand, *raṅga bhōga* has been interpreted in the sense of amusement to be arranged for the deity[70] which would include among other periodical celebrations, dramas and dances too.[71] Owing to the nature of services in which various cultural professional groups were involved as they were closely associated with the functions just discussed, we have clubbed these groups under the above nature of patronage (IVA, ix, 1-25, IVB, ix, 26-135, IVC, ix, 136-154) for the purpose of the present discussion. Finally, the *maṭha* and the priests housed in them representing the ideological moorings of the temple to which they were attached have been studied under a single heading (IVA, vii, x, 1-25, IVB, vii, x, 26-135, IVC, vii, x, 136-154).

In the context of sub-region A during the 11th century A.D. we have reference to 3 instances of the patronage extended by various individuals towards the maintenance of the temple establishment. Thus, we have the grant of some land and an oil mill directed towards a Śivālaya by a *mahāsāmanta* and an *ūroḍeya* in an inscription dated to A.D. 1032 (IVA, viii, 3). In an inscription dated to A.D. 1049, a grant of various measurements of land is made by a *Prabhu* (Śaiva priest) for the repairs of several temples of Śripura.[72] In an earlier inscription dated to A.D. 1033, we have reference to the installation of an image of God Mallikārjuna by a *pergaḍe* (IVA, viii, 5). A little later, in A.D. 1062, reference is made to the renovation of the temple of God Siddeśvara by a *Prabhu* (Śaiva Priest) (IVA, viii, 6). During the 12th century A.D. for the same sub-region we come across only 2 references of the above nature. Among these, in A.D. 1184 the temple of Trikū-ṭa, which consists of the temples of Mācheśvara, Mallikārjuna and Mādhava, was constructed by a *prabhu* and grants of land were made by the *manneya, heggaḍe, daṇḍanāyaka, karaṇa* and various other people belonging to such 'tribal, pastoral groups as *bedaruṁ, janguliya, mādagaru, kuṟība* for the repairs of the above temples (IVA, viii, 21). In an inscription dated to A.D. 1207, the temple of God Telligeśvara, which was constructed by telliga-50, was given various grants in taxes and commodities by *prabhus* and 500 *svāmis* of Ayyavole for its repairs (IVA, viii, 25).

In contrast to the above for the sub-region B, during the 11th century A.D., we have as many as 15 references to the construction and repairs of temples. As early as A.D. 973, we have mention of the construction of the temple of Traipuruṣa by the *brāhmana* donee amidst the village received by him as a grant from the main ruler. Provision was also made here for the repairs of the temple (IVB, viii, 26). In an inscription dated to A.D. 1005, we have reference to a merchant who got the pinnacles of the temple of Gavareśvara constructed and made a grant of cash for the maintenance of the *maṇṭapa* hall of the temple (IVB, viii, 28). In an inscription dated to A.D. 1022, we have reference to a *seṭṭi* as the builder of the temple of Dharmeśvara (IVB, viii, 31). In an inscription dated to A.D. 1022, reference is made to the queen of the royal family as having installed the deity to Traipuruṣadeva and made some grant of land to it (IVB, viii, 32). In A.D. 1029, a Jaina *basadi* is said to have been constructed by a *gāvuṇḍa* (IVB, viii, 34). In another example from an inscription dated to A.D. 1036, reference is made to the construction of the temple of the Traipuruṣas and 12 Nārāyaṇas by a *pergaḍe* who also set up a *garuḍa* column there (IVB, viii, 36). In A.D. 1059 a grant of some *gadyānas* is registered to have been made by a *mahājana* for God Babbaleśvara for the purpose of repairs of the temple among other things.[73] In an inscription dated to A.D. 1060, we have reference to the construction of the temple of Nāgeśvara by a *mahāsāmantādhipati* and the grant of a village is made by the main ruler for several purposes among which the repairs of the temple also figure prominently (IVB, viii, 41). In A.D. 1069, a Jinālaya is supposed to have been built by a merchant (IVB, viii, 44). In A.D. 1076, God Svayambhu Kalidevasvāmi was made a gift of some cash and an oil mill by the local potentate, which among other purposes, was meant for the repairs of the temple (IVB, viii, 50). In an inscription dated to A.D. 1086, we have an interesting reference to the construction of the temple of Dāseśvara by a *nāviḍa* (barber) (IVB, viii, 58). Further, the temples of Viṣnu and Saraswati were supposed to have been constructed by a member of the *mahājanas* in A.D. 1087 (IVB, viii, 59). The temple of God Someśvara is referred to have been built by an *ūroḍeya* in A.D. 1088 and out of various grants made to it, certain amount was to be set apart for the stone work of the temple (IVB, viii, 60). Grants made to the Bauddha *vihāra* in A.D. 1095, by certain merchants also mention that they were to be used for the repairs of the institution among various other purposes (IVB, viii, 62). In an inscription dated to A.D. 1098, reference is made to the construction of a Buddhist *vihāra* by a *seṭṭi* (IVB, viii, 66).

During the 12th century A.D. in sub-region B, we have reference to nearly 16 instances of the patronage extended for constructing or repairing the physical attributes of the temple. We have in this context reference to one *daṇḍanāyaka* who got the image of God Mūlasthāna installed in A.D. 1100 (IVB, viii, 69). In A.D. 1103, reference is made to one *gāvuṇḍa* who got the temple of God Morakeśvara constructed (IVB, viii, 71). In A.D. 1105, the temple of God Brahmeśvara was constructed by a local potentate (IVB, viii, 74). The gift of a garden is registered to have been made by one *gāvuṇḍa* to God Sobhaneśvara, which among other purposes, included its repairs in an inscription dated to A.D. 1105 (IVB, viii, 73). The grant of some land is stated to have been made by a rājaguru for the temple of God Keśavadeva, the purpose for which also included its repairs in an inscription dated to A.D. 1105 (IVB, viii, 75). In an inscription dated to A.D. 1110, God Kammaṭesvara was granted some lime and bronze. This was most certainly meant for the purpose of either, making the deities or, for repairing the temple walls, by various guilds of artisans (IVB, viii, 80). Temples of God Śiva Mahādeva, Mūrti Nārāyaṇa, Chandaleśvara and Sāhasa Bhairava are said to have been constructed by a *brāhmaṇa* functionary. Among these, the grant of a village is made by the main ruler to the temple of Śiva Mahādeva which among its various purposes also included the repairs of the temple (IVB, viii, 81). The renewal of an earlier grant is made towards temple of God Mūlasthānadeva by a *mahāpradhāna* which had among its various purposes indicated that it was meant for the repairs of the temple too (IVB, viii, 90). In this way, between A.D. 1144-A.D. 1178, we have three instances (IVB, viii, 94, 96, 115) wherein the repairs of the temples were invariably effected by the local functionaries. In an inscription dated to A.D. 1179, reference is made to the installation of the deity Keśavadeva by a merchant (IVB, viii, 117). The temples of Chāmeśvara and Māleśvara are stated to have been built by a Sinda chief in memory of his father (IVB, viii, 118). Towards the end of the 12th century A.D. we have two references to the repairs of the temple one made by a functionary (IVB, viii, 129) and the other by the main ruler (IVB, viii, 130).

In sub-region C during the 11th century A.D. we come across nearly 8 instances of grants to the temples which among other things, were meant for the purpose of repairs and upkeep of various shrines located in the temple precincts. We see in this context that the grants in this direction were made by the chiefs of the main ruling family in only 1 instance (IVC, viii, 140) and on the other hand the supra local chiefs dominate the scene as they emerge in this role in nearly 5 instances (IVC, viii, 142, 143, 144, 1145, 146). They are referred to as donors of villages and the income out of this was directed to meet the expenses incurred at the time of repairs for the temple and for various other purposes. In one of these references we also come across an instance of the construction of temple and the installation of deity (IVC, viii, 145) in it by one local potentate in memory of his father. In the other instances we have reference to one *suṅkavergaḍe* who is the stated to be the subordinate of a local potentate and bears the title of a *seṭṭi.* He made grants of taxes and various commodities for, among other purposes, repairs of the temple too (IVC, viii, 139). Further in the 11th century A.D. itself, we have a single reference of its kind of the grant of cash income made by several *gāvuṇḍas, prabhus* and *seṭṭis* who make a grant from the income accrued from each village in Aijie-300 for various purposes of the temple which also included the repairs of it (IVC, viii, 139). During the 12th century A.D. for the same sub-region we have 2 instances of the grants made by the members of the main ruling family which among other things included repairs of the temple (IVC, viii, 149, 152). We further have 1 instance of the mention of *mahājanas*, who were supposed to have installed the deity God Mādhava and set aside some amount for the repairs of the above temple (IVC, viii, 150) and 1 instance of the *mahāmaṇḍaleśvara* who granted income from certain taxes collected from a village which was directed towards the repairs of the temple as well (IVC, viii, 151). It is pertinent to note here that in a majority of cases the temple of God Brahmeśvara receives major attention in the above example which belong to both the 11th and the 12th centuries A.D. We have in this context, nearly 8 references to the above temple (IVC, viii, 137, 139, 142, 144, 146, 149, 151, 152). In fact, the temple of God Mādhava (IVC, viii, 150) has been described as belonging to the Brahmapurigeri of the *mahāsthāna* of God Brahmeśvara.[74]

We have been able to infer upon certain significant trends with regard to the establishment of various temples in the three sub-regions of our study on the basis of above survey. In sub-region A in a majority of cases during the 11th century A.D. grants were directed either, towards repairs or, for the renovation of various temple structures. We come across only one case of installation of a deity by a *pergaḍe* at this stage. It is only towards the end of the 12th century A.D. that we witness in this sub-region the actual construction of temples under operation. However, from these instances we can, at the same time, discern involvement of new groups, wherein, in the first instance, we have reference to the pastoral and hunting groups which suggests the fact that the temple was being constructed at a newly emerging settlement. In the second case, oil mongers who were just beginning to emerge into a powerful socio-economic group, initiated the construction of a temple for their God namely Telligeśvara. A large number of the above instances however clearly signify that sub-region A, in its initial stages, was marked by the existence of already established temple institutions which therefore, required grants for their renovation and repairs. A similar trend can be discerned in the context of the temples of sub-region C too wherein out of a total of 8 instances during the 11th century A.D. it had only one instance of the construction of a temple by a local potentate in the name of his father. On the whole, we find that a majority of the grants were made by various supra local chiefs and the main ruling family members and these were directed towards the renovation and the repairs of various temples of which those of God Brahmeśvara figure prominently. During the 12th century A.D. in this sub-region we see that a similar trend is maintained but it is God Brahmeśvara's temples that have a majority of grants directed to it for its repairs and maintenance and these were made by the members of the main ruling family. We also have at this stage one instance of the installation of deity by the *mahājanas* of the place in the temple of God Mādhava which again belonged to the *mahāsthana* of God Brahmeśvara. The above trends become all the more significant when we take into account our earlier observation that sub-regions A and C had witnessed an active temple building activity much earlier than our period of study, namely during the period of Chālukyas of Bādāmi and the Rāshṭrakūṭas of Malkhed (7th-10 centuries A.D.) In an earlier part of the chapter we have already referred to the fact that the temple of God Brahmeśvara of Alampur is supposed to have belonged to the time of Chālukyās of Bādami.[75]

On the other hand, for sub-region B we find that in the 11th century A.D. itself, a large number of references to the construction of temples and installation of deities have been noted by us above. Out of 15 instances charted out by us and discussed we have observed that references to the construction of various types of religious institutions including the Jaina and Buddhist occur in nearly 9 instances (IVB, viii, 26, 28, 31, 32, 34, 44, 58, 59, 60, 62). During the 12th century A.D. out of 16 references charted by us, we come across 6 instances of construction of the temples and installation of deities (IVB, viii, 69, 71, 74, 81, 117, 118). The remaining other examples were directed towards the repairs and renovation of the temples (IVB, viii, 73, 75, 80, 81, 90, 94, 96, 116, 129, 130). The above evidences are a clear indication of the fact that sub-region B, was marked by a predominance in temple building activity during this period and emerges as a zone of legitimization in the hands of various social groups participating in the above acts. We have also seen in this regard that the rise in the socio-political status of some of the local functionaries and the supra local chiefs was marked by them having the financial resources to build temples. We thus have in an inscription dated to A.D. 1060, temple of Nāgeśvara at Sundi built by one Nāgadeva who had just attained the status of a *mahāsāmantādhipati.*[76] The Akkeśvara temple at Suṇḍi was installed with a deity by Akkadevi, the royal princess of the Chālukya family who ruled over several tracts during the early part of the 11th century A.D.[77] At the local level, we have reference to 4 *gāvuṇḍas* who were supposed to have constructed a Śiva temple at the *agrahāra* of Bannigola in A.D. 1055.[78] In an inscription dated to A.D. 1075, reference is made to a *karaṇa* named Chākimayya, who built the temple of Chākeśvara.[79] In another inscription of the same year, we have reference to one Mārulimayya who belonged to the family of the *pergaḍe* and installed the deity of Māruleśvara.[80] A *brāhmaṇa* functionary called Ravideva, who was conferred several high sounding titles by the Chālukya rulers, got a temple of Svayambhu Śiva constructed at Yehur in association with the *pergaḍe* of the place in A.D. 1077.[81] We come across quite a few references of the nature in the context of 12th century A.D. too. We thus have in an inscription dated to A.D. 1103, which mentions the construction of the temple of God Mōrakeśvara by one Nāki Gāvuṇḍa who named the temple after his family name, the *mōraka kula.* Incidentally, this corresponds to the emergence of the above *gāvuṇḍa* as the ruler *(mahāprabhu)* of Posavūr.[82] The temple of God Brahmeśvara, which was constructed by the Sinda *mahāmaṇḍaleśvara* Barmmarasa in A.D. 1104[83] coincides with the growth in the power of the Sindas of Erambarage which was roughly around this time. In A.D. 1153, we have reference to one Joga Gāvuṇḍa in association with the temple of God Jogeśvara at Rājūr.[84] It is pertinent to note here that the local functionary in this case is referred to as a direct subordinate *(tatpāda padmōpajīvi)* of the supra local chief, which is a clear indication of the rise in the status of the above *gāvuṇḍa.*

In fact, one can clearly discern in the above context a close nexus established between the rise in the status of the local chiefs in the territories of their respective rule which are simultaneously marked by a proliferation of the temple establishments in these areas. We wish to illustrate this with a few examples to vindicate our point. We have already observed in this regard that the emergence of the Chālukyas of Kalyāṇi as the main rulers in independent status was marked first of all, by granting villages as *agrahāras* in the initial stages of their rule.[85] It was among these settlements that we find that there was a significant growth in the temple building activity by the *brāmaṇa* residents. Thus, as early as A.D. 973, conversion of the village of Modeyanūr into an *agrahāra* was marked by the construction of the temple of Traipuruṣas by the *brāhmaṇa* donee.[86] Similarly, the village of Ummachige was converted into an *agrahāra* in A.D. 1012, and was marked by several temple establishments such as the temples of God Someśvara, God Bhagiyabbeśvara (named after the mother of main ruler) Aychagāvuṇḍa's temple (clearly named after the local functionary), and temples of Goddess Beṭṭaḍa Bhāgavati, God Nārāyaṇa and Goddess Mārakabbe Bhaḷāri.[87] Thus, the *agrahāra* settlements during the 11th century A.D. in particular, were mentioned prolifically in the context of various temple establishments located in them. We have an example from an inscription dated to A.D. 1076, to the temples of God Svayambhu Kalidevasvāmi and Goddess Bhāgavati in the context of the *agrahāra* of Niḍgunḍi.[88] Temples of Dāseśvara, Anuveśvara and so on were associated with the *agrahāra* of Kuṛitakuṁte in the inscription dated to A.D. 1086[89] and A.D. 1082[90] respectively. The temple of God Someśvara at the Pulige *agrahāra* was constructed in A.D. 1088.[91]

In the non-*agrahāra* settlements too, we find a similar association with the temple centres which in fact, marks a clear rise in the corresponding spatial context particularly in the 12th century A.D. sources. We have an exception in this regard wherein the settlements of Mulugunḍa and Posavūru emerge as temple settlements as early as A.D. 994. In this context God Mūlasthāna deva of Posavūru is regarded as belonging to God Deveśvara deva of Mulugunḍa. Here, a clear hierarchy seems to have been established in grading temple establishments. In this case, God Deveśvara emerges as having a hold over God Mūlasthāna.[92] It is interesting to note that by A.D. 1103, Posavūru is referred to as the property of God Vīra Nārāyaṇadeva of Mulugunḍa-12 which was a strong hold of the Sindas of the *Kunnūla Vaṁśa.*[93] In the same inscription Posavūru is described as the *baliya vāḍa* of Mulugunḍa-12 and was held on *eka bhoga* (having exclusive familial rights) tenure by one Nāki Gāvunḍa who also built the temple of God Mōrakeśvara there on his family's name. These instances clearly indicate to us that there was an ideological dimension being created to the hierarchical political hold claimed at various levels of chiefs in which there is a clear ascendancy of the settlement of Mulugunḍa held by the Sinda *manneya* (ruler of several villages) over Posavūru which was ruled by a *gāvunḍa*. Therefore, the importance of the temples corresponded to the superior hold of the local chief which was in turn dependant upon the strategic location of the spatial unit held by him. In this case Mulugunḍa emerges as the foremost settlement in the cluster of settlements around it represented through the name Mulugunḍa-12. The temples situated here symbolize a higher level in the hierarchy of the temples located in the settlements surrounding it. By the middle of 12th century A.D. we come across the names of several temples such as those of God Sobhaneśvara (A.D. 1105) God Vidureśvara (A.D. 1144) and so on as located in Mulugunḍa and patronized by a variety of social groups such as the agriculturists, and mercantile groups. We can discern the growth of Narāyaṁgal-12, stronghold of the Sindas of Erambarage, on similar lines during the 12th century A.D. In A.D. 1105 we have reference to the construction of the temple of God Brahmeśvara by the Sinda chief at Nārāyaṁgal.[94] By A.D. 1121, we have reference to God Moṭṭeśvaradeva of Kiru Nārāyaṁgal as attached to the temple of God Sobhaneśvaradeva of Hiriya Nārāyamgal. By the middle of the 12 century A.D. *i.e.,* by A.D. 1144, God Mūlasthāna Brahmeśvara of Kiru Nārāyaṁgal emerges as a major God with several social groups emerging as patrons to it. Nārāyaṁgal-12 figures as an important cluster of settlements among the many territorial units held by the Sinda chiefs of Eranbarage. Thus, the growth in the settlements with a corresponding rise in the growth of the political hold of their respective chiefs and the close association of these with the proliferation of temple settlements can be considered as projection of a symbiotic relationship established between the above elements. In such a set up one realized that the establishment of temples were essentially a conscious effort initiated in the first place by various levels of ruling chiefs to provide an ideological dimension to their politico-spatial expansion in order to seek legitimation for the exercise of their politico-economic control over the local population. The temple on the one hand, represented the dominant strand of ideological hold exercised by the ruling groups and on the other, it provided an institutional focus to the varied local belief systems and thus also acted as in instrument of acculturation by enabling a variety of groups to enter into the purview of state system through the symbol of temple.

By the latter half of the 11th century A.D. we have a significant growth in the participation of various mercantile groups in the temple building activity. In fact, next to the rulers it were the mercantile groups that emerge as builders of various temple institutions as a means to legitimize their professional interests. As early as A.D. 1005, we have reference to one Īśvara Seṭṭi who was supposed to have got the pinnacles constructed for the temple of God Gavareśvara. In an inscription dated to A.D. 1022, one Dharma Seṭṭi was supposed to have built the temple of Dharmeśvara. In A.D. 1069, we have reference to the construction of a Jinālaya by one Māki Seṭṭi. In A.D. 1095, reference is made to a Bauddha *Vihāra* which was said to have been constructed by the group of 18 *seṭṭis*. Apart from these, references to God Śiva in the form of God Kammateśvara (IVB, v, 80), Totigeśvara (IVB, v, 92) (worshipped by the guild of gardeners), Meleśvara (IVB, v, 56) (worshipped by the agriculturist guild) Nakareśvara (IVB, v, 42, 46) (worshipped by the mercantile guild) and Telligeśvara (IVA, v, 25; IVB, v, 135) (representing the interests of the *telligas* or the oil mongers) significantly point to the fact that these temples must have been built to cater to the ideological moorings of various professional groups who begin to figure actively in the inscriptional sources of our study only from the latter half of the 11th century A.D. In such a set up, worship of God Śiva (at times God Viṣṇu too) representing on the one hand, pan-Indian religion of Brahmaṇism or, (better known as Purāṇic Hinduism), and on the other, the ability of this God to transform himself into various forms depending upon the locality of his worship and the social strata seeking legitimation, provides an excellent set of issues to comprehend the various strands of ideological legitimation and integration in the context of our study. We, however, get a better picture of these processes when we take into consideration and have a closer scrutiny of the various patterns of patronage involved in the nature of services performed in the temple institutions for various sub-regions of the present study. We next examine the data available in this regard.

For sub-region A during the 11th century A.D. we have, in the second category of patronage, which was directed towards the worship of the deity, 3 instances in the inscriptional sources charted by us. In an inscription dated to A.D. 1062, grants made by a Śaiva priest were also directed, among other things, towards the performance of the *aṅgabhoga* ceremony (IVA, ix, 6). In A.D. 1070, we have mention of a local potentate who granted some land for the *aṅgabhoga* ceremony of God Mūlasthānadeva (IVA, ix, 8). The grant of the village made by the main ruler towards the temple of God Svayambhu Nāgeśvara and other temples, was directed, among other things for the *nivedya* (offerings) and *pūja* (worship) of the deity (IVA, ix, 10). During the 12th century A.D. for the same sub-region, we have nearly 10 instances of the grants made of the above nature. Of these, in A.D. 1145, a grant of land is registered to have been made by some functionaries towards the *aṅga-bhoga-nivedya* ceremonies of God Mūlasthāna (IVA, ix, 14). In A.D. 1148, gifts of oil and some cash have been registered towards the ceremonies of *nivedya, pūja* and *caitra pavitra* festivals for the God Kalideva by the temple establishment consisting of the *heggaḍe* of the *maṭha* along with the *senabova* and the *telliga* (oil mongers) of the place (IVA, ix, 16). In a much later inscription of A.D. 1173, we have reference to the grant of oil for the *nandādivi* (lamps) and some land for the *nivedya* of God Mahalinga by a local functionary (IVA, ix, 19). In A.D. 1184, we have an interesting reference to the grant of land, house sites, oil mills and so on by the *prabhu, manneya* and other local functionaries which were among other things directed towards the *trikāla* (probably 3 times) *pūja* and *nivedya* of the God. On the other hand, the same God was made grants of house taxes by the headmen of the pastoral groups *(Kuriba gāvuṇḍa)* and hunting groups *(bedar)* along with the *huliya-janguliya, mādagaru* and so on, for the *caitra-pavitra* festival of the God (IVA, ix, 21). In a different inscription of the same year, we have reference to several grants of land, shops, house site, oil mills, taxes and so on made by a *mahāmaṇḍaleśvara* for the purpose of the *aṅga bhoga* and *caitra pavitra* festivals of God Vīra Bayseśvara (IVA, ix, 22). In A.D. 1189 gift of some land was registered to have been made by a *mahāpradhāna* for the *pūja punaskāra nivedya* and *nandādivi* (lamps) of God Nanneśvara (IVA, ix, 23). In another inscription of the same year, the same functionary figures as the donor of some land of God Siryameśvara for the same purposes as above. Certain mercantile guilds also figure as the donors of some oil obviously for the lighting of lamps before the deity (IVA, ix, 24). An inscription of the year A.D. 1207 reports that God Telligeśvara was granted some levies on oil mills and land by the *Ayyavole*-500 and the *prabhus* for the *raṅga bhoga* ceremonies of the God (IVAS, ix, 25).

References to the above kind of patronage emerge in a richer variety of contexts for the sub-region B. We wish to delineate here some of the dominant trends perceived in this regard. During the 11th century A.D. in this sub-region we have come across nearly 19 instances for different types of services rendered in the temple. As early as A.D. 973, we have reference to the provision made for the *nivedya* (offerings), *nandādivi* (lamps) and *nitya pūja* (daily worship) in honour of God Traipuruṣadeva made by a *brāhmaṇa* donee of an *agrahāra* village (IVB, ix, 26). In A.D. 1054, we have reference to one *manneya* whose grant of some cash was directed towards the lamps, offerings and incense in the service of Gods Kalidevasvāmi and Viṣṇudeva (IVB, ix, 39). In an inscription dated to A.D. 1060, we come across reference to the grant of a village of God Nāgeśvara by a local potentate which, among other things, included various types of services rendered to the deity and made provision for the maintenance of different types of professional groups such as the dancing girls, stone cutter, drummer and so on (IVB, ix, xi, 41). In an earlier inscription of the year A.D. 1059, reference is made to the grant of some money by a *mahājana* which included among several of its purposes, maintenance of a *pūjari* and the *aṅgabhoga* ceremonies of God Babbaleśvara.[95] In A.D. 1069, reference of some endowment to God Achaleśvara has been recorded which was made by a Pallava chief which included among others, provisions for the supply of *nivedya* (IVB, ix, 43). In A.D. 1072, grant of oil mills and some gardens are registered to have been made by a *suṅka vergaḍe* and the *nakara* (merchant guild) for maintaining the perpetual lamp *(nandādivi)* of God Nakareśvara (IVB, ix, 46). In a different inscription of the same year, we have reference to the grant of some land, money and oil mill for different Gods by *gāvuṇḍas*, one *seṭṭi* and the body of 1000 for the purpose of *nivedya* (IVB, ix, 47). It is interesting to note that in an inscription dated to A.D. 1075, grant of a village is registered to have been made by the main ruler which was directed among others towards the purpose of personal enjoyment of God Pañchalin, gadeva (IVB, ix, 48). Grants of land have been recorded in an inscription dated to A.D. 1075, which were made by certain local functionaries for the purpose of *nandādivi,* supply of flowers to God Māruleśvara along with the provision made for the maintenance of the *pūjāri* at the temple (IVB, ix, xi, 49). Performance of the *pavitrārōhaṇa* ceremony dominates the purpose of the grant of money made by a local potentate of God Kalidevasvāmi in A.D. 1076. In the same inscription, grants of the queen of the royal family have, among various purposes, been directed towards such services as *dhūpa* (incense) *nivedya* and *nandādivi* of Goddess Bhāgavati who was said to be the *grāmadevata* along with the above God (IVB, ix, 50). The main purpose of the grant of a village by the Pallava chief and Kadamba chief in A.D. 1077, is stated to have been the *aṅga* and *raṅga bhoga* of God Kīrti Someśvara (IVB, ix, 51). The temple of God Svayambhu Śiva in an inscription dated to A.D. 1077, is stated to have been endowed with a grant of a large measurement of land by the main ruler with the purpose of catering to such services as the provision of incense, *nandādivi,* for the procession of the God and the *caitra pavitra* and *nūla prabhaṅda* ceremonies (IVB, ix, 52). The grant of a village to God Achaleśvara is recorded to have been made by the royal queen towards the services of *aṅga* and *raṅga bhoga* of the deity in A.D. 1084 (IVB, ix, 57). Between the period A.D. 1086-A.D. 1088, we have nearly 3 references to the grants directed towards various services of deity which were made chiefly by the *mahājanas* and *brāhmaṇa* (IVB, ix, 58, 59, 60). It is interesting to note that in an inscription dated to A.D. 1095, grants made to a Buddhist *vihāra* by certain merchants mention similar purposes as above for which the grant was made, such as *nandādivi, nivedya* and *pūja* and the maintenance of the *pujari* (IVB, ix, xi, 61).

During the 12th century A.D. for the same sub-region we have a steep rise in the patronage of this kind as we find as many 50 instances of grants directed towards the personal services of Gods at this stage. In this context during the first half of the 12th century A.D. we come across nearly 7 instances of the *gāvuṇḍa/oḍeya/pergaḍe* (various types of village headmen) making various grants to such Gods as Kalidevasvami (IVB, ix, 68), Mōrakeśvara (IVB, ix, 71), Sobhaneśvara (IVB, ix, 73), Bhogeśvaradeva (IVB, ix, 78, 93), Kalideveśvara (IVB, ix, 86) and Mūlasthānadeva (IVB, ix, 96) for the performance of such ceremonies as *aṅga bhoga, nivedya* and, at times, maintenance of *nandādivi* among the purposes. Apart from the above, other functionaries such as the *mahāpradhāna* (IVB, ix, 90) *heggaḍe* of *pannāya* (IVB, ix, 94) figure in 2 instances as patrons of above stated services to such Gods as Mūlasthānadeva. Further, the local potentates figure in 2 instances (IVB, ix, 74, 86) as patronizing such services to Gods like Brahmeśvara and Kalidevasvāmi. On the other hand, the merchants figure in nearly 5 instances as patrons of such specific services as the *aṅga bhoga* (IVB, ix, 78, 95, 96) *nivedya* (IVB, 78, 85, 97) *nandādivi* (IVB, ix, 85, 95, 96, 97), *caitra-pavitra* (IVB, ix, 96) in honour of such Gods as Bhogeśvara, Amriteśvara, Vidureśvara, Mūlasthāna and Mallikārjunadeva. The *mahājanas* figure in 2 instances as patrons of *pavitrārohaṇa* (IVB, ix, 77) and *aṅga bhoga, nandādivi* and *naivedya* ceremonies (IVB, ix, 89) of Gods, Keśavādityadeva and Traipuruṣa. Further, *brāhmaṇa* functionaries figure in 3 instances as patrons of *nivedya* (IVB, ix, 70, 75, 81) *aṅga bhoga, pūja, pavitrārohaṇa* and *nandādivi* (IVB, ix, 75) ceremonies of Gods Somanātha, Keśavadeva, Śiva-Mahādeva, Mūrti Nārāyaṇa and so on. In the second half of the 12th century A.D. for sub-region B itself we come across nearly 10 references to the merchants and their guilds patronizing certain services in the temple. Among these, *nivedya* (IVB, ix, 98, 115, 121), *nandādivi* (IVB, ix, 107, 109, 113, 117), *sthāna pūja* (IVB, ix, 117) *aṅga bhoga* (IVB, ix, 121, 127, 132, 133), and Saṅkrānti festivities (IVB, ix, 121) figure prominently that were done in honour of such Gods as Kavataleśvara, Mūlasthānadeva, Vidireśvara, Keśavadeva, Śankaradeva, Mallikārjuna, Nanneśvara, Billeśvara. Further, artisans/artisanal guilds figure in 4 instances as patronizing worship (IVB, ix, 125), *nandādivi* (IVB, ix, 125), *nivedya* (IVB, ix, 126) *caitra pavitra* festival (IVB, ix,

128) at the Jinālaya, and the temples of God Kammaṭeśvara, God Mōṛakeśvara and Bonteśvara. We have 2 instances of patronage extended by the *ūroḍeyas* (of *agrahāras*) towards *aṅga bhoga* (IVB, ix, 103) and *nivedya* (IVB, ix, 103, 104) of Gods Bhogeśvaraand Keśavadeva. We further have 3 instances of *gāvuṇḍas* who some times figure with the *okkalu* group as patrons of *nandādivi* (IVB, ix, 107, 109, 132), *naivedya* (IVB, ix, 109) and *aṅga bhoga* (IVB, ix, 132) of Gods Goyideśvara Mūlasthānadeva and Billeśvara. The *daṇḍanāyakas/mahāpradhānas* figure in at least three instances as patronizing *aṅga bhoga* (IVB, ix, 105), *nivedya* (IVB, ix, 111, 123), daily worship (IVB, ix, 115, 123) and *caitra pavitra* (IVB, ix, 111, 116, 124) ceremonies of Gods Svayambhu Prasanna Mallikārjuna, Kālika Jyeṣṭha and Mallikārjuna. The Sinda chiefs in 2 instances, and the Kadamba chief in one instance, figure as patrons of *nitya pūja* (IVB, ix, 118) *nandādvi* (IVB, ix, 118), *nivedya* (IVB, ix, 118, 129, 131), and *caitra pavitra* (IVB, ix, 118) of ceremonies of Gods Chāmeśvara, Māleśvara, Svayambhu Paśchima Somanātha and Kalakaleśvara.

For sub-region C, during the 11th century A.D., we have *suṅkavergaḍe* in 1 instance patronizing the *nandādivi* (IVC, ix, 137), *pergaḍe* in 1 instance as patron of *nivedya* (IVC, ix, 138) and the *gāvuṇḍas* along with the *saudhare* and *prabhus* figure in 1 instance as patrons of the *aṅga bhoga* (IVC, ix, 139) of Gods Brahmeśvara and Kukkuṭeśvara. The main ruling family chief emerges in 1 instance as the patron of *aṅga bhoga* and nivedya (IVC, ix, 140) to various deities located in the temple of God Pañchaliṅgadeva. The supra local chiefs belonging to different families such as the Telugu Chola and the Vaiḍumbas on the other hand, figure in nearly 5 instances as patrons of *nandādivi* (IVC, ix, 142, 143, 145, 146) *nivedya* (IVC, ix, 142, 143, 144, 145, 146), *aṅga* and *raṅga bhoga* (IVC, ix, 143, 144), and *pūja* (IVC, ix, 144) of Gods Brahmeśvara, Lakshmaṇeśvara and Bikkeśvara. During the 12th century A.D., for the same sub-region, we came across 2 instances of the queens of the main ruling family patronizing the *nandādivi* and *nivedya* ceremonies of God Brahmeśvara (IVC, ix, 149, 152), 1 instance of the *mahājanas* as patrons of the *aṅga bhoga, nandādivi* and *nivedya* ceremonies of God Mādhava (IVC, ix, 150), 2 instances of the supra local chiefs who emerge as patrons of *raṅga bhoga* (IVC, ix, 151), *nivedya* (IVC, ix, 151, 153) *nandādivi* (IVC, ix, 151, 153) and *abhisheka* (IVC, ix, 153) of Gods Brahmeśvara and Someśvara. Finally, we have reference to several mercantile groups who emerge as patrons of *nivedya* and *nandadivi* ceremonies (IVC, ix, 154) of God Gavareśvara.

An analysis of the above description with regard to the nature of social patronage vis-a-vis rituals/services performed in various temples in the context of their location in different sub-regions of our study enables us to conclude upon certain basic trends involved in the forms of legitimation/integration adopted at various levels of politico-economic functioning during the period under consideration. In sub-region A during the 11th century A.D. we come across mainly three types of social groups who indulge in making grants to cater to the purpose of temple rituals. Among these we have the Śaiva priest (IVA, iv, ix, 6) and the Pallava chief (IVA, iv, ix, 8) who direct their grants for the purpose of *aṅga bhoga* (bathing and clothing the deity) ceremonies in the temple followed by the grants made by the main ruler (IVA, iv, ix, 10) who made grants for the purpose of *naivedya* (offerings) and *pūja* (daily worship). It is pertinent to underscore here that we do not have at this stage any clear indication whatsoever of the involvement of any local authority in this type of patronage system. All the three instances stated above were basically of outside elements trying to carve for themselves some sort of hold in the area under consideration by participating in the local forms of worship. It is, however, during the 12th century A.D. that we get across a variety of social groups who emerge as patrons of different types of rituals in the temple institutions located in sub-region A. Among these we find that the local functionaries predominate the scene followed by artisanal guilds such as oil mongers. We also come across functionaries of the temple establishment, the *mahāmaṇḍaleśvara* and such rulers as the *mahāpradhāna* and so on who figure prominently in this regard. It is pertinent to note here that apart from the above stated names of rituals, we come across in this context certain new rituals along with an increase in the variety of names of Gods. This emerges particularly with regard to the grants made for the performance of the *Caitra pavitra* ceremonies (IVA, ix, 16, 22) and trikāla pūja (IVA, ix, 23). Further, reference to the names of different Gods such as Siriyammeśvara (IVA, v, 24), Nanneśvara (IVA, v, 23) and Telligeśvara (IV, v, 25) towards the end of the 12th century A.D. significantly point to the fact that during this period the expansion of the socio-political base of the temple network was taking place on a considerable scale. In such a context one finds that the local belief systems were increasingly being patronized as can be gauged through their mention in the form of *caitra-pavitra* ceremonies associated with new names of deities and the mention of new groups like the hunters and pastoralists.

The terms *caitra-pavitra* have been considered to constitute two different words wherein the former has been associated with the ceremonies conducted in *chaitramāsa* and *pavitra* emerges in association with the concept of sacred thread.[96] In particular the latter has also been interpreted to mean innesting the image of a diety with a sacred thread. That is supposed to make good all defects and mistakes committed in all *pūjas.*[97] When the contextual nature of the occurrence of these terms is taken into consideration it strongly alludes some sort of initiation of the local deities representing the local belief systems into the main stream of Śaivite ideology as the names of the deities suggest. A large number of examples discussed earlier strongly indicate the chief levels of operation in the realm of ideological integration attempted from above by the politico-economic groups in their attempts to seek legitimation/validation for their interests. Intertwined with this phenomenon was the simultaneous process of the appropriation of local belief systems which led to the integration of various social groups at the local level which can be understood as embedded in it the crucial process of acculturation. The changing symbols of worship which emerge in the form of different names attributed to God Śiva on the one hand, and on the other, the performance of various types of rituals in association with the local groups (such as hunters and pastorlists in this case), have a significant bearing on our comprehension of the processes of integration. Various levels in the operation of the complex processes of ideological integration can, however, be discerned in clear contours in the context of sub-region B wherein we have already discussed above that large scale temple building activity was undertaken by different types of social groups located in the fertile settlements of this area.

During the 11th century A.D. in this sub-region we find a predominance in the *brāhmaṇa/mahājana* patrons (IVB, iv, 26, 58, 59, 60) which is followed by the local potentates (IVB, iv, 41, 43, 50, 51) and the members of the main ruling family (IVB, iv, 48, 50, 52, 56). This firmly attests to the fact that in the initial stages of our study, patronage to the temple establishments gained momentum under the initiative taken by the above ruling elites. The local level of functionaries such as the *gāvuṇḍas* emerge only towards the latter half of the 11th century A.D. and that too only in one instance (IVB, iv, 47). Further, reference to various groups in the context of the names of deities patronized by them becomes a significant pointer towards our comprehension of the nature of legitimation under process. Thus, the *brāhmaṇas* and the *mahājanas* can be seen patronising in a majority of cases such Gods as Traipuruṣa, Viṣṇu, Sarasvati, Rāmeśvara and so on. In all these instances, the names of the Gods pertinently point towards the bias shown by these social groups towards the more orthodox Vedic/Puraṇic creed of worship. In the above context while God Traipuruṣa has been stated to have represented the worship of the Sun God, the others signify various forms of Viṣṇu and his associates.[98] On the other hand, the *mahājanas* can also be seen patronizing various deities named after Śiva such as Babbaleśvara, Dāseśvara and so on. In the latter case, the necessity to take into account the local belief systems must have made it contingent for them to patronize God Śiva. It is significant to note here that in one of these instances, the temple of God Dāseśvara is supposed to have been built by a *nāviḍa* the barber, who is described as the favourite son of *mahājanas*.[99] On the other hand, the members of the main ruling family, the supra local chiefs and other functionaries, including the merchant groups, can be seen patronizing the various forms of Śiva in almost all cases as can be deducted from the names of deities patronized by these groups which have been described by us above. In particular, patronage extended to Goddess Bhāgavati, also termed as *grāmadevata,* by the queen of the main ruling family[100] has a significant bearing on our comprehension of the attempts made by the ruling groups to legitimize their political hold at the sub-regional level through the worship of local Gods.

Such a phenomenon can, however, be comprehended in a better light if we take into account the specific nature of rituals patronized by the above described groups. It is interesting to note that in a majority of the cases of patronage extended towards various temples by the *mahājana* group, provision is made for the *nivedya, nandādivi* and *nitya pūja* ceremonies of Gods on a significant scale. One is here tempted to surmise on this basis the possibility that these aspects were initially introduced by the *brāmaṇa/mahājana* groups and then they came to be accepted, in the long run as the standard symbolizing aspects of worship in the temple which other social groups began to support as well. Further, we have also been able to observe in this regard that we do not come across the performance of the *aṅga-raṅga bhoga* ceremonies (which involves the ritual of bathing the deity in milk and clothing and decorating in rich garments coupled with various types of entertainment including dance and drama provided for the God) almost till the middle of the 11th century A.D. It is, in fact, only in an inscription dated to A.D. 1059, while describing the *mahājanas* patronizing a local deity, God Babbaleśvara, that we get introduced to the above ritual for the first time.[101] In a majority of the instances we, however, come across the patronage of *nivedya* (offerings) to various Gods made by a Pallava chief (1069 A.D.) (IVB, iv, ix, 43), *nandādivi* (lamps) made by a *suṅkavergaḍe* and the mercantile groups (1072 A.D.) (IVB, iv, ix, 46) and again *naivedya* by the *gāvuṇḍas* (1072 A.D.) (IVB, iv, ix, 47). Even in the context of the grants made by the members of the main ruling family, we do not come across the patronage of *aṅga-raṅga bhoga* ceremonies. In an inscription dated to A.D. 1075, the main ruler makes the grant of a village for the personal enjoyment of God Pañchaliṅga (IVB, iv, ix, 48) and in A.D. 1076, grants are made by the sister of the main ruler towards the services of *dhūpa* (incense), *nivedya* and *nandādivi* (IVB, iv, ix, 50). It is only towards the end of the 11th century A.D. that we come across occasional references to the local potentates (A.D. 1077) (IVB, iv, ix, 51) and the queen (A.D. 1084) (IVB, iv, ix 57) including such services as *aṅga bhoga* in their patronage of rituals.

It becomes clear from the above instances that the concept of performance of elaborate rituals in the temple began to gain significant momentum towards the end of the 11th century A.D. By A.D. 1095, in an interesting reference made to the Buddhist *vihāra,* we noted above the mention of the provision being made for the performance of various services such as the *nivedya, nandādivi, pūja* and the *pūjari* by the merchants (IVB, iv, ix, 62). This significantly attests to the fact that certain rituals came to have widespread social acceptance by the beginning the

12th century A.D. and began to be regarded as an important means of expressing one's devotion towards any religious symbol irrespective of the differences in their ideological moorings. However, this crucial step can be considered to have played the most significant role in integrating the wide variety of local belief systems under the dominant strand of belief at this time, namely the Śaivite ideology. By the latter half of the 11th century A.D., we also get introduced to certain rituals which we had earlier observed as associated with the local belief systems. Among these we have the prominent mention of the *pavitrārohaṇa* which was patronized by a local potentate and *chaitra pavitra* and *nūlaprabandha*[102] coupled with the ceremony of the procession of God and the Sankrānti festival, which were patronized by the main ruler. All these were to be conducted at the temple of God Svayambhuśiva, which is mentioned as a newly constructed temple. Their inclusion thus has a significant bearing on our comprehension of the methods of integration and legitimation adopted by various chiefs at the supra local level which was even adopted by members of the main ruling family. The initiative taken by these rulers at this early stage seems to have percolated to the local level politico-economic set up by the turn of the 12th century A.D. wherein we find more and more new social groups patronizing various types of rituals performed in the temple.

Against the above background of changes that took place in sub-region B we need to underline the fact that the proliferation of the local level polity and the expansion of the economic base which led on to unleashing of the forces of commercial growth, were developments that can be seen significantly projected in the nature of the transformation in the ideology. This was mainly as a result of the change in the nature and number of social groups seeking legitimation in the proliferating temple institutions at the local base of socio-economic and political power structure. We have seen from the above descriptions that in the first half of the 12th century A.D. the *gāvuṇḍas* and other village headmen such as the *pergaḍe* and the *oḍeya* dominate the scene as patrons. They are then followed by the merchants, *brāhmaṇa* functionaries, local potentates and the *mahājanas*. The emergence of the first two to the fore front as patrons is particularly significant in the light of the fact that the *gāvuṇḍas* now begin to figure actively in the capacity of rulers of their localities. The important role played by the merchants as patrons in the changing economic scenario as one moves towards commercial activity can be highlighted as well. We have further observed that while the *brāhmaṇa* functionaries and the *mahājanas* to a considerable extent emerge as patrons of such deities as Keśavāditya, Traipuruṣa, Mūrti Nārāyaṇa and so on along side some Śaivite forms of deities, the other social groups invariably figure as patronizing only God Śiva who now emerges with a variety of names as can be gauged through the description furnished above by us. Importantly, among the nature of rituals patronized by various groups during this period, the *nivedya, nandādivi* and *aṅga-bhoga* ceremonies seem to have attained a significant status. At the same time one can clearly discern a crucial change in the nature of rituals being patronized as we now begin to see a gradual increase in the reference made to the ceremonies of *caitra pavitra* (IVb, ix, 96) *pavitrārohaṇa* (IVB, ix, 75, 77). By the second half of the 12th century A.D. these changes seem to have taken a firmer shape wherein we find an increasing number of mercantile and artisanal groups patronizing the above rituals, particularly the *caitra-pavitra* on a large scale (IVB, ix, 112, 118, 124, 128). In fact, we also come across reference to new terms to characterize the performance of the *pūja* ceremony such as *sthāna pūja* (IVB, ix, 117) *nitya pūja* (IVB, ix, 118) and so on which probably depended upon the nature of the deity and its location of worship. Reference to the above forms of temple rituals are, however, made along with the *nivedya, nandādivi* and *aṅga-bhoga* which seem to have got completely entrenched in the concept of temple services. But the increase in the mention of the *caitra-pavitra* ceremonies, albeit in a small way, has wider implications for the gradual shift in the processes of ideological legitimation towards the local base. It is interesting to note at this juncture that we come across the *caitra-pavitra* ceremonies being patronized by the merchant groups in the precincts of the Jaina institution too (IVB, ix, 125). It is in the nature of above evidence which definitely testifies to a crucial shift in the patterns of patronage that we see a projection of the local elements of ideology interfacing with the pan-Indian ideological moorings. While the local rituals begin to be given considerable significance on the one hand, on the other, we see that the *aṅga* and *raṅga bhoga* ceremonies which were not widespread for a major part of the 11th century A.D., emerge as dominating the scene in the hands of local patrons during the 12th century A.D. Both these aspects, coupled with the ever increasing variety of the forms of Śiva worship amply demonstrate the fact that local elements were gaining ascendancy towards the end of the 12th century A.D. in sub-region B.

In the context of sub-region C, on the other hand, we do not get any clear pattern of the various levels of patronage exercised by the politically and economically powerful groups, particularly in view of the limited nature of data available for the 12th century A.D. On the basis of the information available for this sub-region, we have been able to surmise upon an active participation of the supra local chiefs and also of the members of the main ruling family whose grants were normally directed towards the performance of rituals like the *aṅga bhoga, nandādivi* and *naivedya.* These were in honour of God Brahmeśvara in a majority of cases (IVC, iv, ix, 142, 144, 146, 149, 151). Among the other groups who patronized a merchant functionary figures as performing the *nandādivi* of God Brahmeśvara in the middle of the 11th century A.D. and the *gāvuṇḍas* and other local chiefs figure as patrons of *nivedya* and *aṅga bhoga* ceremonies of God Brahmeśvara and God Kukkuteśvara. It is pertinent to note here what we had already observed in an earlier context that sub-region C, emerges essentially as an area of conquest in the hands of both the supra local as well as members of the main ruling family chiefs. Prolific mention of these chiefs in the context of patronage extended by them towards various ceremonies of God Brahmeśvara in particular is a significant pointer towards our comprehension of the attempts made by them for an ideological legitimation of their political hold. Thus on the whole we have hardly any difference in the nature and context of the services and rituals performed in the temple institutions on a sub-regional basis. On the other hand, when we take into consideration the chronological dimension in the patterns of patronage *vis-a-vis* the rituals, one can clearly discern the shift in terms of new rituals *(caitra-pavitra* and so on) gaining greater momentum by the middle of the 12th century A.D. This trend sqarely corresponds to the significant expansion in the social base marked by an emergence in new social groups in the temple patronage network which has crucial implications in our comprehension of the acculturation process operating on a simultaneous plane. It is pertinent to underscore in this regard that it is however the ideological parameters which were firmly rooted in the Kālāmukha doctrine of Śaivism represented by the mention of the powerful trustees to the grants made to various temples located in our area of study that we get a clearer understanding of the powerful role played by the ideology in appropriation and integration of the local belief systems. This beings us to the crucial question of the monastic establishments and the ideology housed in them which, as will be shown below, had a crucial role to play in the ideological transformation of the region under study as a while.

For the sub-region A, during the 11th century A.D., out of 11 instances charted by us, we have 4 references to the *maṭha* or the monastic establishments attached to the temple. Among these, in an inscription dated to A.D. 1032, reference is made to the construction of a *maṭha* by a *mahāsāmanta* and an *ūroḍeya* along with the temple of Śiva (Śivālaya) (IVA, x, 3). In A.D. 1062, we come across, for the first time, reference to *prabhu* Mārasingha, the priest of the temple of Goddess Mahālakshmidevi, who is also described as *Pāśupatāchārya* (*āchārya* of the Pāśupata sect of Śaivism) (IVA, vii, 6). In A.D. 1075, we again come across reference to a priest of Parvatāvali school & branch of the Kālāmukha Tatpurusha Paṇḍita, who emerges here as the trustee (IVA, vii, 10) to the grants of the temple of Svayambhu Nāgeśvaradeva made by the main rulers. We further have reference here to the provision made for feeding the students attached to this *maṭha* (IVA, x, 10). During the 12th century in the same sub-region, we come across nearly 8 references to the priests/*maṭhas* in the context of the patronage extended to them. We thus have in an inscription dated to A.D. 1106, reference to the feeding house located in the Viṣṇu temple (IVA, x, 13). In A.D. 1145, we have mention of one Śūdraka Jiya as the trustee of the grants made by the local functionaries, 8 *hiṭṭus* and a *prabhu,* to God Mūlasthāna (IVA, viii, 14). In A.D. 1147, we have reference to one Gaṅganevve who is supposed to belong to the temple of God Kalideva and emerges as the trustee to the grant of some land made by one *gāvuṇḍa* to the above God (IVA, vii, 15). Towards the end of the 12th century A.D., *i.e.,* between A.D. 1184-A.D. 1207, we come across nearly 5 references (IVA, vii, 21, 22, 23, 24, 25) to various priests such as Amritarāsi Paṇḍita (IVA, vii, 21) trustee to the temple of God Trikuta, Vīra Dāsa (IVA, vii, 22) of the temple Vīra Bayseśvara Lokajiya (IVA, vii, 23) of God Nanneśvara, Kannaguru (IVA, vii, 23, 24), (IVA, vii, 24) of God Siriyameśvara and Nāgarāśi (IVA, vii, 25) who was the trustee of God Telligeśvara.

In sub-region B we, however, come across a greater variety of references to the priests/*maṭhas* attached to various temple institutions. During the 11th century A.D. of this sub-region we have 12 instances of to various types of temple priests. Among these, in the first half of 11th century A.D. we have reference to such priests as Vidyābharaṇa Paṇḍita (IVB, vii, 27), Revabbe Goravi (IVB, vii, 29), Bhāvaśiva Deva (IVB, vii, 33) Devasiṅgha Bhaḷāra (IVB, vii, 37) who emerge as trustees in the context of various grants to such temples as Mūlasthāna deva. Traipuruṣadeva and Bhogeśvara deva. These grants were made by a *manneya* along with a group of *gāvuṇḍas,* by a local potentate and a member of the main ruling family. The above mentioned priests are, however, no where explicity mentioned as belonging to the Kālāmukha sect of Śaivism. Among these, the priest Bhāvaśivadeva is eulogized greatly as the spiritual head of several temples in A.D. 1028. In the second half of 11th century A.D. we come across references to such priests as Someśvara Paṇḍita deva (IVB, vii, 41), Dhruveśvara Paṇḍita (IVB, vii, 42), Someśvara Paṇḍita (IVB, vii, 43, 48, 57), Chikkaṇa Paṇḍita (IVB, vii, 47), Netraśiva Paṇḍita (IVB, vii, 51), Kalyāṇa Śakti (IVB, vii, 55) and Kedāra Śakti Paṇḍita (IVB, vii, 65) who emerge in the capacity of trustees to the grants made to such temples as Nāgeśvara, Achaleśvara, Kalidevasvāmi, Pañchaliṅgadeva, Kīrti Someśvara, Svayambhu Someśvara and so on. The patrons to these temples were chiefly the local potentates (IVB, iv, vii, 41, 43, 51, 55) mercantile guilds (IVB, iv, vii, 42, 47, 53, 65) local functionaries such as *suṅkavergaḍe, pergaḍe* (IVB, iv, vii, 47, 53, 65) and members of main ruling family (IVB, iv, vii, 48, 57). It is pertinent to note here that a majority of the above mentioned priests are described largely as votaries of various Gods whose grants they were entrusted with. During the 12th century A.D. for the same sub-region the number of priests representing monastic establishments attached to the temple institutions increases considerably. In the first half of the 12th century A.D. we have mention of Brahmarāsi Paṇḍita (IVB, vii, 69) Kriyā Śakti Paṇḍita (IVB, vii, 70), Indraśivadevā-chārya, the *rājaguru,* (IVB, vii, 73) Vigreśvara Paṇḍita (IVB, vii, 74), Someśvara Paṇḍita (IVB, vii, 73, 81, 82), Amritarāsi Paṇḍita (IVB, vii, 85, 90), Mallikārjuna Paṇḍita (IVB, vii, 87), Aghora Paṇḍita, the *sthānāchārya* (IVB, vii, 93), Chandrabhūṣaṇa Paṇḍit, the *āchārya* (IVB, vii, 94), Vāmaśakiti Paṇḍita, the *guru* (IVB, vii, 94), and Gaṅgeśvara Paṇḍitadeva the *sthānāchārya* (IVB, vii, 96). A majority of these priests figure as the trustees of the grants made to the temples of Gods Mūlasthāna Kumāreśvara, Mōrakeśvara, Somanātha, Sobhaneśvara, Brahmeśvara, Bhogeśvara, Amriteśvara, Śiva Mahādeva, Svayambhu Trikuteśvara, Mahadeveśvara and Vidureśvara, which are all evidently various names of God Śiva. In this context among the patrons to above temples we have a *daṇḍanāyaka,* a *mahāpradhāna, a heggaḍe* of *pannāya* (IVB, iv, 69, 90, 94), *gāvuṇḍas* (IVB, iv, 70, 71, 72, 78, 93, 96) a *mahāmaṇḍaleśvara* (IVB, iv, 74, 87) and merchant guilds (IVB, iv, 82, 85, 95, 96). Further, in the second half of the 12th century A.D. we come across names of the following priests who figure as holding various titles and again emerge in the capacity of trustees to various grants made to different temple institutions. Someśvara Paṇḍitadeva, the *āchārya* (IVB, vii, 98), Gaṅgarāsi Paṇḍita, the *āchārya* (IVB, vii, 99, 124) Jñanāśakti, the *āchārya* (IVB, vii, 100), Monideva (IVB, vii, 101), Kedāraśakti Paṇḍita, the *sthānāchārya* (IVB, vii, 103), Jaṭaveda Paṇḍita, the *āchārya* (IVB, vii, 107, 110), Ṣuṣaṇa Paṇḍitadeva (IVB, vii, 108), Amritarāsi Paṇḍita (IVB, vii, 109), Tatpuruṣa deva (IVB, vii, 111), Vāmaśakti Paṇḍita (IVB, vii, 115), Siddhāntikāleśvara the *āchārya* (IVB, vii, 116), Gurubhakta deva, the *āchārya* (IVB, vii, 118), Jñanārāśi, Paṇḍita, the *sthānāchārya* (IVB, vii, 119) Agastya Muni, the *āchārya* (IVB, vii, 126), Rudraśakti Paṇḍita (IVB, vii, 128), Siddhānti Chandra Bhūṣaṇa, the *āchārya* (IVB, vii, 134) and Bhāskarāchārya, the *āchārya* (IVB, vii, 135). Most of these priests figure as trustees to the temples of Gods Kavataleśvara, Mūlasthāna, Mōrakeśvara, Bhogeśvara, Goyideśvara, Yigoydeśvara, Mallikārjuna, Vidireśvara, Kālika Jyeṣtha, Chāmeśvara, Meleśvara, Svayambhu Somanātha, Bonteśvara, Svayambhu Trikūteśvara and Telligeśvara. Some of the above mentioned priests such as Monideva emerges as donee and donor and Rudraśakti Paṇḍita emerges as a builder of the temple. Among the patrons of these, we have the prominent mention of merchants (IVB, iv, 98, 115) *gāvuṇḍas* (IVB, iv, 99, 100, 107, 109, 110), a *daṇḍanāyaka,* a *mahāpradhāna* (IVB, iv, 116, 124) *mahāmaṇḍaleśvara* (IVB, iv, 118, 134) and artisanal groups (IVB, iv, 126, 128, 135).

For sub-region C we come across a rich variety of information regarding the Kālāmukha priests of Śaivism right from the middle of the 11th century A.D. Prominent among these are Brahmarāśi Bhaṭṭāraka the *mahāsthānādhipati* (IVC, vii, 137, 139, 142, 144), Lokābharana Paṇdita (IVC, vii, 138), Kāśmira Paṇḍita, the *mahāsthānadhipati* (IVC, vii, 140) Sureśvara Paṇḍitadeva, the *āchārya* (IVC, vii, 141), Sūryarāsi Paṇḍita, the *āchārya* (IVC, vii, 143), Sadyojāta Paṇḍita (IVC, vii, 144) and Someśvara Rāśi Bhṭṭāraka (IVC, vii, 146). These priests emerge as trustees of the temples of God Brahmeśvara, Kukkuteśvara, Pañchaliṅgadeva, Mallikārjunadeva, Lakshamaṇeśvara and Bikkeśvara. Thus, almost all the temple institutions in this sub-region emerge as strong supporters of Kālāmukha Śaivism. Even the two references made to the Jinālaya towards the end of the 11th century A.D. are made in the context of the mention of their priests (IVC, vii, 147, 148). One of these bears the suffix Bhaṭṭāraka which is normally associated with the Brahmanical priests. Among the patrons of the above temples, the supra local chiefs (IVC, iv, 142, 143, 145, 146) and the members of the main ruling family (IVC, iv, 140, 141) figure prominently with a couple of instances of a *suṅkavergaḍe*, a *pergaḍe* and a *gāvuṇḍa* (IVC, iv, 137, 138, 139). During the 12th century A.D. we have reference to Dharaṇīndrarāśi Paṇḍita as the *mahāsthānādhipati* (IVC, vii, 150, 151, 152) of God Brahmeśvara and Keśavarāsi as the *sthānapati* of the Gavareśvara temple (IVC, vii, 154). While the former is described as being patronized in 2 instances by the queens of the royal family (IVC, iv, 149, 152), there is one instance of his patronage by the *mahājanas* (IVC, iv, 150) and in another by the *mahāmaṇḍaleśvara* (IVC, iv, 151). The latter one figures as the trustee of grants made by various mercantile guilds (IVC, iv, 154).

The monastic establishments attached to the temple in the context of our study proved to be one of most crucial arenas where the Śaivite ideology which was dominantly represented by the Kālāmukha creed of Śaivism developed. It began to thrive and became one of the most formidable forces responsible for the spread of the Śaiva cult during the period under study. Traditionally, 4 groups of the followers of the doctrine of Pāśupati (Śiva) have been enumerated and they are the Kāpālas, Kālāmukhas, Pāśupatas and Śaivas.[103] We have significant indications of their presence, in some form or the other, in the inscriptions of the area of under study. It is from among these followers of Śiva that we get introduced to a powerful section of society, who, as the priests to various Śaivite temple institutions begin to command considerable social and political status while symbolizing and performing worship in the temples. It is pertinent to note here that in the area under study we can clearly discern considerable sub-regional variation in the growth and spread of the monastic Śaivite movement. In sub-region A during the 11th century A.D. we have indications of the construction of *maṭhas* attached to the Śivālayas this is exemplified in one of the instances recorded in the descriptions given by us above. Importantly the couple of references made to the Kālāmukha priests in this sub-region has strong indications of a well established monastic movement of Śaivism at least by the latter half of the 11th century A.D. as we find that these Śaivite priests are clearly stated to have belonged to the Kālāmukha/Pāśupata sect. Further, one of them, Prabhu Mārasingha (IVA, vii, 6) even emerges as the donor while the other, Tatpuruṣa Paṇḍita (IVA, vii, 10) is referred to as the trustee of the grants made by the main ruler. It is of some significance to note here that in the context of the description of the Kālāmukha priests, they have been metaphorically eulogized as representing the sun (light) in the darkness spread by the Buddhists *(Bauddhā-dhvanta-bhānave).*[104] At this stage we do not get any clear cut idea of the social base of their patronage but the single reference made to one of the priests in the context of the grants made by the main rulers, alludes to the initiative taken by these rulers in patronizing Kālāmukha Śaivism.

A considered expansion in the social base of patronage extended to the Kālāmukha priests can be well attested in the context of the 12th century A.D. in sub-region A. References to them as trustees of grants made by such varied sections in the society ranging from the local functionaries to professional groups like the oil mongers. It is, however pertinent to note here, that we do not come across any direct reference whatsoever to their Kālāmukha leanings or affiliations. In fact, we have to deduce this through the suffixes attached to this names of priests such as *rāśi* to Amritarāsi Paṇḍita (IVA, vii, 21). Of particular interest in the mention of Śaivite priests of this period is one Vīradāsa (IVA, vii, 22) who has been entrusted with several grants made by the supra local chief to the God Vīra Bayseśvara in A.D. 1184. This priest was supposed to have received the grants on behalf of the *gaṇas* for maintaining the *gaṇa-maṭha.* As the context of their description strongly suggests, the *gaṇas* can be considered to have belonged to the new school of Śaivism and are eulogized as the establishers of the glory of the God Śiva by destroying the Buddhist and Jaina creeds at various places specified in the record wherein the Jaina temples were supposed to have been demolished and the Śiva liṅgas set up at those places.[105] On the basis of the limited evidences available with us we cannot, however, surmise that the Kālāmukha school had a firm and broad base in this sub-region of our study even towards the end of the 12th century A.D. But the evidence of the *gaṇa maṭha* testifies to the fact that there did exist extremely localized forms of Śaivism which often represented the local belief systems projected through dominant cult of Śiva.

On the other hand, the Śaivite priests in the context of sub-region B emerge on a significant scale as weilding considerable popularity amongst a wide section of society. In the first half of the 11th century A.D. we come across certain powerful Śaivite priests as is suggested in particular by the names Bhāvaśivadeva and Nāgasvāmi (IVB, vii, 33) who are greatly eulogized for their position as the heads of several Śaivite temples located at various different places. They even emerge as early as A.D. 1028, as donors of a series of gifts such as cash, gold and land for the purposes of charity. In fact, one of the priests among these, namely, Bhāvaśivadeva, is praised as the spiritual ruler of several villages and so on.[106] It is pertinent to note in this context that none of these priests are directly described as belonging to the Kālāmukha sect of Śaivism. The social base of patronage was also extremely limited in the first half of the 11th century A.D. as we find only a handful references to the social groups such as members of the main ruling family chiefs (IVB, iv, 37), a local potentate (IVB, iv, 29) and the collective group of *gāvuṇḍas* led by the *manneya* of Sinda family (IVB, iv, 27) who figure prominently as patrons. It is pertinent to underscore in this regard that except for the above mentioned Śaiva priests who figure as donors, we find that a majority of them, however, figure on a low key, invariably as trustees to the grants made to the temples. By the second half of the 11th century A.D. one can, however, discern a significant change in the references made to various trustees to the Śaiva temples. First of all one finds that the suffix *'paṇḍita'* begins to be associated with the names of these priests very commonly as can be seen from the list of names charted out by us (IVB, vii, 41-65). Secondly, the social base of their patronage increases substantially as these priests emerge invariably as the trustees to the grants made by such a wide social strata as the local potentates, mercantile guilds, local functionaries, such as *suṅkavergaḍe, pergaḍe* and we also have a few instances of the main ruling family chiefs. At this stage of their mention we importantly come across explicit mention of the Kālāmukha sectarian activities performed by these priest. Further, the context of their mention, establishes their close association with the Śaiva temples and as observers of certain Yōgic practices such as *yama* (restraints), *niyama* (discipline), *svādhyāya* (repetition of the scriptures to one's self), *prāṇāyāma* (controls of respiration) and so on.[107] By the beginning of the 12th century A.D. several significant changes can be gauged in the content and nature of references made to the priests/trustees of the Śaiva temples. In the first half of the 12th century A.D. one sees that there is a distinct growth in the number of references to them as it nearly doubles up when compared to their number in the latter half of the 11th century A.D. We have 8 instances of their mention at this time (IVB, vii, 41, 42, 43, 47, 48, 51, 55, 65), whereas during the first half of 12th century A.D., we come across nearly 14 instances of references made to these priests (IVB, vii, 69, 70, 73, 74, 78, 81, 82, 85, 87, 90, 93, 94, 95, 96). Secondly, there is a significant change in the nature of their references too, as now we find various Śaiva priests referred to through different titles conferred on them which on the one hand, are indicative of the hierarchical relationships established between them and on the other, significantly attest to the fact that they begin to be increasingly recognized in terms of their position held in the temple establishments perse. Thus, we have the mention of such titles as *sthānāchārya, āchārya, guru* and *rājaguru.* Obviously, the last of these terms signifies the close association of these priests with the ruling chiefs of the period of study which must have accorded them a status superior to those functioning merely as temple trustees represented by the first two titles. Further, the social base of their patronage can also be seen significantly expanded with a few instances of the local potentates and several references to such local and intermediary functionaries as the *gāvuṇḍas, heggaḍe, mahāpradhāna, daṇḍanāyaka* and the merchant guilds. We can discern in these intances an increase in the local base of social patronage. It is, however, in the second half of the 12th century A.D. that we begin to get explicit references to the Kālāmukha sect of Śaivite priests who seem to have made considerable in roads by this phase into the social, economic, political and of course, the ideological milieu. The lineage affiliations of the priests of the Śaiva temple begin to be clearly and profusely stated in this period. Thus, in an inscription of A.D. 1179, Gurubhaktadeva of Kallamaṭha is described as belonging to the practice of the Parvatāvali (mountain school) of the Kālāmukhas,[108] while Siddhānti Kāleśvara, the *rājaguru,* of several Sinda chiefs in A.D. 1178, is described as the king of monks among the Kālāmukha teachers of Nagareśvara of Suṇḍi and so on.[109] Along with the continuation in the patronage of the above described social groups, we have now the significant addition of the artisanal groups in the latter half of the 12th century A.D. who also show their affiliation to these sects. On the whole, during this period, the absence in the mention of the main ruling family chiefs as patrons is a significant pointer towards the increase in the patronage at local levels and of the increase in politico-economic power of the Śaivite priests representing the Śaivite ideology.

It is ultimately in the context of sub-region C that one finds the Kālāmukha sect of the Śaivites emerge on a scale and in a state of maturity right as early as the middle of the 11th century A.D. This is attested by the epigraphic evidence available from this period onwards. According to Rajendra Prasad, as early as A.D. 713, in an inscription pertaining to Alampur, located in sub-region C of our study, we begin to get evidence for the establishment of a *maṭha* along with the Śiva temple.[110] Further, an early 10th century A.D. record from Pragaturu, in the environs of Alampur there is a record of gifts of God Lakulīsa, thereby confirming the prominence enjoyed by the Pāśupata cult in this area from a much earlier period,[111] when compared to sub-regions A and B. In fact, high sounding titles such as a *mahāsthānadhipati* that the Kālāmukha priests of this sub-region begin to claim as early as A.D. 1057, establishes their superiority over their counterparts in sub-region A and B. We see in the inscriptional sources of our study, that the *mahāsthānādhipatis* representing the headship of chiefly the temple of God Brahmeśvara of Alampur were extensively patronized by members of the main ruling family. The supra-local chiefs however figure in a majority followed by the mercantile groups and the local functionaries in a couple of instances. The economic and political power wielded by these temple trustees can be seen in their emergence as donors of land[112] through their claims made to the status of direct subordinates of the main rulers[113] in the inscriptional sources of our study. It is interesting to note in the sources of this sub-region that the description of the main ruling family normally begins after the allusion to the spiritual *(rājyam daṇḍu)* sway of the *mahāsthānādhipati.*[114] References to the sectarian affiliations of these priests are also made through the use of high sounding terminology. Thus, in an inscription of A.D. 1069, one Sureśvara Paṇḍita, disciple of Gaṅgarāśi Bhaṭṭāraka, *āchārya* of the God Brahmeśvara of Mosagi, bears among other titles, the titles of Kālāmukha-*samaya saroja-haṁsa* (the royal swan swimming in the lake of Kālāmukha doctrine) and *Lakula siddhānta nayyāyika-naḷini-divākara* (the son lotus of *naiyyayikas* of the *Lakulisa* doctrine). His *guru* is said to be Mallikārjunadeva *darśana-kāraṇa puruṣa* or, the person specially born to create the *darśana* of God Mallikārjuna.[115] In this instance one whole village was granted by the main ruler for the maintenance of the *satra* and the students in the school attached to this temple. In an undated inscription from the Alampur area, roughly corresponding to the 11th century A.D. we have a significant reference to the house of Kālāmukha ascetics *(Kālāmukha tapodhana satrakka)* located in the Siddha Someśvara monastery *(maṭha)* of Alampur which was granted nearly 400 *mattars* of land by the supra local chief.[116]

It has aptly been stated in the context of the above described rise and proliferation of monastic organizations, and the ideological hold exercised by these institutions, that these in effect, "represented the second institutional base for Śaivism and through them all extreme forms and non-conformist elements were integrated into temple organizations and hence as part of social organization."[117] Importantly, the rise of these priestly elements as constituting a significant element of the dominant social strata during this period emerges as peculiar to the socio-economic and political milieu of the early medieval context. The suffixes attached to the names of various Kālāmukha priests, such as *paṇḍita, āchārya* and so on are largely suggestive of the ostensible claims made by them to the *brāhmaṇa varṇa* though this is nowhere explicity stated. In fact even in the contextual references made to these priests they are nowhere explicity stated as belonging to the *brāhmaṇa* social category as is normally done to describe several individual donees that figure in the inscriptional sources of the 11th century A.D. In this regard we have an interesting reference from an early 11th century A.D. inscription, dated to A.D. 1028, wherein mention is made of one Śaiva priest Bhāvaśivadeva who emerges as a very powerful personage having his religious sway over several villages and towns. At this early stage he is nowhere referred to as a *brāhmaṇa.* On the other hand, in the same record we are introduced to one Nāgasvāmi, who is stated to be his disciple and it is pertinent to note here that the latter is eulogized here as the *brāhmaṇa sarvadhammādhikari.*[118] This clearly attests to the strong possibility of these Śaiva priests to have originally represented the priesthood of local cult centres and might have been brought into the main stream of Brahmanical social set up and thereby their close relationship to the *brāhmaṇas* at a later stage. This social change was closely related to the conversion of local cult centres or sports where there was a tree or, pillar within an enclosure and which probably had served as a place of worship before its transformation into a shrine for Śaiva or, Vaiṣṇava worship, more often the former.[119] It is significant to note at this juncture that we do not, however come across any instance of the actual performance of worship by these priests in the temples but they were closely associated with this ideology which emanated from them and enabled them to act initially as managers of the grants made to the temples. Later, their growth into powerful religious personalities enabled them to get established as the *rājagurus* of various ruling chiefs (at the local and supra local levels). Both these above factors had significant implications for the crytallization of the Kālāmukha creed of Śaivism as a potent force subsuming within its fold several local forms of worship. In this sense, these priests designated as *sthānapatis, āchāryas* and *mahāsthānādhipatis,* emerge as representing a distinct social class with well established hierarchical relationships which had their socio-economic and political power rooted in the religious hold that they exercised as a part of the temple institutions. In the inscriptional sources of the period of study, their economic and political role gets well projected as these groups emerge more as the trustees, donors and donees of various grants than merely in terms of upholding a religious ideology. Thus in an inscriptional dated to A.D. 1055 from sub-region C, Someśvararāsi Bhaṭṭāraka, the *mahāsthānādhipati* of the temple of God Brahmeśvara along with his attendants, made a grant of land.[120] As early as A.D. 1014, we come across an interesting reference to the sale of some land by the *sthānāchāryas* of the temple of Jeḍeya Śankara in the context of sub-region B.[121] In sub-region A in an inscriptional dated to A.D. 1100, an *āchārya* of the temple of God Siddeśvara emerges as the donor of some land to a tank.[122] In certain unusual instances these priests have even been described with attributes of rulers. Thus in an inscription dated A.D. 1077, one Netraśva Paṇḍita, incharge of the temple of Kīrti Someśvara is described as skilled in the manifold lore of weapons and conversant with the intricacies of diplomacy. His *guru* Tatpuruṣarāśi is praised as being ably formidable to handle the hostile forces, and a subduer of the pride of the arms of the enemy, supreme in adventure and so on.[123] In another instance of a similar kind in A.D. 1079, we have reference to one Tatpuruṣa Śivachintāyaka who is described as the *rājagurudeva,* the preceptor of the king and who is also described as being supreme in adventure (*sāhasottuṅgam*), formidable to the hostile forces and so on. In the same inscription we are further introduced to one Sūkshmśiva Bhaḷara who was entitled a *pergaḍe* and is described as God Bhairava of the dagger, shatterer of the hearts of the enemy and so on. It is pertinent to note here that he is also termed as the *aṅkakāra* (a title normally held by the generals of the army, who fight on behalf of their superiors in the battlefield) of the above described *guru.*[124] It is of some significance that both the instances cited above belong to the eastern part of sub-region B which emerges as a newly settled region during the period of our study.

The militant nature of the religious ideology is further borne out by the fact that we come across quite a few references in the sources of our study to their avowed hatred for the Buddhist and the Jaina sects.[125] Thus in an inscription dated to A.D. 1184 we have reference to one Vīra-Dāsa, who emerges as the trustee to the temple of God Vīra Baysesvara and is described as the head of a *gaṇa maṭha* which seems to have belonged to the new school of Śaivism. The members of this particular creed of Śaivism are described in the inscription as having established the glory of the God Śiva by destroying the Buddhist and Jaina creeds at several places specified here. After demolishing the Jaina temples, these Śaivities were supposed to have enthroned Śivalingas at those spots with supreme valour.[126] Due to the peculiar life styles adopted by these Śaiva priests which are entirely different from those of the traditional *brāhmaṇa* priests, scholars have been able to conclude upon the fact that the "Pāśupatas appear to have been typically a sectarian movement of social protest".[127] On the other hand, when we take into account the non-Brahmanic origins of these priests, there is a strong allusion to the fact that the Śaiva priests were not protestors or leaders of any dissent movement whatsoever but rather, can be seen as representing a different creed of socio-religious beliefs which was being integrated into the main stream of Brahmanism as a result of the expansion of the state society into new areas of cultivation and habitation. It is significant to note here that several Pāśupatāchāryas had suffixes normally held by the traditional *brāhmaṇas* such as *paṇḍita* and *āchārya*. Also some of their names even depict their interest in bearing close association with the Vedas as is indicated through such names as Jaṭaveda Paṇḍita, and further, the description of these priests as possessing the knowledge of tarka (logic), *Vyākaraṇa* (grammar), Kāvya (poetry)[128] and so on which are normally associated with traditional Sanskrit learning and indicate conscious attempts made by these priests to be accepted in the mainstream. In this regard attention has been drawn by R.N. Nandi towards the 10th century A.D. epigraphic evidence for the Lakulisas. This too bears out the fact that these priests looked to the Vedic *śruti* for guidance and the representation of them as incarnates of God Rudra, who is regarded as a Vedic God with due share in sacrificial offerings and this significantly points to the Vedic character of the Lakulisa sect.[129] On the other hand, the actual names of the Kālāmukha priests such as Someśvara, Mallikārjuna, Kriyāśakti, Siddheśvara and so on bear close resemblance to the names attributed to various forms of God Śiva himself. At times one even sees that priests had the name of the specific deity they were closely associated with as can be seen in the name of Siddhānti Kāleśvara who figures here as the *āchārya* of the temple of Goddess Kālika Jyeṣṭha (IV, v, vii, 116). These aspects of their description evidently provide us with crucial clues of their earlier association with various deities in their tribal form. Along with the increase in the variety of Śaivite deities one also sees an increase in the names of the Kālāmukha priests essentially representing Śaivite ideological moorings.[130] All the above discussed attributes of the Kālāmukha priests with their tribal ideological moorings on the one hand, and on the other, their attempts at associating themselves with the Brahmanical vestiges of religion exhibit a complex level of integrative mechanism under operation "in the formation of a structure which combines heterogeneous beliefs and rituals into a whole even while making or transforming specific elements dominant".[131] In the present context of our study all these led to the crystallization of Śaivite Bhakti ideology with several strands of tribal forms of worship embedded in it and expressed in the form of the names of various local cults and the deities representing them. This is known to us through the reference to some of the social groups which do not commonly figure in the inscriptional sources but which provide us with crucial clues to comprehend the operation of the processes of appropriation and integration of local cults into the brahmanical fold as can be seen from the following examples.

In the later half of the 11th century A.D. which significantly corresponds to the expansion and consolidation of the political hold of the Chālukyas of Kalyāni, we have interesting references to the different cults of Śiva which, in their various forms, are sought to be maintained and patronized by different levels of the ruling elite. We thus have in an inscription dated to A.D. 1060, reference to the construction of a temple of Śiva in the name of God Nāgeśvara by the *mahāsāmantādhipati* Nāgadeva. This chief, with the permission of the main ruler, Someśvara II, makes the grant of a village to the above temple purported to be used for the performance of worship of Śiva and the maintenance of the cult of Śiva. The trustee to this grant was the Kālāmukha priest Someśvara Paṇḍita Deva.[132] 15 years later (A.D. 1075) in the same place, we find another *mahāsāmantadhipati* ruling over the same tract (Kisukad-70) and he now claims to make grants for the maintenance of the cult of Achaleśvara to the temple of God Achaleśvara, another form of Śiva. The next year (1076 A.D.) a Pallava chief, who now claims to rule over the Kisukāḍ-70 tract emerges as patronizing the God Achaleśvara in the same inscription. It is interesting to note that it is the same Kālāmukha priest, Someśvara Paṇḍita who figures as the trustee to the temple in this case as well.[133] In the year A.D. 1075, in a different inscription at the same place, we have the main ruler himself, granting a village for the unkeep of the Pañchaliṅgadeva cult at the temple of God Pañchallṅgadeva. The same trustee figures here too but now his name is changed to Pañchalingadevayya to suit the name of the particular form of Śiva under projection. In a supplement to the same inscription we have reference to one Chākayya the *karaṇa* who makes some grant of land to the above God, now called Ayi (*pañcha*) Liṅga deva for the maintenance of the cult of Chākeśvara evidently another name of Śiva named after the patron.[134] All the above examples aptly testify to the ways in which various local cults, through the intervention of the political chiefs on the one hand, and the Kālāmukha priests on the other, begin to be transformed into translocal idioms. In such a transformation the crucial role played by the Kālāmukha priest is quite evident in the way he signifies at one and the same time, the political and ideological dimensions in the process of the appropriation of local cults. This is indicated in the above case in the way he bears the name of the main ruling family chief in the initial stages, and later gets a new name to represent the Śaivite deity patronized by the main ruler.

The association of the members of the main ruling family in patronizing the deities at Suḍi (where all the above mentioned inscriptions are located) and which becomes the capital of Kisukāḍ-70, one of the most strategically located tract of the area under study, can be seen right from the early 11th century A.D. As early as A.D. 1010 member of the Chālukyan family, namely Akkādevi, figures as ruling over this tract and by A.D. 1054, we have reference to the God Akkeśvara at Suḍi.[135] In A.D. 1075, when the main ruler established the Pañchalinga Deva temple it must have already included in it the worship of the various forms of Śiva such as Akkeśvara, Nāgeśvara, Achaleśvara and Chākeśvara which were all created at various stages. The above discussion clearly brings forth evidence to show that political processes were involved in the appropriation of various local cults and these were, in the main, initiated through the attempts at legitimation made by the newly established rulers which later led to their integration into the fold of Brahmanism as exemplified above in the case of the emergence of God Pañchalingadeva. Another effective example of the politico-ideological dimension can be seen in the rise of the Sindas of Erambarage into formidable supra local force which is depicted in the way their capital Yarambaravi was flooded with various temples of Śiva such as Siṅgeśvara, Rācheśvara, Chauṇḍeśvara, Vikrameśvara and so on. These were all named after the Sinda chiefs and existed along side other temples such as Mūlasthāna, Somanātha and several other monastic establishments as has been illustrated in an inscription dated to A.D. 1178.[136] Apart from these, examples of several names of deities we have come across significantly point to the fact that the appropriation of various cults was taking place on an active scale particularly in the context of sub-region B which had vast stretches of fertile tracts which had not witnessed the complete penetration of the state system prior to the 10th century A.D. The ground here was therefore, fertile for the spread of a new ideology that took into account the local belief system and this took the form of Kālāmukha Śaivism.

Crystallization in the process of cult appropriation can, however, be clearly discerned in the emergence of the Goddess Kālika Jyeṣṭha as the foremost deity in the Kukkanūr-30 tract during the latter half of the 12th century A.D. *i.e.,* in

A.D. 1178.[137] In fact, this is the first time that we come across the praise of the deity and area of its location in such a detailed manner. At Kukkanūr where the temple of the above Goddess is located, nine Svayambhu (self manifest) Śivalingas were supposed to have also been located with an equal number of *śaktipiṭhas*. This place is further eulogized as *Śiva-Śakti-sphūrat sampūta kshetra* (hallowed casket ever radiant with the presence of Śiva and Śakti) and is described as the most sacred place by virtue of its habitation of the great Goddesses Ambika of Ādipiṭha, Purāṇi, Chāmuṇḍi, Mahāmāya, Vasanta, Kāli. Among these the Goddess Kālika Jyeṣṭha, who is stationed in the middle, was considered pre-eminent having such Gods as Brahmeśvara, Gavareśvara, Mūleśvara and Mallikārjuna around her. Of all the Gods and Goddesses around her she is considered to be the most supreme. It is pertinent to note here that prior to this reference we are nowhere introduced to so many forms of Gods and Goddesses at a single place in such a high sounding fashion even at Kukkanūr. All these Goddesses, associated with the cult of Śakti, have been interpreted in various secondary sources, to have constituted an important aspect in the Tāntric-form of worship which became widely prevalent during the early medieval period in several tribal belts of India as whole.[138] In fact though practice of the worship of mother Goddess is supposed to have been prevalent in India from very early times but it has been suggested that its development into a formidable religious force was from the 6th century A.D. onwards and its further crystallization in the form of its literary compilations in the Brahmanical (Kālika Purāṇa, Rudrāyamāla), the Buddhist (cult of Tārādevi) and the Jaina (Yakshi cult) tradition has been attributed to have taken place between the 10th and 11th centuries A.D.[139]

These tāntric deities gained popularity in the latter half of the 12th century A.D. in the context of our study and this has wider implications for our comprehension of the politico-ideological dimensions of the spread in the rural settlements which was taking place on a significant scale during this period as has been seen by us an earlier chapter.[140] In the particular inscription under discussion dated to A.D. 1178, we have reference to the Goddess Kālika Jyeṣṭha with regard to the *mahāpūja* performed for her and the grant of a village made to it by the *adhikāri* of Beḷvola nāḍu, Dhannugi. He bore the titles of *chamūpati* and *daṇḍanātha* and gave this grant along with his family members. The projection of the image of the above Goddess, blown out of proportions in this case, can be comprehended in a better light if we take into account the wider context of the above patronage. It was around this time that the Kalāchuris of Kalyāni were trying to establish their newly acquired independent status as sovereign rulers in various parts of the Chālukyan kingdom and in this their control over sub-region B (particularly the eastern part of it) of our study, owning to its fertile locales, must have proved crucial from the point of view of its economic resources. The tract around Kukkanūr in particular, which we have already seen was renowned for its fertile red soils, was widely contested for by several rulers right from the early 11th century A.D. Under the rule of the Kalāchuris this area rose to greater focus as these rulers on the one hand, grant Kukkanūr as an *agrahāra* to several *brāhmaṇas*[141] and on the other, as we have seen above, they tried to project it as a sacred abode. Through active use of this religious ideology for legitimizing their political hold there is no doubt that the Kalāchuri rulers tried to entrench their control of this area and this can be seen through various other references to them in the latter half of the 12th century A.D. Thus, in an inscription dated to A.D. 1170, we have mention of God Svayambhu Prasanna Mallikārjuna deva who is granted a village by *daṇḍanāyaka* Tejiraja who is described as the foremost ruler of Belvola nāḍu. The above grant was probably made to mark the occasion of his accession to that position. This chief further performed the worship of Svayambhu Mallikārjuna of Kukkanūr with ablutions of 1000 jars of milk to mark the completion of the ritual of bathing the deity with 1000 jars of water. The political dimension of the importance of this elaborate ritual lay in the fact that, several local officials (*karaṇa*) participated in it,[142] Further, the performance of such elaborate religious ceremonies by the above newly appointed chiefs (one among these even belonged to Sahavāsi family from the Kāśmira region) can be clearly understood as a case in political legitimation which required, among other things, identification of the rulers as one among the local populace. The most convenient leverage in this regard can be stated to have been sought in the appropriation of local belief systems which was certainly one of the important reasons responsible for the creation of a sacred image of the Kukkanūr tract on a significant scale by the end of the 12th century A.D. [143]

The political processes involved in the appropriation of local religious symbols initiated in the main, through the attempts made by various newly established rulers at legitimization of their rule, were intricately webbed into the processes of integration/acculturation of several new social elements into the main stream of Brahmanism and the state system it supported. Both these changes were taking place at a simultaneous level at both ends of the social structure. We have a few pieces of evidence explaining the relationship of mainstream brahmanic society with groups living on its margins or completely out side it. It would suffice here to state that these processes resulted out of certain political initiatives grounded in their physiographic and socio-economic setting which we have described above. In an inscription dated to A.D. 1170, we have reference to the *āṭavikas* (forest dwellers) who are mentioned as conquered by the Kalāchuri rulers in their eulogy.[144] As a result of the legitimizing policies undertaken by the rulers these tribes had been subdued militarily and may have been gradually absorbed into the social structure. This can be deduced from another example. In an inscription dated to

A.D. 1184, we have reference to several pastoral/hunting groups such as the *Kuribagāvuṇḍagaḷu, bedarum, huḷiyajanguliya, mādagaru* and so on whose chiefs (*jāti vaggadalu*) emerge as donors of a house tax to the God Trikuta.[145] Among these, while the *kurubas* (a derivative of the Canarese term '*kuru*' meaning sheep) have been equated to mean pastoralists.[146] The term *bedar* is considered to be another term used for *boyas* and therefore are considered to represent for the most part cultivators and herdsmen.[147] The fact that all these groups have been mentioned in the inscription in the context of patrons to temple, suggests pertinently that they had begun to be slowly absorbed into the politico-ideological main stream. On the other hand, reference to these groups as totally separated from other social categories is evidence enough to prove that at this stage these tribal groups still remained on the margins of Brahmanical society. That they granted house taxes to the temple is indicative of the fact that, these social groups seem to have participated in the usual economic support of the ideological institution but their social separatedness was still marked at a distinct level. On the other hand their counterparts in the Andhra region corresponding roughly to the same period, (12th -13th centuries A.D.) namely, the *boyas/herders* have been shown to have emerged as a prominent group of patrons for the large temples of coastal Andhra.[148] The Boyas were also well known for their military might and Suvira Jaiswal draws our attention to a group of Boya *brāhmaṇnas* indicating their acculturation to brahmanical society at all levels.[149] In the context of our study, in an inscriptional of the year A.D. 1196, we have an interesting reference to God Billeśvara, who seems to have represented the interests of the Billa-300 a social group, which was led by one Halla Keta bova[150] as mentioned in this record. Billavas according to Thurston can be understood as bowmen[151] and therefore, must have been part of a large hunting groups. The contextual reference to these groups indicates that they seem to have enjoyed a certain social standing as their God Billeśvara was patronized by a wide variety of social strata particularly constituted of the mercantile groups. In a slightly earlier inscription dated to A.D. 1184, we come across an interesting reference to the term *gaṇas* who were the members of the *gaṇamaṭha* and were led by one Vīra Dasa, their spiritual head. He was the trustee to the temple of Vira-Bayseśvara to which several grants have been made by a *mahāmaṇḍaleś-vara*.[152] All these marginal social groups supported the Śaivite religious ideology but were extremely localised in form and this has some implications for their social composition. It has been suggested elsewhere that when Śiva in the form of Rudra became the deity of the forest tribes, the latter were considered as his *gaṇas*[153] and this is well attested by the epithet *vīra* added to their deity and their priest in the above context.

By furnishing the above examples we have mainly attempted to depict that there were significant movements from the marginal social groups wing on the periphery of agrarian society as a result of the complex processes of legitimation. At the higher levels of social scale also one sees over time, a significant rise in the local ruling lineages into supra local rulers weilding considerable political power over several tracts. The symbols of identity adopted by these chiefs are strongly indicative of their tribal moorings. Most prominent among the supra-local chiefs of the period of this nature were the Sinda rulers of various parts of Karnataka. In particular the Sindas of Erambarage were prominent in the context of the present study. These rulers emerge as constituting the emblem of tiger's crest (*vyāgraha lānchana*) and claim to belong to the Nāgavaṁśa.[154] The association of these chiefs with various animal figures is indicative of their tribal origins. The tribal groups are generally considered to have various names of trees or animals as totemic symbols to differentiate one tribe from the other.[155] Another interesting reference in this regard is furnished in the rise of the Bappura family chiefs in an inscription dated to A.D. 1114. In this record one Dāḍiga of the Bappura family is referred to as the son of Guṇḍa of the Bali *vaṁśa* and appears to have held hereditary claims over the Kisukāḍ tract. It is interesting to note that these chiefs trace their origins to the birth of valiant men from the caverns of mount Kishkindha and had on their family banner the device of an ape.[156] While the claims made by these chiefs to an origin from mount Kishkindha and their genealogy traced to Bali *vaṁśa* are attempts made fictitiously to rise their status by claiming an antiquarian origin, the reality lies in their use of their totemic symbols of animals and it is this that strongly alludes to their origin from an earlier tribal status. R.N. Nandi has drawn our attention to the fact the Vaiḍumbas, who figure frequently in the inscriptional sources of sub-region C in the context of our study, appear to have been originally a totemic tribe. In this context the term Vaiḍumba may be understood as meaning a tribe which considered the *uḍumbura* tree as its totem. These rulers have, according to the author, tried to raise their social position by marrying their daughters into older and more respectable families.[157] Thus, at the higher level of the social structure crystallization of several ruling lineages such as the above has a significant bearing on our comprehension of the processes of acculturation resulting in the politico-ideological aspects of a dominant state system.

It is pertinent to underscore at this juncture that in the context of the present study we do not come across the rise of a regional tradition as has been witnessed in the case of Orissa where the rulers effectively made use of the autotchonous tutelary deities which eventually "underwent a process of Hinduization, the intensity and direction of which usually was directly influenced by the parallel rise of the sub-regional political authority from tribal chieftain ship to Hindu Kingship".[158] In fact, as Kulke has argued it is the cult of Jagannath at Puri, itself an intricate blending of tribal and Brahmanical traditions,[159] that provides an excellent example of the symbiotic relationship established between the political authority and the ritual symbols leading, at every stage, in the simultaneous rise of both the elements as a result of the conscious efforts made by the royal power. The culmination of such a process was then translated into the "emergence of Jagannatha as the *rāṣtradevata* of Orissa par excellence who is said to be "indirectly linked with the deities at sub-regional power".[160] This linkage was similar to what one sees in a political set up. In the present study as has been seen in the case of Sindas of Erambarage the local chieftains could rise only to the level of a supra local power. The nature and forms of legitimation adopted by various rulers (including the main rulers) limited and peculiar to the area under study wherein the growth in the agrarian settlements and the socio-economic power was still in an incipient stage and therefore, local elites during this period were just beginning to emerge. Therefore, this region during the period of study is marked by the strong influence of outside political powers such as the Chālukyas of Kalyāni, Kalāchuris, Yādavas of Devagiri, Hoysalas and so on. In the efforts made by these rulers to carve for themselves productive zones of surplus appropriation, particularly sub-region B of the area under study which was marked by riverine fertile tracts, emerges as a zone of legitimation which sees the rise of several locally entrenched families at various local and supra local levels. It is in fact, these chiefs who had actively participated in the temple building and had developed their patronage networks.

In this regard the role these chiefs exercised was even different form the type of ritual hold that the Chola rulers had exercised over the Kaveri delta through the transactional network[161] created by the construction of the huge temple complexes such as the Brihadiśvara temple at Tanjore. The area under study, on the contrary, essentially witnessed a spurt of building minor temples, each with its local deity and patronage from local elites which prolifically dotted the map of the expanding agrarian base that, in turn was the result of chiefly local initiative.[162] While differentiating between the functions performed by the minor and the major temples, Cynthia Talbot concludes in the context of her study of the Kākatiya period, that the major temple had an edge over the minor ones as the former served as a significant channel for establishing linkages between various types of people. The minor ones, on the other hand, extracted surplus from only a small segment of society of the interior regions and redistributed it among a limited sector.[163] The significance and importance of the role played by the minor temple in establishing local level linkages, in our opinion proved to be a necessary step in the development of linkages on a larger spatial context and this cannot be sidelined. As has been observed in our case study, the minor temple afforded an institutional focus for the hitherto unpenetrated areas and enabled its people to come together and thus form important clusters of settlements of smaller spatial units. They therefore, kept their local identity and, at the same time, integrated with those aspects of Brahmanical Hinduism which suited them most. By projecting the significant role played by the minor temple and the importance attached in its rise in the initiative taken by the local rulers, one is, however, not suggesting here that there were no attempts made by the main ruling family chiefs in the patronage network of the temple institutions in the area of under study. We have seen in this regard that the main rulers did participate at an active level in patronizing the temple institutions largely by giving gifts on a large scale, whereas the construction of the temples remained essentially a local phenomenon. There were very few exceptions to the above trends and this could have been basically due to the fact that the area under study with its tremendous potential for growth in the agarian surplus was marked by a locally entrenched powerful hereditary elite whose support the main rulers required in maintaining their power base in these localities. In order to receive their ideological support they participated more in an indirect way in the gift giving activities of the local temples which were sometimes even named after the main rulers.

On the other hand, the members of the main ruling family played a much more explict and active role in creating the *agrahāra* settlements and patronizing the Vedic learning on a considerable scale. It was in fact in the patronage extended to the temples, firstly by the members of the main ruling family and then, by the *mahājanas/brahmaṇa* functionaries that we get active evidences of the existence of Vedic learning and religion during this period. Thus, in an inscription dated to A.D. 1097, the queen of the main ruling family can be seen granting some land for the purpose of reciting the *Rgveda Khaṇḍika* and *Śāstra Khaṇḍika* (IVA, vi, 12) in sub-region A. It is, however, in the context of sub-region B that we come across a maximum number of references to the patronage extended by the members of the main ruling family towards Vedic learning which can in the first place, be explicitly seen in the creation of *agrahāra* settlements. These are invariably praised for the Vedic knowledge of the residents of the place and over time, the settlements themselves begin to be identified as the abodes of such knowledge. Thus, in an inscription dated to A.D. 1136, we have reference to 20 *mahājanas* of Modanūr who are praised for their knowledge in sacred lore, religious activities, such as the performance of the *Agnisthoma* and other Vedic sacrifices and also for their worship of the Traipuruṣas.[164] On the other hand, in one of its numerous examples, the *agrahāra* of Kukkanūr is eulogized for its natural beauty and its learned inhabitants in Vedas and Vedic sacrifices *(vedādhyariṁ yajñadikshi tariṁ śāstrapurāṇa takka vidarim).*[165] We further have several instances of the performance of Vedic sacrifices by the chiefs of main ruling family. Among these, the performance of *Brahmāṇḍa Kratu* (IVB, vi, 26) which was followed by the accession of the Chālukyas to independent power. The performance of *kōṭi hōma* (IVB, vi, 63) and *Pañchalaṅgala Kratu* (IVB, vi, 64) sacrifices are attributed to the Chālukya Vikramāditya VI. It is pertinent to note here that such sacrifices normally followed grants of villages by the main rulers to individual *brāhmaṇa* personages who performed these sacrifices and then these granted villages were converted into *agrahāra* settlements by granting the same to several *brāhmaṇas* who lived in those settlements. Therefore, the politico-economic dimensions of these ceremonies can be clearly discerned. The performance of these sacrifices come to us from examples located mainly in the eastern part of the sub-region B which constituted the Raichur Doab and which was just beginning to emerge as an actively settled zone. According to Nandi, the above mentioned *dāna* rituals performed by *brāhmaṇas* during the early medieval period seem to confirm the growing awareness of the *brāhmaṇas* on the importance of generating agricultural surplus which was their chief source of livelihood.[166] This is particularly highlighted by the performance of the *Pañchalaṅgalaka* sacrifice which has been considered to be one of the sixteen elaborate *mahādānas* in the *Matsya Purāṇa.* What is of significance to note here is the fact that among the gifts given on the performance of this sacrifice, five sets of wooden ploughs, five pairs of oxen and five plough shares, figure prominently along with 100 *nivaratanas* of cultivable land and villages full of grains.[167] Simultaneously on ideological grounds, the *dāna* rituals were to perform the function of purification and raising the status of the individual[168] who sponsored the sacrifice. Herein lies the role of *dharma* as a purely transcendent authority which was said to be based on supra human revelation of the Veda, the *Śruti.* The transcendence of the Veda was thus guaranteed by putting it rigorously apart from society, out of reach of common man, who was not even supposed to know it.[169] Thus the functional nature of these rituals lay chiefly in elevating the status of the rulers in the eyes of the common people.

The claims made by the ruling chiefs in the context of this study to the *varṇa* status, namely to that of the *kshatriya varṇa* can also be seen in the above light.[170] Thus, on the one hand, patronage extended by the main ruling family chiefs towards the spread of Vedic sacrifices and Vedic learning through a grant of villages and land represented a crucial level in the exhibition of political authority. In the same vein, the imprecatory passages appended to the inscriptions at the end of the text, which normally threaten the violator of the grants, with hell and all sorts of sins and the upholders of the grants with the reward of heaven, can be considered to depict the use of ideology in exercising authority over a large section of population as a means to ensure the safety of grants made by the dominant social groups. In this context Sharma writes, "one of the main reasons why the illusion of hell and heaven was developed very much in early medieval times seems to have been to protect the landed property of the *brāhmaṇas* and others against encroachments by their equally entrenched rivals and also by the mass of the peasantry".[171]

On the other hand, the use of temple institutions to gain legitimacy and appeal to the masses through the appropriation of various cults as has been seen above led to the crystallization of the *bhakti* ideology during this period. This constituted a different level in the attempts at legitimation by the ruling groups. In fact, all the above processes both patronage to the Vedic learning (on a smaller scale) and the use of the *bhakti* medium, to spread Purāṇic Hinduism were definitely not operating on two separate and autonomous levels. On the contrary, these basically indicate the complex processes through which both the local and the dominant (Vedic) ideological institutions were being used by the ruling groups in gaining legitimacy during this formative phase of the formation of regional kingdom and states. The ruling groups during this period were creating a platform for the fusion of these two systems of ideology to evolve into a regional cultural matrix which operated at various levels of society. It was need so as to encapsulate the tribal groups into this structure while maintaining the hold of the powerful landed elites simultaneously. Such a combination of both strands in ideological dimension of control can be seen operating in various areas of popular appeal. Though the temple provided the institutional base to the *bhakti* cult of Śaivism which was operating through the monastic establishments attached to them on the one hand, and on the other, as can be seen in the charts appended to the chapter, these religious institutions were also, in several cases, patronized for the teaching of Vedic knowledge and the performance of Vedic sacrifices, (IVB, vi, 52, 60, 77). In an inscription dated to A.D. 1088 we have very interesting reference to the provision made for the teaching of *Vedas* on the one hand, and on the other, to the recitation of the Śivadharma *Purāṇa* in the presence of God at the same temple.[172] Another platform used by the rulers in particular to display such a fusion of ideological beliefs can be seen in the construction of the genealogical affiliations claiming the origins of the ruling chiefs from the remote past. The genealogical constructs of the Chālukyas of Kalyāni provide one of the typical examples in this direction. In an inscription of A.D. 1112, the Chālukyas claim their descent from both, the solar and the lunar race, the origins of which can be traced back to the time of Manu Svayambhu of the remote past. At the same time, their claims to be incarnates of the boar form of Viṣṇu the Purāṇic God[173] clearly establishes a case of ideological fusion. The medium of expression of all these thoughts, namely the language of the inscriptions, wherein both the Kannaḍa and the Sanskrit script were used simultaneously provided yet another popular platform for the operation of articulating both the pan-Indian ideological moorings in the form of Vedic learning and the local traditions and beliefs that were in the process of being incorporated to Purāṇic Hinduism.

Thus the tremendous potential exhibited by the Brahmanical temple as an institutional base for the varied strands of ideological forces witnessed in the above discussion, enabled it to gear up a wide spectrum of social support and emerge as a mediating space between the forces seeking legitimation and those being legitimized. In such a process, both the local belief systems and the Vedic rituals were being effectively made use of as forces of integration. While the former helped in acculturating the local populace by appropriating their religious cults, the latter helped in creating an aura of superiority required to exhibit the ability of the legitimizer to maintain dominance. It is in these intertwined processes of integration that we have all the crucial ingredients for the shaping of a regional cultural matrix marked by a "movement from within following from the operation of several major historical/societal processes in a regional context"[174] which we have discerned in the above discussion.

REFERENCES

1. The role of the temple is often exaggerated to imply that it was the sole initiator of change in the locality. However, our intention is here to assess its role as a mediator between the religious and secular space of the productive areas that saw its rise in the first place.
2. All these have been considered the ideological dimensions of society during the early medieval period and have been identified on a pan Indian scale. For example B.D. Chattopadhyaya, *The Making of Early Medieval India,* OUP, Delhi, 1994, pp. 28-34. Also see R.S. Sharma *'Problems of Peasant Protest in Early Medieval India', Social Scientist,* 16, 9, September, 1988, pp. 13-15 who suggests crucial areas for our comprehension of various forms of the dominant ideological strands that were under operation during the early medieval period for various regions of India. We do not, however agree that ideological forces should be considered only as the products of the given socio-economic base. We have on the other hand attempted to argue that the economic base itself is relational to change due to the socio political and ideological forces under operation which are expressed through the formation of kin groups, marital relations within them, wars fought by them, forms of legitimation adopted by them and so on. All these helped in unleashing forces of a religious and political dimension which then have a very significant impact on defining the nature of socio-economic change.
3. S. Settar, 'Roots, Relations and Relevance : the Chalukyan Backdrop', in Mulk Raj Anand (ed.), *Marg,* XXII, 1, 1979, p. 11.
4. K.A.N. Sastri, *A History of South India,* Oxford University Press, Madras, 1966 (4th ed.), p. 450.
5. S. Settar, *op. cit.,* 1979, p. 9.
6. *Ibid.,* p. 10. The author further goes on to state that while the Buddhist structures were located prolifically along the east and west coasts of the Deccan, their influence in the mid-Deccan, *i.e.,* in the present Karnataka was at the best nominal and peripheral. The latter area including the whole of southern peninsula was shared by the Jains and Hindus to a considerable extent. See *ibid.,* p. 22.

7. *Ibid.*, pp. 9-10.
8. *Ibid.*, p. 27.
9. Summarised from R.N. Nandi, *Religious Institutions and Cults in the Deccan* (A.D. 600-A.D. 1000), Motilal Banarasidas, Delhi, 1973, p. 1.
10. *Ibid.*, pp. 3-4.
11. K.A.N. Sastri, *op. cit.*, 1966, p. 455.
12. R.N. Nandi, *op. cit.*, 1973, p. 2.
13. *Ibid.*, pp. 2-4.
14. Devangana Desai, 'Art Under Feudalism in India (A.D. 500-1300)', *IHR*, I, 1974, p. 13.
15. K.A.N. Sastri, *op. cit.*, 1966, p. 468-471. According to the author the maturity of Chola architecture found expression in the two magnificient temples of Gangaikonda-colapuram and Tanjore. Of these, the superb Śiva temple of Tanjore, the largest and the tallest of all Indian temples, is considered to be a masterpiece constituting a high water mark of South Indian architecture (p. 468). The credit for bridging the transition from rock architecture to structural stone temples in the South has been attributed to the Pallava rulers by the author. (p. 457.)
16. R. Champakalakshmi, 'Urbanization in South India : The Role of Ideology and Polity', Presidential Address, Section I, Ancient India, *PIHC*, 47th Session, Srinagar, 1986, p. 40.
17. Alladi Vaidehi Krishnamurthry, *Social and Economic Conditions in Eastern Deccan* (A.D. 1000-A.D. 1250), Madras, 1970, pp. 230-239. The author has furnished here a long list of the names of temples which extended from the Ganjam district in north down to the frontiers of Guntur and Nellore in the south.
18. Raichur District, *Census of India*, Series-9, Karnataka, 1981, p. 16.
19. *Ibid.*, p. 16.
20. Raghavendra Rao, 'South Indian Temples', *QJMS, XXIII*, 1, July, 1932, p. 11.
21. Dharwar District, *Census of India*, Series-9, Karnataka, 1981, p. 21.
22. *Ibid.*, p. 22.
23. Bijapur District, *Gazetteer of India* (Mysore State), Bangalore, 1966, p. 480.
24. *Ibid.*, pp. 483-484.
25. *Ibid.*, pp. 514-515.
26. B. Rajendra Prasad, *Chalukyan Temples of Andhradesa*, Abhinav Publications, New Delhi, 1983, p. 10.
27. N. Ramesan, *Temples and Legends of Andhra Pradesh*, Bharatiya Vidya Bhavan, Bombay, 1962, p. 32.
28. *Ibid.*, p. 33-35.
29. S. Settar, *op. cit.*, 1979, p. 17.
30. We have made a detailed analysis of the social context of the patronage in chapter III of the book on *'Social Context'*, see pp. 233-235.

31. Nature of grants to temples has been extensively dealt with in chapter IV of the book on 'Economic context' see pp. 313-321.
32. K. Ismail, *Karnataka Temples : Their Role in Socio-Economic Life,* Sundeep Prakashan, Delhi, 1984, pp. 104-107.
33. Kesavan Veluthat, 'Religious Symbols in Political Legitimation : The Case of Early Medieval South India,' *Social Scientist,* 21, 1-2, January-February, p. 25.
34. R.N. Nandi, *Social Roots of Religion in Ancient India,* K.P. Bagchi and Company, New Delhi, 1986, p. 87.
35. *Ibid.,* pp. 90-91.
36. Widespread popularity of Vaiṣṇavism in various other transformed forms has however, been shown to have gained considerable ground in the post 13th century A.D. era for different regions of the Deccan plateau, such as Maharashtra (K.A.N. Sastri, *op. cit.,* 1966, p. 432) and the coastal Andhra, A.V. Krishnamurthy, *op. cit.,* 19, p. 215.
37. K.A.N. Sastri, *op. cit.,* 1966, p. 435.
38. *Ibid.,* p. 435.
39. The spatial dimension of the temple establishments has been discussed in chapter V of the book on 'Spatial Context' see, pp. 476-488.
40. An increasing participation of the social groups in the temple patronage has been discussed in chapter III of the book on 'Social Context' see. pp. 233-235.
41. 'Inscriptions of Sudi', F., *EI,* XV, pp. 85-94.
42. 'A Stone Inscription of the Sinda Family at Bhairanmatti', *EI,* Vol. III, pp. 230-236.
43. 'Inscriptions of Sudi', D, *EI,* XV, pp. 77-80.
44. 'Inscriptions of Sudi', H, *EI,* XV, pp. 96-100.
45. 'Inscription no. 9', *KI, II,* pp. 25-28.
46. 'Inscription no. 152', *SII, XI,* pp. 189-191.
47. 'Inscription no. 155', *SII, XI,* pp. 194-197.
48. P.B. Desai, *Jainism in South India and Some Jaina Epigraphs,* Sholapur, 1957, pp. 104-109 and pp. 200-205.
49. 'Daddala Inscription', *EI, XXXVII,* pp. 113-116.
50. K.A.N. Sastri, *op. cit.,* 1966, p. 423.
51. 'Inscription no. 56', *SII, XV,* pp. 73-74.
52. Romila Thapar, *'Cultural Transaction and Early India : Tradition and Patronage,* I.H. Qureshi Memorial Lectures, Delhi, 1987, p. 20.
53. In the organized growth of the Saivite ideology influence of Jainism which was a powerful monastic religion has been considered to be quite formidable. See, R.N. Nandi *op. cit.,* 1973, pp. 76-77. This becomes all the more significant when we take into account the widespread construction of the Jaina monastic establishments in the western part of the lower Deccan in the period between the 4th-6th centuries A.D. under the western Gangas. See, Settar, *op. cit.,* 1979, p. 26.
54. R.N. Nandi, *op. cit.,* 1973, pp. 77. One may clearly discern the difference between the monastic establishment of Saivism from its earlier phase (8th-9th centuries A.D.)

wherein the monasteries were a integral part of the temple building itself whereas by the 10th-11th centuries A.D. seperate buildings began to be constructed for the monks to reside (p. 81).

55. R.N. Nandi, *op. cit.,* 1986, p. 96.
56. R.N. Nandi, *op. cit.,* 1973, p. 83.
57. *Ibid.,* p. 83.
58. Champakalakshmi, 'Religion and Social Change in Tamilnadu', in N.N. Bhattacharya (ed.), *Medieval Bhakti Movements in India* (Sri Caitanya Quincentenary Commemoration Volume), New Delhi, 1989, p. 168.
59. Van Troy, 'The Radical Social Protest of the Pāśupatas', *Indica,* 27, 1-2, March, 1990, p. 1. The author has quoted here various Pasupata practices such as bathing with ashes and sleeping on them and other such practices which suggest that brahmanical layers of society in the Gupta period were strongly opposed to them, and their social challenge (p. 2). According to Troy while the prevalence of the Pasupata doctrine of Saivism in the Deccan and South India has been identified from the 8th century A.D. onwards its origins in the North and Central India have been traced back to the inscriptional evidences available there from the 4th century A.D. onwards.
60. P.B. Desai, 'Tantric Cult in Epigraphs', *JOR,* XIX, iv, Madras, 1952, p. 285.
61. B. Rajendra Prasad, *op. cit.,* 1983, p. 9.
62. R.S. Sharma, 'Material Milieu of Tantricism', in D.N. Jha (ed.), *Feudal Social Formations in Early India,* Chanakya Publications, Delhi, 1987, p. 377.
63. This is best exemplified in the work of K.A.N. Sastri, *op. cit.,* 1966, pp. 433-434, wherein he talks in clear terms of a strong 'Hindu revival' as against the earlier Buddhist and Jaina dominance.
64. M.G.S. Narayanan and Kesavan Veluthat, 'Bhakti Movement in South India', in D.N. Jha (ed.), *Feudal Social Formation sin Early India,* Chanakya Publications, Delhi, 1987, p. 366.
65. *Ibid.,* p. 367.
66. R. Champakalakshmi, *op. cit.,* 1989, p. 168.
67. We have discussed this in the chapter III of the book on 'Social Context', see. pp. 238-239.
68. B.D. Chattopadhyaya, *op. cit.,* 1994, p. 28.
69. K. Ismail, *op. cit.,* 1984, p. 77.
70. D.C. Sircar, *Indian Epigraphical Glossary,* Delhi, 1966, p. 276.
71. K. Ismail, *op. cit.,* 1984, p. 77.
72. 'Inscription no. 85', *SII,* XI, pp. 79-82.
73. 'Inscription no. 1', *SII,* XI, pp. 1-2.
74. 'Inscription no. 38', *APGAS,* 3, pp. 126-127.
75. See pp. 556-557.
76. 'Inscription of Sudi', F, *EI,* XV, pp. 85-94.

77. We have referred to these aspects in an earlier chapter. See chapter III of the book on 'Social Context', pp. 158-164.
78. Transcript, *A.R.* no. B 342 of 1957-58.
79. 'Inscription of Sudi', H, *EI,* XV, pp. 96-100.
80. 'Inscription no. 9', *KI,* II, pp. 25-28.
81. 'Inscription at Yewur', *EI,* XII, pp. 269-291.
82. 'Inscription no. 152', *SII,* XI, pp. 189-191.
83. 'Inscription no. 155', *SII,* XI, pp. 194-197.
84. 'Inscription no. 43', *SII,* XV, pp. 56-57.
85. See chapter V of the book on 'Spatial Context', pp. 453-456.
86. 'Inscription no. 11', *HAS,* 18, pp. 57-60.
87. Kotarumachgi Inscription, EI, XX, pp. 64-70.
88. 'Inscription no. 117', *SII,* XI, pp. 117-118.
89. 'Inscription no. 113', *SII,* XI, pp. 154-157.
90. 'Inscription no. 127', *SII,* XI, p. 146.
91. Munirabad Stone Inscription : HAS, 5, pp. 1-12.
92. 'Inscription no. 47', *SII,* XI, pp. 32-34.
93. 'Inscription no. 152', *SII,* XI, pp. 189-191.
94. 'Inscription no. 155', *SII,* XI, pp. 194-197.
95. We have discussed this in chapter IV of the book on 'Spatial Context', see, pp. 215-217.
96. K. Ismail, *op. cit.,* 1984, p. 77-78.
97. K. Iswara Dutt, *Inscriptional Glossary of Andhra Pradesh,* A.P. Sahitya Academy, Hyderabad, 1967, p. 184.
98. K.G. Krishnan, 'Traipurusa-Trikuta Cults in Karnataka', *QJMS,* IV, 1964, pp. 53-56.
99. 'Inscription no. 133', *SII,* XI, pp. 154-157.
100. 'Inscription no. 117', *SII,* XI, pp. 117-118.
101. 'Inscription no. 1', *SII,* W, pp. 1-2.
102. A.V. Krishnamurthy, *op. cit.,* 1975, p. 244. This ritual can be paralleled with the nuli-Punamma performed in the Eastern Deccan which involves the renewing or wearing a new sacred thread on the day of full moon around the deity.
103. David Lorenzen, 'The Kālāmukhas of Śakti Parisad', *ABORI, LII,* Poona, 1972, p. 97.
104. 'Inscription no. 99', *SII,* XI, p. 95.
105. 'Inscription no. 56', *SII,* XI, pp. 73-74.
106. 'Inscription no. 64', *SII,* XI, pp. 53-55.
107. References to the Saiva priests as followers of various ascetic practices described through such verses as *'yamaniyamasvadhyayadhyana dharana mauna nusthana*

japasamadhisampannarappa.' They appear prolifically in the inscriptions of the latter half of the 11th century A.D. For example see, Inscription no, 7, *HAS,* 18, p. 50. English translations furnished in the text have been borrowed from David Iorenzen, *op. cit.,* 1972, p. 112.

108. 'Two Inscriptions from Ron', B, *EI,* XIX, pp. 226-236.
109. 'Inscription no. 13', *HAS,* 18, pp. 63-74.
110. B. Rajendra Prasad, *op. cit.,* 1983, p. 9.
111. *Ibid.,* p. 9 the author further states that the Kalamukhas became a dominant sect from the 9th century A.D. onwards and the *mathas* at Alampur and Papanasi began to wield great influence as can be seen in the way Alampur began to be regarded as the western gateway of Srisaila, a great Kalamukha centre.
112. 'Inscription no. 26', *APGAS,* 3, p. 120.
113. 'Inscription no. 80', *APGAS,* 3, pp. 103-104.
114. See for instance, Inscription no, 12, *APGAS,* 3, pp. 106-107.
115. Transcript, 337/168 of Hyderabad Archaeology and Museums Office.
116. 'Inscription no. 10', *APGAS,* 3, pp. 104-105.
117. Champakalakshmi, *op. cit.,* 1989, p. 167.
118. 'Inscription no. 64', *SII,* XI, pp. 53-54.
119. Champakalakshmi, *op. cit.,* 1989, p. 166. One can clearly distinguish at this stage between the newly emerging priest hood in the temple institutions and the orthodox *brahmanas* known by their generic name *smarta.* In fact, the emergence of the temple priests in the forefront during the early medieval period was supposed to have posed a serious threat to the position of the *smarta brahmanas* who had earlier figured as the major recipients of gifts before the rise of the temples. Herein lies the key to the widespread conflict between the Vedic educated intellectual *brahmanas* and the common practitioners of rituals for the different cults. The former tried to brand the latter as transgressers of Vedic discipline and the latter tried to pick up some intellectual cover by organizing *bhakti* missions and new-intellectual monastic orders as also by preparing elaborate texts in support of their respective cults and its philosophy. (R.N. Nandi, 'Client, Ritual and Conflict in Early Brahmanical Order', *IHR,* 6, 1979-80, p. 115.
120. 'Inscription no. 26', *APGAS,* 3, p. 120.
121. 'Inscription from Navali', *EI,* XXXIV, pp. 164-166.
122. 'Inscription no. 183', *SII,* XI, pp. 242-243.
123. 'Inscription no. 6', *HAS,* 18, pp. 46-49.
124. 'Inscription no. 7', *HAS,* 18, pp. 49-51.
125. These instances have a significant bearing on our comprehension of the acculturation processes which were every much under operation during this period. In this context our attention is drawn the community of *kurubas* (pastoralists) who, according to H.A. Stuart, have a headman or *gauḍa* who acted the part of a *pujari* or priest in all their ceremonies and, at the same time, presided over their tribal meetings and settled disputes (Edgar Thurston, *Castes and Tribes of South India,* I, Asian Educational

Services, New Delhi, 1987, p. 142). In the inscriptional sources of our study we have a couple of instances to the *Kurubas/kuruba gāvuṇḍas* in the context of sub region B, see chapter III of the book on 'Social Context', pp. 241-242.

126. 'Inscription no. 56', *SII*, XV, pp. 73-74.

127. Van Troy, *op. cit.*, 1990, p. 10 observations made by this scholar have been based on literary sources available for a study of Śaivite philosophy which gave importance to the concept of an individual's liberation from the material world through the union of the Pāśupatas with God Śiva.

128. David Lorenzen, *op. cit.*, 112, Reference is also made here to the equation of some of the Kalāmukha priests to the Jaina Philosophers in the description of the former's greatness such as when one of the Śaiva priests Someśvara Paṇḍita's greatness is corresponded with that of the famous Jain logician Akalanka (p. 113). Such comparisons it seems have confused some of the early historians such as J.F. Fleet, as the Kālāmukhas were traditionally supposed to oppose rather then support the Jainas. All this evidently points to the fact that the rivalry between the Jainas and the Kalamukha priests was not on religious grounds alone. As articulated by R.N. Nandi, much of the sectarian tensions and violence which marked the Śaivite and the Jain monastic orders need to be viewed in the context of a low technology and small scale subsistence agriculture which could not provide necessary food surpluses for the ever growing number of monks (R.N. Nandi, *op. cit.*, 1986, p. 97).

129. R.N. Nandi, *op. cit.*, 1973, p. 84. In fact it is the other way round, the contempt shown by the traditional *brāhmaṇas* towards the Śaivite sects is more glaring as can be seen in Rāmanujas 'Sri Bhashya' which contains the only significant non-epigraphic discussion of the Kālāmukha sect (David Lorenzen, *op. cit.*, 1972, p. 97) and it has contemptuous allusions to this creed. According to the text, the Kālāmukhas believed in eating from a skull-bowl, besmearing themselves with ashes of a corpse, eating these ashes, bearing a staff *(laguḍa)*, keeping a pot of win *(sura)* and using that pot for God's worship as the means for securing all desires in that world and the next *(Sribhasya*, ii, 2, 37).

130. The experience in the early medieval Tamilakam region depicts the Kālāmukha sect as one of the 6 Śaivite sects which originated from the *āgamas* of Śaivism, the other 5 were those of the Bhairavaṁ, Vāman, Mahāvratam, Pāśupataṁ and Śaivism. (R.N. Nandi, *op. cit.*, 1973, pp. 84-85). In the context of the present study, there is reference to these priests, of Kalamukha Śaivism, with occassional mention of the Pāśupata tradition and they seem to have been on the rise during this period. According to R.N. Nandi the Kālāmukhas were so called because they adorned their faces with the caste mark of black streak (p. 85). It has been shown in other sources that there were atleast two major divisions in the Kālāmukha order—the Śakti Pariṣad and the Simha Pariṣad. In the area under study, the wide prevalence of the former variety has been attested to (David Lorenzen, *op. cit.*, 1972, p. 97). Further division of the Kālāmukha school into sub-groups such as the Parvatāvali (mountain lineage) and sub-groups of the *santatis* such as Nuavara Koncya Santati Belleya-Santāna, Iṭṭage Santati and so on (*ibid.*, pp. 101-130) have a significant bearing on the extremely local variations of the Śaivite worship which had arisen out of the necessity to incorporate local varieties of worship.

131. B.D. Chattopadhyaya, *op. cit.*, 1994, p. 30.
132. 'Inscriptions of Sudi', F, *EI*, XV, pp. 85-94.
133. 'Inscriptions of Sudi', G, *EI*, XV, pp. 94-96.
134. 'Inscriptions of Sudi', H, *EI*, XV, pp. 96-100.
135. 'Inscriptions of Sudi', C, *EI*, XV, pp. 75-77.
136. 'Inscription no. 13', *HAS*, 18, pp. 63-74.
137. *Ibid.*, pp. 65-67.
138. R.S. Sharma, *op. cit.*, 1987, pp. 382-386. Tantricism and Saivism, according to the author, popularized *puja* and adopted *bhakti* ideology of complete surrender to the God and the *guru* and this was institutionalized by means of temples (p. 377).
139. R.N. Nandi, *op. cit.*, 1973, p. 114.
140. Chapter V of the book on the 'Spatial Context', see. pp.
141. 'Inscription no. 14', *HAS*, 18, pp. 74-79.
142. 'Inscription no. 66', *APGAS*, 3, pp. 73-75.
143. It becomes all the more pertinent to comprehend the crucial role of political legitimation as in its earlier references, Kukkanur is never projected, even in a small measure, as having a close association with any one particular deity.
144. 'Inscription no. 66', *APGAS*, 3, pp. 73-75.
145. 'Inscription no. 58', *SII*, XV, pp. 78-82.
146. Thurston, *op. cit.*, 1987, p. 137.
147. *Ibid.*, p. 180. In the same work it is further stated that Bedar in 18th century were hunters (p. 81).
148. Cynthia Talbot, 'Temples, Donors and Gifts : Patterns of Patronage in Thirteenth Century South India', *JAS*, 50, 2, May 1991, p. 327.
149. Suvira Jayaswal, 'Studies in Early Indian Social History', *IHR*, 6, 1-2, 1979-80, p. 27.
150. 'Inscription no. 211', *SII*, XV, pp. 253-254.
151. Thurston, *op. cit.*, 1987, p. 243.
152. 'Inscription no. 58', *SII*, XV, pp. 78-82.
153. Kanaka Durga and Y.A. Sudhakar Reddy, 'Kings, Temples and Legitimation of Autochthonous Communities, A Case Study of South Indian Temple', *JESHO*, XXXV, p. 162.
154. 'A Stone Inscription of the Sinda Family at Bhairanmatti', *EI*, III, pp. 230-236.
155. R.N. Nandi, 'Clan Name and Social Mobility in the Deccan', *PIHC*, 33rd session, Muzaffarpur, 1972, p. 111. According to the author, the process of acculturation was a phased one. In such a process, the family or it's leader comes into direct contact with the ruling dynasty. Attendant upon this phase is the entry of the personal name and clan name of tribal chief into official documents. In this attendant phase the family often tries to find a suitable position in the status system of the host society. In the context of our study, the Sindas seem to have established marital relationships with the Kadamba rulers at the early stage of their rise (A stone Inscription of the Sinda Family, *EI*, III, p. 231).

156. 'Inscriptions of Sudi', K, *EI*, XV, pp. 105-108.
157. R.N. Nandi, *op. cit.*, 1972, p. 112.
158. Herman Kulke, 'Royal Temple Policy and the Structure of Medieval Hindu Kingdom', in H. Kulke (ed.), *Kings and Cults State Formation and Legitimation in India and South East Asia*, Manohar, 1993, p. 8.
159. Kulke, 'Legitimation and Town Planning, in the Feudatory States of Central Orissa', in H. Kulke (ed.), *Kings and Cults, State Formation and Legitimation in India and South East Asia*, Manohar, 1993, p. 96.
160. *Ibid.*, p. 97.
161. J. Hietzman, 'Ritual Polity and Economy : The Transactional Network of an Imperial Temple in Medieval South India', *JESHO*, XXXIV, 1991, pp. 23-54.
162. Cynthia Talbota, *op. cit.*, 1991, p. 330.
163. One can, at the most, consider the temple of God Brahmeśvara located in sub-region C as exhibiting the vestiges of being a major temple institution. But definitely not on the scale and nature characterizing the Brihadeshwara and the Jagannath temples of Tanjore and Puri respectively. In fact unlike these two temples which were actually constructed to cater to the legitimizing role of the newly emerging rulers of their areas, Brahmeśvara temple was an already existing institution which was made use of by the Chālukyas and other supra local chiefs as a symbol of legitimation and therefore, during the period or our study cannot be considered to represent the interests of any particular ruling family perse. In this context the Chālukyas of Kalyāṇi can be considered to have differed from their predecessors too. They were unlike the Chālukyas of Bādami who had taken the initiative to construct temples on a large scale, and even the Rāshtrakutas, who had taken steps in this direction and were constructed by them in the Deccan region. We, however, do not come across a similar enterprise in the area and period of our study on any significant scale.
164. 'Inscription no. 11', *HAS*, 18, pp. 57-60.
165. 'Inscription no. 10', *HAS*, 18, pp. 54-57.
166. R.N. Nandi, *op. cit.*, 1979, p. 100.
167. *Ibid.*, p. 101.
168. *Ibid.*, p. 95.
169. J.C. Heesterman, 'Power and Authority in Indian Tradition' in R.J. Moore (ed.), *Tradition and Politics in South Asia*, Vikas Publishing House, New Delhi, 1979, p. 63.
170. We have observed in this context that even the local ruling families had claimed *ksatriya varṇa* status We have detailed the *varṇa* status claimed by various social groups in chapter III of the book on 'Social Context'.
171. R.S. Sharma, 'Problems of Peasant Protest in Early Medieval India', *Social Scientist*, 16, 9, September, 1988, pp. 12-13.
172. Munırabard Stone Inscription, *IIAS*, 5, pp. 1 12.
173. 'Inscriptions at Iṭṭaqi', A. *EI*, XIII, pp. 37-58.
174. B.D. Chattopadhyaya, *op. cit.*, 1994, p. 35.

Chart – IV : IDEOLOGICAL CONTEXT

Sub Region A

i	*ii*	*iii*	*iv*	*v*	*vi*	*vii*	*viii*	*ix*	*x*	*xi*	*xii*
S.No.	*Name/Date Dynasty*	*Location*	*Patron*	*Name of the Temple*	*Vedic Learning Rituals*	*Priests/Sects*	*Nature of Patronage*				*Reference*
							Repairs/ Construction	*Rituals/ Festivals*	*Matha*	*Cultural Groups*	
1.	Ins. no. 527 AD 1022.	Muddebihal Tq. Bijapur Dt.	@	Kalideva							*SII*, XV, 357
2.	Ins. no. 61 AD 1024. Chalukyas of Kalyani.	Hungund Tq. Bijapur Dt.	#	Jaina basadi							*SII*, XI, 50-51
3.	Ins. no. 66 AD 1032. Chalukyas of Kalyani.	Muddebihal Tq. Bijapur Dt.	#, @	Śivālaya			maintenance	N.D			*SII*, XI, 57
4.	Ins. no. 68 AD 1033. Chalukyas of Kalyani.	Muddebihal Tq. Bijapur Dt.	@	Bāleśvara Mūlasthāna Deva				AB		@	*SII*, XI, 58-59
5.	Ins. no. 529 AD 1033.	Muddebihal Tq. Bijapur Dt.	@	Mallikārjuna			installation				*SII*, XI, 358
6.	Ins. no. 99 AD 1062. Chalukyas of Kalyani.	Bagalkot Tq. Bijapur Dt.	@	Siddeśwara		Prabhu Marasingha *(pāśupatāchārya)*	renovation	AB	feeding *brāhmanas*		*SII*, XI, 95-96
7.	Ins. no. 107 AD 1068. Chalukyas of Kalyani.	Muddebihal Tq. Bijapur Dt.	@	Baileśvara							*SII*, XI, 104-105
8.	Ins. no. 110 AD 1070. Chalukyas of Kalyani.	Badami Tq. Bijapur Dt.	#	Mūlasthānadeva				AB			*SII*, XI, 107
9.	Ins. no. 113 AD 1074. Chalukyas of Kalyani.	Hungund Tq. Bijapur Dt.	@	Arasara basadi		Āryapaṇḍita (Trustee)					*SII*, XI, 111-112
10.	Ins. no. 116 AD 1075. Chalukyas of Kalyani.	Bagalkot Tq. Bijapur Dt.	>	Svayambhu Nāgeśvaradeva	for the teacher	Tatpurusha Paṇḍita (trustee)		ND, NI, AB, *Puja*	feeding ascetics		*SII*, XI, 239

Key to the Symbols : > : Main Ruler; # : Local Potentate; @ : Functionary; * : *mahājana*; $: *brāhmaṇa*; ~ : Merchant;
A : Artisan; & : Cultural Groups; < : Peasant; AB : *aṅgabhoga*; ND : *nandādipa* (lamps); NI : *Nivedya*.

Chart – *IV* : IDEOLOGICAL CONTEXT

Sub Region A

i	*ii*	*iii*	*iv*	*v*	*vi*	*vii*	*viii*	*ix*	*x*	*xi*	*xii*
S.No.	Name/Date Dynasty	Location	Patron	Name of the Temple	Vedic Learning Rituals	Priests/Sects	Nature of Patronage				Reference
							Repairs/ Construction	Rituals/ Festivals	Maṭha	Cultural Groups	
			@	Svayambhu Kalideva							
11.	Ins. no. 179 AD 1085. Chalukyas of Kalyani.	Hungund Tq. Bijapur Dt.	@	Gunada Bedangi Jinālaya					feeding ascetics		*SII*, XV, 239
12.	Ins. no. 142 AD 1097. Chalukyas of Kalyani.	Badami Tq. Bijapur Dt.	queen of >		Rigveda Khaṇḍika and Śāstra Khaṇḍika						*SII*, XI, 172-173
13.	Ins. no. 190 AD 1106.	Hungund Tq. Bijapur Dt.	@	Viṣṇu					*maṭha*		*SII*, XI, 247
14.	Ins. no. 30 AD 1145. Chalukyas of Kalyani.	Muddebihal Tq. Bijapur Dt.	@	Mūlasthanadeva		Śūdrakjiya (Trustee)		NI, AB			*SII*, XV, 32-33
15.	Ins. no. 34 AD 1147. Chalukyas of Kalyani.	Badami Tq. Bijapur Dt.	@	Kalideva		Ganganavve (Trustee)					*SII*, XV, 41
16.	Ins. no 38 AD 1148. Chalukyas of Kalyani.	Muddebihal Tq. Bijapur Dt.	Temple establishment A	Kalideva				NI, *pūja caitra* pavitra			*SII*, XV 48
17.	Ins. no. 238 AD 1155. Chalukyas of Kalyani.	Badami Tq. Bijapur Dt.	@	Mallikājuna							*SII*, XV 291-293
18.	Ins. no. 88 AD 1150. Chalukyas of Kalyani.	Hungund Tq. Bijapur Dt.	<, ~	Kāleśvara and Āchesvara							*SII*, XV, 114-115
19.	Ins. no. 123 AD 1173. Kalachuris of Kalyani.	Muddebihal Tq. Bijapur Dt.	@	Mahālinga				ND, NI			*SII*, XV, 156

Key to the Symbols : > : Main Ruler; A : Artisan; # : Local Potentate; & : Cultural Groups; @ : Functionary; < : Peasant; * : *mahājana*; AB : *aṅgabhoga*; $: *brāhmaṇa*; ND : *nandādipa* (lamps); ~ : Merchant; NI : *Nivedya*.

Chart – IV : IDEOLOGICAL CONTEXT

Sub Region B

i	ii	iii	iv	v	vi	vii	viii	ix	x	xi	xii
S.No.	Name/Date Dynasty	Location	Patron	Name of the Temple	Vedic Learning Rituals	Priests/Sects	Nature of Patronage				Reference
							Repairs/ Construction	Rituals/ Festivals	Maṭha	Cultural Groups	
20.	Ins. no. 126 AD 1174. Kalachuris of Kalyani.	Muddebihal Tq. Bijapur Dt.	@	Gangeśwara					charity		*SII*, XV, 159-160
21.	Ins. no. 58 AD 1184. Chalukyas of Kalyani.	Muddebihal Tq. Bijapur Dt.	@, ~ all the residents	Trikūṭa		Amritarāsi Paṇḍita (Trustee)	repairs	NI			*SII*, XV 78-82
			bedarum Trikūṭa janguliya māda-garu kuribag-āvuṇḍas				ND				
22.	Ins. no. 56 AD 1184. Chalukyas of Kalyani.	Muddebihal Tq. Bijapur Dt.	#	Vira-Baysesvara		Viradasa (Trustee)		AB-*caitra pavitra* festival	*gaṇa maṭha*		*SII*, XV, 73-74
23.	Ins. no. 147 AD 1189. Yadavas of Devagiri.	Muddebihal Tq. Bijapur Dt.	@	Nanneśvara		Lokajiya (Trustee)		*trikala puja* NI			*SII*, XV, 189
			~	Nanneśvara				ND			
24.	Ins. no. 148 AD 1189. Yadavas of Devagiri.	Muddebihal Tq. Bijapur Dt.	@	Siriyameśvara		Kannaguru (Trustee)		*puja* - ND			*SII*, XV, 190
			~	Siriyameśvara				ND			
25.	Ins. no. 156 AD 1207. Yadavas of Devagiri.	Hungund Tq. Bijapur Dt.	@	Telligeśvara		Nagarasi (Trustee)	repairs	AB			*SII*, XV., 200-201
			~	Telligeśvara							
26.	Ins. no. 11 AD 973. Chalukyas of Kalyani.	Kopbal Tq. Raichur Dt.	>		*brāhmāṇḍa kratu*	$ Revayadvedi Chattopādhyāya					*IIAS*□18, 57-60
			$	Traipuruṣa			repairs and construction	NI, ND daily worship			

Key to the Symbols : > : Main Ruler; # : Local Potentate; @ : Functionary; * : *mahājana*; $: *brāhmaṇa*; ~ : Merchant;
A : Artisan; & : Cultural Groups; < : Peasant; AB : *aṅgabhoga*; ND : *nandādipa* (lamps); NI : *Nivedya*.

Chart – IV : IDEOLOGICAL CONTEXT

Sub Region B

i	ii	iii	iv	v	vi	vii	viii	ix	x	xi	xii
S.No.	Name/Date Dynasty	Location	Patron	Name of the Temple	Vedic Learning Rituals	Priests/Sects	Nature of Patronage				Reference
							Repairs/ Construction	Rituals/ Festivals	Maṭha	Cultural Groups	
27.	Ins. no. 47 AD 994. Chalukyas of Kalyani.	Gadag Tq. Dharwar Dt.	@	Mūlasthānadeva		Vidyābharaṇa Paṇḍita (Trustee)			*vidyādāna*		*SII*, XI, 32-34
28.	Ins. no. 1 AD 1005. Chalukyas of Kalyani.	Yalburgi Tq. Raichur Dt.	~	Gavareśvara			*maṇṭapa* hall maintenance				HAS 18, 39-40
29.	Ins. no 1 AD 1005. Chalukyas of Kalyani.	Gadag Tq. Dharwar Dt.	#	Mūlasthānadeva		Revabbegoravi					*SII*, XI, 36-38
30.	Kotavumachgi Ins. AD 1012. Chalukyas of Kalyani.	Gadag Tq. Dharwar Dt.	$	Several Temples					various types of ascetics		EI, XX 64-70
31.	Ins. no. 58 AD 1022. Chalukyas of Kalyani.	Mundargi Petha Tq. Dharwar Dt.	>, @ ~	Dhameśvara Dhameśvara			construction				*SII*, XI, 48
32.	Transcript AD 1022. Chalukyas of Kalyani.	Manvi Tq. Raichur Dt.	Queen of >	Traipurusadeva			installed the deity				*A.R no.* B.534 of 1961-62
33.	Ins. no. 64 AD 1028. Chalukyas of Kalyani.	Gadag Tq. Dharwar Dt.	$	Traipuruṣadeva	Performed the sacrifices of *agnihotra* and and *dāna* rituals such as *hiraṇya dāna, bhūmidāna* etc.	Bhāvaśiva Deva Nāgasvāmi			*satra and vidyādāna*		*SII*, XI, 53-55
34.	Ins. no. 65 AD 1029. Chalukyas of Kalyani.	Gadag Tq. Dharwar Dt.	@	Jainabasadi			construction				*SII*, XI, 55-57

Key to the Symbols : > : Main Ruler; A : Artisan; # : Local Potentate; & : Cultural Groups; @ : Functionary; < : Peasant; * : *mahājana*; AB : *aṅgabhoga*; $: *brāhmaṇa*; ND : *nandādipa* (lamps); ~ : Merchant; NI : *Nivedya*.

Chart – IV : IDEOLOGICAL CONTEXT

Sub Region B

i	ii	iii	iv	v	vi	vii	viii	ix	x	xi	xii
S.No.	*Name/Date Dynasty*	*Location*	*Patron*	*Name of the Temple*	*Vedic Learning Rituals*	*Priests/Sects*	*Nature of Patronage*				*Reference*
							Repairs/ Construction	*Rituals/ Festivals*	*Maṭha*	*Cultural Groups*	
35.	Ins. no. 4 AD 1032. Chalukyas of Kalyani.	Lingsugur Tq. Raichur Dt.	>	Jagadekamalla Jinālaya							*HAS*, 18 43-44
36.	Gadag Ins. AD 1036. Chalukyas of Kalyani.	Gadag Tq. Dharwar Dt.	@, ~	12 Nārāyaṇas & Traipuruṣas			construction & installation	ND, NI *puja*	feeding *brāhmaṇas*		*EI*, XIX, 217-222
37.	Kilaratti Ins. AD 1046. Chalukyas of Kalyani.	Lingsugur Tq. Raichur Dt.	Younger Brother >	Bhōgeśvara		Devasingha Bhaṭāra (turstee)					*EI*.XXXV, 37-39
38.	Ins. no. 84 AD 1049. Chalukyas of Kalyani.	Gadag Tq. Dharwar Dt.	$	Viṣṇu					feeding guests		*SII*, XI, 77-79
39.	Ins. no. 92 AD 1054. Chalukyas of Kalyani.	Mundargi Tq. Dharwar Dt.	@	Kaidevasvāmi Viṣṇudeva				ND, NI *srikhaṇḍa*			*SII*, XI, 87-89
40.	Ins. no. 94 AD 1059. Chalukyas of Kalyani.	Mundargi Tq. Dharwar Dt.	~	Nagarajinālaya					*āhāradana*		*SII*, XI, 89-90
41.	Ins. of Sudi 'F' AD 1060. Chalukyas of Kalyani.	Ron Tq. Dharwar Dt.	#	Nāgeśvara		Someśvara paṇḍitadeva (trustee)	repairs	NI, ND incense etc.	food for ascetics	& dancing girls & drummers & flute players	*EI* XV, 85-94
42.	Ins. no. 97 AD 1062. Chalukyas of Kalyani.	Gadag Tq. Dharwar Dt.	~	Nāgareśvara		Dhruveśvara paṇḍita (trustee)			feeding ascetics		*SII*, XI, 91-94
43.	Ins. of Sudi 'G' AD 1069. Chalukyas of Kalyani.	Ron Tq. Dharwar Dt.	#	Achaleśvara		Someśvara Paṇḍitadeva (trustee)		NI	feeding ascetics		*EI*, XV, 94-96

Key to the Symbols : > : Main Ruler; # : Local Potentate; @ : Functionary; * : *mahājana*; $: *brāhmaṇa*; ~ : Merchant;
A : Artisan; & : Cultural Groups; < : Peasant; AB : *aṅgabhoga*; ND : *nandādipa* (lamps); NI : *Nivedya*.

Chart – IV : IDEOLOGICAL CONTEXT

Sub Region B

i	ii	iii	iv	v	vi	vii	viii	ix	x	xi	xii
S.No.	Name/Date Dynasty	Location	Patron	Name of the Temple	Vedic Learning Rituals	Priests/Sects	Nature of Patronage				Reference
							Repairs/ Construction	Rituals/ Festivals	Maṭha	Cultural Groups	
44.	Daddala Ins. AD 1069. Chalukyas of Kalyani.	Manvi Tq. Raichur Dt.	#	Girigotemalla Jinālaya			consctuction				EI, XXXVII 113-116
			~	Gingotemalla Jinālaya							
45.	Ins. no. 111 AD 1071. Chalukyas of Kalyani.	Gadag Tq. Dharwar Dt.	@	Baladevajinālaya							SII, XI, 107-110
			*	Baladevajinālaya							
46.	Ins. no. 112 AD 1072. Chalukyas of Kalyani.	Ron Tq. Dharwar Dt.	~	Nakareśvara				ND			SII, XI, 110
			@	Nakareśvara							
47.	Ins. no 122 AD 1072. Chalukyas of Kalyani.	Ron Tq. Dharwar Dt.	@, ~	Kalidevasvāmi Mādeśvaradeva Kāmeśwaradeva		Chikkana Paṇḍita (trustee)		NI			SII, XI, 141
48.	Ins. of Sudi 'H' AD 1075. Chalukyas of Kalyani.	Ron Tq. Dharwar Dt.	>	Pañchalingadeva		Someśvara Paṇḍitadeva		personal enjoyment			EI, XV, 96-100
49.	Ins. no. 9 AD 1075. Chalukyas of Kalyani.	Gadag Tq. Dharwar Dt.	@, *	Maruleśvara				ND, decorations supply of flowers		temple priest to be maintained	KI, II, 25-28
50.	Ins. no. 117 AD 1076. Chalukyas of Kalyani.	Ron Tq. Dharwar Dt.	#	Svayambhukali devasvāmi				pavitrāronaṇa festival	feeding *brāhmaṇas*		SII, XI, 117-118
			sister of >	Svayambhukali devasvāmi & Bhagavati			repairs	ND, NI			
51.	Ins. no. 6 AD 1077. Chalukyas of Kalyani.	Lingsugur Tq. Raichur Dt.	#	Kirti Someśvara		Netrśiva Paṇḍita		AB			Has, 18 46-49

Key to the Symbols : > : Main Ruler; # : Local Potentate; @ : Functionary; * : *mahājana*; $: *brāhmaṇa*; ~ : Merchant; A : Artisan; & : Cultural Groups; < : Peasant; AB : *aṅgabhoga*; ND : *nandādipa* (lamps); NI : *Nivedya*.

Chart – IV : IDEOLOGICAL CONTEXT

Sub Region B

i	ii	iii	iv	v	vi	vii	viii	ix	x	xi	xii
S.No.	Name/Date Dynasty	Location	Patron	Name of the Temple	Vedic Learning Rituals	Priests/Sects	Nature of Patronage				Reference
							Repairs/ Construction	Rituals/ Festivals	Maṭha	Cultural Groups	
52.	Ins. at Yewur B AD 1077. Chalukyas of Kalyani.	Shorapur Tq. Gulbarga Dt.	>	Svayambhuśiva	*homa* and *hali* sacrifies		repairs, fresh plaster	Incense, ND, NI procession *chaitra* festival *nula prabhanda*	clothes food for ascetics		*EI*, XII, 269-291
53.	Ins. no. 7 AD 1079. Chalukyas of Kalyani.	Lingsugur Tq. Raichur Dt.	@, ~	Svayambhu Someśvara		Tatpursha Śivāchintāyaka					*HAS*, *18* 49-51
54.	Ins. no. 127 AD 1082. Chalukyas of Kalyani.	Gadag Tq. Dharwar Dt.	*	Anuveśvaradeva							*SII*, XI, 146
55.	Ins. of Sudi 'K' AD 1084. Chalukyas of Kalyani.	Ron Tq. Dharwar Dt.	#	Pañchalinga		Kalyāṇaśakti (trustee)			food & instruction to ascetics		*Ei* XV, 105-108
56.	Transcript AD 1084. Chalukyas of Kalyani.	Deodurg Tq. Raichur Dt.	<	Mahālinga Meleśvara							*AR*. no., B 665 of 1958-59
57.	Ins. of Sudi 'I' AD 1084. Chalukyas of Kalyani.	Ron Tq. Dharwar Dt.	queen of >	Achaleśvara		Someśvara Paṇḍitadeva (trustee)		AB	feeding education of ascetics		*EI*, XV, 100-103
58.	Ins. no. 133 AD 1086. Chalukyas of Kalyani.	Gadag Tq. Dharwar Dt.	A, *	Pāseśvara			construction	NI, ND AB, wor-ship			*SII*, XI, 154-157
59.	Ins. no. 134 AD 1087. Chalukyas of Kalyani.	Gadag Tq. Dherwar Dt.	*	Visṇu and Saraswati			construction	ND, Sandal flowers incnse			*SII*, XI, 157-160

Key to the Symbols : > : Main Ruler; A : Artisan; # : Local Potentate; & : Cultural Groups; @ : Functionary; < : Peasant; * : *mahājana*; AB : *aṅgabhoga*; $: *brāhmaṇa*; ND : *nandādipa* (lamps); ~ : Merchant; NI : *Nivedya*.

Chart – IV : IDEOLOGICAL CONTEXT

Sub Region B

i	ii	iii	iv	v	vi	vii	viii	ix	x	xi	xii
S.No.	Name/Date Dynasty	Location	Patron	Name of the Temple	Vedic Learning Rituals	Priests/Sects	Nature of Patronage				Reference
							Repairs/ Construction	Rituals/ Festivals	Maṭha	Cultural Groups	
60.	Munirabad stone Ins. AD 1088. Chalukyas of Kalyani.	Kopbal Tq. Raichur Dt.	$	Someśvara	for the priest who has studied Veda		stone work construction	ND, NI food offerings	educating and feeding the ascetics	servants of God *(devara parichārika)*	*IIAS*, no.5 1-12
61.	Ins. no. 137 AD 1091. Chalukyas of Kalyani.	Gadag Tq. Dharwar Dt.	~	Mahālakshmidevi					feeding the *brāhmanas*		*SII*, XV, 165
62.	Ins. no. CXVI AD 1095. Chalukyas of Kalyani.	Gadag Tq. Dharwar Dt.	~	Baudhavihāra & Śri Āryatāradevi vihāra			repairs	ND, NI worship	food and clothes to the mendicants	for *pūjāri* (temple priest)	*IA*., X, 185-190
63.	Transcript AD 1095. Chalukyas of Kalyani.	Devadurg Tq. Raichur Dt.	>		Kōtihōma	Sarvakratu creyana Bhattō pādhyāya somayāji					*AR* no., B661 of 1958-59
			$	Vishṇudeva Rāmeśvaradeva							
64.	Transcript AD 1096. Chalukyas of Kalyani.	Manvi Tq. Raichur Dt.	>		*pañchalingāla kratu*	Vikramāditya Bhaṭṭōpādhyāya Sarvakratu Somayāji					*AR*, no., B 556 of 1961-62
65.	Ins. no. 145 AD 1098. Chalukyas of Kalyani.	Gadag Tq. Dharwar Dt.	@,~,<	Grāmeśvaradeva		Kedaraśakti Paṇḍita (Trustee)					*SII*, XI, 176
66.	Ins. no. 144 AD 1098. Chalukyas of Kalyani.	Gadag Tq. Dharwar Dt.	~	Bauddhavihāra			construction	ND			*SII*, XI, 175
67.	Ins. no. 147 AD 1099.	Gadag Tq. Dharwar Dt.	@	Mādhaveśvara			repairs	AB			*SII*, XI, 178-182

Key to the Symbols : > : Main Ruler; # : Local Potentate; @ : Functionary; * : *mahājana*; $: *brāhmaṇa*; ~ : Merchant; A : Artisan; & : Cultural Groups; < : Peasant; AB : *aṅgabhoga*; ND : *nandādipa* (lamps); NI : *Nivedya*.

Chart – IV : IDEOLOGICAL CONTEXT

Sub Region B

i	ii	iii	iv	v	vi	vii	viii	ix	x	xi	xii
S.No.	Name/Date Dynasty	Location	Patron	Name of the Temple	Vedic Learning Rituals	Priests/Sects	Nature of Patronage				Reference
							Repairs/ Construction	Rituals/ Festivals	Maṭha	Cultural Groups	
	Chalukyas of Kalyani.										
68.	Ins. no. 149 AD 1100. Chalukyas of Kalyani.	Ron Tq. Dharwar Dt.	@	Kalidevaśvāmi				AB, ND			*SII*, XI, 183-184
69.	Transcript AD 1100. Chalukyas of Kalyani.	Shorapur Tq. Gulbarga Dt.	@ *, ~	Mūlasthāna Kumāreśvara Bhonteśvara		Brahmarāsi Paṇḍita	Image ainstalled				*AR. no.*, B 520 of 1960-61
70.	Ins. no. 150 AD 1102. Chalukyas of Kalyani.	Gadag Tq. Dharwar Dt.	@	Somanātha		Kriyāsakti Paṇḍita		NI	maṭha		*SII*, XI, 185-187
71.	Ins. no. 152 AD 1103. Chalukyas of Kalyani.	Gadag Tq. Dharwar Dt.	@	Morakeśvara		jñānaśakti (trustee)	construction	NI, *pūja*			*SII*, XI, 189-191
72.	Ins. no. 153 AD 1103. Chalukyas of Kalyani.	Ron Tq. Dharwar Dt.	A	Kammaṭeśvara							*SII*, XI, 192
73.	Ins. no. 156 AD 1105. Chalukyas of Kalyani.	Gadag Tq. Dharwar Dt.	@	Śōbhaneśvara		Indraśivadevā-chārya (*rajaguru*)	repairs	AB			*SII*, XI, 197-200
74.	Ins. no. 155 AD 1105. Chalukyas of Kalyani.	Ron Tq. Dharwar Dt.	#	Brahmeśvara		Vigreśvara Paṇḍita	construction	worship.ND			*SII*, XI, 194-197
75.	Ins. at Yewur C AD 1105. Chalukyas of Kalyani.	Shorapur Tq. Gulbarga Dt.	$	Keśavadeva (Viṣṇu)			repairs	AB,NI,ND *pūja* Pavit-rārōhaṇa			*EI*, XII, 329-331
76.	Transcript AD 1105. Chalukyas of Kalyani.	Shorapur Tq. Gulbarga Dt.	wife of #	Ugramārtāṇḍa							*AR*.no. B527 of 60-61

Key to the Symbols : > : Main Ruler; # : Local Potentate; @ : Functionary; * : *mahājana*; $: *brāhmaṇa*; ~ : Merchant;
A : Artisan; & : Cultural Groups; < : Peasant; AB : *aṅgabhoga*; ND : *nandādipa* (lamps); NI : *Nivedya*.

Chart – IV : IDEOLOGICAL CONTEXT

Sub Region B

i	ii	iii	iv	v	vi	vii	viii	ix	x	xi	xii
S.No.	*Name/Date Dynasty*	*Location*	*Patron*	*Name of the Temple*	*Vedic Learning Rituals*	*Priests/Sects*	*Nature of Patronage*				*Reference*
							Repairs/ Construction	*Rituals/ Festivals*	*Maṭha*	*Cultural Groups*	
77.	Ins. no 189 AD 1106. Chalukyas of Kalyani.	Ron Tq. Dharwar Dt.	* and several indivi- duals	Keśavāditya- Deva	pārāyaṇa of 2 Vedas			*pavitrā- rohaṇa*			*SII*, XI, 246
78.	Ins. no 158 AD 1109. Chalukyas of Kalyani.	Gadag Tq. Dharwar Dt.	@, ~	Bhōgeśvaradeva Amriteśvara Sarasvati		Sōmeśvara Paṇḍita (Trustee)		AB, NI			*SII*, XI, 201-203
79.	Ins. no 8 AD 1109. Chalukyas of Kalyani.	Devadurg Tq. Raichur Dt.	~	Brahmajinālaya Nakarajinālaya							*HAS*,, 18 51-52
80.	Ins. at Yewur 'D' AD 11 0. Chalukyas of Kalyani.	Shorapur Tq. Gulbarga Dt.	A	Kammaṭeśvara- deva			lime, bronze				*EI*, XII, 332-333
81.	Ins. at Ittagi 'A' AD 1122. Chalukyas of Kalyani.	Yalburgi Tq. Raichur Dt.	@	Śivamahādeva Mūrti Nārāyaṇa God Chaṇḍaleśvara Sāhasabhairava		Sōmeśvara Paṇḍitadeva (Trustee)	construction	personal enjoyment offerings, food,festiv- al, clothes	food, aims		*EI*, XII,, 37-58
			>	Śiva Mahādeva			repairs	NI, ND	stipends	& Dancing girls and attendants.	
82.	Ins. at Ittagi 'B' AD 11 2. Chalukyas of Kalyani.	Yalburgi Tq. Raichur Dt.	~	Svayambhu Trikuṭeśvara Deva Śri Mahādeveśvara		Sōmeśvara Paṇḍitadeva (Trustee) Kriyāśakti Paṇḍitadeva (āchārya)					*EI*, XII, 59-61
83.	Ins. no 167 AD 1032.	Gadag Tq. Dharwar Dt.	@, <	Betteśvara							*SII*, XI, 214

Key to the Symbols : > : Main Ruler; A : Artisan; # : Local Potentate; & : Cultural Groups; @ : Functionary; < : Peasant; * : *mahājana*; AB : *aṅgabhoga*; $: *brāhmaṇa*; ND : *nandādipa* (lamps); ~ : Merchant; NI : *Nivedya*.

Chart – *IV* : IDEOLOGICAL CONTEXT

Sub Region B

i	ii	iii	iv	v	vi	vii	viii	ix	x	xi	xii
S.No.	Name/Date Dynasty	Location	Patron	Name of the Temple	Vedic Learning Rituals	Priests/Sects	Nature of Patronage				Reference
							Repairs/ Construction	Rituals/ Festivals	Maṭha	Cultural Groups	
	Chalukyas of Kalyani.										
84.	Ins. no. 172 AD 1121. Chalukyas of Kalyani.	Gadag Tq. Dharwar Dt.	@, ~	Mūlasthanadeva							*SII*, XI, 220-222
85.	Ins. no. 198 AD 1124. Chalukyas of Kalyani.	Gadag Tq. Dharwar Dt.	~	Viduresvara		Amritarasi-Paṇḍita (*āchārya*) (Trustee)		NI, ND			*SII*, XI, 253-254
86.	Ins. no. 9 AD 1124. Chalukyas of Kalyani.	Lingsugur Tq. Raichur Dt.	#, @	Kalidevesvara				AB,NI,ND incense			*HAS*, 18 52-54
87.	Ins. no. 176 AD 1125. Chalukyas of Kalyani.	Ron Tq. Dharwar Dt.	#	Somesvara		Mallikārjuna Paṇḍita (Trustee)					*SII*, XI, 230-231
88.	Ins. no. 200 AD 1126. Chalukyas of Kalyani.	Gadag Tq. Dharwar Dt.	@, ~	Dasesvara				AB			*SII*, XI, 255-256
89.	Ins. no. 11 AD 1136. Chalukyas of Kalyani.	Kopbal Tq. Raichur Dt.	*	Traipuruṣa	The * are praised for their knowledge in Vedic sacrities such as agnisthōma			AB,ND, NI		*pūjāri*	*HAS*, 18 57-60
90.	Ins. no. 50 AD 1138. Chalukyas of Kalyani.	Gadag Tq. Dharwar Dt.	@	Mūlasthanadeva		Amrutarāsi Paṇḍita (*acharya*)	repairs	NI	*ahāradāna* for ascetics		*SII*, XI, 36-38
91.	Ins. no. 23 AD 1142. Chalukyas of Kalyani.	Gadag Tq. Dharwar Dt.	@	Somesvara				AB			*SII*, XV, 24-25

Key to the Symbols : > : Main Ruler; # : Local Potentate; @ : Functionary; * : *mahājana*; $: *brāhmaṇa*; ~ : Merchant;
A : Artisan; & : Cultural Groups; < : Peasant; AB : *aṅgabhoga*; ND : *nandādipa* (lamps); NI : *Nivedya*.

Chart – IV : IDEOLOGICAL CONTEXT

Sub Region B

i	ii	iii	iv	v	vi	vii	viii	ix	x	xi	xii
S.No.	Name/Date Dynasty	Location	Patron	Name of the Temple	Vedic Learning Rituals	Priests/Sects	Nature of Patronage				Reference
							Repairs/ Construction	Rituals/ Festivals	Maṭha	Cultural Groups	
92.	Ins. no. 5 AD 1143. Chalukyas of Kalyani.	Yalburgi Tq. Raichur Dt.	<	Totigeśvara							*APGAS*, no.9 29-30
93.	Ins. no. 25 AD 1144. Chalukyas of Kalyani.	Gadag Tq. Dharwar Dt.	@, <	Bhogeśvaradeva		Aghora Paṇḍita *(sthānācharya)* (Trustee)		AB, ND			*SII*, XI, 28
94.	Ins. no. 27 AD 1144. Chalukyas of Kalyani.	Ron Tq. Dharwar Dt.	@	Mūlasthāna		Chandrabhu-shaṇa Paṇḍita *(āchārya)* (Trustee)	repairs	AB, NI incense			*SII*, XV, 29-30
95.	Ins. no. 28 AD 1144. Chalukyas of Kalyani.	Ron Tq. Dharwar Dt.	~	Mūlasthāna- Brahmeśvara		Vāmaśakti- Paṇḍita		AB, ND			*SII*, XV, 30-31
96.	Ins. no. 36 AD 1148. Chalukyas of Kalyani.	Gadag Tq. Dharwar Dt.	@, ~	Mūlasthānadeva		Gangeśvara Paṇḍitadeva *(sthānācharya)* (Trustee)	repairs	*caitra-pavitra* AB, ND			*SII*, XV, 43-46
97.	Ins. no. 10 AD 1149. Chalukyas of Kalyani.	Yalburgi Tq. Raichur Dt.	$,~,@,A	Mallikārjuna- Deva	The * are praised for their Vedic learning			ND, NI			*HAS*., 18 54-57
98.	Ins. no. 48 AD 1152. Chalukyas of Kalyani.	Gadag Tq. Dharwar Dt.	@ ~	Kavataleśvara Kavataleśvara		Sōmeśvara Paṇḍitadeva *(āchārya)* (Trustee)		NI NI			*SII*, XV, 64-65
99.	Ins. no. 51 AD 1155. Chalukyas of Kalyani.	Gadag Tq. Dharwar Dt.	@	Mūlasthāna		Gangarāsi Paṇḍita *(āchārya)* (Trustee)			feeding ascetics		*SII*, XV, 67-68

Key to the Symbols : > : Main Ruler; # : Local Potentate; @ : Functionary; * : *mahājana*; $: *brāhmaṇa*; ~ : Merchant;
A : Artisan; & : Cultural Groups; < : Peasant; AB : *aṅgabhoga*; ND : *nandādipa* (lamps); NI : *Nivedya*.

Chart – IV : IDEOLOGICAL CONTEXT

Sub Region B

i	*ii*	*iii*	*iv*	*v*	*vi*	*vii*	*viii*	*ix*	*x*	*xi*	*xii*
S.No.	*Name/Date Dynasty*	*Location*	*Patron*	*Name of the Temple*	*Vedic Learning Rituals*	*Priests/Sects*	*Nature of Patronage*				*Reference*
							Repairs/ Construction	*Rituals/ Festivals*	*Maṭha*	*Cultural Groups*	
100.	Ins. no. 52 AD 1155. Chalukyas of Kalyani.	Gadag Tq. Dharwar Dt.	@	Morakeśvara		Jñānaśakti *(āchārya)* (Trustee)			feeding ascetics		*SII*, XV, 68-69
101.	Ins. no. 50 AD 1156. Chalukyas of Kalyani.	Gadag Tq. Dharwar Dt.	@			Monideva (Donee)					
			Moni-deva	Kavatala Chāvuṇḍeśvara					feeding ascetics		*SII*, XV 66-67
102.	Ins. no. 106 AD 1166. Kalachuris of Kalyani.	Gadag Tq. Dharwar Dt.	~	Chaṇḍeśvara Gavareśvaradeva							*SII*, XV, 136-137
103.	Ins. no. 107 AD 1167. Kalachuris of Kalyani.	Gadag Tq. Dharwar Dt.	@	Bhōgeśvara		Kedāraśkti Paṇḍita *(sthānāchārya)* (Trustee)		AB-NI			*SII*, XV, P 137
104.	Ins. no. 114 AD 1170. Kalachuris of Kalyani.	Ron Tq. Dharwar Dt.	@	Keśavadeva				NI			*SII*, XV, 145
105.	Ins. no. 66 AD 1170. Kalachuris of Kalyani.	Yalburgi Tq. Raichur Dt.	@	Svayambhū-pranna Mallikār-junadeva				AB			*APGAS*, no.3 73-75
106.	Ins. no. 117 AD 1171. Kalachuris of Kalyani.	Ron Tq. Dharwar Dt.	#	Traipurusha							*SII*, XV 147-148
107.	Ins. no. 240 AD 1173. Kalachuris of Kalyani.	Gadag Tq. Dharwar Dt.	@, <, ~	Goyideśvara		Jātaveda Paṇḍita *āchārya* (Trustee)		ND			*SII*, XV, 296-297
108.	Ins. no. 119 AD 1173. Kalachuris of Kalyani.	Gadag Tq. Dharwa Dt.	~	basadi of Balleya Jemayya		Shushana-Paṇḍitadeva *āchārya* (Trustee)					*SII*, XV, 149-150

Key to the Symbols : > : Main Ruler; # : Local Potentate; @ : Functionary; * : *mahājana;* $: *brāhmaṇa;* ~ : Merchant;
A : Artisan; & : Cultural Groups; < : Peasant; AB : *aṅgabhoga;* ND : *nandādipa* (lamps); NI : *Nivedya.*

Chart – IV : IDEOLOGICAL CONTEXT

Sub Region B

i	ii	iii	iv	v	vi	vii	viii	ix	x	xi	xii
S.No.	Name/Date Dynasty	Location	Patron	Name of the Temple	Vedic Learning Rituals	Priests/Sects	Nature of Patronage				Reference
							Repairs/ Construction	Rituals/ Festivals	Maṭha	Cultural Groups	
109.	Ins. no. 121 AD 1173 Kalachuris of Kalyani	Gadag Tq.. Dharwar Dt.	<, ~, @	Mūlasthānadeva		Amritarāsi Paṇḍita āchārya (Trustee)		NI-ND			SII, XV 151-152
110.	Ins. no. 120 AD 1173. Kalachuris of Kalyani	Gadag Tq. Dharwar Dt.	<, ~ @	Yigoydeśvara-deva		Jātaveda Paṇḍita āchārya (Trustee)					SII, XV 150-151
111.	Ins. from Yewur 'F' AD 1174 Kalachuris of Kalyani	Shorapur Tq. Gulbarga Dt.	@	God Mallikārjuna		Tatpurushadeva (Trustee)		AB - NI			SII, XV, 335-336
112.	Ins. no. 241 AD 1174. Sindas of Erambarage	Ron Tq. Dharwar. Dt.	@ * <	Madhaveśvara Madhaveśvara Madhaveśvara			repairs	NI -caitra pavitra festival	satra	@ pujari	SII, XV, 297-301
113.	Ins. no. 125 AD 1174 Kalachuris of Kalyani	Gadag Tq. Dharwar Dt.	~	Asitarakeśava-ditya				ND			SII, XV, 158-159
114.	Ins. no. 12 AD 1175 Kalachuris of Kalyani	Sindhnur Tq. Raichur Dt.	~	Amruthalinga Nakareśvara Manoharachenna -keśva							HAS, 18. 61-63
115.	Ins. no. 131 AD 1178. Kalachuris of Kalyani	Gadag Tq. Dharwar Dt.	~, *	Vidireśvara		Vāmaśakti-Paṇḍita		NI			SII, XV, 167-168
116.	Ins. no. 13 AD 1178. Kalachuris of Kalyani.	Yalburgi Tq. Raichur Dt.	@	Kālikajyeṣtha	Siddhantikākeś-vara (āchārya) (Trustee)		repairs	daily worship	feeding ascetics	& dance master & drummer	HAS, 18, 63-74
117.	Ins. no.135 AD 1079. Kalachuris of Kalyani.	Gadag Tq. Dharwar Dt.	~	Abhinavaprasan-na Keśavadeva and Śaṇkaradeva			Installed the deity Keśavadeva	sthānapūia ND			SII, XV, 174-178

Key to the Symbols : > : Main Ruler; A : Artisan; # : Local Potentate; & : Cultural Groups; @ : Functionary; < : Peasant; * : *mahājana*; AB : *aṅgabhoga*; $: *brāhmaṇa*; ND : *nandādipa* (lamps); ~ : Merchant; NI : *Nivedya*.

Chart – IV : IDEOLOGICAL CONTEXT

Sub Region B

i	ii	iii	iv	v	vi	vii	viii	ix	x	xi	xii
S.No.	*Name/Date Dynasty*	*Location*	*Patron*	*Name of the Temple*	*Vedic Learning Rituals*	*Priests/Sects*	*Nature of Patronage*				*Reference*
							Repairs/ Construction	*Rituals/ Festivals*	*Maṭha*	*Cultural Groups*	
118.	Two Ins. from Ron AD 1179. Kalachuris of Kalyani.	Ron Tq. Dharwar Dt..	#, < entire people	Chāmeśvara and Māleśvara		Gurubhakta deva *(āchārya* (Trustee)	construction	regular worship, ND, *caitra Pavitra* festival NI			*SII*, XIX, 226-236
119.	Ins. from Yewur 'G' AD 1179 Kalachuris of Kalyani.	Shorapur Tq. Gulbarga Dt.	@	Savayamhu Som-anātha deva	Jñānarāsi-Paṇḍita *(sthānāchārya)* (Trustee)				for the maṭha		*EI*, XII, 336-340
120.	Ins. no. 10 AD 1181. Kalachuris of Kalyani.	Gadag Tq. Dharwar Dt.	@	Maruleśvara				ND			*KI*, II, 29-34
121.	Ins. no. 61 AD 1184 Chalukyas of Kalyani.	Gadag Tq. Dharwar Dt.	~	Mallikārjuna				AB, NI, *Sanskrānti*			*SII*, XV, 87
122.	Ins. no. 140 AD 1184. Chalukyas of Kalyani.	Gadag Tq. Dharwar Dt.	Priest Yogisa-haja-nanda	Svayambhu-Mādhaveśvara				NI, NB	feeding *brāhmaṇas*		*SII*, XV, 180-182
123.	Ins. no. 62 AD 1184. Chalukyas of Kalyani.	Gadag Tq. Dharwar Dt.	A, ~	Prasannkeśava Asitarakeśavād-itya							*SII*, XV, 87-88
124.	Ins. no. 64 AD 1185. Chalukyas of Kalyani.	Gadag Tq. Dharwar Dt.	Wife of @ *	Mallikārjuna Mallikārjuna		Gangarāsipaṇḍita *(āchārya)* (Trustee)		*Caitrapavitra* festival NI			*SII*, XV, 89-90
125.	Ins. no. 67 AD 1185. Chalukyas of Kalyani.	Gadag Tq. Dharwar Dt.	A	Nomiyabasadi Sānthinath of Kammatajinālaya				worship *Chaitra pavitra* worship			*SII*, XI, 92-94

Key to the Symbols : > : Main Ruler; # : Local Potentate; @ : Functionary; * : *mahājana*; $: *brāhmaṇa*; ~ : Merchant;
A : Artisan; & : Cultural Groups; < : Peasant; AB : *aṅgabhoga*; ND : *nandādipa* (lamps); NI : *Nivedya*.

Chart – IV : IDEOLOGICAL CONTEXT

Sub Region B

i	ii	iii	iv	v	vi	vii	viii	ix	x	xi	xii
S.No.	Name/Date Dynasty	Location	Patron	Name of the Temple	Vedic Learning Rituals	Priests/Sects	Nature of Patronage				Reference
							Repairs/ Construction	Rituals/ Festivals	Maṭha	Cultural Groups	
				Kammateśvara				ND			
126.	Ins. no. 69 AD 1186 Chalukyas of Kalyani.	Gadag Tq. Dharwar Dt.	A	Morakeśvara		Agastyamuni (āchārya) (Trustee)		NI			*SII*, XV, 95
127.	Ins. no. 70 AD 1186 Chalukyas of Kalyani.	Gadag Tq. Dharwar Dt.	~	Nanneśvara				AB			*SII*, XV, 95-96
128.	Ins. no. 73 AD 1189. Chalukyas of Kalyani.	Gadag Tq. Dharwar Dt.	<, A	Bonteśvara Bonteśvara		Rudraśakti Paṇḍita (Builder of the temple & donor)		*Chaitra-pavitra* festival			*SII*, XV, 99-104
129.	Ins. no. 16 AD 1191. Chalukyas of Kalyani.	Lingsugur Tq. Raichur Dt.	#, @	Svayambhupaś-chima sōmanatha			repairs	offerings			HAS, 18, 83-89
130.	Gadag Ins. AD 1192. Hosyalas of Dwarasamudra	Gadag Tq. Dharwar Dt.	>	Svayambhu Trikoteśvara			repairs, installation	AB	feeding ascetics instruction		EI, IV, 89-97
131.	Ins. no. 74 AD 1194. Chalukyas of Kalyani	Ron Tq. Dharwar Dt.	#	Kalakaleśvara				NI	*satra*		*SII*, XV, 104-105
132.	Ins. no. 210 AD 1196. Hosyalas of Dwarasamudra.	Mundargi Tq. Dharwar Dt.	>, ~	Bulleśvara				AB,ND			*SII*, XV, 252-253
133.	Ins. no. 211 AD 1196. Hosyalas of Dwarasamudra	Mundargi Tq. Dharwar Dt.	~	Billeśvara				AB			*SII*, XV, 253-254

Key to the Symbols : > : Main Ruler; A : Artisan; # : Local Potentate; & : Cultural Groups; @ : Functionary; < : Peasant; * : *mahājana*; AB : *aṅgabhoga*; $: *brāhmaṇa*; ND : *nandādipa* (lamps); ~ : Merchant; NI : *Nivedya*.

Chart – IV : IDEOLOGICAL CONTEXT

Sub Region C

i	ii	iii	iv	v	vi	vii	viii	ix	x	xi	xii
S.No.	*Name/Date Dynasty*	*Location*	*Patron*	*Name of the Temple*	*Vedic Learning Rituals*	*Priests/Sects*	*Nature of Patronage*				*Reference*
							Repairs/ Construction	*Rituals/ Festivals*	*Maṭha*	*Cultural Groups*	
134.	Ins. no. 214 AD 1199. Hosyalas of Dwarasamudra.	Gadag Tq. Dharwar Dt.	#	Svayambhu Trikūṭeśvara		Siddānti-Chahdrabhūshaṇa *(āchārya)* (Trustee)		worship offerings			*SII.* XV, 256-258
135.	Ins. no. 220 AD 1207. Hosyalas of . Dwarasamudra	GadagTq. Dharwar Dt.	~	Telligeśvara		Bhāskarāchārya *(āchārya)* (Trustee)					*SII.* XV, 267-268
136.	Transcript Ad 967 (Rashtrakutas of Malkhed)	Kurnool Tq. Kurnool Dt.	#	Gavareśvara				AB-ND			314/72 of, office of Archeaco-logy and Hyderab-ad.
137.	Ins. no. 19 AD 1057. Chalukyas of Kalyani.	Alampur Tq. Mahabubnagar Dt.	@	Brahmeśvara		Brahmarāsi Bhaṭṭāraka *(mahāsthānādh-pathi (Trustee)*	repairs	ND			*APGAS3*, 114-115
138.	Transcript .AD 1060 Chalukyas of Kalyani.	Alampur Tq. Mahabubnagar Dt.	@	Kukkuṭeśvara		Lokābhāraṇa Paṇḍita (Trustee)		NI	feeding students	& feeding musicians	*A.R.*B72 of 60-61
139.	Ins. no.11 AD 1067. Chalukyas of Kalyani.	Alampur Tq. Mahabubnagar Dt.	@, ~	Brahmeśvara		Brahmarāsi Bhaṭṭāraka *(mahāsthānadhi-*pathi)(Trustee)	repairs	AB			*APGAS* no. 3 105-106
140.	Panchalingala Ins. AD 1068 Chalukyas of Kalyani.	Kurnool Tq. Kurnool Dt.	>	Pañchalinga Deva		Kāsmirapaṇḍits *(mahāsthāna dhipathi* (Trustee)	up keep of various shrines in the temple precincts	AB,offering to various deities			*EI.*, XXXVI 139-143

Key to the Symbols : > : Main Ruler; A : Artisan; # : Local Potentate; & : Cultural Groups; @ : Functionary; < : Peasant; * : *mahājana*; AB : *aṅgabhoga*; $: *brāhmaṇa*; ND : *nandādipa* (lamps); ~ : Merchant; NI : *Nivedya*.

Chart – IV : IDEOLOGICAL CONTEXT

Sub Region C

i	ii	iii	iv	v	vi	vii	viii	ix	x	xi	xii
S.No.	Name/Date Dynasty	Location	Patron	Name of the Temple	Vedic Learning Rituals	Priests/Sects	Nature of Patronage				Reference
							Repairs/ Construction	Rituals/ Festivals	Maṭha	Cultural Groups	
141.	Trancript AD 1069. Chalukyas of Kalyani.	Nandikotkur Tq. Kurnool Dt.	>	Mallikārjunadeva		Sūreśvarapaṇḍita deva (*āchārya*) (Trustee)			*satra*		*337/68 of* Archaeology & Museums Office. Hyd.
142.	Ins. no. 22 AD 1073. Chalukyas of Kalyani.	Alampur Tq. Mahaubnagar Dt.	#	Brahmeśvaradeva		Brahmarāsi Bhaṭṭāraka (*mahāsthāna dhipathi*) (Trustee)	repairs	ND, NI			*APGAS*, no. 3 117-118
143.	Hichapalli Ins. AD 1074. Chalukyas of Kalyani.	Alampur Tq. Mahaubnagar Dt.	#	Lakshmaṇeśvara		Sūryarāsi-Paṇḍita *āchārya* (Trustee)	repairs	AB, NI ND	satra & feeding ascetics		*EI.*
144.	Ins. no 8 AD 1075. Chalukyas of Kalyani.	Alampur Tq. Mahaubnagar Dt.	#	Brahmeśvaradeva		Brahmarāsi Bhaṭṭāraka (*mahāsthānadhi-pathi*) (Trustee)	repairs	AB, NI Pūja			*APGAS*, no. 3, 103-104
145.	Transcript AD 1075. Chalukyas of Kalyani.	Nandikotkur Tq. Kurnool Dt.	#	Bikkeśvara		Sadyōjātapandita (Trustee)	Installed the deity consctruction	NI, ND	*satra*		*AR* no B317 of 37-38
146.	Ins. no 16 AD 1078. Chalukyas of Kalyani.	Alampur Tq. Mahabubnagar Dt.	#	Brahmeśvara		Someśvararāsi Bhaṭṭāraka (*mahāsthānādhi-pathi*) (Trustee)	repairs	NI, ND			*APGAS*, no. 3 107-108
147.	Ins. no. 33 AD 1087. Chalukyas of Kalyani.	Gadwal Tq. Mahabubnagar Dt.	#	Pallavajinālaya		Karakasena Bhaṭṭāraka (Trustee)					*APGAS* no. 3 40-41

Key to the Symbols : > : Main Ruler; A : Art san; # : Local Potentate; & : Cultural Groups; @ : Functionary; < : Peasant; * : *mahājana*; AB : *aṅgabhoga*; $: *brāhmaṇa*; ND : *nandādipa* (lamps); ~ : Merchant; NI : *Nivedya*.

Chart – IV : IDEOLOGICAL CONTEXT

Sub Region C

i	*ii*	*iii*	*iv*	*v*	*vi*	*vii*	*viii*	*ix*	*x*	*xi*	*xii*
S.No.	*Name/Date Dynasty*	*Location*	*Patron*	*Name of the Temple*	*Vedic Learning Rituals*	*Priests/Sects*	*Nature of Patronage*				*Reference*
							Repairs/ Construction	*Rituals/ Festivals*	*Maṭha*	*Cultural Groups*	
148.	Transcript AD 1088. Chalukyas of Kalyani.	Gadwal Tq. Mahabubnagar Dt.	#	Pārśvadeva		Padmanandi Māladhāri (Built the Jinālayi)					*A.R.* B 82 of 60-61
149.	Ins. no. 36 AD 1101. Chalukyas of Kalyani.	Alampur Tq. Mahabubnagar Dt.	Queen of >	Brahmeśvara			repairs	ND, NI			*APGAS*, no. 3, 125
150.	Ins. no. 38 AD 1106. Chalukyas of Kalyani.	Alampur Tq. Mahabubnagar Dt.	*	Mādhava		Dharaṇindrarāsi Paṇḍita *(mahāsthānādhi-pathi) Trustee*	repairs Installation	AB, ND,NI			*APGAS*, 3, 126-127
151.	Ins. no. 37 AD 1107 Chalukyas of Kalyani	Alampur Tq. Mahabubnagar Dt.	#	Brahmeśvara		Dharaṇindrarāsi paṇḍita *(mahāsthānādhi-pathi.)* (Trustee)	repairs	AB, NI, ND			*APGAS*, 3, 125-126
152.	Ins. no. 15 AD 1107. Chalukyas of Kalyani.	Alampur Tq. Mahabubnagar Dt.	Queen of >	Brahmeśvara		Dharaṇindrarāsi paṇḍita *(mahāsthānādhi-pathi.)* (Trustee)	repairs	AB, NI, *Pūja*			*APGAS*, 3, 108-109
153.	Transcript AD 1127. (Telugu Choda)	Kurnool Tq. Kurnool Dt.	#	Someśvara				NI, ND *abhisheka*			*A.R.*B107 of 59-60
154.	Ins. no. 32 AD 1182. Kalachuris of Kalyani.	Alampur Tq. Mahabubnagar Dt.	~	Gavareśvara		Keśavarāsi- *(sthānāpati)* Trustee		NI, ND			*APGAS*, 3 123

Key to the Symbols : > : Main Ruler; # : Local Potentate; @ : Functionary; * : *mahājana*; $: *brāhmaṇa*; ~ : Merchant;
A : Artisan; & : Cultural Groups; < : Peasant: AB : *aṅgabhoga*; ND : *nandādipa* (lamps); NI : *Nivedya*.

RECAPITULATION AND CONCLUSIONS

Our aim in the present thesis has been primarily to focus upon the interaction of the material forces with the political and the ideological structures in determining the status of various social groups in a hierarchical order during early medieval period (A.D. 1000-A.D. 1200) located in the context of a specific spatial parameter (south western Deccan). This has helped us in coprehending not just the nature of social stratification located in the rural settlements of the period, but importantly, it has enabled us to demarcate new regional and social boundaries of research, particularly in relation to the study of local state formation and the evolution of a regional cultural matrix. Viewed from a regional dimension of change, these defy any universalization of specific structural formations and thus, have enabled us to arrive at certain crucial conclusions over various issues related to the specificity of historical change which differ in a large measure from what earlier studies have hitherto had to say on the subject. We have been able to draw our conclusions on the basis of the study having been based largely on the epigraphical sources collected from various journals and periodicals. We wish to underscore in this regard that we have had to make use of the unpublished inscriptional data stored in the forms of transcripts so as to arrive at an indepth picture of various aspects of historical formations which have been divided under various headings listed below.

In the **Historiographical Context (Chapter–I)** of our study we have made an attempt to highlight various Lacunae involved in the interpretations of social structures of the period and region under consideration. In this context we have primarily focussed our attention on a thematic analysis of various issues (society, economy, rural, space and ideology) which we have taken up in the course of our research. We have essentially attempted in this chapter to see how these have been handled by different schools of historical scholarship which have been classified by us under three major headings depending upon the method of approach adopted by them. Thus, under the first category of historical works we have those written in the conventional approach of historical study which gave primacy to facts based on pure observations and guilded by the epistemological moorings of positivism. Secondly, those written under the Marxist method of historical analysis have been taken into account and thirdly, we have focussed on the recent spurt of historical works written with an approach using an inter–disciplinary method but outside the Marxist framework of analysis. In this context we have observed that serious attempts for the study of society during the early medieval period in India were first made by the conventional category of historians. In these works the caste/*varṇa* division was accepted as the only determinant for understanding the division of the social classes for early India. This unconsciously implied that a static order of society based on textual delineations of the social structure was accepted as the social reality for all regions and periods of history by these scholars. The Marxist scholars, on the other hand, have introduced the class dimension of the *varṇa* system and have put forth the paradigm of studying the *varṇa* order in terms of abstractions of actual relations of production. Any deviation from the *varṇa* theory in reality has been looked at by these scholars, from the point of view of breakdown of the traditional system, particularly for the early medieval period. The new historical scholarship, writing from a regional perspective, in particular the writings of B.D. Chattopadhyaya, have brought into focus the untenability of the application of *Dharmaśāstra* categories of social division to comprehend the regional level social formations which, according to the author, are normally described through the economic categories of their existence. Such a realization has marked a significant shift in the earlier historical perceptions of social structure which enables us to come out of the framework of using universal categories to comprehend social formations at specific regional level and thereby come closer to the understanding of historical reality.

At the economic level, the conventional historical scholarship has given an impression of the unchanging nature of the agrarian structure of early India which has been studied totally divorced from the descriptions of corporate institutions and the urban phenomenon. On the other hand, over emphasis laid by the Marxist scholars on studying the change in agrarian structures which have resulted, according to these scholars, from a decline in an earlier urban phenomenon, have generated the impression that the early medieval economy needs to be looked at in terms of its rural character perse. Further, the importance that these scholars have attached to foreign trade in bringing about the ruralization in economy has led to the external stimulus being given undue credence. Against this background, studies conducted by third category of scholars become significant in overcoming the above lacunae in the sense that these have helped us in viewing the economic change during the early medieval period in terms of both the agrarian and the urban phenomenon. Importantly, the latter has been effectively linked upto the former in defining the totality of economic change at a micro–level for various regions of India, during the early medieval period.

The study of the rural set up of early India has undergone similar changes in the interpretative contexts of its analysis. Among these studies the conventional historical works have played a crucial role in essentializing the image of the village in early India through the use of the concept of 'village community'. In such interpretations the unchanging harmonious social structure and the local autonomy were highlighted as important features of village life which was further considered totally closed from outside influence. On the other hand, the Marxist scholars have viewed the transition in the economic structure from the ancient to the medieval as fundamental to comprehend the rural set up of the early medieval period. The rural phenomenon during this period has been understood essentially in terms of the formation of new agrarian relations, in which the land lords figured as the exploiters and the peasants as the exploited. It is against the background of the basic conflict between these two classes that these scholars have argued about the adverse impact of the growing ruralization and self–sufficiency of Indian village communities during the early medieval period. On the other hand, in the works of the non–Marxist scholars writing for various regions of India, the significance of comprehending the rural milieu of the early medieval period in terms of understanding the entire settlement pattern in relationship to the changing social, economic, political, ideological and spatial dimension has been brought to the forefront. This has enabled us to view the village as a node in the development and expansion of rural space and other settlements patterns from one stage to the other rather than understanding it merely in terms of its autonomy or self–sufficiency. Finally, in the last part of this chapter we focussed on the ideological dimensions of the early medieval set up, and historical perceptions of it. The conventional writings on the subject, we suggested, had simply emphasized on describing the religious beliefs and preachings with a moral purpose. This view is presented as though it was unrelated to the social, economic and political context. The Marxists, on the other hand, have viewed ideology as a part of the superstructure emerging as a product of its economic base. However, by giving primacy to the material factors these scholars have tended to underplay the role played by ideology in bringing about the changes at the base of society though they have contributed considerably to our understanding of the inter–relationship between the social, economic and ideological forces. In the works of B.D. Chattopadhyaya and H. Kulke one, however, observed that ideology is looked upon as an integrative force playing a crucial role of change in the socio–economic set up of any given region. Thus, a recognition in the integrative potential of the ideological forces in bringing about economic change has marked a significant shift in the earlier held historical perceptions. This further enabled us to suggest that views on the role of religion in society, in the context of issues raised by the non–Marxist studies that were primarily conducted on a regional level, enhance our understanding of the specificities of complex social relationships. This chapter on the **Historiographical Context** thus provided us with an informed background of the scholarly interventions on the four broad themes of our analysis particularly in the relation to how they have hitherto been analyzed.

In the **Second Chapter (Geo-Political Context)** of our study we had delineated the geographical and political background for the subsequent analysis of the social structure. We had particularly discussed and highlighted the relationship between the geographical configuration of south western Deccan and the nature of political power structure as it emerged in the context of our study. To comprehend various aspects of these relationships in the specific context of their physiographic location, we had further divided our area, which corresponds to the region lying between the Krishna and Tungabhadra, into three sub–regions of study depending upon the local topographical variations. Such a division, coupled with a corresponding survey of the distribution pattern of inscriptional data of our area of research, has enabled us to arrive at certain crucial conclusions regarding the nature of historical geography and its importance for analyzing regional history. Importantly, it has helped us in identifying potential zones of fertile tracts of the early settlements on a sub–regional level. In this context we have observed that settlement sites such as Bādāmi, Pattaḍakal and Aihole of sub–region A and Ālampur of sub–region C had emerged into prominence as temple sites much earlier, *i.e.,* during the early Chālukyan period itself. This stands in contrast to the settlements of sub–region B, most of which had their origins during our period of study. With a large number of inscriptions and temple sites concentrated here for this period, we identified this area as the 'nuclear' area of our analysis as it afforded us with an immense potential to comprehend various structural forces at work. This also helped us explain how these factors gave an impetus in shaping the rural social formations in the newly emerging settlement of this tract. We then compared and contrasted these changes between the various sub–regions. We have further observed in this regard that the impact of the geographical configuration of the area under study can be seen considerably and most conspicuously in the nature of political power structure that evolved at this time.

We have, in this context, the Chālukyas of Kalyāṇi as the most powerful main ruling dynasty for a major part of the period under (A.D. 973–1200) who were followed by the Kalāchuris of Kalyāṇa, Yādavas of Devagiri and the Hoysalas of Dwārasamudra. Each of these ruled different parts of what we have described as south western Deccan and many of them naturally had control of territories outside this region as well. We have observed in this context that while basing themselves in the north of the river Krishna or, to the south of the river Tungabhadra, these rulers tried to wrest the control of the fertile tracts between rivers Krishna and Tungabhadra. In the process they were involved in constant wars among themselves and with other powerful rulers too. In this context we have been able to surmise upon the fact that these urges of the rulers to gain vast stretches of fertile tracts must be linked up chiefly to the geographical configuration of the core areas controlled by the above mentioned dynasties which were either, mountainous or, plateau areas devoid of vast tracts of fertile land to enable a constant flow of agrarian surplus. On the other hand, the Raichur Doab being a fertile a region, was frequently the bone of contention between the plateau kingdoms north of river Krishan and coastal kingdoms of south eastern India and they naturally had the desire to control the entire water way. It is chiefly in the processes of political control which the chiefs of the main ruling family tried to establish over their area of conquest that one can see the region, particularly sub–region B, of our study emerge as a zone of legitimation of political power. We have further been able to note in this context that nature of the political power structure exercised during the early medieval period has been for a long time conceptualized either in terms of centralized (in conventional historical writing) or, decentralized (the Marxist historical writing) notions of polity. It is only in the recent writings, particularly those of H. Kulke and B.D. Chattopadhyaya, that a positive process of state formation during this period has been shown for various regions in India. Importantly, they have put forth the paradigm of looking at the nature of State formation in terms of integration of local bases of power into an over arching State system. It is in the light of these latter views that we have understood the above stated conquering dynasties as having established their rule in their areas of conquest in the first place through the encapsulation of locally entrenched powerful social groups. The local chiefs were integrated into the State structure by conferring upon them various titles of political status. We have pertinently observed in this regard that the emergence of a number of locally powerful ruling lineages on to the political scene coincided squarely with the period of the concolidation of Chālukyan rule in the context of sub–region B in particular. The vertical spread of such a State society has been clearly discerned by us through an analysis of the stratified social relations both at the local and the supra–local levels of their functioning which we have taken up for discussion in the subsequent chapter.

Chapter III (Social Context) of our thesis thus eventually focusses upon the changing nature of the hierarchical social relations established both at the dominant and the subordinate levels of the political, religious and economic contexts of our study. We have been able to arrive at certain crucial conclusions in this regard through the study of various terms used to describe these groups in the inscriptional sources. The mention of dominant social groups in the rural set up of the period has been made mainly as reflected through their political ranks in such terms as *gāvuṇḍas, pergaḍe, heggaḍe* and so on. That these groups were not just political groups imposed from above is underlined by the fact that they had also emerged as donors of various measurements of land in the respective local areas of their dominance. Thus while the designations held by each of these groups indicate for us the political dimension of the nature of stratification, their capacity to make grants is indicative of the economic hold that these groups had to entrench their essential power as owners of land and its resources. Thus, the consequent social power held by the groups is indicated to us through the mention of family names emphasizing their hereditary and lineages ties in the context of description. We have further observed at this juncture that the socio–political relations of these groups at the local level of power did not remain static in nature. This is indicated to us by the fact that some members of these social groups were able to rise to the level of supra–local chiefs from their local roots of power. Thus, for example one of the early members of the family of Kadambas of Karāḍikal who has been referred to as a *manneya, i.e.,* having political-economic control over a group of villages in A.D. 1066, the same person in referred to as a *mahāmaṇḍaleśvara,* ruling over a larger territorial unit such as *nāḍu* ten years later in a record of A.D. 1077. *Manneya*, as is well–known, was a smaller office and the rise of this chief to the position of a *mahāmaṇḍaleśvara* was a clear indication of the rise in his status. We have discussed other similar examples in the chieftaincies of the Sindas, Haihayas and so on. It is interesting to note at this juncture that these supra–local chiefs, termed as *mahāmaṇḍaleśvaras* and *mahāsāmantādhipatis* began to figure actively in the inscriptional sources of our study only from the middle of the 11th century A.D. These chiefs held a position subordinate to the main rulers by owning allegiance to one or the other powerful dynasty and their rise to supra–local power from a local base clearly indicated for us that conferring titles on various locally prominent families by the chiefs of the main ruling family was a through which they could be brought into the political hierarchy of the State.

In this chapter, we further discussed several references which alluded to the local potentates or, *mahāmaṇḍaleśvaras* trying to attain independent status of power at the regional level by claiming the status of the *mahārājādhirāja.* Among these, the most prominent during this period are the Kalāchuryas of Kalyāṇi, Hoysalas of Dwārasamudra and the Yādavas of Devagiri who had been able to attain sovereignty towards the end of the 12th century A.D. It was however, pertinently noted by us, that these rulers did not have their origins in the area of our study. The apex of political power structure in these hierarchical political relations was thus represented by the chiefs of the main ruling family bearing the titles of *mahārājādhiraja, chakravarti* and so on. We have seen in this regard that these groups, having their political hold over wider spatial parameters, had established varying degrees of subordinate relationships with the local and the supra–local levels of power. It was pertinently underscored by us in this context that the exercise of dominance in the area of conquest by the main ruling family depended upon several factors such as their ability to pool resources (military and economic), striking marital relations with the supra–local chiefs, conferring titles or ranks on the locally entrenched powerful groups, employing members of their family as local chiefs and so on. All these we conclude had been crucial for the rise and consolidation of a regional state structure.

We move on in this chapter to discuss how the exigencies of the consolidation of politico–economic set up by various levels of state power, helped in generating an important community in the rural social sphere, namely, the *brāhmaṇas.* Suffixes such as Chaṭṭopādhyāya, Bhaṭṭopadhyāya, Bhaṭṭa attached to the names of some of these *brāhmaṇas,* particularly in the first half of the 11th century A.D , clearly indicated for us that these groups were brought from outside and settled in the rural space of the area under study. They were given grants of villages by the chiefs of the main ruling family to help them in a variety of ways in exercising their dominance at the political level. It also helped in increasing the agrarian base at the economic level and at the ideological level helped in providing legitimation. Consequently, we discussed that these *brāhmaṇas,* also referred to as *mahājanas,* emerged as powerful land owning elites in the *agrahāra* villages and were mentioned in the incriptions, as donees, donors, witnesses, sellers, buyers of land and as protectors of grants. By the latter half of the 11th century A.D. we noted that the mention of the *mahājanas* as donees begins to be slowly out numbered by the mention of individual non–*brāhamaṇa* religious personages who had emerged as the most powerful section of the society owing to their proximity to the temple institution. The temples had, during this period, emerged as the most crucial agent of legitimation in the hands of political groups. These new ideologues, designated as the *sthānapatis* and *mahāsthānapatis* of these temples, we discussed, began to be closely involved in the maintenance, functioning and governance of the temples and thus, we further argued, that they began to emerge as major centers of political and economic power. This in turn, meant that these trustees of the temple grants became the singular most important socially powerful group by the beginning of the 12th century A.D.

Hierarchical social relations of the period, however, get heightened in the context of references made to various social groups who emerge in their economic capacity of functioning which we discussed next in this chapter. Among these, we first discussed the mention of such collective groups as the 60 *okkalu, ugura, mel–sāsivvaru* and so on who had figured as actually participating in various agricultural activities. Through the contextual references made to these groups we have been able to surmise upon their status as of peasant cultivation who enjoyed some sort of usufructuary rights over their area of cultivation. We have also been able to surmise in this regard, on the existence of certain servile sections of society who, however are mentioned in the original sources in an extremely limited manner. Prominent among such references to the servile groups is the mention of the *bhrtya–dāsivargga* (man and woman servants) who were said to be transferred along with the grants of land made to a temple. Along with this, significant allusions made to the existence of some sort of forced labour through the use of the term *biṭṭi* and these examples enabled us to conclude upon the existence of different types of servile groups catering to the services of dominant social strata. In particular, we have been able to conclude on a firmer basis on the subject status of the individual artisans who were mentioned as stone cutters, blacksmiths, goldsmiths and so on and whose services were crucial for the construction and maintenance of the temple institution. By using the term 'subject' essentially to indicate the dependent status of a person to which he was relegated by virtue of the restrictions imposed on him owing to his socio–economic conditions, we have applied it only in relation to a certain category of artisans who functioned outside the guild organization and figured as dependent on the land lords/mercantile groups for their existence. Importantly, on the basis of the relations of socio–economic interdependence established between these professional groups with their patrons (temple institution emerges as a major patron of a variety of these services in the context of our study). We had ventured to comprehend them in terms of *jajmāni* relationships. In this regard we next discussed how almost a similar type of existence prevailed for a variety of cultural professional groups employed in the services of the temple institution and who were remunerated through various measurements of maintenance grants made through the temple establishment to which they were attached. The nature of grant made to these groups, we argued, attests to the presence of a distinct hierarchy among these groups.

Finally, we analyzed the hierarchical nature of relationships present among the artisanal groups who have been discussed in the inscriptions mainly through the mention of guild formations on the one hand, and on the other, through the contextual references made to some of the individual artisans who figure as enjoying an independent economic status. It is, however, only towards the beginning of the 12th century A.D. that we find various artisanal guilds emerging on a considerable scale and with increased prosperity. More importantly, we noted that guild formations figure prolifically in the context of the mercantile organizations in a variety of ways such as the *nakarmu, nānādeśi, tambuliga*–1000, *Ayyāvoḷe*–500 and so on. On the basis of the nature of their references we have been able to conclude upon the fact that in the context of our study, the *nakaramu* emerge as representing the local market networks with agrarian moorings, and the others, figure more as supra–local trading units with wider networks of mercantile activity. Significantly, the fact that the trading groups during the period of study emerged out of a land owning stratum is firmly established through the nature of grants made by them in the context of their emergence as leasors of lands and importantly, through their close association with the families of the *gāvuṇḍas* and, in certain exceptional cases, with those of the *mahājanas.*

A major conclusion that we arrived at in this chapter was to find the mention of various groups in the inscriptional sources invariably through the politico–economic status that they enjoyed in the functioning and governance of society. This, we underline, did not in any way mean that their *varṇa* status was totally side lined. That *varṇa* was an implicit well recognized way of defining social status was most explicitly stated in the inscriptional sources by the importance given to the *brāmaṇas* on the one hand, and on the other, the urges of some of the local lineage groups to establish *kṣatriya* status and the occasional mention of the *caṇḍāla* as the menial category of society. At the same time, we argued that only taking into account the *varṇa* scheme embedded in the *Dharmaśāstra* texts as a criteria for defining social stratification expressed in the formation of distinct peasant groups at the rural level, would preclude us from looking at the problem of regional specificity in social formations marked by the emergence of distinct socio–economic and lineage groups with firmly entrenched local affiliations. This is basically the reason why we have eventually attempted an analysis of various social groups as they are defined in their specific context of the prevalent economic structure. This is most clearly found in the data explicity mentioned in the inscriptions rather than the *varṇa* terminology which is only occassionally used in them.

The next chapter of our book moved on to focus on the **Economic Context (Chapter IV)** in which the above discussed social groups interacted. In the inscriptional sources pertaining to our study, the economic transactions that have been referred to were inextricably related to various types of grants made to religious beneficiaries. In this context we have observed that there was a gradual shift in the predominance of grants of land made in the beginning of our study those of grants of various commodities and coins which began to be made by the latter half of 12th century A.D. Such as change in the economic structure, from a predominantly agarian one to an economy based on commercial activity forms the basis for comprehending the changing social relations of the period under study. We have been able to arrive at a few major observations in this regard which are as follows.

Since it is the nature of rights held in land and their transformation affected through their grants to various beneficiaries that acted as the prime forces in the change of the economic scenario, We have initiated our discussion in this chapter with the question of land rights. We have been able to notice in this context that two principal categories of land holdings, namely *beneficial* and the non–beneficial emerge during the period of study. While the former were held by the *brāhmaṇas* and temples, the latter were held by rich peasant communities. It would be pertinent to state here that in the context of our study, among the recipients of beneficial tenures, it was the brahmanical temples that out number individual *brāhmaṇa* donees. This begins to happen particularly from the second quarter of the 11th century A.D. Grants made to the religious donees were sometimes attached with extensive immunities conferring different kinds of economic, political and even juridical rights which tended to bestow almost total proprietary rights over the lands granted. In most of the cases, however, we noted that these immunities granted were limited to only revenue exemptions and, in some cases, the beneficial land holdings were even required to pay a small amount of revenue to the state. That the non–beneficial holdings were subjected to normal governmental assessment is well attested in the inscriptional sources of our period. We have, in this context, mention of such revenue terms as *siddhāya, aruvṇa, pannāya, banniga–dere, bīravana, manneya–dere, um̐bali* and so on which we discussed in detail as they were prominently mentioned in the records under study.

Further, we elaborated on the fact that there existed private ownership of landed property during the period under study which we found was well documented in the inscriptional sources. First, the main rulers and their family members emerge as holders of extensive rights over lands and villages under their direct control. Secondly, the local potentates such as the *mahāmanḍaleśvara* emerge as the next important social stratum in terms of holding large measurements of landed property. A third strata of the land owning group that emerges throughout the period of study were at a local functionaries and it is characteristic of grants made by this group that they make them to the temple institution almost always in terms of lands and gardens. It was pertinent to underscore in this regard that the rights of sale, gifts, enjoyment generally included among the vestiges of private ownership of property, were seen well exercised by various landowning groups. We have, in this context, references specifying the purpose for which the grants were made throughout the period of our study. This was particularly relevant to analyze the implications of the grants being made from the middle of the 12 century A.D.

In contrast to the non–beneficial tenures and the their individual character of land holdings we observed that the lands in the *brahmadeyas* were held in common and collective grants by the *brāmaṇa* groups to the temples begins to increase by the end of the 11th century A.D. Thus, we argued that as a result of this trend, overtime, the resources of the *brahmadeyas* tended to move slowly to the local deities housed in the temple and this process occurred through the alienation of shares by individual *brāhmaṇas* by granting them to the temple institution. We even have numerous instances of lands being sold by the *mahājanas* for purposes of making grants.

We came to the conclusion that one of the major implications of the land grants made throughout the period by various social groups was the enormous growth in the economic power of the temple institution which gradually began to play the role of the State in assigning collection of taxes and revenues and getting lands cultivated. It was also observed by us that primarily, the control and usage of labour for the effective use of lands for cultivation and other productive purposes, became a crucial factor in the exercise of dominance by the different types of landowners. In the absence of any direct reference made to the groups actually involved in the productive processes, we have been able to conclude upon their existence and their status in the context of the way agricultural production was carried out, from the analysis of the grant of privileges to the beneficiaries and from an analysis of the tax terms mentioned in the inscriptional sources. On this basis we have been able to allude to the existence of a class of tenants, contract producers, hired labourers and those attached to the grants of lands made to the temples. Apart from the use of various kinds of labour and its management for increasing the productivity, the landlords, we have further observed, took important economic measures to improve irrigation techniques resulting in increasing construction of tanks. They also look keen interest to identify the types of soils and which crops could be effectively grown on them. These points are all mentioned while making the grants. The consequent growth in crop–production is clearly attested to and there is increasing mention to a variety of crops which give us an interesting picture of the changing agrarian scenario.

All these changing aspects in production relations and an improvement in agricultural techniques led to a production of surplus and its concentration in the hands of landowning sections. The next set of observations we made in this chapter was with regard to the results of increased agrarian production. An important tendency grew in which various social groups began to invest in trade and commercial activity. This, in turn, brought about a significant change in the socio-economic set up of the region under study. These processes began to gain a greater momentum from the middle of the 12th century A.D. We noted a trend in the emergence of individual merchants and the consequent rise of mercantile bodies from among the landowning sections. This was clearly discernable from the beginning of the 12th century A.D. which also saw a spurt in the mention of various commercial taxes and levies granted to various temple institutions by the functionaries administering them. Significantly, increasing references were made to grant of gold coins expressed through the terms *gadyāna, paṇa* etc. in the inscriptions of the latter part of the 11th century A.D. and throughout the 12th A.D. This led us to conclude that there was a clear emergence of a monetized market economy, wherein even the revenue over land began to be charged in terms of *gadyānas* or coins. In this context we made significant note of an increasing reference to the minting establishments. Through a close analysis of the mercantile activity in the context of our study, we argued that the emerging economic scene betrayed signs of a limited nature of the urban phenomenon in the sense that the trading activity of the period was still in an incipient stage with the agrarian features juxtaposed closely with the commercial transactions. In such a situation one has attempted to characterize the commercial spurt in the area under study in terms of a stage in rural–urban continuum. We have pertinently underscored in this regard that with the gradual shift in the economic activity marked by a limited commercial growth, the temple emerges as a major consumer of various articles of merchandise. Coupled with this the temple also began to play the role of an employer for various artisanal and professional services performed in the temple precincts. Thus we conclude that the temple becomes the focal point for agrarian, commercial and artisanal production with social groups involved in various economic activities, all trying to seek validation by participating in the gift giving and temple management functions. We further concluded that the temple emerged as a centre of a complex of nucleated settlements. A comprehensive understanding of all phenomena revolving around the temple was, however, next placed in its spatial dimension and then, in its ideological context. We focus on these aspects in our next two chapters namely, **chapters V and VI** of the thesis.

In **Chapter V (Spatial Context)** from the inscriptional sources of our study we have taken up the descriptions of various types of settlements that were mentioned. It has been noted by us that while at times, some of these settlements themselves form objects of grants, they were mostly described to us either, in the form of boundaries to land grants or, as the location for the grants of lands and other commodities made. We detailed in this chapter types of nomenclature used to describe the physical space during the period under study. In this exercise *ūr, grāma, pura* and *paṭṭaṇa* had figured prominently and were invariably mentioned as located in the context of the *nāḍu,* which has been explained by us as the broadest settlement unit. It was further elaborated that while the larger number representing *nāḍus* indicated a higher level in the settlement structure, the smaller number attached to them such as Mulugunḍa–12, Kisukād–70, Bāgaḍage–70, Kukkanūru–30, Toragare–60 and so on represented an intermediate stage of evolution of these settlements clusters. This, we argued, was a transition in the broad settlement area from a local to supra–local level and ultimately, leading to the formation of a region mostly expressed through such terms as Kuntala *deśa.*

A major part of this chapter, however, was focussed upon a comprehension of the hierarchical nature of the settlement patterns which has been obtained by us through an analysis of the suffixes attached to individual settlements, coupled with the contextual references made to these in terms of the socio–economic activity operating in them. We noted that suffixes such as *palli, vāḍa, ūr, grāma* and *paṭṭaṇa* figure prominently in the context of settlement names. *Palli* we described, has been equated to mean a pastoral or tribal settlement, *vāḍa* to mean an enclosure of a village, *ūr,* defined in the sense of planting new places and *grāma,* equated to mean a village settlement perse, defined as referring to a consolidated agricultural community, distinguished from other types of settlement patterns. We argued that while all these terms could be used to define broadly a rural spatial structure, the term *paṭṭaṇa* was the singular most important term used to describe a market place, or a prosperous city. Apart from a discussion of these suffixes attached to the spatial terminology which largely indicated for us the settlement character, we have also pertinently observed in this context that the usage of certain suffixes which primarily connoted the physical features of the locality or, the area to which they are attached. Thus, for instance, *guṇḍa* in Nīruguṇḍa, *gere* in Purigere, *giri* as in *Eṭagiri, kallu* as in Koppakallu, *gola* as in Bennigola and so on were important place names defining the ecological context in which they were located. The terms *giri* and *koṇḍa* have been equated to mean a hill or mountain, *kere* to mean a tank and *kallu*, denoting a stone was simply indicative of a stony or rocky nature of the place.

Thus, on the basis of a variety of contexts in which the settlements were mentioned in the inscriptions of our study, we have been able to surmise upon the fact that the normal rural or urban settlement is much too complex to be encapsulated by generic terms like *grāma or pattaṇa*. In such a situation we have observed that while the lines of demarcation between all these settlements cannot always be drawn with unequivocal sharpness, these could, however, suggest to us in broad terms, the potentiality of a settlement to evolve certain typical characteristics at a given point of time which did not remain static and definite. We have argued to show that they underwent significant changes in the nature of their organization through the influence of a host of factors. An analysis of the contextual references made to various settlements in the inscriptional sources has enabled us to conclude upon the fact that it is the *ūr* and the *grāma* suffixed settlements that stand out particularly in their richness and their complex settlement structure. Secondly, we have also been able to observe in this regard that a large majority of the settlements mentioned in the sources were rural in character and that only some of these gradually head towards an urban like environment by the latter part of the 12th century A.D. when they begin to be characterized as *paṭṭaṇas.* It has further been noted by us that even the nature of rural space was changing over time. This, we noted, was possible to argue on the basis of an increase in the mention of the names of various types of rural settlements which was strongly suggestive of a significant expansion, on the one hand, of the agrarian base. On the other, the fact that some of these were able to emerge to the forefront as important centres of temple settlements underlined the point that there was a significant improvement and increase in the agrarian production which enabled them to maintain various religious establishments on a considerable scale.

These changes have been explained by us as largely an outcome of the urges exhibited by rulers at various levels, who in exercise of their socio–political authority, tried to carve for themselves their spheres of politico–economic influence both at the local and supra–local levels of state power. Therefore, we have been able to argue in this regard that there was a prolific emergence of a particular settlement unit into an *agrahāra, rājadhāni, nelevidu, bhaṭṭa–grāma, mahāgrāma* and so on in the fertile tracts of the area under study. The location of temple centres, depended in a large measure on the political initiative in this direction which often tended to coincide with the rise in the family of the ruling chiefs extending patronage to it. It is in these processes of political control that one has been able to crucially relate the emergence of some *grāmas* as nodes in a cluster of rural settlements surrounding them such as Kukkanūr–30, Muluguṇḍa–12, and so on which again get interlocked with each other to form supra–local territorial units such as the *nāḍus* marked, at every stage, by various levels of political authority. In this regard we have been able to surmise upon an exercise of basically three levels of political power over the settlement structure under consideration. In this pattern the *gāvuṇḍas* mark the primary stage of political authority, followed by the *manneyar* (ruling over several villages) at the secondary level and at the apex of the power structure emerged figure the main ruling family chiefs, who in the initial stages of our study (11th century A.D.) tried to appoint certain powerful chiefs from among their kith and kin.

By the turn of the 12th century A.D. we, however, see a distinct change in the exercise of political authority in the local bases of power, wherein the *manneya* now emerge as the supra–local chiefs and the *gāvuṇḍas* still figure as an important socio–economic and political force to be reckoned with at the primary level of political power in rural settlements. A perceptible change can, however, be seen in the mention of several newly emerging functionaries with high sounding and compound titles who can be located between the supra–local and the local authorities as the representatives of the former. On the basis of the contextual references to the exercise of actual political authority held by these chiefs we have been able to surmise upon the fact that there was considerable amount of adjustment made between the supra–local and the local authority in sharing the political power over the rural space. In such a set up it was definitely the latter who had an edge over the former owing chiefly to their hereditary claims of economic power rooted at the local power structure. We thus conclude that in the light of the high degree of interaction that existed between various settlements established at the political, economic and social levels of integration, represented by the *agrahāras* and the temple settlements comprehensions of the rural settlements of this period as insulated and closed from the outside world have no historical basis whatsoever. Therefore, the transformation of the physical space into a viable productive zone and its subsequent growth into an ideological space marked a crucial phase in the evolution of settlements structure during the early medieval period. It is in this wider context of spatial changes that we have attempted to comprehend the growth in certain pockets of commercial centres amidst the widespread prevalence of rural settlements as products of essentially the proliferation and expansion of agrarian settlements which was taking place on a considerable scale throughout the period of our study. This was marked by a simultaneous increase in the grants of land and villages on a significant scale to the temple institutions. We finally focus on all dimensions of this aspect in **chapter VI** of the thesis.

In **Chapter VI (Ideological Context)**, we have essentially focussed upon the fact that to analyze the significant implications of the enormous growth in the socio–economic and political power in the temple during this period, one needs to take into consideration the crucial role of the ideological moorings conserved in them. This, we argue, is needed because they, in turn, had far reaching effects on the socio–economic change that marked the area of our study during the early medieval period. In the process of such a study we have been able to comprehend various significant issues related to the legitimizing and the acculturating role of the temple institution at various levels of state and social structure. The interrelated aspects of such an analysis have also included a comprehensive understanding of the complex dimensions of ideological manifestations operating at such diverse levels as the religious, social political and economic phenomena expressed, on the one hand, in the form of Purāṇic compilations, juxtaposed with Vedic rituals and *varṇa* ideology and, on the other, through the descriptions of genealogies embodied in the *Praśastis* of dominant social groups coupled with the imprecatory verses that provide another crucial dimension of the ideological process during this period. As such, our study touched upon all the above stated phenomena and this has enabled us to arrive at certain significant inferences in the context of the legitimizing role played by the temple institutions *vis–a–vis* their patrons who represented the hierarchical relations of the politico–economic structure of the period. First of all, we have observed in this context that the early medieval period was marked by a growth on the one hand, of an intense emotional *bhakti* to Śiva or Viṣṇu and on the other, of an outspoken hatred for the Buddhists and Jains. Particularly, the dominance exercised by the Śaivite sectarian ideology of Kālāmukha–Pāśupata variety, through its organized monastic establishments attached to the temple institutions, can be considered to demonstrate, on a substantive basis, the operation of the actual socio–political processes. These, in turn, helped in the crystallization of several more varieties of Śaivite ideology and also some forms of Śāktism, Tāntricism and so on which actually represented an absorption of local belief systems in the context of our study. We have seen in this regard that the growth in the political hold of the local chiefs was marked by a proliferation of temple centres as well. As a crucial implication of this symbiotic phenomenon, we have been able to surmise upon the fact that the establishment of the temples was eventually a conscious effort initiated, in the first place, by various levels of ruling chiefs to provide an ideological dimension to their politico–spatial expansion and thus seek legitimation for the exercise of their politico–economic dominance over the local population. On the other hand, patronage extended to various Śaivite institutions by different socio–economic groups such as the agriculturists, traders and the mercantile groups can be seen on an increasing pace around the beginning of the 12th century A.D. wherein the increase in the variety of the names of deities corresponded squarely with names of the social groups that installed them or patronized them. All these descriptions were clearly indicative of a significant expansion in the social base of temple patronage, which we argue, had crucial implications in the acculturating process operating on a simultaneous basis through the appropriation of the local cults and the consequent absorption of the local tribal groups at various levels of the social structure.

We have been able to identify these processes at three levels. Firstly, at the socio–religious level we saw such a process operating in the integration of the Kālāmukha priests with their tribal ideological moorings into the vortex of the temple establishment wherein the tribal deities and the ideology that they represented had attained an institutional basis which began to gain social recognition on a large scale by the middle of the 12th century A.D. Further, at the political level we have been able to identify the processes of acculturation operating in the crystallization of various local lineages of power at the supra–local level of the state structure. This is revealed in the use of various totemic symbols on the one hand, and on the other hand, by them actively participating in the construction of temples. This normally coincided with the attainment of considerable political eminence by these locally entrenched ruling lineages. This has been considered by us as depicting significant tendencies in a pattern of acculturation resulting largely out of the integrative mechanisms adopted by the dominant state system, represented by powers who came from outside, as did most of the main ruling families. At the other end of the social structure, we have reference to several pastoral/hunting groups who begin to emerge as patrons to certain temple institutions and thus represent yet another level of absorption of social groups into the politico–ideological mainstream. We have pertinently noted at this juncture that in the context of our study, we do not come across, on any considerable scale, the rise of local state structure to a regional level as has been witnessed in the case of Orissa during the early medieval period. On the other hand, the processes of local state formation in the context of study was only demonstrated in the rise of local chieftaincies from a local to supra–level. It is in the hands of these rulers that the temple institutions emerge actively as tools of legitimation and integration. Another important conclusion we arrived at was that the chiefs of the main ruling family figure as actively patronizing the Vedic belief system by indulging in elaborate Vedic sacrifices and creating *agrahāras* and also extending support to the Vedic learning in the temple institutions. Thus, the support extended to these diverse belief systems, we have observed, enabled these rulers to claim a superior status in the eyes of the common people. We also noted that members of the main ruling families also patronized local beliefs of the areas under their control as their own. These two processes of integration can thus be considered to represent two sides of the same coin wherein a common platform for the fusion into a dominant ideology was being simultaneously created to evolve into a regional cultural matrix which operated at various levels of society. The *Praśas* of the ruling groups and the imprecatory verses in the inscriptional sources, were the more authoritative mediums of expressing this application and operation of the dominant ideology over a pervasive and syncretic belief system.

On the basis of above discussions in each of the chapters of the book we have been able to arrive at the following conclusions on the nature of the socio–economic and politico–ideological structure of early medieval south western Deccan enabling us to complete this micro–level study on social stratification and rural settlements.

We have seen in our discussion that the period under study witnessed a highly stratified social structure at various levels of its socio–economic formation. We have attempted in an overall sense to draw attention to the interpretative perspective that the nature of the polity and the dominant ideology of the time interacted with the social and economic system of the period in bringing about the particular character of social stratification. As has been already pointed out in the beginning of our discussions that the social groups involved in the administration of the period, had earlier been viewed either, in terms of belonging to a centralized bureaucratic structure by the conventional historians or, in terms of being feudatories in a decentralized polity trying to entrench themselves in the rural space by the Marxist scholars. We have, on the other hand, argued with the help of our study, that it were primarily the dominant social groups, located chiefly at the local and supra–local levels, that formed an integral part of the political power structure of the area under study. The land lords at the local level were able to exercise a great control over the population of their localities by virtue of their ownership of land and their subsequent involvement in the local political structure. It was these social groups who entrenched themselves in terms of the local and supra–local landed elite, and who formed an integrated state structure of the period. This was done, mainly through the conferment of titles and ranks upon them by the main ruling family who needed a viable base at the local levels to maintain their political authority.

Towards the beginning of the 12th century A.D. we have found that more and more new terms emerge to describe the dominant social groups in the process of our study. This would then imply that new bases of power were brought into the vortex of state structure by the main ruling family. Simultaneous to this phenomena was the expansion in the economic and spatial milieu of the social structure through the grants of land and villages by various levels of state power. Apart from helping in the agrarian expansion and the strengthening of the State system at the local levels, the religious beneficiaries of various grants, also helped in the crucial process of acculturation. Thus, the enormous growth in the Brahmanical temples as land lords significantly coincided in the context of our study with the spread of the *bhakti* cults. Their success was much dependent on the institutional base provided by the temple. The proliferation of the local forms of *bhakti* ideology also had the support of the local bases of power on an extensive scale and those of the main ruling family chiefs to a limited extent. While we have argued that the latter were, unabashed patrons of Vedic learning and religion. Changes in the social structure were primarily related to the broader changes in the land relations, but at the same time, we cannot conclude that the change was totally independent of the dominant ideology and the political system of the time. Thus, it is the relationship between the ideological and the material factors which enabled us to explain the totality of societal organization and change.[1] We wish to further state that in our efforts at the identification of the elements responsible for social change and social stratification, in the context of our study we have been able to arrive at certain crucial conclusions over various issues involved in the nature of state formation and the shaping of the socio–cultural matrix at a regional level.

In this regard one can conclude, first and foremost, that there was the crystallization of the elements of localism dominating the scene at various levels of the socio–economic and politico–ideological structures. We have observed in this context that despite the knowledge and experience in the *varṇa* based division of society as is represented through the significant mention of the *brahmaṇa varṇa* followed by an occasional reference made to the *kṣatriyas vaiśyas and caṇḍala,* the accent is, however, on the description of various social groups in terms of the familial affiliations they claimed, or, with the occupational status represented by them. We have in this context reference to such terms as the *heggaḍe gāvuṇḍa manneya* and so on who represent a nexus of the dominant politico–economic interests and the reference to various agriculturist/cultivating groups is made through the use of such terms as the *okkala, ugura, mel–sāsivvaru* and so on and these social groups, with this particular terminology, can be only be identified on a regional basis. Similar is the case with the various artisanal groups such as the *kammaṭa, akkagale* and the mercantile groups such as the *nakara, taṁbūliga seṭṭi* and so on who represented local artisanal and mercantile interests. It is these hard core categories of social divisions, rooted in the socio–economic ethos of their specific physical setting that provide us with effective clues to comprehend the hierarchical nature of regional social formations as they actually operated. Any attempts at comprehending these groups only in terms of the universal and bibliocentric categories of the *varṇa* divisions, which were based on an all India level, would preclude us from comprehending the actual nature of their stratification. This, we argue, can be understood effectively through the references made to them in the context of their descriptions in the inscriptional sources which was very rarely done through the use of *varṇa* categories especially when local land owning peasant groups were being described. Thus, we conclude in this regard that, "normative values have to be juxtaposed with social reality"[2]. It is only then that the contribution of each aspect, i.e. caste *(varṇa)* and class will enhance the study of "alternative traditions" and provide us with a clearer image of what we regard as "established traditions". It is essentially being emphasized here that though *varṇa* may not have been a explicit category of description in the original sources, it cannot be ignored. At the same time, power and class cannot be undermined in assessing the nature of social stratification. We have further been able to conclude that the processes of local State formation were effectively demonstrated in the rise of local chieftaincies from a local to a supra local level as a result of their interaction with the dominant State system. Closely intertwined in these processes was the introduction of small scale irrigation systems by these elites which helped in the expansion of the productive base at the rural level and also the rise of various spatial units into clusters of settlements at the local and supra–local levels. All these were significant pointers to the efforts made by the local State system to improve and expand their politico–economic urges to gain an effective control over their localities.

Importantly, the elements of localism can be most effectively demonstrated in the processes of acculturation that operated at various levels of socio–political structure. We have been able to depict, in this context, that there were significant movements from the local levels which got precipitated in the formation of local lineages at the political level and in the absorption of various pastoral/hunting groups at the other end of social structure. Kālāmukha priests representing various forms of local belief systems provide an excellent example of integrative processes operating at the local levels of State formation. In fact, the success of Śaivism as the most popular form of ideological manifestation in the context of our study depended, to a large measure, on its ability to adapt itself to various local situations that cropped up in the positive expansion of the settlement patterns that matched with a corresponding increase of deities in the form of God Śiva. However, it is in the context of the construction of temple institutions which acted as the mediating space in such an integration that we have been able to discern the operation of local State formation on a substantial level. We have observed in this regard that our area of study essentially witnessed the spurt in minor temples which prolifically dotted the map of the expanding agrarian base which was a product chiefly of local initiative. Forms of legitimation adopted by various rulers (including main rulers) have been understood by us as peculiar to the area of our study wherein the growth in the agrarian settlements and socio–economic power was still in an incipient stage marked by the strong influence of outside political powers such as the Chālukyas of Kalyāni, Kalāchuris, Yādavas of Devagiri, Hoysaḷas and so on. We wish to reiterate here what we had stated in an earlier chapter that it is chiefly in the efforts made by these rulers to carve for themselves productive zones of surplus appropriation in the area under study, particularly in sub–region B which was marked by riverine fertile tracts that this emerges as a zone of legitimation. It is not surprising therefore, that this sub–region also sees the rises of several locally entrenched families at various local and supra–local levels. It was eventually these chiefs who participated in the temple building activity and the extensive patronage networks. We also conclude that the ever changing pattern of various dimensions of the regional culture cannot be studied totally independent of the changes at the pan–Indian level. We have seen that the formation of the region was a result of the fusion of both the internal and external stimuli of change represented by the urges to the claim to *brāhmaṇa* status by the Kālāmukha priests as has been noted in the suffixes of their names such as Paṇḍita, Āchārya and so on. At the supra local level the occasional attempts at claiming *kṣatriya* status and the patronage extended to Vedic learning in the temple institutions by the main ruling family chiefs are all manifestations of such a cultural fusion in which regional elements begin to take shape through local assimilation as well as through the adoption of trans–regional idioms.[3]

Our major contributions in terms of historical research have been basically at two levels—empirical and theoretical. At the empirical level we have been able to expand the data base of our knowledge by using hitherto unresearched material. These sources have been critically analyzed and presented through well–formulated charts. At the theoretical level we have been able to view the social change as emerging out of an interaction of a host of historical processes that cannot be viewed as independent of each other as determinants of any historical change.

The empirical contribution of this study are new in the way. They have been presented in the extent to which the minutest details have been highlighted. Some of the earlier published epigraphs had been used for reconstructing a political history of this region as part of the larger territorial entities or in the form of political dynastic history. Our study has shown that even the most conventional understanding of history in terms of political history should be done to highlight the political exigencies and imperatives at the local level. It is the rural elite emerging from small localities primarily as owners of land that ultimately forge ties with supra–local and regional levels of power to give a particular character to State formation. Similarly, inconventional historiography large temples have been studied in all their grandeur detailing the magnificence of their architectural marvels. In contrast to this our study has contributed to an understanding that the temple has to be seen as much a part of the economic and social history as it has been of the religious and artistic history of early medieval times. This could once again only be done by moving away from major temple sites and looking at even the small localities where temples were located to ultimately view them in relationship with each other.

Most of our endeavours in writing this regional study were possible because we methodologically chose to divide the whole area into three sub–regions for enhancing the empirical specificity. This we suggest is a major contribution of our study because when liked to our seminal understanding of the importance of historical geography, it enabled us to present elements of both homogeneity and hetrogeneity for almost all aspects of social, economic, spatial and ideological analysis. Thus, while staying close to the descriptive dimensions at the beginning of each chapter we found difference of terminology and nomenclature, and more pertinently, of quality and size confronting us. We have been able to present these variations, at a glance in the charts accompanying each chapter. Though, we must admit, that we set out do to this exercise to look for uniform variables within sub–regions and across sub–regions.

Our efforts at theoretically enriching the debates in historical scholarship, first and foremost, hinge on our contribution of looking closely at a part of the period of transition commonly known as the early medieval. Undoubtedly, the 11th and 12th centuries A.D. witnessed changes which we consciously chose to focus on as important markers of this transition. Thus throughout each chapter we contrast the 11th century conditions from the 12th century ones to comprehended this specificity. Change in time was most clearly visible on the surface manifestations of economic and political activity. Thus we have argued how the totally agrarian milieu of the 11th century gave way to an urban like environment in the 12th century, and on the political front, this saw the assertion of local chieftaincies and powerful landed and commercial elites who entrenched their hold over localities with greater certainty in the 12th century. Though social and ideological change is less crystallized in perceiving it, nonetheless our method of viewing this from the perspective of changes in settlement hierarchy enabled us to conclude on a qualitative change from the 11th and 12th centuries in these two aspects of historical transition as well. It would be pertinent to state here that while Vijayanagara rule over this area of study has been much researched, our contribution to highlighting the above–mentioned changes in pre–Vijayanagara times would positively contribute to enhancing the historical discussions of transition from early medieval to medieval.

This leads us on to the final point we wish to make. It is well recognized that India is a country where multiple layers of regional identity are preserved and conserved. However, it is often erroneously projected that these identities only emerged out of conflict and thereby, have to be maintained as such by highlighting their unique qualities, generating at times, on the negative sides, elements of parochialism and isolationism. Our study has theoretically argued that regions gain their particular identity as much due to conflict, as they do because of interchange of ideas and integration of values. Whereas, the former was necessary to define the acquisators of power at the rural levels in terms of stratified relations of dominance and sub-ordination, the latter enabled a cohesiveness to develop linking up the south western Deccan effectively to the Indian civilization ethos. Secondly, pre–modern India is most frequently projected as being overtly spiritual and therefore, unable to define space for the operation of the political and economic spheres of activity. Theoretically, we have vindicated this stand to argue vehemently that the ideological and material forces in pre–modern India were so inter twined that to separate the secular from the religious domains of activity would miss the complex texture of specific historical reality in the innumerable regions of India. Whereas, our study of a region is apparently an attempt to separate, our concern to highlight the positive forces of integration has been to consciously focus on the inseparability of the profane and the material pillars of India's total past.

REFERENCES

1. Frank Perlin, 'The Material and the Cultural : An Attempt to Transcend the Present Impasse', *MAS,* 22, 2, 1988, p. 383.
2. B.D. Chattopadhyaya, *The Making of Early Medieval India,* Delhi, OUP, 1994, p. 32.
3. Romila Thapar, *Cultural Transaction and Early India : Tradition and Patronage,* Delhi, 1987, p. 440.

BIBLIOGRAPHY

1. (A) ANNUAL REPORTS

Annual Report on Epigraphy for 1965 and 1966 (Epigraphy Series), Government of Andhra Pradesh, Hyderabad.

Annual Reports of South Indian Epigraphy, (1887–1951).

Annual Reports of Indian Epigraphy.

Annual Report of the Mysore Archaeological Department, Bangalore (1908 Onwards.)

Annual Report of the Archaeological Survey of Mysore, Dharwar.

Progress Report of Kannada Research Institute, Dharwar.

1. (B) EPIGRAPHIC SOURCES

A Corpus of Inscription in the Kannada Districts of Hyderabad State, ed. by P. B. Desai, Hyderabad 1958.

A Corpus of Inscriptions in the Telangana Districts of H.E.H. the Nizam's Dominions, ed. by P. Sreenivasachar, the Nizam's Govt., Calcutta, 1940.

A Corpus of Inscriptions in the Telangana Districts of Andhra Pradesh, Govt. of A.P., Secunderabad, 1956.

Andhra Pradesh Government Archaeological Series nos. 3, 9, 13.

Copper Plate Inscriptions of Andhra Pradesh Government Museum, ed. by N. Ramesan, Vols. I & II, Hyderabad, 1962.

Corpus of Telangana Inscriptions, ed. by M. Somasekhara Sarma, Govt. of AP, Hyderabad.

Epigraphis Indica, Vols. III to XXXVI, Inscriptions edited by J.F. Fleet, Lionel D. Barnett, R.S. Dikshit, G.S. Gai, R.S. Panchamukhi, N. Lakshmi Narayana Rao, V.V. Mirashi and R. Kulkarni, Published by ASI, Calcutta, 1895–1965.

Epigraphia Andhrica, Vols. I–V, edited by P. V. Prabrahma Sastry and N. Mukunda Rao, Epigraphical Series no. 11–12, Govt. of AP, 1975–1988.

Historical Inscriptions of Andhra Pradesh, ed. by Robert Sewell and K.S. Aiyangar, Madras, 1932.

Hyderabad Archaeological Series, Hyderabad.

Indian Antiquary, Vols. VI to XVI : Inscriptions edited by J.F. Fleet, Swati Publications, Delhi, 1984 (rp.).

Karnataka Inscriptions, Vols. 1–3, edited by R.S. Panchamukhi, Vol. IV edited by A.M. Annigeri and Vol. V edited by P.B. Desai and B.R. Gopal, Dharwar, 1941–1961.

Select Epigraphs of Andhra Pradesh, Hyderabad, 1970.

Select Stone Inscriptions of Andhra Pradesh, ed. by P.B. Desai Govt. of AP, Hyderabad, 1962.

South Indian Inscriptions, Vols. XI, XV, XVII and XX from the Bombay Karnataka Series and Vol. X Telugu Inscriptions of Andhra Pradesh, Archaeological Survey of India.

The Kannada Inscriptions of Andhra Pradesh, (ed. by P. Sreenivasachar and P.B. Desai), Govt. AP, Hyderabad, 1962.

Topographical List of Inscriptions of the Madras Presidency, ed. by V. Rangacharya, Vols. 1–3, Madras 1919.

II. BOOKS (SELECT READINGS)

Altekar, A.S. — *History of Village Communities in Western India,* OUP, Bombay, 1927.

———— *The Rashtrakutas and Their Times,* Oriental Book Agency, Poona, 1934.

Appadurai, A. — *Economic Conditions of South India (1000 A.D.–1500 A.D.),* Madras University Historical Series, 2 Vols., Madras, 1936.

Appadurai, Arjun — *Worship and Conflict under Colonical Rules,* Orient Longman, New Delhi, 1983 (2nd ed.).

Aruna, A. — State Formation in the Eastern Deccan, Bharatiya Kala Prakashan, Delhi, 2000.

Basham, A.L. — *The Wonder That Was India,* 3rd Revised ed., Sidgwic & Jackson, London, 1967.

Beteille, Andre — *Inequality and Social Change* (A Ramaswamy Mudaliar Lectures), OUP, Delhi, 1988.

Bhandarkar, R.G. — *Early History of the Deccan : Down to the Mahomedan Conquest*, Asian Educational Services, New Delhi, 1985 (2nd ed.).

Bhattacharya, N.N. *Ancient Indian Rituals and Their Social Context,* Delhi, 1975.

Braudel, Fernand *Civilization and Capitalism, 15–18th cen., the Perspective of the World,* III, Fontana, Great Britain, 1984.

Carr. E.H. *What is History?,* Penguin, Harmondsworth, 1977.

Chattopadhdyaya, B.D. *Coins and Currency Systems in South India* (A.D. 225–A.D. 1300), Munshiram Manoharlal, New Delhi, 1977.

——— *A Survey of Historical Geography of Ancient India,* (K.H.R. Publications), New Delhi, 1984 (Ist ed.).

——— *Aspects of Rural Settlements and Rural Society in Early Medieval India,* (S.G. Deuskar Lectures on Indian History and Culture), New Delhi, 1990.

——— *The Making of Early Medieval India,* OUP, Delhi, 1994.

Chattopadhyaya, Sudhakar *Some Early Dynasties of South India,* Motilal Banarasidas, Delhi, 1974.

Chopra, P.N. Ravindran, T.K. Subramanian, N. *History of South India,* Vol. I, S. Chand and Co. Ltd., New Delhi, 1979.

Chaudhuri, A.K. *Early Medieval Village in North Eastern India (A.D. 600–1200),* Punthi Pustak, Calcutta, 1971.

Coomaraswamy, A.K *Spiritual Authority and Temporal Power in the Indian Theory of Government,* American Oriental Society, 1942.

Crane, R. (ed.) *Regions and Regionalism in South Asian Studies : An Exploratory Study,* Duke Univ., 1966.

Das, D.R. *Economic History of the Deccan* (Ist–6th Century A.D.), Munshiram Manoharlal, Delhi, 1969.

Desai, Dinkar *The Mahamandalesvaras Under the Chalukyas of Kalyani,* Bombay, 1964.

Desai, P.B. *Jainism in South India and Some Jaina Epigraphs,* Jaina Samskriti Samrakshaka Sangha, Sholapur, 1957.

——— *History of Karnataka,* Kannada Research Institute, Dharwar, 1970.

Dikshit, D.P. *Political History of the Chalukyas of Badami,* Abhinav Publications, New Delhi, 1980.

Dikshit, G.S. *Local Self Government in Medieval Karnataka,* published by S.S. Wodeyar, Dharwar, 1964.

Dubreuil, G.J. *Ancient History of the Deccan,* Pondicherry, 1920.

Dumont, L. *Religion, Politics and History in India* (Collected papers in Indian Sociology), Mouton Publishers, Paris, The Hague, 1970.

Elphinstone *Report on Territories Conquered from the Peshwa,* Oriental Publishers, Delhi, 1973 (rp.), First Published in 1821.

Fleet, J.F. *The Dynasties of the Canarese Districts of the Bombay Presidency from the Earliest Historical Times to the Musalman Conquest* of A.D. 1318, Bombay, 1896.

Fox, R.G. *Kin, Clan, Raja and Rule, State–Hinterland Relations in Pre–Industrial I*ndia, Bombay OUP, 1971.

———— (ed.) *Realm and Region in Traditional India,* Vikas Publishing House Pvt. Ltd., New Delhi, 1977.

Fuller, C.J. *Servants of the Goddess : the Priests of a South Indian Temple,* University Press, Cambridge, 1984.

Ganapathi, R. *Subordinate Rulers in Medieval Deccan,* Bharatiya Kala Prakashan, Delhi, 2000.

Gopal, B.R. *Minor Dynasties of South India : Karnataka*, Vol. I, New Era Publications, Madras, 1982.

Gupta, Dipankar (ed.) *Social Stratification,* OUP, Bombay, 1992.

Gururajachar, S. *Some Aspects of Economic and Social Life in Karnataka (A.D. 1000–A.D. 1300),* Prasaranga, Mysore, 1974.

Haynes, Douglas, Gyan Prakash *Contesting Power and Every Day Social Relations in South Asia,* OUP, Delhi, 1991.

Ismail, K. *Karnataka Temples : Their Role in Socio-Economic Life,* Sundeep Prakashan, Delhi, 1984.

Jha, D.N. *Studies in Early Indian Economic History,* Annapurna Publications, New Delhi, 1980.

Kamat, Jyotsna — *Social Life in Medieval Karnataka,* Abhinav Publications, New Delhi, 1980.

Kane, P.V. — *History of Dharmasastra,* Bhandarkar Oriental Research Institute, Poona, 1868 (2nd ed.).

Karashima, N. — *South Indian History and Society (Studies from Inscriptions A.D. 850–A.D. 1800),* OUP, Delhi, 1984.

__________ *Towards a New Formation* (South Indian Society Under Vijayanagara Rule), OUP, Delhi, 1992.

Kosambi, D.D. — *An Introduction to the Study of Indian History,* Popular Prakashan, 2nd revised edition, Bombay 1985.

Krishna Murthy, A.V. — *Social and Economic Conditions of Eastern Deccan (A.D. 1000–A.D. 1250),* Secunderabad, 1970.

Kukle, Hermann — *Kings and Cults, (State Formation and Legitimation in India and South East Asia),* Manohar, Delhi, 1993.

Kuppuswamy, G.R. — *Economic Conditions in Karnataka (A.D. 973–A.D. 1336),* Research Publications, Series No. 22, Dharwar, 1975 (1st ed.)

Lahiri, Nayanjot — *Pre Ahom Assam (Studies in Inscriptions of Assam Between the 5th and the 13th centuries A.D.),* Munshiram Manoharlal, New Delhi, 1991.

Lal, Makhan — *Settlement History and Rise of Civilization in Ganga–Yamuna Doab (1500 BC–300 A.D.),* B.R. Publishing Corporation, Delhi, 1984.

Ludden, David — *Peasant History in South India,* OUP, Delhi, 1989.

Mahajan, Malati — *A Cultural History of Maharashtra and Goa (from Place–Name Inscriptions),* Sundeep Prakashan, Delhi, 1989.

Mahalingam, T.V. (ed.) *Mackenzie Manuscripts* (Summaries of Historical Manuscripts in the Mackenzie collection), Univ. of Madras, 1972.

__________ *Administration and Social Life Under Vijayanagar,* University of Madras, Madras, 1975, 2nd ed.

Maine, Henry Sumer — *Village Communities in the East and the West,* B.R. Publishing Corp., Delhi 1985 (rp). First Published in 1913.

Mangalam, S.J. *Historical Geography and Toponomy of Andhra Pradesh,* Sundeep Prakashan, New Delhi. 1986.

Marriott, McKim (ed.) *Village India : Studies in the Little Community,* University of Chicago Press, Chicago & London, 1986 (rp.), First Published in 1955.

Marwick, Arthur *Nature of History,* Macmillan Press, London, 1989 (2nd ed.).

Mukunda Rao, N. *Kalinga Under the Eastern Gangas (900 A.D.–1200 A.D.),* B.R. Publishing Corporation, Delhi, 1991

Mulay, Sumati *Studies in the Historical and Cultural Geography and Ethnography of the Deccan (Based Entirely on the Inscriptions of the Deccan from 1st–13th Cen. A.D.),* Deccan College Dissertation Series, Deccan College, Poona, 1972.

Nandi, R.N. *Religious Institutions and Cults in the Deccan (A.D. 600–A.D. 1000),* Motilal Banarasi Das, Delhi. 1973.

__________ *Social Roots of Religion in Ancient India,* K.P. Bagchi and Company, Calcutta, 1986.

Narayanan, M.G.S. *Reinterpretations in South Indian History,* College Book Home, Trivendrum, 1977.

Narayana Rao, Velcheru Shulman, David and Subrahmanyam Sanjay *Symbols of Substance, Court and State in Nayaka Period Tamilnadu,* OUP, Delhi, 1992.

Parasher–Sen Aloka *Social and Economic History of Early Deccan, (Some Interpretations),* Manohar, Delhi 1993.

Powell, Baden *Indian Village Community,* Longmans, Green and Company, London, New York and Bombay 1896.

__________ *The Origin and Growth of Village Communities in India,* Unity Book Service, New Delhi, 1986 (rp.), First Published in 1899.

Ramachandra Rao, C.V. *Administration and Society in Medieval Andhra (A.D. 1038–A.D. 1538),* Manasa Publications, Nellore, 1976 (1st ed.).

Ramachandra Rao, P.R. — *Alampur : A Study in Early Chalukyan Art,* Akshara, Hyderabad, 1977.

Rai, G.K. — *Involuntary Labour in Ancient India,* Allahabad, 1981.

Ramesan, N — *Temples and Legends of Andhra Pradesh,* Bharatiya Vidya Bhavan, Bombay, 1962.

Ray, H.P. — *Monastery and Guild* (Commerce Under the Satavahanas), OUP, Bombay, 1986.

Rea, Alexander — *Chalukyan Architecture,* Archaeological Survey of India, Madras, 1896.

Richards, F.J. — *Mugal Administration in Golconda*, Claredon, Oxford, 1975.

Saletore, B.A., Aiyangar S.K. — *Social and Political Life in the Vijayanagara Empire (1346 A.D.–1646 A.D.),* Vol. II, B.G. Paul and Co., Madras, 1934.

Sarma, R.G. — *Sri Brahmesvara Kshetra Mahatyam,* Alampur, 1958. (in Telugu).

Sastri, K.A.N. — *A History of South India from Prehistoric Times to the Fall of Vijayanagara, OUP*, 4th ed., Madras, 1987.

Sarma, M.R.K. — *Temples of Telingana,* Hyderabad, 1972.

Sastry, P.V.P. — *Srisailam its History and Cult,* Srisaila Devasthanam, Srisailam, 1990.

Satyanarayana, K. — *A Study of the History and Culture of the Andhras,* Vol. 1, People's Publishing House, New Delhi, 1982.

Seshagiri, B.S. — *Bombay–Karnataka–A Geographical Survey,* Belgaum, 1941.

Shanta Kumari, S.L. — *Agraharas in Ancient Karnataka,* Karnataka University, Dharwar, 1970.

Sharma, R.S. — *Social Change in Early Medieval India (A.D. 500–A.D. 1200)* (The First Devaraj Chanana Memorial Lecture), Delhi, 1969.

———— — *Indian Society : Historical Probings : In Memory of D.D. Kosambi,* New Delhi, 1974.

——— *Sudras in Ancient–India (A Social History of the Lower Orders Down to Circa A.D. 600),* Motilal Banarasidas, 2nd ed., Delhi, 1980.

——— *Indian Feudalism (A.D. 300–A.D. 1200),* Macmillan India Ltd., New Delhi, 1980, 2nd ed.

——— *Perspectives in Social and Economic History of Early India,* Munshiram Manoharlal, New Delhi, 1983.

——— *Urban Decay in India (300 A.D.–1000 A.D.),* Munshiram Manoharlal Publishers, New Delhi 1987.

Shastry, T.L. (ed.) *Ancient Indian Tradition and Mythology,* Vol. 21, ii, Motilal Banarasidas, Delhi, 1982.

Shrimali, K.M. *Agrarian Structure in Central India and the Northern Deccan (A.D. 300–A.D. 500),* Munshiram Manoharlal Publishers, Delhi, 1987.

Singh, R.L. (ed.) *India : A Regional Geography,* UBS Publishers Distributors Ltd., New Delhi, 1987.

Singh, Upinder *Kings, Brahmanas and Temples in Orissa,* An Epigraphic Study A.D. 300–1147, Munshiram Manoharlal, New Delhi, 1993.

Sircar, D.C. *Landlordism and Tenancy in Ancient and Medieval India as Revealed by Epigraphical Records,* Lucknow, 1969.

Spate, O.H.K. *India and Pakistan, A General and Regional Geography,* Munshiram Manoharlal Publishers Pvt. Ltd., New Delhi, 1984 (1st Indian ed.).

Srinivas, M.N *India's Villages,* Asia Publishing Home, Bombay, 1977.

——— *Dimensions of Social Change in India,* Allied Publishers, Bombay, 1978.

——— *Dominant Caste and other Essays,* OUP Delhi, 1987.

Srinivasan, T.M. *Irrigation and Water Supply in South India (200 B.C.–1600 A.D.),* New Era Publishers, Madras, 1991.

Stein, Burton *Essays on South India,* Vikas Publishing House, New Delhi, 1976.

——— *Peasant State and Society in Medieval South India,* OUP, Delhi, 1980.

Stokes, Eric — *The English Utilitarians and India*, OUP, Delhi, (First Pub. 1959), 1982 (rp.).

Subbarao, B. — *Personality of India : Pre and Proto Historic Foundation of India and Pakistan,* Second edition, Baroda, 1958. (2nd edn.).

Sundaram, K. — *Studies in Economic and Social Conditions of Medieval Andhra (A.D. 1000–A.D. 1600),* Triveni Publications, Machilipatnam, 1968.

Thakur, V.K. — *Historiography of Indian Feudalism,* Patna, 1989.

Thapar, Romila — *A History of India,* Vol. I, Penguin Books, Harmonds Worth, 1977.

——————— *Ancient Indian Social History,* Orient Longman, New Delhi, 1978.

——————— *From Lineage to State,* OUP, New Delhi, 1984.

——————— *Cultural Transaction and Early India : Tradition and Patronage,* OUP, Delhi, 1987.

Thurston, Edgar — *Castes and Tribes of South India,* I–IV, Asian Educational Services, New Delhi, 1987.

Trigger, Bruce (ed.) — *Time and Traditions. Essays in Archaeological Interpretations,* Edinburgh University, Edinburgh, 1978.

Venkaramanayya, N. — *The Eastern Chalukyas of Vengi,* Vedam Venkatanarayana Sastry and Bros., Madras, 1950.

Venkata Ratnam A.V. — *Local Government in the Vijayanagara Empire,* Publishers, Mysore, 1972.

Veluthat, Kesavan — *Brahman Settlements in Kerala,* Sandhy Publications, Calicut, 1978 (Ist ed.)

——————— *Political Structure in Early Medieval South* India, Orient Longman, Delhi, 1993.

Wittfogal, Karl — *Oriental Despotism : A Comparative Study of Total Power,* New Haven, 1959 (Reprint).

Yadava, B.N.S. — *Society and Culture in Northern India in the 12th Cen. A.D.,* Central Book Depot, Allahabad, 1973.

Yazdani, G. — *The Early History of the Deccan,* OUP, New Delhi, 1982.

III. ARTICLES (SELECT READING)

Alam S.M. — 'The Historic Deccan–A Geographical Appraisal', in Bawa, V.K. (Ed.). *Aspects of Deccan History,* Hyderabad, 1975, pp. 16–29.

Altekar, A.S. — 'Society in the Deccan', *JIH,* XXX, I, Trivandrum, April, 1952, pp. 57–66.

Appadorai, A. — 'Kings, Sects and Temples in South India (1350–1700)', *IESHR,* 14, no. 1, 1977, pp. 47–73.

————— 'Right and Left Hand Castes in South India' *IESHR,* Vol. XII, nos. 2–3, 1974, pp. 216–259.

Baden Powell, B.M. — 'The Study of the Deccan Villages, Their Origin and Development', *JRAS,* 1897, pp. 279–299.

Barnett, Stephen, A. — 'Approaches to changes in Caste Ideology in South India', in Burton Stein (ed.), *Essays on South India,* New Delhi, 1976, pp. 149–180.

Basavaraja K.R. — 'Agraharas in Medieval Karnataka', *JKU,* 1960, pp. 106–114.

Bernhard, Kolver — 'On the Origins of the Jajmani System', *JESHO,* XXXI, 3, October, 1988, pp. 265–285.

Buyres, T.J. and Mukhia, Harbans — 'Modes of Production and Non–European Pre–colonial Societies : The Nature and Significances of the Debate', *JPS,* Vol. 12, Nos. 2 and 3 Jan.–April, 1985, pp. 1–18.

Champakalakshmi, R. — 'Peasant State and Society in Medieval South India' (Review Articles), *IESHR,* Vol. III, nos. 3 & 4, July–Dec., 1981, pp. 411–426.

————— 'South Indian History and Society : Studies from Inscriptions, A.D. 850–1800' (Book Review), *SIH,* 2, 2, July–Dec., 1986.

————— 'Urbanization in South India : The Role of Ideology and Polity,' Presidential Address, Section I, *PIHC,* 47th Session, Srinagar, 1986, pp. 1--58.

————— 'The Study of Settlement Patterns in the Cola Period Some Perspectives,' *Man & Environment,* 14 no. 1, 1989, pp. 91–101.

——————— 'The State in Medieval South India : Emerging Perspectives', *PAPC,* 13th Session, Sri Sallam, 1989, pp. 263–276.

——————— 'Religion and Social Change in Tamil Nadu (A.D. 600–A.D. 1300)', in, N.N. Bhattacharya (ed.), *Medieval Bhakti Movement in India,* Sri Caitanya Quincentenary Commemoration Volume, New Delhi, 1989, pp. 162–173.

——————— 'A Framework for South Indian Polity (Review Article)', *The Book Review,* XVIII, 6, June, 1994, pp. 4–6.

Chaturvedi, B.N. 'The Origin and Development of Tank Irrigation in Peninsular India', *Deccan Geographer,* 6, 2 (July–December), 1968, pp. 57–85.

Chakrabarti, Kunal 'The Sacred and the Profane in Ancient Indian Myth and Literature,' *SIH* 5, 1, 1989, pp. 143–158.

Change K.C. 'Settlement Patterns in Archaeology', *An Addison-Wesley Module in Anthropology, Module, 24,* 1972, pp. 1–26.

Chattopadhyaya, B.D. 'Trade and Urban Centres in Early Medieval India', *IHR,* 1, 2, 1974, pp. 203.

——————— 'Coinage in Early Medieval Andhra', *JAHRS,* XXXV, Hyderabad, 1971, 61, pp. 245–250.

——————— 'Origin of the Rajputs : the Political, Economic and Social Processes in Early Medieval Rajasthan', *IHR,* III, 1976–77, pp. 59–82.

——————— 'Political Process and Structure of Polity in Early Medieval India : Problems of Perspective', Presidential Address, Section I, *PIHC,* 44th Session, Burdwan, 1983, pp. 25–63.

——————— 'Urban Centres in Early Medieval India' in, Sabyasachi Bhattacharya and Romila Thapar (ed.) *Situating Indian History,* OUP, Delhi, 1986, pp. 8–68.

Choudhary, R.K. 'Visti (Forced Labour) in Ancient India', *IHQ,* XXXVIII, 1 March, 1962, pp. 44–59.

Commander, Simon 'The Jajmani System in North India : An Examination of its Logic and Status Across Two Centuries', *MAS,* 17, 2, 1983, pp. 283–311.

Dandekar, R.N. 'Some Trends in Indian Historiography', *JBBRAS,* New Series, 49–51, Bombay, 1979, pp. 97–139.

Dharma Kumar 'Private Property in Asia, The Case of Medieval South India', *CSSH,* VII, 2, 1985, pp. 340–366.

Derret, J.D.M. 'Rajadharma', *JAS,* XXXV, 1976, pp. 597–609.

Desai, Devangna 'Art Under Feudalism in India (A.D. 500–1300)', *IHR* 1, 1974, pp. 10–17.

Desai, P.B. 'Tantric Cult in Epigraphs' *JOR,* XIX, iv, Madras, 1982, pp. 285–288.

Dikshit, G.S. 'Trade Guilds under the Chalukyas of Kalyani' *PIHC,* 1951, pp. 122–125.

———— 'Mahanadu', in *S. Srikantha Sastry Felicitation Volume,* Geeta Book House, Mysore, 1973, pp. 92–96.

———— 'Group Organisation in Medieval Karnataka', *JKU* (Humanities), 1, pp. 59–64.

———— 'Constitution of Trade Guilds in Medieval Karnataka', *JKU (Humanities),* III, pp. 53–57.

———— 'The Okkalu', *JKU* (Humanities), IV, pp. 58. ff.

———— 'Some Aspects of the Working of Local Assemblies in Medieval Karnataka'. *JKU* (Social Sciences), 1, pp. 107–110.

———— 'Numerical Suffixes of Territorial Divisions in Medieval Karnataka', *JIH,* XLI, pp. 235 ff.

Dirks, Nicholas B. Political Authority and Structural Changes in Early South Indian History, *IESHR,* XIII, April–June, 1976, pp. 125–157.

———— 'Ritual and Resistance : Subversion as a Social Fact' in Douglas Haynes and Gyan Prakash (ed.), *Contesting Power and Everyday Social Relations in South Asia,* Delhi, 1991, pp. 213–238.

Fox R.G. 'Varma Schemes and Ideological Integration in Indian Society', *CSSH,* 11, 1969, pp. 27–45.

Gadgil V. 'The Village in Sanskrit Literature', *JBBRAS,* Vol. II, (New series), London, 1926, pp. 150–166.

Ganesh, Kamala — 'Jajmani Relations in Tirunelveli District. A Case Study of the Kottai Pillaimar 1839–1979,' *IESHR,* XXII, 2, 1985.

Ghoshal U.N. — 'Ownership of the Soil in Ancient, India: The Evidence of Certain Texts Discussed', *IHQ,* II. Calcutta, 1926, pp. 198–203.

Gopal, Lallanji — 'On Some Problems of Feudalism in Ancient India', *ABORI,* LIV, Poona, 1963, pp. 1–31.

Govind, Vijay — 'Some Aspects of Village Administration as Gleaned from Sukranitisara, *JAHRS,* XXX, Rajahmundry, 1964–65, pp. 71–84.

Gunavardana, R.A.L.H. 'Social Function and Political Power : A case Study of State Formation in Irrigation Society', *IHR,* IV, 2, 1978, pp. 259–273.

———— 'The Analysis of Pre–Colonial Social Formations in Asia in the Writings of a Karl Marx,' *IHR,* Vol. 2, 1976, pp. 365–388.

Gurukkal, Rajan — 'Medieval Land Rights : Structure and Pattern of Distribution', *PIHC* 39th session, Hyderabad, 1978, pp. 279–284.

———— 'Aspects of the Reservoir System of Irrigation in the Early Pandya State', *SIH,* New Series, 2, 2, 1986, pp. 155–164.

———— 'Towards the Voice of Dissent :Trajectory of Ideological Transformation in Early South India', *Social Scientist,* 21, 1–2, Jan.–Feb. 1993, pp. 2–22.

Gururajachar. S. — 'The Vira–Bananuas of Karnataka (A.D. 1000–A.D. 1300).' *Studies in History and Culture* (P.B. Desai Felicitation Volume), Karnataka University, Dharwar, 1971, pp. 76–84.

Gyan Prakash — 'Writing Post–Orientalist–Histories of the Third World Perspectives from Indian Historiography', *CSSH,* 32, 2, 1990, pp. 387.

Hall R. Kenneth — 'Peasant State and Society in Chola Times. A view from the Tiruvidalmarudur Urban Complex', *IESHR,* XVIII, 3 & 4, 1981, pp. 393–410.

Habib, Irfan — 'The Peasant in Indian History'. General President's Address, *PIHC,* 43rd Session, Kurukshetra, 1982, pp. 3–47.

——— 'Classifying Pre–Colonial India', *JPS*, (Special issue) Edited by T.J. Byres and Harbans Mukhia 12, 2 & 3, Jan–April, 1985, pp. 44–53.

——— 'The Social Distribution of Landed Property in Pre–British India', in Sharma, R.S., Jha, V.N. (ed.) *Indian Society : Historical Probings,* Peoples Publishing House, New Delhi, 1985, pp. 3–37.

Heesterman, J.C. 'Power and Authority in Indian Tradition', in R.J. Moore (ed.), *Tradition and Politics in South Asia,* New Delhi, 1979, pp. 60–85.

Heitzman, James 'Socio–Economic, Formations in Pre–Modern South East Asia,' *JPS,* 13, 1, 1985, pp. 47–60.

——— 'Temple Urbanism in Medieval South India,' *JAS,* 46, 4, 1987, pp. 791–826.

——— 'State Formation in South India, A.D. 850–A.D. 1280', *IESHR,* XXIV, 1, Jan.–March, 1987, pp. 35–62.

——— 'Ritual Polity and Economy : The Transactional Network of an Imperial Temple in Medieval South India', *JESHO,* XXXIV, 1991, pp. 23–54.

Inden, Ronald 'Hierarchies of Kings in Early Medieval India', *Contributions to Indian Sociology',* (New Series), 15, 1–2, 1981, pp. 99–125.

——— 'Orientalist Constructions of India', *MAS,* 20, 3, 1986, pp. 401–446.

Jaiswal, Suvira 'Studies in the Social Structure of the Early Tamils', *Indian Society : Historical Probings,* New Delhi, 1974, pp. 124–155.

——— 'Changes in the Status and Concept of Sudra Varna in Early Middle Ages', *PIHC,* 41st session, Bombay, 1980, pp. 112–119.

——— 'Varna Ideology and Social Change' *Social Scientist,* 19, 3–4, 1991, pp. 41–48.

Jha D.N. 'Temples as landed Magnates in Early Medieval South India (A.D. 700–A.D. 1300)', in Sharma, R.S. Jha, V. (ed.) *Indian Society : Historical Problings.* New Delhi, Peoples Publishing House, 1974.

Jha, Vivekanand — 'Varnasamkara in the Dharmasastras : Theory and Practice', *JESHO,* 13, 3, 1970, pp. 273–288.

__________ 'Stages in the History of Untouchables', *IHR* July, 1975, pp. 14–31.

__________ 'Social Stratification in Ancient India : Some Reflections', *Social Scientist,* 19, 3–4, March–April, 1991, pp. 19–30.

Joshi S.B. — 'Etymology of Place Names Patti–Hatti Some Observations on the History of Maharashtra and Karnataka', *ABORI,* XXXIII, Poona, 1952, pp. 41–56.

Kanakadurga, P.S.
Sudhakar Reddy, Y.A. — 'Kings, Temples and Legitimation of Autochthonous Communities : A Case Study of South Indian Temple' *JESHO,* XXXV, 1992, pp. 145–166.

Karashima, N. — 'The Village Communities in Chola Times : Myth or Reality', *JESI,* VIII, Dharwar, 1981, pp. 85–96.

Karve, Iravati — 'The Indian Village', *BDCRI* (Taraporewala Memorial), 18, Poona, 1958, pp. 73–106.

Kennedy, Richard — 'Status and Control of Temples in Tamil Nadu', *IESHR,* June–Sept. 1974, pp. 260–269.

__________ 'The King in South India, as Chieftain and Emperor' *IHR,* III, 1 July, 1976.

Kosambi, D.D. — 'Early Stages of Caste System in Northern India,' *JBBRAS,* New Series, XXII, London, 1946, pp. 33–48.

__________ 'What Constitutes Indian History', *ABORI,* XXXV, Poona, 1954, pp. 194–201.

__________ 'On the Development of Feudalism in India', *ABORI,* XXXVI, Poona, 1955, pp. 258–269.

__________ 'Origins of Feudalism in Kashmir', *JBBRAS,* New Series the Sardhasatabdi commemoration, 311 & 312, London, 1956–57, pp. 108–120.

Krishnan, K.G. — 'Traipurusha–Trikuta Cults in Karnataka', *QJMS,* IV, Bangalore, 1964, pp. 53–56.

Kulke, Hermann — 'Kshatriyaization and Social Change. A Study in Orissa Setting', Devadas Pillai (ed.), *Aspects on Changing India* (Studies in honour of Professor G.S. Ghurye), Bombay, 1976, pp. 1–12.

——— 'Royal Temple Policy and the Structure of Medieval Hindu Kingdoms', in Eschmann, A, Kulke, H and Tripathi, G.C. *The Cult of Jagannath and the Regional Tradition of Orissa,* South Asian Institute, Delhi, 1978, pp. 127–130.

——— 'Fragmentation and Segmentation Versus Integration? Reflections on the Concepts of Indian Feudalism and the Segmentary State in Indian History,' *SIH,* V, 2, 1982, pp. 21–25.

——— 'Maharajas, Mahants and Historians : Reflections on the Historiography of Early Vijayanagara and Sringeri in Vijayanagara City and Empire', *New Currents of Research,* Vol. I, University of Heidelberg, 1985, pp. 120–140.

Kuppuswamy, G.R. 'Role of the Mahajanas in the History of Medieval Karnataka', *JKU* (Social Sciences) VI, 1970, pp. 61–66.

Mahaligam, T.V. 'The Nolamba Pallavas', *JIH,* XXXVI, 1, Trivandrum, April, 1958, pp. 131–141.

——— 'Village Communities in South India,' in T.V. Mahalingam, *Readings in South Indian History,* S.P. Gupta and K.S. Ramachandran (ed.), Delhi B.R. Publishing Corporation, 1977, pp. 94–105.

Mayer, Peter 'Inventing Village Tradition : the late 19th century Origins of the North Indian "Jajmani System". *MAS* 27, 2, 1993, pp. 357–395.

Mishra, R.N. 'Village Life and Settlements in the Light of Vakataka inscriptions', in B.N. Pande and B.D. Chattopadhyaya (ed.), *Archaeology and History,* Vol. II, Delhi, pp. 643–644.

Mookerji, R.K. 'Local Self Government in Ancient India', *QJMS,* VIII, no. 3, Bangalore, 1917–1918, pp. 223–242.

Morrison, Kathleen D.
Sinopoli, Carla M. 'Economic Diversity and Integration in a Pre–Colonial Indian Empire', *World Archaeology,* 23, 3, Feb., 1992, pp. 335–352.

Mukhia, Harbans 'Was there Feudalism in Indian History?' Presidential Address, *PIHC,* 40th Session, Waltair, 1979, PP. 229–280.

————	'Peasant Production and Medieval Indian Society', *JPS,* 12, 2 and 3, Jan–April, 1985, pp. 228–251.
Murthy M.L.K.	'Environment, Royal Policy and Social Formation in the Eastern Ghats of South India, A.D. 1000–1500', Presidential Address, *PIHC,* 53rd session, Warangal, 1993, (Cyclostyled copy).
Murthy, T.S.N.	'Corporate Life in Medieval Andhra Villages', *Itihas,* VI, I, Hyderabad, 1978, pp. 63–69.
Nagaraju, S.	'Beginnings of Telugu Literature : A Socio-Historical Approach,' Presidential Address, *PAPHC,* 11th Session, Nagaram, 1987, pp. 1–25 (cyclostyled copy).
————	'The place of J.F. Fleet in Western Contributions to Indological Studies in Indian Culture.' Published by Professor Ramachandra Rao Felicitation Committee, Bangalore, pp. 327–337.
Naik, A.V.	'Inscription of the Deccan : An Epigraphic Survey,' *BDCRI,* IX, 1–2, Poona, 1948, pp. 1–148.
Nandi R.N.	'The Boyas–Transformation of a Tribe into Caste', *PIHC* Bhagalpur Session, 1968, p. 971.
————	'Clan Name and Social Mobility in the Deccan', *PIHC,* 33rd Session, Muzaffarpur, 1972, pp. 111–117.
————	'Origin of the Vira–Saiva Movement', *IHR* II, 1, July, 1975, pp. 32–46.
————	'Client Ritual and Conflict in Early Brahmanical Order', *IHR,* 6, 1979–80, pp. 64–118.
————	'Growth of Rural Economy in Early Feudal India' Presidential Address, *PIHC,* 45th Session, Annamalai Nagar, 1984, pp. 1–72.
Nanda Kishore, K.	'Hydraulic Agriculture in Peninsular India (300 B.C.–1300 A.D.)', *PIHC* 40th session, Waltair, 1979.
Narayanan, M.G.S.	'Trends and Prospects in Historiography', Presidential Address, section 1, *PIHC,* 39th Session, Hyderabad, 1978, pp. 12–40.
————	'South Indian History and Society (studies from Inscriptions, A.D. 850–A.D. 1809)', by Karashima, N. Review Article, *Tamil Civilization,* 3, 1, 1985, pp. 57–71.

——————— 'A Critique of the History of South India and a Proposal for a New Conceptual Framework', *PSIHC,* 7th Session, Madras University, 1987, pp. 9–14.

Narayanan, M.G.S.
Veluthat, Kesavan 'Bhakti Movement in South India' in Jha, D.N. (ed.) *Feudal Social Formations in Early India,* Delhi, 1987, pp. 348–375.

Panchamukhi, R.S. 'The Historical Remains of Pattadakal', PKRB, Dharwar, 1948, pp. 52–56.

Parasher-Sen, Aloka 'Feudal Formations' *Social Scientist,* 171–172, Aug.-Sept., 1987, pp. 122–125.

——————— 'Recent Historical Writings on Early Indian History upto A.D. 500, Some Theoretical Implications', *Seminar,* October, 1987, pp. 44–48.

——————— 'Early History of Andhra Some Interpretations', *PAPHC,* 9th Session, Kurnool, 1988, pp. 184–191.

——————— 'The Village Given to Us : Intellectual Constructions of the Village Community in Historical Writing', in Alok Bhalla and Peter, J. Bumke (ed.) *Images of Rural India in the 20th Cen.,* Sterling Publishers, New Delhi, 1992, pp. 17–37.

——————— 'Nature of Society and Civilisation in early Deccan', *IESHR,* 29, 4, 1992, pp. 437–477.

——————— 'Temple Girls and the Land Grant Economy, (8th–13th centuries A.D.)', in Aloka Parasher (ed.) *Social and Economic History of Early Deccan,* (Some interpretations), Delhi, 1993, pp. 158–239.

Pathak, R.S. 'Vedic Rituals in Medieval Period : An Epigraphic Study', *ABORI,* XL, Poona, 1959, pp. 218–230.

Perlin, Frank 'State Formation Reconsidered', *MAS,* 19, 3, 1985, pp. 415–480.

——————— 'The Material and the Cultural : An Attempt to Transcent the Present Impasse', *MAS*, 22, 2, 1988, pp. 383–416.

Pramila, K. 'Landholding Pattern in Early Medieval Telangana' *APHC*, Tenali, 1994, pp. 46–48.

Prasad, O.P. — 'A Study of Towns in Karnataka on the Basis of Epigraphic Sources (A.D. 600–A.D. 1200)', *PIHC,* 38th Session, 1977, pp. 57–60.

Rai, G.K. — 'Forced Labour in Ancient and Early Medieval India', *IHR*, 3, 1976–77, pp. 16–41.

Ramaswamy, Vijaya — 'Some Inquiries into the Conditions of Weavers in Medieval South India', *IHR*, 6, 1979–86.

Ramudu, M. — 'Tank Irrigation under the Rayas of Vijayanagara–Some Theoretical Considerations', *PAPHC* (13th Session), Srisailam, 1989, pp. 76–80.

Rawlinson, H.G. — 'A Century of Oriental Research', *ABORI,* VI, i, Poona, 1924–25, pp. 41–49.

Ray, Niharanjan — 'Rural Urban Dichotomy in Indian Tradition and History', *ABORI,* LVIII & LIX, Diamond Jubilee Volumes, Poona, 1978, pp. 863–892.

Reddy, M.P.R. — 'Village Communities in the Eastern Deccan', *Itihas*–VI Hyderabad, July–Dec., 1978, pp. 63–79.

Rouse, Irwing — 'Settlement Patterns in Archaeology', in Ucko P.J. Tringham R., and Dimbley D.W., *Man Settlement and Urbanism,* London, Duckworth 1972, pp. 95–107.

Rudra, Ashok — 'Against Feudalism', *EPW*, Vol. XVI, no. 52, Dec. 26th, 1981, pp. 2133–2146.

Sastri, K.A.N. — 'Grama an Examination of a New Interpretation, the *JOR,* Vol. IV, Part III, Madras, July–Sept., 1930, pp. 211–225.

Samuel, Raphel, — 'What is Social History?', *History Today,* March, 1985, pp. 34–44.

Settar, S. — 'Twentieth Century in Ancient India', Presidential Address, Ancient India section, *PHIC*, 43rd session, Kurukshetra, 1982, pp. 57–91.

———— — 'Roots Relations, Relevance, the Chalukyan Backdrop',in Mulk Raj Anand (ed.), *Marg,* XII, I, pp. 10–30.

Sharma, R.S. — 'Reconstruction of Ancient Indian History', *ABORI,* LV, Poona, 1974, pp. 1–8.

———— — 'Indian Feudalism Retouched' (Review Article), *IHR*, 1, 2, Sept., 1974, pp. 320–330.

———— 'Problem of Transition from Ancient to Medieval in Indian Society', *IHR*, 1, 1974, pp. 1–9.

———— 'Problems of Social Formations in Early India', Presidential Address, Section I, *PIHC,* 36th session, 1975, pp. 1–11.

———— 'How Feudal was Indian Feudalism' in Jha, D.N. (ed.), *Feudal Social Formation in Early India,* Chanakya Publications, Delhi, 1987, pp. 165–197.

———— Material Milieu of Tantricism', in D.N. Jha (ed.), *Feudal Social Formations in Early India,* Chanakya Publications, Delhi, 1987, pp. 377–388.

———— 'Problem of Peasant Protest in Early Medieval India', *Social Scientist,* 16, 9, 1988, pp. 3–16.

Shettar, Ashok 'Aspects of Agricultural Expansion in Early Medieval Southern Karnataka', In K. Veerathappa (ed.), *Studies in Karnataka History and Culture Proceedings of the Karnataka History Congress*, Mysore, 1987, pp. 70–78.

Shulman, David 'The Enemy within : Idealism and Dissent in South Indian Hinduism' in S.N. Eisenstadt, Reuven Kahane and David Shulman (eds.), *Orthodoxy, Heterodoxy and Dissent in India,* Mouton Publishers, New York, 1984, pp. 11–55.

Stein, Burton 'Integration of the Agrarian System of South India' in R.E. Frykenberg (ed.), *Land Control and Social Structure in Indian History,* Madison, 1969.

———— 'The State and Agrarian Order in Medieval South India : A Historiographical Critique' in Burton Stein (ed.), *Essays on South India*, New Delhi, 1976 pp. 64–91.

———— 'Circulation and the Historical Geography of Tamil Country', *JAS,* XXXVII, no. 1, Nov., 1977, pp. 7–26.

———— 'The Segmentary State in South Indian History', in Fox, Richard G. (ed.), *Realm and Region in Traditional India,* Vikas Publishing House, New Delhi, 1977, pp. 3–51.

———— The Segmentary State in South : Interim Reflections', *Seminar paper on State Formation in Pre–Colonial South India,* Delhi, March, 1988, (Cyclostyled Copy).

Stein, Burton, Byres, T.J. and Mukhia, Harbans — 'Politics, Peasants and the Reconstruction of Feudalism in Medieval India', *JPS,* 12, 2 and 3, Jan.–April, 1985, pp. 54–64.

Shrimali, K.M. — 'Religion, Ideology and Society', Presidential Address, Section, *PIHC,* 49th session, Karnataka University, Dharwad, 1988, pp. 1–51 (Reprint).

———— 'Cash Nexus on Western Coast, A.D. 850–1250 : A Study of the Silaharas' in Jha, Amal Kumar (ed.), *Coinage, Trade and Economy* (3rd International Colloquium, January, 8th–11th, 1991, pp. 178–193.

———— 'Reflections on Recent Perceptions of Early Medieval India', Presidential address, (sec. v) *PAPHC*, 18th session, Tenali, 1994, pp. 124–130.

Singh, K.S. — 'Technology and Acculturation : the Brahmanical Model Reconsidered', *Social Science Probings* 2, 1, March, 1985, pp. 20–34.

Singh, Yogendra — 'The Changing Pattern of Social Stratification in India', in Srinivas, M.N. (ed.), *Dimensions of Social Changes in India,* Bombay, 1977, pp. 137–154.

Sinha, Nandini — 'A Study of State and Cult: The Guhilas, Pasupatas and Ekalingaji in Mewar, Seventh to Fifteenth Centuries A.D.,' *SIH,* 2, 1993, pp. 161-179.

Sinopoli, Carla M. Morrison Katheleen D. — 'Dimensions of Imperial Control : The Vijayanagara Capital', *American Anthropologist,* 97, 1, March, 1995, pp. 83–95.

Sister Licyria, M. — 'Emergence of Brahmanas as Landed Intermediaries in Karnataka, A.D. 1000–A.D. 1300', *IHR*, 1, 1974, pp. 28–35.

Smith, C.T. — 'Historical Geography : Current Trends and Prospects', in Chorley R.J. and Haggett, P. (ed.), *Frontiers in Geographical Teaching,* London, 1965, p. 133.

Smith, M. Ronald — 'Power in Ancient India : Kingship and Authority' *ABORI, XXXIX,* i–ii, Jan.–April, 1958, pp. 1–33.

Srinivas, M.N. 'The Social System of Mysore Village', Mckim Marriott (ed.), *Village India : Studies in the Little Community,* Midway reprint, Chicago, 1986, pp. 1–35.

Subbarao. B. 'The Geographical Factor in Andhara History and Archaeology', *BDCRI,* IX, 1–2, Poona, December, 1948, pp. 167–183.

Subbarayalu, Y. 'The Place of Ur in the Economic and Social History of the Early Tamil Nadu (From A.D. 750 to A.D. 1350)', in A.V. Narasimha Murhy and B.K. Guraraja Rao (ed.), *Rangavali : Recent Researches in Indology, Sri S.R. Rao Felicitation Volume,* Sundeep Prakashan, Delhi 1983, pp. 171–177.

———— 'The Chola State and the Agrarian Order–Some Clarification', Paper Presented to the Seminar on the State in Pre–Colonial South India, Centre for Historical Studies, 28th–30th, March, 1989, pp. 21 (Cyclostyled Copy).

Subramanyam, Sanjay 'Writing History "Backwards, South East Asian History and the Annales" at the Cross Roads', *SIH,* 10, 1, 1994, pp. 131–145.

Sundaram, K. 'The Balanja Merchant Community of Medieval Andhra (A.D. 1300–1600 A.D.). *JOR*, XXX, Madras, 1963, pp. 13–27.

———— 'The Vaisya Community in Medieval Andhra (A.D. 1000–A.D.–1600)', *JAHRS*, XXX, Rajahmundy, 1964–65, pp. 11–20.

———— 'The Artisan Community of Medieval Andhra (A.D. 1000–A.D.–1600)', *JIH,* XLIII, ii, Trivandrum, Dec. 1965, pp. 905–915.

Talal, Asad 'Is there a History of Peoples Without–Europe? (A Review Article)', *CSSH,* 29, 1987, pp. 594–607.

Talbot, Cynthia 'Temples, Donors and Gifts : Patterns of Patronage in 13th Century India', *JAS*, 50, 2, 1991.

———— 'Political Intermediaries in Kakatiya Andhra, 1175–1325', *IESHR,* XXXI, 3, July–Sept., 1994, pp. 262–289.

Tarafdar, M.R. 'Trade and Society in Early Medieval Bangal', *IHR*, IV, 1978, pp. 274–286.

Tejaswini, Yarlagadda — 'Social Groups and Economic Change (7th–13th centuries A.D.)', in Aloka Parasher Sen (ed.), *Social and Economic History of Early Deccan (Some Interpretations)*, Delhi, 1993, pp. 158–239.

Thakur, V.K. — 'Trade and Towns in Early Medieval Bengal (c.A.D. 600–A.D. 1200)', *JESHO*, XX ii, June, 1987 pp. 196–220.

Thapar, Romila — 'Dissent and Protest in Early Indian Tradition', *SIH*, L, 2, July–Dec., 1979, pp. 177–195.

__________ 'Genealogical Patterns as Perceptions of the Past', *SIH*, New Series, 7, Jan–June, 1991, pp. 1–36.

Thyagaraju, A.S. — 'A Study of Telugu Places Names', *JAHRS*, XXII, 1952, pp. 182–184.

Tringham, Ruth — 'Introduction : Settlement Patterns and Urbanization' in, *Man, Settlement and Urbanism*, Duckworth, London, 1972, pp. xix, xxviii.

Troy, J. Van — 'Radical Social Protest of the Pasupatas', *Indica*, 27, 1–2, March, 1990, pp. 1–10.

Vasantha Madhava, K.G. — 'Agarian Structure in Coastal Karnataka', (1400–1800), *Indica*, 21, 1, March, 1984, pp. 90–96.

Veluthat, Kesavan — 'Royalty and Divinity; Legitimisation of Monarchical Power in South India', *PIHC*, 39th session Hyderabad, 1978, pp.

__________ 'The Temple Base of the Bhakti Movement in South India', *PIHC*, 40th Session, Waltair, 197, pp. 185–194.

__________ 'Religious Symbols in Political Legitimation : the Case of Early Medieval South India', *Social Scientist*, 21, 1–2, Jan.–Feb., 1993, pp. 23–33.

__________ 'The "Early Medieval" in Indian History', *The Book Review*, XIX, 3, March, 1995, pp. 4–5.

Venkata Rama Ayyar, K.R.R. — 'Medieval Trade Craft and Merchant Guilds in South India', *JIH*, XXV, 1, Trivandrum, 1947, pp. 269–280.

Venkateswara Rao, T. — 'Local Self Government in Medieval Andhra', *JAHRS*, Vol. XXXI, Rajahmundry, 1965–66, pp. 113–123.

——— 'The Gaundas in Medieval Andhra', *Itihas,* Vol. IV, Hyderabad, Jan–June, 1976, pp. 75–81.

Yadava, B.N.S. 'Immobility and Subjection of Indian Peasantry in Early Medieval Complex', *IHR,* 1, 1974.

——— 'Problem of Interaction Between Socio–Economic Classes in the Early Medieval Complex', *IHR*, 3, 1976–77, pp. 43–58.

Yasoda Devi. V. 'The History of Andhra Country 1000 A.D.–1500 A.D. Subsidiary Dynasties', *JAHRS,* XVIII, Rajahmundry, 1951, pp. 33–110.

——— 'The Krishna–Tungabhadra Doab (1000 A.D.–1335 A.D.)', *JAHRS, XXXII,* Hyderabad, 1971–72, pp. 94–101

IV. GAZETTEERS/CENSUS REPORTS

Andhra Pradesh District Gazetteers : (Mahaboobnagar Dt.), Hyderabad, 1976.

Andhra Pradesh District Gazetteers (Kurnool Dt.), Hyderabad, 1974.

Gazetteer of Bombay Presidency, (Bijapur District), Bombay, 1884.

Gazetteer of Bombay State (Dharwar District), Bombay, 1959.

Gazetteer of India, Mysore State (Bijapur and Gulbarga Districts), Bangalore, 1966.

Gazetteer of India, Mysore State (Raichur District), Bangalore, 1970.

Imperial Gazetteer of India, Provincial Series, Hyderabad State, Calcutta, 1909.

Imperial Gazetteer of India, Provincial Series, Bombay Presidency, Vol. II, Calcutta, 1909.

Madras District–Gazetteers, Gazetteer of Anantapur, Madras, 1905.

The Imperial Gazetteer of India, Vol. I, London, 1881.

Census Reports of India–Andhra Pradesh State Series–2, Mahboobnagar and Kurnool Districts, 1981.

Census Reports of India–Karnataka State Series–9, Gulbarga and Dharwar and Raichur Districts, 1981.

V. ENCYCLOPAEDIA/DICTIONARIES/ATLASES/THESES

Davis C. Collins, *An Historical Atlas of the Indian Peninsula,* OUP, Delhi, 1949 (2nd ed.).

Encyclopaedia Britannica, Micropaedia, Vol. III, University of Chicago, 15th edition, 1977.

Hasings, James (ed.), *Encyclopaedia of Religion and Ethics,* Vol. VI, New York 1974.

Hornby, A.S. *Oxford Advanced Learner's Dictionary of Current English,* Delhi, 1987.

Kittel, F. *A Kannada–English Dictionary,* Basel Mission Book and Tract Depository, London, 1894.

13 September 1995 Margaret and Statley, James *Harper Dictionary of Hinduism,* Harper and Row Publishers, New York, 1817.

Moore W.G., *A Dictionary of Geography* (Definitions and Explanations of terms used in Physical Geography), Penguin Books, Great Britain, 1973, (rp.).

Schwatzberg, Joseph, E. (ed.), *A Historical Atlas of South Asia,* The University of Chicago Press, Chicago, 1978.

Sills L. David, (ed.), *International Encyclopaedia of Social Sciences,* Vol. I and II, Collier–Macmillan Publishers, London.

Sircar, D.C., *Indian Epigraphical Glossary,* Motilal Banarasi Das, Delhi, 1966.

The Oxford School Atlas, 26th edition, OUP, Delhi, 1986.

Williams, Monier, *A Sanskrit–English Dictionary*, Oxford, 1960.

Prameela, K., '*Economic and Social Conditions* of *Telangana (A.D. 1000–1323)',* Ph.D. Dissertation Nagarajuna University, Guntur, 1988.

Venkateshwara Rao, T., *'Local Bodies in Pre–Vijayanagara Andhra',* Ph.D. Dissertation, Karnataka University, Dharwar, 1975.

Talbot, Cynthia, 'Gifts to Gods and Brahmins, A Study of Religious Endowments in Medieval Andhra', Ph.D. Dissertation, the University of Wisconsin, Madison, 1988.

INDEX

A

abhidhāne grāma 270
abhyantarasiddhi 191
Achaleśvara 272, 332, 356, 365
āchārya 116, 196, 202
achchupannāya 109
aḍake 212
Ādipiṭha 367
āgama 331
Agnishtoma 372
agrahāra 10, 15, 16, 22, 34, 38, 114, 115, 129, 191, 192, 195, 201, 202, 209, 213, 258, 264, 265, 266, 267, 268, 269, 270, 274, 277, 278, 280, 281, 283, 284, 285, 291, 296, 297, 337, 343, 372, 416
— *chūḍāmaṇi* 280
— *agrahāra Muḍinūr* 281
ahikārika 93, 95, 96
Aijamunnūralūralu 268
ainnūrvāru 130
Akkādevi 111, 196, 290, 293, 333, 334, 342, 366
akkasāle 121, 217, 218, 219, 420
akkasāleyar 122, 217
Akkeśvara 333, 342
Alam, S. M. 68
Allahulirasa 137
Altekar, A.S. 21, 33, 53, 54, 55, 73, 93, 108, 188
Alva 197
Amarāchārya Bhaṭṭāraka 113
Ambika 367
Amritarāsi Paṇḍita 356, 357, 359
aṅgaḍi 131, 214, 215
aṅgaḍidappa 215
aṅaḍi-okkalu 215
anādipaṭṭaṇa 274, 296
aṅga-bhoga 126, 328, 346, 347, 348, 349, 352, 353, 354, 355
angaḍiya nakaraṁgalu 128
ānikāra 131
aṅkakāra 363
Annama Gavuṇḍa 209
Anuveśvara 344
Appadorai, A. 123
appayanavīḍu 290
araṇya 262
arasara basādi 334
arasu 92, 93, 129
Arthaśāstra 33
Arthur Marwick 20
aruvaṇa 132, 193, 195, 205
aruvattokkalu 117
Ashok Shettar 208
Asokan 54
aṣṭabhōga 192
āṭavikas 368
āya 194
ayangadees 31
Aycha Gāvuṇḍa 295, 343
Ayi 365
Ayiseṭṭiya Jinnoja 121
Ayyandeva 102
Ayyāvoḷe 115, 128, 129, 132, 214, 339, 346

B

Babbaleśvara 339
bāḍa 270, 271

baḍagi 121, 217
— *Kammarar* 122, 218
baḍagitānakkaru 218
Baden Powell 32
balañjadādi paṭṭaṇa 274, 296
balbñja 132
Bāleśvara 332
Bālikabbe Gauḍi 198
Bali *vaṁśa* 370
baliya 267, 283
— *agrahāra* 269
— *bāḍam* 286
baliyagrāma 269
baliya vāḍa 266
banajiga 128
baṇañju 262
banañjuvaṭṭaṇa 274
Bannigola *agrahāra* 282, 290
Bappura family 103
Basavaraja, K.R. 73, 74
Baudha *vihāra* 334, 345
bāvi 208
beḍaruṁ 135, 339
benniṟke 197
Beṭṭaḍa Bhāgavati 343, 352
Bhāgiyabbeśvara 343
Bhakti ideology 41, 331
— movement 331
Bhandarkar, R.G. 8, 53
Bharata 53
Bhāratavarsha 33
bhaṭṭagrāma 209, 269, 270
bhattamāṁ 118, 203
Bhāvaśivadeva 356
Bhoga 99
— -Gāvuṇḍa 197
Bhogeśvara 332, 348
bhritya-dāsi varga 120, 204
bhukti 336
Bhuvanakosha 53
bīḍu 211
Bikkeśvara 333, 349
Billeśvara 332, 348, 349, 369
bīra 133
bīravaṇa 193, 194
biṭṭa 267
biṭṭi 120, 138, 204, 410
Bonteśvara 332, 349
Bopparasa 292
brahmadeya 26, 31, 36, 37, 38, 189, 193, 201, 202, 262, 282, 283, 294, 412
brāhmaṇa 9, 14, 22, 23, 24, 27, 35, 36, 78, 79, 80, 110, 111, 113, 114, 115, 135, 136, 137, 138, 189, 191, 192, 193, 198, 201, 202, 203, 209, 269, 270, 291, 335, 348, 352, 364, 372, 373, 411, 420
— -militia 75
Brahmeśvara 333, 340, 341, 343, 349
Brihadiśvara temple 371
Burnett, Lionel, D. 8
Burton Stein 36, 76, 260

C

caitra pavitra 346, 347, 348, 350, 353, 355
caityas 56, 328
caṇḍāla 138, 411, 420
Chākamma 199
Chākeśvara 333, 343
Chākimayya 333, 343
Chālukyan dynasty 67, 328
— ruler 61, 62, 67
— temple 61
— territories 67
chāmarada sūḷe 125
Chāmeśvara 332, 349
Champakalakshmi, R. 78, 129, 132, 213, 215, 329
Chāmuṇḍi 367
Chandaleśvara 340
Chandarasa 196
Chandrabhūṣaṇa Paṇḍita 357
Chandoja 123
Chauṇḍeśvara 366

Chattopadhyaya, B.D. 78, 79, 80, 81, 113, 214, 273, 404, 407
Chaṭṭapayya Nāyaka 109
Chāvuṇḍa 130
Chavuṇḍamayya 199
Chola kingdom 69
Chola polity 26
Choudhury, A.K. 257
chronological dimension 91
chulāyata 92, 93
Cutus 55
Cynthia Talbot 78, 81

D

Dāḍiga 103
dakṣiṇa 53
dakṣiṇāpatha 53, 54, 55
Dāmodara Seṭṭi 130
Dāmoja 123
dāna 373
daṇḍa 192, 194, 206
daṇḍanāyaka 108, 109, 111, 135, 340, 368
Das, D.R. 69
Dāseśvara 344, 351
Dāsimayya 282
Dāsiseṭṭiya Bammoja 121
Deccan Peninsula 29
Desai, P.B. 8, 39, 334, 336
devadānam 36, 189
devalaka brāhmaṇa 135
Devangana Desai 329
devargge parichārikar 120, 204
devigere 280
dhānya 212
Dharma Kumar 188, 189
Dharmaśāstra 24, 25, 28, 138, 404, 411
Dharma Seṭṭi 345
Dharmeśvara 332
dhora kula brāhmaṇa 136
Dhoroja 124
Dhoyipayya 130
dhūpa 347
digvijaya yātra 107
Dikshit, G.S. 73, 74, 99, 261
Dikshit, S.K. 8, 34
Dubreuil, J. 53, 54

E

ekabhōga 100
Ekalingāji 81
ekku varge 281
Emmanuel le Roy Ladurie 9
Eṭagiri 415

F

Fernand Braudel 52
Fleet, J.F. 8
Fuller, C.J. 124

G

Gabbūr 211
gadde 207
gadyāna 115, 120, 124, 193, 207
galduge 207
galeya 117, 118, 119
gāṇa 218
gāṇada tere 218
Gaṇapojana 123
gaṇdhasāli 210
Ganga 70
Gangara Chāvuṇḍamaya Nāyaka 109
Gaṅgeśvara 332
garuḍa 339
gātrigaru 128, 130
gātrigas 132, 133
gātuka 212
gauḍa 264
gauṇḍi 199
gaura-kere 209
gavares 132, 295
— *gātrigas* 132, 133
Gavareśvara 332, 333
gāvuṇḍa 11, 22, 28, 92, 93, 94, 95, 98,

99, 100, 101, 102, 103, 109, 117, 118, 130, 139, 192, 194, 195, 196, 197, 200, 271, 289
gāvuṇḍa volada 197
gere 15, 263
geri 276
Ghai, G.S. 8
Ghatapanadi, S.G. 120, 204
ghaṭikāsthāna 127
ghoṣaka 257
ghoṣe 257
Ghoshal, U.N. 188, 190
giri 257, 262
Girigotemalla Jinālaya 334
gola 262, 267
gotra 91, 135
Goyideśvara 332
grāma 10, 11, 15, 34, 264
grāmabhoktṛ 94
grāmadevata 264, 352
grāmakūṭa 93, 94, 95
grāmapati 94, 95
gūḍem 258
guṇada beḍangi 334
guṇḍa 262
Gururajachar 203, 205

H

Haihaya chiefs 103, 109
— *kula* 137
— of Raichur 70
hālika 119
halli 262, 264, 265, 266
haṇa 118
Haṭṭagara 103
heart land Deccan 68
Heitzman 201
hejjuṁka 194, 197, 205, 215
herder 369
Hermann Kulke 40, 78, 79, 81
hiriya 286
— *-akkasāle* 218
hola 99
Holla 99
— *Gāvuṇḍa* 292
Hosavūr 267
Hoysalas 62, 65, 68, 105
— of Dwarasamudra 65, 67, 68, 69, 105, 192, 270, 406, 408
— of Raichur 70
huligajañguliya nāvikaru 135

I

idaṅgai 27, 28
Ikṣavāku 55, 62
Indian Feudalism 74, 77, 102, 204
Indo-Gangetic plain 188
Iriva Nolambādhirāja 104, 111
Ismail, K. 39
Īśvara Seṭṭi 345

J

Jagannātha 40, 79, 370, 371
Jaina affiliation 312
— monks 273
— sect 332
Jajmāni 122, 410
Jakkiyabbe 134, 199
James Heitzman 78
janada prabhu 93
janguliya 339
jaragina doni 218
— *tere* 218
Jaṭadeva Paṇḍita 357
Jātaka 53
jāti 21, 28, 90, 138
Jayaswal, K.P. 188
jeṣṭhāṁśada bhūmi 198
jinālaya 271, 334
Jñānaśakti 357
Joga 110
— Gāvuṇḍa 200
joyisa 92
Jyāmatūru 267

K

Kadamba chieftain 139, 196, 296
— family 102
— lineage 139, 293
Kākatiya polity 81
Kalāchuri monarch 112
Kalakaleśvara 332
Kālāmukha sect 116, 335
— doctrine 335
— Śaivism 17, 38, 39
Kāli 367
— age 39, 40
Kalideva 332, 346, 347, 348, 356
Kālideveśvara 348
Kālika Goddess 332
— Purāṇa 367
kalkuṭiga 217
kalkuṭṭiga goṭṭali 217
Kallamaṭha 361
Kalleśwara temple 329
kallu 15, 262, 263, 267
kāluva 208, 209
kambhada sūḷe 125
kaṁchagāra 131, 217, 218
— *goṭṭali* 217
kamma kula 135
kammaras 219
kammaṭa 121, 213
Kammaṭeśvara 332, 340, 345
kammaṭi adhikāri 131, 219
Kammaṭida Jinālaya 334
kammaṭi kāru 219
kāmyani 336
kanna 134
Kāpālika 336
kaśyapa gotra 201
kara 193, 207
— *bhūmi* 285
karaṇa 92, 94, 95, 96
Karashima, N. 26, 27, 77, 78, 188, 202
karaṇikas 28
Karhad 113
Karikāla 104
kariya keyi 207
— *keyye* 280
kariyanela 207
Karl Marx 32, 188
karpūraṁ 211
karṣaka 119
karsha 262
kāruka 218
Kāśi Viśveśvara 329
Kaṭarasa 103
Kaṭṭale 103
kaundinya gotra 136
Kavataleśvara 332
Kāveriballabha 104
Kāvya 257
kelawāḍi 209, 293
kemmanna kuṇi 207
keṇi 219
keṇikaram 131, 219
kere 263
Keśadevara Bammoja 121
Kesavan Veluthi 75
Keśavāditya 353
Keśvādityadeva 348
Ketoja 123
khar 210
kharvāta 257
kheta 257
khetaka 257
kīl-jātiya 281
kināsa 24
Kirti Someśvara 116
kiru kulaya 212
kisukāḍu 207, 280
kisu mattar 207
kola 263
komaṭi 139
koṇḍa 257
koṇḍalli-koṭṭalli 211, 212
Koralaguṇḍa 101

Kosambi, D.D. 188
kōṭi hōma 372
Kovara Gāvuṇḍa 197
Kriyā Śakti Paṇḍita 356
krośa 262
kṣatriya 22, 135, 137, 420
— *pavitra* 137
— *vaṁśa* 137
— *varṇa* 137
kubera 132
Kukkuṭeśvara 333
kula kamala 137
kulakaraṇi 92, 94, 95
kuli 120
kulkuṭiga 121
kumbāra 131, 193, 217
kunnula vaṁśa 102, 136, 291
Kuntala *deśa* 260
Kuppuswamy, G.R. 4, 23, 29, 114, 203, 207, 214
kuṟība 339
— *-gāvunḍugaḷum* 135, 369
kuriṁbana 134
Kuṛitakuṁte 295
Kusuva family 103
kuṭumbiṭṭi agrahāra 282

L

Lakmādevi 134
Lakshmaṇeśvara 349
Lākula 335, 362
Lakulīsa 361
lenas 56
Liceria, M. 113
Linga 98, 284
Lokāditya 200
Lokamānikaseṭṭi 109
Lokkigadyānu 213
lokkipon 213
Lokkiya-visa 213
Lokkuṇḍi 213
Lucien Febvre 1

M

Mācheśvara 338
mādagāra 135, 339
Mada Nāgi Seṭṭi 130
Maddūr 211
Mādhava 338, 341
mahājana 9, 11, 14, 22, 114, 115, 116, 119, 120, 134, 201, 202, 203, 204, 264, 265, 281, 282, 337, 341, 351
Mahālakshmi 332
Mahāliṅga 332, 346
mahāmaṇḍaleśvara 72, 101, 105, 107, 110, 200, 292, 341, 347, 350
Mahāmātya 93, 108
Mahāmāyā 367
mahānāḍu 211, 274
mahānakaraṁigalu 133
mahāprabhu 98, 99, 100, 289
mahāprabhuvini 134
mahāprachaṇḍa 288
mahāsāhaṇi 111
mahāsāmantādhipati 72, 101, 105, 196, 202, 339, 408
mahāsthānādhipati 116, 362, 363
mahāvaḍḍavyāvahari 131
Mailayya 134
Maine, H.S. 32
Māki Seṭṭi 345
mālagāra 12, 193, 217, 218
Malati Mahajan 257, 258
Malegatti Śivālaya 329
Mallikārjuna 332, 338
Mallikārjunadeva 333
Malloja 121
maṇḍapa 328, 338
mānevergaḍe 95, 108
Mangalam, S.J. 262
Mangalūra *halli* 284
māṇi 124
manneya 92, 94, 95, 100, 101, 102, 195, 196, 268, 287, 293, 339, 408

manneya svāmya 282
manneyar 200, 287
mānya 191
Mārakabbe Bhaḷāri 343
Mārasinga Gāvuṇḍa 200
Marc Bloch 1
marchland Deccan 68
Mark Wilks, 32
Maruleśvara 332, 333
Marxian methodology 76
Marxist 5, 13, 23, 25, 26, 28, 30, 35, 40, 41, 74, 75, 76, 119, 336, 404, 405
maṭha 115, 116, 193, 328, 335, 337, 355, 356
Matsya Purāṇa 53, 373
mattar 123, 124, 125, 126, 192, 193, 195, 196, 202, 203, 214
Maunara Śridhara 113
Mauryan Empire 75
— period 33
meli 118
— *-sāssivvaru* 117, 118, 139
meṅkalu 134
menṭe 117
menti 120
Metcalfe 33
Minakshi temple 124
Miṇiṅjige 267, 269
Mishra, R.N. 257
Mitākshara 109
Molleya Saṁka Gāvuṇḍa 200
mōraka kula 100, 292, 333
Morrison, Kathleen D. 31
Mountstuart Elphinstone 32
Muḍiyanūr 281
mukti 336
Mūlasthāna 193, 340, 341, 366
Mūlasthānadeva 283, 332, 340, 346
mūliga 206
mūligadere 206
mummurridaṇḍas 127, 129, 132, 133, 211, 214, 295
Munro 32
Mūrti Nārāyaṇa 340, 353
murttage family 100

N

nāḍapergaḍe 96, 100
nāḍa-seṭṭi guṭṭa 127
nāḍu 26, 33, 36, 37, 76, 77, 112, 259, 260, 261, 293, 294, 408
naivedya 338, 346, 347, 348, 350, 354
Nāgadeva 333
nagara samudāya 271
Nāgavarmarasa 102
Nāgeśvara 332, 333, 356
nakaraṅgaḷu 130
nakara samūha 127, 128, 289
Nakareśvara 345, 347
Nāki 98, 99, 100, 101
— Gāvuṇḍa 200
Nalayira Prabandhaṁ 331
nāl-gāvuṇḍa 100, 101, 102, 103, 200
— *-prabhu* 100, 290
nānādeśi 127, 128, 129, 130, 211, 214, 274, 295, 410
nandādivi 338, 346, 347, 348, 349, 354
Nandi, R.N. 75, 119, 188
Nandini Sinha 80
Nanneśvara 332, 350, 356
Narayanan, M.G.S. 75
Nationalist writers 73
Nāṭyaśāstra 53
Navalinga group 329
nāviḍa 193, 217, 282
Nāvile figure 283
nāyaka 108, 121, 197
nelevīḍu 278, 290
Netra Śiva Paṇḍita 116, 363
Nilakantha Shastri 334
Nolamba Pallavas 103, 111, 112, 287
Nolambavāḍi 112
nūlaprabandha 353

nyāsa 114

O

oḍeya 348, 353
Oja 121
Ojana 123
okkalu 22, 24, 117, 118, 119, 120, 193, 195, 296, 409
okkala 24, 118, 119, 131, 139, 267, 289, 420
okku 117

P

pādapadmopajivin 105
pāḍuvāribaggam 124
paliyam 258
palli 10, 11, 15, 34, 257, 259, 261, 264, 265, 266, 268
palligrāma 257
pallika 257
paṇa 117, 193, 212, 213, 215
Pañchalaṅgala Kratu 372
Pañchaliṅga 332, 352
— *grāma* 271, 275
Pañchalingadeva 332, 333, 349, 356, 365
Panchmukhi, R.S. 8
pannāya 194
paraiya 28
parjāgāvuṇḍa 28
pasalu 207
pasāyita 92, 94, 95, 96, 97
Pāśupata 8, 335, 336
parekara 123, 126
pārta 123, 126
patram sūḷe 125
paṭṭana 11, 15, 127, 132, 259, 261, 264, 416, 417
paṭṭa sālega 218
— *-sūtraṁ* 211
pejjuṁku 215
Pemāḍi 112
pergaḍe 11, 92, 93, 94, 95, 96, 197
Permadi Jayasiṅgadeva 136
piṇḍadāna 203
pola 271
polimera 265
Positivism 20
potail 31, 32
prabhākara 114
prabhu 92, 93, 94, 95, 96, 97, 98, 197, 200, 338, 339
pradakṣiṇa 328
praja 197
pramukha karaṇa 92
— *ubhayanānādeśi* 128
praśasti 327
praviṣṭa vāda 267
prithvīvallabha 105
priya putra 282
Puilge *grāma* 278
pujā 124, 347, 348, 349, 350, 352
pūjāri 347, 348, 352
pūjasiva āchārya 124
Pulige 281
Purāṇas 53, 257
Purāṇic Bhakti 38
— God 374
— Hinduism 16, 374
— sect 41
Purāṇism 38
Puvvaravalli 275

Q

quit-rent 193

R

Rācheśvara 366
Rai, G.K. 120, 204
rājadhāni 262, 271, 278, 290, 416
— *paṭṭaṇa* 274
rājas 40
raṅga-bhoga 126, 338, 346, 352, 353, 354

Rāshṭrakūṭa chiefs 105
— dynasty 62, 73, 104
— of Malkhed 106
— ruler 105
rāṣṭradevatā 371
Ray Chaudhari, H.C. 53
regaḍy 207
Revabbe *goravi* 134
Revaya Dvedi Chattopādhyāya 113, 135, 278
Ṛgveda Khaṇḍika 372
Romila Thapar 112, 335
Rudra 369
Ryotwari system 188

S

Sabhyasachi Bhattacharya 1
sādada pergaḍe 290
Sāhasa Bhairava 340
Sahavāsi 111
sāiga okkala 212
Śaiva *Āgama* 335
— priest 200
— *Siddhānta* 331
Śaivism 16, 38, 41, 116, 331, 335, 336, 356, 359, 360, 366, 374
Śaivite ideology 335, 350, 417
sakara 211
śakti pīṭha 336
sālega 122, 193
sālyakshetra 207
samastabhuvanāśraya 105
samastādeyasahitaṁ 191
samasta nakara 127
— *nakaraṁgalū* 132
saṁskāra 40
samudra 208
saṅdhivigrahi 108
Śaṅkaradeva 348
Saṅkimayya 295
Sankrāṅti festival 353
Saraswati 332
Saratavūra 283, 288
sarvabādhaparihāraṁ 191
sarvābhyantarasiddhi 282, 283
Śāstra Khaṇḍika 372
Śātavahana 55, 56, 75, 186, 327
satra 199
Satyāśraya 67
saudhare 96
saurabhaṁ 285
savakaṭṭu karu 131
Selagara 267
senabova 93, 94, 96
senādhipati 108, 110
seṇigaru 131, 218
serfdom 204
seṭṭi 127, 128, 132, 133, 203, 209, 214, 215, 272, 273
Shrimali, K.M. 35, 257
siddha 194, 336
Siddhānti Kāleśvara 361
siddhāya 194, 195
Siddheśvara 332
śikhara 328
Sindas 70, 100, 102, 102, 106, 139, 196
— Bopparasa 136
Sindāra-gere 209
Sindavāḍināḍ 293
Sinda Vikramādityarasa 112
Siṅgeśvara 366
Sinopoli, Carla M. 31
Sircar, D.C. 8, 102, 128
siri vāgilu 287
Sirivūra 283, 288
Siriyammeśvara 332, 350
Śiva 332, 333, 334, 336, 345, 351, 355, 365, 366, 369
Śivadharma *Purāṇa* 374
Śiva Mahādeva 340
Śivālaya 332, 338, 355
śivāta 196
Sobhaneśvara 340, 344

social stratification 90
soḍorevaḍiyara 92, 93
Someśvara 333
soṅṭe 218
Spatial Context 10, 15
Śridhara Bhaṭṭa 278
śri khaṇḍakke 211
Sṛitis 257
Śruti 373
sthala vritti 270, 271, 275
sthānāchārya 116, 202
sthānāpati 116, 202
stūpas 56, 328
Subbarayulu, Y. 77
śūdra 22, 27, 137, 138, 139
sūḷe 123
sūḷevala 126
śulkadaṇḍa 191
Sumati Mulay 53
suṁka 192, 193, 194
Sundaram, K. 217
Suṇḍi 130, 131, 203, 271
suṅka 212, 213, 215, 283
suṅkada pergade 290
suṅkaveragaḍe 92, 93, 109
Suvira Jaiswal 135
Svayambhu 201
— Kalidevasvāmi 339, 343
— Paśchima Somanātha 349
— Prasanna Mallikārjuna 349
— Śiva 332, 347, 353

T

takkilu 207
tala samastha 127
tāmbuliga seṭṭi 118, 128, 130, 131, 134, 295, 420
Tamilakam region 77, 78, 260
taṁtrapālu 109
Tarafdar 213
tatpādapadamōpajivi 72, 103, 109, 110, 117
Teggina Irappa 329
tejaḥsvāmya 192
telikis 22, 27
telligaraivattokkalu 122
telligas 121, 134, 193, 199, 217, 345
Telligeśvara 332, 334, 339, 341, 350
Thurston 369
Thyagaraju, A.S. 257, 258
Tippaya Nāyaka 198
tīrtha 277
— *yātrā* 40
toṁṭa 117, 200
toṁṭigalu 118
Totigeśvara 332, 345
Traipuruṣa God 332, 343, 353
tribhoga 283
tribhogābhyantarasiddhi 191
trikāla 346
Trikūṭa 332, 369
Tumbula 211
tuppaka 217

U

ubhayanānādeśi 133, 211
ugura 28, 117, 118, 139, 409, 420
uguruli 118
Uṁbalam 194
uṁbali 412
Ummachigen 281
ūr 10, 11, 15, 33, 34, 37, 259, 262, 267, 268, 269, 271, 278, 414
ūroḍeya 92, 94, 201, 282, 339, 355
— *volada* 201
ūruṁ 129
uttama bhoga bhūmi 285, 292

V

vāḍa 10, 11, 15, 34, 38, 259, 261, 262, 266, 267, 268, 271, 278, 414
vaḍḍarāvula 194, 205, 215
vaḍḍarāyakas 109

Vaiḍumba 70, 103, 137
Vaiṣṇavism 16, 38, 41, 331
vaiśya 22, 24
Vākāṭaka economy 35
— inscription 257
— ruler 186
valaṅgai 27, 28
valasa 258
valgaḍlu 207
valli 262, 264, 265
vaṇiga mahājana 130
varṇa 21, 22, 23, 28, 90, 91, 135, 136, 137, 138, 327, 337, 404, 420
vāvi 263
Vedānta 331
Vedic age 188
— sacrifices 113, 135, 373
vellala 331
velpura 127
Venneyya Bhaṭṭa 135
vibhu 290
Vidureśvara 332, 344
Vidyābharaṇa Paṇḍita 356
Vigñāneśvara 201
vihāra 56, 328, 339, 340
Vikramaditya 107, 112
Vikrameśvara 366
Vincent Smith 188
vipra 270
vipragrāma 269, 270, 272, 171, 278
vīra-baṇañju 139
vīra-baṇañju dharma 133
Vīra Baseśvara 332, 346
Vīradāsa 359, 364, 369
Vīra Nārāyaṇadeva 344
viśayapati 93, 95
Vishṇu Bhaṭṭa 113, 135
Viṣṇu 332, 333, 334, 345, 351
Viśwāmitra gotra 135
volāl 271
vṛṣṭi 25, 120, 204
vyāgraha lāñchana 102
vyākaraṇa 114
vyudhabhūmi 207

W

Wiser 122
wāḍi 257
wāḍigrāma 257

Y

Yadava, B.N.S. 119, 204
Yādavas 7, 62, 65, 69, 105, 270, 406
Yakshi cult 367
Yasoda Devi 104
Yazdani, G. 53, 54
yogapīṭhās 127, 132
Yogeśvara 329
Yogeśvari 336

***